F

THE SOUTH THROUGH TIME

THE SOUTH THROUGH TIME

✻ *A History of an American Region* ✻

JOHN B. BOLES
Rice University

PRENTICE HALL, Englewood Cliffs, New Jersey 07632

Library of Congress Cataloging–in–Publication Data

Boles, John B.
   The South through time : a history of an American region / John B.
Boles.
      p.   cm.
   Includes bibliographical references (p.   ) and index.
   ISBN 0–13–825050–2   ISBN 0–13–157306–3 (v. 1)   ISBN 0–13–157314–4 (v. 2)
   1. Southern States —History.   I. Title.
F209.B65   1995
975—dc20   94–3343
                                                               CIP

Acquisitions editor: Steve Dalphin
Editorial/production supervision and
   interior design: Joan Powers
Cover design: Ray Lundgren
Buyer: Nick Sklitsis
Copy editor: Mary Kinsella
Photo editor: Lorinda Morris-Nantz
Photo researcher: Barbara Scott

Cover credit: *Bottom photo,* Houston, Texas; *top photo,* Ives after painting by W.A.
Walker, Library of Congress.

© 1995 by Prentice-Hall, Inc.
A Simon & Schuster Company
Englewood Cliffs, New Jersey 07632

Printed in the United States of America
10 9 8 7 6 5 4 3 2 1

ISBN 0-13-825050-2

Prentice-Hall International (UK) Limited, *London*
Prentice-Hall of Australia Pty. Limited, *Sydney*
Prentice-Hall Canada, Inc., *Toronto*
Prentice-Hall Hispanoamericana, S.A., *Mexico*
Prentice-Hall of India Private Limited, *New Delhi*
Prentice-Hall of Japan, Inc., *Tokyo*
Simon & Schuster Asia Pte. Ltd., *Singapore*
Editora Prentice-Hall do Brasil, Ltda., *Rio de Janeiro*

Dedicated to my teachers
at the public schools of Center, Texas, 1949–1961;
Rice University, 1961–1965;
University of Virginia, 1965–1969;
and, with love, to Nancy, David, and Matthew

Contents

CHAPTER 2
The National South *79*

CHAPTER 3
The Southern Nation *177*

CHAPTER 4
The Colonial South *337*

CHAPTER 5
The American South   *450*

Preface

For at least a half century southern history has been arguably the most robust field in the entire discipline of American history. The last twenty-five years have been especially fruitful, and a number of topics—slavery, women's history, the rise of sharecropping, the causes of Populism, and the impact of World War II, to name only a representative few—have undergone revisions in interpretation so fundamental that what was generally accepted just a generation ago is now rejected, replaced with a significantly different interpretation. This abundance of writing and the vigorous interpretative debates that have resulted have been exhilarating to professional historians, but much of the exciting new findings and viewpoints has been confined to scholarly articles and monographs, dissertations, and papers at academic meetings. The lay reader, the student, and the historian not specializing in the history of the South find it difficult to stay abreast of new writings.

Even specialists in the history of the South often discover that the amount of publications appearing in only a portion of the field, say slavery or the Civil War, is so extensive that it precludes keeping up with the entire field. And much of the most impressive new scholarship, methodologically innovative investigations of very narrow topics, is not fitted into the larger context of southern history. A reader must either remain content with, in effect, core samples of the new scholarship on the South or undergo a daunting regimen of reading in order to comprehend the larger contours of southern history. My purpose in planning this book was to be both inclusive and interpretative in my account. Perhaps having taught in Louisiana and Texas moved me away from seeing southern history as Virginia or Carolina writ large. My intended audience is the advanced undergraduate reader and the large public of lay historians—that plentiful group of well-read amateurs who are fascinated by the past. Of course, I hope that my academic colleagues approve of my distillation of a generation of scholarship and agree with my portrayal of the South's history, but even more do I hope that these pages whet the reading appetite of students and general readers. One of the real glories of American historical scholarship since World War II has been the field of southern history. I hope these pages reveal my debt to the work of two generations of diligent scholars and accurately represent their scholarship to a broad audience.

J.B.B.

Acknowledgments

I hardly know where to begin or end this section. For almost three decades I have been reading in the field of southern history and attending the annual meetings of the Southern Historical Association. In addition, for a quarter century I have had students, undergraduate and graduate, who have prepared papers, given in-class reports, asked probing questions, and often offered fresh ideas. After more than a decade as managing editor of the *Journal of Southern History* I have also read more than a thousand submitted manuscripts. From all of these sources I have learned. In addition I have done specialized reading and research on topics that particularly intrigued me. However, in a book of synthesis such as this, I am most dependent on the scholarship of others. I hope that I have fairly, accurately, and succinctly borrowed from their work and sensibly related all the pieces to the whole.

My family aided me by putting up with my work habits and taking care of things I neglected, as did the wonderful staff of the *Journal of Southern History*—Patricia Dunn Burgess, Evelyn Thomas Nolen, and Julia Cabanis Shivers. Allen J. Matusow, dean of humanities at Rice University, and George E. Rupp, then president of the university, provided me with a year of released time during which a substantial portion of the manuscript was written. My colleagues at Rice have created a very supportive research environment. Several graduate students assisted me in the final stages: Anya Jabour researched illustrations; Angela Boswell checked the bibliographical citations; Jennifer Payne corroborated obscure spellings; and Melissa Kean helped with the proofreading. The six outside readers chosen by the press made valuable corrections and suggestions. Elizabeth Hayes Turner, Lynda Crist, Mary Dix, and Eric Walther read portions of the text and offered sound advice. The text benefited from an extraordinarily careful reading by Evelyn Nolen, who saved me from many infelicitous phrases. I am particularly grateful for her assistance, both with this book and daily at the *Journal*. My younger son once asked me to dedicate this book to our family dog. I have resisted that well-intentioned request.

THE SOUTH THROUGH TIME

❋ CHAPTER 1 ❋

The Southern Colonies

THE FIRST SOUTH

What has come to be known as the American South is a geographical expanse of enormous diversity, stretching from just north of the Chesapeake Bay to the semitropical tip of the Florida Keys and westward beyond the rugged hill country of central Texas. Most of the region lies below the isotherm that marks an annual average temperature of 60 degrees Fahrenheit, though Kentucky, Maryland, Virginia, and the mountainous highlands of the Appalachians and the Ozarks have colder climates. Much of the South, with the exception of the western portions of Texas along with Oklahoma and Missouri, receives forty inches of rain or more annually, and this rain often falls in torrential bursts that seem to attack the soil and everything on it with supernatural fury. The soil of the South is ancient, for the area escaped the last glaciation; blazing sun and penetrating rains have assaulted the South's mountain backbone and worn and rounded its once rocky peaks. The relatively thin soils of the hillsides have been partly leached of life-supporting nutrients by the heavy rains of millennia, and the warmth of the long summers has speeded up the organic decay of the resulting clays. Much of the more fertile soil has been washed into the dark loam of the bottomlands bordering the creeks and rivers. The long growing season, the ample rainfall, and the unevenly fertile soils all play shaping roles in the region's long history of agricultural exploitation.

The American mainland was isolated from the remainder of the continental land masses for most of prehistory, but several times in the last fifty thousand years or so, when the earth's climate cooled and huge glaciers covered much of North America, the lowered sea levels revealed a land bridge connecting Siberia with Alaska. Over that temporary umbilical cord Asian peoples in several widely separated migrations entered a pristine continent, beginning perhaps as long as forty-five thousand years ago, truly discovering a New World many centuries before adventurous European seafarers ventured west. These intrepid hunters and gatherers of Asian ancestry spread southward, eventually populating both American continents. Precisely when these first American explorers and settlers entered what we today call the South is not clear, but archaeological evidence from scattered sites suggests their presence between twelve and fifteen thousand years ago.

Very little is known about the earliest human inhabitants of the region, a group sometimes called "early men," but after about 11500 B.C. men and women of a slightly more advanced cultural level emerged. These Paleo-Indians, apparently moving eastward across the plains, were nomadic hunter–gatherers who had mastered the use of grooved (fluted) stone spearpoints. The Paleo-Indians hunted the large animals that grazed on the plains—horses, camels, mammoths, and an earlier version of the bison—either by driving them off cliffs or by thrusting their spears into them at very close range, perhaps surprising the game at water holes. Rude stone tools have been found, implements to butcher meat and scrape skins. These early hunters almost certainly ate some plants, seeds, and fruit, but they were not agriculturists. Their population probably grew with explosive speed in the new land because their journey across the Alaskan land bridge and the Arctic isolated them from the prolific disease environment of the Old World. This disease filter, along with the apparently abundant big game of the plains, may have made the Americas an unusually propitious location for human settlement. Within relatively few centuries the Paleo-Indian population seems to have spread across much of the two continents. But because of both climatic changes and the hunting pressure of the expanded human population, the large animals upon which the Paleo-Indian culture depended were slowly depleted—the animals simply became extinct by 7000 B.C. or so. The drier climate may also have meant that the better hunting lands shifted eastward even as the size of the available game became smaller. As the meat supply changed in size and location, the human culture had to adjust. The result was the development, beginning at around 8000 B.C., of another Indian cultural tradition, the Archaic.

The Archaic tradition proved to be extremely durable, lasting in some isolated regions until after Europeans arrived in the New World. The Indians of this tradition learned more efficient ways of exploiting their environment, and with the slight increase in leisure and skills there appeared for the first time polished rocks used for adornment, stone pipes used for ritualistic smoking, and definite burial ceremonies. Using small javelins or darts hurled with spear-throwers (sticks that were essentially extensions of the arm), these Indians hunted a great variety of small animals (as compared to the mammoths, bison and so forth of an earlier age) including bear, fox, turkey and other fowl, squirrel, opossum, and especially deer. While exclusively the men hunted, men, women, and children gathered nuts, seeds, berries, roots, and shellfish (especially mussels). Some Archaic tradition Indians became semi-sedentary, tending to stay near proven sites of mussels, for instance. As certain groups began to specialize in region-specific food sources, tribal differences and a sense of territoriality evolved. In several regions, for example along the Savannah River in Georgia as early as 2000 B.C., these Indians learned to make pottery, mixing vegetable fibers with the clays before firing to gain additional strength.

Precise dates cannot be given for the origin of the next phase of Indian culture, but what is known as the Woodland tradition began to emerge about 1000 B.C. along the valleys of the Mississippi and Ohio rivers. This new tradition represented a series of cultural refinements of patterns that had developed in the latter stages of the Archaic tradition, apparently with a few admixtures from Indian cultures to the South in Mexico. No sharp break with the Archaic emphasis on hunting and gathering occurred, but slowly, and at different rates in different subregions of the Southeast, the people of the emerging Woodland tradition began to utilize more efficiently a greater variety of methods for acquiring foods, and the whole panoply of their culture unfolded.

While minor improvements were achieved in hunting, the signal advances came in the gathering of seeds, advances that represented the emergence of agriculture for the first time in the American South. In those portions of the middle South where deciduous trees—hickory, walnut, butternut, chinquapin, and oak—predominated, nuts and acorns became increasingly important as a food source, and underground storage pits for these nuts and the seeds of various grasses came to be used, suggesting a more sedentary life. For the first time homes of relative permanence were constructed. Hunting continued, perhaps even as the primary food supply, but slowly native plants, such as the sunflower, sumpweed, and chenopodium, came to be cultivated for their seeds rather than merely gathered in the wild, and these initial farmed crops grew best in the well-watered and fertile bottomlands near rivers.

Toward the end of the Archaic period two plants, squash and the bottle gourd, first domesticated in what is now Mexico, diffused into the American

South, and Woodland tradition people came to cultivate them, eating the squash and using the dried gourds for storage containers and dippers. About 200 B.C. a small variety of corn, called tropical flint, also came to be cultivated, although it faded away, probably for climatic reasons, by 400 A.D. In certain areas of the South people who deviated somewhat from the rudimentary plant cultivation of the Woodland tradition thrived on other food sources, especially fish and shellfish. The Calusas of southwestern Florida, for example, were not primitive farmers but rather gatherers of shellfish, leaving one refuse heap (what archaeologists call a midden) more than a quarter mile square and twelve to fifteen feet high. Yet the point is that improvements in food production or collection allowed the growth and concentration of Indian populations and the development of semipermanent villages, both of which made possible the flowering of Woodland cultural traditions.

The people of the Woodland tradition made much wider use than before of pottery, but now the clay was tempered with crushed rock or grit, not vegetable fibers. The vessels were frequently decorated, and styles came to be associated with the various tribal groupings that were developing. Archaeologists have discovered many items intended to be worn as body decorations—stone or copper gorgets that were suspended from the neck by cords, varieties of earrings, small cylindrical "cymbals" that were attached to the elbows and knees, and bracelets. Decorative and perhaps ritual artifacts made of nonnative materials, such as mica, copper, even grizzly bear teeth and obsidian from the Rocky Mountains, have been unearthed, suggesting that a vast trade network linked the Woodland Indians of the Southeast with cultures elsewhere across the continent. Mortuary ceremonies, which had first appeared among the people of the Archaic tradition, grew enormously in complexity in the era of the Woodland tradition. Items for body decoration, pottery (that had been "killed" by having a hole knocked in it), smoking pipes, even sacrificed dogs and, for chiefs or their spouses, the bodies of close servants were interred with the dead. It seems clear that some kind of religious conception of an afterlife had arisen.

Graves were often covered by huge mounds, and in fact the mound building of the Indians of the Woodland tradition is their best known cultural activity. Mounds were built for a range of ceremonial purposes other than burial, but their exact use and meaning are unknown. The mounds from the period that have been found are in a variety of shapes and sizes; some are geometrical in design, while others are in the shape of animals. Several are hundreds of feet in length and from five to fifty feet in height; occasionally a series of smaller mounds surrounds one very large mound, perhaps on top of which was once a temple. One can imagine ceremonies of great complexity and sophistication occurring on or around these mounds, attended by numbers of participants and directed by ritual specialists. The colossal dimensions of some of the mounds, for example, those at Poverty

Point in Louisiana or Kolomoki in Georgia, and the recognition that they were built one basketful of dirt at a time suggest both the substantial population of the Woodland Indians at certain locations and the relative permanence of their villages. Despite these cultural and physical achievements and for reasons that are unclear, the Woodland tradition began to fade in the central South around 700 A.D., and the elaborate burial ceremonies ceased.

Indian life, of course, evolved with no sudden discontinuities from the past, with the Woodland tradition persisting longer on the fringes of the South. Indeed, remnants of the Archaic tradition lingered in certain areas, as along the Texas Gulf Coast where Spanish traveler Alvar Nuñez Cabeza de Vaca as late as 1530 encountered extremely primitive hunter–gatherers who barely eked out a mosquito-infested existence on low coastal islands. Nevertheless, between 700 and 900 A.D., beginning in the fertile floodplains bordering the Mississippi River from present-day St. Louis to Vicksburg and thence eastward in the moist river valleys of the region, a still more advanced Indian society developed out of the Woodland tradition. This new culture, the Mississippian tradition, was the most culturally and socially advanced Indian civilization in all of North America and was at its very apex at the moment of initial European contact with the New World.

The basis of the Mississippian tradition was an agricultural breakthrough that allowed substantial population growth, which in turn required political organization to control the labor, defend the limited amount of arable riverine soils, and promote the elaboration of cultural and religious forms. The key was the introduction between 800 and 1000 A.D. from MesoAmerica of a new species of maize or corn, called eastern flint, that grew prolifically in the rich, moist bottomlands, and, about the same time, the parallel introduction of "pole" beans, typically grown among the corn stalks. (The seeds of both may have been spread by Aztec traders, called *pochetecas*.) Corn is the ultimate domesticated crop, so adapted to human cultivation that it cannot survive wild, but grown alone it exhausts the soil and consumed alone it is a dietary disaster, for it contains a bonding agent that fixes an important vitamin, niacin, in such a manner that it can not be effectively digested, resulting in the protein deficiency disease pellagra. The growing of beans intercropped with corn solved the soil problem, for as a legume the bean plant resupplied nitrogen to the land. Consequently the Indians could grow corn interminably without fertilizer and still maintain their crop yield. Moreover, by eating beans with their corn (often together in a dish called succotash) the Indians had a source of niacin that negated the one nutritional disadvantage of corn. Indian cultivation of native plants, such as sunflower and sumpweed, declined significantly, although squash continued to be grown and eaten. Corn would prove to be the major cereal crop of the South for the next thousand years, until our own century.

By 1200 A.D. the Mississippian tradition, with its agricultural successes, sustained numerous Indian towns, even cities; one settlement near the confluence of the Missouri and Mississippi rivers reached a population of nearly forty thousand, larger than any American city at the time of the American Revolution. Most villages and towns were, of course, much smaller, but the point is that rich crop production allowed a kind of agricultural–urban society to develop in the South before Columbus. These towns were near the rivers with their fertile soils that were enriched annually by spring floods, and the villages and towns, often surrounded by protective moats or palisades, had nearby garden plots worked primarily by the women and large fields further away that were cleared by the men. The men also did the preliminary breaking up of the soil for the garden plots, using hoes whose blades were made of stone, conch shell, or the shoulder blade of a large animal.

Men and women working together cultivated the large fields by making small hills several feet apart. Then, after digging a hole in the center of the hills with a pointed stick, a seed kernel of corn was dropped in and covered, probably with the foot. As the corn grew, the dirt was piled around the stalk, and the hill both protected the roots and helped retain the moisture. These large village fields were owned and tilled communally, with the work decisions made by the chiefs and village elders. Surplus crops were stored in communal granaries. Organization was required both to order the labor routines and to devise military plans and fortifications to protect the relatively limited supply of rich bottomland so important to food production. Out of this necessity came the various Indian confederacies, headed by powerful chieftains, such as, Powhatan in Virginia and the Queen of Cofitachequi in South Carolina, whose authority and immense wealth so impressed Hernando de Soto in 1540.

Many of the villages also contained pyramidal mounds, sometimes of huge size, with flattened tops on which temples and other ceremonial structures were built. Often these pyramids faced grand plazas, and crowds of Indians congregated there to hear soaring orations, participate in rituals of religious, agricultural, or military import, and witness rough-and-tumble competitive games that themselves had communal religious meaning. Although there were significant regional differences among the Indian groupings in the South, with variations in the degree of hunting and fishing that complemented the growing of crops and stylistic differences in the decorations of the plentiful pottery, basketry (made of grasses and reeds, split canes, or pine straw, as baskets made by slaves would be later), ornamental jewelry, and deerskin clothes, the similiarities among the general participants in the Mississippian tradition are more important than the local particularities.

Across much of the region, uniformities of decorative style and religious ceremonies—what anthropologists label the Southeastern Ceremonial Complex—are testimonies to the prevalence of one general cultural system. Despite variations, one encounters the Corn Mother goddess again and

again, and throughout the region the Green Corn festival, or busk, was celebrated after the new crop ripened. There were other profound cultural similarities, one being the general matrilineal nature of the Mississippian Indian
tradition. Mothers were primarily responsible for child rearing, and the children belonged to her clan: the mother's brother was more important to the
children and more responsible for their training than was their biological
father, who was of another clan. Several language families existed in the
South, but their similiarity is suggested by the fact that the interpreters
accompanying de Soto were apparently able to communicate with Indians
from Florida to Texas, as was Cabeza de Vaca on his long journey from
Florida to Texas and thence to Mexico.

Nevertheless, the pervasive Mississippian tradition was not everywhere
equally dominant. On the western fringes of the South, in present-day central
Texas, for example, it was too dry for the riverine agricultural complex of
corn and beans, and hunting–gathering Indians there depended heavily on
buffalo. In sandy coastal regions, not just near Galveston Island where Cabeza
de Vaca had such unpleasant experiences with hunger, cold, and mosquitoes,
but along much of the Gulf Coast and on the Florida peninsula, the soil
would not support extensive agriculture. As a result, the smaller Indian populations there were heavily dependent on fishing. The southeastern Indians of
the Mississippian tradition had the largest and most settled population in
North America; the Indians of the western plains and the Northeast were
much less agricultural and depended far more exclusively on hunting, fishing, and gathering. The Algonquians of the Powhatan Confederacy of Virginia came from Canada and were a transitional group, being more dependent on hunting than Indians deeper south but more adept at growing corn
than Indians to the north (or the English at Jamestown!).

A typical Indian male of the Southeast in 1500 was more a village-
dwelling farmer than a forest hunter, though there is much evidence that
during certain seasons of the year, when agricultural chores were limited,
southern Indians (especially the men) shifted temporarily into a hunting
mode to supplement their grain diet. Women performed most of the agricultural labor. The bow and arrow had become the primary weapon, and fires
were used both to drive the game toward the hunters and to keep the underbrush cleared so that game—mainly deer—would have good grazing and
could be seen easily by the hunters. Early European explorers and settlers
often remarked on the park-like nature of the forests, with the tall trees
standing clear of underbrush, and occasionally Europeans at sea reported
smelling smoke before land could be sighted. One long-range result of this
Indian practice of burning the woods may be the prominence in much of the
South even today of pine forests, for the thick-barked pine with its seeds that
will germinate on top of the soil can survive fires better than other native
southern trees. The southern pine pulp wood industry of the twentieth cen-

tury may owe its existence at least in part to Indian hunting techniques that predate Columbus's voyages.

Yet the very success of the Mississippian tradition contributed to its decimation in the century after initial European contact. The cold Arctic barrier to Asian microorganisms kept American Indians relatively free of diseases. Consequently the agricultural prowess of the Indians of the South resulted in substantial population growth—their numbers in 1500 probably exceeded two million (more than the population of the South in 1800)—and most of them lived in towns or were in regular contact with others either through attendance at ceremonies or games or via overland traders. The European invaders from the Old World, having been in contact with Asia for centuries and having thereby encountered, suffered from, and gradually domesticated a rich diversity of diseases, unsuspectingly brought with them to the New World a series of plagues to which they were largely immune but to which Indians were pitifully susceptible. The concentration of population promoted the spread of disease among southern Indians. Shortly after 1500 the seaboard South began to receive unwelcome microorganisms from shipwrecked Europeans, interloping slavers looking for Indians to capture, and explorers and would-be colonizers under the flags of Spain, France, and England; and almost at once diseases previously unknown to the Indians began to wreak havoc with their populations and societies. De Soto reported Indian towns ravaged by disease by 1540. The resulting epidemiological disaster might very well have halved the total southern Indian population by the time Jamestown was settled in 1607—certainly the Indian cultures were seriously crippled before permanent English settlement began. That Indian cultures nevertheless evolved and survived in part at least is testimony to their resilience. The Indian population continued to drop precipitously, falling to around 200,000 by 1685 and plunging further to less than 60,000 in 1790, about 3 percent of the pre-Columbian population.

THE OLD WORLD DISCOVERS THE NEW

This largely unintentional demographic disaster might suggest otherwise, but European exploration and settlement of the North American mainland in general and the South in particular was slow, halting, and essentially unsuccessful for more than a century. Columbus, of course, never reached the northern mainland; it was almost a decade after his 1492 contact with West Indian islands before even the peninsula of Florida was known by Europeans to exist, and they did not suspect at first that it was connected to a whole continent to the north. Not until Juan Ponce de León sailed along its eastern shore and rounded the tip in 1513 was its size comprehended. Before the possibilities of Florida and the mainland were understood, the Spanish discovered the wealth that could be obtained first in Mexico under Hernando Cortés, Marqués de Valle, in 1519 and later in the Andean highlands at the ruthless hands of Francisco Pizarro. For a hundred years or more Spain's attention was directed toward the fabulously rich gold mines of Mexico and South America. The initial Spanish settlements and port towns of the Caribbean were little more than provision stations for the vessels transporting Europeans to the fortune-producing regions and returning from there with cargoes of treasure to the mother country. The exploration and initial settlement of the American South occurred almost as an afterthought, was of secondary concern, and came to be considered of some importance only when tentative French and English explorations along the southeastern seaboard in the 1560s posed a potential threat to the Spanish seaborne commerce that normally sailed via the Gulf Stream northward from Cuba and then skirted the Florida and Carolina coasts before turning eastward to Spain.

Spain did not completely forget the region between Florida and Mexico in the fifty years after its mining operations in South America began, but the arduous explorations into the region and the several short-lived attempts to establish permanent toeholds proved extraordinarily unpromising. Ponce de Léon himself made a futile attempt at settlement with two hundred colonists on the Gulf Coast of the Florida peninsula in 1521, but fierce Indian opposition (Ponce de Léon was wounded by an arrow) brought a quick end to the planting. Later that year Lucas Vásquez de Ayllon made a quick and illegal incursion on the Atlantic Coast of Florida seeking Indians to enslave, and his appetite for permanent settlement of the mainland was whetted. Five years later, having sailed along the southeastern coast as far north as Cape Fear, he landed with five hundred Spanish men and women, numerous black slaves, and livestock at a location between present-day Savannah and St. Helena Sound (in South Carolina) and established a town called San Miguel de Gualdape, but again spirited Indian opposition along with disease soon forced the settlement to be abandoned.

In 1528 the red-bearded Pánfilo de Narváez, a former rival to Cortés who, out-generaled in Mexico, sought to recoup his honor in another theater of the New World, came ashore near Tampa Bay with six hundred men, some women, slaves, and friars, planning to conquer and convert the native inhabitants. Harassed once more by Indians, the ill-led expedition, disintegrating as it traveled, finally made its way to the Florida panhandle. In desperation the survivors built four boats and fled from Apalachicola Bay, hoping to make their way along the Gulf Coast back to Mexico. Storms at sea ravaged the makeshift flotilla, and ultimately a handful of explorers, including second-in-command Cabeza de Vaca, wrecked on a low sliver of sand, Galveston Island. After spending some time in coastal Texas as a trader and presumed medicine man, Cabeza de Vaca and three others, including the black Estévanico, set forth westward by foot in 1534, hoping against hope to reach Spanish settlements in faraway Mexico. Two years later, after thousands of miles and incredible adventures, the troupe made contact with Spanish officials on the western coast of Mexico! Gradually Spain was accumulating information—sometimes exaggerated and fallacious—about the land to the north, but as yet it did not invite serious colonization. In 1524 Giovanni da Verrazzano, flying the French flag, sailed southward from New England as far as Cape Fear, and in 1527 the Englishman John Rut skirted the eastern coast from Labrador to the Florida straits, but they landed only temporarily for provisions. Pirate hideouts and shipwrecks brought additional Europeans ashore, but other than spread their diseases to the Indians and thereby convince them that invading Europeans were up to no good, little effect came of these random visits. Such brief, often accidental, sojourns did not alert Europeans to any obvious advantages of occupying the mainland.

Hernando de Soto, wealthy from fifteen years of service in Central America and Peru, also dreamed of power, and despite the horrendous experiences of Spanish explorers in Florida, he imagined an empire there. In 1537 King Charles V granted de Soto a charter to conquer the region at his own expense, with the king due half the gold and precious stones that might eventually be found. On May 25, 1539, de Soto with six hundred soldiers, more than a hundred black slaves, two hundred horses, and three hundred pigs (which were driven along as a slow-moving food supply throughout the subsequent journey) landed in Florida just south of Tampa Bay, beginning what turned out to be a four-year, several-thousand-mile exploratory and plundering escapade stretching from Florida to South Carolina then westward and southward to near Mobile and then, discovering and crossing the Mississippi River, northwestward toward Arkansas, south again into Louisiana, and then west into Texas. De Soto's men overcame extraordinary obstacles of terrain, exhaustion, and occasionally ferocious Indian battles, usually provoked by de Soto's callous mistreatment. While he did not find the kind of bullion wealth he had seen in Peru, de Soto did visit Indians who displayed the highest achievements of the Mississippian tradition: large towns, massive ceremonial mounds, extensive corn fields, and handsomely decorated pottery, gorgets, and deerskin clothes.

De Soto, like most contemporary Europeans, regarded everything he saw—including people—as fair game to take, and as he did he left a trail of enemies and devastation across the South. Well treated by the prospering Cofitachequi of South Carolina, he angered them by kidnapping their queen's niece (de Soto thought she was the queen herself). Soon his brutal reputation preceded him; and Tascalusa, the great chief of the Choctaw Indians near Mobile, by ruse enticed de Soto and his men into a stockade in October 1541 and then attacked them. De Soto lost many men and most of his horses, baggage, and the pearls taken from the Cofitachequi; the Choctaw suffered grievous losses, too, but de Soto's expedition was in complete disarray. It wandered almost without purpose, and the Spaniards continued looking for what they knew not. Fever killed de Soto in May 1542, but his successor, Luis de Moscoso, somehow held the entourage together. After perils and privation Moscoso got them back to the Mississippi, where they built seven boats, stole two Indian dugouts, floated down the river, and ultimately set out into the Gulf. By the fall of 1543 some three hundred survivors, together with a hundred Indian captives, reached Panuco, on the northeastern coast of Mexico, with de Soto's grandiose vision of an empire in tatters. The hardships encountered and the absence of easily obtained riches in the interior of the region permanently discouraged the Spanish from planning significant development there—the area was essentially written off.

By the late 1550s, however, while French privateers were obtaining provisions along the coast of the southeastern mainland and threatening the treasure-laden homewardbound Spanish ships, the Mexican viceroy determined that a clear Spanish presence was needed in the area. Tristán de Luna was chosen to establish a shore base at Santa Elena (present-day St. Helena Sound), and in 1559 Luna's forces entered Florida's Pensacola Bay, expecting to march over land to the South Atlantic coast. A hurricane struck, Luna was forced to move inland, and somewhere near the Alabama River in 1560 he founded a small town settlement; but after about a year (the longest Spanish occupation to that point on the mainland) supplies were exhausted, and evacuation was planned. Luna's authority crumbled, the rescue vessels were delayed, and the expedition foundered. Later in 1561 Spanish naval commander Pedro Menéndez de Avilés entered for the first time the great bay today called the Chesapeake, but Spanish success on the mainland was still ephemeral.

The Spanish concern that France was casting imperial eyes toward the coastal South were not unfounded. For several decades French privateers had operated out of the region, plundering Spanish shipping, but French Huguenots saw a New World colony both as a possible refuge from Catholic persecution at home and an opportunity to strike a blow against Spanish Catholicism abroad. Consequently, in 1562 Jean Ribault, an experienced French pilot, with the tacit approval of the king, set forth with two ships and 150 men, René Goulaine de Laudonnière second in command, intending to plant a permanent Huguenot settlement in striking distance of the Spanish shipping lanes. They first landed at Anastasia Island off Florida and ascended the nearby St. Johns River for a short distance before deciding to move northward. Scouting the coast, they finally entered St. Helena Sound, and there, near the present site of Port Royal, established Charlesfort. Ribault and Laudonnière returned to France to raise more funds and attract more men; the soldiers left at Charlesfort ran out of food, and the resulting starvation led to cannibalism and eventually the collapse of the settlement (an English privateer rescued the survivors and returned them to France). Ribault prepared a report to the French officials in an effort to further his plans, and this report, soon translated into English, gave Queen Elizabeth's subjects their first rosy portrait of the American Southeast.

Supplies and settlers were collected, and in 1564 Ribault and Laudonnière tried again. This time they chose to plant their would-be colony on the banks of the St. Johns River in Florida, establishing Fort Caroline in mid-1564. Food soon ran short again, and the French had difficulty obtaining as much corn as they hoped for from the nearby Saturiba Indians, but the absence of visible Spanish opposition lulled them into false security. The Spanish, however, quickly learned of their presence—a Spanish squadron had already discovered the ruined Charlesfort—and the skilled Pedro Menéndez de Avilés, who had previously explored Chesapeake Bay, on June 29, 1565, left Spain on a mission to locate and destroy Fort Caroline. Two months later he landed at Anastasia Island, naming the site San Agustín, and made preparations to rout the French. Following a preliminary skirmish or two, in late September Menéndez attacked Fort Caroline by land, slaughtering most of the defenders. Luckily for posterity, artist Jacques Le Moyne was one of the few who escaped; his drawings have provided wonderful documentation of Indian housing and clothing. But the abortive French outpost was destroyed, and the vengeful Menéndez completed his mission by reinforcing his initial landing site at San Agustín; this turned out to be the first continuous settlement by Europeans (and a handful of African slaves) on the North American mainland.

Pedro Menéndez may have been brutal, but he was a very able leader and the real founder of the Spanish South. He envisioned a Spanish North American empire sweeping southward from the Chesapeake, around the Florida peninsula, then westward along the Gulf Coast all the way to Mexico. He of course did not succeed in establishing such an empire, but he did transform the defeated Fort Caroline into a Spanish settlement named San Mateo and brought farmers with their livestock there from his home in northern Spain; he reestablished the Spanish presence in the region of Santa Elena by constructing and garrisoning a fort, San Felipe, on Parris Island; and he caused more settlers, slaves, livestock, and provisions to be provided for San Agustín. Menéndez also intended to convert the Indians to Christianity, though his was not a gentle conception of the gospel. Consequently he welcomed Catholic missionaries, fourteen of whom arrived at one time in 1568. Yet the Spanish presence was not without opposition, both from Frenchmen with long memories and from Indians who chafed at the heavy-handed methods of the Jesuit missionaries and the secular settlers whose demands for corn seemed impossible to satisfy. Just the year before, in 1567, the French commander Dominique de Gourgues had re-sacked San Mateo for revenge. By the end of the decade, however, a small chain of Spanish military and missionary outposts were sprinkled along the coast in present-day South Carolina, Georgia (on the sea islands particularly), and Florida. Only San Agustín proved to be permanent, but Spain's claim against rival European powers that she owned and controlled the entire region was reasonably legitimate.

From the viewpoint of strategists back in Spain, Menéndez's envisioned empire was useful primarily as a symbol of Spain's claim to the mainland and as a protector of Spanish shipping interests against English and French pirates and privateers. In reality, the Franciscan missionaries who replaced the Jesuits in 1573 were more successful religious colonizers than military planners. Sir Francis Drake devastated San Agustín when he attacked in 1586 and revealed just how precarious the isolated Spanish garrisons were. (Drake destroyed everything that he did not think useful for the English colony on Roanoke Island off the coast of North Carolina; by the time he arrived there the initial colonizing effort had failed, and Drake took the survivors of Roanoke back to England.) The missionaries through hard experience had learned to temper their demands that the Indians completely give up their own culture and become religious dependents—when pushed too severely the Indians fought back. Under the leadership from 1594 to 1610 of Francisco de Pareja, the Franciscan missionaries effectively created a viable Christian community among the Indians.

Pareja understood the Indians' rule of matrilineal succession and was able to position pious female chiefs in the principal coastal tribes. The Spanish missionaries had long encouraged the Indians to live in towns near the mission centers, and under Pareja each center established a school. Pareja learned the Timucuan language, translated a catechism and a book of religious instruction, and proceeded to train a cadre of Indians. No longer were the Indians seen simply as an obstruction or as suppliers of food; the rudiments of a genuine Spanish-Indian hybrid Christian culture was emerging. Misunderstandings still existed, in part because the Franciscans fully believed their European and Christian ways were superior to Indian ways, but for the time and place the degree of mutuality was notable. In 1606 the bishop of Cuba visited Florida, where more than thirty members of the Franciscan order had prepared approximately two thousand Indians to be accepted by the bishop into the Catholic faith. Florida and Georgia had become more a mission field than a significant cog in the Spanish military and economic empire and as such did not command the level of importance they might otherwise have had in the halls of government. Consequently, even though Spanish officials heard rumors of English colonizing activity to the north first in the mid-1580s and then, more threateningly, in the years after 1607, no effective countermeasures were mounted. And thus the impetus of history shifted to England and the upper South.

ENGLAND ESTABLISHES A NEW WORLD COLONY

Today it seems difficult to comprehend why England for so long was so little interested in the possibilities of the New World. Walter Ralegh (his spelling), an adventurous rascal whose intellect and curiosity roamed all spheres, in 1584 finally received a patent from the Crown for the southern latitudes north of the center of Spanish activity. Ralegh and promoter–publicists, such as the Hakluyts (father and son), little knew what might be found or grown in the region, though they expected that, since its latitude was similar to that of the Mediterranean, it could supply England with Mediterranean products—wine, olive oil, sugar, spices, oranges, and so on. In April 1584, in order to determine the potential of the region, Ralegh sent forth two ships to reconnoiter. The experienced pilot Simao Fernandes on July 13 put the ships in at Roanoke Island. For several weeks the English examined the region, and the artist John White and the young Oxford scholar Thomas Harriot, who were part of the expedition, produced artistic and verbal portraits that would ultimately shape English opinion about the New World. Before departing to England the explorers persuaded two young Indians, Manteo and Wanchese, to return with them in order to learn English.

Once in England, Ralegh used his own charm, the testimony of White and Harriot, and the appeal of Manteo and Wanchese to drum up support for his New World plans. He courted Queen Elizabeth by naming the region Virginia in her honor, but the Virgin Queen offered only a ship and some supplies, not the full energetic support of the government. Nevertheless, in the spring of 1585 another expedition set forth, under the command of Sir Richard Grenville with Ralph Lane, who had relevant experience in Ireland as governor of the colony. After a series of small blunders, 108 men were eventually landed on Roanoke Island in the late summer of 1585; Lane and the men built a fort and associated cottages, expecting reinforcements in both men and supplies in 1586. Food shortages soon developed, however, then discontent, so that when Sir Francis Drake arrived in June 1586, exuberant from having leveled San Agustín, Lane and the cheerless survivors forsook the infant colony and returned to England. Within a few weeks Lord Grenville and the long-awaited reinforcements arrived, but the settlers had abandoned Roanoke. Lord Grenville stationed a small party of men there essentially to serve as placeholders, but in truth Ralegh's initial colony had failed.

That might have ended the matter, but Thomas Harriot had already begun in early 1587 to write glowingly of the prospects for colonization, and John White seemed absolutely enamored of the place. Harriot and others began to tout the pleasures of smoking tobacco, which they saw as an exportable crop. Ralegh was reengaged, several influential merchants put up

Fig. 1. A drawing of Indian settlers in Virginia, as seen by Ralegh's expedition in 1585. (Theodor de Bry, engraving after the water color by John White, 1590; The British Library)

funds, and in May three vessels set sail again, with John White the appointed leader. The intention was to visit Roanoke, pick up the few men left by Lord Grenville the previous summer, then seek a better location somewhere in the Chesapeake. At the last moment the pilot, Fernandes, blaming the lateness of the season but probably eager to return to plundering Spanish shipping, refused to carry them beyond Roanoke, so White and the settlers set about refurbishing the homes left by the initial colonists. Shortly thereafter, on August 24, White's daughter Eleanor, who had married one of the company assistants, Annias Dare, gave birth to a daughter, christened Virginia, the first English child born in the New World. Three months later John White left his beloved colony and family members to return to England to arrange for additional settlers and supplies.

As fate would have it, war soon broke out between Spain and England, and all available ships and trained personnel were required to prepare for the expected Spanish Armada and, after its defeat, to guard against reprisals. Three long years elapsed before White could return to Roanoke. Finally, on August 18, 1590, he and his reinforcements arrived at the fort. It was deserted, the houses were burned, and only the word CROATOAN was found carved on a door post. Since the agreed-upon symbol of distress was not located, the settlers had presumably moved southward a few miles to Croatoan Island (now called Ocracoke). After White had not returned within a few months or even a year, the Roanoke survivors might very well have moved north toward the Chesapeake. There is some evidence that the so-called Lost Colonists lived among the Chesapeake Indians near the James River and intermarried with them until they perished in the 1606 massacre of the Chesapeakes by the Powhatan Indians on the very eve of the planting of the first permanent English settlement nearby.

Ralegh's abortive colony at Roanoke was to have an immense influence. Even as its remaining settlers were perhaps contemplating moving to Croatoan Island, in England Thomas Harriot was publishing *A briefe and true report of the new found land of Virginia* (1588), which played up the potential of the new land; within two years the younger Richard Hakluyt had brought out his *Principall navigations of the English nation* (1589) and, under the auspices of Theodor de Bry in Frankfurt, a full-fledged illustrated report (1590) utilizing the words and illustrations of Harriot and White. Alert Englishmen now had available persuasive rationales for moving more energetically toward establishing a New World empire to rival Spain's. The Lost Colonists were also not forgotten, either in literature or by adventurers; several voyagers, perhaps even Christopher Newport, sailed along the coast and into the Chesapeake Bay searching for them. Perhaps it was this experience that would lead Newport, in 1607, to command the *Susan Constant*, the *Godspeed*, and the *Discovery* into the bay and up the James River.

Certainly it was a collection of old hands from the Roanoke adventures—Ralegh, Harriot, Richard Hakluyt the Younger, Sir Thomas Smith, and others—who stoked merchants' interests in the commercial possibilities of a new settlement in Virginia. The movement gathered in momentum until it led in 1606 to a royal charter establishing two joint stock companies, the Plymouth and the London, under a common council. While the Plymouth Company was assigned roughly the northern half of the coast, the grant of the London Company (more commonly called the Virginia Company) lay to the south, between the 34th and 41st degrees of latitude. Hopes mounted, commercial prospects were considered and profits anticipated, funds were raised, settlers were signed up, and on December 20, 1606, the three ships, with Captain Newport in overall command, raised anchor and made their way down the Thames, the Atlantic and the New World before them. Four months later the small convoy entered the Chesapeake. Two weeks were spent seeking a site that seemed hidden from easy Spanish discovery and at the same time easily defensible. On May 13, a location was selected, a small peninsula on the north bank of the James River, sixty miles inland from Cape Henry. Here, at what turned out to be a swampy, unhealthful site, Jamestown was established.

The four-month voyage from England was relatively uneventful; only 1 of the 105 passengers died (39 of the 144 on board the three ships were crew members). Bickering developed among the leaders, however, and John Smith was put under arrest on the ship. Once the settlers were ashore and opened the Virginia Company's sealed directions, they found that Smith had been appointed by officials back in London to be one of the company officers—the resulting friction between the strong-willed, arrogant, and usually practical Smith and other officers plagued the fledgling colony for years. But there was work to be done. Quickly the men set about building a triangular fort, a company storehouse, a church, and a series of huts, and just as promptly the nearby Paspahegh Indians indicated their opposition. As one of the company officials wrote, "The people used our men well until they found they began to plant & fortefye, Then they fell to skyrmishing & killed 3 of our people." Apparently, at first the Indians thought this was but another of those European temporary visits for ship repair and provisioning. When they realized that the intruders intended to stay, Indian hospitality was withdrawn.

The several Indian tribes were loosely joined together into the Powhatan Confederacy, and as Chief Powhatan of the Pamunkey tribe came to understand the English mission, he became increasingly unfriendly. But for a while Powhatan's people traded corn to the men of the fort, many of whom, being soldiers, perfumers, goldsmiths, and the like, were unable and unwilling to till the soil even at the pain of starvation. In those first few weeks the marsh-like peninsula was aswarm with activity, with some corn being planted and preliminary explorations made. The well-intentioned but inept Edward Maria Wingfield was chosen president of the colony, and on June 22 Captain Newport weighed anchor for England, planning to bring back more colonists and supplies to what he expected to be a thriving community.

When Newport returned on January 2, 1608, he found only 38 survivors from the original 104 colonists. Internal feuding had disrupted the settlement, many of the men were extraordinarily ill-chosen as pioneers, there were shortages of food, troubles with the Indians, and rampant disease. Probably the leading causes, then and for a decade, of the demoralizingly high death rates were typhoid, dysentery, and salt poisoning, all exacerbated by the ecology of Jamestown. The James was a tidal river, meaning that its broad mouth was essentially a part of the saltwater Chesapeake Bay. As the tide rose, the water level of the lower James rose, and salt water mixed with fresh water made the river brackish for miles inland. In the winter and spring the heavier flow of fresh water meant good drinking water for Jamestown, but in the drier summer months the flow slackened and salt water seeped westward past the settlement. Not only did the salt penetrate the land and contaminate the wells that were later dug, but the boundary between salt water and fresh water in the river served as a plug that, worsened by the rightward deflection of the current caused by the earth's rotation, trapped organic wastes and fecal matter along the shore of the settlement—spreading the typhoid and dysentery epidemics late each summer, diseases that provide very little subsequent immunity to former victims. The slow salt poisoning also led to lassitude and irritability, precisely the traits that the beleagured colony least could afford.

Luckily for the Virginia Company, Captain John Smith took charge of the Jamestown colony in 1608. John Smith was a man who still looms larger than life, in part because of his brilliantly boastful prose and in part because his skill, courage, and charisma largely justified his arrogance. Before coming to the New World in his late twenties he had experienced incredible adventures in eastern Europe, but nothing he did was more important than holding the Jamestown colonists together, almost against their will, in 1608. He forced them to work building houses and planting corn, persuaded the Indians to supply still more corn, dispersed some of the settlers away from the deadly Jamestown peninsula, and explored the lower reaches of the Chesapeake. On one of his earlier scouting journeys in 1607 he had been captured and imprisoned by an Indian chief named Opechancanough, brother of Powhatan. Smith already had learned the Indian language, and when he was brought to Powhatan, he soon gained the chief's favor. After a ritualistic mock sacrifice (an event Smith later extrapolated into the chief's favorite daughter, Pocahontas, saving him by throwing herself between him and a menacing weapon), Smith was accepted into the tribe and eventually brought back to Jamestown. Smith capitalized on this experience to improve relations with the Indians, at least as long as he was the commander.

Under the leadership of Smith the colony limped along, helped by a visit in June 1609 of a vessel captained by Samuel Argall who sold the men wine and biscuits, a welcome relief from their monotonous diet. Earlier in the year the Virginia Company had been given a revised charter that broadened the boundaries of their New World claim and strengthened the role of the company's governor. With firmer recognition from the crown the Virginia Company was transformed from simply a private investment to a royal venture, and Jamestown's success became a point of national pride. New investors in the company were secured—they promptly elected Thomas West, Lord De La Warr, as governor—and additional settlers, including women and children, were attracted.

In May 1609 the 600 or so new settlers, men and women, aboard nine ships with the new interim governor, Sir Thomas Gates, set sail for Virginia, but a hurricane disrupted the journey and shipwrecked Sir Thomas and the passengers of his ship on Bermuda. They thrived on the island and gave William Shakespeare the plot for *The Tempest*, but Gates's arrival at Jamestown was delayed for almost a year. One of the smaller ships sank in the storm. Meanwhile, six of the remaining ships in the convoy made it to the Virginia colony in August 1609, having brought too few supplies and arrived too late in the season to plant additional corn. The seventh ship, the *Virginia*, reached the settlement two months later. The result of this augmentation of seven ships and approximately 300 new colonists was disastrous, and disease, famine, and perennial bickering once again nearly destroyed the colony. Much of the precious food supply was commandeered for the ships' crews on their return voyage to England, further crippling the colony.

Opposition to Smith arose, which he probably could have overcome but for a gunpowder explosion that wounded him so seriously that he was forced to return to England in October, leaving approximately 350 colonists behind in Virginia. With his steady hand gone, the affairs of the colony quickly deteriorated: the coming winter became known as "the starving time," and by May 21, 1610, when Sir Thomas Gates finally arrived from Bermuda, only about 60 settlers survived at Jamestown (Ironically, another three dozen or so colonists had earlier moved downstream to Point Comfort, and they apparently had sufficient food. The settlers at Jamestown, including at least four women and two children, were too ill to travel to Point Comfort for supplies, and the few able-bodied men, fearful of Indian attack, could not leave the women and children unprotected at Jamestown in order themselves to go to Point Comfort for food.). The situation looked so bleak at Jamestown itself that Gates decided to abandon the colony. By June 7 all were aboard the four small ships available, leaving Jamestown abandoned and the grand experiment failed. Unbeknownst to them, the day before, Lord De La Warr, with three ships, more settlers, and an abundance of supplies had entered the mouth of the James River; the next day he met the evacuees and they all turned around and returned, reestablishing Jamestown on June 8, 1610.

Lord De La Warr provided effective leadership, putting the men at Jamestown once more to purposeful work, even developing three small settlements away from the unhealthful peninsula. De La Warr also communicated optimism to company officers in London, news they were able to use to gain additional settlers and supplies. Illness forced De La Warr to return to England in March 1611, but Sir Thomas Gates replaced him as governor and brought another capable leader, Sir Thomas Dale, to serve as marshall. These two experienced military men vigorously enforced the new company disciplinary code, the *Lawes Divine, Morall and Martiall* (1612), and though disease continued to take a heavy toll, gradually the colony was learning to grow corn and beans in the Indian style. Relations with Powhatan improved somewhat, especially after 1614 when one of the colonists, John Rolfe, married Pocahontas. Still the long-term economic base of Jamestown was clouded, but in 1614

Rolfe also sent the first four barrels of cured tobacco leaves to England, heralding the economic salvation of the Virginia Company.

English gentlemen and trend-setters since Sir Walter Ralegh in the late 1580s had fancied tobacco, but they preferred the sweet-scented leaf grown in the Spanish Indies to the harsh "byting taste" left by the smallish plant grown by Indians in the vicinity of Jamestown. Rolfe saw an opportunity before him. He began in 1612 to experiment with growing different varieties of the West Indies species on Virginia soil and trying out various methods of curing the leaves so they could be shipped to England. After two years of trial and error he produced a crop he deemed exportable. Sir Thomas Gates himself took the four barrels with him to England and found a ready market. The Virginia tobacco was still inferior to that of the Spanish islands, but it did sell and the demand for it seemed inexhaustible. Local company officials soon had every available hand and every cleared acre, even the roads, devoted to the cultivation of the habit-forming weed that King James fiercely denounced, and by 1618 the Jamestown settlers shipped almost fifty thousand pounds of tobacco to England. Ironically, while overemphasis on growing tobacco at first worsened the tendency not to grow enough food in the colony to allay occasional starvation, soon the need to seek more tobacco land forced the settlers to spread up the James River and away from disease-ridden Jamestown peninsula, ultimately improving the chances for survival.

Of course no one could foresee in 1614 the ultimate result of perfecting tobacco cultivation, much less the health implications of its use, but prescient company officials such as Sir Edwin Sandys could see that those living in Virginia needed greater incentive. Until 1617 the Virginia Company owned all the land in the colony, and the profits, if there were ever to be any, would be distributed to company investors. The actual settlers consisted of investors and company servants working to pay off their transportation costs, but there was no individual ownership of land. In 1617 the company changed the rules and granted 100 acres of land outright to all freemen who had arrived before 1616, with company servants receiving their land after fulfilling their terms of service. As an incentive to new investors, they were to be granted 100 acres for each share purchased in the company and—to increase immigration and staple crop production—would receive the right to patent (obtain) after a small fee an additional 50 acres for every tenant or servant whose passage to Virginia they paid. This head-right system, so called because land was granted per "head" imported to the colony, raised funds for the company, caused a huge increase in the number of persons settled in Virginia, and provided a strong incentive for those of wealth and success to see their future in terms of the long-term development of Virginia. A formula for success had been found even if its ultimate implications were still imperfectly understood: with more land one could grow more tobacco and with the profits transport more servants, for which one received more land on which to grow more tobacco.

Hence the mechanism for transforming the colony from an experiment into a thriving reality had been found.

More reforms were forthcoming. Sir Edwin Sandys became head of the Virginia Company in 1618 and pushed for further changes. Not yet convinced that tobacco would be the boom crop it turned out to be but sure that the path to prosperity involved staple crops of some sort, Sandys sought to attract even bigger investors to Virginia. Experienced colonists were given huge grants of land and local political authority if they would develop large-scale plantations, and the promoters who responded founded such mini-colonies as Berkeley and Flowerdew plantations. Sandys also realized that the draconian military discipline of the *Laws Divine, Morall and Martiall* had to be moderated and the rule made more similar to that in the mother country. A new governor, Sir George Yeardley, was appointed, and when he arrived in 1618 to take office he brought a new governmental plan. The various settlements and independent plantations were directed to elect representatives, or burgesses, to meet in Jamestown with Yeardley, and on July 30, 1619, the group assembled in the church for five sultry days to debate and make laws for the colony (subject to the approval of the company in London). Thus was begun the tradition of local representative government in the English New World colonies.

Sandys further recognized that for Virginia settlements to prosper and to be more like home, a significant number of women had to be available as wives. Never one to delay, Sandys arranged for a shipload of ninety marriage-able women to arrive in Virginia within the year; they chose husbands who only had to repay the company the cost of their transportation from England. Another portent of the future was the arrival of a Dutch man-of-war, desperate for provisions, in the James in 1619. These Dutch traded twenty-odd "Negars" for necessary food and water. There may have been several blacks already in the colony, and practically nothing is known of what befell these clearly documented arrivals of 1619, except that full-blown slavery did not evolve for another half century. But the simultaneity of the arrival in the same year of representative government and black laborers should escape no one's sense of irony.

Nor should the reforms of the decade following John Rolfe's initial experimentation with the tobacco plant mislead us into thinking that the colony was finally on a smooth path to prosperity for the stockholders of the Virginia Company. Dissension still characterized the local government, disease and famine continued to plague the struggling population, and profits remained a dream. At least, following Rolfe's marriage to Pocahontas, Indian relations seemed better. But Pocahontas suddenly died in 1617, her father Powhatan followed her to the grave the following year, and his brother Opechancanough, with an abiding hatred of Europeans, succeeded him as the great chief of the Indian confederacy. The gradual growth of the

Jamestown colony persuaded Opechancanough of the fundamental threat the Europeans posed to the Indian culture, and he carefully bided his time, waiting for the right moment to strike back in a concerted effort that he hoped would drive the invaders from his soil for all time.

Friday, March 22, 1622, was the day chosen for the attack, and the Indian warriors struck with intentional vengeance, killing 347 settlers, a third of the colony's white population. The suddenness and ferociousness of what was labeled the "Massacre" stunned the settlers, then they responded with equal ferocity in a bitter war that continued for half a decade. (Twenty-two years later an aged Opechancanough made one last effort to eradicate the European settlement, but by then the strengthened whites were able to smash the Indian uprising with such finality that thereafter Indians posed no threat to the colony's survival.) The Virginia colony survived, but its near annihilation was the final straw to company stockholders back in England who had been misled by Sandys into thinking the experiment was closer to bringing returns on their investments. Even King James was disgusted and initiated a suit in 1623 that resulted in the Virginia Company's charter being voided. James was moving toward putting the colony under direct royal control when he died on March 27, 1625, and six weeks later King Charles I, his successor, proclaimed Virginia to be a royal colony.

For the next half century Virginia was at the periphery of the Crown's attention, and in the shadow of this neglect the colony developed its own governmental institutions while its economy solidified on the basis of tobacco and its population finally began to show sustained growth, increasing from about 1,500 whites in 1626 to a total white and black population in the mid-1670s of slightly more than 40,000. King Charles did not specify that the Virginia Assembly, dating from 1619, was to continue to be called into session, but the first royal governor, Sir Francis Wyatt, and his successors did in fact call the burgesses to meet. Whatever royal officials might have thought in England, the General Assembly's lawmaking functions were useful on the local scene, and recognition of its utility caused Virginia leaders to pressure Charles into legally sanctioning it in 1639. Actually, the General Assembly had three constituents—the royal governor, his appointed Council, and the elected burgesses. At first the Council served as the basic court for the colony and sat with the burgesses, but by the middle of the century the Council began meeting separately and gave up its jurisdiction over lesser civil cases to county courts. In 1634 Virginia was divided into eight counties, each of which had local officials, such as a sheriff, justices of the peace, constables, and a clerk to record wills, deeds, and court proceedings. The county court had first jurisdiction over most civil cases, and the Council sitting as the "Quarter Court" had jurisdiction over felonies.

The county as a unit of government and its institutions and officers became the focus of colonial life. Courts soon performed a variety of administrative as well as judicial functions; serving as sheriff or justice of the peace became the normal stepping-stone by which rising leaders—determined by wealth, family, and character—gained experience and support for election to the House of Burgesses; and the emerging legal system, based on English common law adapted to the local situation, gradually created among the increasingly far-flung settlers a tenuous sense of community that directed their loyalties away from the Crown and Parliament and toward the House of Burgesses. The House of Burgesses itself, now sitting separately from the Council and made up of locally elected representatives whose interests were primarily local, gradually expanded its functions, responsibilities, and autonomy. The locus of government came inevitably to be the county and the representatives in Jamestown. Sir William Berkeley, the royal governor from 1642 to 1676, acquiesced to these developments and in fact tended to identify with the interests of the colonists.

MARYLAND

Virginia was not the only colony to be caressed by the gentle waves of the broad Chesapeake or the only English settlement whose success was dependent upon European addiction to tobacco. But the background of the planting of this other colony to the north was different. George Calvert, a young Oxford graduate, quickly gained the favor of King James I and rose through a series of appointments to become Secretary of State and gain a lucrative pension. Long inclined toward overseas enterprises and an early investor in the Virginia Company, Calvert in 1620 bought stock in a syndicate planning a colony in Newfoundland, and for several years thereafter he devoted himself and a part of his fortune to a vain attempt to develop a settlement named Avalon there. In 1625 he announced his conversion to the Catholic faith and had to resign his government position, though James raised him to peerage as Lord Baltimore. Thereafter Calvert, Lord Baltimore, began to plan a colony in warmer regions both to augment his fortune and to serve as a refuge for fellow Catholics.

He pressed the king for a charter granting him land somewhere in the Chesapeake and even went out to Jamestown to scout the territory in advance. But Calvert's Catholicism made him unpopular, and even the king resisted his entreaties. Calvert was persistent, by now thinking of a site north of the Potomac in the region he had named Maryland to honor Queen Henrietta Maria. At last, just several days before his death in April 1632, Calvert's request passed the first hurdle, the privy seal. Two months later, on June 20, 1632, the charter was bestowed to his son, Cecilius Calvert, Lord Baltimore, granting the younger Calvert as proprietor practically imperial authority over a domain of almost seven million acres, reaching from the Potomac northward to the fortieth parallel; in return for this virtual kingdom, Lord Baltimore and his descendants were to pay the king, each Easter, two arrowheads in rent—this was more like a feudal fiefdom than a modern joint-stock company.

Calvert promptly began organizing to get his project underway, raising money, recruiting settlers, and arranging for transport. Finally, on November 22, 1633, aboard the *Ark* and the *Dove*, the 150 passengers—including two Jesuits (members of a Catholic order established in 1534 and devoted especially to missionary work)—left the familiar coast of England and set out for the shores of the Chesapeake some three thousand miles distant. Four months later, Annunciation Day by the church calendar, March 25, 1634, the tiny convoy anchored off St. Clements Island near the tip of the broad land mass between the mouth of the Potomac and the bay proper of the Chesapeake, and there erected a huge cross fashioned from the trunk of a tree. Within days Calvert was exploring the banks of the Potomac and found a likely location where the St. Mary's River emptied into the Potomac. The friendly Yaocomico Indians bartered the site, including their wigwams and planted cornfields, for an assortment of metal tools and bolts of cloth. Thus the Maryland settlers, spared the privations of the early Virginians and able instantly to take advantage of the European demand for tobacco, whose cultivation and marketing the Virginians had pioneered, were with relative ease able to develop a thriving, prosperous colony.

Maryland did not develop as an exact replica of Virginia—the presence of a minority of Catholics caused some differences, including the famous Act of Toleration of 1649 whose primary purpose was to guarantee toleration by the majority Protestants of the Catholics for whose benefit in part the colony was originally settled. But the Maryland story is remarkably similar to that of the older colony to its south. For example, the local Maryland Assembly grew in authority, officially became a body separate from the Council in 1650, and came to defend provincial interests against the proprietor as did the Virginia House of Burgesses against royal interference. A system of local counties, with the usual officers, was organized, and a strong local court system developed. Eventually the Anglican Church was established as the official, state-supported religion in Maryland (1702) as it had earlier been in Virginia (1610). In both colonies, there being no resident bishop, the local vestrymen came to control the churches, recruiting ministers, managing the church finances, and caring for the poor. These vestrymen—local planters of at least some wealth and good family—were of the sort who often progressed from being justices of the peace to assemblymen, and as such their religious and governmental leadership cemented their dominance of local affairs. These men, pragmatic and localistic in their concerns, identified with the needs of those involved in commercial agriculture—tobacco—and helped set the tone of colonial Chesapeake society.

CREATING A TOBACCO ECONOMY IN THE CHESAPEAKE COLONIES

The cultivation, marketing, and fluctuating price of tobacco in large part shaped the history of the Chesapeake region. *Nicotiana tabacum* required a great deal of human effort to grow, and planters had to devise a labor system to provide and control the necessary workers. At first, white indentured servants from England were the laborers of choice, making possible the tobacco boom of the mid-seventeenth century that finally proved the region had a viable economic future. Then, by 1700, black slaves came to dominate the labor market and changed forever the future of the South. The marketing mechanisms that arose to sell the tobacco obviated the need for urban centers, though changes in the eighteenth century brought the development of small commercial villages. The ups and downs in the price tobacco growers received for their output led to efforts to increase productivity, regulate the quality of the tobacco marketed, and seek crop diversification. Hence the growing and selling of tobacco affected nearly every aspect of life in the Chesapeake.

A tobacco planter first had to clear the field of trees, often only girdling them Indian fashion and cultivating amid the dead trunks. Then, apart from the main fields, a rich bed was prepared for the tobacco seeds, taking care to protect the tender plants once they sprouted from the frost by covering them with cloths or leaves. The actual fields were formed by using a heavy hoe to mound the soil into small hills—again, Indian fashion—arranged in rows; when the weather was warm enough, the slips from the seedbed were transplanted to the hills. Then the fields had to be worked with hoes to keep weeds from taking over, and tobacco worms, green-horned little monsters with voracious appetites, had to be picked off the maturing tobacco plants. Secondary shoots called "suckers" grew from the base of the stalks, and these had to be cut away else they steal nutrients from the parent plant. Toward the end of the summer, the full-grown stalks were cut and hauled to curing barns to be dried, and, after the proper amount of curing, the leaves were picked off and carefully packed in wooden barrels called hogsheads that, fully loaded, often weighed over five hundred pounds. The whole process took from February to November, each step required tedious labor, and the timing of each stage—when to transplant the slips, for example, or how long to cure the leaves—determined the quantity and the quality of tobacco produced. The crop put a premium on both menial labor and agricultural skill. Successful planters, understanding the role their skill played in producing a profitable crop, grew in self-confidence and optimism, increasingly sure of their ability to make decisions about a wide range of human activities.

Not even John Rolfe could have estimated the English and European demand for tobacco, first to be smoked in pipes, then, as fashions changed, consumed as snuff. Initially, tobacco was an expensive luxury item, but the growth in the Chesapeake production (from four barrels in 1614 to sixty-five thousand pounds annually in the early 1620s to more than twenty million pounds per year by the 1670s) resulted in a very significant reduction in its price. As the cost fell, consumption increased, seemingly without end.

Productivity gains by Chesapeake tobacco growers, however, made up for the falling price per pound. The pioneer planters sought to meet the growing demand and did everything they could to increase production. But since tobacco was such a labor intensive crop, the most severe obstacle to expanded production was the lack of available hands to work in the fields.

In Virginia the English population had not grown rapidly enough to provide surplus workers; the Indians, understandably unfriendly and their numbers decreasing rapidly because of disease, provided no ready source of labor. The English were aware of slavery, including the bondage of Indians and Africans, but they associated slavery with "backward" Mediterranean and Catholic societies like Spain and were determined not to succumb to such practices. After all, more than a century of sustained population growth in England itself, combined with the agricultural revolution that forced hundreds of thousands of former serfs off the manors, had produced what many English observers called a massive surplus population. Indeed, one of the rationales that publicists such as the Hakluyts had advanced for erecting overseas empires was that they could absorb these "surplus" people and put them to productive work. The English strongly preferred to replicate in the New World as much of the homeland as they could, including familiar English workers who shared their language and folkways. Slavery was deemed "un-English," at least by the molders of opinion—hard-pressed tobacco growers in Virginia may have been somewhat less fastidious about the race or status of their workers. Through the apprenticeship system and debt peonage, the English had experience with forced labor—the labor of a person controlled by another for a set term of years until an obligation was met. This prior experience, combined with the head-right system that granted land to those who could transport people to the colony, provided a way to solve the labor shortage in Virginia and Maryland caused by the demand for tobacco.

In the course of the half century following 1630, about seventy-five thousand white men, women, and children came to the Chesapeake region from England, and perhaps as many as three-fourths of the migrants came as indentured servants. These servants had their transportation provided to Virginia or Maryland; once there, the indenture—essentially a legal agreement to work for a set number of years determined by a person's age, gender, and skills—was purchased by a landowner who then, while recognizing certain basic rights of the servant, could set the servant to work at any task the landowner chose until the cost of the indenture was paid off. Since the purchaser of the indentured servant's labor received a free grant of land for each person brought to the colony under indenture, and since the profits that could be earned by growing tobacco allowed the planter to repay the cost of his investment in two years or less, the region was at last primed to boom. And boom it did; planters clamored for additional land and servants and every effort was made to maximize efficiency and profits.

Indentured servants were drawn from a wide swath of English society. Some were the younger sons and daughters of the lower gentry class and others were paupers; the majority lay between these extremes, though more toward the lower end of the spectrum. The great majority were young men, who outnumbered women servants by about four to one. The population boom that England had enjoyed since 1450 had decreased opportunities at home and lowered wages; young men and women saw several years of labor in the Chesapeake as an acceptable burden to bear in order to obtain their own land and a chance to make a better life. The lack of economic opportunity in England was severe enough to cause young workers to leave the world they knew and risk disease, overwork, potential abuse, and perhaps death in a strange new world.

The life that many found here was worse than they had anticipated. Illness brought death to many before they ever fulfilled the terms of their indenture, and occasionally ruthless and unprincipled planters took hard advantage of them. The work was often unremitting and difficult; the climate could be infernally hot and muggy in the summer and bone-chillingly cold in the winter; insects bedeviled workers and made sleep sometimes almost impossible; and the virtual loss of contact with friends and loved ones back in England led to homesickness and despair. The groupings of servants on farms and plantations were typically quite small, and visiting with servants on other plantations, separated not simply by miles but by vast forests scarcely penetrated by roads and by innumerable creeks and rivers not yet bridged, was a daunting task. Localized community life often emerged, but in spite of adversity. The broad tidal rivers, whose mouths were many miles wide for a long distance inland, divided the tidewater region into long, narrow peninsulas of land (called necks), further isolating the scattered outposts of settlement. The vastly uneven sex ratio, at least for the first two or three generations, aggravated by the paucity of roads and resulting isolation, meant that many indentured servants, even after gaining their freedom, could never find a spouse and gain the comfort and sense of home that a marital partner and children can provide. One result of this was limited population growth, which of course perpetuated the need to import indentured servants to labor in the tobacco fields.

The Chesapeake of the mid-seventeenth century does not fit the popular stereotype of the colonial South, with magnificent brick mansions lining the James and York rivers, their interiors filled with beautiful furniture and staffed with a retinue of black slaves. Not only were blacks few in number in, say, 1650, with only about a thousand in the entire Chesapeake, but the white planters lived on a scale far below what visits to existing eighteenth-century colonial mansions lead one to expect. Most so-called planters were in truth large farmers who lived in unpretentious houses of perhaps two ground-floor rooms that were sparsely furnished with furniture made by someone on the farm, and the several indentured servants slept in a large attic or in a lean-to attached to the main house. The servants probably took their meals with the planter (and his wife, if he were so lucky to have one), though, if present, a servant woman would do most of the cooking.

On small farms, women did very little field work, even if they were indentured servants. Gathering, washing, and preparing vegetables and fruit for meals was extremely time consuming. The typical farmer's wife may have spent as much as two hours daily grinding corn with a pestle and mortar to make meal. Often cider was brewed, and dairying—milking the cows, churning the butter, making cheese—took hours. Men usually slaughtered the hogs and beeves, but women finished the process by rubbing the meat with salt and then smoking the pork in the chimney and pickling the beef in barrels of brine. Laundry and housecleaning were also strenuous tasks, even though seventeenth-century standards of cleanliness seem to have been quite low. The making and mending of clothes probably occupied most evenings. The farmer's wife supervised the servant girl, if there were one, but performed many of the household chores herself. Certainly the farmer himself supervised the field work of the male servants and worked in the field beside them.

Before about 1660 those indentured servants who survived their period of service could expect, upon gaining their freedom, to purchase land, plant tobacco for themselves, and begin sharing in the prosperity of the tobacco boom; perhaps, if they lived long enough, they could buy the labor of new indentured servants and obtain additional head rights. With more land and more bountiful harvests, the former servants soon began to move up the ladder of social respectability, too. For forty or fifty years, as long as relatively inexpensive land remained available on the waterways, it was possible for at least some former servants to make the transition from servant to freeman to planter. Even those who did not do quite so well came to own small farms, build modest homes—maybe with dirt floors and unglazed windows, but homes, nevertheless, on their own land—an ambition few could entertain back in England. Clearly the more prosperous farmers who were importing indentured servants and patenting more land were in the process of creating a gentry class separate from the masses of farmers, and service as a local justice of the peace or on the vestry cemented their sense of community leadership and provided them with the reputation to solidify that leadership. But the economic difference between the wealthy planters and the middling farmers was less than it would ever be again. This relative equality of social condition and the near universal involvement in the cultivation and marketing of tobacco would later make possible the development of a solidarity of white interests that would shape southern society for three centuries.

Not all white indentured servants were so lucky. Many died before gaining their freedom, and many of those who survived had neither the skill, luck, good health, or ambition necessary to succeed. The price tobacco fetched fell gradually from 1630 to 1680, and while well-managed farms and plantations could always prosper by becoming more efficient, beginning freemen often could not survive the learning curve that such efficiency required. The margin for error was tiny, and one miscalculation or an unfortunate illness or a fire could doom a beginning farmer to failure. For whatever reason one failed, few other chances were offered. One might have to become a tenant farmer or a wage laborer simply to survive, and the surplus income such employment provided seldom allowed one to purchase land or servants. Of course some freemen overcame incredible obstacles and made extraordinary steps up the socioeconomic ladder; more failed and slipped down a rung or two. By 1650 the increasing cost of land near the waterways made economic progress for those at the bottom of the ladder increasingly difficult.

Certainly, by English standards, there was an abundance of land in the Chesapeake, but the thin soil was easily exhausted and tobacco demanded much from the land. After three crops productivity began to fall, and after six to ten years the soil was effectively exhausted. Successful planters and farmers realized very early that obtaining far more land than they could cultivate at any one time was the surest hedge against the day when they would have to abandon their current cropland as "old fields" (soon grown over with hedge grass and scrub pine). Those who could afford to buy more land or to have it granted to them for bringing over indentured servants guaranteed their (and their descendants') future prosperity. Those who were unable to buy the increasingly expensive land either had to find work as tenant farmers or wage laborers or move further west, but there the difficulty of transporting the heavy hogsheads of tobacco mitigated against tobacco culture. Even younger sons of property-owning farmers and planters found it necessary to move westward and southwestward in search of well-situated and arable acres, competing with the declining number of Indians on the frontier for land.

In the Piedmont many small farmers depended more on corn and livestock than on tobacco, though small amounts were grown there. Eventually, those who stayed behind in the Tidewater would, by the mid-eighteenth century, increasingly turn to wheat, which did better on nutrient-poor soil than did tobacco. Many indentured servants served their time only to find that the scarcity of cheap land deprived them of the upward mobility for which they had come to the New World. Freedom meant still more years of working for someone else as a tenant farmer or hired hand; finding a spouse was still difficult. Wasn't life after servitude supposed to mean more than poverty and loneliness? These freemen were understandably restless, frustrated, and not a little alienated from the emerging ruling class of increasingly prosperous planters and farmers who had engrossed most of the land near the waterways.

This discontent caused rebellion in Virginia in 1675 and 1676 and rocked the colony to its core. The trouble began in Stafford County in the Northern Neck between the Rappahannock and Potomac rivers in July 1675 when a group of Indians belonging to the Doeg tribe took some hogs from a white man named Thomas Mathew, whom they claimed had failed to pay them for goods. Mathew and his men promptly chased the Indians, took the hogs back, and killed several Indians to boot. The Doegs retaliated and killed one of Mathew's servants. This outraged Mathew and other whites in the Northern Neck, and with a force of men they went after the Doegs, tricked them into a parley, and murdered a king and ten braves. Almost incidentally the whites then encountered a group of uninvolved Susquehannah Indians and killed fourteen of them before realizing they were not Doegs. The Susquehannahs then retaliated against the Virginians. Sir William Berkeley, the governor of Virginia, sent a militia of Virginians and Marylanders to quell the revengeful Indians, but the Susquehannahs escaped and disappeared into the trackless forests, emerging now and then to vex the whites in hit-and-run attacks. The Indians were too few, all of them combined, to fight the whites now in a frontal attack. These intermittent forays, though, terrorized the whites on the frontier, and they appealed to Governor Berkeley for a swift and effective response.

Governor Berkeley, for his own reasons, decided that a defensive posture was the best policy, and he persuaded the assemblymen in Jamestown to establish a line of forts manned by soldiers recruited from the Tidewater counties. Settlers on the frontier, threatened by the Indians and desiring the Indians' land, wanted to attack them aggressively, having decided that the only good Indian was a dead one. An upstart newcomer to the country, Nathaniel Bacon, emerged as the leader of the party who wanted a more aggressive Indian policy. One of Bacon's indentured servants had been killed in a raid by the Susquehannahs, but more than anger seemed to motivate him in his vengeance toward the Indians. Bacon was an unscrupulous, power-hungry young aristocrat who inflamed popular fear of the "red men" into a frenzy of hatred. He took advantage of this widespread animosity and poor white discontent with the political-economic establishment to weld together a mob to stabilize the frontier by destroying the Indians.

Governor Berkeley distrusted Bacon's ragtag army and believed that friendly Indians benefited the colony. Berkeley discountenanced Bacon's forces and removed him from his seat on the Council, and in order to defuse the tension Berkeley called for the election of a new assembly. Bacon ignored the governor and proceeded to make war against all Indians indiscriminately. This disobedience was more than Berkeley could overlook, so he issued a

"Declaration and Remonstrance," making clear that Bacon was a rebel against the government and hence involved in treason. But supporters of Bacon apparently won the majority of assembly seats. When Bacon himself arrived in Jamestown to take his seat in the House of Burgesses, Berkeley outsmarted and captured Bacon, who then confessed to wrongdoing. Having reestablished his authority, the governor promptly pardoned Bacon—Berkeley did not have the public support to do much else, but he sought to turn his necessity into a victory. Bacon soon left Jamestown and proceeded to crusade against the hapless Indians; when Berkeley again remonstrated, Bacon issued a "Declaration of the People" attacking Berkeley's favorites and calling upon men of every class to plunder and put back in their proper places those individuals who had improperly prospered because of their connection to the governor.

A small-scale but vicious civil war broke out. Both sides offered freedom to the servants and slaves belonging to their enemies, if they joined forces to help crush their former masters. The troubles came to a head when Bacon's forces burned Jamestown to the ground on September 19, 1676. Before the situation could deteriorate much further, Bacon died of dysentery on October 26. Without his leadership the rebellion petered out, for it had no focus beyond killing Indians and aggrandizing Bacon's ego. Bacon's so-called rebellion did show that whites of all classes could be cemented together by their common racism—hatred of Indians. And it showed that social disorder among the whites themselves could get out of hand if the alienated, poor whites, ever increasing in numbers, combined with the scattered black and Indian slaves. The specter of social chaos loomed over the Chesapeake.

In this context of increasing numbers of propertyless white freemen, the labor force in the Chesapeake gradually began to shift toward a dependence on black slaves. The transition was unplanned, halting, and shaped by a variety of factors; the practice of buying blacks as servants for life—slaves—seemed to outrun legal guidelines for a while and forced the assemblies gradually to devise laws that controlled the behavior of the slaves and protected the "property rights" of the slaveholders. No one at the time understood the full implications of the region's development into a slave society. In retrospect, it is clear that a labor force that never became free would not compete for land, that a labor force composed of blacks who were deemed barely human could be controlled with a harshness considered inappropriate for Englishmen, and that the potential threat of a black servile rebellion could be turned into a rationale for all whites of every class to unite to protect their common interests. Clearly the Chesapeake region was in the midst of a change of enormous consequences for its future. But the change came about in a series of small decisions and as the result of impersonal forces that no one fully comprehended. The future is never clearly glimpsed by those about to enter it.

THE RISE OF SLAVERY IN THE CHESAPEAKE COLONIES

The identities and the subsequent histories of the twenty or so blacks who were unceremoniously disembarked in Jamestown in 1619 are unknown; two censuses taken in Virginia in 1624 and 1625 reveal the presence of twenty-two and twenty-three blacks respectively, but their relation to the original number is problematic. The black population increased very slowly, in part because the English colonists had a clear preference for white servants. The Englishmen coming to the New World already felt they were venturing into the unknown and they wanted to hold on to as much of the familiar ways of the motherland as they could. Blacks from Africa seemed to them the strangest possible people—there was even some question about their humanity—and the ethnocentric English, connoting evil and inferiority to *black* people, did not want themselves surrounded by unknown workers who spoke incomprehensible languages. Moreover, the English associated slavery with "backward" Mediterranean societies. Since whites were plentifully available to come to the Chesapeake as indentured servants, there was no reason to shift to the most foreign servants of all. For complex reasons, including the great distance from Africa to the Chesapeake—which increased basic transportation charges—and the strong demand for black slaves in the West Indian sugar islands that drove up their price even more, the initial cost of black slaves was significantly higher than the price of white indentured servants. In the 1620s and 1630s black slaves might live no longer than most whites in the New World, which meant that the slaves' higher price could not be amortized over a lifetime of labor. Cheaper, more familiar, available white servants were the laborers of choice for tobacco growers along the shores of the Chesapeake Bay for more than a half century.

Despite the clear preference for whites, a sprinkling of blacks arrived in the region in the two generations after 1619. The small market for slaves in the region disinclined the large slaving vessels direct from Africa from coming to the Chesapeake and peddling their human cargoes from one isolated plantation wharf to the next. Hence slaves via the West Indian islands usually ended up in the tobacco colonies only as an incidental result of maritime commerce with the Caribbean. But many tobacco growers, knowing the strength of the demand for slaves in the sugar colonies, assumed that only slave rejects or troublemakers would be offered for sale in the Chesapeake, which discouraged them from purchasing those few slaves tendered for sale. Nevertheless, by the late 1650s there were perhaps as many as one thousand blacks in Maryland and Virginia.

The legal status of these blacks varied widely. Some were clearly slaves for life, others were servants for a set term (like white indentured servants) who gained their freedom if they lived long enough, and still others may have arrived free. Some native-born blacks of mixed parentage were declared free by laws establishing legal status according to the status of the father (in Maryland for a few years) or the mother (in Virginia). Still other blacks earned enough money to purchase their freedom or had it bestowed upon them for meritorious service. The court records show that several blacks who had previously been in England, had learned the English language, and had been baptized in the Christian faith successfully sued their owners for freedom. (One of the English rationalizations for enslaving Africans was that they were "heathen"; the logical converse was that Christians, even black Christians, should not be slaves.) But, however they obtained it, freedom was a condition that set black freemen apart from slaves and servants. Free blacks, such as Anthony Johnson of Virginia and later Maryland, could own property, testify in court against whites, vote, serve on juries, pay taxes, borrow money and extend credit to others, be fined and win court decisions against whites, even, for a while, own black and Indian slaves and the indentures of white servants. Not until 1670 did Virginia legislate that "no negro . . . though baptised and enjoyned their owne ffreedome shall be capable of any such purchase of christians [i.e., whites]." This 1670 proscription against black control of white labor was the first flagrant indication of discrimination against free blacks.

The rights extended to free blacks in the first fifty years of their presence in the Chesapeake suggest an openness to the society that contrasts sharply with the racial mores of later centuries. The contrast is even more boldly etched when one examines the relationships between black slaves and white indentured servants in the period before the early 1670s. The huge majority of field workers in the Chesapeake before 1670 were whites, and strong hierarchical attitudes carried over from England caused the land owners and independent farmers to label servants, tenant farmers, and propertyless laborers of all kinds as an undifferentiated "lower sort." The tobacco boom created a exploitative mentality, worsened by the falling tobacco prices throughout the seventeenth century that put a premium upon maximizing efficiency. The tendency among many planters importing indentured servants and engrossing land was to mine the land profligately for several years before abandoning it and to extract as much labor from the white servants with as little expense as possible. Lifetimes were short, the market price of tobacco was falling, and indentures lasted only several years and then the servants were gone. Out of this mixture emerged a callousness toward the servants who were with an owner only temporarily, a harsh, get-it-while-you-can attitude that some Chesapeake planters had previously adopted during a sojourn in Ireland. The first black servants and slaves in the tobacco colonies were cast into this maelstrom of greed and rigorous discipline.

Because there were few blacks scattered amidst a far larger population of white servants and because many of the blacks had already been slaves in the West Indies and had become at least partially acculturated, planters seemed to consider them simply additions to the lower-class work force, with relatively little attention paid to their being black. White servants were less expensive than slaves, so consequently whites were not spared the most difficult or dangerous tasks. In fact, white servants and black slaves (the terms were not clearly differentiated in the early seventeenth century) usually worked together at the same tasks, suffered similar discipline, ate the same food, slept in identical quarters, were subject to the same illnesses, played and caroused together, and ran away together. Masters perceived both as troublesome property that needed constant supervision; black and white laborers tended to see one another as fellow sufferers and friends. Many Africans became quite Europeanized in the mostly white society. These comparatively benign racial relationships continued as long as the black population was small.

English pride in things English became inflated during and after the reign of Elizabeth, with the converse of this pride being an aversion to non-English cultures and people. The English, who disliked even the Irish, hated and were suspicious of the Spanish, and quickly grew shockingly inhumane toward the Indians, certainly were prejudiced against those most foreign of all, the Africans. The Africans' very blackness, associated as that color was in Western culture with evil and terror, made their vast difference from the English only more visible and indelible. Yet such an automatic predisposition to denigrate Africans was more an abstract, superstitious dislike of the unknown and the different—a generalized and passive prejudice—than a systematic racism that shaped every black–white interpersonal relationship. But the existence of this background prejudice surely made easy the acceptance of perpetual slavery for Africans. The Chesapeake planters who bought blacks from the Caribbean or directly from Africa justified their actions as buying people who were already enslaved; the planters rationalized that they were not guilty of putting men and women in bondage but were merely changing the location of where they toiled. For almost a half century the handful of blacks did not threaten the whites or seem so unassimilable and different as to activate the passive prejudice into pervasive racism. That would occur as the seventeenth century came to a close.

By the mid-1660s laws first began to be drawn up that treated black slaves differently. What would be the status of the offspring of interracial sex when one of the parents was a slave? Virginia in 1662 legislated that all children born henceforth as the result of miscegenation would have the legal status of their mother. The children of slave women, stated a Maryland law of 1664, were to serve for life, and those white servant women who married slave men would themselves serve as slaves for the lifetime of their husbands, and any offspring would likewise be slaves (intermarriage itself was not yet made illegal). What would the status of a slave be who could prove he or she was a baptized Christian? Owners' property rights over these Christian slaves were made less precarious in 1667 by a Virginia statute that made clear "that the conferring of baptism doth not alter the condition of the person as to his bondage or freedom." These laws reveal something of the openness of the society before their passage and suggest that attitudes toward blacks were in flux on the eve of their great expansion in numbers.

The evident preference of the English tobacco planters in the Chesapeake for white indentured servant laborers did not alter after 1660, but the available supply and relative cost of both whites and blacks changed significantly. Beginning around 1640 or 1650 the two-century-long population growth spurt in England came to an end, and this meant, slightly less than two decades later, that the age cohort of English most likely to be candidates for indentured servanthood decreased. This drop in population growth was accentuated by the Great Plague that struck England in the mid-1660s. The combined result was a shortening of the supply of workers in England and a marked increase in wages, further increased by the expansion of job opportunities in construction following the Great Fire of 1666 that leveled a huge area of London. There simply came to be fewer young English people who felt it necessary to come to Virginia or Maryland to get ahead. Then and in the decades that followed the development of other colonies—the Carolinas and especially Pennsylvania—there were strong competitors for the decreasing numbers of willing white migrants. Servants became harder to obtain and potential importers had to try to make their condition in the Chesapeake more attractive by shortening their period of service, effectively raising the price of indentured servants. Labor-hungry tobacco planters lowered their qualifications and accepted as servants people they would have refused a decade or so earlier—younger males, more women, Irishmen, the almost totally unskilled laboring poor, and finally, even convicts. In their desperation they reconsidered enslaving the Indians.

In the context of this insufficiency of workers, in 1674 the Royal African Company (the joint-stock company authorized in 1672 to engage in the slave trade) began direct shipments of slaves from Africa to the North American mainland, marginally lowering their costs to planters strapped by low tobacco prices. From that year on, increasing numbers of slaves were sold in the Chesapeake, and, while most were still probably purchased via the West Indies, a larger volume than previously estimated now appears to have been imported directly from Africa. After 1698, when the Royal African Company's twenty-six-year monopoly on the exclusive right to import slaves directly from Africa to the North American mainland was ended by a parliamentary act and numerous enterprising merchants with smaller vessels—more appropriate to the kind of plantation-to-plantation slave peddling that existed in the Chesapeake—entered the trade, the slave imports to the region reached flood-tide proportions. The demand for white indentured servants still existed, but in the midst of their unavailability the planters turned to the increasingly inexpensive African slaves.

As the planters learned when to import slaves so as to minimize their death rates, the comparative costs of slaves amortized over a lifetime of service versus the several years of servants' indentures fell even further. Buying slaves came to be seen not just as necessary but economically advantageous. Slowly it dawned on planters that the offspring of slaves were themselves slaves, an additional advantage. Moreover, slaves never became free to compete for land or grow tobacco independently and further depress the price. Since they came involuntarily, slaves did not have an opportunity to choose the colony to which they would come: they represented a steady source of labor. Planters inadvertently seem to have stumbled upon a solution to a number of their social problems. Beginning in the 1670s slave imports shot upwards, increasing with the passage of years. More were imported between 1695 and 1700 than during the preceding twenty years, and more were imported between 1700 and 1705 than during the preceding eighty-one years. Within a decade the Chesapeake became a slave economy, with enormous implications for everyone involved. By 1700 other regions in the South were also developing a similar labor system, though based on a different staple crop.

CAROLINA: A BARBADIAN COLONY ON THE MAINLAND

The Spanish had early shown interest in settling in what is now South Carolina, but their several attempts to establish outposts near Port Royal Sound had all come to naught. After the English settlement at Jamestown showed signs of success, other Englishmen looked at the territory stretching southward from Virginia to the northern boundary of Spanish Florida, but the civil war that disrupted England diverted attention and investment away from the southeastern coast. Not until the restoration of the monarch in 1660 was England again prepared to entertain colonizing activities to the south of Virginia, and then only because an enterprising and influential group of royal supporters, led by Sir John Colleton, a Barbadian planter, persuaded King Charles II to reward their support of the Crown with a generous gift of land and authority. In 1663 Charles II granted a huge expanse of land, named Carolina in his honor, to eight of his favorites, including Colleton and Sir Anthony Ashley Cooper, later Lord Shaftesbury. Two years later the proprietors were given another charter broadening their governmental authority. (Carolina was divided into North and South Carolina effectively in 1691, officially in 1712.)

The proprietors, hoping to attract settlers, quickly issued a Concessions and Agreements that promised virtually complete self-government to the colony by means of an elected assembly, religious freedom (matched at the time only by Rhode Island), and practically free land based upon a head-right system similar to that in Virginia but giving the early arrivals up to 150 acres for themselves and for each dependent they brought to Carolina. The first attempts in 1665 and 1667 to establish settlements failed, though William Hilton (hence Hilton Head Island) and Robert Sandford were engaged to sail along the coastal region and scout the terrain and waterways for prospective sites for colonization. Sandford left an adventurous young surgeon, Dr. Henry Woodward, in the vicinity of Port Royal in 1666 to indicate the legitimacy of the "purchase" of the Indians' land. Woodward soon learned Indian languages, explored far into the interior, was captured by the Spanish and taken away to San Agustín, was rescued by a pirate, and eventually returned to South Carolina to become an interpreter and mediator between whites and Indians for several decades. His knowledge of the back country and his connections with a variety of Indian peoples laid the background for the lucrative trade in deer skins that proved to be so important to the Carolina economy after about 1690. But in the first years after receiving their charter the proprietors, perhaps inhibited by the Great Plague of 1665 and the Great Fire of London, did little else to advance their empire in Carolina. It was to be Anthony Ashley Cooper who would push the group into action after 1669.

During that year Ashley Cooper (Lord Shaftesbury), helped by his close friend John Locke, composed an elaborate and utopian scheme of government for Carolina, called the Fundamental Constitutions, that combined older conceptions of landed nobility, leetmen (serfs), and restricted representative government with the new idea of religious toleration, but it never was fully put into effect. Turning from ideas to action, Shaftesbury convinced the other proprietors to put up enough money to organize an expedition, which he proceeded to get underway. In August 1669, three ships carrying about one hundred colonists set out from England and, by way of Ireland and Barbados, finally arrived on the Carolina coast just north of present-day Charleston. They slowly worked their way southward to Port Royal, but once there the marsh-like environs and a persuasive Indian convinced them to sail north again to a site on the west bank of the Ashley River—the Indian apparently believed the presence of beholden Englishmen would protect his people from the warlike Westo tribe. Here Charles Town was first established; in 1680 it was moved down river to the tip of the peninsula separating the Ashley and Cooper rivers, where they come together, as latterday Charlestonians love to say, to form the Atlantic Ocean. (Charles Town was renamed Charleston in 1783.)

Most of the eight proprietors had some connection to Barbados, that miniscule English island in the Caribbean that by the mid-seventeenth century was producing fabulous amounts of sugar. The tropical climate and disease-ridden environment of Barbados discouraged white servants, and the wealth easily made possible the purchase of slaves; consequently the labor force of Barbados quickly became African. In 1650 there were 15,000 slaves there, by 1660 the number had climbed to 34,000 only to zoom to 52,000 by 1670, outnumbering the whites (whose numbers had begun falling in 1630) by 8,000 that year. The enormous profits to be earned by sugar cultivation led the wealthiest planters to monopolize practically all the land, squeezing off the island smaller farmers and white servants who had served out their time. So lucrative were the returns from growing sugar that planters ceased growing foodstuffs, finding it more profitable to buy them elsewhere. Hence there was pressure to find both a settlement for displaced Barbadians (some of whom were quite prosperous but in search of new opportunities) and a source of food and lumber products. Those motives shaped the proprietors' plans for Carolina, which was intended in a real sense to be a colony of a colony.

The proprietors focused on the southern portion of Carolina, from Cape Fear to the Savannah River, and they solicited settlers from Barbados and older English colonies to the north, along with Huguenots from France. The colony grew slowly at first, though it never had a starving time as had Virginia, and the pioneer settlers experimented with a variety of products associated with the Mediterranean—silk, olives, grapes, and citrus crops—all of which proved to be failures. Early attempts to cultivate rice and indigo were also unpromising. But soon the colonists found that simply growing mundane foodstuffs—corn, peas, hogs, and cattle—and selling them to provisions-starved Barbados was a sure path to prosperity. Carolina also had bountiful forests; lumber, shingles, and barrel staves found a ready market in the Caribbean. In 1686 Dr. Henry Woodward, who was ill, arrived in Charles Town carried on a litter, and accompanying him from a long trek in the Indian territories to the west were one hundred and fifty Indians porters laden with deer skins, which inaugurated the lucrative Carolina fur trade. Within little more than a decade, more than 50,000 deer skins annually were being exported to England.

Most of the original settlers in Carolina were poor, small farmers and freemen "out of their time" from Barbados and similar migrants from Virginia, with a smattering of people from New England, England, and even France, seeking opportunity or religious freedom. Some wealthier planters from Barbados arrived, few in number but a portent of the future in that they came with their slaves and, more important, a ready acceptance of the idea of a slave-based economy. John Colleton, himself a Barbadian planter, had provided for the control of slaves in the colony by inserting in the Fundamental Constitutions a clause that "Every freeman of Carolina, shall have absolute power and authority over his negro slaves, of what opinion or Religion soever." In a real sense Carolina was born a slave society in principle; unlike Virginia, its acceptance of the idea of slavery did not evolve over half a century. However, for the first decade and a half, most whites in Carolina could not afford to purchase slaves. As in Virginia, white indentured servants were cheaper than slaves, and in fact the much smaller volume of trade in Carolina and the absence of a dominant export crop like tobacco meant not only that the necessary wealth required to purchase many slaves did not exist but also that the correspondingly small market for slaves there lessened their supply and elevated their cost. In the 1670s the number of white servants entering Carolina outnumbered the number of black slaves by more than six to one.

Nevertheless, as the economy of Carolina began to prosper—with the trade in deer skins to England and in food and livestock to Barbados leading the way—the need for laborers began to outstrip the supply of white immigrants from England. The demographic developments in late seventeenth-century England that dried up the number of potential indentured servants bound for the Chesapeake affected Carolina, too. Some Indians from relatively nearby tribes were captured and enslaved or sold to the West Indies in return for black slaves, but Indians could not solve the labor needs of the 1690s. The increasing efficiency of the African slave trade, however, was, after the 1680s, lowering the costs of slaves in the West Indies. The larger demand for slaves in the Chesapeake about this time began to attract slaving ships directly from Africa. So, as Maryland and Virginia shifted from a servant economy to a slave economy in the 1680s and 1690s, the blacks they purchased increasingly came straight from Africa. In Carolina the smaller demand for slaves, which discouraged the transatlantic slave ships, and the large scale of the provisioning trade to the West Indies meant that most initial slave imports to Charles Town came from the islands. The 200 blacks in 1680 in what is now South Carolina increased to 1,500 in 1690 and to 2,400 by 1700, by then vastly outnumbering the number of white servants.

After 1700, Carolina, like the Chesapeake colonies to the north, was a slave society. This shift to slave labor in Carolina occurred before any significant change in the nature of the Carolina economy, although after the late 1690s the successful cultivation of rice caused a tremendous increase in the colony's wealth, led to an enormous proliferation in the number of slaves, and circumscribed the work routines of the majority of the blacks. But before the rice boom that transformed (South) Carolina after 1700, the first generation of Carolina slaves were set to work in the more open conditions of a mixed economy. Slaves worked with whites of various origins at a variety of tasks: growing corn and peas for export to Barbados; cutting timber in the forests for lumber, shingles, and barrel staves; working in the infant naval stores industry providing pitch and tar for British shipping; and herding cattle in the woods and rounding them up in cow pens for the beef market at home and in the West Indies. Slave herdsmen may have been the pioneer cowboys in the South. In this varied economy of the pioneer days in Carolina, blacks and whites worked together and socialized together not truly as equals but with a greater degree of harmony than they did for two-and-a-half centuries thereafter.

From the beginning, the Carolina proprietors had hoped to recoup their investment by discovering a bonanza crop like tobacco or sugar that could be grown there and profitably sold in England. Agricultural experiments were made in the first decade of settlement with a number of plants, including rice and indigo, but nothing seemed commercially viable. About 1690, improved rice seeds from Madagascar and the East Indies were introduced and, after several years of trying different techniques of cultivation, rice farming became profitable. Approximately four hundred thousand pounds of rice were exported in 1700, 1.5 million pounds in 1710, and by the middle of the century 50 million pounds were being shipped annually. Initially rice was grown on regular, well-watered soil, with no enormous start-up costs, though the labor needed to keep the moist rice fields weeded put extreme pressure on the available supply of slaves imported from the West Indies. The swift expansion of the rice crop caused a demand for slaves sufficient to attract large slaving vessels directly from Africa, which slightly lowered the price for slaves. The profits from rice allowed planters to buy even more slaves. Accidentally at first, then by planter preference, the increased importation of slaves from the Grain Coast of West Africa brought blacks whose expertise in planting and growing rice helped expand rice cultivation in the South, which of course strengthened still more the demand for slaves. Simultaneously, the naval stores industry expanded, especially after England began in 1705 to offer bounties for tar, pitch, turpentine, ships masts, and the like produced in Carolina. The resulting naval stores boom, which lasted for two decades, brought additional profits that could be reinvested in slaves. Consequently, the market for slave laborers mushroomed.

For a while the demand for slaves outpaced the Africa trade's ability to adjust, and in the fifteen years following 1700 the number of Indian slaves increased significantly. In fact, in 1708, the year blacks first outnumbered whites in what is now South Carolina, the population of Indian slaves equalled one-quarter of the black population. In part, this magnification of the trade in Indian slaves, which had been miniscule in the seventeenth century, was made possible by the huge trade network that had arisen as a result of the deer skin trade; trade connections were now made through friendly local Indians to Indian nations as far away as the Mississippi River, and most of the Indians made available as slaves came from regions in the West. The Indian slaves, living among and marrying black slaves, had a cultural impact on the emerging black culture still not fully understood, but important as it was, the trend toward enslaving Indians was short-lived. Partly because they were frightened by the expanding scale of Indian slavery, many of the hitherto passive local Indians, confederated with tribes more distant, struck back at the whites in 1715 in what is known as the Yamasee War and almost fatally destroyed the white settlement, causing the whites to abandon for a while perhaps one-half of the cultivated area. This seems to have been the Carolina

Indians' last-gasp effort to protect their own way of life from destruction, but it failed, and the white countermeasures essentially succeeded in eliminating the Carolina Indian population. In the midst of the war the Carolina assembly passed an Indian Trading Act that sharply restricted dealing in Indian slaves.

In the future the servile work force in Carolina would be blacks from Africa and, after about 1730, their Carolina-born descendants. The increasing number of Africans from the Grain Coast utilized their expertise with rice to teach white Carolinians improved techniques for its planting and cultivation. As the rice industry matured and became more efficient, it shifted from dry-land cultivation to fresh-water swampy regions for irrigation to flood the fields to kill the grass and, finally, after mid-century it shifted once more to tidal-swamp areas in the lowcountry.

Here the sluggish rivers became passive agents of an ingenious irrigation system. When the tide of up to eight feet came in along the South Carolina and Georgia coasts, it caused the fresh water in the lowcountry rivers to back up and rise also. By constructing an elaborate network of levees, sluice gates, and ditches, planters could open the gates at high tide and flood their fields—thereby killing the grass—and then, when the river levels were down, they could reverse the process and drain the fields. The moon's gravitational pull, in effect, irrigated the rice fields. But such a system required tremendous start-up and maintenance costs, the necessary labor was backbreaking, and only blacks were thought to be capable of performing it. Nevertheless, the profits were enormous. Coastal Carolina soon became like a black country—black slaves on manorial-sized plantations greatly outnumbered whites, and slaves were assigned almost exclusively to agricultural tasks. The old mixed economy with a degree of white–black equality in the workplace was a thing of the past. Carolina, like the Chesapeake, in the early eighteenth century had become a full-fledged slave society.

THE NORTHERN PORTION OF CAROLINA

The Carolina proprietors' attention was focused on the southern portion of their New World investment, and the rice and later indigo grown there brought great wealth to the colony. The northern half of their land grant, the portion between Virginia and Cape Fear, never loomed large in the planning sessions of the proprietors. For one thing, the long range of barrier islands stretching from the southern tip of the Chesapeake Bay all the way to the mouth of the Cape Fear River made the entire coast of northern Carolina inhospitable to shipping. The islands themselves, the shifting sand bars, and the shallow inlets with no natural harbors all discouraged coastal exploration, especially when contrasted with the inviting harbors along the

Ashley and Cooper rivers and in the vicinity of Port Royal. This lack of attention meant that northern Carolina developed with little assistance from the proprietors and, although the region was sparsely settled until about 1725, thereafter it developed through a rich stream of migration from Europe, persisted in an increasingly profitable mixed economy, and by 1790 was second in population among southern colonies only to Virginia.

The chief geographical feature of the northernmost part of Carolina was Albemarle Sound, a large salt-water bay separated from Virginia by the aptly named Dismal Swamp. Nevertheless, by the 1650s Virginia settlers, seeking additional tobacco land, began to push southward from Norfolk. In 1655 Nathaniel Batts established a home on the western shore of Albemarle Sound, becoming the first permanent white inhabitant in all of Carolina. Batts himself traded with the Indians for deer skins, but the region soon had other former Virginians who grew tobacco; in fact, the region around Albemarle Sound eventually was more tied to the tobacco economy of the Chesapeake than to the provisioning trade and later rice industry of southern Carolina. Even before Carolina was granted to the proprietors, the Albemarle region had begun to be settled as a colony of Virginia, with small farmers and servants who had fulfilled their indentures coming in search of inexpensive land. While Albemarle grew in the shadow of Virginia, the colonization efforts further south faltered.

After the formal organization of Carolina the proprietors desired population growth and economic development, but for several years their promotional schemes were tentative and ill-focused. Later, under the leadership of Lord Shaftesbury and with the expansionist plans of many Barbadians, economic activity centered on the region near Charles Town. But in the early 1660s several abortive attempts were made to establish settlements to the north. In late 1662 and early 1663 two small groups of Puritans from Massachusetts, who had employed Captain William Hilton to bring them south, settled on the banks of the Cape Fear River, but for reasons unknown they abandoned the region in the spring of 1663. Later that year several Barbadians hired Hilton to explore a settlement site for them, and in 1664, under the leadership of John Vassall of Barbados, a group of Barbadians also planted a small village on the Cape Fear, but with the loss the following autumn of a ship bringing supplies, then trouble with the Indians, this infant colony struggled, eventually collapsing in 1667.

Meanwhile, the white population grew steadily in the Albemarle region, and by 1665 the area had its own local government and an agreement with the proprietors that a local assembly would represent the interests of the citizens. A decade later, when Thomas Miller, a deputy governor and customs collector appointed by the proprietors, was deemed to have overstepped his authority, Albemarle citizens, led by John Culpeper, rose in rebellion, arrested Miller, called a new election, and put up such a peppery defense of their interests that the cautious proprietors backed down from punishing them. From the time of this "Culpeper Rebellion" in 1678 until the American Revolution a century later, a strong tradition of local rule persisted in the Albemarle region.

The tobacco economy penetrated Albemarle and tied many farmers there into the marketing system, but throughout the region tobacco did not dominate as it did in tidewater Virginia and Maryland. In part because of the absence of deep-water harbors and hence dependence on shipping by way of Norfolk, settlers in the Albemarle region were less committed to trade with England and practiced a more diverse local economy. Tobacco was grown as a money crop, but farmers quickly learned to grow corn, peas, beans, cattle, hogs, even fowls for their own food and for trade either to Virginia, the rice farmers to the south, or especially to the West Indies via shallow-draft boats not suitable for transatlantic commerce. The growing economy propelled the expansion of the colony beyond the vicinity of Albemarle Sound, leading to the organization in 1696 of Bath County between the Sound and the Pamlico River. After 1705 the Naval Stores Bounty Act, passed by Parliament that year, benefited the independent farmers of northern Carolina as it did those near Charles Town, and the naval stores industry, complementing tobacco and food production, brought hitherto unknown prosperity to northern Carolina. Of course, prosperity and a thriving, diverse economy attracted more settlers.

Around 1704 and 1705 a group of French Huguenots moved into Bath County from Virginia, and this firm indication of growth prompted the local assembly in 1706 formally to incorporate Bath as the first town in northern Carolina. Within several years more Huguenots from Virginia arrived. Moreover, word of the region had apparently already spread to Europe, and by 1705 Swiss merchants in Bern were forming a joint-stock company and drawing up plans for a colony in Carolina. Simultaneously, war, economic deprivation in the Palatinate region of Germany, and an extraordinarily cold winter persuaded thousands of Palatine Germans to leave their homeland. Many fled to London, from whence some later migrated to Ireland and New York while others awaited opportunity elsewhere in the New World. Eventually, Baron Christoph von Graffenried came to head the Swiss company, and he purchased from the Carolina proprietors thousands of acres of land between the Neuse and Cape Fear rivers. Graffenried transported some Swiss settlers and contracted to settle 650 Palatines from London in the Swiss territory. Plans momentarily went awry, there were food shortages, and the Tuscarora Indians resisted the European takeover of their traditional lands, but despite adversity Graffenried finally succeeded in establishing a town and colony on the banks of the Neuse River. He named the town Neuse-Bern after his home city in Switzerland, but English settlers soon anglicized this to New Bern. New Bern prospered, more Swiss and Germans followed, and they, along with additional Huguenots, gave northern Carolina a rich ethnic diversity and a devotion to a mixed economy that neither the tobacco region to the north nor the rice-growing region to the south could claim.

By 1715 rice cultivation had spread to the Cape Fear region, but, like tobacco in Albemarle, it complemented the economy rather than dominated it. Most of the settlers in the region from Albemarle Sound to the Cape Fear River were practical farmers simply trying to make a living with no concern for how they might some day fit such labels as subsistence farmers or commercial planters. They tried to produce most of their own foodstuffs and everything else they needed—subsistence farming—but they also grew some tobacco and rice for English markets and funneled them through the harbors at Norfolk or Charles Town; others produced pitch and tar for the naval stores bounty when crop needs allowed it. They learned to profit by selling surplus corn and livestock to tobacco and rice planters and to hungry Barbadians; they were even known later to drive herds of cattle, hogs, and turkeys northward to Baltimore and Philadelphia. Hence they participated in commercial production to a degree, but they claimed some independence from the marketplace.

Another industry, even more individualistic, brought income to the region hidden behind the Outer Banks. Large ocean-going vessels could penetrate the dangerous shoals of the barrier islands only at great peril to themselves, but swift, shallow-draft pirate vessels could dart in and out, hide in innumerable inlets, and attack the slower, more cumbersome ships laden with valuable goods. Independent maritime opportunists, with no allegiance to England, Virginia, or Carolina but only to their own fortunes, made the northern coast of Carolina for about a decade after 1710 the center of North American piracy. No more colorful group ever plied the coastal waters than pirates, such as the brute Edward Teach, called "Blackbeard," or Stede Bonnet, the "gentleman pirate," who as a well-educated and wealthy retired British army major set up his pirating headquarters along the Carolina coast. The British navy finally captured them both, hanging Bonnet in 1718 and killing Blackbeard after a fierce battle the same year. The heyday of Carolina pirating had ended.

Six years earlier, in 1712, Carolina had been divided: South Carolina became a separate royal colony, while North Carolina continued under the administration of proprietors until 1729. But long before Carolina's formal division, North and South Carolina had forged different economies and different societies. Even so, North Carolina with its mixed economy profited from growing tobacco and rice and from selling foodstuffs to the more staple-crop-dominated colonies on either side of it. North Carolina was still a part of the mercantilist world system that bound England and its colonies by means of markets and credit. As North Carolina grew and prospered, its population swelled by migrations from Europe and by white servants "out of their time" from Virginia and Barbados, it, too, came to import a few black slaves. Four of the early settlers who came to the Albemarle region from Virginia in 1663 are known to have brought several slaves with them, and the earliest regulations of the proprietors protected the rights of slaveholders. Yet North Carolina was very slow to import slaves. While some tobacco and less rice was harvested in the seventeenth century, it was marketed via Norfolk and Charles Town, with relatively little maritime connection with the slave trade. Corn, livestock, and naval stores brought prosperity to farmers, but little of the surplus income necessary to purchase slaves, and the scale of the farming and naval industry and such trades as cooperage did not exhaust the available supplies of labor. North Carolinians accepted the idea of slavery, and at times wished they had the wherewithal to acquire more slaves, but the colony developed as a yeoman economy. As late as 1712 there were only approximately 800 slaves in the region—a decade after the Chesapeake and South Carolina had become slave societies. More slaves would come later, but in the early eighteenth century North Carolina stood apart from the fully commercialized economies on her borders.

THE LATIN SOUTH

The South's history after 1607 is often thought of as the progress of English settlement across a grand sweep of a continent occupied only by decreasing numbers of Indians, and the presence of French and Spanish settlers is only incidentally noted as background to the Louisiana Purchase and later to the controversy over the annexation of Texas. Yet the cultures of Spain and France left a deeper impress on the region from Florida to Texas than the short shrift given them in most histories suggests. European wars and rivalries affected Spanish and French attempts to establish mainland colonies as much or more than indigenous problems did, and, in fact, these Old World rivalries shaped the timing of both the beginning and the end of Spanish and French control of large portions of the present-day South.

Initially, the Spanish in Florida were little bothered by the English colony at Jamestown. By 1607 Florida was primarily a mission field for the Franciscans whose series of mission outposts at Indian towns swept from San Agustín to the northernmost Sea Islands of Georgia, called Guale after a local Indian chief. The Franciscans had real success in pushing their missions into West Florida, and by 1674 when Bishop Calderon visited, there were thirty-two missions in Florida and more than thirteen thousand officially Christian Indians. But though faraway Jamestown had posed no problem for the Spanish, the establishment in 1670 of Charles Town was a different matter. Within less than a decade Carolina traders and fur trappers were crossing into Guale and gaining influence over the Indians, who found it hard to turn away from British goods. English and French pirates also raided the isolated missions in coastal Guale, forcing the Spanish to abandon Georgia and try to hold on to their threatened missions in northern Florida. British-armed Indians made periodic raids on the Spanish missions, culminating in 1702 and 1704 when Governor James Moore of South Carolina invaded Florida and, assisted by Indian allies, devastated the missions near San Agustín and in the Apalachee region; neither the missions nor Spanish authority ever completely recovered in Florida. Already another European rival, France, had begun to threaten the Spanish presence from the west.

In the early seventeenth century Cabeza de Vaca and Hernando de Soto had traveled through Alabama, Mississippi, Louisiana, and Texas, but their difficult experiences had not led to serious attempts to plant permanent settlements in the region; Spain used their travels only to claim the territory. At the western edge of the tenuous empire there were some tentative Spanish missionary activities, with missions established in the vicinity of Santa Fe in 1598 and efforts made to spread Christianity near the upper Nueces River and in the Edwards Plateau region of Texas after 1600; the oldest permanent settlement in Texas began in 1681 at the mission outpost at Ysleta, near present-day El Paso. Except for these settlements far to the west, Spain neglected the entire region from the Rio Grande to the Escambia River in West Florida, seeing neither a military nor an economic reason to become more involved. Then France entered the area, and the entire geopolitical situation changed.

The French empire in Canada had seemed so remote that it could not affect Spanish interests. But the French, with their intrepid fur trappers and explorers, had begun to seek a warm-water river route southward from Canada; in 1673 Father Marquette and Louis Jolliet had followed the Mississippi River down to where the Arkansas River joined it, and nine years later, in 1682, René Robert Cavelier, Sieur de La Salle, floated all the way to the Gulf via one of the Mississippi's several mouths, staking a French claim to the region. That would have been provocation enough for the nervous Spanish, but after returning to Canada and then to France, La Salle in 1684 with a small colonizing expedition set forth for the Mississippi to plant the beginning of a French empire. La Salle miscalculated the location of the mouth of the Mississippi and instead landed on the Texas coast at Matagorda Bay. There, on a tributary of the Lavaca River, La Salle built a small garrison named Fort Saint Louis in February 1685. This tiny French outpost on the edge of Texas failed, with La Salle himself leaving with a handful of men heading on foot toward Canada in search of reinforcements. One of La Salle's own men killed him in eastern Texas in an argument over how to share the sparse food supply; the remainder of the men straggled on to Canada, while Indians made short work of the remnant of the French forces at Fort Saint Louis. Thus ended the French empire in Texas, a chimerical empire at best.

The Spanish, who soon heard exaggerated rumors of a French invasion somewhere along the Texas coast, feared the worst and imagined their hitherto neglected territory—already harassed on the east by the English—being attacked at its very center by another European rival. Determined not to have its empire nibbled away, the Spanish mounted efforts to locate and to destroy the French settlement. The French had deserted Fort Saint Louis before the Spanish under Governor Alonso de Leon of Coahuila discovered its ruins in 1689, but in a chance meeting with a band of Tejas Indians (from whom the name Texas came) from eastern Texas the Indians asked de Leon to establish a mission for them. De Leon must have been flabbergasted, but in the next few years two Catholic missions were located in eastern Texas. However, disease, food shortages, and the lackadaisical interest of the Indians caused the missions to be abandoned in 1693. With the French seemingly out of the picture by then, Spain again forgot about Texas for two decades, until, once more, the French appeared on the scene.

La Salle had died in Texas in 1687, but his memory was kept alive in France. In late 1697 a friend of his, the Sieur de Remonville, wrote a convincing report to the Count de Pontchartrain, the French Minister of Marine, to the effect that bountiful opportunities existed for France if she would but establish a colony in Louisiana, the land bordering the Mississippi River that La Salle had named in honor of King Louis XIV. The king and his ministers accepted Remonville's argument and chose a young French Canadian explorer, Pierre le Moyne, Sieur d'Iberville, to lead an expedition of four ships and two hundred persons to the vicinity of the mouth of the Mississippi. D'Iberville raised anchor on October 24, 1698, and after a voyage of three months he had reached the western coast of Florida. Finding a small Spanish garrison at Pensacola Bay, he continued westward, first touching Dauphin Island off Mobile Bay but finally anchoring at Ship Island, near Biloxi Bay.

Leaving the bulk of his force there, he and his brother, Jean Baptiste le Moyne, Sieur de Bienville, sailed on in search of the Mississippi, entered one of its mouths on March 2, 1699, and made their way upstream to where they saw a red pole standing on the east bank of the mighty river. The red pole was of course an indication of Indian habitation, but European explorers seldom considered Indian territorial claims as binding. Naming the spot Baton Rouge, they continued upstream some distance further to make certain it was the Mississippi; satisfied that it was, the two brothers returned to Ship Island by different routes. D'Iberville moved his people from Ship Island to the mainland and at the site of today's Ocean Springs, Mississippi, established a palisaded garrison, Fort Maurepas, in May 1699. This settlement proved unsuccessful and in 1702 the fort was abandoned and the garrison moved to Mobile Bay; later, it was moved again and finally located at the site of modern Mobile in 1711. Believing it was important to erect a barrier against Carolina fur traders and trappers, the French in 1717 established Fort Toulouse at the juncture of the Coosa and Tallapoosa rivers, just north of the present city of Montgomery.

D'Iberville died in 1706, before the Gulf Coast colonies could be called a success, but over the next decade and a half new efforts were made to build forts and set up trading stations both to buy deer skins from the Indians and to present a barrier to the English fur trappers ranging far west from Carolina. In pursuit of these policies a permanent French settlement was made at Natchitoches in 1714 and at Fort Rosalie at the site of Natchez in 1716, and Bienville founded the colony's first town, New Orleans, on the bank of the Mississippi south of Lake Pontchartrain in 1718. The original town, what is now known as the Vieux Carre or French Quarter, was disease-ridden and flood-prone, but with it the French were finally firmly established in Louisiana. The economy depended on exchanging cheap European goods with a variety of Indian groups for valuable deer skins; the French did not establish significant agricultural production.

All these activities of the French caused little stir in Spain and Mexico until the summer of 1714 when a group of French traders, led by Louis Juchereau de St. Denis, suddenly appeared at a Spanish presidio (garrison) and mission on the Rio Grande and asked to open trade between French Louisiana and Spanish Texas. After all, said St. Denis, France and Spain were now at peace, and the Louisiana governor wanted to reopen the missions in eastern Texas. The startled Spanish commander arrested St. Denis and sent him to Mexico City, but St. Denis charmed the viceroy into appointing him the leader of a Spanish expedition sent to reestablish a Spanish presence in eastern Texas. Subsequently in 1716 and 1717 a string of six Fransican missions and a presidio were founded in east Texas, near present-day Nacogdoches and San Agustín, with the last one, Los Adaes, actually located across the Sabine River in Louisiana, only fifteen miles west of the French post at Natchitoches. In 1718 the Spanish authorities directed that a supply depot be set up half way between Mexico and the eastern missions, so Governor Martin de Alarcon of Coahuila established a mission (later called the Alamo) and the town of San Antonio—the same year, more than five hundred miles to the east, that New Orleans was founded.

The very next year, though, a French force, hearing that hostilities had resumed between France and Spain in Europe, attacked the Spanish mission at Los Adaes, causing the entire Spanish population in eastern Texas to flee westward to the stronger presidio at San Antonio. The French did not occupy the vacated eastern Texas, leading Mexican officials to push into the area again in 1721, reestablishing the original presidio and missions and building a strong fort at Los Adaes, which became the Spanish capital of Texas for the next fifty years even though it was in Louisiana. This half century marked the heyday of Spanish Texas. The economy of the Spanish borderlands was based far less on agriculture than on livestock—hogs, mustangs, and especially cattle. In the Southeast particularly Spanish breeds of cattle and hogs later interbred with English stock. In the late nineteenth century descendants of the original Spanish mustangs were the mount of choice for ranchers in Texas—those icons of the American West, cowboys.

A number of towns and missions were founded in Texas after 1721, some 2,500 people were permanently settled, and the governor even attracted a group of colonists from the Canary Islands. Spanish place names, ranching techniques and terms, the concept of a homestead law that exempts a person's home from seizure for debt, the idea that husband and wife jointly share their property—these and other aspects of the Spanish heritage made a permanent impress on Texas. In the midst of this success, in 1762, France ceded Louisiana to Spain, and with the foreign threat removed, the Spanish withdrew their missions and presidios from eastern Texas in 1772 and concentrated on the region near San Antonio. Some of the settlers who had been forced to leave eastern Texas wished to return, and eventually, in 1779, they went back to the site of Nacogdoches and laid out the present town there. For the next fifty years, occasional explorers, adventurers, promoters, pioneers, and scoundrels from Louisiana and points east came to Texas and settled there, with tensions simmering until a rebellion ultimately broke out in 1836. While the Spanish controlled Louisiana and New Orleans, two disastrous fires in 1788 and 1794 destroyed the original French buildings of the Crescent City. The presently existing Vieux Carre was rebuilt by the Spanish, which explains why the "French" Quarter largely exhibits Spanish architecture. Otherwise, French culture, especially the system of Napoleonic law, persisted in Louisiana. Spain later ceded Louisiana back to France, and Napoleon began to do business with negotiators acting on orders from President Thomas Jefferson. But that, and even the coming of the Acadians to Louisiana, belongs to another part of our story.

THE FOUNDING OF GEORGIA

The southern boundary of colonial Carolina was vague, and the English and the Spanish disputed the line. Clearly the Spanish had explored the coastal region from Florida all the way to the Port Royal region of South Carolina long before the English appeared and had established settlements and missions along the coast and especially the Sea Islands of the region they called Guale. Before 1700, however, Indian allies of the Carolina fur traders and marauding pirates had driven the Spanish from Guale all the way back to the vicinity of San Agustín, and Governor James Moore's 1702 and 1704 raids had even further diminished Spanish authority in northern Florida. After 1704, the Spanish posed no real threat to the thriving English population in

South Carolina. But the unprecedented French encroachment on the Gulf Coast awakened the Carolinians to a potential threat as surely as it spurred the Spanish in Mexico to respond. French garrisons at Mobile, Natchitoches, Natchez, and then Fort Toulouse in central Alabama clearly endangered the lucrative Carolina trade in deer skins with Indians all the way to the Mississippi River, and the French establishment of New Orleans in 1718 near the mouth of the Mississippi and the seizing of Pensacola from the Spanish in 1719 suggested that the French planned to connect their Gulf Coast settlements with their fur trading empire in Canada. Carolina saw more than its fur trade being disrupted by the French in the South. And there was always the possibility that the Spanish in Florida could be reinforced and become more aggressive.

These concerns in Carolina about the dangers inherent in the uncontested French presence on the Gulf and the remnant of Spanish authority in Florida were reinforced in 1715 and 1716 by the Yamasee War, when a confederacy of Indians made one final effort to drive the English out. Carolinians were quick to see French and Spanish complicity in the designs of the Indians, further persuading the authorities in Carolina that steps had to be taken to put a barrier between their communities and the enemy, prevent the Gulf and Canadian French settlements from being linked, and safeguard Carolina fur trade routes to the west. All these purposes could be served by occupying and fortifying the disputed land between the Savannah and Altamaha rivers.

In 1717 a Scottish baronet, Sir Robert Montgomery, proposed that he be allowed to establish a new colony to be named Azilia south of the Savannah River. He intended to produce Mediterranean products such as wine and silk there, and the citizen–soldiers who settled Azilia would be able to resist the French, Spanish, or Indians. Montgomery wrote two promotional tracts extolling the benefits of the region. The Crown approved the idea, but the necessary funds were not forthcoming, so no Azilia ever materialized. In 1724 a Swiss merchant, Jean Pierre Purry, also proposed a settlement south of the Savannah, but again financial problems delayed any action until 1730, when he established a short-lived settlement on the north bank of the river. Nevertheless, these colonizing plans and failures indicate that people in Carolina and abroad saw both an opportunity and a need to occupy the disputed territory. In 1720 a detailed report on the military importance of the region was submitted to the Board of Trade in London; the Board of Trade subsequently authorized the building of a fort at the mouth of the Altamaha River. Fort King George was erected there, though it was ill supported and ultimately abandoned in 1727. South Carolina's first royal governor, Robert Johnson, was convinced of the need to establish a strong English presence between Carolina and Florida, and in 1729 and 1730 he began to spell out a program of creating fortified townships throughout the region, with citizen–soldiers to work the fields and defend the settlements. Certainly the air was filled with plans and proposals to attract new settlers to the region, raise crops that did not compete with South Carolina's rice, and establish a defensive barrier between Carolina and European rivals.

These needs turned out to mesh with the reform desires of a group of English philanthropists led by Sir John Perceval and James Oglethorpe. In 1729 Oglethorpe was named to head a parliamentary committee to investigate abuses in the penal system; what he found opened his eyes to the need for providing a charity colony for the poor rather than a debtors' jail. As Oglethorpe became more involved in the issue, he came into contact with a wide range of reformers, including Dr. Thomas Bray, perhaps England's leading philanthropist. Out of this mutual concern eventually arose a group of men, influenced by both Bray and Oglethorpe, that organized to address several moral responsibilities: evangelizing among slaves and Indians, creating libraries, and establishing a charity colony for the deserving poor. With Perceval's help, Oglethorpe raised funds for a charitable colony, having already chosen the region now being called Georgia (after King George II) for the site. Perceval and Oglethorpe were also petitioning the king for a charter on behalf of the group now called the Georgia Trustees. The charter was finally issued in 1732.

The trustees were authorized to govern the colony for twenty-one years, after which it would revert to the Crown. As Oglethorpe and the others proceeded to raise funds for the enterprise, the contagion of reform spread. Economic dislocations were producing many "worthy" poor who, through no fault of their own, were unemployed: farmers, artisans, and tradesmen. The proposed colony came to be seen as a way of providing all these unfortunates an opportunity for a new life. The debtors in prison, on whose behalf Oglethorpe had first worked, seemed forgotten. By this time Oglethorpe was so caught up in the plans that even before adequate monies were raised he announced he was going with the first colonists to Georgia. Never really officially named the governor of the colony, Oglethorpe's natural abilities and forceful personality made him the leader of the experiment from the moment the *Anne*, with a little over a hundred passengers, left England on November 17, 1732. A child, christened Georgius, was born en route, with Oglethorpe serving as godfather.

The *Anne* reached Charles Town in mid-January 1733. Oglethorpe went ahead to scout out a site for settlement, and two weeks later, in February, the colonists disembarked at a high bluff on the south side of the Savannah River, seventeen miles from its mouth. The location was fortuitous: easily defended, not subject to flooding, relatively healthy, and the nearby Indians, the Yamacraws, were friendly. John Musgrove, a South Carolinian, already had a trading post on the site, and he and his mixed-blood wife, Mary, smoothed relations with the Yamacraws. Oglethorpe treated them and other

Indians fairly, in fact becoming a good friend with Tomochichi, the Yamacraw chief, who helped insure peace with the larger Creek confederacy of Indians.

The settlers first lived in four large tents, but within a week and a half Oglethorpe and Colonel William Bull laid out the town of Savannah, using a grid pattern with open public squares regularly spaced throughout. That pattern still gives the city a special charm. There was illness and death the first summer, but supplies were sent by the trustees, the Indians helped, and the colony was a success. The trustees transported additional settlers—impoverished but "worthy" men and women and practically no debtors from emptied prisons. The reform image of Georgia spread throughout Europe and within a year others seeking a new chance in life requested to come.

In 1733 Lutherans who had been persecuted by the Catholic church in Salzburg were granted permission to immigrate to Georgia, with the Reverend Samuel Urlsperger serving as their intermediator. Led by Reverend John Martin Bolzius, the first group of Salzburgers, fewer than a hundred, arrived in Savannah in the spring of 1734, made their way some twenty miles northwest of Savannah, and established the town of Ebenezer on a creek six miles distant from the Savannah River. The site proved inaccessible and the surrounding soil unproductive, so the town was relocated to the Savannah River. In subsequent years more Salzburgers arrived, hard-working farmers and devout Lutherans all. After an initial period of hardship and disease, the Salzburgers began to prosper, and their presence attracted additional settlers—some transient, most permanent—to Georgia, giving the colony by the mid-eighteenth century a substantial German-speaking population and a cluster of German folkways. Two small groups of Moravians arrived in 1735 and 1736, but as pacifists in a land where there was always a perceived threat by European and Indian enemies, the Moravians were not well received. By 1740 most of them had left for Pennsylvania. Sensing a need for citizen–soldiers who could both farm and fight, the Georgia trustees recruited a group of Scottish Highlanders—known to be aggressive defenders of their property and way of life—with the result that by 1741 several hundred had come, most of them settling in the town they established, Darien, at the mouth of the Altamaha River, the more-or-less accepted boundary between English and Spanish authority.

In less than a decade Georgia gave the appearance of prosperity, and its reputation for a salubrious climate (based more on promotional literature than meteorological or demographic data) and an openness to European victims of oppression and poverty attracted settlers from England, Germany, Switzerland, Wales, Scotland, and Ireland. One of the nation's earliest Jewish communities began in Savannah when, in the summer of 1733, an unannounced ship arrived bringing a number of Jews from England. They had no rabbi, but they soon founded a synagogue, called Mickva Israel, and practiced their faith. The early Georgians, their numbers increasing, soon felt secure enough to begin to protest Oglethorpe's paternalistic leadership and several of the restrictions placed on their society by the well-meaning trustees. This sense of independence gained added strength after a spasmodic little war with the Spanish in Florida between 1738 and 1742. Oglethorpe attacked the Spanish at San Agustín and the Spanish invaded St. Simon's Island near the mouth of the Altamaha only to be driven back for good—eliminating the danger of foreign invasion.

Safe from danger, the colonists began to think about their long-term prosperity. The trustees wanted to maintain Georgia as a charitable preserve for the worthy poor and objected to the idea of particularly successful farmers controlling huge blocks of land. So the trustees assigned land to individual farmers in small parcels that they could hold for their lifetimes; the land could not be sold and could be conveyed only to their male heirs. If there were none, the land reverted to the trustees. Pressure from the colonists led the trustees to change the restrictions prohibiting female inheritance in 1742, and farmers were allowed to lease land. This did not satisfy local farmers, whatever the philanthropists in London might have thought, and further protests led in 1750 to a removal of all restrictions against land utilization, farmers being given the right to hold it in fee simple and buy or sell it as they wished.

In 1735 the trustees had also issued regulations prohibiting African slavery in Georgia, banning the use of rum or other strong drinks, and restricting trade with the Indians. The trustees saw Georgia as a moral experiment. They intended to transport there persons in unfortunate circumstances, then train them in ways of thrift and morality so they would become upstanding citizens. Such an experiment required, the trustees believed, the prohibition of spirituous drinks, which often led to intemperance and abuse, and the disallowance of slavery, which was bad in and of itself and also tempted slaveowners with idleness and a hunger for extravagant profits. Good relations with the Indians were necessary both for safety's sake and a sense of fairness, hence trade with the Indians had to be closely regulated. But despite the moral and practical rationales for these rules, the settlers soon came to chafe under them. The restrictions against rum and brandy proved impossible to uphold, and they were soon honored mainly in the breech and became a dead letter by 1742. South Carolina Indian traders who had long carried on a lucrative business in deer skins objected all the way to England about the restrictions on how they conducted their relations with the Indians, and gained some concessions. The restrictions were gradually emasculated and finally lifted at the beginning of royal control of Georgia in 1752.

When the small-scale production of wines and silk failed, the Georgia farmers wanted to reject the utopian agricultural schemes of the trustees and adopt the hugely profitable system of rice cultivation pioneered in South Carolina. In the mid-1730s Carolina rice production had moved from the moist highlands to the coastal lowcountry, where the tidal rise and fall of water in the rivers could be used, by means of levees, gates, and ditches, to augment the cultivation of rice. Such an irrigation system required immense amounts of labor under extremely unpleasant conditions. Recognizing the strenuousness of the work and seeing the wealth slavery was bringing to South Car-

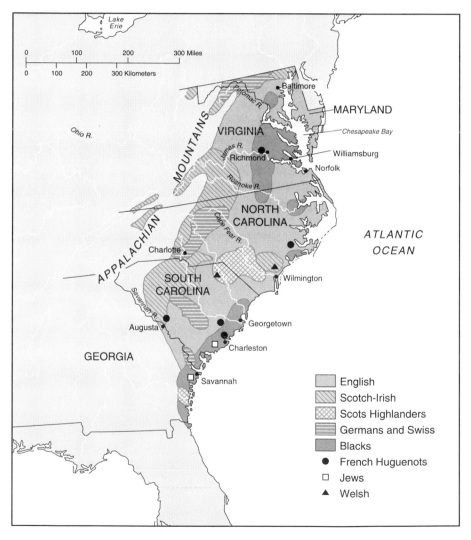

Map 1. Early settlements in the seaboard South.

olina, Georgians began to clamor for slaves to perform the offensive labor. In the face of restrictions they sought ways to circumvent the law, often leasing slaves for ninety-nine years from South Carolina "owners" and paying the entire rent in advance. Others simply brought in slaves in flagrant disregard of the law. This agitation to end legal proscription of slavery began in the late 1730s and rose to such a pitch that the trustees in 1750 were forced to revoke the 1735 prohibition.

By 1750 Georgia had transformed itself from a fragile new settlement placed between South Carolina and vague enemies in the south and west to a prosperous colony that, as a mirror of its northern neighbor, produced a profitable agricultural export for the world market. No longer primarily a charitable experiment for the worthy poor, Georgia, while open to Europeans fleeing from oppression and hunger, was now enslaving black Africans as fast as she could afford them. It was not a reformer's ideal of small independent farms but a booming plantation society that emerged in the newest American colony.

THE CHARACTER OF THE MID-EIGHTEENTH-CENTURY SOUTH

There was no one "South" in the mid-eighteenth century, no unified region that had a sense of self-identity. In the Chesapeake region tobacco culture created a commonality of interests that united much of Maryland, tidewater Virginia, and the Albemarle area of North Carolina, and this Chesapeake society shared a number of characteristics that made it an identifiable subregion of the South. Similarly the rice and indigo economies of coastal South Carolina and Georgia produced a Carolina society different from the Chesapeake in a number of ways. Yet both these regions whose way of life was based on the large-scale production of staple crops for the international market shared a number of features that both set them apart both from the northern colonies and from the later settled, more mixed economies of their own "back country." This region stretched from the western edge of tobacco cultivation in Maryland and Virginia to the Piedmont and the Great Valley running southwestward through Virginia into North Carolina.

These back settlements continued into the south-central portion of Virginia below the James River, characterizing much of North Carolina and most of the territory of South Carolina and Georgia beyond the lowcountry. The land west of the mountains, which would later become Kentucky and Tennessee, was the hunting ground for several major Indian tribal groups, and though fur trappers and traders from the French settlements in Canada and from Virginia and even South Carolina knew the region, it was, before 1750, still Indian country. The spread of tobacco cultivation, slavery, and the eventual rise of King Cotton would soon integrate most of the non-mountainous back country settlements into the slave-labor/staple-crop dominant South. In a sense the back country was a transitory phase between pioneer settlement and full involvement in commercial agriculture, though some aspects of the early economy persisted and coexisted with boom-time cotton production.

There was yet a fourth region, the Latin South, an area greater in size than the back country settlements combined with the Chesapeake and Carolina societies, and this region—sweeping from Florida through present-day Alabama, Mississippi, Louisiana, Arkansas, and Texas—was controlled by the French and Spanish, with presidios, missions, and towns sprinkled from San Agustín on the Atlantic coast to Pensacola and Mobile on the Gulf to the commercial entrepot of New Orleans on the Mississippi onward to San Antonio in central Texas. Though there was subsistence agriculture and trading for deer skins, and some commerce, the Latin South was—with the exception of south Louisiana—more a region under light military occupation for reasons of international rivalry than a colonial empire being settled by Europeans. International treaties and negotiation would ultimately deliver the region—with the exception of Texas, which was annexed as an independent nation—to the United States as an important new area of the American South.

There is a temptation to see the southern colonies of about 1750 as the faint but sure image of the later "Old" South of about 1850, which in this view represents only the more complete manifestation of traits visible almost from the beginning. This temptation makes studying southern history much like watching a Polaroid picture develop before one's eyes, with the passage of time serving to bring into clearer focus what was there in rudimentary form from the beginning. There was, of course, great diversity in the overall region in 1750, and even within the boundaries of individual colonies like Virginia there were tobacco- and wheat-growing areas with different labor needs, a developing Piedmont with these two crops but also substantial corn and livestock production, and then a broad western valley that had Scotch-Irish and German settlers with religions, languages, and agricultural practices different from the English and slave societies to the east. North Carolina and Georgia had even greater ethnic diversity. Actually, the Old South was more diverse than is commonly realized, but its very image of homogeneity suggests how different from the mosaic-like South of 1750 it was.

There is a related temptation, given the distinct nature of the South in 1850 as compared to the rest of the nation—and, in fact, as compared to the post-emancipationist British empire—to assume that the southern region looked equally atypical in 1750. In a larger New World context, the southern mainland colonies were exactly what England desired and expected colonies to be—regions where, because of different climate, crops and naval stores could be produced that did not compete with the homeland but rather supplied goods England would otherwise have to trade outside her empire to obtain. From the vantage point of London, the southern colonies, utilizing slave labor to grow tobacco, rice, and indigo, looked similar to the West Indian islands' producing sugar. New England, to the contrary, with its fisheries and commerce, was the atypical New World colony, the distinctive region whose differentness required explanation. But New England or the northern colonies in general were not set apart from the South in 1750 on the issue of slavery. At that date, slavery existed in every colony, from Massachusetts to Pennsylvania, with Connecticut, New York, and New Jersey each possessing significant numbers of black slaves engaged in agricultural pursuits. The labor force of no colony north of Maryland was dominated by slaves, and no northern colony had what could be called a slave society, but a traveler in 1750 from Massachusetts to Georgia might very well have perceived that the institution differed only by degree in the southern climes. That vague, almost unexpressed similarity both to New England and to the English island colonies helps explain why the American South did not develop a strong sense of separate identity with substantially different interests until the early nineteenth century.

The two dominant subregions of the eighteenth-century South were the tobacco society of the Chesapeake and the rice–indigo society of the Carolina–Georgia lowcountry. These two subregions dominated the southern colonies economically and politically, and the gentry culture that emerged in each helped define and shape the entire society for generations. Likewise, the slave cultures that developed in the Chesapeake and Carolina subregions shaped the future evolution of African-American society in the South. The back country and Latin South developed later and differently; their histories will be told in time. But the white gentry and the black slave cultures in the staple-crop producing regions so significantly molded the southern historical experience that their characters must be outlined in detail, beginning with the gentry.

At close inspection the differences between the Chesapeake and Carolina societies loom large, but from a more distant perspective the differences look like variations on a theme and the two societies seem to merge. An accurate portrayal should blend these viewpoints, recognizing the significant points of societal and economic divergence but emphasizing how there was a convergence of white, wealthy cultural responses. Members of the gentry class from either subregion would have felt at home in the other, understood the central values, and agreed upon the status of the black population. The long-term profitability of commodity production made possible the evolution of the gentry classes in both areas, and the increasing stability of the population affected the timing of the gentry's emergence.

In the late-seventeenth-century Chesapeake, the most successful tobacco farmers began to move into positions of dominance, controlling local political offices and sitting on the vestries of the Anglican church. With their tobacco profits these increasingly affluent farmers could afford to bring over more servants or slaves and hence patent additional land, safeguarding against the effects of soil exhaustion. Those who patented the land conveniently near the waterways had a clear advantage, and with their growing prosperity they could afford further expansion; with fresh soil and cheap transportation, plus slight advantages of scale in buying and selling by means of their commission merchant in England, they often by their greater efficiency could advance their relative position even when the tobacco price fell. Such individuals who were hardworking, skilled, and lucky enough to live a moderately long life, could amass fortunes and achieve positions of influence in their neighborhoods. Their children started out from privileged positions and, if they were also skilled, hardworking, and long-lived, could achieve both political and economic power.

The social and economic dominance of the Chesapeake gentry began in the late seventeenth century, but the high mortality rates circumscribed the ability of many men to realize their potential, and many infants and children never lived to inherit their estates. Parents often died, leaving their orphaned children to be reared by relatives or court-appointed guardians. Adults who lost a spouse usually remarried, with the result that households were filled with stepchildren; some children had a succession of stepparents. For much of the seventeenth century the large preponderance of white men over white women made it difficult for many men even to establish a family, and in this kind of society, with unsure families and short life spans, even quite substantial fortunes were often not translated into the kind of long-term familial wealth that provides the foundation for a gentry class. At the end of the seventeenth century and in the first two decades of the eighteenth century, the sex ratio began to equalize because the small numbers of American-born children were divided equally by gender.

These youngsters, coming of age in the New World, were healthier and better able to find spouses than their parents and soon were having children. Death rates were still high, but nothing like those of the first generation, and family life became more stable. Parents could expect to live to see their adult children, who sometimes even knew their grandparents. Estates could be preserved and passed on, and marriage, which often combined estates, was as much a matter of business negotiation as it was of true love. Powerful families whose names brought political and economic preference arose, and influence and wealth—strengthened through carefully calculated intermarriage—enabled the scions of such families to enhance their holdings of land and slaves. Demographic stability among powerful families was directly related to the onset of large-scale slaveholding. This slow process of lowered mortality, equalizing sex ratios, stabilizing families, and the resultant consolidation of wealth and influence in a relatively small number of families occurred at slightly different times in the Chesapeake and in Carolina. There were local variations even within the same subregion, but by the second quarter of the eighteenth century in both areas dominant families had arisen whose cultural, economic, and political influence would shape the social terrain.

There were popularly elected lower houses in the governmental structures of all the southern colonies (in Georgia after it became a royal colony), and there were both government-appointed and locally elected officials in the counties, but deference was as much a part of eighteenth-century politics as democracy. On the imperial level, the rise to power of the local assemblies was extremely important and, as a fillip to local control, the strengthening of the assemblies was a prerequisite for the later American Revolution. But the very importance of the colonial assemblies raised the stakes of election; for all its localistic and even democratic tendencies, the eighteenth century was still not modern. Society was assumed to be hierarchically arranged, with royalty and nobility at the top (absent in America), followed by the upper class, the middling class, then the lower orders. It was accepted practically without question that those of the upper and upper-middling class—those born into or who had earned the rank—had the responsibility and the duty to govern, and those beneath them in rank expected to be governed by their social "betters" (who supposedly were better informed and wiser) and seldom aspired to reach beyond their rank and compete for the reins of government.

Such nearly universally held assumptions meant that the families preeminent in wealth were preeminent in politics, and that the heads of household were schooled to rule the plantation and the family in the image of Old Testament patriarchs, and likewise to stand ready to serve the broader populace in the halls of government, when chosen. By today's standards the franchise was severely limited—women and blacks were automatically excluded, and only white men over age eighteen who met modest property requirements could vote—but still the franchise was broader than anywhere in England or Europe. There was no secret ballot: on election day the voters convened at the courthouse or other public place and, with the candidates seated at a table before them, identified themselves when their name was called by the clerk and announced their choice. In one sense this was the most personal kind of politics, a face-to-face participation in choosing one's representative. The candidates, however, were not representative of everyman; they were from the gentry class of prominent families, having usually already proven their mettle one way or another through previous service in an appointed position such as justice of the peace or perhaps through a term on the local vestry. Though all of the same class, the candidates on the basis of their local reputation or prior service presented themselves to the electorate to be chosen or not.

Such personal politics made modern campaigning impossible; at the most a candidate could treat the populace with drink and barbecue as an indication of his generosity and social "right" to govern—George Washington learned how to earn the respect and votes of his fellow citizens with peach brandy. But phony rhetoric and false posturing counted for little; the candidate's family connections, affluence, man-to-man honesty, and character were all important. All in all, the system worked quite well as a method to select and get elected the most capable and respected leaders who understood both their own interests and the interests of most of their electors, whom they knew as people and neighbors, not as abstractions.

Wealthy planters, with reserves of land, a plentiful and stable labor supply, a long line of credit from their English commission merchants, and political power at home were in a good position to solidify their economic position by enacting legislation that benefited themselves and by developing new technologies for growing old crops or experimenting with lucrative new crops. In Virginia and Maryland great efficiency in growing tobacco had already been achieved, but stagnant prices in the first quarter of the eighteenth century led colonial leaders to seek political solutions. Virginia tried in the 1720s to stem overproduction by a system of regulating how many tobacco plants planters could grow, and production did fall, although a series of natural calamities might have had more to do with the decline than had the government limitations. Many powerful planters came to believe that inferior grades of Chesapeake tobacco, poorly packed with trash and dirt in the hogsheads, gave all Chesapeake tobacco a poorer reputation than it deserved and kept prices low.

The remedy, pushed hard and effectively by Governor William Gooch of Virginia, was a tobacco inspection act (put into effect in 1732) that required all tobacco to be government inspected (unacceptable tobacco was destroyed), stored at public warehouses, and shipped in standardized barrels, and detailed records were to be kept to minimize smuggling. The warehouse receipts for stored tobacco were allowed to circulate as legal tender—previously, the actual tobacco had been transferred to pay for debts. Small farmers with perhaps less skill, poorer land, and little slave labor claimed discrimination. Certainly, the new procedures favored the interests of the great tobacco planters, but tobacco prices did inch upward under the new regulations, and the industry became more rationalized. After extensive debate, Maryland in the 1740s followed with its own version of a tobacco inspection act. The Chesapeake economy remained dominated by tobacco throughout the colonial period, even as some planters, disillusioned with tobacco and the vagaries of its price, began to move toward grain cultivation, especially wheat. As the Revolutionary Era began, wheat was growing in influence and would eventually play a significant role in the economic development and urbanization of the Chesapeake.

By the 1740s South Carolina planters were also faced with falling prices for rice. Many planters had already begun to shift from dry-land cultivation of rice to the tidal irrigation areas. Though the initial costs of preparing such fields were so high that only the most successful planters in the first place could afford to adopt the technique, the increases in efficiency and production promoted the creation of a group of superplanters of extraordinary wealth. These planters could, by their increased agricultural efficiency, survive in a time of declining prices caused largely by their own overproduction, but the disruptions in the world market caused by King George's War further complicated their dilemma. Rice is a bulky crop to transport and requires inexpensive shipping. Wartime shipping risks drove up the cost of maritime insurance, which in effect pushed even lower the price growers received for their rice. As the price plummeted in the 1740s, production began to fall, with the amount shipped at the end of the decade one-half that of 1740. The resulting rice depression led planters to seek alternative crops, and the crucial breakthrough was achieved by the young daughter of the governor of Antigua.

George Lucas of Antigua owned plantations near Charles Town, on Wappoo Creek, and there his sixteen-year-old daughter, Eliza Lucas, decided to experiment with indigo seeds sent to her by her father from the West Indies. Her first two crops failed because of frost and worms, but in 1741 she succeeded with a Carolina crop that rivaled the best West Indian indigo. By saving these seeds and replanting them, Eliza Lucas was able to distribute seeds to planters in her neighborhood by 1744. With the demand high for the blueish-purple dyestuff because of the booming English textile industry, England in 1748 began to offer a bounty for indigo. Valuable in proportion to its volume, capable of being grown on the high dry ground where rice was no longer cultivated and harvested at times other than when rice was harvested, indigo proved to be an ideal alternative crop. Its production soared, reaching 50,000 pounds in 1750 and more than a million pounds by 1775. But in the same way that the costly infrastructure required of tidal rice cultivation favored the development of fabulously rich rice planters, the manufacturing costs of indigo further concentrated wealthholding.

Indigo, whose color has in the form of blue jeans become a worldwide symbol for American youth and independence, was a plant originally domesticated in India and grown in South Carolina primarily by slaves. Several times in the late summer and fall the leaves of the plant (which has a powdery coating from its blossoms) were cut off and carefully placed in a wooden vat filled with water and urine—the urine collected from the slave quarters in tubs. The water–urine mixture caused the steeping indigo leaves to ferment, after which the smelly liquid was drained into a lower vat. The plant stems were carried away to be used as fertilizer, but the liquid was beaten and agitated with paddles until it began to foam, then oil was sprinkled on the froth to make it subside. When the indigo maker decided the moment was right, lime water was poured into the vat. This caused the liquid to turn purple and

Fig. 2. The different forms of transportation of tobacco. (New York Public Library)

begin to granulate, and the particles slowly settled to the bottom of the vat, with the excess liquid drawn off. This wet solid matter, called indigo mud, was scooped out and placed in linen bags, then hung out to dry partially. When the mud reached the consistency of paste, it was spread out on wide planks to dry even further. Then the dried indigo granulate was cut into small rectangular "bricks" about the size of dominoes and packed in barrels to be sent to England. The whole process required equipment, skill, and much very unpleasant labor, but the rewards to the planter were great. Indigo and rice made possible the magnificent plantation homes and town houses of the Carolina lowcountry and Charles Town.

By the middle of the eighteenth century in both the Chesapeake and the Carolina lowcountry (and increasingly the Georgia lowcountry, which can be thought of as but an extension of South Carolina) the stable prosperity and family structure of the wealthier class of planters had produced a recognizable southern gentry. There were important differences in the two slave-owning societies, but more important were the similarities. The Chesapeake was the older society, with a substantially larger population, and the wealth of the aggregate tobacco region was greater, although the rice-growing lowland of South Carolina was richer per capita. The locus of the community in the Chesapeake was rural: tobacco's voracious appetite for soil nutrients forced planters to claim huge estates, and the need to be near the waterways resulted in plantations being strung along the rivers and estuaries. Miles of forests often separated the various plantations, and transportation was provided by boats—homes and churches in Tidewater Virginia and Maryland usually faced the water routes.

Trading towns and villages were slow to develop because the great planters each had their own wharf and from there shipped their tobacco to commission merchants in London. The commission merchant would sell the tobacco, reimburse himself for purchases the planter had made the previous year or two and take out a carrying charge, then purchase goods for the tobacco planter on credit predicated on the following year's crop and ship the goods back directly to the planter's wharf. The largest planters often helped market the tobacco of the smaller producers in their neighborhood and received goods from the commission merchant, which the planters in turn sold to the farmers. Consequently, opportunities for Chesapeake storekeepers or artisans were so limited that there was little economic reason for towns to emerge.

After the Tobacco Inspection Act took effect in 1732, tiny villages sometimes developed near the public tobacco warehouses—perhaps a tavern was built next door. Also, after the 1730s Scottish factors began to locate in the Chesapeake, especially in Virginia, and they changed how tobacco was marketed. The factors bought the tobacco directly from the grower in Virginia, paid him on the spot for his crop, stored it in local warehouses, then shipped the tobacco in large lots to Glasgow. They bought store goods in bulk and shipped them back to Virginia, established local stores near their warehouses, and from the stores supplied the needs of the planters and farmers. Tiny commercial villages began to appear near the waterways of Maryland and Virginia after mid-century, and Norfolk grew into a marketing and transshipping center, but the Chesapeake gentry defined themselves in rural terms. At best, they styled themselves English country gentlemen.

Scattered along the waterways and separated from one another by the almost trackless forests, outnumbered by servants, tenants, small farmers, and slaves, wealthy planters sought ways to set themselves above the middling crowd and make a visible statement about their wealth, political power, and aspirations to leadership. Perhaps, too, they wanted to overawe those beneath them and thus earn, in a deferential society, the right to lead. For these reasons, and because they aped their English role models, Chesapeake planters by the second quarter of the eighteenth century began to build handsome country mansions whose size and architectural grandeur spoke tangibly to their owner's importance. (In ways the planters could have only imperfectly recognized, the size of their houses may have helped maintain their authority over their slaves: in many African societies only the tribal chief lived in a two-story house, whose very height, towering over the common people's huts, symbolized his eminence.) By their dress, by their hauteur, by their fine horses and carriages, by their ostentatious betting at horse races and cock fights, the powerful planters exhibited their claims to colonial leadership. Marriage between propertied families sealed political alliances as surely as it protected inheritances, and the habit of visiting among kin and social equals countered the loneliness of rural habitation at the same time that it welded together the gentry's sense of political and cultural hegemony. Powerful, competitive men perceiving a need to act in consort required ways of deflecting intragroup tensions, and in the colonial Chesapeake good manners, graciousness, and sociableness smoothed the gears of social intercourse.

Chesapeake planters were practical men, not intellectuals, though certainly many of them had great intellect—in that sense, John Marshall was the truer ultimate product of colonial Virginia than was Thomas Jefferson. Social grace—being a good dancer, for example—and skill at witty conversation and repartee took one further than the smell of midnight oil, but knowing how to mix and find compromise among powerful and self-important men was a valuable political art the Virginians especially learned well. Those skills, honed in the affairs of daily life, combined with a habit of command learned by controlling slaves, would give Virginians disproportionate political influence in the two generations following 1775. In Annapolis, the only Chesapeake town with a stable urban population—Williamsburg swelled to town size only when the assembly was in session—there was a sparkling if limited urban ambience, with theatrical productions and music in season, and a social organization, the Tuesday Club, where urbane colonial gentry, led by Dr. Alexander Hamilton, met to dine, debate, and descant, usually with humor, on a variety of topics sacred and profane. But this was hardly a leisure society. Even the wealthiest planters were first and foremost *planters*, concerned with the management of slaves and the cultivation and marketing of crops. Yet it is important to recognize that the most successful planters were more entrepreneurial in orientation than the agricultural connotation of the word *planters* suggests. They were alert to changes in the market and open to new profitable crops—whether indigo in South Carolina or wheat in Virginia. They would tinker in commerce, land development and speculation, or other ventures when opportunity offered itself. The Chesapeake's was a working gentry—agricultural businessmen, not philosophers—and when in the decades after 1760 they found themselves drawn to consider issues of politics, local, practical matters framed their considerations of statecraft.

The Carolina rice (and indigo) society was newer than the Chesapeake society, with real wealth and family stability coming after 1725. Because of the capital needed to start rice cultivation or indigo manufacture, only the better-off planters could even begin to compete, and the fortunes that could be earned accelerated their ability to expand their holdings of both land and slaves. So a smaller percentage of the white population in South Carolina owned slaves, and they owned substantially more. Poor whites and slaveless farmers were squeezed out of the rice-growing region—in the Chesapeake, planters, farmers, and tenants lived intermingled—with the result that isolated white planter families lived on plantations of sometimes thousands of acres amid huge numbers of slaves. The blacks outnumbered the whites in the Carolina lowcountry by margins as high as twenty-to-one, producing an edginess, even fear, on the part of many whites, an instant desire to protect one's honor, pride, and "right" to command that would mark South Carolinians down to Fort Sumter.

This lowcountry, with its vast fields flooded with stagnant water, was an Eden for mosquitoes, and though no one understood the connection, malaria was pandemic for whites. Carolina was, the saying went, "in the spring a paradise, in the summer a hell, and in the autumn a hospital." Africans, however, possessed a degree of immunity to malaria and seldom got the disease or had a mild case, further proof, if the whites needed any, that somehow blacks were naturally suited to be slaves working in the rice fields. Planters quickly learned by sad experience that it was healthier in the summer and early fall to move to Charles Town. There, in the brisk sea breezes, disease seemed to be blown away—no one suspected that it was the mosquitoes that in fact were blown away, but the effect was the same. After the loneliness of rural plantation life and the atmosphere of tension tinged with fear because of the surrounding majority of blacks, life together with fellow planters in Charles Town was gay indeed.

Magnificent town houses, often built a single room wide and stretching back from the street with a piazza down the side to maximize the cooling and health-giving breezes, gave Charles Town a splendor and urbanity unmatched in America. The social life and hospitality displayed to visitors in the rural Chesapeake were on exhibit for all to see in lively Charles Town. Theater, lending libraries, dining clubs, and musical societies (the St. Cecilia Society is the oldest musical organization in North America) gave a sheen to social life in Charles Town that reminded some visitors of London. The planters and their ladies strolled about and rode carriages in a splendor of dress and equipage that told their social class and significance to all onlookers. Conspicuous consumption was their game, and a serious game it was. The South Carolina lowcountry was the most aristocratic region in the South, and the government of the colony was the least concerned to give the lower orders a degree of participation. Here was deferential politics in its most uncompromising form, and the show of wealth and power was meant to keep the poor upcountry whites in their place as much as it was hoped to overawe and keep under control the black majority.

Charles Town was a real city, not just the dwelling place and parade ground of the planting gentry. It was the largest colonial city south of Philadelphia, with a population over 10,000, and it was a major seaport—a visitor in 1773 reported 350 sailing ships in harbor and said the "number of shipping far surpassed all I had ever seen in Boston." In addition to the thousands of hogsheads of rice and indigo shipped to England, substantial amounts of corn, livestock, and timber products were sent to the West Indies. Each year, prodigious amounts of deer skins were exported from Charles Town, and from the earliest days of the city it lay on the route of maritime shipping via the Gulf Stream from the West Indies to England, and many ships lay in for provisions and repair. Here, too, were merchants, artisans, and shopkeepers plying their trades, and a polyglot population consisting of members from most European countries, along with a large, skilled slave population. Understandably, even though its economy depended upon rural production of agricultural commodities, the Carolina gentry felt themselves to be an urban, urbane people. But in their attitudes toward slaves and who should exercise political and cultural power, the Carolina gentry stood shoulder to shoulder with their Chesapeake counterparts.

THE DEVELOPMENT OF A SLAVE CULTURE

The gentry, of course, owed the grandeur of their lifestyles not just to their business acumen and broad acres but to the labor of tens of thousands of slaves, most of whom were black. Far-reaching changes occurred in the slave workforce between 1700 and 1750, transformations that immeasurably altered the experience of the bondspeople. By the second quarter of the eighteenth century, the slave population became self-sustaining; the indigenous population growth outnumbered slave imports, which began to make possible the development of the slave family and a flowering of slave culture. With the growth of the slave population also came significant changes in white attitudes toward blacks, and the legal restrictions against slaves hardened, but ironically the beneficial developments in the slave quarters countered many of the harsh aspects of white treatment. To a surprising degree, slaves carved out their own special world, often coexisting spatially with whites but with a degree of cultural autonomy whites seldom comprehended. Whites and blacks living cheek-by-jowl together for two centuries borrowed a whole range of attitudes and behaviors from each other, often never fully realizing the degree of their interrelationship. The result was in many ways a biracial culture, with both on occasion borrowing from the Indians in their midst. Red, white, and black living close together and in tension with one another created a hybrid southern culture. Indians and blacks had more cultural autonomy than formerly was acknowledged and they affected each other and the dominant white culture—and in turn were affected by it—in subtle and profound ways historians have still not completely plumbed. The slave experience, so central to understanding the history of the region, was fundamentally transformed in the mid-eighteenth century.

Before about 1700, when the number of blacks in the Chesapeake and Carolina was quite small and they were scattered among a working class of white indentured servants or worked side by side with their owners, a surprising degree of harmony existed between blacks and whites. There was a general English predisposition to see blacks—indeed, anyone not English—as inferior, but as long as there were relatively few blacks and they seemed relatively acculturated, this potential for harsh racism was only occasionally activated. Lower-class white workers and black slaves interacted with apparently little racial consciousness, and the owners of labor—indentured or chattel—treated all workers essentially the same. This seventeenth-century harmony was short-lived, for as the number of slaves rapidly increased in the 1690s, then became a torrent after 1700 in both the Chesapeake and Carolina, racial attitudes rapidly changed. Not only were there more slaves, but they were coming directly from Africa. Hitherto, most imported slaves had spent some time in the West Indies and had to a degree been acculturated, but far larger numbers of far stranger Africans were beginning to dominate the work force. These exotic African slaves were called "outlandish" to distinguish them from the acculturated, American-born slaves called "country-born."

By the end of the first decade of the eighteenth century, black slaves outnumbered whites in many Tidewater counties of Virginia and in South Carolina as a whole. Blacks now appeared threatening, and the English predisposition to see slaves as vastly inferior, perhaps even subhuman, came into play. The result was a spate of laws passed between 1690 and 1715 in both slave regions that significantly downgraded the legal status of slaves. Slaves were no longer seen as individual co-workers but increasingly as indistinguishable members of a degraded and despised alien work force. With slaves perceived as property more than as persons, it became easier in this hardening racial atmosphere for whites to treat slaves with a harshness and an impersonalism almost unthinkable in the mid-seventeenth century.

The continued prosperity of both tobacco and rice cultivation led to increased slave imports, and during the middle decades of the eighteenth century more Africans entered the colonies than at any other time before or later. The increasing Africanization of the slave population led to even harsher racial attitudes—whites casually treated blacks more inhumanely in these years than ever before, and worse than they did after about 1800. Brutal whippings were more common in these years than they were later, though the brutality extended throughout society and was not confined to slaves. These were years in which sailors were whipped within an inch of their lives for minor infractions, felons were publicly hanged and their heads impaled on pikes for all to see, white and red captives in Indian wars were scalped or burned alive by both sides, and lower-class whites fought, bit, and gouged eyes with reckless abandon. In terms of laws and white behavioral patterns, the second and third quarters of the eighteenth century were the nadir of slave–planter relationships.

It is but another of the many ironies of southern history that events in the slave quarters were so changing the lives of most blacks that in the midst of hardening white attitudes the conditions for slaves were actually improving—not because of white actions but rather because slaves creatively learned to cope with the exigencies of bondage in a raw new world. As the influx of African imports grew to flood proportions, many slaves, uprooted from their traditional societies, found themselves culturally adrift in the New World and often unable to speak the language of the other slaves with whom their lot was cast—West Africa contained hundreds of different culture groups with mutually unintelligible tongues. Slaves quickly created a pidgin language composed of fragments of African languages, some English, and perhaps some Spanish, Dutch, and Portuguese, the languages of the principal slave-trading nations. This pidgin became the lingua franca for communication with fellow slaves and with the whites. Slowly, as the slaves became acculturated, the pidgin evolved in the direction of standard English, though peculiarities of syntax and pronunciation remained. In regions, such as the Sea Islands, where there was little direct contact with whites, the pidgin language became the mother tongue of the American-born (i.e., creole) slaves, and in this creolized form it became known as Gullah in South Carolina and Gee Chee in Georgia. This pidginization process, whereby slaves from various African societies with differing experiences in the New World created a "new" hybrid language that allowed them to communicate with one another, was but the earliest example of a process of culture-creation by American slaves. The resulting tongue, neither truly African nor truly English but rather African-American, was a makeshift adjustment to the realities of slavery that, by allowing slaves to talk, broke down the isolation and loneliness that left them so alienated and bereft of a sense of human community when first sold in America. A common language was the first step toward creating an African-American community.

Before a significant African-American community could develop, there had to be a significant number of blacks living separately enough from the white majority to have at least a degree of cultural elbow room. In the first two or three generations of the slave presence in the southern colonies there were so few blacks and they lived in such small groupings so intermingled with white indentured servants that much of their Africanness was bleached out of them. Many individual blacks isolated on small plantations had almost no contact with other blacks; there were very few African women, so family formation was very difficult. A population of mostly young black males seemed to have little need for their traditional cultural rituals and had little possibility of sustaining them if they felt their loss. Since the ritual specialists in Africa were nearly always elderly people, there was no market for them in the New World. The multiplicity of African tribal groups and cultures made it difficult for American slaves to find persons who shared their precise cultural outlook. The result, throughout most of the seventeenth century, was a small slave population whose African roots almost dried up.

In the final years of the seventeenth century the rising tide of slave imports from Africa began to change the nature of the slave community in profound ways, and the import figures continued to grow, peaking in the mid-eighteenth century before declining in the last quarter of the century. (The trade would be legally ended in 1808.) This fresh injection of African people and African culture came at a moment when the early slave population, previously Europeanized, was beginning to grow indigenously and seek cultural roots. These two simultaneous developments led to a flowering of African-American culture in the eighteenth-century South, a culture more Europeanized than slave cultures in the West Indies and Latin America, yet more Africanized than recognized until very recently. The key to this transformation of the slave experience in the southern colonies was indigenous black population growth during the age of slave imports, which in the New World colonies occurred only in the American South.

In the first decades of the importation of blacks, the slave population in the Chesapeake and Carolina suffered a net population loss; as with the whites, the population grew slowly only because of substantial immigration, with annual deaths far outnumbering births. This failure of the indigenous population to grow was primarily caused, for whites and blacks, by disease and by an imbalance in the ratio of men to women. No population consisting overwhelmingly of males can sustain population growth, and the importers of laborers (whether servants or slaves) preferred young males. The relatively few women did not live long enough in the early years to have many children, while the restrictions against white servant women getting pregnant (the penalty was having their time of service extended) and the rigors of the passage on the slaving ship, which often left slave women unable to conceive until after a year or two of recuperation, further restrained indigenous population growth. Yet the few children who were born and survived to adulthood were acculturated to the American environment and healthier than their parents had been, and their sex ratios were essentially even. The result, initially, was a small group of American-born slave women who could bear more children over a longer period of time; and the second generation of creole children, still healthier, when they became adults found it much easier to find mates.

The developing colonial societies also built roads and established ferries, making travel less difficult and increasing the range of potential marriage partners with whom slaves came into contact. As the slave (and general) population grew and the size of slaveholdings expanded, more potential mates were available. With prosperity came more adequate food supplies—the starving times were past. The slave women also may have abandoned the African practice of nursing children for three years or more and (because plentiful food in America allowed women to provide their toddlers nourishment other than milk, because black males felt that sex with a nursing mother was taboo and therefore pressed for a shorter nursing time, or because slave women simply chose to or were forced by their white masters to emulate the white women) adopted the English practice of weaning their children at about one year of age. Since lactation and nursing acts as a natural contraceptive, the decrease in the length of nursing contributed to a very significant increase in the number of black births. Hence the increased number of children of the American-born or creole slaves made possible the beginning of slave population growth, and the effect was cumulative.

In the first decade and a half of the eighteenth century, many Indian women were enslaved in South Carolina, further increasing the availability of spouses for black males. (The Indians apparently taught the slaves much about the foods easily grown in the South, for certainly blacks adopted and soon made their own such Indian vegetables as corn, beans, peas, squash, and pumpkins, and such native foods contributed to the improved diets of all southerners.) Throughout the colonies from Maryland to South Carolina the growing presence of slave women and the increase in life expectancy slowly changed the outlook of adult slaves. Now they could anticipate not just several lonely years of unrequited toil but a spouse and family, and love and companionship became possible for southern slaves even in the midst of a life of bondage and hard labor. By the second quarter of the eighteenth century, population growth through reproduction had begun in the Chesapeake and in Carolina, and slaves living in family groups were becoming normative. The increase in the size of average slaveholding meant that, while formerly an owner's one or two slaves probably lived in the attic or slept in the kitchen or a lean-to attached to the house, the ten or more slaves lived in their own small houses separate from the main house and, in the evenings, out of sight and to a degree beyond the supervision of the whites. In this niche a surprisingly autonomous slave culture soon took root.

A slave population consisting of parents and children was incidentally easier for the owners to control, for slave men were not likely to run away or participate in rebellious activity that might cause repercussions for their wives or children. Undeniably the companionship and love that slaves found in their families made bondage more endurable, and parents, now that they had children to nurture, explored ways to recreate in America some semblance of the rituals—half remembered but still meaningful—traditionally used to ceremonialize significant events in the lives of their children. At this moment, when slave families were realizing anew the importance of traditional culture, the rise of African imports provided a fresh injection of African beliefs and practices. There were no ritual specialists present, and the precise ingredients of the rituals, specific to each African tribal group, were non-existent in the South; furthermore, the variety of tribal groups represented by the slave population meant there was little agreement on the exact nature of the rituals. But there emerged a common recognition that such events as births, reaching adulthood, and death, needed ceremonial authentication, and this common need led to the creation of synthesized, hybrid cultural expressions that were—like the pidgin language that arose—neither truly African nor Anglo but rather African-American. Perhaps it should be pointed out that while slaves borrowed, adapted, and subtly transformed much from Indians and whites, the borrowing went in both directions. Whites, too, found their own culture—their music, food, language—benefitted from the interchange. To a degree not always recognized, what historians and journalists even today call southern culture is surprisingly biracial in origin.

As though there was a sort of African grammatical principle embedded deep within, slaves from a variety of African locations and in diverse southern settings came to express their African-American culture in their music, their patterns of naming their children, their funeral customs, and their body language, in the motifs woven into their baskets and sewn into their quilts, in their conceptions of the proper size and shape of their housing, in their attitudes toward kinship, and in myriad other ways. A sense of cultural autonomy told them they were not empty vessels filled at the whim of whites but rather were a people who though in bondage had a personality, an existence, an inner self beyond the corrupting effect of enslavement. Out of this came a sense of pride and self-worth that helped most slaves survive bondage, even at its eighteenth-century worst, with a degree of dignity and integrity left intact. While the laws and white attitudes became increasingly harsh, these developments in the slave quarters ameliorated the lives of most slaves.

By 1750 slaves performed the bulk of the menial agricultural labor in the wealthy tidewater and lowcountry regions where tobacco, rice, and indigo were produced for export, but they always worked at a variety of other tasks as well. Slaves cleared land, herded livestock, fished, worked in the naval stores industry, and served in the maritime trade, often utilizing skills first learned in Africa. Many slaves had experience in wood and metalworking in Africa, skills readily transferable to carpentry, cabinetmaking, and blacksmithing. As planters learned that trained blacks could perform such artisanal trades, there came to be even less use of white servants and less need of villages where artisans plied their crafts. As the diversified economy in the Chesapeake region especially created an increased demand for slave men to be trained as artisans, slave women were increasingly relegated to field work. The largest plantations became almost like independent little fiefdoms, and the slave quarters on such plantations became practically African-American villages. The architectural ensemble of the master's house, a separate kitchen building, the overseer's house, the several slave houses, along with barns, sheds, and other outbuildings made the large plantations more imposing parts of the landscape than the scattered crossroads villages strewn across the South.

In the Carolina lowcountry the average holding of slaves was much higher, and since the owners spent a good portion of the year at Charles Town, leaving the plantation under the control of an overseer, slaves in the rice-growing region had less contact with whites and consequently had greater control of their everyday lives. Blacks outnumbered whites in the lowcountry by margins of up to twenty-to-one, and large-scale importations of Africans continued longer in this region than elsewhere; consequently, the slave population of lowcountry South Carolina and Georgia was far denser and more heavily Africanized than slave populations anywhere else in the colonies. The task system of labor, whereby slaves in the rice-cultivation regions were given a set amount of work to perform—a mutually agreed upon "task" that most slaves could finish by early afternoon after which their time was their own—allowed lowcountry slaves a degree of autonomy over their physical and cultural lives unmatched by slaves elsewhere. Black culture in this region was more heavily characterized by African attitudes than in the Chesapeake, and far more Africanized than the general slave population in the nineteenth century.

In the Chesapeake, where the average size of slaveholdings was smaller, where many more whites lived and worked amid the slaves, and where the slaves' work routines were not set by an agreed-upon task, following the completion of which the slaves could own their own time, slaves were more completely under the supervision of whites. The result was a black population less culturally separate; African attitudes certainly affected white practices to a degree and shaped the slaves' borrowing of social and cultural patterns from the whites, but the general culture of Chesapeake slaves was far more Anglicized than was that of the lowcountry and Sea Island district to the south. The slave cultures of the Chesapeake and Carolina were as different as the respective gentry cultures were, but in the early nineteenth century, as slavery followed the cultivation of cotton across the back country into the Latin South from western Georgia to east Texas, these two slave cultures were blended together into an antebellum slave culture that closely resembled the Chesapeake model—the only exception being the sugar-growing region of south Louisiana, which demographically resembled the Carolina lowcountry.

The eighteenth century began with slavery as a newly evolving solution to the labor needs of the staple-crop regions of the South, but by mid-century slavery had emerged as a bedrock of the entire coastal South. At this date, whites were still uneasy about the looming presence of blacks and treated them with a degree of harshness and inhumanity that both reflected and legitimated the white fear about being surrounded by and often outnumbered by slaves. White racial attitudes hardened even as cultural developments in the slave community were ameliorating the lives of most blacks. Blacks succeeded in creating pockets of cultural autonomy in the midst of white control and generally had adequate food and housing, which, though small, cramped, and barely protective in winter, was not much different from that of many poor whites. But slaves did not have the freedom to shape their own lives. Slaves could not simply move west to try their lot in a new region when life got them down where they were. And that, the absence of freedom, the lack of choices and mobility—not the size of their huts or the number of calories in their meals—was the true measure of bondage. But in the mid-eighteenth century, in many ways the nadir of black–white relationships, the beginning of an African-American community had been established, and out of it arose an African-American culture that would serve to insulate many blacks from the most debilitating aspects of three centuries of bondage. That was a human achievement of the first order.

THE SOUTHERN BACKCOUNTRY

The total population of the southern colonies in 1750, Maryland to Georgia, was approximately 525,000. The racial breakdown suggests only about 5,000 Indians still survived, but there were 210,000 blacks (almost all of whom were slaves, though there were several hundred free blacks who were either the descendants of seventeenth-century free blacks or were former bondspeople freed by their owners usually for meritorious service) and 310,000 whites. A tiny percentage of the whites were of the class labeled gentry, possessors of many hundreds of acres of land and dozens of black slaves. This propertied aristocracy was disproportionately influential in local colonial politics, and their attitudes toward government, slavery, commerce, and the law helped shape the contours of southern history. To a significant degree, southern leaders both economic and political would be drawn from their ranks. But the southern gentry were few in number. The majority of whites in 1750, as in 1850, owned no slaves, and most slaveholders possessed fewer than five slaves. This great spectrum of whites, ranging from small slaveholders living in the tidewater and lowcountry to slaveless farmers in the Piedmont and mountain valleys to propertyless tenants and day laborers in the developed portion of the region and hardscrabble settlers in the backcountry, represented the majority of whites. Their story is less well known than that of the wealthy planters and slaves, but their contribution to the history of the South is equally great.

Only in the narrow, flat lowcountry of coastal South Carolina and Georgia were practically all whites slaveholders. Even in those colonies, beyond that special region where the ebb and flow of the ocean's tides could be harnessed to serve the needs of rice cultivation, many poor whites lived in the interstices of the plantation economy, growing corn and peas and keeping hogs and cattle, mainly for their own consumption but occasionally for sale either to rice or indigo planters who miscalculated their food needs, to the expanding urban population of Charles Town, or to markets in the West Indies. Still other whites, sometimes aided by a slave or two, found work in some aspect of the timber industry, perhaps making shingles or barrel staves. These whites often owned their farms, lived in log cabins, raised large families, hoped some day to be able to buy slaves, and, by their lights, prospered. Compared to the brick town houses and social graces of the aristocrats of Charles Town, these plain people appeared to upper-class travelers to be dirty, uncouth, immoral, and violent, but such descriptions suggest more about the class biases of the writers than about the lifestyle of the plain folk.

Throughout the tobacco-growing region of the Chesapeake many small slaveholders and slaveless farmers lived in the shadows of the great mansions facing the broad rivers. Again the dwellings and lifestyle of these people seem primitive when juxtaposed to the baronial estate of a William Byrd at Westover, but they were much better off than the British peasantry and their quality of life was similar to that of their later pioneer descendants across the South and West. Their homes were small, perhaps one or two rooms with a dirt floor, and their clothes were homespun. Furnishings were simple and homemade, and people were accustomed to growing and preparing most of their own food. In addition to grain and livestock, which they ate, perhaps selling any surplus, they often planted several acres of tobacco to earn spending money. Those with more hands, either slaves or older sons, planted proportionally more tobacco. Like most small farmers, they first took care to provide enough food for their families and slaves, if they owned any, and then with the land and labor left over they planted a cash crop. The tenant farmers worked land rented from the great planters and they, too, emphasized food production but grew enough tobacco to pay their landlord.

North Carolina was dominated by such small planters and farmers, growing mixed crops and laboring in the timber and naval stores industries. Life was unpolished and sometimes hard, but it was usually not, as William Byrd suggested in the 1720s and 1730s, brutish. He called the inhabitants of North Carolina "Wretches" living "in a dirty State of Nature" and described a crowded overnight stay in a cabin ("pigged . . . together") with his party of travelers as being "littered down in one room, in company with my landlady and four children." But many of these farmers, adapted to exploiting whatever small opportunities came their way, were willing to endure hardship and poverty while carving out a life for themselves and their children, and when soil exhaustion and the increasing aggrandizement of the best lands by the powerful planters lessened their prospects in the tidewater and lowcountry, they were ready to move westward into the Piedmont and on toward the back country, where they joined another migration from the north. By 1750, in many ways the most dynamic portion of the South was the Piedmont and back country, a region of new opportunity for small farmers from the eastern sections and new immigrants from Europe by way of Pennsylvania.

Fur traders and occasional hunters had crossed the first ridge of mountains and had entered the broad valley running southwestward from Pennsylvania all the way to the Carolina and Georgia uplands before 1730, but it was in that year that permanent settlement of the valley by Europeans began. A group of Germans trekked from Pennsylvania in 1730 following the Shenandoah Valley south and settled near present-day Luray, Virginia; within several years, thousands more Palatine Germans, then Scotch-Irish from Ulster, and English Quakers, and an assortment of other pioneers traveled down the valley and by mid-century were peopling the interior of Virginia, North and South Carolina, and, by the Revolution, northern Georgia. These hardy pioneers, often Lutheran or Presbyterian, practiced a mixed agriculture, growing grains and keeping cattle, and hunted to complement what they could raise. Poor but industrious, they built sawmills and grist mills on the numerous rapids, mined iron ore and lead, sent hogs and cattle by foot to the markets to the east, made a living however they could. Not a few prospered and enjoyed upward mobility.

Let the example of one family suggest the nature of this migration. The Calhoun family from the Scottish highlands had, early in the eighteenth century, migrated to Ireland. Frustrated after a generation, the family moved to Pennsylvania and settled near the Maryland line. When the elder Patrick Calhoun died in 1741, he had an estate of £150 along with livestock and land. But within several years the Calhoun family, hearing of better opportunities to the south, picked up and moved to Augusta County, Virginia, near the North Carolina border. By the 1750s the Calhouns owned three thousand acres and were cultivating two hundred. But then an Indian raid discouraged them, so four Calhoun brothers (sons of Patrick) and their families, along with their elderly mother, moved again in 1756 to western South Carolina, near the settlement named Ninety-Six. By the mid-1760s elder son Patrick was emerging as a local leader, and in 1770 he married a Scotch-Irish woman named Martha Caldwell. At the outbreak of the Revolutionary War, Patrick was an elected member of the state assembly that voted for independence. And by 1790 Patrick Calhoun owned thirty-one slaves, thousands of acres of land, had great herds of cattle, sheep, and hogs, and grew many acres of corn, wheat, and oats. He also had a young son named John Caldwell Calhoun, of whom more will be heard.

This western territory beyond the Piedmont was new country, so there were no established families and no entrenched political power bases to control the local government, but courts and the other sinews of government soon appeared and, although there was frequent turnover of officeholders, the governmental institutions were stable. The turnover meant less social chaos than social mobility; within one or two decades certain families emerged better off than others, while some younger sons from the plantation region arrived with the wherewithal to purchase larger acreages and even buy slaves, but the economy of the valley remained mixed agriculture. In the Piedmont or in other regions east of the mountains left undeveloped before 1725 or so, as the farmers and small slaveholders grew more prosperous and increasingly became involved in tobacco cultivation, their needs for credit and for marketing their cash crops drew them inexorably into closer contact with the older, better established regions of the colony. Commercial agriculture in the form of tobacco gradually integrated the newer portions of the Chesapeake with the earlier settled regions. Later, cotton culture would serve the same purpose in the early nineteenth century: help create a unified economy and outlook from South Carolina all the way to Mississippi and even Texas.

The relatively egalitarian society that developed in the back country proved adaptable to a variety of terrains and climates. With simple log cabins, a willingness to grow whatever the soil and seasons allowed and on a small enough scale that slaves were not necessary, and a desire to go wherever opportunity seemed to beckon, the settlement pattern of the back country, after incorporating the cultivation of cotton, eventually spread throughout much of the South. Backcountry egalitarianism was a characteristic only of the first generation. Quickly an incipient upper class began to develop and take leadership positions. These enterprising leaders wanted not to perpetuate frontier patterns but to adopt the social structures of the more established East, including courts, schools, churches, and economic institutions. For example, backcountry settlers and their descendants obtained slaves as soon as they could afford them, for they seldom opposed slavery per se. The comparative absence of slaves in the region was a matter of economics, not ideology; whites everywhere shared the view that blacks were natural slaves and a sound, proper investment. The profits from upland cotton would after 1800 seal the dominance of slavery in the antebellum South.

The backcountry was never as geographically isolated as it has sometimes been presented. During the first decades, as settlement moved down the valley, the mountains served to set the region off to a degree, but even then there were economic, cultural, and kinship ties both to Pennsylvania and to the coastal regions. For example, the wealthy Tidewater planter and land speculator Daniel Dulany visited western Maryland in 1744 and witnessed firsthand the stream of German settlers and some of their well-managed farms, and instantly saw the potential they offered. Subsequently the entrepreneurial Dulany patented 20,000 acres of choice western land, sold it (often on credit) in family-farm-sized parcels to Palatine settlers, and set aside some 7,000 acres on which to establish Frederick Town. Giving artisans and tradesmen town lots at rates they could not turn down, Dulany bet on the increasing population and prosperity of the entire region to raise the value of his remaining lots and farm property. Soon Frederick Town was a booming success, and Dulany still richer, proving his skill as a land and town developer.

On other occasions the influence went from west to east, as in Virginia where a Scotch-Irish Presbyterian minister from the valley, William Robinson, hearing in 1743 of a small-scale "Lutheran" revival developing in Hanover County, just north of Richmond, traveled east to bring the movement under the auspices of the Presbyterian Church. In rural Hanover County a group of people, hungry for the fellowship of a church community, had begun to meet together in each other's houses, and lacking a minister, read from an old book of Martin Luther's sermons and a more recent publication of the sermons of George Whitefield. Moved simply by hearing the sermons read, a localized spiritual awakening erupted. Robinson accurately saw this as a missionary opportunity, came east to preach in person to these religiously starved farmers, and effectively proselytized them from their tentative association with Lutheranism or Anglicanism to his own Presbyterian faith.

The continuing influence of Pennsylvania was exhibited in many ways, but nowhere more spectacularly than in the development of the Moravian community in North Carolina. The Moravians, a pietistic group originally from Saxony, had settled for a few years in Georgia, but after the threat of war with Spanish Florida had moved to Pennsylvania in 1740. Their initial two settlements there, Bethlehem and Nazareth, proved very successful. In 1752 the Moravian leader, Bishop August Gottlieb Spangenberg, came down the valley to select a site for a new southern settlement. He found the mountains impressive but for farming liked the rolling, well-watered terrain of the North Carolina Piedmont, and he made arrangements in 1753 to purchase one hundred thousand acres there. In the fall of that year an advance party of Moravian farmers, carpenters, and other craftsmen arrived at a place soon called Wachovia to build the infrastructure for the later, more substantial migration. More Moravians soon came south by foot and by wagon, motivated by their religion to work hard and build a new life, and the region prospered. Church leaders regulated commerce, often set prices, and helped maintain among the Moravians a firm sense that they were a special people. The trading town of Salem was established in 1766, but the industrious farmers and craftsmen of the settlement had long before brought stability and profits to the German-speaking community on the Piedmont.

The backcountry and the Piedmont in 1750 were the newest portions of the South, the most ethnically diverse, the most politically and socially egalitarian, the least tied to slave labor—a matter of affordability, however, not ideology—and with the greatest range of economies. During the period from 1750 until the Revolution this region was also the most rapidly growing part of the South, with a population in 1776 reaching 250,000. In 1750, however, there was still no sense of a "South" that encompassed the entire region. Interests were either local—defined by immediate needs, kinship, and ethnicity—or agricultural—defined by the particular marketing requisites of the major crop, tobacco or rice. Slavery was dominant in a good portion of the Chesapeake and in the Carolina–Georgia lowcountry and present to a degree everywhere, but the institution of slavery in and of itself did not set the South apart in 1750 from the other English mainland and island colonies. From the perspective of London the whole South in mid-century seemed more internally stable, more prosperous, more militarily safe from European rivals than ever before. Willingly absorbing settlers from England and elsewhere and producing valuable raw products for the mother country, the South represented the ideal English colonies in 1750. The region had come a long way from the tragic, mistake-ridden days of the lost Roanoke colony or early, deadly Jamestown. The future seemed bright indeed from England's perspective, and from the colonies', in the mid-eighteenth century.

❈ CHAPTER 2 ❈

The National South

Because writing history is a retrospective art, an author knows in advance the conclusion of his story, and the plot outline seems so clear that the early portions of a narrative often serve merely to set the stage for what logically follows. Were one able to look at history prospectively, with no foreknowledge, its development would appear more disjointed. Promising projects turn out to founder, seemingly insignificant irritants grow into major problems, completely unforeseen issues arise to divide people and fuel discontent. Of course, no one can really write about the past as though the outcome was unknown to the writer; one must be alert to contingency, however, and demonstrate that certain historical actions or attitudes emerge from a welter of influences.

Nowhere is this problem more pressing than in writing about the coming of the American Revolution. One must begin to talk about its causes in a subtle way, recognizing that what are now seen as causes were completely overlooked or misunderstood by contemporaries; yet one must realize that, from the vantage point of contemporaries, nothing is predestined or predetermined. Again and again the human actors in history are caught unaware. At a number of occasions another decision, another action, another practical outcome, would have affected subsequent history in unfathomable ways. All one can do is to try to determine what in fact did happen in a specific time and place and attempt to relate in a causal fashion the multitude of persons, perceptions, and actions—placed in a variety of contexts—that make the events understandable. Historiography is not a science, it is not predictive; rather, it is a creative written reenactment of a portion of what is known to have occurred, an attempt to give life and meaning to commonly accepted data on the past.

The cumulative events of the 1750s and early 1760s did not lead to the colonial rupture with Great Britain, although the result of those developments helped produce a political climate in the 1770s out of which revolutionary sentiment emerged. No one in 1760 or 1770 or even as late as 1775 understood what lay beyond the threshold of their time. Yet to understand why things happened as they did in the compact and tumultuous half-decade before 1776 one must look at the evolving relationship between the maturing colonies and an increasingly hard-pressed mother country. People on both sides of the Atlantic misunderstood the others' situation and incorrectly assigned malevolent intentions to unexceptionable actions. In a sense London had never really comprehended what life was like and what settlers needed in the New World, and colonists had always chafed under what they interpreted as England's arrogance and ignorance. This potentially explosive mutual antagonism had for over a century been defused by the colonists' dependence on English supplies and protection and by England's failure to rule efficiently and rationally her overseas empire. But both English neglect and colonial dependence began to change in the mid-eighteenth century, imperceptibly at first, and no one sensed any long-term implications.

VIRGINIA'S FIRST QUARRELS WITH ENGLAND

Virginia was by far the most populous of the southern colonies, with one-third of the region's total population; and the volume of its overall maritime commerce far outranked that of any other colony. Virginia's age, stability, wealth, and size gave it a sense of self-importance that no other southern colony could entertain in 1750. Yet that same wealth and power brought it increasingly to the notice of a newly attentive England in mid-century. For several decades England had neglected supervision of its American colonies, but following the conclusion in 1748 of King George's War, the nature of British politics changed: a new group of leaders emerged, determined to administer the affairs of empire with fresh vigor and purpose. George Dunk, the Earl of Halifax, was appointed head of the Board of Trade and set forth to regulate commerce and fulfill what had always been a theoretical responsibility of the board—oversee and ratify colonial legislation. Independent of Halifax's coming to office, the Virginia assembly had begun in its 1748 and 1749 sessions to overhaul and codify the colony's laws. This was seen as routine legislative housekeeping, and the newly worded laws were printed and placed in force before they were reviewed formally by the Board of Trade and then ratified by the Privy Council. From the Virginia viewpoint such oversight was unnecessary because it had not previously occurred and, furthermore, these were not new laws but simply a recodification of older statutes. But this *was* a new Board of Trade. Under Halifax it was aggressively fulfilling its theoretical responsibilities to review colonial legislation. Consequently, after considering the Virginia statutes until 1751, the Board of Trade finally responded. It disallowed ten laws, accepted seven provisionally, accepted fifty-seven, and sent three back to the assembly for colonial reconsideration. To Virginians this response to their recodified laws was an unprecedented and unnecessary degree of interference in the legislative process of a stable, mature, responsible colony, and it rankled them considerably.

Simultaneously, another unsettling issue arose in Virginia. In 1749 the popular royal governor Sir William Gooch—who empathized with the colonists—returned to England, to be replaced two years later by Robert Dinwiddie, a meticulous Scottish businessman concerned first with royal interests and then with his own. Seeing the population growth in western Virginia and the related boom in land patents, Dinwiddie believed that he could better regulate land sales and, at the same time, fatten his own account by charging a fee for validating a land patent. He chose as his fee a widely circulated Spanish coin, the pistole, worth 18s. 6d.—as one historian has written, "roughly the purchase price of a cow." This charge hit small farmers and settlers very hard, and many powerful colonists with extensive land speculations were outraged because they hoped to profit from selling parcels of their holdings to small farmers. Virginians accurately perceived the pistole fee not as an essential and legitimate imperial regulation but rather as a way to line the pockets of an arrogant royal bureaucrat; it would limit the settlement of the West and was, even worse, a flagrant infringement of a people's right not to be taxed, not to have their property taken, without their consent! Urgent and forthright remonstrances were made to the Privy Council, which technically ruled in favor of the governor's levying such a fee. In practical terms, however, the governor's fee-charging prerogative was limited so extensively that, in essence, the council's ruling supported the colonials. Virginians would later have reason to remember the controversy, their direct complaints, and the favorable outcome, and they drew predictable conclusions about the efficacy of such remonstrances.

By the time the pistole argument was settled, the colonies and England were being drawn into an American war against the French and their Indian allies. In the midst of that conflict another dispute arose in Virginia over colonial control of local financial matters. For years the Anglican clergy in Virginia had been paid in tobacco—16,000 pounds of the leaves annually. In the mid-1750s two years of bad harvest had raised the price per pound of tobacco, giving the clergy what amounted to a significant increase in salary. To relieve the taxpayers the Virginia assembly in 1755 and again in 1758 had passed what came to be called the Twopenny Acts, which allowed the salaries to be paid not in the actual poundage of tobacco but rather at the rate of two pence per pound, a fair rate historically but substantially less than what tobacco fetched in the years of short harvest. The 1758 act had been in force for twelve months when the angry clergy decided to fight it—in part because the act had not formally been submitted for Privy Council approval but also because it deprived the clergy of what they saw as their legal due. The Reverend John Camm went to England and asked not simply that the current act be disallowed but that both Twopenny Acts be declared null and void from their inception, leaving open the possibility for suit to recover lost income. The Privy Council merely disallowed the acts—disregarding part of the Virginia clergy's request—but went on to chastise the assembly and Governor Francis Fauquier for not adding a suspending clause that kept the act from taking effect until the Board of Trade approved it. Camm returned to Virginia and along with other clergy tried to sue for recovery of their salaries, in the process antagonizing Governor Fauquier and further convincing colonists that nothing but trouble would be the result of increased involvement by the Board of Trade in local fiscal matters. In passionately arguing against the claims of the Reverend James Maury—a young minister who sued in the Hanover County court for the full value of his salary—a young lawyer named Patrick Henry first became known as a forest-born Demosthenes, and in the heat of the moment he claimed that by disallowing the Twopenny Act the king had forfeited claim to obedience from Virginians.

So far these minor antagonisms were primarily restricted to Virginians, though Marylanders, saddled with fees and levies to several layers of proprietary officeholders that more than doubled the effective cost of local government, had begun to resent what seemed unfair charges. The enmity of Maryland and Virginia toward English officialdom would grow under the pressure of military events, for arrogant English military officers rankled colonial militia officers, and increased wartime expenses caused colonists to insist on local control of governmental purse strings.

THE FRENCH AND INDIAN WAR AND ITS CONSEQUENCES

Both England and France claimed the broad expanse of land in the Ohio Valley—England by virtue of the earliest colonial boundaries of Virginia that had no western limits and the occasional traders and trappers from Pennsylvania and Virginia who traversed the region and on behalf of whom the area was "purchased" from the Iroquois in 1744. French claims to the region had begun with the assertion by René Robert Cavelier, Sieur de La Salle, of France's title in 1679, but more practically French trade with the

Indians gave some substance to her contention. Neither nation had permanent settlements there, though some English expansionists professed to see a French desire to link her Canadian and Louisiana territories via a broad swath of land through the heart of America that would also serve as a barrier to England's fulfilling her imperial ambitions in the New World. A group of land promoters and speculators, most from Virginia's Northern Neck—the area between the Potomac and the Rappahannock Rivers and the colony's gateway to the West—organized the Ohio Company in 1749 and were granted outright two hundred thousand prime acres above the Ohio River with the promise of three hundred thousand more once they successfully settled a hundred families on the land. The French in Canada responded by sending a small military party led by Captain Celoron de Blainville on a path roughly south from Lake Erie through westernmost Pennsylvania, marking a putative French boundary by burying metal plates inscribed with France's claims to the Ohio Valley.

This evidence of France's resolve to hold the territory prodded the Ohio Company of Virginia into quick action. The company had built a storehouse on the Virginia banks of the Potomac across from the site of present-day Cumberland, Maryland, and in 1750 increased the shipment of goods to and from the Indians in the general area. Colonial officials, hoping to solidify the English position on the northwest frontier, called a treaty parley for June 1752. The French were not sitting still: the Marquis Duquesne had meanwhile become governor of Canada, and, having ambitious plans for the disputed territory, he set out to build three forts to establish French claims. Governor Dinwiddie of Virginia, of the pistole fee controversy, hoped to prosper from his office and was an investor in the Ohio Company. He recognized that inaction might enable France to realize her imperial aspirations in the Ohio Valley. After receiving vague approval from the English secretary of state, the earl of Holderness, Dinwiddie at the end of October 1753 sent a confident, twenty-one-year old militia major, George Washington, to warn the French that they were trespassing on Virginia soil. The French officer at Fort Le Boeuf coolly rebuffed Washington's warning and sent him home empty-handed. But Washington's published account of the affair brought him instant fame and fanned the temper of the Virginians.

Caught up in the pistole fee controversy and feeling put upon by their own governor, the Virginians were quick to take offense at another insult and one from a foreign enemy at that. In this situation Governor Dinwiddie was on their side, and he obtained permission from the council to raise two hundred militia to protect workmen who were building a fort at the confluence of the Monongahela and Allegheny rivers. Finally, in April the militia, numbering fewer than the authorized two hundred men, under the command of Major Washington set out for the construction site, but they quickly learned that the French had overrun the place, destroyed the small fort, and started

building a far greater one to be named Fort Duquesne. Washington continued cautiously northward; on May 28 he surprised a small advance party of
French soldiers and killed or captured all but one of them. Expecting retaliation from the main French forces, he retreated a few miles to the south to a
place called Great Meadows and fortified his camp as quickly as possible, calling it Fort Necessity. On July 3, 1754, the larger French forces arrived, Washington's Indian allies melted away as they approached, and in the midst of a
fearful rainfall the French soundly defeated Washington's troops lying in
watery trenches. At midnight Washington surrendered, and with one rain-
splattered document he in effect turned the whole Midwest over to the
French.

Until now the skirmishes between English and French forces in the
Ohio region had been planned and executed by local officials, but London
began to comprehend that the future of their New World empire might be at
stake. War was not yet formally declared against France, but an experienced
military man, General Edward Braddock, with two regiments of regular
British troops, was dispatched to Virginia and arrived in February 1755.
Haughty, brusque, and generally contemptuous of all colonials, General
Braddock condescended to offer Washington, who had been promoted to
colonel, a position as aide-de-camp with a temporary commission as captain—Washington did not accept the demotion but agreed to serve as a volunteer. Braddock huffed and puffed and made arrangements to march overland with wagons and artillery and to hack a road through the wilderness, all
the way to Fort Duquesne.

The pace was excruciatingly slow. On July 9, just short of their destination, Braddock's men were making their way through a narrow, heavily
wooded valley with steep cliffs. Suddenly the hills came alive with Indians and
French soldiers masquerading as red men. The bullets rained down upon the
Redcoats, and, breaking all the rules of formal European warfare, the French
and Indians hid behind trees and rocks and raked the English with deadly
fire. Confusion and panic reigned, with Redcoats bumping into each other
and unable to take bead upon the now-you-see-them, now-you-don't enemy.
After the retreating English were able to take the measure of the day, they discovered a casualty rate of 70 percent, and Braddock himself was fatally
wounded. His second-in-command retreated to Fort Cumberland in Maryland
and began to make plans for his winter quarters in safe Philadelphia even
though it was only July. The mighty British army, even its experienced soldiers,
could be defeated in the wilds of America. Colonists and the government in
London were shocked by the spectacle. For the next three years the British
suffered a number of defeats along the frontier, and Indians, armed by the
French and angered by the relentless move westward of land-hungry, English-
speaking settlers, raided frontier farmsteads and forced hundreds of western
pioneers to give up their homesteads and move to safer territory in the East.

As the frontier blazed, the colonial assemblies were pressured to provide both men and money to continue the fight. Maryland, Virginia, and North Carolina, the colonies closest to the French threat, grudgingly supplied militia, though they found it irritating to serve under British officers who were often ignorant of American realities and condescending toward colonists. Funds were provided by the legislatures, and the local assemblymen pushed for more control over how the monies were to be spent. The Maryland assembly, for example, having long felt aggrieved by the levies paid to proprietary officials, used the wartime emergency to force Governor Horatio Sharpe and the proprietary court to allow military expenses to be taken from funds that otherwise would have fattened the proprietary coffers. The colonists found in the war a way to flex their fiscal muscles and were discovering, in the face of metropolitan condescension, the birth of a new sense of local patriotism. It would be too much to say that American nationalism or southern sectionalism emerged in the mid-1750s—after all, the Plan of Union worked out by delegates from seven colonies at a conference at Albany, New York, in June and July of 1754 had tentatively suggested a kind of intercolonial central government only to have all seven colonies reject their proposal—but it would be fair to suggest that events proved to many colonists that they were the equals of Englishmen and should be accorded the same respect and legal rights by the mother country. They were colonials geographically but Englishmen culturally and politically, and they were increasingly ready to say so.

For more than two years the encounters between the French and Indians had been a backwoods American affair, but by the late spring of 1756 the conflict spread to Europe, England formally declaring war against France on May 18, 1756. The British command was inept, but in December William Pitt came to power as secretary of state for the southern department and leader of the House of Commons. Pitt was an eloquent, supremely confident man, with a sharp intellect that quickly penetrated to the heart of matters. He understood that this was not simply another in a string of minor battles but was instead a great war for an American empire, and he realized that the major theater would be the American continent itself. Such a prize required energy, money, and young, aggressive, able military leaders. Pitt was more than willing to do what was required. Paying German mercenaries to fight for the British in Europe, Pitt poured men and supplies into North America, capably utilized the superior British navy, and promoted the officers that he sensed could seize the victory.

Like a great ship, a nation changes its direction slowly, but with Pitt at the helm the shift surely occurred, and the British began to defeat the French on the battlefield. In 1758 the mighty French fortification at Louisbourg on Cape Breton, the Gibraltar of the New World with thirty-foot high stone walls and 250 cannons, fell to Major General Jeffery Amherst. Later that year General John Forbes captured Fort Duquesne and rebuilt the burned fortification as Fort Pitt (later Pittsburgh). The pace picked up in 1759. Fort Niagara fell to the British in July, and Amherst won Forts Ticonderoga and Crown Point in July and August; then in September came one of the greatest victories in the annals of military history. Under the inspired command of thirty-three-year-old James Wolfe, a British expedition had descended the St. Lawrence River to Quebec. There atop the bluffs lay the city ably defended by General Louis Joseph de Montcalm. After two months of cat-and-mouse skirmishes Wolfe found a way to lead his troops up the steep cliffs, and at two o'clock in the morning of September 13 his forces set out, climbed the path, and surprised the French on the Plains of Abraham at the western fringes of the city. The French, finally aware of the presence of the British forces, approached Wolfe's men in a set-piece operation like those described in contemporary European military manuals, and in a murderous set of volleys the British devastated the French. Both Wolfe and Montcalm were killed in the fierce fighting, but on the windy plains above the St. Lawrence the contest for the American empire was really settled. England was triumphant in her world-wide war in that and the next several years, and reports poured in to London of victories in India, Cuba, Spain, and the Philippines. For England and France, all that remained of the war in North America after 1760 was a series of mopping-up exercises before the peace was signed in 1763.

The Indians, however, had plans of their own. The Cherokee, one of the four large groups of Indians remaining in the Southeast, lived in the mountainous region of western North and South Carolina, northern Georgia, and what is now eastern Tennessee. In the course of the war they had become increasingly disenchanted with the British military and angered by colonial encroachments on their lands, especially four forts that had been established in their territory. Small-scale border skirmishes erupted in the spring and summer of 1759, and a peace delegation of Cherokee headmen were rudely treated in Charles Town by Governor William Henry Lyttelton of South Carolina. As tension escalated, Lyttelton helped raise a militia force of 1,300 men and marched west to quell the incipient uprising, but bad weather and an outbreak of smallpox prevented him from doing little more than taking a few hostages that he held for ransom. In February 1760 the Indians attacked Fort Prince George in westernmost South Carolina where the hostages were held, and after the battle the soldiers slaughtered all their Indian captives. The Cherokee retaliated with a vengeance, raiding frontier villages and pushing the line of white settlement eastward a hundred miles. Lyttelton, already making plans to accept the governorship of Jamaica, essentially threw in the towel and requested help from the Crown. General Jeffery Amherst in Philadelphia dispatched Colonel Archibald Montgomery with two regiments of British soldiers to settle the matter.

Montgomery's heart was not in the assignment. Several years earlier, in the winter of 1757–1758, during a scare that the French might invade Carolina, Montgomery had been sent to Charles Town with 1,700 regular troops, overloading the few military barracks and forcing unwilling citizens to quarter troops. The mutual ill will between Montgomery and many Carolinians had not lessened, and Montgomery half-blamed the locals for their Indian difficulties. The troops marched westward to Fort Prince George, destroying five Indian towns on the way and killing perhaps seventy-five warriors. As the terrain became rougher and his wounded increased, Montgomery decided that he had accomplished his mission and withdrew—the Carolinians and Indians said retreated—to Charles Town. The emboldened Indians had already surrounded Fort Loudoun (near present-day Knoxville, Tennessee) and stepped up their siege; with Montgomery departed and supplies gone, the garrison surrendered to the Cherokee chiefs on August 8, 1760. The next day, remembering the butchering of their own six months before at Fort Prince George, the Indians surprised their white captives, murdered thirty-five, and divided the rest among themselves as hostages. Whatever Montgomery wanted to believe, peace was not at hand.

With Lyttelton gone to Jamaica, acting governor William Bull, Jr. decisively moved to pacify the frontier. He simultaneously raised a new provincial regiment and a party of mounted rangers headed by Frances Marion and Henry Laurens and successfully appealed to General Amherst again for military assistance. Amherst sent a detachment of regular troops commanded by Lieutenant Colonel James Grant, who had been second-in-command under Montgomery. Grant was more favorably disposed toward the Carolinians and was impressed by the vigor and sense of purpose shown by Governor Bull. In command of combined forces of 2,800 men Grant moved to chastise the Indians; as he marched west in the summer of 1761 Grant's army destroyed approximately fifteen Indian towns, burning their crops and pushing perhaps as many as five thousand Cherokees out of their homes and into the forests. The Indians further in the interior, seeing what they had in store, sent a peace delegation to Charles Town in September 1761. The negotiations were confused: the Cherokees refused to accept one clause—that four warriors be executed—that most Carolinians thought essential in order to claim a sort of symbolic victory, but, in a spirit of compromise marked more by rancor than harmony, a kind of makeshift peace was achieved. No Cherokees were executed. The treaty, which was signed on December 17, 1761, included a boundary line separating Indian and white settlements. Grant was unfairly blamed for the flawed treaty, and he came to feel the colonists were incompetent ingrates. The real results of the treaty negotiations were smoldering Indian hatred for the southern whites, British contempt for colonials, and increased South Carolinian resentment of the typically arrogant crown officers. The southern Indians were still positioned between contending European powers, and this would prove to give the Indians some leverage to play one side off against the other.

In late 1760 King George II died, and his grandson, George III, ascended to the throne. More assertive in governing than his grandfather, George III moved toward ending the war with France and pressured headstrong Pitt out of office. Meanwhile, victories around the globe forced England's enemies to accept terms of peace that ratified the new grandeur of the British empire. France ceded to England all claims to North America except for New Orleans and Louisiana west of the Mississippi, which she awarded to her ally Spain, in part as compensation for Spain's loss of Florida to the English. (Earlier in the war, in 1755, the English had deported some six thousand French inhabitants from Nova Scotia, called Acadia by France. These Acadians were scattered throughout the southern colonies, where they were unwelcome, but most eventually got to the bayou country of southern Louisiana. With their name corrupted to "Cajuns," they survived with much of their language and culture intact into the twentieth century.) The Peace of Paris of 1763 left England supreme on the entire eastern half of the American continent and the thirteen colonies free of any real foreign threat for the first time in their history. Despite the manifold tensions that had developed between the colonists and the mother country in the course of the long war, the Americans participated in the common outpouring of English pride over the great imperial victory that the Peace of Paris represented.

BRITISH IMPERIAL ADJUSTMENTS TO VICTORY

England enjoyed a surge of patriotism in 1763, but thoughtful men there foresaw troubles on the horizon. The sun never set now on the British empire, but England had no powerful allies in all of Europe. And while the military victories of 1759 to 1762 had been remarkable, they had been purchased at a heavy cost. England's debt had soared to £130,000,000, and taxes in England had risen to new and worrisome levels. Moreover, all the new territory in North America had to be administered and defended. What if French citizens in Canada revolted against their new rulers, or the Spanish forces in Louisiana sought to conquer the lightly settled region between the Mississippi River and San Agustín (St. Augustine after 1763), Florida? To guard against that exigency it was deemed necessary to place British troops in various Canadian population centers, at Forts Niagara, Detroit, and Michilimackinac in the Midwest, and at St. Augustine, Pensacola, Mobile, and near the lower Mississippi—all at great expense. Perhaps all this military preparedness was an overreaction to only a slight and mostly theoretical threat, but after these steps were taken new sources of revenue would have to be found.

At the same time, remembering the tendency of northern Indians to side with the French and the brutality of the late Cherokee war in the South, George III's government moved to prevent future Indian troubles. In 1762 two royal superintendents for Indian affairs were appointed, William Johnson for the northern region and, briefly, Edmund Atkin, then John Stuart, for the southern Indians. Both Johnson and Stuart were unusually able men, and Stuart had earned the respect and affection of the Cherokees. The two men attempted to control such matters as trade between Indians and whites and prevent the worst abuses. By the spring of 1763 George Grenville had become George III's chief minister, and he, along with the earl of Shelburne, head of the Board of Trade, sought to stop the major cause of Indian–white conflict, the white seizure of Indian lands. As a result of their leadership a royal proclamation was issued in October 1763 that created three new colonies— Quebec and East and West Florida—and, more important, drew an imaginary line down the crest of the Appalachians, at the headwaters of all the eastward flowing streams, and decreed that all territory to the west of the line was off-limits to settlement by whites. Many farmers, traders, and adventurers in the southern colonies saw the Proclamation of 1763 as a high-handed and unwelcome interference in their aspirations to move west and take whatever land they wanted—not as a reasonable and fair temporary solution to conflicts over Indian lands. The British solution to the Indian problem seemed more appropriate from the perspective of the benches of Parliament than from the banks of the Peedee.

England's postwar revenue needs led the Grenville ministry to explore a variety of measures to rationalize the economic relationship between the mother country and the mainland colonies with the aim of better administration and enhanced revenues. The first step was the so-called Sugar Act, more accurately and correctly named the American Revenue Act, which passed Parliament in the spring of 1764. Using good mercantilist logic the Crown had long attempted to regulate trade between the colonies and the rest of the empire, beginning with the Navigation Acts of 1660. The colonies accepted the legitimacy of such imperial trade regulations, which were intended to keep all trade revenue within the British Empire. To pressure the mainland colonies to buy molasses from British West Indian islands rather than French or Spanish, the Molasses Act of 1733 had placed a stiff tariff on non-British-produced molasses (the colonists used it primarily to make rum), but the colonists, by smuggling and bribery, negated the effect of the act. The Sugar Act of 1764 halved the levy to three pence per gallon and strengthened the efforts at collection. To a degree this would help British molasses producers, and to whatever extent colonists preferred to buy the French or Spanish molasses (in return the French and Spanish planters bought slaves, lumber products, and provisions from the colonists and provided them with hard money like the Spanish pistole), the levy on non-British molasses would fill

England's tax coffers. Clearly the Sugar Act had two purposes—a traditional regulation of imperial trade and an innovative effort to raise revenue in America. The revenue portion of the act, once it was understood as a new development, came to rile American consumers.

Even so, the levy might have been unexceptionable except that it was soon lumped by Americans with a series of other new acts, all of which put new restraints on Americans and suggested an ominous new direction being taken by the British government. The Currency Act of 1764, which prevented the colonies from issuing paper money, decreased the supply of hard coinage, which, prior to the passage of the act, could be obtained by exchanging paper currency. Of course, the better enforcement of the Sugar Act decreased the supply of foreign coinage and exacerbated the deflationary effect of the Currency Act. Unconnected with the purpose of these acts but soon grouped with them was the Quartering Act of April 1765, which in fact affected only a minority of mostly northern cities; the principle, however, of requiring citizens even against their wishes to quarter and provision British troops was again interpreted as a new and menacing exercise of imperial power. But the action of Grenville's ministry that inflamed colonial leaders throughout the length and breadth of the land had been passed the month before, in March 1765, and no one in England anticipated the ensuing controversy in part at least because English taxpayers had been paying a higher version of the new levy for more than two generations. So Grenville expected the Stamp Act to be an easy method of raising revenues in America, all the proceeds of which would be earmarked to pay a portion of the expenses of the British troops stationed there by the Crown for the colonists' defense.

The Stamp Act required that a tax stamp ranging from a halfpenny to ten pounds be purchased and affixed to all legal documents, licenses, newspapers, pamphlets, almanacs, insurance policies, playing cards, and dice. The stamps would be distributed by specially appointed stamp collectors, and violators would be tried in admiralty courts where, since juries were not involved, convictions could be expected. Whereas the other postwar acts had affected only portions of the colonies, the Stamp Act left no region untouched and most severely affected the very people—merchants, lawyers, publishers—most able and prepared to object. Grenville had unknowingly opened the proverbial Pandora's box, and the controversy that waxed and waned for the next decade ultimately led to the American Revolution.

THE SOCIAL CONTEXT OF REVOLUTION

Today, long removed from the passions of the time, the colonial unrest that escalated from written remonstrances to armed rebellion seems out of proportion to the limited nature of British taxation and regulation. But contemporaries did not experience the changes in British policies with the clinical objectivity of an outsider. Rather, pulled and pressured by the tensions and doubts rending the apparent stability of their societies, American colonists perceived slights and dangers where later observers see only misunderstandings. No doubt the colonists overreacted, which in turn caused the imperial officials to overreact. In the course of the political arguments and protests that followed one on top of the other, the whole axis of the colonial world shifted.

The decade between the passage of the Stamp Act in 1765 and the gunfire that shattered the quiet of the village green of Concord on April 19, 1775, has too often been portrayed simply as an intensifying series of Parliamentary actions met by colonial protests, a ping-pong match of politics with one's attention focused first on one court, then the other. Yet the cultural ambiance of the colonies must be understood before sense can be made of the colonial perception of the epochal events of the moment. Political irritations *were* piling up at an unprecedented rate. In addition to the Proclamation of 1763, which restricted westward migration, and the Sugar Act and the Currency Act and the Quartering Act and now the Stamp Act, local annoyances—old and new—continued to vex.

Marylanders still felt the proprietor's men took an indefensible amount of money from them in the way of fees for which no real service was rendered. In North Carolina, western settlers particularly were galled at the £16,000 expended in the late 1760s on an extravagant palace for the royal governor at New Bern. In Virginia, the Reverend James Maury, still fighting the Twopenny Act in what had come to be called the Parsons' Cause, was suing for his salary and provoking the oratorical wrath of Patrick Henry. In South Carolina, the new governor, Thomas Boone, refused to administer the oath of office in 1762 to newly elected assemblyman Christopher Gadsden, presumably because of Gadsden's criticism of the British commanders in the recent Cherokee war. When the South Carolina assembly went ahead and declared Gadsden elected, Governor Boone precipitously dissolved the legislature! The Carolinians appealed all the way to London, and Boone ultimately resigned and left for England in 1764, but the enmity lingered. The house had long considered inviolable its right to decide its own membership—how dare a royal governor try to interfere with such a traditional English right.

Yet this chain of local and international political events occurred in a social context that aggravated their significance, for colonists saw the events against a backdrop of unsettling cultural worries: political and economic events were interpreted and understood by colonists whose mood was subtly affected by a malaise of complex origins. Good times and bad times are seldom simply a measure of statistical indices but rather a cultural rendering of that data. And in the third quarter of the eighteenth century many colonists sensed that their affairs were going badly. There was a downside to this so-called Golden Age of the American colonies.

After 1750 or so the growing prosperity of the colonies and the lengthening life spans had resulted in more families sufficiently wealthy and stable to send their sons to England for an education. These youths, understandably proud of their family's success and their homeland's increasing maturity, found that the English condescended to them as colonial bumpkins and disparaged their home colonies as cultural backwaters. There was enough truth in the insults to make them doubly hurtful. Most youths abroad reacted defensively and their colonial patriotism increased. Henceforth they would be quick to spot other English slights, and there were plenty during the French and Indian War, when English officers disdained to learn from more experienced colonial militia officers, and after 1763, when imperial decisions took little account of colonial attitudes.

The prosperity that indirectly led to colonial students' suffering British insults also led to colonial worries about disturbing changes in the character of the home society. Beginning in the 1750s there came to be a growing concern among many southern whites about corruption, extravagance, and moral decay gnawing at the heart of the society, a mindless male preoccupation with luxury and horse racing and cock fighting with attendant gambling that seemed to value ostentatious consumption and immediate gratification more than virtue and a responsible stewardship of resources. Political dissenters in England were developing a language of discourse about such matters, finding numerous examples of corruption, luxury, irresponsibility, and self-serving political action at home, and these dissenters—journalists such as John Trenchard and Thomas Gordon—employed a vocabulary wherein words like *duty, honor, virtue,* and *moderation* were used as antonyms to actual, concrete malefactions. This whole way of interpreting political life has come to be called the ideology of Republicanism, and it became a motif that would run through American political life for at least a half century. As the planter elite and other shapers of public opinion in the southern colonies read English social criticism in periodicals like the *Spectator* and innumerable pamphlets, its portrayal of the English scene was given credence by the increasing degree to which it seemed to describe tendencies in the colonies. When, upon the death in May 1766 of John Robinson, the beloved and longtime speaker of the Virginia house and treasurer of the colony, it was discovered that he had essentially embezzled £100,000 from the government and loaned the monies to friends and political associates, the worst fears of corruption came home. Such self-revelations jolted reflective colonial leaders and sharpened their resolve to stand on guard against other threats to the commonweal.

While certain planters and their spokesmen detected a moral or even a spiritual dimension to the perceived increase in corruption in Virginia after the 1750s, a more profound religious critique of the society would soon be made by a trio of religious dissenters. The weak Anglican establishment inadequately responded to the population growth in the Piedmont and in the region south of the James River, and in fact the religious flabbiness of the church and its identification with the planter elite who constituted its lay leadership did not position it well for ministering to the needs of the back country. Beginning in the 1740s a group of Presbyterian evangelicals began to gain converts, and under the leadership of several gifted divines such as Samuel Davies, it worked out a modus operandi with the legally established Anglican Church that freed it from most of the restraints placed on non-established churches. However, when a cadre of evangelical Separate Baptists from Connecticut entered north-central North Carolina in 1755 and began missionary forays into southern Virginia, the Anglicans met a formidable cultural foe. The lower-class Baptists were egalitarian and biracial, and they opposed the luxury and corruption and competitiveness and pride associated with the planter establishment. In their biting critique of the Anglican-planter-establishment way of life they offered a counter example, a privatized community of fellow believers who disdained opulence and show, whose religion was demonstrably emotional and personal (with foot washings, hand shakings, and embraces of the beloved), who rejected the authority of the civil courts and disciplined their own evildoers in church disciplinary proceedings. The Baptist repudiation of establishment racial and religious mores and their withdrawal from the authority of the official church and court to settle affairs among themselves threatened the fragile control of the political-religious establishment; attempts to throttle Baptist growth only strengthened their convictions. They became indefatigable opponents of the state-supported church and advocates of what became known as the American tradition of the separation of church and state. When the Church of England itself developed an evangelical wing of Wesleyan exhorters after 1770, the Methodists, the entire image of late colonial religious order appeared to be coming unraveled, one more instance of the sense of disorder and potential for chaos that appeared to threaten the whole society beginning in the 1760s.

Another of those threats of chaos, and one that southern planters tried desperately to push beyond their consciousness, was the fear of slave rebellion. In the wealthiest portions of the Chesapeake Tidewater and the South Carolina–Georgia lowcountry the majority black population was a constant, if seldom publicly articulated, concern. In some regions of the lowcountry slaves outnumbered whites by as much as twenty to one. Here the memory of the Stono Slave Revolt of 1739 kept fears alive and perpetuated a regimen of harsh controls. Slaves had little reason to identify with the existing order; would they be tempted by outside forces—French, Spanish, or whatever—to turn against the powers that be in a bloody insurrection? This fear of strangers in their midst who were potential co-conspirators against the public peace had motivated those South Carolinians in 1756 who were alarmed by the presence of one thousand exiled Acadians—would these Frenchmen "join with the negroes"? Any instability, any crack in the political control of the dominant whites, could threaten the whole social establishment and lead to chaos and ruin.

The political establishment's degree of control over the society, which had a surface appearance of strength in the 1760s—because of the ascendency of the lower houses of representatives, the system of courts and justices of the peace, and the colonial militias—was in fact fragile not only because of the evangelical splintering of the religious hegemony and the presence of large numbers of slaves but also because of real social and political unrest in the western portions of North and South Carolina. In South Carolina the rush of settlers to the back country outpaced the ability and certainly the desire of the lowcountry-dominated colonial government to provide the infrastructure of stable government: convenient courts, schools, and adequate representation in the colonial legislature. The South Carolina backcountry was in chaos. The social dislocation that followed the Cherokee War was made worse by the presence of bandits and gangs—sometimes called "white Indians"—who raided the farms of settlers and threatened to turn much of the South Carolina frontier into a lawless no-man's-land.

In 1767 and 1768, groups of law-abiding farmers, primarily those with high economic standing, began to organize to put down the disorder and institute the stabilizing forces of regular government, including a demand that their section be represented in the colonial assembly. By 1768 these Regulators, as they were called, had quelled the unrest, but in the heat of the moment they perhaps went too far and enforced their own sense of social morality too rigorously. The colonial government came to agree that the Regulators were pushing too hard for change and tentatively went along with a counter-movement called the Moderators, led by Joseph Coffell. Coffell's true colors soon became clear: he was the leader of a gang of ruffians who wanted to retaliate against Regulator "good government" actions. Both sides gathered supporters in early 1769 for a showdown, and in March over one thousand men assembled in what is now Newberry County, presumably for a pitched battle. At the last moment colonial authorities, having learned more about Coffell's tactics, withdrew their support and commanded the Moderators to disperse. Moderates in the movement persuaded them to do so, and bloodshed was averted. The Moderators disbanded, the Regulators had made their point, the lowcountry establishment made some accommodations (including greater representation), and order was restored to the backcountry. But the lowcountry leaders understood the fragility of the peace and recognized that they had to give consideration to the interests of the westerners in order to earn their support. Clearly the possibility for future social unrest existed and had to be guarded against.

The specter of internal social disorder was also raised in western North Carolina. There the colonial assembly had extended a bare-bones system of local government, but a small group of political appointees dominated the system. Backcountry spokesmen felt these appointed agents were corrupt and concerned more with feathering their own nests than with serving the hard-pressed families on the frontier. Much of their disfavor was aimed at Edmund Fanning, a native New Yorker and favorite of the royal governor, who simultaneously held a variety of political offices in Orange County. Fanning represented the kind of government official who had no real stake in the community he supposedly served. The issue was not the absence of government but rather ill-administered government, symbolized by the enormous amount expended in the late 1760s on the elaborate governor's palace in New Bern. Angry backcountry men began to organize in 1768 as self-appointed Regulators, and there followed a season of rioting, closing down of courts, and general opposition to the colonial government. When Governor William Tryon attempted to restore order, a virtual civil war erupted. In September, Tryon, with 1,400 militiamen, overawed a much larger body of Regulators near Hillsboro, but nothing was settled.

In the months that followed, Regulators continued to use violence and intimidation to protest the administration of justice and the alleged unfairness of taxation and representation in the backcountry, and Tryon, rather than seeing the justice of many of their claims, tried to quash the uprising. Tensions rose, Regulators in several counties announced their intention to pay no more taxes, and Tryon—even though he had already accepted the position of governor of New York—decided to act swiftly to end the unrest once and for all. With 1,400 militiamen he marched to a site near Great Alamance Creek and there confronted on March 16, 1771, some 2,000 Regulators. Tryon's men were better organized and armed, and within two hours they had routed the Regulator forces. Twelve leaders were captured, tried for treason, and convicted; six of these were hanged and the others pardoned by the governor. Tryon then offered to pardon all the rest of the rebels who would put down their arms and accept the authority of the government. Several thousand later moved to Tennessee, but the great majority of Regulators remained in North Carolina and submitted to the colonial government even while they harbored feelings of resentment. Some adjustments were later made by the authorities to redress the westerners' grievances, but the North Carolina backcountry remained a sore spot on the body politic. It reminded the colonial establishment that all was not well and remained a potential threat to the peace of the commonwealth.

The presence of slaves in all the southern colonies fueled fears other than those of rebellion and social disorder, for abstract terms like *freedom* and *independence* took on a very tangible meaning for whites surrounded by blacks who had no freedom and no independence. Independence meant freedom from the control of others, and being subject to the control of others meant slavery pure and simple; no whites better understood the full horrors of slavery than southern slaveholders. But capture in Africa was not the only way to slavery; one who was greatly in debt was ultimately subject to the control of others. The real evil of luxurious living and wasteful gambling was that it easily led to debt and then subservience to creditors. One beholden to another was hardly a free actor in the political world. White southerners tried in their interpersonal relationships to deny this implication of debt, and gentlemen creditors were loath to collect their debts aggressively because they fancied the debt as a kind of bond of friendship between equals—to demand repayment was tantamount to asserting that the debtor was not a gentlemen.

But while among themselves southerners accepted this polite conceit, they feared—even if they wanted to deny it—that their British creditors had a different conception of credit. To push too hard to collect one's debts was, in the minds of southern planters, to cast aspersions on the debtors. Following the economic dislocations at the conclusion of the Seven Years' War, when hard-pressed English merchants and commission agents began to push harder than ever for prompt repayment, planters—whose entire style of commercial agriculture was based on long-term credit—misunderstood the intentions of their creditors and interpreted the mounting pressure of debt as a conspiratorial method of gaining control over Americans, ultimately perhaps a way of enslaving them. Imagined fears based on the real events of practical life gave concrete meaning to the political abstractions about independence.

Greed and corruption were real, as was the desire for power, and ultimately the virtue of its citizens—putting the good of one's government ahead of personal gain—was the only salvation of a body politic. The colonists' reading of political events at home and abroad gave credence to their reading of the literature of Republicanism, and they viewed Parliamentary actions after 1765 through the spectacles of English dissent, giving them a point of view that magnified the perception of a British conspiracy against colonists' liberties. Southern slaveholders were extraordinarily sensitive to any conceivable threat that they themselves might be politically enslaved; they became vigilant to British action that might hint at such a future. In this mood they responded to the Stamp Act in 1765.

THE ROAD TO REVOLUTION

Grenville's Stamp Act was one of the greatest miscalculations in history. Grenville thought the Americans, after a little grumbling, would pay the tax, which, because it was easy to collect, would be a painless and efficient way to raise revenue. The colonists proved far more sensitive about their rights and alert to perceived threats than Grenville imagined. In 1764 James Otis of

Massachusetts had published a widely read pamphlet entitled *The Rights of the British Colonists Asserted and Proved* that spelled out in convincing argument why taxation without representation was wrong; southerners were particularly quick to see that if a government could take away one's property (by taxes), one was subject to the control of others and would be a bondsman as surely as an African slave. This intellectual hyperbole came to be accepted as an ideological truism in the decade after 1765. Even before the Stamp Act was passed colonists got wind of it, and the Committee of Correspondence of the Virginia house sent protests to England in which it asserted that Virginians were "not subject to any taxes but such as are laid on them by their own consent, or by those who are legally appointed to represent them." Taxing them otherwise was to make them "slaves." Grenville was undeterred by such remonstrances; after all, he had expected some protest.

When word reached Virginia in May 1765 that the new levies had passed Parliament despite colonial objections, the burgesses were near the end of their session. There was no instant reaction, perhaps because official confirmation of the act's passage had not arrived and probably because the colonial leaders had not had time to reach a consensus on the proper way to respond to the implicit threat the act represented. But fiery Patrick Henry, under forty years of age and seated in the house as recently as May 20, rose on May 29, just before the session was to close, and with a torrent of oratory persuaded the barely one-quarter of the members who were present to act as a committee of the whole and pass five resolutions critical of recent Parliamentary behavior. These resolutions argued that from the founding of the colony the people of Virginia possessed the immutable rights of all Englishmen, including the right not to be taxed without their consent—"the distinguishing characteristick of *British* freedom" was the way the fourth resolution put it. Two more radical resolutions, essentially demanding civil disobedience to thwart such taxing proposals, were defeated by the house. In fact, the political old hands objected to Henry's resolutions, and it was only his cascading rhetoric that flooded their disagreements beneath a rising tide of patriotism. In this May 29 speech, citing Brutus and Caesar, Henry seemed to call for the execution of George III, and in the heat of the moment Henry said what William Wirt later reconstructed as: "If this be treason, make the most of it."

A contemporary French traveler who heard the speech wrote that Henry just as quickly backed down from such radical sentiments and apologized, but the ringing phrases and the spirit of rebellion against so-called tyrants continued to reverberate throughout the hall and down through history. Consciously or not, Henry was pioneering a new form of political rhetoric, borrowed from the evangelical ministers. Varying the tone and timber of his voice, making skillful use of pauses, then bolting forth with clamorous, lightening-like flashes of oratorical brilliance, Henry sought to excite the listeners' emotions, to move them to a decision, to jolt them out of old habits of thinking. This was a newly democratic use of speech for political purposes; the older style of political oratory was calm, balanced, with detail piled on top of telling detail until logic demanded a single conclusion, the whole adorned with classical allusions and learned asides understandable only to the intended small audience of elite, educated leaders. The force of Henry's rhetoric carried the day, even if, as Thomas Jefferson once wrote, after the powerful drama of the moment passed one hardly knew what Henry had actually said.

Newspapers in the other colonies reprinted all seven of the Henry resolutions as though all had passed, spreading and even intensifying the colonial resolve not to accept the turn of imperial events. The various southern legislative houses, except for that of Georgia, adroitly controlled by Governor James Wright, all passed similar resolutions essentially denying that Parliament had the right to tax the colonists without their freely given consent. The precise timing of the legislative action was determined by when they were called to meet, and the exact tenor of the various resolutions were shaped by many factors, but clearly colonial public opinion made a significant shift following the Stamp Act news. In June the Massachusetts house issued an invitation to the other colonies to send representatives to a Stamp Act Congress to meet in New York City the following October—the Stamp Act was scheduled to take effect November 1. Governor Francis Fauquier prevented the Virginia house from choosing official delegates by refusing to reconvene it, and Governor Wright of Georgia similarly prevented that colony's participation. But Crown officials could not stem the tide of public opinion. Delegates from the other southern colonies met in New York with representatives from six northern colonies, accepted a Declaration of Rights and Grievances that included opposition to taxation without representation and the use of admiralty courts to enforce the Parliamentary laws in America, and sent notice that they did not accept the British conception of "virtual" representation, which argued that Americans were somehow represented in Parliament by members residing in England. Shortly after the congress was adjourned Maryland's Daniel Dulany completely exploded the British position as casuistry in a scholarly dissertation entitled *Considerations on the Propriety of Imposing Taxes in the British Colonies, For the Purpose of Raising a Revenue, By Act of Parliament* (1765).

Dulany's pamphlet was written for learned readers, but the essence of his argument on behalf of local, constituent representation was widely accepted. If Britain could tax people without their consent, could it not by the same logic take other liberties with their freedom; could it not make them do as it wished? As a group of North Carolinians wrote to Governor Tryon, "submission to any part of so oppressive and (as we think) so unconstitutional" an act would be "a direct inlet for slavery." Taking their cues from earlier English dissenters, Americans guarding the ramparts of their freedom against Parliamentary assaults began calling themselves "Sons of Liberty" and rallying around Liberty Trees and Liberty Poles. In Boston, in Annapolis, and in Charles Town stamp collectors confronted angry crowds and backed down. These were not wild and out-of-control mobs of rowdies and ruffians but well-organized pressure groups of artisans and property owners often led by substantial men, and the crowds were utilized like a battering ram to knock down the authority of British officials. Samuel Adams in Boston was the premier American agitator and propagandist against British actions, but energetic Christopher Gadsden in Charles Town was a close second.

Sentiment against Britain escalated as an intercolonial boycott of British goods spread throughout America. The boycott offered thoughtful colonists who had been worried about the spread of luxury and vice a way to strike simultaneously against both external and internal threats. By the fateful first of November, when the Stamp Act was to take effect, it was voided in effect by the colonial opposition in every colony but Georgia. (East and West Florida, new English territories since 1763, had so few English settlers they were hardly more than military garrisons, and the army officials at St. Augustine, Pensacola, and Mobile saw to it that the very limited shipping met the Stamp Act requirements.) Everywhere else courts were closed, newspapers either did not print or did so without the hated stamps, and ports shut down. The act was a dead letter by the time it was supposed to come to life.

In the midst of this brewing controversy King George III dismissed Grenville in a complicated quarrel involving the king's mother, and in July 1765 Grenville was replaced by the Marquis of Rockingham, who was far more sympathetic to the American view. Pressured at home by British merchants, who were being hurt by the American embargo, Rockingham moved cautiously to gain Parliamentary support to repeal the Stamp Act. A majority of members thought the act was either impractical or unfair, and Rockingham won enough support to repeal the act on March 17, 1766, by agreeing to accept passage of a companion bill, the Declaratory Act, which stated that Parliament had the authority to pass laws regarding the colonies "in all cases whatsoever." Colonists were so exultant over the end of the Stamp Act and so quick to see it as a peaceful victory of protest and principle over Parliamentary error that they dismissed the Declaratory Act as a meaningless face-saving gesture. In that the colonists were wrong. But Parliament was also wrong in choosing to believe that the colonists had objected only to internal taxes and were not opposed to external (that is, related to regulating maritime trade) taxes. Following this logic, Rockingham sought further to mollify the colonists by reducing the three-pence-per-gallon levy on non-British molasses to one pence on every gallon imported, regardless of origin. This could not be seen as regulative of trade and was purely a measure to raise money—a portentous change in tariff policy—but the colonists were so relieved over the Stamp Act victory and so unburdened by the one penny tax that they did not protest. This silence misled the British.

Within months after the Stamp Act repeal the Rockingham government fell out of favor with George III, who in August 1766 asked William Pitt to put together a new ministry. Now titled the earl of Chatham and as intellectually able as ever, Pitt was soon forced by a severe attack of the gout to retire. In his absence, Charles Townshend, the chancellor of the exchequer, came to dominate the government; his judgment was as flawed as his energy level was high. The British people themselves were substantially taxed, and neither they nor their representatives were pleased that the Stamp Act repeal meant that the Americans would be practically untaxed. Misled by the external versus internal tax issue and the apparent acceptance by the colonies of the one pence tax on all imported molasses, Townshend in May and June of 1766 pushed a new plan through Parliament just before he died. The Revenue Act placed a levy (external tax) on all glass, lead, paint, paper, and tea imported into the colonies. Associated with this was the organization of the Board of Customs Commissioners to be located at Boston to enforce the new levies and the establishment of three additional superior vice-admiralty courts in Boston, Philadelphia, and Charles Town (supplementing the one already in Halifax, Nova Scotia) to see that British justice was done. Incidentally, to punish New York for dragging its feet on carrying out the Quartering Act of 1765, the colonial assembly was suspended until the colony met the terms of the act. Townshend proposed to use the monies raised to pay royal officials in the colonies, freeing such officials from dependence on, and hence control by, the colonists.

The Townshend acts did not cause an instant firestorm of protests the way the Stamp Act had, but gradually the opposition arose, often orchestrated by merchants. Once again nonimportation emerged as a real and symbolic form of protest, and the call for boycotting British goods and making do with American homespun appealed to the colonial uneasiness about luxury and waste that it was feared could destroy their society from within. A life of simplicity was a moral as well as a political good. Simple living conformed with ideas about disinterested virtue, an existence that looked to the common good rather than individual self-aggrandizement. Images of British corruption and extravagance were easily contrasted with American wholesomeness, and what many colonists interpreted as British efforts to take away Americans' property and freedom came to be seen as a logical outcome of British corruption; clearly, power corrupted and corruption led to a hunger for power. In the hands of Sam Adams the political protest was a campaign for political liberty and for moral purity, and in subtly different shades the American movement against the Townshend acts took on the coloration of a moral crusade.

John Dickinson's *Letters from a Farmer in Pennsylvania*, first serialized in colonial newspapers in the winter of 1767–1768, effectively put the whole struggle in the context of the rights of mankind, not just British rights, an idea that blossomed in time. The Massachusetts legislature passed a strongly worded circular letter protesting the Townshend Acts, and royal objections to the letter only emboldened other colonial legislatures to endorse its sentiments. Meanwhile British custom officials enforced the acts with a heavy hand, producing opponents even among moderates. In South Carolina the legislature tweaked John Bull's nose by authorizing a contribution of £1,500 sterling to a British fund to support the notorious John Wilkes, a radical gadfly who provoked George III to distraction—this legislative act outraged royal officials. Sam Adams continued to stoke the unrest in Boston, leading local Sons of Liberty to so aggravate the authorities that two regiments of redcoats were sent to the city to keep the peace, raising all kinds of alarms about the evils of standing armies in peacetime. It was only a matter of time before trouble broke out, and when it did in March 1770, mostly because of colonial provocation, Sam Adams and a marvelously propagandistic drawing by Paul Revere made the so-called Boston Massacre a byword for British tyranny throughout America.

By 1770 every colony but New Hampshire was participating in an increasingly effective boycott of British goods. The British government had been in disarray since Townshend's death in 1766; but finally in 1769 a government of the "King's Friends" was formed, and in January 1770 George III named Lord North his first minister. Although Lord North was more hardworking than brilliant, he recognized that the Townshend duties were costing more in plain money than they were bringing in and that their cost in ill will was enormous. By spring he had persuaded Parliament to repeal all the duties except the three-penny-per-pound levy on tea, which was retained as a matter of principle—actually, nine-tenths of the tea consumed in the American colonies was smuggled Dutch tea anyway, so this tax burden was negligible. American protests dried up, the nonimportation agreement collapsed, and an uneasy peace settled upon the colonies.

The next three years were relatively uneventful. In June 1772 Rhode Island radicals burned a British patrol boat, the *Gaspée*, that had run aground, convincing British officials that colonials were incorrigible troublemakers. Later in that year and in early 1773 the assemblies of Massachusetts and Virginia formed committees of correspondence within the individual colonies and among them; soon this method of keeping themselves informed of what was happening elsewhere linked all the colonies. Slowly, almost without realizing it, a sense of intercolonial identity was emerging. Sometimes Virginia was in the forefront, sometimes Massachusetts, and occasionally South Carolina, and one colony would respond to the leadership or the need of another, but there was little recognition of distinct regional interests and instead a sense of American interests began to form.

Lord North shattered the calm, his hand forced by events in India. The East India Company, a British-chartered monopoly, which had friends in the highest places of government, was threatened with bankruptcy in the early 1770s. If the company collapsed, trade with India and the governing of English territories there would be endangered. Meanwhile, 17 million pounds of tea sat in the company warehouses while the American colonists illegally consumed huge amounts of cheap Dutch tea. North concocted a scheme too clever by half: British tea was expensive because it first had to be unloaded in England, where a twelve pence duty was collected, then transshipped to the colonists by independent tea merchants, where the three penny American duty was collected. North proposed to refund the twelve pence tax on the tea sent to America and to allow the monopolistic East India Company to bypass independent tea dealers and sell the tea directly. North reasoned that even by keeping the American three penny tax the new marketing procedure would make East India tea substantially cheaper than the smuggled Dutch tea. Colonists, he assumed, would gladly pay the small duty and drink British tea, providing a welcome market for the hard-pressed East India Company to rescue it from the brink of bankruptcy. Everyone would benefit, North supposed.

North completely misread the political pulse of the colonies. Conditioned by a decade of controversy to be vigilant toward the slightest threat to their freedom and suspicious of British intentions with regard to colonial liberties, the colonists—led by local merchants being bypassed by East India Company agents—instantly saw the Tea Act of May 1773 as a subtle plot against freedom. The real cost of the cheaper tea was colonial acceptance of British monopoly, first on tea, but then on who knew what? The colonial reaction was quick, for the committees of correspondence provided protesters in all the colonies with intelligence of what was happening elsewhere. Each colony tried to match, if not outdo, the other in their standing up against this evident sneak attack on their cherished liberty. Southern slaveholders knew intimately of what slavery consisted, and they were ever alert to the smallest indication that British actions might circumscribe their liberty. The rumor of a slave rebellion conjured up fears of British collusion; the decline in the price of tobacco seemed understandable to planters—who identified their own worth with the value of their crop—only if there was a conspiracy to downgrade the leaf and force growers into debt; and the rising pressure on planters to pay their debts came to be seen as plot to make Americans subservient to their creditors. Fears of real or potential internal unrest (the religious challenge to the establishment in Virginia and the memory of the Regulator movement in the Carolinas, for example), combined with what seemed to be a concerted British policy to restrain the traditional liberties of the colonies, created a mood of tense watchfulness.

A new generation of colonial leaders was also emerging, men such as

Thomas Jefferson, born in 1743, who had entered upon the political stage only after Britain had begun to tighten the imperial restrictions. The emerging political leadership cut their teeth on opposition to British policy, and maturing after the French threat to the West was removed, they tended to have a grander vision of the ultimate American empire, a vision that could hardly be reined in by bureaucrats in London. Poised to protect American colonial interests, leaders in all the colonies saw the Tea Act as an insidious Trojan Horse; acceptance of the ostensibly harmless act would be the wedge by which Britain would take control of more of the colonial economy, with the end result a form of economic bondage—slavery would not be far behind.

In every colony except Georgia, where Governor Wright still maintained obedience to England, irate colonists in all walks of life refused to buy the British tea. East India Company agents felt the brunt of public antagonism expressed in mass meetings, and the agents cautiously withdrew from the market. Colonists prevented ships from unloading the tea and agents from selling it. In Charles Town the tea was simply unloaded into a warehouse with no effort made to sell it (it would later be sold and the profits turned to the revolutionary cause). The Tea Act had everywhere been blunted by the exercise of public displeasure. Then, on a dark December night, a group of radical Bostonians took the opposition one step further. Masquerading as Indians, they boarded an English ship at anchor in the harbor and threw the tea overboard, a symbolic slap in the face of Parliamentary authority.

Even many Americans thought the Boston protestors had gone too far by destroying property, but the British were first shocked, then outraged. These upstart colonial lawbreakers had to be disciplined, and disciplined harshly, before matters got out of hand. Lord North, with the king's support, convinced Parliament to pass in April 1774 what the colonists dubbed the Intolerable Acts. The port of Boston was closed until the East India Company was reimbursed; royal officials would henceforth be tried in England; the Massachusetts council would no longer be elected by the lower house but appointed by the crown, as would sheriffs and judges. The British army moved troops into the city and citizens were required to board them by the terms of a tough new Quartering Act. (Incidentally, Parliament also passed the Quebec Act in 1774, liberalizing the governance of the Canadian province of Quebec, and this act was in British eyes totally unconnected with events in Boston. But colonists saw British concessions to French citizens and the Catholic church in Canada as an additional menace.)

Again Lord North misread colonial sentiment. From Boston to Charles Town colonial opinion swung to the support of the Bostonians; supplies were gathered and sent to relieve those harmed by the closing of the port—more than two hundred barrels of rice came from South Carolina and even Georgia. The committees of correspondence sprung into action—what should be done to protest this gross infraction of American freedom? A clear sense of proto-nationalism was emerging: colonists in Maryland, Virginia, and South Carolina felt themselves symbolically attacked by the actions taken against the people of Boston, and they responded in unison as Americans. One colony's action emboldened other colonies to act: in October 1774 Marylanders not only prohibited the tea ship *Peggy Stewart* from unloading its cargo but caused the ship to be burned, one-upping the Bostonians.

When the Massachusetts government proposed in June 1774 that all the colonists send delegates to a "continental" congress to meet at Philadelphia that September, a momentous step was taken. By the time the fifty-five delegates from twelve colonies (Georgia being the only hold-out) gathered, most had read pamphlets by Pennsylvanian James Wilson, *Considerations on the Nature and Extent of the Legislative Authority of the British Parliament* (1774), and by Thomas Jefferson, *Summary View of the Rights of British America* (1774), both of which argued that the colonies were subject only to the Crown, not Parliament—legislative authority lay at home. Late that summer, before going to Philadelphia, George Washington had written that a line of demarcation had to be drawn separating British and colonial authority. Though he wished that this determination could be put off, "the crisis is arrived when we must assert our rights, or submit to every imposition," until—and note again the specter of bondage that so haunted southerners—"custom and use shall make us as tame and abject slaves, as the blacks we rule over with such arbitrary sway."

The First Continental Congress rejected calls for a truly continental government but passed a Declaration of American Rights that conceded Parliamentary authority only to regulate commerce and truly imperial matters; all else was to be left to colonial assemblies. The congress also called for a Continental Association to enforce an effective and wide-ranging boycott of British goods and also a prohibition of exports to England—South Carolina and Georgia won a concession to be allowed some leeway on rice exports. No colony lost sight of its particular circumstances, but together the colonies were groping toward a nationhood that for the moment at least subsumed all mean regionalism; a second Continental Congress was scheduled to meet in May 1775. By the winter of 1774–1775 the Maryland and Virginia conventions—extralegal colonial governments circumventing the control of the royal governors—were calling for volunteer militiamen to organize and begin training. Massachusetts minutemen were already doing so and were collecting munitions and supplies.

Some Virginians cautioned moderation, a wait-and-see attitude, and in response to these men Patrick Henry once more electrified the assembly with words probably something like: "Gentlemen may cry peace, peace—but there is no peace. The war is actually begun! . . . Is life so dear, or peace so sweet, as to be purchased at the price of chains and slavery? Forbid it, Almighty God! I know not what course others may take; but as for me, give me liberty, or give me death!" Whatever he actually said, the meaning was overwhelming, and the resolution to put Virginia in an active defense posture passed. The point of no return was about to be reached. As John Adams recalled long afterwards, "The Revolution was in the minds of the people, and this was effected, from 1760 to 1775, in the course of fifteen years before a drop of blood was drawn." But bloodshed was not far off in the spring of 1775.

A month after Henry's stirring oration, British General Thomas Gage, hundreds of miles to the north in Massachusetts (where he was also governor), hearing of minutemen stockpiling arms, was ordered to make a preemptive strike at Concord. He set forth Major John Pitcairn with approximately seven hundred British soldiers on the night of April 18, 1775, hoping to squelch the rebellion before it started. Paul Revere and two other riders learned of the plans and rode into the countryside spreading the alarm. Early on the morning of April 19 Pitcairn and his troops entered Lexington, five miles from Concord, and found about seventy minutemen lined up on the village green. Commanded to lay down their arms, the village militia began to do so when suddenly a shot came as out of nowhere. The redcoats responded with a withering volley of fire, and eight minutemen lay dead on the lawn. The redcoats pushed on to Concord, but the forewarned Americans had removed the supplies. After a bloody skirmish at Concord's North Bridge the disappointed British began the tortuous trek back to Boston, with three to four thousand quickly assembled minutemen firing at them, it seemed, from behind every tree and fence. General Gage lost almost half his men en route, and the shots fired that day reverberated across the continent and throughout the world.

The echoes were still audible when the Second Continental Congress met in Philadelphia in May 1775. Moving quickly to "adopt" the forces near Boston as an American army and naming Virginian George Washington as commander-in-chief, the "continental" nature of the conflict was openly legitimated. Most colonists remained hesitant to break irrevocably from England and professed loyalty to the king, blaming the troubles on ill-advised ministers. The Congress passed a "Declaration of the Causes and Necessity of Taking up Arms" that made clear that their "cause is just," and for that reason they affirmed their commitment to take up arms, if necessary, "being with one mind resolved to die free men rather than live like slaves." This read like a throwing down of the gauntlet, but it was quickly accompanied by the Olive Branch Petition begging George III to keep Parliament at bay until some kind of peaceful reconciliation could be discovered. King George was undeterred by the conciliatory petition. Events tumbled out of control. Even as the Congress was meeting, American forces under the command of Ethan Allen and Benedict Arnold were taking Fort Ticonderoga in New York, and in mid-

June a reinforced General Gage attacked the Massachusetts minutemen assembled on Breed's Hill; the ensuing battle, incorrectly called Bunker's Hill, was a blood-soaked victory for the British. Washington soon arrived, took charge, and after months of wintry stalemate the British evacuated Boston on March 17, 1776.

Throughout the colonies the conflict in Massachusetts was widely interpreted as a symbolic attack on all white Americans' freedom by a British government gone mad. Many Americans were cross-pressured; conditioned by language and habit to remain loyal, they felt threatened by their interpretation of recent British actions. On May 29, 1775, the *South Carolina Gazette* printed an inflammatory extract from a letter written earlier in England in which thousands of weapons were described as being sent to America to be provided to "N———s [Negroes], the Roman Catholics, the Indians, and the Canadians." The letter sent a chill down the spine of undecided Carolinians and inched them toward revolution. In November, Governor Dunmore of Virginia issued a proclamation granting freedom to "all indented servants, Negroes or others" who would "bear arms" and join "His Majesty's Troops." Dunmore had earlier offended Virginians by seizing the powder magazine at Williamsburg and was soon attempting to rule from shipboard while cruising Chesapeake Bay.

On December 8, 1775, a small American contingent routed a British force at Great Bridge, ten miles south of Norfolk—the second battle of the American Revolution. The retreating British troops moved back into Norfolk, but then Dunmore disbanded his few black troops, gave up the city, and evacuated his soldiers, accompanied by local Tories, to his ships. In order to render Norfolk useless to the Patriots, Dunmore bombarded the city from his ships in the harbor on January 1, 1776, and sent in raiding parties to burn houses. Patriot forces then completed the destruction of the city, presumably to prevent it ever being of use to Dunmore as a base of operations. The animosity toward the British was reaching a fever pitch in some quarters. Even in Georgia the tide of public opinion was turning; Governor Wright, who had seemed until now uniquely able to throttle American opposition to Parliamentary arrogance, had lost the battle for control of public sentiment and soon had to slip away for his own safety. At this moment, in January 1776, on the very cusp of change in popular allegiance, a blockbuster pamphlet entitled *Common Sense* was anonymously published in Philadelphia.

Its author, Thomas Paine, a ne'er-do-well recent immigrant from England, proved to be an extraordinarily gifted pamphleteer who perfected with the written word the techniques Patrick Henry had pioneered so brilliantly with the spoken. Here was no learned dissertation for the erudite but rather a hard-hitting, blunt attack on the king—"a royal brute"—and his policies written in a muscular vernacular whose concrete of imagery seared its message in the minds of common Americans. Tens of thousands of copies of *Common Sense* were soon circulating, and in every colony it was discussed and debated. Public opinion was undergoing a seismic shift.

The Continental Congress had become the quasi-national government—it issued paper money, established an intercolonial postal service under Benjamin Franklin, set up a committee to negotiate with foreign nations, declared American ports open to all nations except Britain, and in May 1776 advised all the colonies to sever their relationship with Britain and organize separate state governments. After all that had happened this final step remained difficult for many delegates, but on July 2, 1776, after several weeks of debate, the assembled delegates in Philadelphia adopted the forthright resolution offered by Richard Henry Lee of Virginia: "RESOLVED, That these United Colonies are, and of right ought to be, free and independent States, that they are absolved from allegiance to the British Crown, and that all political connection between them and the State of Great Britain is, and ought to be, totally dissolved." The passage of this resolution officially cut the umbilical cord that bound the colonies to their mother country, but the Congress felt such a momentous break with the past needed to be explained to the world. Accordingly, early in the discussion of Lee's resolution the Congress appointed a five-man committee headed by thirty-three-year-old Thomas Jefferson to prepare the document. Jefferson had, in John Adams's apt phrase, a "peculiar felicity of expression," and practically overnight he penned a brilliant statement that with only minor changes was accepted by the Congress on July 4. Less a history of the revolutionary movement than a philosophical lawyer's brief for the cause, Jefferson eloquently summarized the American state of mind and persuasively put the case for their independence before the court of world opinion. Jefferson did not innovate—his "all men are created equal" carried the eighteenth-century meaning that all white male citizens in the colonies had equal political rights with the white male citizens of England, and the intellectual orgins of his ideas, ranging from John Locke to the Scottish Common Sense philosophers, were widely known to educated colonists—but the declaration contained seeds of wisdom whose fruition Jefferson could not have comprehended. The equality phrase would be expanded in later centuries to encompass the rights of all people, irrespective of race or gender. In 1776, however, Jefferson was intent primarily on writing a defense of the American political position, and the list of charges against the king was more than three times the length of the philosophical first two paragraphs. It was in the nineteenth and twentieth centuries that this powerful document came to be seen as the philosophical ideal of the American nation.

Thomas Jefferson.
(New York Public Library)

THE FIGHT FOR INDEPENDENCE IN THE SOUTH

In 1775 the British saw New England generally and Massachusetts specifically as the cause of their American troubles, and for three years the primary aim of their military strategy was to isolate and subdue the rebellious New Englanders. From the beginning, British strategists believed there was significant pro-British sympathy in the southern colonies. A show of British strength, they believed, would bring these colonies to the aid of royal authority and secure the South for His Majesty. In truth, there was much reluctance to break with England in the South: government officials of course were pro-British, as were many merchants who feared disruption of commerce and appreciated the British markets and bounties on such products as indigo. Some wealthy planters also identified with the cause of the Crown, and in certain regions specific ethnic groups, such as the Scottish Highlanders in North Carolina, were pro-British. Many former Regulators in the North Carolina Piedmont identified the Patriot planters to the east with the political establishment that had participated in the misrule of the western areas; but most Regulators were less pro-British than anti-East. In many regions very local concerns determined the stance persons took as the rupture with England neared; after the break, the presence or absence of either one of the competing armies influenced how people sided. Terrorism or indiscriminate violence or stealing of one's cattle and corn by either army could easily turn victimized settlers into enemies, at least until the other army acted similarly. Perhaps 15 percent or slightly more of the southern white population were Loyalists, or, as the Patriots called them, Tories.

A quick show of force by the British army might have gained the base Loyalist population and overawed many others who were as yet unsure, but England squandered this early opportunity because it misunderstood the seriousness of the conflict with America until it was too late, and by then the decision had been made to concentrate on New England. The rumors in May 1775 in Charles Town that the British were conspiring to arm the slaves for a revolt against their owners solidified the lowcountry planters against the British, and the same happened in Virginia in November after Dunmore's proclamation raised the specter there of slave revolt. As the news spread into Maryland and North Carolina of Dunmore's supposed machinations, England looked ever more like an unscrupulous tyrant. In the South Carolina Piedmont bands of Loyalists began hostilities against Patriot supporters in the late fall of 1775, only to be crushed in mid-winter by Colonel Richard Richardson, who had gathered four thousand Patriots and secured much of the back country and Charles Town. Dunmore was also blamed for the burning of Norfolk on New Year's Day 1776, making the British cause look barbaric—depriving women and children of shelter in the depth of winter.

Perhaps taking heart from Dunmore's incendiary success, about fifteen hundred Scottish Highlanders and Piedmont Loyalists—called by North Carolina Governor Josiah Martin in early 1776 to help put down the rebellion—began to move toward Wilmington, North Carolina, expecting help from the British navy and redcoats. Neither assistance arrived, but at Moore's Creek Bridge a thousand Patriot troops, having removed the flooring from the bridge and greased the supporting beams, subjected the Loyalists to deadly fire in the dim morning light of February 27, 1776, as they struggled to cross the high-banked creek on the slippery beams—the Loyalists were crushed and scattered, and the region secured for the Patriots. In a vain attempt to reverse this series of disappointing developments British General Henry Clinton and Commodore Peter Parker decided they could take Charles Town and give heart to Loyalist Carolinians. But the British naval operation to capture Sullivan's Island at the entrance to the harbor at Charles Town was a comedy of errors. British mistakes combined with the resourcefulness of Patriot leaders John Rutledge and William Moultrie and the surprising resilience of the palmetto log fortifications on the island led to another

British defeat in the South in late June and early July. So far England had not dispatched many troops to the South, and events there had proved sorely disappointing to the British.

England's real emphasis in the opening years of the Revolution was New England, but the March 17, 1776 evacuation of Boston forced British strategists to look toward the Middle Colonies as the way to isolate and defeat the Massachusetts Patriots. In the spring of 1776 the British, led by the brothers General William Howe and Admiral Richard Howe, occupied New York City. By late fall they had pushed Washington's outmanned army southward through New Jersey into Pennsylvania. Only a surprise Christmas Day 1777 victory over a Hessian garrison at Trenton, New Jersey, followed by a stunning victory on January 5 at Princeton, prevented Washington's army from collapsing. In the late spring of 1777 General William Howe moved to take Philadelphia; after defeating Washington at Brandywine Creek, the British settled in to hold Philadelphia for the duration of the war. As fall came, Washington prepared to go into winter quarters in nearby Valley Forge. Meanwhile, a British decision to let General John Burgoyne come south from Lake Champlain, hoping to cut New England's lines of communication and its provisions from the Middle Colonies, resulted in a surprise victory for the Americans on October 17, 1777, at Saratoga, New York. The real result of this Patriot triumph was that, by suggesting a possible American victory in the war, it convinced France, still smoldering from defeat at the hands of the British a decade and a half earlier, to sign on February 6, 1778, a treaty of alliance with the infant United States. With the Patriots still controlling Boston, General Howe having resigned and been replaced with General Henry Clinton, who then moved from Philadelphia and engaged in a long standoff with General George Washington at New York City, the British war aims were stalemated.

In March 1778 the British ministry decided to break the stalemate by focusing attention on the South, where, they assumed, the potential for Loyalist support suggested that a relatively light application of military force might produce substantial results. The theater of war thus shifted southward in 1778. Although the decision was made in the early spring, it was not until late November that General Clinton sent Lieutenant Colonel Archibald Campbell south with 3,500 men to join Brigadier General Augustine Prevost marching north from Florida to attack Savannah—the British had been led by the former royal governors to believe that such a move would awaken latent Loyalist supporters. Within a couple of months the British not only had taken Savannah but also had the surrounding lowcountry under control. In the spring several abortive efforts were made to move north along the coast and take Charles Town, but these efforts were curiously halfhearted and ineffective. Clinton—preoccupied with holding New York and the Middle Colonies—made one slight feint toward the Chesapeake, but, worried about

French naval activities in the West Indies, he hesitated to make a bold move and frittered away most of 1779. Finally, two days before Christmas, Clinton left New York for South Carolina, finished preparations for a siege of Charles Town that began on April 1, and on May 12, 1780, forced General Benjamin Lincoln to surrender the city and over 5,500 defenders, the greatest loss of American troops during the entire Revolution. A victorious Clinton left for New York in June, leaving General Charles Cornwallis as his successor.

Cornwallis meant to subdue the Patriot forces in the interior and put an end to the war. Moving quickly to the west, he engaged an American force commanded by General Horatio Gates at Camden and routed the Patriots. Emboldened by this easy success to think that even without reinforcements he could sweep across the backcountry chastising the Patriots and energizing Loyalist uprisings, Cornwallis was unprepared for the fierce hostility he met. In part because British officers, such as Banastre Tarleton and Patrick Ferguson, used brutal violence against the Patriots and thus created a backlash and in part because many so-called Loyalists were loyal only when redcoats were in their midst, Cornwallis learned that the more territory he conquered the more ephemeral was his control. Patriots and others outraged by British excesses fought back with a bloody vengeance. On October 7, 1780, a force of more than a thousand Patriots, led by William Campbell, surprised the hated Ferguson and his troops at Kings Mountain and destroyed them, ignoring their attempts to surrender. With Clinton still fixated on New York City and hesitant to spare more than a few troops for the South, Cornwallis—determined to pacify the backcountry and awaken the presumed Loyalists who only awaited a British show of force—decided once more to move to the west. He had hardly begun his new offensive before Tarleton was decisively defeated at the Battle of Cowpens, but recovering, Cornwallis continued to pursue two able southern leaders, Daniel Morgan and Nathanael Greene, through the western Carolinas, finally winning a Pyrrhic victory at Guilford Court House on March 15, 1781. Over a quarter of Cornwallis's troops were wounded or killed, and his army was so crippled that he could not return to the offensive. Instead he withdrew down the Cape Fear River to rest and lick his wounds at Wilmington.

Across the backcountry Patriot and Loyalist/British forces clashed and slashed with ruthless abandon; here the Revolution was a true civil war, and the normal rules of war were forgotten as each side returned barbarism for barbarism. Francis Marion, whose first experience in fighting had been in the Cherokee conflict two decades earlier, was an especially able tormentor of the British. Operating out of bases in the lowcountry swamps, he waged effective guerrilla warfare and lived up to his nickname, the Swamp Fox. With the backcountry out of control and after more than two years of effort, Clinton and Cornwallis had little more than a narrow strip of safe territory along the coast. Cornwallis still harbored dreams of uncovering substantial Tory sup-

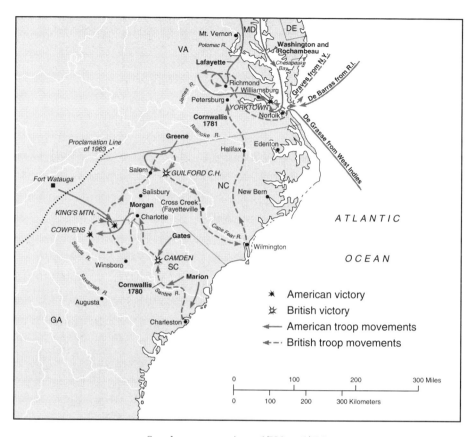

Southern campaigns, 1780 to 1781

port among the hills and small farms of the Piedmont, and, stymied until now in Carolina, he became convinced he had to invade Virginia less for its own sake than to stop supplies from reaching the rebels in the Carolinas. He had not yet comprehended that the whole British conception was flawed; there was no Loyalist majority in the hinterland ready to rise. Rather, the British army, despite having conquered large sections of the South, never really controlled any area beyond where its troops were at any given moment. The potential Loyalist population was an illusion that misled the British into thinking that they could win the South without a massive introduction of British forces.

Thus misled by his assumptions, Cornwallis invaded Virginia in May 1781 and combined General Benedict Arnold's troops with his own. For several months the British forces, now numbering more than seven thousand, made punishing raids throughout central Virginia, almost capturing Thomas

Jefferson and the Virginia legislature near Charlottesville and forcing Governor Jefferson to escape across the mountains. The American forces in Virginia were ably led by the Marquis de Lafayette and General Friedrich Wilhelm von Steuben, and when Patriot General Anthony Wayne arrived with reinforcements, Cornwallis began to move eastward and shift into a defensive posture on the Yorktown peninsula a scant dozen miles from Jamestown, where the whole English adventure in the New World had begun. Cornwallis expected to be reinforced at Yorktown by the arrival of British naval forces, but that was not to be.

Britain still ruled the seas, but for a combination of reasons Admiral Thomas Graves arrived in the vicinity at the end of August only to discover that French Admiral François Comte de Grasse had earlier sailed in from the West Indies, arrived at Yorktown, and landed three thousand troops to aid Lafayette and was simultaneously thwarting Cornwallis from making a maritime escape. After a short skirmish in early September, Graves gave up the area and sailed north. Several months before, in May 1781, George Washington had finally convinced the French commander General Comte de Rochambeau to join his forces in Newport with Washington's forces near New York City, but before they could move against Clinton, Washington and Rochambeau were informed that de Grasse was sailing toward the Chesapeake. Making a feint toward New York City to keep Clinton off guard, Washington and Rochambeau quickly moved the bulk of their troops to the Chesapeake. By the time they arrived, de Grasse had dispatched his troops and was able to use a portion of his fleet to ferry the forces of Washington and Rochambeau to the James River, landing them on September 18.

Now the combined American forces—Lafayette and Wayne's men, plus those of Washington and Rochambeau—numbered sixteen thousand, more than double the forces of Cornwallis. With de Grasse controlling the seas, the combined American forces began to move down the peninsula on September 28. They were near enough to Cornwallis's troops by October 9 to commence the bombardment. Five days later, first American and then French troops stormed outlying British breastworks. On October 16 Cornwallis's troops attempted two sorties against the advancing army, but were soon thrown back. Cornwallis toyed with the idea of trying to escape across the river, but a sudden storm swept the first boats down the river. When the bombardment resumed the next morning, Cornwallis realized his situation was hopeless. On October 17, 1781—four years to the day after the British defeat at Saratoga—Cornwallis signaled Washington asking for a twenty-four-hour armistice to discuss the terms of surrender. Washington offered two hours. Cornwallis hoped for leniency; Washington demanded complete surrender. Two days later, almost eight thousand British troops laid down their arms as a British military band played a whimsical nursery tune: "If cats should be chased, / into holes by the mouse; / If mammas sold their babies, / To gypsies for half a crown; / If summers were spring / And the other way round; / Then all the world would be upside down."

Though naval skirmishes would continue in the West Indies for months, the heavy fighting on the mainland was finished. Britain's last lingering hopes for victory were dashed, as Lord North realized when he got the disappointing news from Yorktown. "O God! It is all over," he said again and again. However, the war in the South persisted, not at a boil but at a low simmer. The cities of Charles Town, Wilmington, and Savannah were still held by British troops—more of them in South Carolina and Georgia than there had been in Cornwallis's army. Although the British troops were severely demoralized following Yorktown, General Nathanael Greene's Patriot forces—recently victorious in a major battle at Eutaw Springs, South Carolina, on September 8, 1781—were too exhausted and undermanned to follow up that victory with a quick assault against them. Nevertheless, by January 1782 the British had retreated to the vicinity of Charles Town and Savannah. The low-country was the scene of vicious, small-scale, almost personal terroristic warfare between Tories and Patriots. No set-piece battles occurred, but personal scores were being settled. Greene's forces inexorably tightened the noose around Charles Town, as did General Anthony Wayne's around Savannah. In July 1782 the British evacuated Savannah, and during the summer British General Alexander Leslie began to evacuate Charles Town, taking away some 3,800 Loyalists and 5,000 slaves. On December 13, 1782, the British troops themselves began boarding the ships ready to transport them away, and evacuation was complete the following day. As the British rear guard marched to the wharves to depart, American infantry followed only two hundred yards behind. Later that day General Greene triumphantly led a parade of Continental soldiers down King Street. The American Revolution was finally over.

Progress was also being made on the diplomatic fronts. In March 1782 Lord North had resigned, to be replaced by a ministry more friendly toward the United States. American peace negotiators had long been in Paris, and the terms of the 1778 alliance with France required that no separate peace be signed. The crafty Americans, however knew that France wanted an independent but weak America; sensing that Britain would prefer to keep France at arm's length from the new United States, the Americans struck a separate treaty with Great Britain on November 30, 1782. The British, hoping to wean the Americans away from the French, were generous. They recognized American independence and ceded to the United States all the former British territory east of the Mississippi, bounded on the north by the Canadian border and on the south by the Florida territories, which were ceded to Spain by another treaty. The definitive Treaty of Paris, also signed after France had ceased hostilities with England, was concluded on September 3, 1783. The United States would begin its career as an independent nation, not as thir-

North America in 1783

teen small states hugging the Atlantic but as a land-rich empire sweeping westward a thousand miles.

SLAVERY AND THE AMERICAN REVOLUTION

In May 1775 white citizens of Charles Town and vicinity had been outraged by the *South Carolina Gazette*'s reprinting of a letter written in England that mentioned English arms being sent to America for the use of slaves and Indians, for in the lowcountry and in the back country the threat of either a black or a red uprising was a constant worry. South Carolinians knew whereof they feared. Indian warfare on the frontier a decade and a half earlier had pushed white settlement back to the east, and certainly the relations with

Indians in the ensuing years—unscrupulous white traders cheating them and white farmers homesteading on traditional Indian lands—had done nothing to turn the Indians into friends of the white southerners. But for most whites, certainly those in the Chesapeake Tidewater and the Carolina–Georgia low-country, where the slave population was concentrated, the most immediate threat was that of a slave rebellion, especially one fomented and armed by nefarious British agents.

Of course slaves had rebelled against their owners without conspiring with the British, as South Carolinians with long memories certainly knew. Most slave rebellion was passive—refusing to accept all of the white man's culture and holding on to at least a degree of black autonomy. Some was individualistic—running away, breaking a tool, slowing one's work pace. Nevertheless, whites must have understood, even if they tried to deny it to themselves, that blacks had good reasons to rebel against their white masters. Blacks understood full well what absence of freedom meant, and while the few literate slaves no doubt occasionally caught a glimpse of the newspapers and pamphlets fulminating against slavery, many others heard indiscreet whites disparaging slavery and proclaiming the virtues of freedom. The whites were discussing the loss of political freedom, not black bondage, when they attacked slavery. But black slaves saw that what was good for the white goose was good for the black gander. Slaves needed neither political pamphlets nor British agents to teach them the evils of bondage, but many were emboldened by both to seize the opportunity offered by social and political disruption to improve their status.

In April 1775, the month of Lexington and Concord, a group of Virginia slaves had come to Governor Dunmore and offered their services in return for freedom. Dunmore hesitated to take an action so offensive to white Virginians at that time, but his position deteriorated to the point of desperation. By November, he was willing to offer freedom to those slaves and servants who would transfer their allegiance to the Crown. Dunmore's army was routed so quickly by Patriot forces at the battle of Great Bridge that his "Ethiopian Regiment" had little military significance. Virginia slave masters tightened the controls over their slaves, removed them from sensitive areas, and tried to convince them that the English hoped to hoodwink the slaves into coming within their grasp, then the redcoats would ship them to a far worse bondage in the West Indies. Despite these defensive measures, many slaves risked everything to flee to the British armies. After 1778, when the theater of war shifted southward and there were active British forces in Georgia, the Carolinas, and Virginia, thousands of southern slaves joined the British armies, sometimes almost overwhelming military logistics by their numbers and need for housing and food.

The British had little or no commitment to emancipation as a principle, but they saw liberating the slaves of Patriots as a useful military strategy. The

British used slave labor to build fortifications, to forage for food, to drive teams of oxen, to cook for and wash for and serve the troops. Other slaves served as pilots to guide British boats through the labyrinthine waterways of the coastal South, as scouts who intimately knew the wooded terrain, as spies who could ferret out information about Patriot troop movements. The British sometimes treated their black allies as simply contraband, giving them as slaves to officers and enlisted men as reward for meritorious service. Before Yorktown but especially afterwards, as British troops and Loyalists evacuated the South, thousands of blacks who had joined the Loyalist cause—perhaps as many as 50,000—left with them, destined for freedom in Canada and Sierra Leone and for bondage in the West Indies. The issue of departing slaves embittered British–United States relations for a half century because in southern eyes the British were expected to return all property seized in the course of the war, including the slaves whom Britain had promised freedom in return for service. Liberation had never been a war aim for the British but rather a means to an end. Yet the realities of the situation presented them with a moral dilemma: to dismiss the promises of freedom and callously return the blacks to their vengeful former owners seemed grossly dishonorable. Once the return of such "property" came to be seen as involving their honor, the British balked and refused to desert their black refugees, to the wrath of the southern whites. While most black allies departed with the British, some chose to remain in America, either fleeing to the North (and Canada) or preferring to stay with loved ones in the South. No doubt some blacks took advantage of the chaos of war to emerge as free blacks in southern towns and cities.

Not all slaves sided with the British. For complex motives some served the Patriot armies, again doing duty as foragers, laborers, spies, everything but actually bearing arms. (In fact, there may have been a few slaves who served as soldiers in Maryland). Some may have hoped such service would gain them the appreciation of their owners and perhaps even emancipation; some may have feared even worse bondage at the hands of the redcoats. In February 1782 John Laurens of South Carolina proposed that 2,500 slaves drawn from the estates of Loyalists be drafted into the Patriot army under the command of white officers. The state assembly rejected his resolution—probably assuming the war was too nearly over to justify such a radical move. For the great majority of slaves in the South, the revolutionary settlement that led to independence for the United States and the beginning of what Jefferson once called the "empire for liberty" for whites left most blacks more firmly in bondage. To a degree the ideals so eloquently expressed in Jefferson's Declaration of Independence found their way into the hearts and minds of some slaveholders, as did the evangelical belief that in God's eyes all persons were equal, with the result that in the immediate postrevolutionary South more than a few slaveholders freed their slaves; the number of free blacks in the South increased severalfold between 1776 and 1790, by which time they totaled more than 32,000, a number that almost doubled again in the next decade.

In the states north of the Mason-Dixon line (a line that had been surveyed in 1767 by Charles Mason and Jeremiah Dixon to settle a long-standing boundary dispute between Maryland and Pennsylvania), where slavery had always existed but had never been an essential element of the colonial economies, a process of gradual emancipation had been initiated by Pennsylvania in 1780 and would be culminated by New Jersey in 1804. The result, even by the mid-1780s, was to set the South apart as the region of human bondage, a bondage made more permanent by the fact that political control of the South and its increasingly peculiar institution now lay in the hands of southern slaveholders themselves and their representatives. American independence and home rule ensured that nonresident legislators would not be able to end slavery by legislative fiat, as Parliament did for British West Indian slavery in 1833. Black slavery and white freedom were strengthened by the outcome of the American Revolution.

INDIANS AND THE AMERICAN REVOLUTION

South Carolinians' fears of an Indian attack stimulated by the inflammatory letter reprinted in the *South Carolina Gazette* in May 1775 were not solely evoked by memories of the bloody Cherokee War of 1760–1761. Knowledgeable leaders from Virginia to Georgia knew that developments outside the commonly accepted boundaries or the lines of settlement of the original thirteen colonies made the region beyond the backcountry a powder keg of competition between European powers, and between them, resident Indian nations and westward and southward pushing colonists. The vast territory south of the Ohio River all the way to the Gulf Coast, bounded on the west by the Mississippi River and including Florida, had been ceded to England in 1763. France's governance of this empire had been almost nonexistent; four major Indian nations—the powerful Cherokee and Creek in what is now eastern Tennessee and the southern Appalachians to Florida, the Choctaw in southern Mississippi, and the Chickasaws in northern Mississippi—occupied the region before 1763, and they continued to farm and hunt there after the treaty pen was laid aside. England tried by the infamous Proclamation of 1763 to regulate the incursions by land-hungry white farmers and speculators, hoped the Indian superintendent John Stuart could placate white traders and Indian deer hunters, and basically tried to hold back the tide of white settlement. This effort predictably failed, with the eventual disposition of the region not fully determined until after a half century of turmoil, intrigue, and conflict.

Before 1763 the Indians of the region knew white colonists only to the extent that they were participants in the voluminous and lucrative trade in furs and deer skins. Almost imperceptibly the Indians had gotten accustomed to European goods—cloth, metal implements, guns, and, sadly, rum—and they determined to trade with whomever could keep the supply firm. While this steady incorporation into the larger European commercial world was destructive to the traditional Indian cultures, Indian leaders themselves accepted the bargain. But when after 1763 whites became no longer content simply to profit from the deer trade and began to enter the region in significant numbers with expectations of permanent settlement, Indians quickly perceived the danger to their way of life. White settlement beyond the older, accepted boundaries began in a major way when England in 1764 organized Florida into two colonies, East and West Florida.

At first the British army established garrisons at Mobile and Pensacola, but within a decade hundreds of settlers from the other southern colonies, from England, and from New England moved into West Florida in the vicinity of Mobile and Pensacola and especially in the fertile bottomland along the east bank of the Mississippi from below Baton Rouge to Natchez, the site of the old French Fort Rosalie. Because the Spanish controlled New Orleans and its immediate surroundings on the east bank of the Mississippi nearer its mouth and denied the English settlers of the Natchez District access to the port, the economic growth of these initial Mississippi settlements was slow, but it did result in a population of perhaps 2,500 whites and 600 slaves in West Florida within a decade. And it did, from the Indian perspective, give Europeans a potentially threatening toehold in the region. The development of East Florida, with its poorer, sandy soil, was slower and was confined to a strip of settlement along the coast from the mouth of St. John's River to just south of St. Augustine. Several expansive colonization schemes were mounted, only to fail.

Farmers, small planters, and ambitious land speculators, along with a rag-tag assortment of ruffians, scoundrels, and barely civilized hunters and trappers had long pushed at the western edge of settlement in North and South Carolina; by the early 1760s many in the South Carolina Piedmont were beyond the range of effective government institutions while settlers in western North Carolina chafed under what they took to be the unresponsive rule of officials appointed by self-absorbed eastern Carolina bigwigs. In both colonies the rapidly growing backcountry population was outracing the ability of the older ruling establishment to provide adequate and fair government. These internal law-and-order disputes were eventually settled in a fashion after the Regulator movements in both colonies, but the root of the problem, pell-mell westward migration, continued, and Cherokee and Creek Indians bore the brunt of the scramble for land. The diplomatic skills of John Stuart led to the Treaty of Hard Labor in 1768 wherein the Cherokees and the Creeks accepted a boundary line, but few whites ever felt bound by the agreement. Virginia hunters and land speculators never accepted the terms worked out at Hard Labor, for they already had greedy eyes on the fertile lands of the west. By the mid-1760s Virginia farmers were exploring and settling river valleys far in the mountainous interior, with settlements in what are now West Virginia and eastern Kentucky and Tennessee. From the banks of the Ohio to the shores of the Gulf, from the headwaters of the Savannah to the mouth of the Mississippi, wherever perceptive Indian leaders looked they saw the inexorable western advance onto their traditional hunting lands by would-be permanent white settlers.

Once the troubles between Britain and the colonies had escalated into actual combat at Lexington and Concord in the Spring of 1775, both British officials and colonial leaders began to calculate the potential effect of Indian involvement and began to maneuver to try to gain Indian allies. Both sides assumed the other would try to preempt Indian support by buying them off; consequently both began to treat the Indians with goods and trinkets. Governor Dunmore in Virginia and Loyalist leader Thomas Brown in South Carolina hatched plots to arm the Indians and have them raid the frontier. British Indian Superintendent John Stuart hoped to prevent or at least lessen such interracial warfare, knowing how vicious it could be, but suspicious Carolinians had already forced him to flee Charles Town and seek refuge in St. Augustine. Stuart wanted to put a damper on Indian unrest and at most have them do battle only in consort with British regulars.

The Cherokees, however, had a mind of their own; they were angered by years of encroachment by colonists and felt cheated by the 1775 Treaty of Sycamore Shoals, which formalized a "purchase" by a group of North Carolina speculators of a huge tract of land between the Kentucky and Kanawha rivers. In the summer of 1776 hundreds of Cherokee warriors murderously attacked white squatters in eastern Tennessee, western Virginia, and the western borders of both Carolinas and Georgia. Rumors of British aid and the presence of British arms—the Indians had bought weapons from them for many years—gave substance to colonial fears of British collusion. This was no isolated Indian raid but one part of the battle with the British for independence. Interpreting the Indian uprising in such a way, even backcountry settlers who had no quarrel with the mother country were transformed into supporters of the revolutionary cause. During the late summer and fall the states of Virginia, North and South Carolina, and Georgia sent nearly six thousand militia to crush the Cherokee. Hopelessly outnumbered, most Cherokees made peace in May and July 1777 and ceded to the new states a large part of the Indian hunting ground. One Cherokee leader, Dragging Canoe, was especially resolute; he and his followers fled west to the vicinity of Chickamauga Creek. Gathering other diehards, they organized themselves into the Chickamauga tribe and continued to fight until the very end of the war—Dragging Canoe persisted as a foe of the whites until his death in 1789. But the united militia of the southern states had broken the back of Cherokee resistance, and the other Indian tribes of the South, including the Creeks in southwestern Georgia and northern Florida, were largely intimidated by the ferocity and effectiveness of the southern counterattack.

There were, nevertheless, occasional Indian raids, and the British persisted in plying the Creeks with trade goods in an attempt to keep them actively hostile toward the Patriots. But in 1779 Spain too declared war on England, leading ambitious Governor Bernardo de Galvez of Louisiana to attack the British outposts in West Florida. The garrisons at Manchac, Baton Rouge, and Natchez fell almost instantly, and by March 1780 Galvez (after whom the island of Galveston off Texas is named) had captured Mobile. The hard-pressed British used all their influence with their Indian allies to persuade the Indians to aid them in trying to protect the British position in West Florida. After several attempts, and augmented with forces from Cuba, Galvez succeeded in taking Pensacola in May 1781 despite a spirited Indian-British defense.

The Spanish offensive in the Southwest and the necessity for the British to respond spared the southern states from Indian attacks in the West in the very period when British military strategy shifted to the southern theater. Had it been otherwise, the British might have found far more success in their attempt to squelch Patriot sentiment in the South and awaken Loyalist support. In the far West the small American settlements in the Kentucky territory suffered several devastating raids from Mingo and Shawnee warriors from north of the Ohio River until George Rogers Clark smashed the British outposts there in 1778–1779. All told, in the South as a whole the Indians proved to be less of a military factor than Patriots had feared in 1775 but enough of a menace to fuel preexisting white hatred for Native Americans; white southerners in the new nation would not hesitate to push Indians from their traditional hunting lands and considered them vermin fit only for extermination. White enmity toward the Indians was one part of the heritage from the colonial and revolutionary past.

CREATING THE NEW NATION

The American Revolution was multifaceted, but at its core was an effort to redefine the parameters of political authority. In part because of the inner logic of the developing argument with England after the early 1760s, it was unanimously accepted that the ultimate locus of political authority inhered in the people. The tradition of local government, based on the territorial unit of the county with justices of the peace, sheriffs, and juries drawn from its citizens, gave tangible meaning to popular rule, and the accumulating prestige and power of the lower houses of assembly in all the colonies was based on the assumption that direct representatives of the people, chosen from specific geographical districts, were the truest conduit through which people might consent to their government. Borrowing from the dissent tradition in England and from their own experience, Americans honored the right to private property, believed that no one should be deprived of any portion of their property through taxation unless they or their agents so approved, and were jealous of their liberty, a word packed with meaning but especially evocative of freedom from the arbitrary or despotic control of others. Southerners surrounded by their black slaves had an immediate reminder of what the absence of liberty meant and were as a result extraordinarily sensitive to any potential threats to their own freedom.

At its core the revolution was a constitutional debate over how a diverse and far-flung people might be governed, a debate requiring instant practical solution at several levels once the decision was made to dissolve the political connection with England. The journey from dependent colonies to independent states within an independent nation took more than a decade, solicited an impressive outpouring of political thought, and proceeded by fits and starts, but the destination reached in 1787 represented a remarkable achievement for a nation of only three million inhabitants. The southern states were disproportionately responsible for choosing the itinerary and for suggesting the constitutional destination, in fact, for creating the new nation.

Two sets of governance problems had to be addressed in 1776: new local governments for the individual colonies now that they were breaking away from the Crown and some kind of overarching structure of government binding the states together into a continental or national association able to coordinate personnel and purposes in the face of military conflict with England. Virginia—as the most populous and the oldest colony and the one with the most distinguished stable of political theorists—played the lead role in state and national constitution making. First on the agenda was the easier task, creating new forms of state government. In May 1776 the Continental Congress, the extralegal informal governing committee of the colonies in rebellion, instructed the various colonies to frame new governments "under the authority of the people," not the Crown or some distant proprietor. Virginia took the lead, drafting the first state constitution and one that would have much influence in the other emerging states.

The Virginia constitution, written in the heady days of early summer 1776 by a committee of delegates sitting in the Virginia Convention—the extralegal transmutation of the old House of Burgesses—was mainly the work of George Mason, and it represented the political viewpoint of colonists angered by what they interpreted as the executive tyranny of the king and eager to defend the prerogative of the legislature. The constitution approved by the convention on June 29 was very much a creature of its times. Only two weeks before the convention had passed a Declaration of Rights (a prototype bill of rights) that clearly placed sovereignty in the hands of the people, and that idea was implicit in the new constitution even though the framers were careful to filter the vox populi through mechanisms intended to restrain temporary enthusiasms. The constitution provided for executive, legislative, and judicial branches, but the balance of power was clearly tipped toward the legislative. Colonial experience with the discretionary power of Crown officials and the fear of executive tyranny as outlined in Republican ideology were the root of their preference for legislative predominance. The General Assembly, consisting of a House of Delegates and a Senate, chose the governor, and he did not have the power to dissolve or adjourn the Assembly. The ability to initiate legislation was confined to members of the House; the Senate could not even propose revisions to money bills. Property requirements still existed for voting, and the western counties remained underrepresented. This cautious document, resting power in the hands of the peoples' representatives, reflected the era's concerns about the power to tax and the fear of a strong executive.

Thomas Jefferson, off in Philadelphia preparing to write the Declaration of Independence, wished he were in Richmond to do what seemed the more important work—not to summarize what people felt but rather to set one's hand to the once-in-a-lifetime task of fashioning a new plan of government from the lessons both of history and of recent experience. He sent letters to friends in Richmond, proposing a better balance between the several branches of government and suggesting that not a regularly convened convention but only a specially called one should have the authority to rewrite the rules of government. By October 1776 Jefferson was sitting in the new House of Delegates elected by his constituents in Albemarle County, and for a decade Jefferson and like-minded legislators such as James Madison introduced and guided through the legislature a series of bills that extended the liberties of white Virginians and made the state a laboratory for liberal government.

The exigencies of the revolutionary war delayed many of the reform efforts—for example, the complete revision of the legal code—and Madison had to push many of the bills through the Assembly because by then Jefferson was serving as the American minister to France. Entail and primogeniture were abolished, the range of crimes punished by death was drastically cut back, and a Bill for Establishing Religious Freedom—a cause especially dear to Jefferson—was finally passed in 1786 after much controversy and the bitter opposition of the Anglicans and others who deemed government support necessary for the survival of religion. One counter-proposal was to prorate the distribution of state support among the various denominations according to their membership—hence establishing religion in general rather than one particular church. Jefferson fought this compromise, but Jefferson was not alone. Madison's aid—intellectual and political—in achieving religious freedom was inestimable, and their joint achievement was one of the landmarks of the entire revolutionary era. Here Virginia was far ahead of Massachusetts and most of the rest of the Western world. Fourteen centuries of church-state partnership, dating from the reign of Emperor Constantine, were reversed, and the result proved to be beneficial for both government and religion. The US tradition of the separation of church and state really dates from the efforts of Jefferson and Madison—assisted by the Baptists in eighteenth-century Virginia. Devoid of government funds, the churches had to become both more vigorous and more atuned to the people's needs, and the result has been enormous vitality on the part of religious denominations in this nation.

Jefferson's hopes for a bill providing for the gradual emancipation of slaves and a bill providing for public schooling for all children, on the contrary, were dashed, but Virginia had partially pointed the way toward the future. Before the war ended every state had a new constitution, though some merely excised offending references to the king and England from their colonial charters, and each celebrated the power of the lower house, weakened the power of the governor, stated that the basis of sovereignty was the people, and most had some form of a bill of rights. In 1779 and 1780 Massachusetts pioneered in the election of a specially called convention to frame the principles of government and provided that the newly drafted document would have to be ratified by the people through a form of popular vote. The Virginia principles and the Massachusetts process would be employed again in 1787 on behalf of all the states.

In addition to providing for appropriate new governments for the individual states, the second administrative problem that had to be addressed in 1776 was devising a form of superintending structure that could coordinate the thirteen separate state governments into some kind of unitary entity for certain purposes while at the same time recognizing their autonomy in other areas. A careful balancing of authority was required, but the understandable hesitancy to create a powerful central government in America at the moment the states were opposing what was felt to be overweening central authority in London led to an unwieldy and impotent confederacy of states. In 1776 most people's loyalty was to their state, not to some inchoate consolidation of American provinces. Perceptive people understood that British threats against the liberties of citizens of one state were in a sense threats against the liberties of all, and common sense suggested there needed to be some sort of concerted opposition to such threats. But no one could really conceive of a modern nation consisting of thirteen disparate former colonies with differing economies, diverse people, and varied histories. In the maelstrom of war the Patriot leaders groped toward a solution to problems as tangible as shoes and blankets for soldiers at Valley Forge and as metaphysical as the indivisibility of political sovereignty. It was one thing for a committee of wise men to devise a plan of government, another to get it ratified by thirteen states protective of their authority, and still another to make the system work in difficult times.

Richard Henry Lee's resolution of independence, passed by the Continental Congress on July 2, 1776, had called for a plan for forming a continental confederation, and within two weeks a committee chaired by John Dickinson of Pennsylvania produced a draft of the "Articles of Confederation and Perpetual Union." Strenuous debate embroiled the congress, for Dickinson's proposal gave to a centralized Congress more power than delegates were yet ready to approve. Many other wartime issues demanded consideration by the Continental Congress, so the Articles were not always the center of attention, but after sixteen months of on-again, off-again deliberation, the Articles of Confederation were adopted by the Continental Congress on November 15, 1777, and the document was transmitted to the thirteen states for the mandatory unanimous ratification before it would take effect. Maryland, fearing eventual domination by states like Virginia that had vast claims to western lands, refused to accept the new government unless the western lands were ceded to the common government. Virginia finally relented, Maryland ratified, and the Articles of Confederation Congress on March 1, 1781, became the formal ruling body of what was for the first time called "The United States of America." For almost five years the Continental Congress had struggled to govern the embattled fledgling nation, and the Continental Army had suffered inconveniences, shortages, and dispiriting hardships as a result. Now, with the war ironically almost over, a new governmental structure was in place.

The Articles created essentially a confederation of thirteen co-equal states, with each state annually sending a delegation to the Congress that was in effect a continuation of the Second Continental Congress. In the Congress each state had one vote, and, indicative of Americans' fear of a strong central authority, power was concentrated almost exclusively in the continental legislature. There was no separate executive leader; rather, various congressional committees whose membership changed served a quasi-executive function. This enhanced Congress had the sole authority to make treaties and declare war—in other words, conduct diplomacy—to manage a postal service, to coin and borrow money, to regulate Indian affairs, to mediate interstate disputes, and it could requisition soldiers and money from the states—the states could decide whether to honor the requisitions or not. Given the sentiment in defense of local autonomy and the insistence that liberty meant freedom from the control of distant authority, much less the inexperience of any of the Americans with any real form of consolidated government, the Articles of Confederation represented a striking step toward a national ruling authority.

It was an ingenious effort to divide the real powers of government in such a manner as to protect the local autonomy of the individual states in most areas and transfer other powers to a superintending continental government. In addition to this theoretical breakthrough, the Congress in its few years of existence had at least one notable legislative achievement, the Northwest Ordinances of 1784, 1785, and 1787 that provided for the orderly settlement of the land in the former Ohio Territory, guaranteeing freedom of religion, underwriting public schools, prohibiting slavery in the vast region north of the Ohio River (although there was a fugitive slave provision to return runaways to southern owners), and establishing a process by which these territories could make the transition from frontier colony to full statehood. Yet the Articles had several fatal flaws. While the Congress could requisition soldiers and money from the states, it did not have the power to enforce its requests. The states were free to ignore the requisitions or to meet them partially. Since the states were jealous of their authority and always unwilling to tax themselves, much less to send the revenues off to a faraway Congress that would spend the monies elsewhere, the Articles failed to raise the necessary revenues to run the government. It was as much a failure of local will, but one purpose of a national government is to compel people to support activities that benefit the common good, not just the immediate local interest. The Articles were also cumbersome, requiring the approval of nine states for major decisions and demanding unanimous consent for amending the Articles themselves. Even when obvious problems arose and were recognized, sufficient political will could not be motivated to correct the structural inadequacies of the Articles of Confederation government.

It has been to easy to blame the Articles for some of the difficulties and confusion of the 1780s. The American nation was undergoing tremendous economic, demographic, social, and political changes in the years after 1781, and no imaginable government would have been able to cope with the stresses and expectations without controversy. During the war thousands of small producers had been drawn into the effort to provide for the army, resulting in a commercial revolution. Commerce had hitherto been seen primarily as exchanging goods between nations and colonies, but now local trade, between small producers and consumers, came to be seen as a legitimate and highly prosperous enterprise. The volume of local commerce as farmers and artisans began to produce for the markets increased significantly, greatly increasing the need for a stable currency and for uniform port regulations.

The southern staple crop producers experienced a number of shocks: Chesapeake tobacco growers, finding their British markets limited, had sought European buyers and had accelerated the prior shift from tobacco cultivation to wheat. The lowcountry rice growers were cut off from their lucrative British West Indian markets and in fact never completely recovered, and indigo production, now devoid of the profitable British bounty, collapsed. Southern planters too had to cope with the loss of as many as 50,000 slaves to the evacuating British armies. Simultaneously, perhaps 75,000 white Loyalists left too, though many eventually returned, but their emigration produced an economic and political vacuum in many localities and opened up opportunities for the Patriots who remained. Rapid migration westward began, swelled by former soldiers rewarded with land warrants in Kentucky and elsewhere. To some observers it seemed as though the older states were emptying into the transmontane regions, crowding the Cumberland Gap and rafting down the Ohio River. New questions began to be raised about the morality of slavery; in fact, the northern states set underway a variety of legal procedures that would soon end the institution in every state north of the Mason-Dixon line.

All of these changes would have stretched any government's ability to govern; the Articles of Confederation soon came to be seen as incompetent to meet the exigencies of the age. Had the Patriots risked everything to win their independence, only to see that very independence sink beneath an avalanche of local problems? Even within individual states disputes over how to treat the confiscated property of Loyalists, how to raise state taxes, and how to accommodate the increasing surge of commercial activity led to bitter factionalism, with the common good seemingly forgotten in the rush to take care of narrowly provincial interests. States discriminated against one another in commercial regulations and fees. "A spirit of *locality*," James Madison complained, was negating "the aggregate interests of the community." Without the ability to tax there was no way the Articles of Confederation Congress could meet its financial obligations, even pay the interest on the wartime debt. Astronomical inflation was devastating to many farmers and to those on relatively fixed incomes.

After the war rising imports of foreign goods threatened to overwhelm the infant American manufacturers, and Britain in the far Northwest and Spain in the Southwest made noises about holding on to territory that by treaty clearly belonged to the new United States—but without the ability to demand troops, what could the Articles of Confederation Congress do about this foreign threat in its backyard? In 1784 Spain closed the Mississippi River to American trade, crippling the economy of the settlers in Kentucky and Tennessee and threatening the western dreams of Carolinians and Georgians. New Yorker John Jay exacerbated the problem when in 1785–1786 he negotiated a treaty with Spain that accepted the limitation on American usage of the river in return for opening up markets in Spain for New England fisheries, so infuriating all southerners that they prevented the treaty's being ratified by the congress.

Then in the summer of 1786 farmers in western Massachusetts, pushed to the breaking point by inflation and higher taxes and fearing their homes would be seized in payment of debt, revolted and attacked civil courts where foreclosure proceedings were to take place. Led by Daniel Shays, the rebellion grew so intense that the governor had to call out state forces led by a former Revolutionary War general to quell the unrest—all this in Massachusetts, whose model constitution of 1781 had been ratified by the people by popular vote! Was the whole revolutionary settlement coming unraveled? Was the American experiment in liberty dissolving in chaos and rebellion? Was private greed overwhelming the public good? Thoughtful men pondered these questions deeply in late 1785 and 1786.

In 1888 the historian John Fiske, borrowing a phrase from graduate John Quincy Adams's 1787 Harvard commencement address, described this period of the mid-1780s as "the critical period of American history," and that label has stuck. In fact many contemporaries perceived events of the era in exactly that fashion, and even though subsequent studies have shown that it was more a period of change and economic adjustment than of real crisis, their perceptions shaped their responses to the age. Problems on the state level—debt stay laws, state paper currencies that rapidly plummeted in value, harmful navigation acts pitting one state against another—were more disturbing than the inadequacies of the Articles of Confederation, but many leaders came to see the weaknesses of the Articles as symptomatic of the general problem. Somehow the excesses of localized democracy exhibited by the state legislatures and the understandable fear of an overstrong executive (a fear embodied by the directionless congress) had to be overcome without destroying the states or creating a new form of tyrannical authority. Again it would be southerners who would point the way toward the future.

In early 1785 delegates from Maryland and Virginia, meeting at Alexandria trying to settle a dispute over navigation on the Potomac, realized that practical good could result from such discussions, and the meetings were moved to George Washington's home at Mount Vernon and delegates from Delaware and Pennsylvania were invited. These negotiations were so promising that the group recommended that the Virginia legislature invite all the states to send delegates to a meeting scheduled for Annapolis, Maryland, in September 1786 to discuss common problems. Only five states sent delegates to the Annapolis convention, but two of the delegates, Alexander Hamilton of New York and James Madison of Virginia, seized the opportunity to argue for a general meeting not simply to discuss commercial difficulties but to consider amending the Articles of Confederation. Hamilton and Madison were energetic and persuasive; they convinced those present to call for delegates to meet in Philadelphia the following May. The Confederation Congress meeting in New York City was cumbersome and slow to act, but in February it took notice of the coming convention and authorized it to revise and amend the Articles.

All the states but Rhode Island eventually named delegates to the convention—a total of seventy-four. As the May 14 scheduled opening date drew near, the men began straggling into Philadelphia, but the opening had to be delayed until May 25 for there to be delegates present from seven states—enough to do business. Eventually fifty-five delegates attended the convention, though they were never all there at the same time. The group as a whole was remarkably young—the average age was forty-two even with the presence of Benjamin Franklin, eighty-one years old and near the end of his remarkable life. Several of the giants of the age were absent: thoughtful Thomas Jefferson and John Adams were serving the Confederation as ministers to France and England, respectively, while Sam Adams was not chosen by the Massachusetts legislature and Patrick Henry, who was chosen, said he "smelt a rat" and decided not to come. But those present nevertheless represented the most able group of American statesmen ever assembled: Alexander Hamilton, Roger Sherman, Elbridge Gerry, James Wilson, Gouverneur Morris, Edmund Randolph, James Wilson, George Mason, George Washington, and James Madison. Most were well educated, were aristocrats, had served in the Continental or Confederation congresses, and fully one-third had fought in the Continental army, a nationalizing experience where they had seen the common good repeatedly neglected because of provincial jealousies and shortsightedness. All in all, it was a remarkable assemblage of leaders, learned in the writings of history and political science and in the school of practical experience, determined to put aside petty divisions and to work for the national purpose.

On the opening day the twenty-nine delegates present elected George Washington president of the convention, recognizing that his immense prestige would give their deliberations added credibility. Understandably concerned that rumors and press reports could cripple honest airing of all the issues at stake and lead to grandstanding, the convention also decided to shut the windows and keep their collective mouths closed as well when they were outside the hall, conducting their official discussions in secret. Then on May 29 Governor Edmund Randolph of Virginia presented the first of a series of proposals that came to be known as the "Virginia Plan," the first of which was that the delegates should exceed their limited directions to propose amendments to the existing frame of government and instead create an entirely new national government. Some delegates hesitated; this was a bold proposal, but urged on by Hamilton and others, the convention adopted Randolph's resolution "that a national government ought to be established." In any such general meeting he who arrives with a well-thought-out plan can dominate the proceedings, and the Virginia delegation came intellectually armed with a plan presented by Randolph but authored by James Madison, truly the Father of the Constitution. Madison was the greatest political thinker of the age: only five feet four inches tall and weighing less than a hundred pounds, soft-spoken and always dressed in black, he was a physical snippet of a man but an intellectual giant.

As the delegates began to consider the proposals made by Governor Randolph, the revolutionary nature of Madison's conception of the new government became clear. His plan called for the creation of a strong general government, not a loose confederation of independent states; this national republic would overlay the state governments and in specified ways have legal precedence, including the right to exercise power directly over individuals living in the various states. Madison proposed a strong executive and a bicameral national legislature, the lower house of which would be popularly elected with the states' representation being proportional to population. This lower house would in turn elect the upper house, and both houses together would elect the national judiciary. The national legislature would have the power to pass virtually any laws required by the welfare of the several states and disallow state laws—neither of these two powers were ultimately included.

Most delegates were willing to accept much of Madison's scheme; most realized that a new superintending government had to be given far more powers than the Confederation allowed, particularly the right to levy taxes, regulate commerce, and enforce national laws. But many delegates were taken aback by the full extent of power Madison was willing to transfer from the states to the national government, and those from small, underpopulated states feared that proportional representation in such a powerful national legislature would allow large states like Virginia too dominant a role. The issue here was small state versus large state rather than North versus South, but the acrimony of the debate threatened to terminate the proceedings early in the game. Wiser heads predominated, with a committee appointed to consider the Virginia plan and the so-called New Jersey plan pushed by William Paterson that called for states having equal representation; while the committee dealt with the matter of representation the convention as a whole could continue to discuss the entire range of issues raised by Madison's proposals. Ultimately the Great Compromise provided a solution: a lower house based on proportional representation and an upper house wherein each state had two votes.

Meanwhile the convention had solved other, related problems that reflected regional self-interest. Finally it was decided to count the slave population in the proportion of three-fifths both with regard to the apportionment of direct taxes and the calculation of representation in the lower house of the national legislature. The commercial North wanted the national government to have full authority to regulate interstate and foreign commerce and make treaties, but the South feared such authority could be used to place export taxes on their tobacco and rice and worried that control of trade and treaties could be employed to end the slave trade or place prohibitive taxes on the importation of additional slaves. South Carolina and Georgia were particularly alarmed over these possibilities, though every southern state was concerned to protect its self-interest, as was every northern state. Different economies in the regions produced different conceptions of proper policy; after long and hard debate a series of compromises resulted. It was agreed in favor of the South that the national congress would not interfere with the international slave trade for twenty years and would not have the power to impose export taxes, and a two-thirds vote would be required to ratify treaties; in return, northern commercial interests were mollified by an agreement that a simple congressional majority would obtain on bills to regulate all commerce.

As the discussion continued throughout the hot, humid summer behind closed windows, with delegates coming and going, a number of complicated issues were raised, debated in detail, and compromised, but withal Madison's basic plan shaped the proceedings. Too much has been made of the differences between the delegates; in large outline the majority accepted Madison's assumptions about what needed to be done. Madison lost on the national legislature's ability to disallow state laws, but in a general sense he carried the day. Madison wanted a strong executive elected by the people. Because everyone assumed George Washington would be the first president, the convention accepted an executive possessing more powers than otherwise might have passed, and the election procedure adopted, that of the electoral college, was intended more to address the presumed inability of any candidate to muster support in several states (no one predicted national political parties, much less organs of mass communication) than to remove the choice one step from direct election.

Madison won on the idea of a government balanced between three independent branches, with elaborate checks to prevent any one branch from trampling on the liberties of the people. Moreover, arguing that the people were ultimately sovereign, not the states or the Confederation Congress—a subtle political move that bypassed the potentially adverse opinion of state and continental legislatures unlikely to want to give up so much of their power to a new national government—Madison and his allies persuaded the convention to call for ratification of the new plan of government by specially elected state conventions, with approval of only nine states (not the paralyzingly unanimous support required to amend the Articles of Confederation) necessary for the Constitution to take effect as the legal government.

The national government proposed by the Philadelphia convention in the summer of 1787 had a far stronger president and central legislative body than anyone could have imagined in 1776 or 1781. Yet there were all kinds of safeguards to protect the liberty of the people. Certainly one of the perceived enemies the convention delegates identified was an excess of local democracy in which the greater good was sacrificed to particular interests. Because the national government limited such prerogatives as state stay laws (postponing the repayment of debts) and navigation acts and currencies, the Constitution has been called a conservative document that ended an age of dynamic democracy begun in 1776. But to describe the Constitution in such fashion is to misunderstand its origins. In 1776 and even a decade earlier, as troubles developed between the colonies and the mother country, a group of leaders, cosmopolitan in outlook and optimistic about the ultimate destiny of the American colonies, struggled to define the proper constitutional relationship between the colonies and England. Determined to defend the rights and liberties of the white citizens of America, they risked revolution to create a political world wherein white Americans could enjoy "life, liberty, and the pursuit of happiness." In pursuit of that political world they had to experiment with continental consolidation, resulting in the Articles of Confederation.

When new problems at home and abroad arose that seemed beyond the capability of that government to solve, leaders of the same general outlook as in 1776—cosmopolitan, optimistic, and activist in temperament—came to the fore to define the issues once more and attempt to find a new political solution. In a real sense the world had changed more than the goals of the American nationalists had changed, and in both critical periods, the early 1770s and the mid-1780s, nationalistic southerners, particularly Virginians, were in the forefront of the movement for national action. Certainly southerners in 1787 were conscious of their special interests—slavery, to be sure, but also the regional dependence on export crops and the navigation needs on the Mississippi of westerners—but so were spokesmen for northern commercial and fisheries interests. The point is not that southerners were aware of their own economic interests but that they on most issues were willing to compromise in order to shape a powerful new national government. Southerners in 1787 were nation-makers, not narrow sectionalists, and they were most hopeful about the long-range outlook for America.

But for all the boldness and optimism represented by the Constitution that the Philadelphia convention produced, signed and approved by thirty-nine delegates on September 16, 1787, it meant no more than the paper it was written on until it was ratified by the people of at least nine states through specially called conventions. Until that happened, the Confederation government remained in force and the Constitution was simply an idea on paper with no more effectiveness than a good intention. For the next year a political debate raged across the length and breadth of the land, a debate as intense and on as high an intellectual plane as the political discussion of the early 1770s, with the stakes equally as large. The defenders of the new Constitution won an initial symbolic victory by styling themselves the Federalists, suggesting that their opponents were simply naysayers with no valid proposals for dealing with what seemed the manifest problems of the age. The opponents, burdened with the name Antifederalists, tended to be men of a more localist orientation, were less expansive in their expectations for America's future, and often lived in regions less dependent on trade and commercial agriculture and hence did not expect to be particularly benefited by commercial regulations and treaties or a uniform currency or taxes that would be collected. Other Antifederalists were fearful of the power of the president, imagining a person other than George Washington turning the office into a quasi-monarchy. The strong Congress with powers to enact enforcement legislation they could similarly imagine tyrannizing the people with tax collectors and a standing army. And where, they asked, was a Bill of Rights guaranteeing certain essential rights necessary for the people to remain free? Some of these arguments were disingenuous, the conservative ruminations of men with local loyalties who could scarcely conceive of a national government without evil centralizing tendencies. Many southern Antifederalists did honestly fear for the future of slavery under the new Constitution. They felt that consolidation with the northern states would come to mean that southern interests— by which they primarily meant slavery—would be sacrificed. State and local rights to whites were seen as the only guarantees of the preservation of slavery.

Yet the Antifederalists in general had neither the education nor the influence of the Federalists; they had no one to match the prestige of Washington, no one who could write as convincingly as Alexander Hamilton, John Jay, and James Madison, whose essays, published serially in New York in the winter of 1787–1788 (and later collected as *The Federalist*), provided a brilliant defense of the Constitution. And Madison, who was there at Philadelphia, could reassure southern doubters that the new constitution was not a Trojan horse for abolition. The first five states to call ratifying conventions— Delaware, New Jersey, Georgia, Pennsylvania, and Connecticut—quickly accepted the Constitution. In Pennsylvania there was controversy, but the Federalists easily prevailed. The vote was closer in Massachusetts, but after promising to work for amendments approximating a bill of rights the Federalists were victorious in February 1788. Maryland and South Carolina overwhelmingly gave their approval in April and May, respectively; then, following astute Federalist politicking and mobilization of forces, New Hampshire ratified the Constitution on June 21, 1788, giving the new government the necessary nine-state approval.

But neither New York nor Virginia, home of the two staunchest Federalists, Hamilton and Madison, had ratified the Constitution, and everyone knew that New Hampshire's vote meant nothing unless these two powerful, populous, and economically dominant states accepted the new government. Virginia held the key to genuine acceptance of the Constitution, and once more the future of the nation seemed to depend upon the political leadership of that bellwether state. The debate in Virginia was scintillating, the whole state conducting a seminar in political theory led by Patrick Henry and George Mason on the negative and James Madison and Edmund Pendleton arguing in the affirmative. Henry's rhetoric as always was an awesome force, but the Federalists won the war of intellect and had an ace in the hole, George Washington. Washington's support converted Edmund Randolph, who at the tail end of the Philadelphia convention had suffered a failure of nerve and refused to sign the Constitution until he saw how the political winds were blowing. With the promise of adding a Bill of Rights as the first order of business for the new government, the Federalist heavy artillery in Virginia won the pitched battle in a close vote, 89 to 79, on June 25.

Messengers were promptly dispatched to New York, where Hamilton was engaged in a holding action against the Antifederalist forces of Governor George Clinton. When word arrived that New Hampshire and Virginia had ratified within four days of one another, giving the Constitution a solid ten-state approval, and with the promise there too of a Bill of Rights, the opposition faded and the Federalists won a close victory on July 26, 1788. With New York and Virginia behind the Constitution, ultimately unanimous approval was virtually assured. North Carolina had originally turned down the Federalists but reconsidered and overwhelmingly approved the Constitution in November 1789 after the Bill of Rights was submitted; stubborn, faction-ridden Rhode Island—evidence that republicanism worked worst in small empires exactly as Madison had argued in Federalist Number Ten—threatened with designation as a foreign country, relented and approved the Constitution by a narrow vote on May 29, 1790, more than a year after Washington had been inaugurated as the first president of the United States. A new age had begun in America, and the South was at the forefront of national developments.

THE SOUTH AND THE RISE OF POLITICAL PARTIES

The first new Congress of the United States was to open in New York City on March 4, 1789, but not until a month later did both houses have a quorum present. Then, according to the procedure outlined in the Constitution, the electoral college ballots were counted. As everyone expected, George Washington was unanimously elected president, with John Adams the vice-president. Following a long journey from Mount Vernon, lionized at every step, Washington was inaugurated on the balcony of Federal Hall in New York on April 30, 1789, beginning the initial term of the first president. Washington was a southerner and a slaveholder, but he was, as president, foremost a nationalist. He had witnessed firsthand at Valley Forge and elsewhere the real costs of narrow provincialism and localism, and in his support of the Annapolis and Mount Vernon conventions, as well as his presence at the Philadelphia convention that drafted the Constitution, he had put first the good of the nation. It was as an American more than as a southerner or a Virginian that Washington constructed his administration, choosing able men—many of whom had served with him in the Continental army—from every region to try to establish the infant republic on a solid footing. Washington understood that his every decision created a precedent for the future;

he knew there were European powers who did not wish the new nation well; he remembered the problems of debt and the powerlessness of the executive in the Confederation government. Washington intended to do everything in his power to make this government a success.

One measure of a leader's confidence is the caliber of the people he appoints as advisers. Washington chose two brilliant but dissimilar men, Alexander Hamilton and Thomas Jefferson, for the two major cabinet positions, secretary of treasury and secretary of state respectively. Jefferson was more the passive intellectual who believed that government best protected the liberties of its citizens by limiting its supervisory role; for Jefferson intellectual assent to the high purpose of the Constitution and its associated Bill of Rights should be the flux that wielded popular support behind the new government. Hamilton, the embodiment of economic man, was less sanguine about popular sentiment. For him not idealism but economic interest was the key to creating support for the government. Make it in the self-interest of the powerful to protect the government; lofty ideals and metaphysical abstractions might have been motivating forces for a Jefferson, but they were a weak reed upon which to try to erect the structure of a government. Hamilton greatly admired the British financial system, and he passionately believed it was only by implementing certain aspects of British fiscal and commercial policy that the United States would survive the vicissitudes of statehood in a hostile world. Hamilton was incisive and persuasive, and he had the practical George Washington's trust in a way that philosopher Jefferson did not. Hence in the critical first years of policy-making Hamilton shaped the government to an extent never again equalled by an unelected figure.

This is not the occasion for a detailed analysis of Hamilton's Federalist program; suffice it to mention four magisterially argued reports to Congress in 1790 and 1791 laying out an approach to stabilize the public credit, calling for the establishment of a national bank modeled after the Bank of England, proposing a national mint, and advocating a plan for stimulating manufacturing in the United States. The two most controversial aspects of his plan dealt with the national and state debt and the bank. Everyone understood the importance of dealing with the debt, which after all had largely toppled the Confederation government, but Hamilton's solution favored one part of the population disproportionately. He proposed paying off the debt owed to foreigners (uncontroversial), then assuming all the debt owed to United States citizens either by the various states or the Confederation, rolling them into one, then replacing the old, depreciated notes of credit with new ones, at full value, backed by the new government. The new government revenues from customs duties and excise taxes would be sufficient to pay the interest due, and owners of certificates would support the new government with all their energy because only its success would guarantee the eventual repayment of their certificates at full value—hence it was to their self-interest for the government to be a resounding success. And since the rich and powerful had through speculation and business acumen wound up with most of the old depreciated certificates, the government by this policy would garner the support of the very people best able to guarantee its success. All in all, it was a brilliant policy, and richly advantageous for some states and some people.

But not for southerners. Most southerners invested in slaves and land, not paper certificates, and Hamilton's plan to them looked like a scheme to enrich speculative northern merchants at the expense of the common folk who had loaned the Continental government monies at its moment of greatest need in the depth of the Revolutionary War but had later sold the bonds at greatly reduced rates to wealthy speculators. Moreover, such states as Virginia and Maryland had paid off their debts; Hamilton's plan would utilize national funds in part raised in the South to pay off the northern states' debts. From Jefferson's perspective and that of James Madison, and many other southerners, Hamilton's so-called national plan, which Washington had bought hook, line, and sinker, unfairly benefited one portion of the nation and a tiny minority of the population. Only after prolonged debate did Madison agree to throw his support in the House of Representatives behind a slightly modified version of the assumption plan, and he did this because, at a dinner party arranged by Jefferson, Hamilton had agreed in return to use his influence to see that the national capital, after a ten-year stay in Philadelphia, would be moved to an as yet unchosen location on the Potomac—in the South.

At the very beginning of their political differences Madison and Jefferson were willing to compromise with Hamilton, but attitudes soon hardened. Madison in the House emerged as the leader of the opposition to Hamilton's proposal to establish a national bank because it too seemed to favor the interests of a northern, commercial minority; moreover—and this became the essential arguing point—it seemed to Madison and Jefferson clearly unconstitutional. To assuage the fears of the opponents of the Constitution in 1787 and 1788 Madison had assured the doubters and naysayers that the Constitution gave to the central government only those powers expressly enumerated. And here, to support his national bank, Hamilton was arguing that the Constitution carried the implication to do things not literally spelled out. Jefferson and Madison developed a tradition of "strict interpretation" of the Constitution because they feared the centralizing tendencies implicit in Hamilton's plan would get out of hand, with the major casualty ultimately being the liberty of the people.

It should be remembered that while Hamilton was no warm democrat and doubted the judgment of the people, his goal was not self-enrichment but the strengthening of the United States—that was what recommended his policies to Washington. But Hamilton's high-handedness and his contempt for public sentiment frightened Jefferson, the principled democrat. Hamilton pursued sound policy in using an armed militia of 13,000 to quell the Whiskey Rebellion in western Pennsylvania in 1794 and make the point emphatically that this government could enforce the law, but to those who were suspicious of Hamilton's motives it looked frighteningly like an exercise in military dictatorship. Hamilton's proposal to stimulate and protect manufacturing in America would aid the nation's commerce and make her less dependent on European goods, but the protective tariffs would work against the interest of the staple-crop-exporting South. It was not simply that Jefferson and Madison were knee-jerk supporters of the South and hence critical of Hamilton's pro-northern stance. Rather, Jefferson and Madison sincerely believed that the tenor of Hamilton's plans would tilt the United States toward the English mode of government, with powerful commercial and banking interests corrupting the people, privileging certain entrenched interests, and nipping the growth of popular liberty in the bud. The diplomacy of the Washington administration, with Hamilton and negotiator John Jay essentially circumventing Secretary of State Jefferson and giving in to England on most issues, further infuriated those still resentful of England's arrogance. Here was no petty squabble over political tweedledum but, in Jefferson's view, a contest for the future of American freedom.

Although during the first Congress James Madison had been eager to establish a strong role for the office of the president and to insure the energy and success of the new government, he quickly broke with the Federalists on the matter of Hamilton's plan to refund the debt and the assumption of the states' debts. Madison believed the original holders of the certificates of debts (bonds), not their present owners—northern speculators—should be rewarded; after all, the original bond owners had in effect advanced money in hard times to finance the Revolution. And Madison thought assumption of the state debts was grossly unfair to those states, mostly southern, who had already repaid their debts. At first this difference of opinion between Madison (and Jefferson) and the administration was simply a dispute about policy, but as the full scope of Hamilton's plan became more clear, especially the proposed bank, Madison and Jefferson took the lead in developing a group in clear opposition to the direction Hamilton and Washington were taking the nation.

Madison and Jefferson used the terminology of the 1770s: they represented the "country opposition" defending the "republican interest" against the self-aggrandizing policies of the "court party." Suddenly it was again for Jefferson and Madison a battle for the soul of the country, with the interests of the people (and slaveholding planters!) posed against the corrupt interests of money jobbers and government placemen. Debt, associated in 1770 with a British plot against American liberties, again seemed associated with dangerous tendencies to consolidate powers in the central government, erect an unconstitutional bank, and impose import duties to benefit only a tiny proportion of the public. Certainly the policies Madison and Jefferson opposed were policies unfavorable to the South, but the important point is that at this time, the 1790s, Jefferson and Madison attacked the offensive policies because they saw them as inimical to the proper course the Republic should take. Some members of the "court party" even went in for elaborate government pageantry, fancy carriages for the president, and addressing the president as "His Highness." Was this not evidence of a monarchial plot? Jefferson and Madison sought in the 1790s to establish the government envisioned in 1776 as modified by the Constitution of 1787; Hamilton hoped to push beyond that limited government and establish a futuristic nation state with far-ranging federal-business cooperation. Hamilton really foresaw a diversified, capitalistic economy, agriculture balanced with trade and manufacturing. Jefferson and Madison, still nationalists, and agrarians, still democrats, not yet sectionalists, could barely comprehend and certainly not accept Hamilton's vision of America that seemed so to reflect aristocratic British policies that enriched a few at the expense of the many.

Jefferson and Madison were truly intellectuals, but they proved themselves again to be effective politicians and organizers of men; Jefferson later pioneered the role of president as party leader. Both men possessed enormous personal charm, and they used their personalities as well as their ideas to develop an opposition group. In 1791 they helped establish a newspaper, the *National Gazette*, edited by Philip Freneau, to editorialize on their behalf; in 1792 Madison and Jefferson took a "botanizing" trip up the Hudson River during which they helped solidify support among such New Yorkers as Governor George Clinton and Aaron Burr, and through letters and friendship with many southerners they succeeded by the election of 1792 in making their views known via the "candidacy" of Clinton for the vice-presidency. No one could imagine challenging Washington, but the "Jeffersonian" support for Clinton presaged the evolution of a party, a bugaboo term that at the time was equated with a self-serving little faction deemed antithetical to the common good. But though the idea of party was still anathema, Jefferson and Madison were, like it or not, willing to admit it or not, on the verge of creating the first party, labeled Republican—soon there would be wily political managers like John Beckley of Pennsylvania, who printed voting guides and the like. Congressional voting was not yet divided along strict party lines, but the lineaments of a clear difference in opinion about the future course of the nation were becoming increasingly visible.

Even with the respected George Washington at the head of the administration, political differences were dividing the nation into recognizable positions, but the positions were not narrowly regional—note that the Jeffersonians included New Yorkers Clinton and Burr and the Pennsylvania political operative Beckley, while there were merchants in Charleston and Richmond especially who supported the Federalist program. The differences represented contrary visions about the role of government in the new nation, and by their own lights Jefferson and Madison were as true nationalists as Hamilton; they simply weren't as consolidationist as he was. Neither were the issues dividing the two developing "parties" entirely domestic. Europe was aflame with the French Revolution, and the boiling conflict between England and France quickly involved the United States because each of the belligerents tried to interdict seaborne trade to the other. Hamilton had pronounced pro-British sympathies, while Jefferson was just as pro-French philosophically. Many wealthy southern planters and merchants, fearful both of Jefferson's partiality toward the French and the egalitarian tendencies of his politicies, were strong Federalists in the late 1790s.

The international situation could not have been more prone to exacerbate the political differences that already existed in the United States, and when a brazen French agent, "Citizen" Edmund Genet, came to the nation, traveled through the South trying to recruit American sailors and soldiers for the French cause and, after George Washington rebuffed him, sought to go over Washington's head and appeal to the American public, even Jefferson was outraged. The public outcry over Genet's shenanigans were matched by furor at British actions on the high seas; in theory, French intentions toward American shipping were as unpalatable, but England had the naval strength really to enforce her plans, which she did by stopping American vessels, taking off sailors of British birth, and forcing them into the British navy—this "impressment" was particularly galling to Americans.

Both the Jeffersonian Republicans and the Hamiltonian Federalists had reasons to justify their tilting either toward the French or the British. But by the end of 1793 Jefferson felt he could no longer serve in the administration; certainly as secretary of state he was being undercut by Hamilton, although Jefferson did accept Washington's Neutrality Proclamation—an act of practicality, because the president knew as perhaps neither Hamilton nor Jefferson could how disastrous involvement in a major European war would be for the young nation—as the best policy following the Genet fiasco. Washington accepted Jefferson's resignation in late 1793, and Jefferson felt more free to emerge as the leader of the political opposition. Jefferson and those who thought like him were upset by the clear pro-British favoritism shown by the Jay Treaty (submitted to the Senate in June 1795) and its equivocation on the southern demand for British compensation for slaves carried away during the American Revolution, but southern interests were partially mollified by Pinckney's Treaty signed with Spain in 1795 and ratified by the Senate in 1796. South Carolinian Thomas Pinckney had negotiated an agreement whereby Spain accepted the 31st degree of latitude as the northern boundary of West Florida and more importantly agreed to open the Mississippi to American traffic, with a renewable three-year license to use the port city of New Orleans. (England had ceded Florida to Spain in 1783).

In the midst of acrimonious political debate and recrimination, George Washington, having served two terms, decided in 1796 not to seek reelection. His eloquent Farewell Address, largely a rewrite by Jay and Hamilton of a draft prepared by Madison in 1792, warned of the dangers of "permanent alliances" with European powers and of "geographical discriminations—*Northern* and *Southern, Atlantic* and *Western*—whence designing men may endeavor to excite a belief that there is a real difference of local interests and views," but it did little to dampen the political fires that were raging. The Federalists ran John Adams for president and Thomas Pinckney for vice-president, while the Republicans presented Thomas Jefferson and Aaron Burr for the two offices. Adams won by three electoral votes, but Jefferson outpolled Pinckney, so Jefferson won the vice-presidency. This division presaged continued conflict, as did the fact that Hamilton had by now broken with Adams and intended to carry on essentially a hyperfederalist program within the administration but independent of the president.

When the French, irritated by the Federalist leanings toward the British, picked up the tempo of their attacks on American shipping, the Hamiltonian faction pushed for war. Adams desired peace and sent three diplomats to France to try to defuse the situation. After the French agents (code-named X, Y, and Z) bungled the effort by trying to extort a bribe from the American diplomats, Americans were rightfully outraged. Political passions boiled over: newspapers were mushrooming in number and they splattered charges and countercharges across their pages; Hamilton's friends pushed for an expansion of the army to resist foreign dangers and crush internal opposition to their policies; angry fingers were pointed at political enemies who were either called French radical agents or British monarchists. In the heat of the XYZ affair the Federalist-dominated Congress passed the Alien and Sedition Acts, lengthening the nationalizational process for foreigners (and hence delaying their right to vote), expanding the president's police powers over aliens, and severely cracking down on the right of political opponents to criticize the ruling administration. Plans were laid vastly to increase the army, with Hamilton in charge.

The United States seemed on the verge of civil war in the late 1790s: events were tumbling out of control. Hamilton saw a chance to rid the nation of Jeffersonian Francophiles, while Jefferson himself feared liberty was as much at risk as it had been in 1776. Jefferson and Madison turned to the states as liberal bulwarks against what they saw as the tyrannical machinations of the Hamiltonian central government. Jefferson and Madison wrote a series of resolutions, passed by the Kentucky and Virginia legislatures respectively, that argued that the states retained the right to judge the constitutionality of federal acts and the right to intervene between individuals and the national government to prevent the exercise of inappropriate federal power. Later the Kentucky and Virginia Resolutions would be applied by a new generation of southern leaders to protect not liberty but primarily the right to own slaves. But in 1798-1799, as the Jeffersonians and Federalists were nearing what looked more and more like internal war, pudgy, supersensitive, stubborn John Adams—long a foe of standing armies and a dedicated friend of the government he had helped establish a generation before—broke with his partisan advisers, swallowed his pride and anger over the XYZ insult, and sent a new peace message to France. There had been a sea change there, and First Consul Napoleon Bonaparte was now in charge. Bonaparte had other fish to fry than war with the United States, so he agreed to terms in 1800, ending the so-called quasi-war between France and America.

The Hamiltonian Federalists were furious at Adams, who had in fact put the nation's interest above his (and their) political fortunes. The "high" Federalists no longer had a "patriotic" rationale to crush their domestic opponents. The high Federalists' break with Adams in the election year led, despite all Hamilton's scheming, to the election by the House of Representatives of Thomas Jefferson as president, with Aaron Burr as vice-president. Adams had saved the peace but sacrificed his incumbency; Jefferson, who hated face-to-face conflict, sought to conciliate the nation and lead by the force of his ideas. A precedent as important as any established by Washington was made by the election of 1800. Political power, political control of the government, was peacefully transferred following the result of the popular vote. As a result of what Jefferson called the revolution of 1800, a new tone would be set by the new administration. For the next twenty-four years the presidency would be held by a Virginian. During that period southerners led the nation, and for the majority of the time the top of the administration at least was firmly nationalistic even though the conception of central governmental power differed from the Hamiltonian view. Yet even as southern presidents guided the nation, forces were at work beneath the political surface that presaged an era not far removed when regional interests would supersede nationalism. At the very summit of southern nationalism there were developments underway that would—although no one fully understood it at the time—prepare the soil in which the seeds of southern sectionalism would eventually germinate.

THE FIRST WEST

At the conclusion of the American Revolution in 1783, almost two centuries after Sir Walter Ralegh's first attempted English colony on Roanoke Island, practically all Anglo and African southerners still lived within several hundred miles of the Atlantic Ocean, and the roster of southern states still included only the former English colonies sweeping southward from Maryland to Georgia. Yet to the west of this South there lay an immense territory, greater in size than the original colonies, that was bounded by the Ohio River to the north and the Gulf of Mexico on the South, and would ultimately extend westward beyond the Mississippi. Within a generation after the Revolution this great expanse of land would become a real, functioning part of the South, settled largely by migrants from the Atlantic states and adding her wealth in soil, natural products, and crops to the economy of the region. This empire, from which eventually grew seven new states, would turn out to be the very heart of what has come to be known as the Old South although in 1860 it was in reality the "new" South as compared to the older seaboard states. Even before the Revolution this largely unknown frontier region, occupied by Indians and traversed by white long hunters and deer skin traders, began to enter the consciousness of southerners. Its history would soon become integral to the history of the larger South of which it soon formed a colorful part.

The identity and date of the initial Anglo-American intrusion into Kentucky is unknown, but by the 1750s there were occasional adventurers and hunters in the region. In 1750 Dr. Thomas Walker rediscovered an Indian pathway through the Appalachians in far southwestern Virginia—a gap first located by Gabriel Arthur in 1674—and it would be through this Cumberland Gap that many of the first settlers would enter the West. Daniel Boone, a strongly built, soft-spoken, highly skilled frontiersman, was one of those who came to know what the Indians called "the dark and bloody land" in the late 1760s and early 1770s, and in September 1773 Boone led a group of pioneer families through the Cumberland Gap into Kentucky only to have an Indian raid so discourage the people that they retreated to Virginia. The following June a hardy band of adventurers led by James Harrod established a small settlement by building several cabins and planting some corn fields near the headwaters of the Salt River, then departed back east across the mountains. In their absence Indians destroyed the unoccupied settlement, but Harrod's party returned in May 1775, found other whites already rebuilding the cabins, joined them, put up a palisade, and founded Harrodstown (later Harrodsburg) as the first permanent white settlement in Kentucky.

At about the same time in North Carolina an unscrupulous entrepreneur, Richard Henderson, was planning a trans-Appalachian empire. In March 1775 he conferenced on the banks of the Watauga River with a large gathering of Cherokees—who really did not hold title to nor control the Kentucky territory—and after giving them £10,000 in goods signed the Treaty of Sycamore Shoals giving him what he took to be legal claim to a huge portion of Kentucky. Envisioning a fourteenth colony (though both Virginia and North Carolina later voided his private purchase agreement with the Indians), Henderson hired Daniel Boone to lead settlers on behalf of the Transylvania Company; by May 1775 Boone had helped Henderson lay out the pioneer settlement at Boonesboro in the center of Kentucky and with a team of axmen cut a primitive road (Boone's Trace), eventually a part of the famed Wilderness Road leading from Virginia through the Cumberland Gap to the heart of the Kentucky Bluegrass region.

Kentucky represented a long, arduous journey over rough terrain for pioneers from Virginia and North Carolina, and during the late 1770s marauding Indians, armed by the British, made life one of constant vigilance and death. Governor Henry Hamilton, the British commandant of the Ohio Territory, from which the Indians staged their raids, was called by the Indians "Hair Buyer" because of his rewarding them for the scalps of Kentuckians. But after the 1778–1779 military successes in the Northwest of George Rogers Clark, the Indian dangers lessened. Not until the Indian defeat in 1794 at the Battle of Fallen Timbers in northern Ohio would the Kentucky frontier be safe for settlement, but before then the numbers of pioneers pouring through the Cumberland Gap and soon descending the Ohio River by raft and flatboat would transform Kentucky from a sparsely settled frontier outpost into the first trans-Appalachian (and second new) state in 1792 (Vermont had been admitted as the fourteenth state in 1791).

The territory just to the south of Kentucky, which would be organized as the state of Tennessee in 1796, actually had permanent white settlers before Kentucky, but being more inaccessible from the east its population grew more slowly. As pioneer families from North Carolina pushed gradually westward through the mountain valleys and hollows of the far northwestern extremity of the state, they began to appear west of the mountains along the Holston and Watauga rivers. Some of these westering families were refugees of the Regulator movement after their defeat at the Battle of Alamance in 1771, but the first transmontane families had built their cabins in 1769 and 1770. These early settlers in the hills and valleys of eastern Tennessee came from North Carolina, Pennsylvania, and Virginia; by 1772, after the colonial government of North Carolina had failed to establish any sort of local government for them, a group of settlers along the Watauga and Nolichucky rivers had organized themselves into the Watauga Association to provide some semblance of democratic order on the frontier. Finally recognizing the growth of the western settlements, North Carolina in 1776 incorporated the Watauga region and all of the eventual state of Tennessee into Washington County, North Carolina—a remnant of the ancient colonial charter whereby the Carolina boundaries had no precise western limit.

Not all of Tennessee was settled by "osmosis" by families from eastern regions gradually moving west. As with the initial Kentucky settlements, in 1779 a long-distance leap was made out to the Cumberland River region by pioneers led overland by a rough-hewn frontier entrepreneur named James Robertson. A few months later, in early 1780, another contingent of families, led by John Donelson, floated on flatboats down the Kentucky River to the Ohio, thence to the Cumberland River, and then poled their boats up it to the site of Nashville (originally Nashborough). Both Robertson and Donelson were agents working for Richard Henderson, who had earlier planned the Transylvania colony in Kentucky; after his land purchase of Kentucky from the Cherokees had been voided, he had been given as consolation a 200,000-acre grant of land in the Cumberland River country, so he shifted his colonial ventures southward. This second Tennessee settlement, some two hundred miles west of the Watauga–Holston area, quickly prospered, leading North Carolina in 1783 to divide the original Washington Country and name the western part, incorporating the Nashville area, Davidson County.

In that very year (1783) the Watauga–Holston settlers, harassed by Indian attacks and land-grabbing speculators and faced with what they considered an unresponsive state government that was in the process of ceding them to the Articles of Confederation government that seemed equally uninterested in their needs—and led by charismatic John Sevier—declared their independence and established the State of Franklin in the mountainous counties of what is now eastern Tennessee. For four years there were in effect rival governments in the area, with competing sheriffs and courts, conflicting land claims, and bloodshed. North Carolina in 1784 repealed the land cession to the Confederation government and worked thereafter to put down the Sevier-led rebellion. Sevier was captured by state authorities and imprisoned but soon escaped; finally in 1788 the Franklinites ceased their separatist rebellion, North Carolina ceded the territory to the new national government, and in 1790 Congress organized the region below Kentucky into the Territory South of the River Ohio under an appointed territorial governor, William Blount, himself an accomplished land speculator, seated at the new capital village of Knoxville in the former Franklin area of eastern Tennessee. The territory's growth in population and prosperity was such that in 1796 Tennessee became the sixteenth state in the American union.

Contemporaries were astounded at the rate of development of the transappalachian territories after 1783, when Revolutionary veterans rewarded with land grants were added to the normal migration. For the first decade Indian raids were a constant threat, and the earliest settlers for reasons of defense grouped their cabins together within fenced compounds called stations. As more families came, additional cabins would be constructed within sight of the fortifications, and often men took their long rifles to the fields for protection against surprise attacks. Families often came west in caravans, traveling together for safety's sake, and the first order of business would be to build the palisaded station, temporary huts, then the small fields of corn planted amid girdled trees. For the first year or two families ate corn, the produce of a small garden, and whatever game or fish the countryside provided, and no money crop was raised—this was, for many of the first families in Kentucky and Tennessee, true subsistence living. Perhaps by trapping or hunting some pelts or skins were obtained that could be shipped east for money. But this frontier subsistence stage passed quickly; huts were replaced with log cabins, stations became villages, and soon the surge of new settlers would provide markets for the surplus corn of the prior settlers. Blacksmiths, store owners, and mill owners promptly found calls for their services.

For one observing the steady stream of wagons moving through the Cumberland Gap or the flotillas of flatboats down the western river systems, it seemed the older seaboard settlements were emptying themselves westward. Thousands of Virginians and North Carolinians went searching for the fertile lands and fresh opportunities they heard praised by western publicists. These immigrants from the seaboard South brought their social, political, racial, and religious views with them, transplanting the slave plantation system and tobacco growing in Kentucky and Tennessee. The territories were divided into counties with sheriffs and justices of the peace, schools and churches were either founded or desired as quickly as possible, and families who were either luckier, more skilled, or started out with more resources soon came to form the top of a social and political hierarchy that replicated society east of the mountains. By the time of statehood both Kentucky and Tennessee had become western versions of their mother states, dependent on commerce down the Ohio River and then the Mississippi for their economic prosperity. American concerns about the right of passage down the Father of Rivers all the way to the Gulf was no diplomatic conceit in the 1790s but a necessity driven by the growth of population beyond the Appalachians.

THE OLD SOUTHWEST

The great expanse of land between the southern border of Tennessee and the Gulf of Mexico had a tangled history in the four decades after 1763, when most of it was transferred to England by the treaty that ended the French and Indian War. Within forty years France, Spain, England, and the United States claimed the territory, although most of it was in reality controlled by Indians, but through diplomacy and war this region too became a part of the Old South, with white settlers, black slaves, and a new crop—cotton—gradually integrating this frontier with the older South of the seaboard. In 1759 France began to perceive that she might lose her North American empire, and rather than see her archrival England gain all of France's New World territory, France in 1762 ceded Louisiana (which included West Florida) to her ally Spain. By the terms of the Treaty of 1763 all the land east of the Mississippi to the Appalachians came to England, and in a separate treaty Spain ceded West and East Florida to England and all of Louisiana east of the Mississippi except the Isle of Orleans that surrounded New Orleans. In 1763 Britain organized the two Floridas as territories, with the northern border of West Florida at the thirty-first parallel. At first the British saw little of value in this new possession, with the small port towns of Mobile and Pensacola in West Florida being rundown, miserable little villages of insignificant promise, and the boundary at the thirty-first parallel denied either town much of an agricultural hinterland. By 1764 the British Board of Trade corrected this by moving the northern boundary of West Florida to the 32nd degree, 28 minutes north latitude, from where the Yazoo River met the Mississippi east to the Chattahoochee River. This gave West Florida profitable farm lands above the coast, and it put the fabulously fertile lands near Natchez within the territory.

Only a few French settlers remained around Mobile and Pensacola, barely eking out a living by raising cattle and producing some naval stores. But the British quickly realized that the countryside near Natchez, soon organized as the Natchez District, had real agricultural promise. Liberal land grants were extended to prospective settlers, and a steady stream of migrants from the seaboard colonies were attracted. When the American Revolution began, a significant number of southern Loyalists fled the conflict and came to the Natchez District, bringing their slaves and establishing plantations. By 1780 the vicinity of old Ft. Rosalie, established by the French in 1716, had acquired a pronounced English character. Yet this bucolic existence would soon change, for Spain declared war against England in 1779, and Governor Bernardo de Galvez of Spanish Louisiana quickly attacked and conquered the British outposts along the Mississippi River; by 1781 he had taken Mobile and Pensacola and controlled the whole of West Florida. The British farmers and planters in the Natchez District—most of them refugee Tories from South Carolina and Georgia—now found themselves under Spanish rule.

The treaty negotiations in Paris that ended the American Revolution did not tidy up the details of this portion of the conflict. According to Britain's treaty with the United States, the new nation was given all of Britain's possessions between the Appalachians and the Mississippi all the way to the thirty-first degree of latitude, the original (1763) northern border of West Florida. In a separate 1783 treaty Britain ceded West Florida to Spain without mentioning the northern border, but in 1764 the British Board of Trade had moved the border to 32 degrees, 28 minutes so West Florida would contain the valuable Natchez District. So that slender strip of land between latitudes 31 degrees and 32 degrees, 28 minutes was claimed both by the United States and by Spain—but Spanish forces had conquered it, had it under control, and intended to maintain their authority; there was little the United States could do but protest. Not until the Pinckney Treaty of 1795 did Spain give up its claim, and during the twelve years of disputed sovereignty Spain lightly ruled the Natchez District.

The population grew so that in 1788 the Spanish crown appointed

Manuel Luis Gayoso governor of the district. Gayoso, who spoke fluent English and had married an American wife, realized that most of the settlers were American and that arbitrary rule might drive them to unite with the United States and rebel against the fragile Spanish authority. Consequently Gayoso ruled with a benevolent hand, and Spanish bounties for tobacco and indigo production, along with prodigious cattle ranching, brought prosperity to his satisfied subjects. There was no outcry for the Spanish to leave in 1795, and in fact the Spanish garrison did not leave the Natchez District until March 1798, the year in which the United States Congress organized the whole region from the Appalachians to the Mississippi (north of the border of West Florida) as the Mississippi Territory. For several years Winthrop Sargent from New England served as territorial governor, but President Jefferson replaced him in 1801 with William C. C. Claiborne. Claiborne was an able and well-liked administrator, and he helped establish the kind of governmental institutions that led to population growth and economic development.

There was no steady, even march of settlers from east to west across the Mississippi Territory. At first the most substantial development lined the eastern banks of the Mississippi River, then pockets of settlement sprang up near Huntsville and Madison County in the northern part of the Alabama portion of the territory. Creeks, Cherokees, and Choctaws still occupied major sections of the region, and white settlements were largely confined to the interstices between the Indian nations, whose presence slowed the evolution of the territory into statehood. Real growth would not come until after the War of 1812 when there would be a land rush for the fertile acres. In the tumble of events after 1815 Mississippi would gain statehood in 1817, the eastern portion of the former territory would be reorganized as the Alabama Territory, and Alabama itself would be granted statehood in 1819. Soon there would be massive efforts to remove the Indians from the area, an effort that proved fatal to many Indians and destructive of their cultures. But few southern whites had time to care about the Indians, for Alabama and Mississippi were becoming the heart of the Old South and cotton profits and the value of slaves pushed other concerns far from the consciousness of most whites. Nothing counted on the raw cotton frontier but profits.

William C. C. Claiborne had long since moved from Mississippi to Louisiana, where President Jefferson appointed him territorial governor in 1803 after its surprise purchase; Claiborne would become the first elected governor of the State of Louisiana in 1812. France had ceded Louisiana west of the Mississippi River, along with the Isle of Orleans (New Orleans), to Spain back in 1763. The French inhabitants, whose opinion about the turn of events had never been asked, resisted the transfer. In 1768–1769 they revolted against the small Spanish garrison sent to rule them, provoking Spain to send in General Don Alexander O'Reilly, an Irish soldier of fortune presently serving Spain, to crush the rebellion. O'Reilly, never one hesitant to use force, arrived in New Orleans with twenty-four ships and two thousand troops and emphatically established Spanish rule. But the colony of Louisiana, despite the tobacco, indigo, cattle, and other agricultural products, including sugar after 1795, along with extensive trade with various Indian groups for deer skins, never proved profitable to Spain, and its population remained culturally French in every way. The four decades of Spanish rule left no impress except place names and, ironically, the architecture of the Vieux Carre in New Orleans.

Don Bernardo de Galvez was the most able of the Louisiana governors under Spanish rule, and he aggressively pursued the imperial aims of the mother country during the American Revolution, for it was Galvez who so effectively attacked Britain on its southwestern flank, conquering Natchez, Mobile, and Pensacola, and all of West Florida. In reward for his successes Galvez was promoted to the vice-royalty of Mexico in 1785, and while the population and agricultural production of both Louisiana west of the Mississippi and the disputed territory around Natchez increased, the administrative and defensive expenses to Spain outweighed the agricultural proceeds. In the final analysis, the rulers of Spain four thousand miles away were less interested in the region and the right to ship goods down the Mississippi than were the ambitious leaders of the southern and western United States. In response to those unequal pressures Spain had relinquished its claims to the valuable Natchez District (east of the Mississippi River) to the United States in the treaty negotiated by Thomas Pinckney in 1795, including the navigation rights to the Mississippi all the way to its mouth.

The disposition of this whole region, rich in history and invaluable as the natural entrepot to the interior of the continent, would be settled not by the settlers at hand or the forces they could raise but by diplomats in Europe. Napoleon persuaded Spain to give Louisiana back to France by the terms of the secret Treaty of San Ildefonso in 1800, but of course the United States soon learned of the transfer. Thomas Jefferson was inaugurated in March 1801 and by reputation and sentiment he was pro-French, but more than that, Jefferson was passionately devoted to the United States. He realized that France, imperiously led by Napoleon, dreamed of reestablishing her New World empire and saw Louisiana as a wedge both to stop the westward development of the United States and as an éntrée into the nation's interior. Another worry of Jefferson's was that in the advent of British–French European hostilities Britain might seize New Orleans and Louisiana, and certainly that was no pleasant prospect to Jefferson. Jefferson was willing to side with Britain to prevent French control of the mouth of the Mississippi, or vice versa.

But with no American army of significance to defend America's interests, Jefferson first tried diplomacy, hoping to purchase the Isle of Orleans (and West Florida) from France. Developments beyond Louisiana or Paris soon intervened. France's intentions in Louisiana were dependent upon a firm way station in the West Indies, but the slave rebellion in Santo Domingo threatened to consume all of the French military. With expenses and casualties mounting rapidly in the West Indies, Louisiana daily grew less attractive to Napoleon and its use as a gambit for regaining a French empire on the American mainland seemed increasingly farfetched. After all, the West Indies were more important to France than a hypothetical colony in Louisiana. Jefferson's envoy in France, Robert Livingston, had already offered two million dollars for New Orleans but gotten no deal. Before the second American envoy, James Monroe, arrived, Napoleon reevaluated France's New World prospects and decided to cut his losses. On April 8, 1803, Livingston was offered all of Louisiana (one third of the continent!) for one hundred million francs. Livingston was stunned, and when Monroe arrived the two began haggling over the offer, ending up on May 2 signing the terms to the greatest real estate bargain in history: almost 400 million acres for sixty million francs, or fifteen million dollars, about four cents per acre.

Jefferson was as unprepared for the bargain as were Livingston and Monroe, and he had strong Constitutional scruples against such an expansion of diplomatic power. But Jefferson was both a dreamer and a practical man; he understood the significance of removing a European threat and spreading the authority of the new nation from the mouth of the Mississippi all the way to Canada and westward to the Rocky Mountains and beyond to the Pacific Ocean. Swallowing his Constitutional doubts, Jefferson pushed the purchase treaty through the Senate on October 19, 1803, doubling the size of the United States (and acquiring some fifty thousand hesitant new inhabitants). Two months later American troops under the command of William C. C. Claiborne assembled in what is now called Jackson Square in New Orleans; French and American officials signed the final papers inside the ancient government building called the Cabildo. Shortly thereafter the signatories stood on a Cabildo balcony as the French flag was lowered and the American flag raised. With that ceremony America's future in the New World was made secure, and territory for a multitude of additional states, including Louisiana itself (1812), Missouri (1821), and Arkansas (1836). By 1803, then, except for Florida and Texas, which both entered the Union in 1845, the geographical boundaries of the South were drawn. The stage was set for the expansion of the South into what was at the time called the Southwest: the states of Alabama, Mississippi, Louisiana, and Tennessee. Two export crops new to the region, cotton and sugar, along with slave labor, would be the energizing forces that would propel the development of the Old South across the entire region, from the Piedmont of the Carolinas and Georgia to beyond the west bank of the Mississippi River.

THE RISE OF COTTON

Cotton is an ancient plant, described as early as the first century by the Roman historian Pliny as being grown in Egypt to make comfortable garb for the priestly class. Varieties of the plant were known in Europe as botanical curiosities for more than a millennium, but it was not until the seventeenth century that its fibers came to be desired to make clothing. For one thing, wool growers in England had sought to prevent the importation of finished cotton goods, cloths with names like calico (after Calcutta), madras (Madras), and muslin (Muslim) that suggested their Asian or Euro-Asian sources. By the early eighteenth century, however, entrepreneurs in England had begun importing raw cotton fiber and creating an indigenous cotton textile industry to meet the demand for cheaper cloth. Because the cotton industry was new in England, tradition-bound guilds were less able to control its direction and prevent the development of labor-saving machinery. The result, following John Kay's invention of the flying shuttle in 1733, was a series of technological advances leading to the factory system that revolutionized the production of cotton goods. The expanding English population after 1750 pushed up the demand for the ever-cheaper cotton cloth, and the booming textile factories had an unquenchable demand for raw cotton that far outstripped the world supply.

Minute amounts of cotton had been grown on the American mainland since the settlement of Jamestown in 1607, and many farms and plantations cultivated small patches for domestic use. White farm women as well as slave women knew how to pick, clean, card, and spin cotton into thread and then weave it into cloth. Some upland farmers even sold excess cotton to planters whose slave women made cloth for slave consumption. But difficulties in growing cotton and in processing the cotton once harvested did not make it commercially feasible on a large scale. Several species of cotton were known in the South before the Revolution: a hardy green-seed variety that would grow in practically any soil but whose short lint adhered tenaciously to its fuzzy seed, and a smooth, black-seed variety with a longer lint that was easier to separate from the seed but whose cultivation was severely limited by its unfortunate susceptibility to a fungus popularly known as the rot.

Before the Revolution planters throughout the South used what was known as a roller gin—sometimes called a "churka" after the earlier device, the "charkha," developed centuries before in India—to separate the seeds from the lint. The roller gin consisted of two cylinders turned toward one another by means of a gear, operating like an old-fashioned wringer washing machine. The cotton lint (of the black seed variety) was inserted from one side, and as the turning rollers pulled the lint through, the narrow gap between the rollers would not admit the seeds, which in effect were squeezed out of the cotton. This roller gin, however, was ineffective with the green seed cotton, which had to be laboriously hand-separated from the seed. Still, as inefficient as the process was, there existed in the South a small cotton economy, and during the Revolutionary era boycotts of British goods, it became the patriotic fashion to wear homegrown and homespun cotton clothing. Southerners of both races were familiar with the crop well before it transformed the region's agricultural economy.

In 1786 and 1787 several planters in coastal Georgia obtained seeds of a variant of the black-seed cotton grown in the Bahama Islands; the seeds of this more rot-resistant, long-staple cotton were apparently introduced to the mainland by returning Loyalist refugees who had fled the fighting of the American Revolution. This new cotton grew famously on the Sea Islands of South Carolina and Georgia, and, ginned either by hand or by roller gins, found a ready market in England. This "sea island cotton" began the first cotton boom in the South; between 1784 and 1791 British imports of southern cotton increased 216 percent, and they would double again by 1800. Clearly hand and roller-ginned cotton could not meet such a growing demand even if sea island cotton cultivation could have been expanded into the upland. Shrewd planters observed the rising cotton prices and contemplated the wider geographical range of the green-seed cotton whose commercial possibilities were limited only by the difficulty of separating its short staple from its tenacious seeds. In addition to these planters who desired to diversify by cultivating cotton, many small farmers from Virginia and Maryland—former tobacco growers—had moved into upland South Carolina and Georgia. These small farmers were already acquainted with commercial production of staple crops, and in fact they brought tobacco cultivation south too. By 1792 Georgia was the third-ranking tobacco exporting state. These newly settled tobacco farmers were quick to see the economic potential offered by the green-seed cotton. They knew how to cultivate the crop and were alert to the demands of the market; only the difficulty of removing the lint from the seed slowed their wholesale transition from tobacco to cotton. In this situation many would-be inventors set themselves to the task of devising a mechanical gin adapted to the peculiar characteristics of green-seed cotton.

Several people achieved the breakthrough almost simultaneously, a situation that ultimately prevented the inventor of record, Connecticut-born Eli Whitney, from capitalizing on his contraption. In 1793, while the young tutor was visiting Mulberry Grove, the Georgia plantation of the late Nathanael Greene, he "heard much of the extreme difficulty of ginning cotton." As Whitney wrote later that year to his father, "There were a number of very respectable gentlemen at Mrs. Greene's who all agreed that if a machine could be invented that would clean cotton with expedition, it wuld be a great thing both to the Country and to the inventor. I involuntarily happened to be thinking of the subject and struck out a plan of a Machine in my mind." Whitney's idea was brilliantly simple, a significant refinement of the old roller gin. He added wire teeth to one͂ roller and rotated it in such a fashion as to grab and tear the lint from the seed of cotton fed into a slatted box whose gaps were too narrow to allow the seeds to be pulled through. Another roller, with small brushes, whisked the separated lint from the teeth of the first roller.

Thus, Whitney had made an inexpensive, workable, and easily duplicated improvement of the roller gin. The result was that upland-grown green-seed cotton could now compete for the expanding British market for raw cotton staple. Rapid improvements, especially circular saws replacing the wire teeth, by Whitney and others multiplied the efficiency of the gin, with the ultimate result that cotton soon became the most promising money crop in Piedmont South Carolina and eastern Georgia. The combination of the upland farmers' and planters' knowledge of both the cultivation of cotton and the nature of commercial agriculture, the strength of the English demand for the fiber, and the success of the technological breakthrough represented by Whitney's gin would wreak an economic revolution in the South.

In the decade following 1793 millions of acres of fertile land became available for enterprising (some would say greedy) southern farmers. Between 1783 and 1796 a series of treaties with Indians opened central and western Georgia to the advance of agriculturists, and land speculation further beckoned cotton growers. Fraud and avarice were the hallmarks of the land grants in the Yazoo River country of Georgia, but the final result was the westward march of the cotton frontier. Cotton cultivation quickly leapfrogged across the Indian nations to the Anglo settlers in the Natchez District. Farmers here had earlier experimented with a Siamese variety of black-seed cotton, especially after insects had destroyed the future prospects of indigo cultivation. Since many of the early Natchez farmers were Loyalists who had fled Georgia and South Carolina, they had contacts with planters in the seaboard region. News of the cotton gin quickly spread westward, and Whitney's basic machine was so simple that it was easily replicated near Natchez by 1795, the year the disputed land claims between Spain and the United States were settled by the terms of Pinckney's Treaty. Within a short time Mississippi had entered the modern cotton age, and when, in 1798, the Mississippi Territory (including present-day Alabama) was formally organized by the United States, the advance of the fluffy staple all the way to the Father of Waters was assured. Cotton cultivation required no expensive infrastructure (like rice or indigo) to begin, harvested cotton could be stored inexpensively without danger of spoilage or of being consumed by vermin, and because its value in relation to its weight was high, it was relatively cheap to transport, making it an advantageous crop to the small farmers who pioneered its spread across the

South. Large planters followed in their wake but never pushed out the small producers; even so, most cotton would be grown on large plantations by slaves. More than anything else, cotton and slaves would create the Old South.

Cotton, however, was not the only crop amenable to slave labor in the deep South. Almost simultaneous with the development of the gin in 1793, the growth of the British demand, and the settlement of new territories to the west that ushered in the age of cotton, advances in the cultivation and manufacturing of sugar in Louisiana were occurring that would turn southern Louisiana (and, for a decade and a half before the Civil War, the lower Brazos River bottomlands in Texas) into a region of wealthy sugar plantations employing thousands of slaves. Sugar cane had been introduced into Louisiana by Jesuit priests, but the growing season even in southern Louisiana was not long enough really to mature the cane. Many French planters fleeing the rebellion-torn Santo Domingo had brought their slaves and knowledge of sugar cultivation with them in the early 1790s, just as insects were ravaging the infant indigo industry in Louisiana and the Natchez region.

But the nine-month growing season allowed the sugar growers only to make syrup from the immature cane. The normal sugar manufacturing process, with which the émigré planters were familiar, did not produce marketable sugar from such cane. In 1795, after many experiments, a French émigré planter near New Orleans, Etienne de Boré, successfully developed a process of crystallizing sugar from the juice of immature cane. The new process allowed the other émigré sugar growers, and native planters who emulated their success, to begin a lucrative new industry in south Louisiana. By 1801 to 1802 as many as seventy-five sugar plantations were producing between four and eight million pounds of brown sugar annually to supply the American appetite for sweets. The territory acquired by the United States in 1803 was entering a prolonged sugar boom, with most of the labor performed by slaves. The size, the wealth, and the work routines of the Louisiana sugar plantations served to differentiate Louisiana from the rest of the South, but the important point is that, before 1800, technological breakthroughs at both ends of the South—by Eli Whitney in Georgia and by Etienne de Boré in Louisiana—made possible the remarkably rapid rise of a slave–staple crop society in the lower South.

THE GREAT REVIVAL IN THE SOUTH

Within several years near the beginning of the nineteenth century the territorial acquisitions had been made and the agricultural crops and related finishing processes had been developed that, along with slave labor, would allow the expansion of the South from the Atlantic seaboard all the way westward to Sabine River, the still vague border with Spanish Texas, which was administratively a province of Mexico. Of course, no one could anticipate that Texas would eventually become a part of the Old South, even though, as early as 1807 when the American explorer Zebulon M. Pike, fresh from his trip through the West and northern Mexico, was crossing Texas and nearing the Louisiana border, he encountered a handful of "American emigrants" who were "introducing some little spirit of agriculture near to Nacogdoches and the Trinity [River]." No doubt these American settlers beyond the edge of the South in east Texas were typical of thousands more who moved westward and southwestward in leaps and bounds, often traveling in wagon caravans with neighbors and relatives to carve out small farms in the beckoning frontier. Building log cabins, girdling the trees, planting corn, beans, peas, and squash, hunting and trapping to supplement their diet and provide clothing, putting in a few acres of cotton when they could see a way to get it to market, these farmers whose roots lay in the Piedmont and backcountry of the former seaboard colonies represented the advance agents of southern society and culture. Close behind them were wealthier emigrants, often sons of planters sent out with a group of slaves to build rude shelters and plant the initial crops preparatory for a more substantial migration of family members and slaves the following year. Beginning with pockets of settlement along the Mississippi River, the Tennessee River, the hinterland of Mobile, and infilling as prosperity—and, later, the retreating Indians—allowed, the people, the culture, the society of the seaboard South ineluctably spread to the Sabine River and farther in the years after 1800.

Southern culture and society in the early nineteenth century consisted of more than a devotion to slavery and cotton and an exaggerated sense of personal independence. An entire constellation of attitudes, practices, fears, and hopes characterized the Anglo settlers who were busily winning the Southwest, and this culture had been forged in the decades before 1800 even as it came to fruition later. A distinct southern religious heritage was an important aspect of this culture, and religion was one of the several influences that ultimately set white southerners apart from their fellow Americans in the North. An intense series of evangelical revivals erupted in the South in 1800 and soon enveloped the entire settled region, reshaping the religious contours of the South and developing a regional religious *mentalité* that helped define the southern character.

A religious revival does not occur in a vacuum. Several prerequisites must be met before a general religious awakening—like the Great Awakening of the late 1730s and early 1740s in the Middle Atlantic and New England colonies—can occur; there has to be in place a network of churches and ministers, there must exist a prevailing belief system—shared ideas about God, people, and redemption—and there must be a sense of religious crisis, a feeling that there exists a powerful need to invigorate the spiritual life of a community. A series of small revivals during which the Presbyterian, Baptist, and Methodist churches were planted in colonial Virginia between 1740 and 1776 began the process that would eventually transform the religious history of the South. These limited revivals, and others like them in South Carolina and Georgia, were the necessary preliminaries to the genuine, region-wide revival that would occur at the very beginning of the new century.

In each of the southern colonies the Anglican Church was the official established church, but in none of them did it minister effectively to the majority of the population. Parishes were too large, given the inadequate transportation network of the time, to make regular attendance at worship convenient. Anglican priests had to be ordained in England, and the difficulties in attracting talented, caring ministers to serve in parishes that sometimes seemed to them to lie beyond the pale of civilization made church participation even less appealing to the laity. The wealthy, often worldly planters who controlled the church vestries set the tone of the worship experience, giving it a reserved, emotionally arid character that to the common folk often smacked of elitism. When in the quarter century before the Revolution evangelistic Presbyterians, Baptists, and Methodists, in that order, began to preach and organize dissenting churches in the region, they found a warm and ready audience among the poorer whites and slaves who had felt condescension and a strong hint of social authoritarianism at the hand of the Anglican establishment. In no colony was the evangelical alternative approved of by officialdom, and the Baptists and Methodists, who were far more emotionally demonstrative and egalitarian than the Presbyterians, seemed especially threatening. Particularly in Virginia and North Carolina the civil authorities used strong-arm tactics in a vain attempt to put down the religious rebels, but as so often happens persecution enhanced the zeal of the evangelicals and, by forcing many literally to flee the region, actually accelerated the spread of Baptist preachers into Kentucky, Tennessee, and the backcountry of South Carolina and Georgia.

Had the American Revolution not occurred in 1776, Virginia and neighboring southern states might have experienced a Great Awakening-type religious revival then, for two of the prerequisites for such an event were in place: a series of churches of the major evangelical denominations had been founded along with a contingent of evangelical ministers, and the very existence of the churches and ministers were evidence that at least a segment of the population had accepted an evangelical world view. Yet the third prerequisite, a shared sense of religious crisis—a situation that, the faithful believed, could be rectified only by a special act of Providence—had not been fulfilled. True, the earlier Presbyterian and Baptist revivals had cooled off, and the Methodist movement was crimped by the outbreak of hostilities, but most evangelicals expected the Revolution, once completed, to usher in an era of political liberty and religious expansion. The wartime delay, even decline, in religious activity, was presumed to be temporary.

That optimistic expectation seemed confirmed when, in the mid-1780s, a revival began in central Virginia. What made this development especially heartening was that, for the first time, all three denominations experienced revivals simultaneously and in the same region. On a small scale, the 1785–1788 Virginia revival seemed like a Great Awakening both in intensity and in universality. But the grandiose expectations were soon dashed when the local revival faded. In fact, throughout Virginia and the South the decade after the mid-1780s was disastrous for the state of religion. Several reasons have been advanced to explain why religious growth faltered after the initial indications of expansion. The late 1780s, which saw the Constitution written, fiercely debated, then ratified, with a new government soon in place, was an era when political concerns replaced religious ones for many people. The southern economy had been severely disrupted in the final years of the Revolution, and economic affairs—rebuilding barns, fences, and irrigation systems; working out new markets for staple products; adjusting to the new demands for land and slaves after the invention of the cotton gin—became an understandable preoccupation for many persons. The trans-Appalachian frontier was now open, and thousands, many of whom were Revolutionary War veterans possessing land bounties from the government, were making the trek westward with their families. This massive migration actually left some seaboard regions depopulated, and on the frontier the onrush of settlers outpaced the ability of institutions such as churches to keep up even as churches to the east were nearly emptied. For these and, no doubt, other reasons, the decade that had opened in 1785 with such religious promise had within just a few years turned into a season of despair.

This despair only deepened as the years passed, and fears of deism and infidelity (stoked by news and rumors of the revolution raging in France) were soon added to more prosaic worries about religious indifference and decline. As one reads the letters and diaries of ministers and laypersons in the early 1790s, it becomes apparent that a perceived "religious declension," a sense of crisis, gripped many believers. For many settlers in the western regions, separated from relatives back east, worried about Indian attacks, missing the fellowship and mutual comfort provided by a supportive religious community, the absence of a local church often contributed to a feeling of social bereavement that produced a hunger for supportive institutions. The myth of the happy frontier, populated by adventurous, independent-minded extroverts exuberant about their prospects for success, hides the unattractive side of life, particularly for women: terrible loneliness, monotony, drudgery, sickness, and death. Life was hard and took its toll on the human psyche. Such conditions obtained across the rural South, but especially so toward the west, and these conditions were kindling awaiting a religious spark.

Religion plays many roles in any society, and one of its major functions is to provide an explanatory system for the joys and tragedies of life. There is a deep human desire to find a larger purpose for the myriad dramas of daily life, and this purpose religion can provide. Not just the ultimate mystery of death but the everyday concerns of living cry out for a context of meaning. For an age when religious interpretations of all human events were far more prevalent than today, we should not be surprised to discover that many ministers and laypersons desperately sought a religious explanation for the perceived spiritual crisis of the 1790s. Why, after the early revivals planting the seeds of the evangelical denominations before the Revolution, then the fleeting promise of an interdenominational revival in the mid-1780s, was religion in serious "declension" in the final decade of the century?

Clergy pondering this problem began with the axiomatic assumption that God was all-knowing and hence was purposely chastising the churches and their members for some error or sin. As quickly as the problem was posed ministers had a list of supposed faults: a rampant preoccupation with crops, slaves, and land; too much trust in human endeavor as revealed in resort to war and statecraft; negligence in the spiritual life as the dreary details of hardscrabble existence on the southern frontier crowded contemplation and devotion out of the conscience. Hence God had sent the "declension" to teach people the errors of their ways. Once people recognized their transgressions, were contrite, communicated their sense of repentance to God with days of fasting, and prayed for deliverance, they could—or so many ministers wrote and preached—confidently expect God to lift His displeasure and send a renewal of religious vitality. Over and over ministers throughout the South in the mid-1790s expressed their confidence that God was a loving and forgiving God who would hear and respond to their heartfelt requests. What had started out as an attempt to understand their perceived dilemma ended up as a hopeful expectation of what they typically called "deliverance."

It is one thing to talk of abstract causes, societal tensions, and perceived crises, and another to explain how, at one time and place, a broad social movement is set underway. Ultimately history must come down to particular people acting in a specific place at a precise moment. Luckily, the pivotal individual in this story can be identified and his catalytic role described. The Reverend James McGready, a man of imposing size, piercing eyes, and penetrating voice, was the person who provided the vital nexus between the background causes and the actual historical movement. A North Carolina Presbyterian minister who had created a stir in the Carolina Piedmont, McGready moved to the Kentucky frontier in the winter of 1795–1796. He had come to know firsthand the religious disappointments of the age, and confident that contrite, prayerful Christians could prevail upon God to redeem the times, he organized prayer and fast societies among the members of his three tiny congregations and fed them a steady diet of hope. Almost accidentally at a

Saturday night service in June 1800 attended by the most devout parishioners from all three churches, an extremely emotional Methodist preacher was allowed to preach to the emotionally drained members. He alternated crying and shouting, startling the normally sedate Presbyterians, when suddenly at the rear of the church a woman began shouting and collapsed in tears. Like an electrical charge, excitement swept through the congregation, and people to the right and left, in unconscious imitation, broke out in uncontrollable sobs. McGready himself, never having experienced such a scene, stood back in amazement, but he quickly concluded, as did countless others in the South who soon heard about the meeting, that here, before his very eyes, was the sign, long prayed for and fervently hoped for, of a Providential deliverance of the region from the grasp of irreligion and apostasy.

Interpreting this event as a minor miracle, McGready quickly determined to make the most of the opportunity presented. No sooner had the worshipers departed than he began laying preparations for an even grander occasion the following month, July 1800, at his Gasper River church. Notice was sent far and wide, with everyone invited to come prepared to camp out so services could continue until another miraculous outburst occurred. It is hard to overestimate the effect these preparations and the rumors of the previous meeting had on the rural people scattered across the lonely frontier. Desiring to recapture the sense of congregational community they warmly associated with the past (or back east across the mountains), and led by years of sermons to expect some day a glorious renewal of religious fervor, an almost palpable sense of expectation welled up among many of the people. This only increased the more they heard about and imagined the novel events in June. As the appointed date in July neared, the excitement reached fever pitch. Many hundreds came to the Gasper River church, camping among the trees awaiting a miracle. The size of the crowd, the numerous ministers in attendance, the pent-up hope, all worked together to produce an incredible religious revival. An unprecedented number of people—slave and free together—gathered from far and near, providing their own shelter, to attend the huge outdoor religious meeting and hear a non-stop barrage of sermons from teams of ministers.

Like a self-fulfilling prophecy, the Gasper River meeting, the first of many so-called camp-meetings that were to become a staple of southern religious life, galvanized churchpeople into vigorous activity. Emboldened ministers elsewhere announced that the long-anticipated revival had at long last begun and scheduled massive outdoor religious services themselves. The pace of religious activity accelerated, and camp meetings within three years spread across the entire South: the Great Revival was in full swing. Given its geographical extent, its interdenominational appeal (though after a while the camp meeting became primarily a Methodist institution, with Baptists staging revivals in individual rural churches and "protracted meetings" in towns), the intensity of the religious fervor, and the numbers of persons added to the church roles (membership doubled and tripled in some areas), this was the South's first great awakening. The huge camp meeting held at Cane Ridge, Kentucky, in August 1801, attended by, according to contemporary estimates, upwards of 20,000 persons, for many people symbolized "the mighty work" being done by God in the South. In the two decades after the Great Revival evangelical Protestantism moved far beyond the cabins of the common folk in the backcountry and the frontier and became overwhelmingly the dominant form of Christianity in the South.

What were the cultural consequences of the Great Revival; what difference did it make for the South? The three popular denominations, in their desire to maximize conversions and minimize interdenominational conflict in the midst of the revival, recognized that theological precision and sophistication were unnecessary, even counterproductive. Because it worked, southern churches were for a century and a half to pride themselves on a simple Biblicism that hardly extended beyond Scriptural literalism and the emotionally wrenching story of the crucifixion and the need to "give one's life to the Lord." Southern evangelicalism began and ended with the conversion experience. In large part because one's conversion was considered to be entirely a matter between an individual and God, with no place for mediating institutions, southern evangelicalism was strikingly privatized and individualistic.

Obviously, groups of converted individuals united together in congregations, and these local communities of the faithful played a powerful role in the cultural life of the people. For example, women found in church life and organization a unique arena for self-expression and mutual growth, and working with other women for a common cause contributed to the growth of a separate women's culture. The early evangelical churches also eagerly reached out to convert the blacks and bring them under the sacred canopy of the church, really beginning the remarkable growth of Christianity among the slaves—a development of signal importance, as we shall see later. But the sense of community within the churches seldom extended beyond the local congregation, with a felt responsibility for the larger society noticeably weaker in the South than in the Northeast and Midwest, where the lengthened shadow of Puritanism left a strong societal dimension to popular religion. Outside the South revival zeal often led to social reform; in the South the presence of slavery, which all other southern institutions had to acknowledge, forced southern churches to develop an exquisite ability to distinguish between things of this world and the other. Ministers attacked personal sin but felt constrained to defend regional institutional arrangements.

Ironically, southern evangelicals who began in the eighteenth century as dissenters outside the establishment and critical of it became, early in the nineteenth century, defenders of the status quo. Evangelical religion linked the newer subregions of the South with the older seaboard states and crossed class and race boundaries. As much as cotton or slavery, a common form of religious expression helped create a solid South in the early nineteenth century. Much of the vaunted localism and exaggerated individualism, along, paradoxically, with cultural and social conformity, that are often listed as characteristics of the South arose from the dominant religion. Southern sectionalism would soon find fertile soil in this localism and conformity, and religion would be one of the factors ultimately entering a wedge between the South and the nation.

THE AGE OF JEFFERSON

From the post–Civil War perspective of the twentieth century the history of the American South is often presented as the story of an eccentric region that ultimately became so incompatible with the North—the normative American region—that it broke off to form the Southern Confederacy. In many ways this is a distortion of the historical reality, for throughout much of early American history the North, with its Puritan origins and urban–commercial character, was the atypical area, and it changed more in the six decades after 1800 than did the South. With not a little justification the South would come to believe the rest of the nation had so transformed itself that the South had reason to withdraw from it in a conservative revolution. Certainly in the colonial period the staple-crop producing South was more the model of what England expected of New World colonies than the North was, but at no time was the South more the normative region of the nation than during the half-century following the beginning of troubles with England.

In Thomas Jefferson, Patrick Henry, and George Washington, Virginia produced the Pen, the Voice, and the Sword of the Revolution; Madison was the Father of the Constitution; and Washington was the precedent-setting first president. For twenty-four consecutive years after 1800 Virginians controlled the presidency (and John Marshall dominated the Supreme Court for those years and a decade longer). Southerners set the national agenda, fought a second war with England while New England sulked and plotted secession, and liberally welcomed immigrants and new western states. This was the high point of the national South, when southerners were at the liberal forefront of the nation and sought to protect the Republic from foreign threats and internal intrigue. This was the Age of Jefferson, when the size of the nation doubled and its ascendency in this hemisphere was proclaimed. But in the South too this was an era of change, and beneath the surface of national political leadership there were forces at work that would turn the South from national to local and then sectional concerns, foreshadowing the development of a separate southern nation in 1861.

For most politically literate southerners in 1801 Thomas Jefferson represented the sum total of their political philosophy: that government is best that governs least. For Jefferson and most of his fellow southerners the activist policies of the Hamiltonians—a national bank, incentives for manufacturing, a funded debt tying the economic interests of the mighty to the political fortune of the ruling administration, and heavy-handed intervention to throttle public dissent—were anathema. For Jefferson, Madison, and many southerners, Hamilton's policies seemed to favor the North at the expense of the South, and moreover, seemed an attempt to mold the American economy too closely along British lines, benefiting a privileged few. At this near remove from 1776 many southerners still associated British ways with corruption and tyranny. Once in power Jefferson scaled down the size and cost of the government and let such hated laws as the Alien and Sedition Acts expire without being enforced. A rigorous policy of retrenchment resulted in a federal government that, exclusive of a military of fewer than four thousand men, in terms of budget and personnel was smaller than many universities today. For Jefferson the power of ideas was the force that held the nation together, along with a geographical expanse—his vaunted empire for liberty—that would allow the untrammeled movement of white farmers across the West where they could pursue happiness free from the contaminating influence of cities or commercial greed.

There were contradictions in Jefferson's philosophy and blind spots in his vision, and despite his idealism he was a crafty political animal who pioneered the role of the president as the head of his political party. An aristocrat by birth but a democrat by intellectual persuasion, he was slow to understand that slaveholding planters, rather than unpretentious yeomen, would set the tone of his region. But for all his localism, for his attachment to Monticello with its vista to the West and his love affair with Albemarle County, Jefferson was a nationalist of the highest order. His vision of the historical role of the United States knew no bounds, for its banner was freedom ultimately for all mankind. (Though he felt that blacks were as yet far from ready, he believed Indians were at the threshold of being able to merit liberty.)

Jefferson was an enormously complex man. He idealized the nation as an agrarian republic, but he understood the necessity of trade and commerce. Aware of the writings of Adam Smith, he came to see that the seeking of private interest, properly harnessed, could result in social benefit. No backward looking farmer, he experimented with new kinds of plows and seeds, sought to open up commercial markets in Europe for American agricultural products, and promoted the building of canals to link the valley of Virginia to the Chesapeake ports. Rather than prohibit manufacturing and commerce, he wanted it balanced so that no one privileged group or region would dominate, and he sought also to balance commerce and agriculture. In subtle ways his views shifted, and while Hamilton's sophisticated economic policies looked backward to England, Jefferson's in the long run more truly came to foreshadow modern American liberal capitalism. Particularly in the booming urban areas of the Mid Atlantic region, ambitious artisans and would-be entrepreneurs seized upon Jefferson's egalitarian policies as a mechanism to challenge entrenched political and economic interests. In the cities Jeffersonianism unleashed democratic, modernizing social and commercial forces in ways that Jefferson himself was not prepared fully to comprehend. Jefferson was of course committed to political and intellectual freedom, but just as strongly he was committed to the freedom of individuals through exertion and enterprise to prosper economically.

In the South Jeffersonianism tended to reflect a somewhat nostalgic image of plain farmers and plantation gentry mildly suspicious of urban enterprise. But both city artisans and country agriculturalists shared an antipathy toward the British monarchy, privileged (and often assumed to be corrupt) merchants, and banking practices that seemed to favor only a fraction of the population. And Hamilton and the Federalists were associated with exactly those institutions and policies. Jefferson's philosophical opposition to the Hamiltonian program allowed him simultaneously to appeal to the artisans and working men of the cities as well as to the planters and small farmers of the South. It is but one of the ironies of the Jefferson administration that over a period of decades his economic vision more shaped the northern economy than it did the South as a whole. True, Baltimore, Richmond, and Norfolk grew rapidly in size as flour processing and shipping centers as a result of agriculturalists in the region responding to the growing European demand for wheat (and hence higher prices), but the full implications of the commercial revolution being set underway were not realized for decades.

Jefferson led his region (and the nation) more by the power of his luminous personality than by the almost millennial (and sometimes contradictory) nature of his nationalistic and egalitarian vision. A charming conversationalist with a nearly limitless curiosity and an unmatched breadth of learning, Jefferson could speak with authority to farmers and philosophers and win the affection of both. He downsized the scope of the federal government, democratized the style and substance of governing, and opened opportunities for individual commercial enterprise.

Jefferson's folksiness and identity with the soil recommended him to southerners high and low who failed to share his metaphysical devotion to the idea of the American nation. He seemed to be, and he was, one of them, and yet he was more. Most southerners accepted Jefferson and his intellectual and political entourage at the top of the ticket—Madison, Gallatin, Monroe, and others—even when the administration advanced policies with which they disagreed. Jefferson was a living symbol of American independence and Nationalism who commanded respect and affection from most southerners even while political and economic developments were producing localistic concerns at odds with the nationalistic tilt of the president. The commercial revolution underway in the North would eventually open a breach between the regions. Moreover, the proliferation of elective offices, the perfection in the South and West of political practices such as the use of circular letters to congressional constituents, and the changing role of the political leader as the spokesman and agent of the people, not their chosen better who substituted his wisdom for their myopic self-interest, would eventually force political leaders in the South to be more narrowly atuned to the views and prejudices of the local voters, especially when, after 1816, the threat of European entanglements lessened and Americans turned inward. But despite these localizing tendencies, *at the presidential level* the South during the years of the Virginia Dynasty represented the nation.

Jefferson was, then, philosophically a nationalist but operationally a localist; hence he could defend the idea of an "empire for liberty" but oppose John Marshall's judicial decisions that strengthened the central authority of the Supreme Court and the federal government. Most southerners could agree with Jefferson's conception of a weakened government because to them enhanced federal powers might eventually reach into the states and threaten the institution of slavery. Yet Jefferson was exceedingly complicated, composed of idealism and pragmatism in equal parts, and capable of changing his opinion when conditions warranted. A strict constructionist of the Constitution, he swallowed his scruples (albeit with difficulty) when the opportunity to purchase Louisiana arose. A spokesman for the liberty of man, he was a lifetime holder of slaves. A spokesman for agrarian values, he often championed commerce and trade. Opposed to the use of military force, he sent a naval squadron to chastise the Barbary pirates in North Africa. But Jefferson's willingness to take action in order to try to achieve an idealistic purpose met with mixed success. Fearful, for example, of the effect on Indian culture of the rapacious greed of unprincipled whites, he forced the Indians westward and tried to entice and then coerce them to accept white attitudes toward land and property. He thought such forced change was better than imminent genocide, but the long-range result of his removal policies (as carried to fruition by Andrew Jackson, who hated Native Americans) was still the destruction of the Indian cultures. Jefferson's greatest political failure came as he tried to deal with the commercial and naval complications of the British–French conflict in Europe.

American maritime trade with England and France, and especially their West Indian empires, had boomed since the mid-1790s when the Napoleonic wars broke out, making the United States the world's leading neutral carrier of goods. Nowhere was this trade more lucrative than shipping the exports of the French and Spanish sugar islands in the Caribbean back to the mother countries in Europe. The British victory by Admiral Horatio Nelson over the French and Spanish at Trafalgar in 1805 gave the English unrivaled control of the seas, strengthening French markets for American neutral shipping. In truth such American trade had always been in violation of England's so-called Rule of 1756 (which denied to neutral nations the right to trade during times of war with belligerent nations whose ports had not been open to the neutral nations in peacetime), but American shippers had developed the practice of carrying the goods to an American port, unloading them, paying the requisite duties, then reloading them, receiving a rebate of the duties, and shipping the goods to France—such "broken" voyages technically met the requirements of the British Rule of 1756.

England had long seen the fiction of such transshipments, and in the *Essex* decision in 1805 a British admiralty court ruled that only if a shipper could prove the cargo had not been meant for France in the first place would such vessels not be subject to seizure. Emboldened by recent naval successes, Britain simultaneously began to enforce a blockade of France by confiscating the cargoes of American ships and, even more galling to Americans, search them for sailors of British extraction, "impressing" those found and putting them into service in His Majesty's Navy. From the British perspective they were catching deserters, but in the eyes of Americans the high-handed British were kidnapping American sailors on the open sea, a flagrant slap in the face of American sovereignty and a slight to her national honor. United States sentiment boiled, but Jefferson was opposed to military action and idealistically thought the proscription of trade with England would be an effective alternative to armed combat. The administration pressured Congress to pass the Nonimportation Act of 1806, which threatened to limit British imports unless she changed her policies. However, Britain scarcely budged when Jefferson's negotiators pushed for a shift in policy. As if to demonstrate British arrogance, in June 1807 *H.M.S. Leopard* ordered the US frigate *Chesapeake*, in open waters off Norfolk, to heave to, raked her decks with gunfire when she did not, then boarded her and seized four sailors. The American public was absolutely outraged. Had Congress been in session, there surely would have been a declaration of war. By this time through a series of decrees England and France had effectively blockaded each other and put all American shipping at risk. Jefferson, still hoping to find a substitute for war in settling international conflict, was able to persuade Congress to pass an Embargo Act on December 27, 1807, stopping American trade with the entire outside world. France and England were little affected, but American shipping interests were devastated, and New England's ports, lacking the domestic or coastwise trade of such cities as Philadelphia, Baltimore, and Charleston, were especially hard hit. Opposition to Jefferson flared in New England, and Jefferson left office in March 1809 with his administration in near ruin even as southerners still supported him. That southern support enabled Jefferson's lieutenant, Secretary of State James Madison, to succeed him in the presidency.

As Jefferson was leaving office his party, the Jeffersonian Republicans, replaced the despised Embargo Act with the more narrowly focused Nonimportation Act of March 1, 1809, which restricted trade only to France and England and promised to lift the embargo to whichever side lifted its blockade to American shipping to Europe. Madison too was devoted to what Jefferson had called a "candid and liberal experiment" in "peaceful coercion," but the Nonimportation Act proved impossible to enforce and the loss of revenue from trade duties crippled the government. Trying still to make trade an effective substitute for war, nonimportation was replaced with Macon's Bill No. 2 in May 1810. Taking another tack, this bill opened trade with both England and France but promised that if either of the belligerents lifted their proscriptions against neutral trade, then the United States would place an embargo against the other nation. Desperate to find some sign of success in this beleagured policy, Madison interpreted what he took to be a slight change in French policy as movement toward freeing commerce with neutrals (actually Napoleon seems to have snookered Madison with an empty gesture toward repeal of the existing restrictions). In March 1811 the administration slapped nonimportation on trade with England.

France was as guilty of ill will and evil intentions toward the United States as England, but the reality of British naval power made England in fact the greater malefactor. Moreover, Jefferson and Madison both had had a smoldering dislike of England since 1776, and those embers had been kept alive in the 1790s by the pro-British tilt of Hamilton, their common political foe. Britain still seethed over the results of the American Revolution; her arrogance toward the United States and the fear that she might want to put down her upstart child made many Americans quick to see her actions as an insult to American honor and a real threat to American independence. This disposition to be suspicious of Britain was fanned by Indian troubles in the Ohio Territory. Pressured by land hungry white settlers, the Indians in that region had combined under Tecumseh to be a genuine threat, but Americans interpreted the natural defensiveness of the Indians as proof of British involvement. In November 1811 General William Henry Harrison routed a group of Tecumseh's braves (under the leadership of his brother, The Prophet) near the Tippecanoe River in Indiana, but Tecumseh—on a secret mission to the South to create an alliance of southern Indians to resist further white settlements—lived to fight another day. With rumors of British-aided Indian wars in the West and the continuing embarrassment of British impressment of American sailors, Madison sensed that war with England was inevitable if America's independence and pride were to be protected. When Madison, acting on that judgment, asked Congress in June 1812 to declare war on Great Britain, the South—ever alert for any slight to personal or national independence and led by such aggressive young congressmen as

John C. Calhoun and Henry Clay—overwhelmingly voted for war while New England opposed the measure. In large part the War of 1812 was the nationalistic South's war.

THE WAR OF 1812

Despite the bellicose talk and the failure of a series of trade restrictions that seemed to leave war as the only alternative to national humiliation, the United States was comically unprepared for war in early 1812. Republican retrenchment had meant a reduction in the size of the military forces, citizens were unwilling to pay taxes for any purpose, the nation was deeply divided over the declaration of war, and the charter of the Bank of the United States, the only significant national financial institution, had been allowed to expire in 1811. Madison had book learning but no military experience, and he did not possess Jefferson's uncanny political skills. The result was a predictable rash of military defeats, with Oliver Perry's naval victory on Lake Erie in October 1813 and William Henry Harrison's defeat (and killing) of Tecumseh at the Battle of the Thames in southern Ontario in the same month the only glimmers of hope for the Americans. By early 1813 the British navy had the American navy bottled up, and Britain's preoccupation with Napoleon in Europe seemed the sole factor preventing American defeat.

After Napoleon abdicated in early 1814, Britain turned her whole attention toward the United States, planning a two-pronged attack against her former colonies. The first, a major move south from Canada, was surprisingly thwarted by American victories at Niagara in July and at Plattsburg near Lake Champlain in September. But in between these two American successes a group of British regulars, supported by the navy, had invaded Maryland, scattered American defenders at Bladensburg, and entered Washington, DC, where on August 24, 1814, they torched the Capitol and the White House and forced the Madison administration literally to run. The following month the British turned toward Baltimore, a hated center of privateering activities against the British navy, but their invasion was halted when, after a fearful bombardment, Fort McHenry refused to fall. Even though eyewitness Frances Scott Key wrote the "Star-Spangled Banner" in celebration, the American situation still looked bleak. A crack British force, fresh from defeating Napoleon, was planning an assault on New Orleans and within a month New England dissidents, unhappy with southern influence over national policies, were calling for a meeting in December at Hartford, Connecticut, to propose a New England secession and a separate peace.

In August 1814 the United States sent a team of peace commissioners to Ghent, Belgium, to negotiate with the British. The British commissioners, expecting word of victory from their new offensive, stalled and presented the Americans with a harsh set of demands. The American negotiators refused to accept the demands, in part at least because two of them, Henry Clay and John Quincy Adams, had severe differences over the British proposals. Finally word arrived of the unexpected American victories at Niagara and Lake Champlain, and with her European position in flux, England reconsidered the difficulties of defeating the sparsely settled, decentralized United States and decided to lessen her demands for peace. The result, an agreement signed on Christmas Eve, 1814, at Ghent, left the major issues—impressment and maritime rights—unresolved and simply restored the status quo from before the war. The treaty, worked out by appointed commissioners, of course meant nothing until it was formally ratified by both governments. England still harbored hopes for the invasion force heading toward New Orleans. On board the ships commanded by Admiral Alexander Cochrane (with army troops under the leadership of General Edward Michael Pakenham) were the staff for a complete civil government, including an attorney general, a judge, a colonial secretary, and a superintendent for Indian affairs; a proclamation disclaiming the Louisiana Purchase as fraudulent; and a plan to name General Pakenham the governor of a new British province. If Pakenham were victorious, the Americans would be ousted from the region, the British reinstalled, and the tide of history since 1776 reversed. A treaty might have been signed, but it did not have to be ratified until after word came from New Orleans, and the British were confident that news would be bracing.

Even after 1803 United States hegemony over much of the territory in the Southwest remained fragile. Most of the Mississippi Territory was controlled by Indians—the Creek, Cherokee, Choctaw, Chickasaw, and Seminole—and Spain continued a tenuous hold on West Florida. As early as 1804 groups of Louisianians were plotting to seize at least a portion of West Florida from Spain; they soon staged a mini-revolution there, proclaimed the region's independence, and asked that it be annexed by the United States. The administration ignored the request, in part because negotiations were under way with Spain on West Florida and related issues, including the western boundary of the Louisiana Purchase. The sovereignty over West Florida continued to be problematical; finally, in October 1810 President Madison issued a proclamation claiming that West Florida was a legitimate part of the Louisiana Purchase and setting the boundary line at the Perdido River (between Mobile and Pensacola). Two years later, six days after the Orleans portion of the grand purchase was admitted to the Union as the state of Louisiana, the disputed West Florida territory from the Mississippi to the Pearl River was added to the state of Louisiana (the so-called Florida parishes of Louisiana). The region from the Pearl to the Perdido River was assigned to the Mississippi Territory, but no immediate steps were taken to drive out the Spanish settlers until the War of 1812 made the presence of even the weakest foreign garrison a potential threat. Then in April 1813 General James Wilkinson made a slight show of force at Mobile, whereupon the Spanish surrendered and the US took control.

The Indian presence in the Mississippi Territory was a far more serious threat to United States hegemony in the area than the sprinkling of Spanish settlers along the Gulf. In the fall of 1811 the great Shawnee chief Tecumseh, accompanied by two dozen Shawnee warriors, had come south into the present-day state of Alabama to rouse the Creeks to fight against further white intrusions. Most Creeks rejected Tecumseh's impassioned call to arms, but many younger braves, calling themselves "Red Sticks" because of their painted war clubs, took up his banner. Tecumseh visited other Indian nations and had some success with the Seminoles, too. In 1813 the Creeks struck against the white settlers with victories at Burnt Corn and Fort Mims in Alabama. Militia from the Mississippi Territory, from Georgia, and from Tennessee were soon engaged in a general war against the Creeks.

Late in the year the Tennessee forces, aggressively led by Major General Andrew Jackson, began a vicious campaign southward from Huntsville through central Alabama, defeating the Creeks in a series of one-sided victories. Jackson paused during the dead of winter to rebuild his supplies and receive reinforcements, then in early 1814 he began a hard-fought trek toward the Horseshoe Bend on the Tallapoosa River, where a thousand Creek warriors were ensconced. There in late March Jackson annihilated the Indian army. Only a minority of Creeks in the region were actually opposing Jackson, but Old Hickory was an implacable foe of Indians. He continued hostilities at the negotiating table, forcing all the Creeks, even the friendly majority, to accept the harsh Treaty of Fort Jackson on August 9, 1814, whereby they ceded some 23 million acres of land in central and southern Alabama and southern Georgia to the United States. This treaty not only opened up a vast region to white settlement, but it effectively ended the Indian military threat before England turned its military attention toward the Southwest and New Orleans.

In the course of prosecuting the War of 1812 England originally intended to move a fleet into Pensacola (Spain only nominally controlled East Florida), then mount an overland attack on New Orleans by way of Mobile. But in April 1813 the Americans had occupied Mobile, and in late 1814, with ever strengthening rumors about an imminent English invasion through Pensacola—and a tiny preliminary British force already occupying the port city—General Andrew Jackson decided to take swift action. With some three thousand troops he easily captured Pensacola after sharp skirmishing in the city streets. Meanwhile, with the conclusion of the Napoleonic wars, England suddenly had more troops and ships at her disposal. Disdaining a frugal campaign along the Gulf coast, she decided to mount a major invasion force from Jamaica under Admiral Cochrane and General Pakenham. Because of

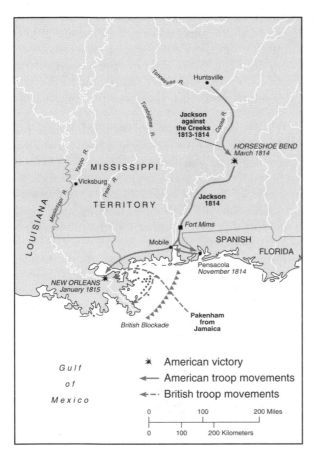

Southwest campaigns,
1813 to 1815

the difficulties of sailing up the Mississippi some hundred twisting miles to New Orleans, the British decided to enter the city from the east through shallow Lake Borgne and a swampy network of bayous. Jackson had hurried a contingent of troops overland to New Orleans, arriving on December 1, 1814, only three weeks before the 1,600 British reconnaissance troops began to gather some seven miles below the city on the narrow peninsula of land bounded on one side by the Mississippi River and on the other by the nearly impenetrable swamps.

Had the British moved promptly, before Jackson acquired reinforcements and established a line of defense, the Red Coats might have won the city. But Pakenham delayed in anticipation of assembling a much larger force as the British laboriously moved men and material across the swampy terrain from Lake Borgne. This buildup of British forces allowed Jackson to put together a defensive army composed of regular soldiers, sharpshooting militiamen from Kentucky and Tennessee, two battalions of free blacks from New Orleans (south Louisiana had a numerous and proud segment of population known as the free people of color), patriotic pirates associated with Jean Lafitte, and friendly Creek Indians. Positioning themselves behind a canal (which they flooded) linking the river with the swamps, and building a mud-and-log rampart shoulder high, Jackson's men awaited the British advance.

Early on the fog-shrouded morning of January 8, 1815, the Red Coats moved, but as a breeze blowing from the river rolled back the fog, devastating cross fire from Jackson's artillery began to wreak havoc. Then the riflemen behind the ramparts, whipped into a frenzy by Jackson's exhortations and the military band playing "Yankee Doodle," began a deadly fusillade. In five furious minutes the British army was decimated, although shooting continued for over an hour. Pakenham and another general were killed, and dead soldiers lay in heaps across the battlefield; the heart of the army was broken before the survivors could even retreat. When the firing stopped, the British had suffered over two thousand casualties, the Americans a mere seventy-one. The greatest battle in American history to date was over. True, it occurred two weeks after the signing of the Treaty of Ghent on December 24, 1814, but that treaty would not go into effect until both sides exchanged ratification. Jackson's victory at New Orleans clinched the decision—Britain's hopes of getting another foothold in North America were dashed—and the English ministry and the United States exchanged ratification of the treaty on February 17, 1815. Without the victory Britain might well have sat on the treaty and prosecuted the war further. So the Battle of New Orleans was not simply an empty victory, a patriotic media event, but the anchor that ensured the outcome of the war.

THE SOUTH EXPANDS WESTWARD

Throughout much of the nation word arrived of the acceptance of the Treaty of Ghent and Jackson's seemingly miraculous victory at New Orleans almost simultaneously, and there was a veritable explosion of nationalistic fervor. Jackson instantly became a nationwide hero, the would-be New England secessionists were completely discredited, and American honor was unfurled for the world to see. The Madison administration had been rescued from military unpreparedness and an excess of government decentralization by the victories of the last few months of the war. Learning from recent mistakes, Madison pushed for a series of Hamilton-like measures whose necessity had been proved by wartime exigencies. A second Bank of the United States was established in 1816 with a twenty-year charter, and even southerners like John C. Calhoun advocated a program of protective tariffs so infant American manufacturers could survive the dumping of cheapened English goods. The warm afterglow of wartime patriotism suffused the nation for several years.

In the South the combination of the victory over the British, the Indian land cessions of 1814 followed by additional cessions in 1816 in northern Alabama and 1818 in western Tennessee, and the American occupation of West Florida, opened the floodgates of migration to the bountiful territory between the Mississippi River and the Georgia border. Before 1812 there had been a substantial migration to Louisiana, to the Natchez District, to the hinterland of Mobile, and to Huntsville, where the Tennessee River dipped south into Alabama, but that emigration paled beside the mighty tide of settlers moving west after 1816. Travelers reported seeing thousands of people on the roads, with so many caravans of wagons and cattle headed for settlement that publicists in the seaboard states worried about depopulation.

The Land Act of 1800 had provided for the sale of public lands in lots of 320 acres at two dollars per acre, payable in four annual installments. The minimum purchase size was halved in 1804, and thousands of small farmers along with planters and speculators sunk their savings and the promise of future crops into a mad frenzy of land purchases. The so-called Great Migration transformed the Mississippi Territory in the four years following 1815. The fertile land and the long growing season made cotton a fabulously lucrative crop, particularly for those who had slaves and could multiply the amount of land they could cultivate. Plain farmers and slave-owning planters alike literally mined the soil for several years as a boom mentality took over. All who could were buying land on credit and expanding the scale of their agricultural operation. The population of the Mississippi–Alabama territory expanded from 40,352 in 1810 to 222,311 in 1820, with Mississippi entering the union as a state in 1817 and Alabama in 1819.

The advance of United States citizens into new regions included settlers moving into the area bordering north central Florida, still under Spanish control. When Seminole Indians from Florida skirmished with white settlers, General Andrew Jackson was authorized to punish the Native Americans. Jackson needed no prodding as he eagerly pursued the Indians back into Florida in early 1818. When he found them cowering near the Spanish fort at St. Mark's, he promptly captured the fort and summarily executed two British citizens he found there on the pretense that they were provoking the Indian raids. Then he followed the fleeing Indians toward Pensacola and captured the Spanish fort there. Back in Washington, DC, President Monroe and Secretary of War John C. Calhoun (not to mention the Spanish and British embassies) were appalled by Jackson's exceeding his authority by leaps and bounds, but Secretary of State John Quincy Adams, bogged down in negotiations with Spain to purchase Florida, adroitly persuaded the administration not to censure the hotheaded Jackson. The evident ease with which he had run roughshod over the weak Spanish garrisons in Florida sent an unmistakable signal to Spain. Adams pushed hard for an agreement; in February 1819 he struck a bargain. By the terms of the Adams-Onis Treaty, Spain gave up its last claims to West Florida, ceded East Florida to the United States (it was organized as a territory in 1822), and agreed upon a western boundary to the Louisiana Purchase all the way to the Pacific—Spain gave up the far Northwest in order to hold on to Texas—all in exchange for the United States' assuming up to five million dollars in claims held by American merchants against Spain dating back to the Napoleonic wars. The territorial Old South was complete now except for Texas.

THE RISE OF SOUTHERN SELF-CONSCIOUSNESS

The era of ebullient westward expansion soon came to a crashing halt, and it did so in such a manner, and in conjunction with such other events, that the effect was to alter fundamentally how the South saw itself in relation to the rest of the nation. A great fault line developed across the historical landscape, and along that fissure the nation would eventually break apart. But only the beginning tremors were felt in 1819 and 1820. The opening up of virgin land in the West and the pent up demand for cotton textiles in war-torn Europe had fueled the march of cotton and slavery, with the result that the production of cotton in the United States increased from 146,290 bales in 1814 to 349,007 bales in 1819, and at the beginning of that year cotton was fetching more than thirty cents a pound. This heady prosperity and the expectation that it would continue forever led farmers, planters, and speculators to demand loans to purchase more land and slaves, and a proliferation of banks—the new Bank of the United States, state banks, and local banks—was only too glad to supply the funds with little thought given to maintaining a safe ratio of holdings in gold and silver to extended loans. Then the whole house of cards came crashing down: the European demand for cotton was exceeded and the price of cotton plummeted. Suddenly farmers and planters could not meet their notes. To make things worse, the mismanaged Bank of the United States got new directors in early 1819 and decided to retrench, calling in too quickly loans extended to local banks. The resulting credit crunch forced the smaller banks to pressure their debtors, the already hard-hit cotton growers, to speed up their repayment. Much of the South and West plunged into the worst economic depression of the young nation's history, and eager to find a scapegoat for this Panic of 1819, many southerners fixed on the financiers of the Bank of the United States, headquartered in Philadelphia. The economic interests of the North, it now seemed patently obvious to bankrupt southern farmers, were antithetical to the prosperity of the South.

Compounding this southern animosity toward the national bank was a controversial Supreme Court decision by supernationalist John Marshall that was easily interpreted by touchy southerners as a potential fatal blow to the rights of individual states, which southerners already saw as the surest defense of the institution of slavery. In his 1803 *Marbury* v. *Madison* decision that rebuked Jefferson, Chief Justice Marshall had staked out the Supreme Court's sole authority to determine the constitutionality of federal legislation, but the importance of that decision was little recognized at the time. More worrisome to southerners was the case of *Fletcher* v. *Peck* (1810), in which the Supreme Court overturned a series of Georgia laws that were attempting to correct the fraud that followed in the wake of land claims along the Yazoo River—Marshall defended not the corruption of the land speculators but the sanctity of contracts.

Yet this anti–states' right decision had come while James Madison was still popular and while the nation was still united in the midst of threatening maritime entanglements with England and France. But when, during the economic collapse of 1819 that already awakened southern fears of centralizing northern economic prowess and distrust of the national bank, Marshall struck down a Maryland law that attempted to punish (by taxation) an obviously corrupt local branch of the Bank of the United States, it seemed to many southerners that Marshall was espousing a dangerous policy. The power to tax was the power to destroy, argued Marshall, and he went on in broad language to defend the constitutionality of the bank that, he said, was implied by the "necessary and proper" clause of the Constitution. Such a bold and loose construction of the Constitution frightened white southerners, who could imagine such interpretations leading to a federal assault on their institution of slavery.

What welded the issues of the Panic of 1819 and the hatred of the Bank of the United States and the fear of the implications of Marshall's constitutional pronouncements together into a perceived major threat against the South was the explosive topic of restricting the spread of slavery. Not since the Northwest Ordinance of 1787 had limiting the practice of slavery been an issue in American politics, and white southerners were convinced the Constitution undergirded forever their right to own humans as property. The Ordinance also set forth a model procedure by which territories would, through a series of three steps determined by their population, make the transition to statehood. In 1812, when Missouri (a part of the original Louisiana Purchase) was elevated to the second grade of territory in this three-stage process, a Pennsylvania congressman, Abner Lacock, introduced a motion to prohibit slaves from the territory, but his motion was easily defeated. Four years later Missouri ascended to the third grade of territory, and in 1817 its citizens began petitioning Congress for statehood. A House committee on April 3, 1818 reported an enabling act for her admission; the following day

Congressman Arthur Livermore of New Hampshire proposed a constitutional amendment to prohibit slavery in any future state—New Englanders, reflecting the sentiment of the abortive Hartford Convention, still feared the future dominance of a slave-holding West and South. Livermore's resolution failed, but the enabling act for Missouri never got any further than the Committee of the Whole. Then Congress recessed without deciding the issue.

When the Fifteenth Congress reconvened in November 1818, a resolution was presented for the admission of Illinois as a state from the original Northwest Territory. Representative James Tallmadge, Jr., of New York bitterly opposed the resolution because the proposed state's constitution did not expressly prohibit slavery—in Tallmadge's view a clear violation of the Northwest Ordinance. Nevertheless, the House approved the Illinois resolution. Before Speaker Henry Clay of Kentucky could present to the House on December 18, 1818, a resolution from Missouri's legislators seeking permission to adopt a constitution and become a state, the American Convention for Promoting the Abolition of Slavery, and Improving the Condition of the African Race, held an emergency session in Philadelphia. There a special committee prepared a petition that, when enough time had elapsed to collect a goodly number of signatures, would be presented to Congress requesting that slavery be prohibited in all new states and territories.

As the new year began, premonitions of the impending controversy quickly occurred. In January another Quaker State representative, John Sergeant, introduced an opaque resolution instructing the Judiciary Committee to study an ordinance guaranteeing certain basic civil and religious rights to all inhabitants of the territories. William Lowndes of South Carolina was one of those who espied the real antislavery intentions of the resolution, which was tabled. Quite clearly the admission of Missouri was becoming entangled in a gravely important issue that had never before been publicly acknowledged: the expansion or containment and eventual demise of slavery. For opponents of slavery, Missouri, most of whose boundary was shared with Illinois, seemed a logical extension of the Northwest Territory; for southern proponents of slavery, Missouri's location west of the Mississippi River made it an essential symbol of slavery's right to expand westward. Pressure seemed to be building up as legislators, considering principles and politics, jockeyed for position. Yet still no one was prepared for what was to happen.

The House, sitting as a Committee of the Whole, took up the bills introduced to form Missouri (and, incidentally, Alabama) into states. There was no controversy about Alabama; it obviously would be a slave state, and, as the twenty-second state, it produced an equal balance between slave and free states. But Missouri was a different matter, and how it came in would now shift the balance of power in the Senate. During consideration of the Missouri Enabling Bill on February 13, 1819, Representative Tallmadge stood up and moved to amend the bill to prevent the further introduction of slaves into the state and to provide for the eventual emancipation of the present slave children. With this bombshell the divisive issue was broached, for the first time, openly on the floor of Congress. Southern congressmen were quick to denounce the Tallmadge amendment, but they were outvoted. By a strict sectional vote the House on February 17 passed the controversial amendment, but it failed in the Senate ten days later. When Congress adjourned on March 3, the festering issue of Missouri lingered.

The new Congress gathered in December 1819, but passions had not cooled. In the ensuing debates all the pro and con arguments about slavery heard in later decades were rehearsed, and the intensity of feeling about the issue frightened moderates. Northerners openly argued that slavery was in contradiction to the Declaration of Independence and had no legitimate place in America's future. White southerners just as fervently believed that their freedom included the freedom to own slaves, and in fact they defined their liberty in terms of the right to hold bondspeople. The raw tensions dividing the nation stood revealed like an inflamed wound whose covering bandage had been ripped off.

Into this dilemma stepped a determined Henry Clay in early 1820, and using the powers of his office as Speaker of the House and his marvelously

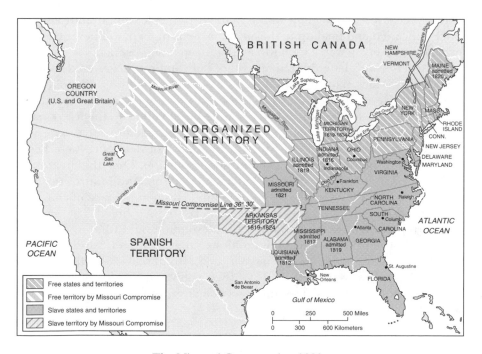

The Missouri Compromise, 1820

winning personality he devised a series of compromise measures that with shifting majorities narrowly survived the votes of the Senate and the House. The resulting Missouri Compromise is well known: the far northeastern territory of Massachusetts was admitted as the free state of Maine to match the admission of Missouri as a slave state, and slavery was prohibited from the remaining portion of the Louisiana Purchase that lay north of the southern boundary of Missouri, latitude 36 degrees, 30 minutes. South of the line (the Arkansas Territory including the eventual state of Oklahoma) slavery would be legal. At the time the Great Plains were viewed as a desert inhospitable to settlement, so the disparity in size between the two portions of the Louisiana Purchase did not seem unreasonable. The Senate balance was maintained, slavery would be disallowed in most of the existing United States territory, but slavery's theoretical acceptance in the trans-Mississippi region was symbolically realized. (In 1821 Clay had to work his magic again to dissuade the Missouri legislature from severely discriminating against free blacks.) Sectional peace was restored, at least on the surface, by the settlement of the Missouri issue. But Thomas Jefferson's foreboding April 1820 letter to a congressman from the former District of Maine would prove hauntingly prescient: "This momentous question, like a fire-bell in the night, awakened and filled me with terror. I considered it at once as the knell of the Union. It is hushed, indeed, for the moment. But this is a reprieve only, not a final sentence. A geographical line, coinciding with a marked principle, moral and political, once conceived and held up to the angry passions of men, will never be obliterated; and every new irritation will mark it deeper and deeper."

As Jefferson's letter hinted, the veneer of compromise covered seething sectional tensions. For at least a decade southern politics and politicians beneath the level of the presidency had been growing increasingly localistic. The number of elective offices had expanded tremendously, the use of partisan electoral techniques had been perfected, and congressional letters to constituents appealed to local issues. The politics of deference were being replaced with political subservience to public opinion. Only the great prestige of the Virginia Triumvirate of Jefferson, Madison, and Monroe enabled them to maintain the facade of southern nationalism in the face of constricting patriotism, but these aging men were the last of their breed. The younger southern politicians were not sons of the Revolution but rather of the partisan 1790s, when the sectional animosities of the Alien and Sedition Acts—and the states' rights Kentucky and Virginia resolutions—were the shaping events. The controversies of 1819 to 1820 cultivated the long-planted but until then dormant seeds of southern sectionalism, and their eventual harvest would be bitter indeed.

CHAPTER 3

The Southern Nation

Movies and popular fiction have created a series of vignettes about life in the Old South that have indelibly fixed the place and era in the American mind. These images of stately mansions, gallant southern gentlemen and their ladies, lazy, sallow-faced, poor white trash, and contented slaves at work in boundless fields of cotton have proven remarkably impervious to the undramatic work of historians. Paradoxically there is another popular version of the Old South, and it is a kind of perverse mirror image of the first: this South is populated by uniformly evil white planters with an eye for the "wenches"; plantation mistresses lusting for slave men; poor whites envious of the planters and filled with hatred toward all blacks; and robust slaves constantly seething with rebellion. Of course neither bundle of stereotypes fully captures the genuine South of the decades between the end of the second war with England and the American Civil War, but as with all stereotypes they contain a confused hint of several truths along with their many distortions.

Americans have long been fascinated with the South of this era, when slavery set it apart from the rest of the nation and cotton was king. Yet while the South changed in the years after 1820, its growth was evolutionary, unlike the fundamental transformation that created a new North in those same decades. As immigration, the beginnings of urbanization and industrialization, the transportation revolution, and other forces of modernization were remaking the North, the South came to appear, and so felt itself to be, increasingly different from the rest of the nation. The South has often been portrayed as growing apart from the North. But the perception of the changing South was an optical illusion, for in fundamental ways its earlier tendencies were only intensified, and it was the North that moved in new directions. Nevertheless, the result was the same: to many contemporaries the United States seemed to be becoming two dissimilar civilizations, with opposed interests.

The use of the phrase "the South" projects a false uniformity upon a region of great diversity, even within individual states, but it especially hides the differences between the older seaboard states, from Maryland to Georgia, and the newer "cotton" South that stretched from western Georgia to Louisiana and, after 1845, into Texas. The thin soils of the upper seaboard South had been depleted by nearly two hundred years of tobacco cultivation there, and the rice and indigo plantations of lowcountry South Carolina and Georgia never regained their pre-Revolutionary prosperity. The younger sons of landowners had to look elsewhere for their economic future, and poorer whites also sought cheaper land and better opportunities beyond their birthplaces. After 1815 millions of acres in what was then called the Southwest were opened to white settlement. The new lands beckoned many energetic or desperate settlers, and cotton, a kind of fluffy gold, its price long maintained by the hungry looms of England, proved to be a powerful engine driving the southern economy across the fertile acres of Alabama, Mississippi, and Louisiana. The dominant money crop was new, cotton instead of tobacco or rice, but the markets were still mostly foreign and the laborers were still white yeoman and black slaves. It was as though the system worked out over decades in the seaboard South simply shifted southwestward to the frontier, with only the crop changed. In agricultural societies the peculiarities of a crop—its cultivation and harvesting—determine much of life. Even church revival meetings were scheduled for after lay-by time, when crop labor needs diminished. In order to understand the South, one must know the nature of its farm products.

THE AGRICULTURAL ECONOMY OF THE OLD SOUTH

The old seaboard South lost population only in a relative sense, simply growing more slowly than the states to the west, and Virginia and South Carolina continued to set the tone for much of southern political and cultural life throughout the period. Tobacco and rice continued to be grown there, and planter families continued to live comfortably. The more perceptive planters experimented with new agricultural techniques, especially after the mild depression of the 1830s. In order to increase their yields, agricultural societies, fairs, periodicals, and reformers, such as Edmund Ruffin, promoted crop rotation; the use of lime, manure, and marl (a naturally occurring soil deposit heavy with calcium carbonate, good for lime-deficient land) on depleted fields; better livestock breeding practices; and more accurate accounting methods. In much of Piedmont Maryland and Virginia the larger plantations had long ago shifted to wheat cultivation, and small farmers, landowning yeomen, came to dominate tobacco production with their small, five- or ten-acre crops. The Virginia and North Carolina tobacco industry was invigorated in the final two decades of the antebellum period by the production of "bright yellow tobacco," whose curing process, using charcoal as fuel for heating and drying the leaves, had been discovered by a slave named Stephen in North Carolina in 1839. But even tobacco moved west, beginning with early Virginia pioneers to Kentucky; in 1839 the aggregate production of Kentucky and Tennessee was more than Virginia's and almost double that of Maryland and North Carolina combined.

The western states of Kentucky and Tennessee, and later Missouri, came to dominate the cultivation and processing of another crop, hemp, whose demand was related to the expansion of cotton farming. Ginned cotton was pressed into rectangular bales, then covered with bagging and secured by ropes. Both the cotton bagging and the bale ropes were made from hemp fibers. Hemp, a plant originally from Asia, grew particularly well in the famed Bluegrass region of Kentucky and in the environs of Louisville; its tall stalks, twice as high as a man, were cut with a special knife and allowed to lay in the fields, rotting in the dew and late fall rains. In early winter the partially decayed stalks were broken into inch-long segments by a hinged handtool and the internal fibers pulled out, leaving the broken husk of the stalks in piles to be burned at night in fires whose smoke gave the evenings a peculiarly pungent smell. The collected fibers were spun into thread and woven into cloth or rope at local factories. Cutting and breaking the stalks was especially demanding labor, and (as one would expect) slaves were employed in every step of hemp production. The majority of slaves in Kentucky were in fact employed in some aspect of the hemp industry, and hemp, more than tobacco, gave the Bluegrass State a slave economy.

Even in colonial days the British, needing ropes for its navy, had tried without much success to encourage hemp production by offering bounties to American farmers—and it was grown in all the southern colonies—but the farmers could make more money from tobacco. After the Revolution, Congress sought to promote the crop by placing a levy on imported competing fibers, and hemp production boomed with the expansion of cotton cultivation. Southern hemp was in truth far inferior to the fibers of water-rotted Russian hemp and hemp rope and bagging from Manila and Scotland, but southern producers, led by Henry Clay, who had married into a wealthy hemp-growing family, had the political clout to maintain its tariff protection.

After the Civil War hemp bagging was replaced with jute bagging, and today hemp is an outlaw crop, grown surreptitiously throughout the rural South as a source of marijuana and hashish.

Clearly the South as a whole did not practice monocrop agriculture, and no individual planter grew only a money crop to sell on the open market—even the most profit-oriented plantation grew some vegetables, kept livestock and poultry for home consumption, and exchanged some products and services in the local economy. The Old South as a whole was self-sufficient in foodstuffs, unlike the post-Civil War South. Yet despite substantial cereal and livestock production, cotton came to dominate the Old South's economy, its labor force, and its state of mind the way no other crop did. There is no understanding of the Old South without a knowledge of the cultivation and marketing of cotton, but an exclusive focus on cotton production fails to reveal the complex nature of southern agricultural society. Historians often describe the Old South as being either capitalistic or non- or precapitalistic, farmers as being either subsistence agriculturalists or producers for the market, but historical reality rarely fits such neat categories. In most situations these classifications blend together in various mixes, and comprehending the past is easier if it is not forced to fit contemporary labels.

Cotton was admirably suited to the climate of the South, for it requires a growing season of slightly over two hundred days, and most of the South below the thirty-seventh parallel (except in the higher elevations of the mountains) had frost-free seasons of such duration. Moreover, cotton thrives best with a rainfall distribution that provides sufficient spring moisture but not so heavy rain as to rot its roots or cause the stalks to grow too rapidly and too tall, summers with plentiful afternoon showers to keep the mature plants healthy as they begin to bud, and relatively dry late falls so that hard thunderstorms would not knock the opened cotton bolls to the ground. Much of the lower South stretching westward from central Georgia and South Carolina all the way beyond the Sabine River into eastern Texas is blessed with such precipitation characteristics, making it the land for cotton. The imperishability of cotton and its relatively high value relative to its volume permitted isolated producers to transport it to market affordably, even when the trip by wagon took days. Cotton's suitability for transportation allowed slavery to expand far beyond the coastal and tidewater enclaves where it had mainly existed in colonial days. The development of shallow-bottomed steamboats that could navigate the smaller southern rivers also enabled cotton producers to sell their crops at innumerable intermediate market towns or country stores scattered across the hinterland. The steamboats with their broad decks piled high with bales ferried their cargoes to port cities, such as New Orleans and Mobile, where the cotton was pressed into still more compact bales in preparation for transshipment to the North or to England. Throughout the antebellum period the dollar value of cotton exports to Europe represented over half the total United States export trade. Cotton was a major reason for the growth and prosperity of New York City as a port.

From the white viewpoint, cotton was well suited to cultivation by slaves because the mature plants were short enough for planters or overseers to easily see and supervise slaves working in a vast field. But cotton was also a very democratic crop. Its cultivation required no expensive network of dikes, flood gates, and canals as did rice; there were no appreciable economies of scale, so a small family farm could grow cotton about as efficiently as a large slave plantation could; and cotton's imperishability, unlike sugar cane, permitted small producers to spend several weeks accumulating enough of the

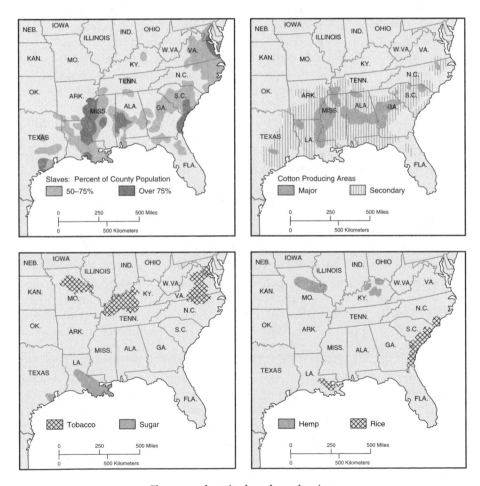

Slavery and agricultural production

crop through several pickings (because the bolls did not ripen all at once) to make up a wagon load to haul to the gin. Once ginned, cotton could be warehoused for months without spoilage. Hence cotton could be grown profitably at any scale. Small farmers, so-called subsistence farmers, could plant a few acres of cotton as a money crop to complement their emphasis on food crops and livestock.

Small farmers sometimes depended on larger growers to gin and market their cotton in return for a tiny percentage of the output, but just such relationships helped create a community of economic interest. True, the farmer might own no slaves, but his shared involvement in cotton cultivation produced a commitment to the staple in common with the wealthy planter. The simultaneity of effort—planting, chopping, and picking—involved in growing cotton knew no class boundaries, and small farmers and large planters simultaneously performing identical labor created an imagined community, a sense of "we" cotton growers, that bound white southerners together. Many a politically acute planter knew how to appeal to this cross-class identity when familiarly conversing with small farmers on court days or around a crossroads store. The farmers, proud of their egalitarian relationship to their more wealthy neighbors, acknowledged the planters' right to hold political office even as the officeholder acknowledged the plainfolks' right to make the ultimate electoral choices.

Cotton was an easier crop to cultivate than tobacco, rice, and sugar. Unlike tobacco, which had to be transplanted from the seed bed to the field at just the proper moment and whose leaves had to be stripped and cured just so in order to achieve a high-grade product, a successful cotton harvest was more dependent on the climate of a particular year than on a series of judgments by the grower. Tillage of cotton was not nearly so unpleasant and disease-ridden as working in the rice fields of coastal South Carolina and Georgia, flooded as the fields were for long periods of time with stagnant, malodorous water. The cotton fields were "broken" with a large turning plow in early spring, then plowed into rows or ridges about three feet apart. A light plow was used to cut a small trench in the top of the rows, and cotton seeds were usually dropped by hand into the trench. A harrow was then used to cover the seeds with a thin layer of soil. The seeds sprouted in a week or ten days. Hoes were used to thin the cotton plants and chop the grass from the tops of the rows between the cotton plants, while shallow-scraping, winged plows were used to throw a layer of soil over the grass on the sides of the row, killing the grass that would otherwise steal nutrients from the cotton plants. Cotton fields were cultivated (plowed) three or four times before mid-July, after which the cotton stalks were too large to allow the mule or horse to pull a plow down the middle of the row—the crop was now "laid by" until harvest time.

And while the picking of cotton was laborious and required going over the fields several times as successive bolls opened to reveal their lint, the work—though the temperature was often hot, the dried bolls could cut pickers' hands, and the leaves sometimes stung their skin—was nevertheless not nearly so backbreaking as the frenzied effort to harvest ripe sugar cane before it spoiled. In fact, cotton was not especially labor intensive until harvest; when the first bolls began to ripen, farmers and planters would shift every available hand to picking. Since the cotton did not rot or spoil—rain often forced delays till the staple dried out—and the bolls continued to open for several months, the busy picking season could last three months or more. But the discrepancy between the amount of labor required to plant and cultivate cotton as opposed to the labor to harvest it provided cotton growers more an opportunity than a problem.

Any number of agricultural laborers—a small farmer working beside a son or a large contingent of slaves—could cultivate more cotton than they could pick, which placed an upper limit on the acreage farmers planted in

Slaves are shown picking cotton with an overseer on a horse watching over them. (National Archives)

cotton. Even though every available hand, including those (the wives of small farmers and most house slaves of grand plantations) not normally assigned to field work, was put to the task of picking, the labor force could not be expanded enough to harvest the maximum acreage that could be cultivated. There was no significant standby population of white workers or excess slaves that could be temporarily employed by hard-pressed cotton growers in the peak picking season. (Only in very special situations was it possible for planters to hire additional slaves in picking season, although for particular jobs in the off season—clearing new land in the winter, for example— planters could augment their workforce by hiring on the short term slaves from nearby plantations.) Every cotton grower at whatever the scale of opera- tion understood this picking restraint; it simply was wasted effort and expense to plant and cultivate cotton that could not be harvested. Hence growers planted only the acreage that they could reasonably expect to be able to harvest. The obvious result, since a slaveowner's labor force remained con- stant, was that most cotton plantations had excess labor capacity much of the year.

One canard formerly leveled against the economy of the Old South was that the region so emphasized cotton production that it had to import a sub- stantial portion of its food supply from the Midwest. That interpretation was flawed, and the Cotton South as a whole could maximize its cotton produc- tion without going hungry because of the asymmetrical labor needs of the primary money crop. Practically all farmers and planters had far more land than they cultivated in any given year, and even their amount of improved land was greater than the acreage devoted to cotton. With "surplus" land and "surplus" labor, a food crop that could be planted, cultivated, and harvested around the labor cycle demanded by cotton could be grown for an insignifi- cant additional cost—it was virtually free. Corn was just such a crop. It thrived in the southern climate, could be planted before or after the cotton had to be planted, its cultivation needs were minimal, and it could be harvested before or after cotton or in between the multiple pickings of the cotton. Since growing corn did not interfere with growing cotton, plantation owners could utilize their excess land and labor to make their operation essentially self-sufficient in foodstuffs. Corn was not the sole food crop, for there were substantial acres given over to peas, sweet potatoes, and beans, but corn was essential to the southern economy, not only making plantations more prof- itable but also ensuring that slaves in general obtained an adequate diet. In addition, corn was used to feed, or especially fatten, hogs, the primary source of meat in the South. In 1859, the year of the largest antebellum cotton har- vest in the South, more southern acres were planted in corn than in cotton.

Corn was a more ubiquitous crop than cotton because practically every farmer, from the wealthiest planter to the poorest tenant farmer, planted it as the primary food crop for himself, his family, and his livestock. The small family farm, with no slaves, was far more common in the Old South than the plantation, and most family farms emphasized production for the table before production for the market. This is not to say that family farmers were totally removed from the market, for they showed surprising ingenuity in selling surplus goods and often planted several acres of cotton to make money. But their first concern was keeping food in the mouths of their families and livestock, and sole dependence upon the proceeds from cotton to purchase food was simply too risky. Hence farmers devoted most of their acreage to corn, peas, sweet and white potatoes, peanuts, squash, beans, and occasionally fruit trees. They kept hogs that foraged in the woods for roots and nuts for most of the year; in winter, or just before they were butchered, the hogs would be fed or fattened on corn. Similarly small farmers usually had cattle, which, like the hogs, grazed the unfenced pasturelands and woods for most of the year and were fed corn (or peanuts or cowpeas) only in the dead of winter; and a variety of poultry. Southerners of both races and every economic level also supplemented their diet with game and fish.

Aggregate level data about the number and distribution of slaves and various agricultural products corrects one prevalent misconception about the South—that practically all whites were slave owners and grew only cotton. On the matter of slave ownership the census figures are unambiguous. Only a minority of whites—about one-third in 1830, decreasing to one-quarter in 1860—owned any slaves at all, and most slaveholders possessed too few slaves to be considered plantation owners. Only 12 percent of all slaveholders qualified as planters (owning twenty slaves or more) in 1860, and substantially less than 1 percent, or about 2,300 families out of a total white population of eight million, owned one hundred or more slaves and constituted the planter aristocracy. The mythical owner of a Tara—the plantation in *Gone With the Wind*—was less common in the South of 1860 than a millionaire is today.

Not only did a minority of whites own slaves, but a minority of the slave owners owned the bulk of the bondspeople. In the South the major component of wealth was property in slaves, so, as one would expect, wealth distribution was unequal, but, interestingly enough, not as skewed toward the richest decile as in northern urban areas. The weathiest decile of slaveowners also, and quite understandably, produced a vastly disproportionate amount of the cotton grown in the South. These two facts—that a wealthy planter minority dominated both the slave-owning and cotton-producing statistics—combined with evidence from the census that many nonslaveholding farmers grew little cotton and emphasized food production, have helped popularize the view that there were two Souths existing side by side, or at least within the same general region. This view suggests that the slaveholders, capitalistically involved in the international market for cotton, whose price was set by the demands of Liverpool, had one set of economic principles, whereas the nonslaveholders, only incidentally growing cotton, lived on the whole in regions separate from the areas of large cotton plantations and pursued an old-fashioned, cashless, barter economy communal lifestyle removed from the demands of the marketplace. A variant of this interpretation holds that the planters themselves, enmeshed in paternalistic relationships with their slaves and tied to the soil, were similarly removed from the modern, capitalistic principles of the world market and were not profit maximizers and cold calculators of the main chance. One interpretation points to the prevalence among the papers of planters of copies of Thomas Affleck's printed *Plantation Record and Account Book* to prove the economic rationality and hence capitalistic orientation of planters. However, another interpretation emphasizes that often the model account books were not filled in with the plantations' financial records, which suggests the precapitalistic orientation of the planters.

Such large-scale typological analyses of the South as summarized above in oversimplified form have been quite fruitful in stimulating research on the southern economy and society, but the result of much of this new scholarship has been to lessen the persuasiveness of either of the broad-gauged interpretations of the nature of the South. The problem, plainly stated, is that the South refuses to fit neatly either of the positions; the planters at one moment acted with clear capitalistic resolve and at the next they partook of an older conception of economic and labor arrangements, bartering with neighborhood farmers and engaging in cashless swaps of labor and services. Slaveless farmers far removed from the capitalistic, market tentacles of Liverpool and New York would at the nearest country store sharply bargain surplus corn or beeswax and ginseng gathered in the woods for either cash or goods or drive a herd of hogs to Augusta or Charleston with full awareness of the relationship of the price of cotton to what they could expect to get from their pigs. Perhaps the focus should not be on the metaphorical South as a whole but instead narrowed down to snapshots of the crop choices and market behavior on plantations and farms of different sizes in an attempt to understand, on the most nitty-gritty level, how the agricultural society worked.

This task is frustratingly complex because the South is enormously diverse, and it is nearly impossible to define a typical plantation or farm. Even within a single county there will be differences in soil type, terrain, and accessibility to transportation routes that will make marked differences in the crops grown or, more precisely, the mix of crops grown. Individuals in absolutely similar situations will make different choices, and factors ranging from family size and gender and age mix to the number of slaves available help determine the crop decisions made by heads of household. Allowing for this variety, it is possible in general terms to suggest the interrelatedness of most kinds of agricultural units in the antebellum South and to describe a spectrum of economic behavior ranging from nearly "true" subsistence farming on the one hand to nearly "true" capitalistic production for the world market on the other. Practically every southern farm, whatever its size and crop or range of crops, lay in the broad central portion of that spectrum, blending aspects of self-sufficiency and market awareness.

Not only were such family farmers dependent upon cooperative planters to gin and market their cotton; they also found plantations to be occasional markets for their surplus corn, potatoes, beeves, and hogs. Many farmers, including those with several slaves, had a clear commercial orientation and produced prodigious amounts of corn and raised significant numbers of hogs or cattle specifically to market to plantation regions or to the South's towns and cities. Hog Mountain Road that enters Athens, Georgia, today from the north is a reminder of earlier days when hogs were driven from the lower reaches of the Appalachians to the markets of Augusta and the plantation region beyond. Food production was a major part of a thriving mixed economy in many regions of the South, as we will see later. In special circumstances planters would hire the labor of white farmers for specific chores. Often small farmers would borrow money from wealthier planters, and planters often offered, through their broad contacts with merchants in regional marketing towns, to make special purchases on behalf of neighborhood farmers. A clear economic nexus, born of a cooperative spirit, commonly tied slaveless farmers to the affluent planters in their midst. In addition to race, a community of interests bound slaveholder and slaveless farmers together in the antebellum South.

Some case could be made for corn being the defining crop of the Old South, not only because it was so widely grown but because of its essential role in the preferential diet of southerners. Eaten shelled or on the cob, boiled, fried, or baked, turned into corn liquor or hominy or grits, the basis of corn bread and hoecake, or converted into pork (or, less commonly, into beef), even half burned and ground into an abominable ersatz coffee, corn and corn-fattened pigs were the mainstays of the southern diet. But, despite the culinary dominance of corn, a far better case can be made for cotton as the crop that made the Old South. Cotton was *the* money crop, more than four-fifths of all slaves were involved in its cultivation, it brought great wealth to the region, and it was the supposed dependence of the North and England upon southern-grown cotton that ultimately gave the South the chutzpah to attempt to form a separate nation. But the economic influence of cotton reached beyond those actively involved in its cultivation, and only a few people in the region, white or black, no matter how distantly removed from the fertile cotton fields themselves, were not drawn into the economic orbit of King Cotton. Dependence on cotton and, indirectly, on slavery characterized every region of the South. The sway that cotton held over Dixie was not limited to a narrow minority of wealthy slaveowners or even to those farmers who actually grew cotton

The South consisted of a number of subregional economies, yet in different ways all were brought into the supraregional cotton economy. The hemp crop's relationship to cotton is immediately obvious, but in subtle ways the enormous profits that came from cotton production—its cultivation, its ginning, its further compression into dense bales at the port cities, its purchase on the international market—dominated the local mixed economies. Cotton was not grown in Maryland and hardly at all in Virginia, and it was an insignificant crop in Kentucky, but the Cotton South of the Lower South created a strong demand for the products of the border states, tying their economies to the fortunes of cotton. Kentucky, for example, did not just export hemp products southward. Kentucky's mixed farm economy produced large surplus crops of corn, thousands of bushels of which were transported by wagon to Tennessee and into Alabama and Mississippi, while even more was sent by flatboat and steamboat down the Mississippi River to be sold in river towns and to sugar plantations in Louisiana—such profits could be garnered from sugar cultivation there that it made sense to buy cheaply transported foodstuffs from upriver and to maximize the acreage devoted to cane.

Kentucky, along with Missouri and Tennessee, also utilized its corn harvests to feed cattle, hogs, and especially horses and mules, which were exported to the cotton-growing states. In the last decades of the antebellum era tens of thousands of mules were shipped annually from these three states to the cotton belt, and in the South as a whole in 1860 there were almost one million mules (and over 2 million horses) being used as draft animals. Cotton cultivation drove the demand for horses and mules, and supplying the demand provided a brisk economy in the upper South. Thousands of small farmers, some with slaves, had horse and mule farms, grew thousands of bushels of corn (and oats, barley, and other feed grains) to feed their stock or purchased the feed from still other farmers and participated in a trade network that involved breaking and training the animals and driving them overland to the southern markets. These farmers were not growing cotton and most owned no slaves, but the well-being of the cotton economy was indispensable to their livelihood.

Most cotton plantations raised most of their own food supplies, but in the aggregate they still represented a substantial market for the surplus grains and livestock produced by farmers who were not primarily cotton growers. Again, this was particularly true for the Louisiana sugar plantations and for the rice and sea island cotton plantations along the coast of South Carolina and Georgia. Thriving trade networks involving wagoners bringing corn, hay, potatoes, barley, wheat, various fruits, butter, and honey developed between the coastal staple-crop producers and the small farmers toward the interior who specialized in mixed agriculture. These farmers also grew prodigious numbers of hogs and cattle, even ducks and turkeys, that were driven along established roads or trails to market. Again these animals traveled on foot from their region of provenance to the region of consumption, and they had to be fed along the way. En route there were farmers who specialized in grain production aimed at supplying the needs of the hog drovers who herded hundreds of hogs at a time from regions like the Appalachian counties of western North Carolina to buyers in South Carolina. Such hog farmers and indeed everyone ancillary to the trade and those sending corn or barley or honey to plantation markets understood that it was profits from cotton that provided the demand for their products, and they spoke as knowledgeably and with as much interest of the price of cotton as did the cotton nabobs themselves. In an unusual case, stock growers in Arkansas in the 1850s drove thousands of cattle overland to sell them for high profits in the California gold fields.

The major southern markets for the grain and livestock of the upper South were not the cotton belt plantations but rather the coastal shipping towns in the coastal South sweeping from North Carolina all the way to New Orleans and later Galveston, Texas. The South was, of course, overwhelmingly rural, but this rural, raw-product-producing South depended on port cities to sell its cotton, rice, and sugar either to the North or to a variety of European, South American, and Caribbean nations. The urban populations in Charleston, Savannah, Mobile, and New Orleans, with all the intermediate towns in between, imported their foodstuffs from the southern hinterland. In the immediate vicinity of the towns there were truck farms for fresh vegetables and such perishables as eggs and milk, but the bulk of food—wheat milled into flour, corn, hogs, cattle, even poultry—were imported from regions in the interior where cotton was not the dominant crop. Most of the grain consumed in the southeastern urban areas came from North Carolina, Virginia, and Maryland, while New Orleans distributed grains from Kentucky, Missouri, and Tennessee via the Mississippi River to Gulf Coast towns. Even so, southern markets could not consume all the corn and especially wheat grown in the upper South; consequently more grain from Virginia and Maryland was sent to Midwest urban markets and to eastern metropolises such as Philadelphia and New York than was sent to deep South coastal cities.

A whole congeries of trade networks, credit arrangements, and reciprocal agreements tied together the regions and subregions of the South. While the small farmer simply brought his several bales of cotton to an obliging planter or the local country store, the planter's crop (and usually the cotton aggregated by the country stores) was marketed through a factor, a jack-of-all-trades economic agent. Working from a base in a major cotton-shipping city, the factor kept abreast of the prices that the various staple crops were bringing in the world market and contracted with planters (and store owners) to ship their cotton to the cotton market and there sell it to buyers either in the North or in England. For this essential service the factor charged a brokerage fee of .5 to 2.5 percent and another 2.5 percent or so as a commission. Other fees were charged for hauling, insurance, wharfage, and so on, amounting to perhaps 6 to 9 percent of the value of the cotton.

Factors also acted as buying agents in the port city from wholesalers there or in New York for products desired by the rural planters and storekeepers; on many occasions the planters through their agents bought goods for the small farmers in their midst whose scale of operation did not permit them to have their own purchasing agent. Occasionally such planters virtually served as storekeepers for local farmers, and indeed some such planter–merchants emerged after the Civil War as full-time store operators who extended credit to the neighboring farmers and sharecroppers. Factors also secured loans for their planters, and often they were themselves the source of credit via drafts through secured by the planters' future crop. There were factors who abused their knowledge of the cotton market and others who cheated the cotton growers, but on the whole factors served an important economic function, connecting rural agricultural producers with the world market both to sell their crops and to purchase goods unavailable in the local economy.

To the extent that the larger planters sold their cotton through factors based in port cities and purchased most of their goods through their factors from merchants located in the major cities, the system worked against local country stores and market towns in the interior. But the country stores served a vital function for the small farmers, who after all far outnumbered the wealthy cotton planters. Country stores stocked a wide range of goods that could not or only with great difficulty could be produced locally: all kinds of dry goods, laces, gloves, hats; boots and shoes; glassware, tools, nails, cutlery; lead, lamp oil, medicines; coffee, spices, sugar, and tea; even toys, firecrackers, and books. Country stores often contained the post office, had newspapers for customers to read, were a center of political discussion, and often had attached facilities for ginning cotton or milling corn. The store goods were sold for cash or exchanged for "country produce," which the storekeeper then sold to other farmers who were short of food or sent the produce to sell in towns or cities further removed.

Small farmers, those without slaves or only a few, whose cotton output would never have justified a gin of their own, often brought their wagonloads of cotton to the local store and there sold it for cash or exchanged it for store goods. The storekeeper, if he had a gin, would gin the cotton or, if not, sell it in bulk to factors who marketed the cotton exactly as they would that handled for large planters. While planters would buy most of their goods through their factors, they often had occasion to purchase immediate needs from the local country store. And while the planters' credit was supplied by their factors, usually the storeowners offered credit to the smaller producers, arranging the credit in such fashion as to tie the farmers' future crops and needs to the store.

Two sorts of markets existed in the antebellum South. Cotton (and to a lesser extent, tobacco and some grains) was ultimately intended for the international market, where prices were set by the world demand and communicated by such means as the *New Orleans Price-Current*, a business newspaper scanned eagerly by the cotton factors. There existed an equally vital local market, dominated by the country stores, whereby small farmers exchanged their surplus products either for cash or goods. Prices or exchange rates were worked out in face-to-face bargaining, goods were exchanged for services and vice versa, and the storekeeper often did either the initial processing of the agricultural product or found buyers or processors elsewhere and essentially linked the small local market to a larger regional or even international market. A country storekeeper bartering goods for hogs, then sending the hogs to Charleston where the price they fetched was related to the price of cotton, served as the medium through which the world market, many times removed, affected the lives and standard of living even of farmers in the backcountry, growing only foodstuffs, who had little consciousness of the market economy.

Many economic transactions were entirely between individuals, with no store, no factor, no external institutions or agents involved at all. One individual would sell or trade surplus corn, or pigs, or butter, or any of a hundred items to another for money, another product, or the promise of future labor or services. Many transactions that resulted in the exchange of services or skills were carried out in the cooperative spirit of community neighborliness, with the assumption of mutual benefit and reciprocity. Barn-raisings, log-rollings, and corn-huskings were only the most obvious examples of occasions in which real labor was exchanged without immediate recompense, but on many occasions farmers across the economic spectrum shared labor and skills—perhaps at hog butchering time, or to build a fireplace. Similarly a farmer's wife might help another at canning time, or with spring housecleaning, or with sewing, quilting, or washing. Economic life consisted largely of hundreds of such exchanges of labor and services for money or goods.

Planters—and much more so the smaller farmers practicing mixed agriculture—were betwixt and between modern capitalism and older agrarian attitudes that emphasized barter, cashless exchanges of services, and a spirit of communal cooperation marked by face-to-face relationships. For that reason different interpreters have called the South capitalistic or precapitalistic, but in truth it betook characteristics of both and had throughout its history since the development of commercial agriculture. Certainly planters were acquisitive, stayed abreast as best they could of the price of cotton, concerned themselves with the price of land and of slaves, and sought within limits to maximize their income. Countless commentators—travellers, journalists, humorists, preachers, to name but a few—have remarked on the planters' concern with making money, have complained about their aggressive speculation in land

Engraved design on a Confederate fifty dollar bill, exemplifying how the economy was based on agriculture.

and slaves, and have described their preoccupation with getting ahead. Yet few planters seem to have sought economic success solely for profits alone; harking back to earlier values, they talked of land and slaves as giving them independence—echoes of the Revolutionary-era republicanism that suggested that dependence on others was the absence of real freedom and the essence of slavery. They talked of land as guaranteeing the future independence of their children, of giving them a stake in life.

These same planters would participate in community activities of shared labor that bespoke an attachment to an old ethos of mutuality and interdependence. When small farmers or tenants ran short of food—often because they did not own or work enough land to grow sufficient food, especially in a poor season—planters would provide relief for bartered services or even, in a spirit of *noblesse oblige,* expect no remuneration. And farmers engaged in a mixed agricultural economy, supplementing their crops with honey or ginseng or animal pelts traded at the country store, and bargaining a day's labor for store goods or other services, were ingeniously taking advantage of their surpluses and skills to hold on to their few acres or acquire the extra money to purchase land of their own. They, too, equated land with independence, and they sought not wealth for the sake of wealth but instead to achieve a competency—a comfortable existence, not beholden to anyone.

SOUTHERN WHITE SOCIETY

Planters and plain folks were tied together by this web of common and community interests. The multiplicity of goods and services exchanged on the various local markets again and again established a real economic nexus between all actors at whatever scale in the economy. In the local community where most interactions took place, kinship also tied people of every economic level together. Planters had kin who were small slaveholders, nonslaveholding farmers, probably tenants (often unmarried sons who had not yet gained their inheritance), even hired laborers. And, conversely, poor farmers had relatives who were slave owners. Often young men would own no slaves, but as they lived longer and accumulated property, they could realistically anticipate joining the slaveholding minority. Moreover, the fact that nearly all farmers and planters grew corn and most grew at least some cotton created a commonality of interests.

Localism was another powerful force in the antebellum South, and for many people their entire lives were lived out within a very circumscribed geographical area. One married within the neighborhood, attended a local church and democratically mingled with all the members, met as equals at the voting booth, and had a first-name acquaintance with everyone in the community. Local politics was a dance between deference and egalitarianism; nonslaveholding farmers treasured their independence (grounded in their land ownership) and expected to be treated in such a way as to respect their dignity even as they tended to esteem the skills and business acumen of their economic betters and acknowledge that esteem in political deference. Much of antebellum politics involved winning the support of influential local leaders in the expectation that their prestige would sway the support of the common voters in their community. Voting was often determined by intensely local factors, and kinship, community ties, and church affiliation shaped politics more than knowledge of national issues did.

Like gravity, racism was a force always present in southern white society even when most actors were unaware of its pull. It is unnecessary to posit racism as the sole or primary flux welding lower-class, slaveless whites together with the wealthy, slaveholding minority to form a solid South on the matter of protecting slavery in the secession crisis. A commonality of economic interests, ties of kinship, a strong sense of localism, and a politics of deference are just some of the features of antebellum southern society that created a strong degree of white solidarity. But racism did serve as another agent that bound whites together. Since the late seventeenth century, political rhetoric and statutory law had made clear that all whites, even the meanest, were legally superior to all blacks, and that sentiment had developed a logic of its own, shaping behavior in a multitude of ways that erected a wall of racist assumptions between whites and blacks. An educated, genteel planter and his wife might have nothing but private disgust for a propertyless or disreputable white in their neighborhood and have real affection for some of their slaves, but they would be careful in their public behavior to do nothing that might suggest a criticism of the racial line that divided society. Whites who owned no slaves usually wished they did and anticipated doing so, and they certainly supported slavery as a means of controlling the blacks in the South. Slavery as an institution existed in every part of the South, even in the decidedly nonplantation areas, and racism did serve, at the subconscious level, to put all whites together in a common category separate from all blacks. But for everyday purposes it was not racism but a wide-ranging community of interests that created southern white culture.

Southern whites may have shared a commitment to the cotton economy and have ultimately found a sense of brotherhood and sisterhood grounded in a racist distinction from blacks, but that is not to say all whites shared the same lifestyle or that there were no class-like economic distinctions within the antebellum South. An outside observer, unaware of how the interests of a mule farmer in Kentucky were related to the prosperity of a black belt cotton farmer in Mississippi, might even have erroneously assumed that the gradations between whites denoted a greater difference than that which separated propertyless whites from slaves. When everything else failed, the presence of black slaves united whites into a self-defined ruling race, but there were ranks among the rulers. According to the stereotyped view familiar to movie fans and readers of pulp fiction, all whites were either planters and mistresses living in white-columned mansions surrounded by fields white with cotton that stretched from the magnolia-shaded verandah to the river banks, or, conversely, were desperately poor, lazy trash who preferred moonshining to farming and dwelled in an antebellum version of Dogpatch. It has proved almost impossible to root out these misconceptions from the popular imagination.

The South was so varied in 1830 or 1860 that it is difficult to capture its essence through descriptive vignettes of "typical" white persons without the necessary number of descriptions multiplying into dozens. Tobacco plantations and small farms still were dominant in Virginia and Maryland, although wheat was now a major crop and Richmond and Baltimore were among the nation's leading flour-milling centers, with growing markets for their exports in the West Indies. The ease with which wheat harvesting was mechanized— Cyrus McCormick invented his reaper in Virginia in 1834—lessened the dependence on slaves and the resulting excess in their numbers led to large-scale slave exports to the booming cotton southwest. The growing urban areas in Maryland and Virginia, including Norfolk, Washington, DC, and Petersburg, supported substantial truck-farming operations, and increasing numbers of slaves either worked on such farms or were employed in non-agricultural jobs in the cities. Maryland had moved so beyond the older slave-based tobacco economy that in 1860 almost half (49.1 percent) of the blacks in the state were free.

Along coastal South Carolina and Georgia and on the Sea Islands rice and sea island cotton continued to bring profits, and this region, with its extremely high black-to-white ratio, was the most plantation-dominant region of the entire South and perhaps the most atypical. Planters and farmers grew hemp in parts of the upper South, and along the lower Mississippi River (and the Brazos River in Texas after it became a state in 1845) there were capital-intensive sugar plantations. The interior South, especially the more isolated areas, were mixed farming and livestock growing regions. But the heart of the Old South was the broad swath of cotton-growing counties stretching from central and western Georgia and upcountry South Carolina across central Alabama and Mississippi, spreading out along the Mississippi River delta and sweeping through central and northern Louisiana into eastern Texas and southeastern Arkansas. Quite obviously the work routines, crop mixes, average farm size, and profit levels differed according to the dominant crop in the region.

Yet the diversity continued from the state down to the county level, and this point bears repeating. Even within a given county differences in soil type, terrain, and access to rivers or roads determined what crops if any were grown and at what scale. A state like South Carolina would have a coastal region with extremely large rice plantations; a region beyond the tidewater reaching into the Piedmont with cotton plantations of hundreds of acres intermixed with much smaller cotton farms, nonslaveholder farms, and significant production of food crops; and in the far northwest farms in the foothills of the Appalachians growing no cotton but rather a rich mixture of corn, barley, oats, and hay. With the exception of some communities in the most isolated mountain valleys that were settled at the very end of the antebellum period, slaves were to be found everywhere, though in greatly varying numbers. Not only were slaves employed everywhere, even in the Appalachian highlands of the southern states, but small farmers, including nonslaveholders, were also found everywhere, even in the regions where the largest rice or cotton plantations were concentrated. Nonslaveholders and slaveholders, and slaves and family farmers coexisted throughout the South. In the wealthiest plantation belts, tiny farms were located in the interstices between larger agricultural units; nowhere did rich planters completely push family farmers away from the best land.

There really was no "typical" southern region, but in a general sense—outside the narrow bands of rice cultivation and sugar cultivation in South Carolina, Georgia, and Louisiana—about one-third of the whites were members of slaveholding families. In the richest section of the cotton belt in Alabama and Mississippi, perhaps three-fourths were slaveholders. South-wide in 1860 one-quarter of whites owned slaves. Most slaveholders owned fewer than six slaves, and if we accept the ownership of twenty slaves as the lower size limit of a plantation, throughout the entire South in 1860 there were but 46,264 plantations—out of a white population of slightly more than eight million. This meant that, outside of the richest plantation belts, roughly

10 percent of the white families were planters, although the minority of larger slaveholders held more actual slaves than did the majority of smaller slaveholders. Of the 70 percent or so of nonslaveholding whites, the great majority owned their own land, though their acreage was far less than that of slaveholders. (Because there were few agricultural laborers to be hired, the purchase of slaves was generally the only way to enlarge the number of acres in a farm beyond what family members could work. With slaves, the only practical limit on acres under cultivation was the number of slaves one could buy, and as a result the average-sized agricultural unit was larger in the South than in the North.)

In most regions of the South approximately 10 to 15 percent of adult white males did not own land. Some were farm laborers, usually young unmarried males working for more prosperous farmers; often these young men had not yet inherited their share of their parents' land, and when they did, or as they through hard work gradually were able to buy a few acres, they entered the landowning population, married, and began to raise a family. Occasionally landless white men were plantation overseers working in the employ of a planter; overseers could with some optimism look forward to par-laying their agricultural skills and wages into a farm of their own some day. Still other landless farmers, perhaps as many as 10 percent of the population in some areas, were tenant farmers, renting land for which they paid a share of the crop. Like the unmarried farm laborers, the tenant farmers (who often had families) were occasionally related to the owner of the land they rented, and they could expect, with good health and some luck, to be able eventually to buy a farm for themselves, perhaps further into the interior or further west. Land ownership and slave ownership was positively related to age; success followed years of hard work, good judgment, and the smile of dame fortune, or, a southerner would have been more likely to say, divine providence. Those who did not own slaves or land could entertain prospects of eventually doing so, and many who had moved up the ladder of success could remember their lean days and had friends and relatives who still only hoped to join the property-holding class.

If one can imagine a local antebellum southern community, there would be constant interrelationships between whites of every economic level and relationships between the whites and slaves. In mountain neighborhoods fewer owned slaves—perhaps 10 percent of the heads of household—and the average-sized holding was smaller. But slaves would be employed there in every aspect of the local economy: farming, livestock raising, mining. Kinship, innumerable exchanges of goods and services, membership in the same churches, and common interest in the prospects for cotton minimized the potential for class conflict, especially when there was a common resolve that slavery was an appropriate way both to gain wealth and to control the "real" underclass. Only during the strains and dislocations of the Civil War were there revealed the potential fault lines of social division that had always laid beneath the calm surface of the white community, rending the civil compact. Before the wartime stress precipitated social division, southern society had exhibited the paradox of great inequalities in wealth but with an egalitarian ethos that bound most whites together into a republican brotherhood that treasured land ownership, exalted the idea of individual independence, and claimed a common stake in the "southern way"—at this time a euphemism for the institution of slavery.

Some wealthy Virginians or South Carolinians, often the younger sons of great planters, migrated westward to carve new plantations out of the Southwest. The normal process was for the man, with a handful of slaves, to come out early, build a temporary house and slave quarters, and plant an initial crop of cotton and corn. After harvest the young planter would return to the seaboard, gather up his wife (who often went grudgingly) and children, take his portion of his parents' slaves, and in a wagon caravan of black and white families, all their household belongings, cattle, hogs, and horses, journey west to the new homesite. Such migrations produced instant cotton plantations, with an unmistakable scent of seaboard aristocracy and often an almost tangible condescension toward the roughness of frontier society and manners. Only this tiny minority of planter aristocrats, mainly in the Tidewater and lowcountry of the seaboard South, and their scions widely scattered across the cotton-growing South, had homes of real grandeur, dressed in the finest clothes from London and Paris, had libraries stocked with everything from the classics to agricultural tracts to Sir Walter Scott, and maintained the facade of aristocracy in the midst of a democratic society. The antebellum mansions visited by tourists today were extraordinarily atypical.

Once settled in Alabama or Mississippi, these transplanted "Virginians," who frequently lived up to the aristocratic image that appellation carried in the Southwest, were forced to have numerous interactions with the mixed society that constituted their community. Thomas Dabney, who had migrated to Mississippi from Virginia in 1835, conducted himself there, like the proverbial Englishman having his afternoon tea in the heart of the jungle, exactly as a transplanted country gentleman. But when he went to help a small farmer whose cotton had "gotten in the grass" and gloved, sitting astride his horse, directed the labor of his twenty slaves, Dabney discovered that the farmer was, rather than thankful for the assistance, insulted by Dabney's aristocratic mien. As Dabney's daughter later described the event:

> The man said that if Colonel Dabney had taken hold of a plough and worked by his side he would have been glad to have his help, but to see him sitting up on his horse with his gloves on directing his Negroes how to work was not to his taste. [Dabney] heard a long time after these occurrences that he could have soothed their wounded pride if he had asked them to come over to help him to

raise his cabins. But he could not bring himself to call on two or three poor white men to work among his servants when he had no need of help.

There were few such unacculturated aristocrats as Thomas Dabney in the cotton-growing South.

Throughout the antebellum period the South that lay to the west of Georgia had a fluid, mobile social structure, and many slaveless pioneers cleared a patch of land, used the logs to construct a rude log cabin, grew enough corn to feed their family and livestock, and made quick profits from cotton planted in fabulously fertile virgin soil. With those profits they invested in more land, bought a slave or two, and the next year doubled their cotton harvest. In a rapid upward spiral of purchasing land and slaves, and by staying healthy, some pioneers within a decade or two moved up the economic ladder, even becoming planters by the time they reached middle age. By now the original log cabin had been enlarged with perhaps a shed added on the back, then another cabin connected to the first with an open porch or breezeway in between—a dogrun house—and eventually, as the cotton prosperity continued, the roofs were raised, second floors added, a porch supported by columns was extended across the front of the house, and finally the logs were covered with plank siding. Presto! Posterity points backward to an ancestry of planter aristocracy. But history adds that the line dividing slaveless pioneer from small slave-owning farmer from proud planter was thin indeed, and fundamental values changed little.

The poor white southern farmer has not fared well in the popular mind. Since the days in the eighteenth century when William Byrd and Charles Woodmason described them as prone to fighting and drinking, having no ambition, and living in dirty, cramped cabins with large broods of ill-mannered children, they have variously been described as sneaky, lawless, immoral, snuff-dipping, and incurably lazy. Such views persist today, with the farmers portrayed as a species of wild, boorish, loud-mouthed, lazy Celt, quick to fight, a kind of living fossil from the windswept highlands of the northern and western fringes of Britain. Actually, circumstances, not genetics, molded the plain folk of the Old South.

Southern white farmers shared much in terms of basic values and outlook with the middling farmers of Pennsylvania or Illinois. Yeomen farmers in the South worked reasonably hard, they varied their crops according to the terrain and soil, they were adept at many skills—could tend cattle and split rails, gather beeswax and hunt animal pelts, butcher a hog and raise a little cotton. They gardened some; the women quilted, made butter and soap, sewed and spun, quieted babies and fed their families; and men and women alike gossiped and discussed local politics and went to Sunday meeting when a church was near. They grew much of what they needed, traded for what they could not grow, augmented their tables with wild game and fish, hoped to get ahead and buy more land, and occasionally saw their way clear to purchase a slave.

In their willingness to hold bondspeople they were somewhat unlike Midwestern farmers, but that was more a matter of location than fundamental cultural difference. Contemporary travelers from the North often mistook the absence of sturdy barns and solid fences for poverty and laziness, not understanding that the southern climate did not demand winter shelter for animals who, in any case, were grazing unfenced in the bountiful southern woodlands and canebrakes. Southern cattle were, it is true, smaller than their northern counterparts, but that was because the mild winters did not kill the tick that spread a debilitating infection to the livestock—a microorganism, not ignorant herdsmen, was responsible for the scrawny size of southern cows.

Not every pioneer prospered. Mobility went both ways, and in any ten-year period demarked by the federal census, about 40 percent of the inhabitants in a given county moved away. Those who stayed, the persisters, tended to be those who were moving up the economic scale as they grew older. Some of those who left eventually found prosperity in their new location, perhaps the next state west. As genealogists have found over and over again, many of their ancestors were born in Georgia or South Carolina, had one or more children born in Alabama, others in Mississippi, and were ultimately buried in Louisiana or Texas. Some whites never made it into the landowning class and spent their entire (often relatively brief) lives as hired farm laborers, unskilled workers in a southern city, or tenant farmers scrambling to make ends meet after paying off their landlord in agricultural produce. But the great majority of whites who survived into middle age ended their lives as at least small landowners. Of course there were some who suffered downward mobility. A bad crop year, sickness, a fire, failed judgment, alcoholism, poor loans, overextended credit, any number of situations could cause small landowners, even owners of a slave or two, to lose their land and have to sell their slaves. Larger landowners could sell off some acreage or, if they held substantial numbers of slaves, could sell several to stave off bankruptcy, but the marginal farmers and small owners often had no other recourse when times were bad but to give up their property and try to start over again, perhaps beginning as a tenant farmer or moving west to "squat" on unclaimed land. Everyone in the Old South knew, perhaps were even kin to, people who had moved up the ladder of success and those who had slipped several rungs. Mobility in either direction usually strengthened the commitment to cotton—and secondarily to slavery—as the avenue to greater success or at least a comfortable independence in old age.

PLANTATION SLAVERY IN THE OLD SOUTH

Many people seem to believe slavery was invented in the American South, either to cultivate the tobacco that legend tells us was planted even in the streets of Jamestown or to plant and pick the cotton after Eli Whitney's gin made it profitable. Slavery of course has a history far antedating Jamestown—the Bible, for example, is replete with references to slavery—and it has been employed in most societies all over the world. Slavery has been an attractive source of labor when war has incidentally provided captives from another nation or ethnic group—rather than kill them, it was reasoned, put them to work. In most societies, those enslaved represented a race or tribe or nationality different from the masters, although in several societies—ancient Greece, for example—no stigma of racial inferiority was attached to slavery per se; it was simply a category of unfree existence. Slaves were often quite skilled and respected, and the slave labor force included people from a wide variety of national or racial backgrounds. The harshness of slavery varied greatly, from relatively humane Greece to the barbarous salt pits of medieval Arabia.

Slavery in the American South was not the result of war captives being put to work instead of to death (although some Indians had been so enslaved in the seventeenth and early eighteenth centuries). Rather, the need for a cheap and stable, though portable, labor force drove the demand for slaves once the available supply of white indentured servants began to dwindle in the late seventeenth century. After settlement had pushed beyond the narrow confines of the Tidewater, the increasing availability of inexpensive farm land made it impossible to employ a permanent class of landless, white farm laborers; they could too easily move west, squat on unclaimed land, and aspire to upward mobility. The relative ease of land ownership put upward pressure on wages for day laborers and made their presence at harvest time uncertain. Planters of tobacco, rice, and indigo wanted a cheap, stable source of laborers under their firm control, laborers who would remain in place until the planter decided to move his operations or divide his work force among several farms. As explained earlier, black slaves "solved" the primary labor needs of white agriculturalists, and the abundant demand for their crops provided the wherewithal to buy Africans. The disruptions of the Revolutionary Era momentarily stalled the expansion of the slave-based agricultural system, but the spread of cotton cultivation after 1793, combined with the opening up of millions of acres of fertile soil in Alabama, Mississippi, and Louisiana, ensured the maturation of the slave economy across the deep South. Cotton allowed slavery to spread far beyond the limited confines of the tidewater and sea islands and enter into and affect every region of the South, including the mountain highlands, and in every area slaves were put to profitable use. Economics, not war, drove the expansion of slavery.

During the years when substantial numbers of slaves were being directly imported into the South from Africa, the initial act of enslavement in Africa may have been related to war, although by 1700 the Caribbean and South American demand for slaves, combined with the continuing Arabian demand, had helped to transform the indigenous African slaving networks into brutal wholesale markets for bondspeople, with wars conducted for the sole purpose of acquiring slaves. But by the end of the first quarter of the eighteenth century more slaves were being born in the South than were being imported from Africa. Even as African imports peaked in the mid-eighteenth century, the slave population was becoming increasingly Americanized in terms of nativity. For a combination of reasons, white planters learned that it made sense to allow their slaves to live in family groupings of their own making, with slave population growth a predictable result. Such slave management was prudent economically and morally, the slaves were more content and less troublesome, and home-grown slaves seemed far less strange and threatening to the whites who were often nearly surrounded by a sea of black faces. Even before the 1808 congressional ban on additional imports of Africans, the southern slave population had become predominantly American-born, and this tendency increased every year thereafter.

The character and tone of race relations varied with the demographic makeup of the population. In the mid-1600s, when there had been very few slaves and they lived and worked amid a labor force of white indentured servants, relationships between white and black workers had been comparatively harmonious. Then, after 1700, as the relative number of slaves in the workforce suddenly grew astronomically, with a significant upsurge in the absolute number of slaves imported directly from Africa who seemed especially alien to the whites, race relations grew markedly more harsh. Legal black codes to control the behavior of slaves proliferated, slave revolts (like that along the Stono River in South Carolina in 1739) and rumors of revolt led to ever more severe restrictions on black autonomy, and frightened whites sought through exaggerated demonstrations of their power to overawe the slaves into cowed subservience. Eighteenth-century South Carolina represented the nadir of race relations within the institution of American slavery.

Despite the oppressive nature of white–black interactions during this century of great change, social and cultural developments were underway that would result in a significant amelioration of the physical treatment of slaves by the early decades of the nineteenth century. One factor was simply that the white population grew accustomed to having blacks around them; the black presence came to be seen as normal, not threatening, and years of mutual interchange produced a series of tension-reducing mechanisms and social behaviors—owners learned a "habit" of command and slaves an etiquette of deference—that smoothed interpersonal relationships. In truth, an increasing majority of slaves were American-born, English-speaking, acculturated workers who understood (even if they did not accept) what was expected of them and through a complicated social calculus managed to render to their master what he deemed his due while at the same time they held back a portion of their psyche in order to maintain a sense of their own identity and self-worth. Accordingly, white planters learned what they could reasonably expect from their slaves and generally did not push beyond mutually accepted definitions of proper service because to do so was to risk activating an entire range of slave behavior stretching from feigned illness or minor sabotage and work slowdowns to running away and violence.

Basic attitudes toward slaves as persons also shifted in the last quarter of the eighteenth century. Most slave owners who became familiar with the natural rights philosophy of the Revolutionary Era did not extend its benefits so far as to free their bondspeople, but a residual effect of discussion about the rights of mankind was a growing tendency to perceive blacks more as people than as beasts of burden. The simultaneous growth in the evangelical movement, with its emphasis on all peoples' having souls and being precious in the sight of God, also had a tendency to change how whites perceived the blacks in their midst. The evangelical denominations that grew to dominate the South in the nineteenth century welcomed slave members, and slaves often made up a substantial portion of rural church membership. Whites saw slaves attending church, singing hymns, being tearfully affected by sermons—with the result not that racism ceased but was subtly transformed.

Blacks came increasingly to be seen as childlike, as existing in an environmentally arrested stage of development. As such they were deemed appropriate for bondage, for control by a "superior" race, and for being described as permanent children rather than as recalcitrant savages. Whites spoke of their slaves' "childlike faith" or "childlike simplicity" or "childlike irresponsibility," never consciously realizing that their conceptual infantilizing of their slaves was one way of mediating white guilt about enslaving persons with souls and, at least arguably, some claim on a natural right to freedom. If one convinced oneself that slaves were a race of permanent children, then one could rationalize depriving them of adult freedom. Most slave owners never worried about the morality of slavery in principle—they might have objected to outrageous examples of mistreatment or perhaps the separation of infants from their mothers—and simply accepted the presence and utility of slaves as societal givens. When their consciences were touched in particular circumstances or they encountered an explicit criticism of slavery as an institution, then the metaphor of slaves as children served as a kind of societal expiation. Churchgoers often defended slavery as the process by which God conspired to bring the Gospel to his black children.

This species of racist thinking could be debilitating to blacks, especially to the extent that some slaves came to accept at least the essentials of the white view, but it also helped domesticate American slavery. Slaves perceived as children rather than savage beasts were treated with less physical harshness, interpersonal relations were filled with less suspicion, and a certain looseness in control was accepted in the mid-nineteenth century that would have been unthinkable a century earlier. Children after all are human, and real human affections sometimes bound whites to individual blacks, and vice versa. Slavery in the nineteenth-century South differed from that in ancient times because almost all the southern slaves were of black ancestry, and blackness was associated with inferiority. Only thus could the white support of slavery for blacks be unhypocritically harmonized with support of democracy for whites only.

While it is true that not all southern slaves toiled on plantations—thousands of slaves lived and worked in cities—the great majority were agricultural workers, approximately nine out of ten. The circumstances of slaves' lives were as varied as those of whites, with some slaves being the sole bondsperson on small farms and still others being part of a veritable village of several hundred slaves. The distribution of bondspeople across the southern landscape varied greatly, and although most slave owners owned only a handful of slaves, most slaves lived on plantations of more than twenty slaves. This apparent paradox requires explanation. Of the 385,000 heads of household who owned slaves in 1860, almost 49 percent possessed fewer than five slaves, and only 12 percent of all slaveholders qualified as planters—that is, held twenty or more slaves. Substantially less than 1 percent, or about 2,300 families, owned one hundred or more slaves and constituted the planter aristocracy—out of a white population of eight million. During the last antebellum decades slave ownership became more concentrated in the hands of a smaller percentage of whites. The percentage of all southern families who owned slaves fell from thirty-six in 1830 to thirty-one in 1850 and to twenty-five in 1860, and the size of slaveholding was increasing. Those who owned fewer than five slaves decreased from 50.2 percent of all slaveholders in 1850 to 48.5 percent in 1860, and those owning more than twenty increased from 10 to 12 percent. Yet the 12 percent of the farming units employing twenty or more slaves in 1860 represented over half the total number of slaves—one plantation of fifty or eighty slaves would have more bondspeople than a dozen small farms with one or two or four slaves each. Hence while the typical slaveowner was a farmer with only several slaves, the typical slave—62 percent of those in the deep South in 1860—lived on a plantation.

What difference did it make to a slave man or woman what size farm or plantation he or she lived on? At one time it was thought that conditions were much harsher on large plantations in Mississippi or Alabama than on small farms in the upper South, but such a characterization may have been more the result of the admonitory threat of slaveowners to sell their slaves to a different region if they misbehaved than of reality—and the slaves so cautioned probably dreaded the separation from loved ones more than the implied worsening of their living and working conditions. In many ways slaves, given such a Hobson's choice, might have preferred bondage on a large plantation. At least there one would find in the slave quarters some semblance of a slave community at the end of the workday. The presence of numbers of fellow slaves would allow the nurturing of a separate black culture, especially in the evenings when the blacks cooked and ate their dinners; cared for their children; talked, sang, and entertained each other; courted and worshiped and practised folk crafts away from the meddling eye of their owner or overseer. In a sense there was safety in numbers, an ability to be oneself without constantly being on guard against a comment or gesture that could be perceived as disrespectful or threatening by whites. Companionship and marriage was easier on large plantations, and the wealth of such a master could provide a cushion against bad crop years that might force a smaller, less solvent, slave owner to sell some of his slaves and thereby disrupt families.

On half of all slaveholding units the number of blacks was four or fewer, and the slaves lived almost in the constant presence of whites. Often, if there was only one slave and 20 percent of all owners held just one bondsperson—she would be a domestic worker who did or helped with the cooking and washing and perhaps worked in the garden or dairy. Such a slave would probably live in the slave owner's cabin, either in a lean-to or in the attic, and would spend most of the day and evening in direct communication with her owner. If the slave were male, he would work in the fields side by side with the owner. It is true that such close interactions often partially broke down racial stereotypes and led to friendship within the constraints allowed by the extant racial etiquette, but just as often such familiarity could lead to contempt, though the slave had to conceal his or her sentiment. Work routines tended to be more varied and hence possibly more interesting on small farms than on large plantations, where work was often specialized, and the slaves turned their hand to whatever tasks needed to be done throughout the year. The variety of jobs on farms may have in part made up for the closer white surveillance that was possible, but surely the absence of a group of fellow blacks with whom one could nightly converse and confide with a sense of ease and safety must have been a lonely existence. The personalities and character of everyone involved—white as well as black—made an immense difference in such intimate arenas, and mutual respect, even something approaching love, was present on rare occasions, even as, on equally rare occasions, there was absolutely brutal and pathological treatment of slaves. Usually behavior lay near the midpoint of that spectrum, with a blend of humanity, self-interest, and socially prescribed decorum moderating the worst abuses of slave ownership. Yet even under the best owners slaves were legally defined as property, could be sold to settle estates, and had practically no civil rights recognized by the courts; their marriages were not valid in law, and they suffered under an all-enveloping canopy of racist thought.

On larger farms and small plantations slaves were generally able to carve out a greater degree of autonomy if for no other reason than numbers provided the camouflage of anonymity. The majority of slaves living in plantation groupings lived, usually in family units, in log cabins of one room, perhaps sixteen feet square—the same-sized cabins white pioneers and slaveless farmers lived in. It wasn't square footage of dwelling space but the absence of freedom that really set slaves apart. These cabins were sometimes haphazardly grouped near the barns and other dependencies, but more often they were constructed in two parallel lines, forming a kind of village street. Stretching out from the back or to the side of the cabins would be fences made of interwoven sticks that penned several pigs or chickens, with other fences surrounding a small garden planted in collards, peas, gourds, corn, yams, squash, and other delectables. Perhaps there would be a community outhouse, though just as likely the bondspeople simply had to go in the woods. On nearly every plantation slave women cooked for their own families in their own fireplaces. Occasionally planters with an acute concern for efficiency would propose a central kitchen, but most slave women, tired as they were at night, preferred cooking and caring for their own loved ones in their own cabins, and around those simple hearths much of African American culture was both created and preserved.

Work routines for slaves varied according to gender, crop, season, size of plantation, and master. On farms and very small plantations most black women were heavily engaged in domestic chores throughout the year and shifted to field work during the months of heaviest need—planting, then hoeing and chopping, and finally picking. Only the atypical giant plantations had a permanent corps of house servants; most women worked in the fields when needed but in off season or on days when it was too wet or too cold for outside chores they spun thread, wove cloth at the loom, canned vegetables or fruit, washed and mended for the white family and for their own family, and there was always the dairy to be attended to—butter to churn, cheese to make—and eggs to gather. Slave women were also usually parents, and in their limited free time after feeding and clothing their children they taught them survival skills, not just how to cook or sew but how to practise the skills of dissimulation and deference necessary to survive psychologically as a chattel slave.

For cultural reasons reaching far back in time male slaves had fewer parenting responsibilities; in fact, slave fathers and husbands occasionally lived not with the mother or wife but on an adjoining farm or plantation, and the masters recognized midweek and weekend visiting rights. This practice was a reflection both of a common African heritage whereby women and children lived in minivillages separate from where the men lived and a practical accommodation to the southern situation; often slave owners did not possess enough slaves for them to find spouses at home, and even if they had, love knows no such artificial boundaries as property lines. Moreover, slave men and women may have preferred a separation of work places because it was particularly emasculating to the slave men to have to acquiesce to other (white) men controlling and disciplining their wives and children. But despite this custom of slave women and children living "abroad" from the father, most slaves lived in family units. Especially if one remembers that in Africa the men often lived apart from the family, then the majority of slave children would have spent at least their early years in a family grouping that they would have considered normal.

On farms and small plantations male slaves worked at a variety of jobs; besides the tasks associated with crop cultivation, there were hogs and cattle to tend, fences and barns to mend, new fields to clear, and firewood to cut and split. On larger plantations some labor specialization arose, with certain men designated as livestock handlers or wagon drivers or plowmen, although slave women sometimes plowed too. Even such crafts as blacksmithing, coopering, and carpentry were assigned to skilled slaves on the very largest plantations. Most slaves, though, were jacks-of-all-trade who could be expected to do nearly every imaginable farm chore. The length of the work day varied according to the season and the press of the need: on short winter days the hours of light limited work to nine or ten hours even on farms with the hardest driving owners, while in late spring, when after a spell of rain the grass threatened to take over the crop, slaves might for several days be in the fields for twelve or fourteen hours. Cold, inclement weather would keep most slaves indoors—except, of course, to milk the cows, feed the livestock, and carry in firewood—and rainfall even in the heart of the crop season could prevent slaves from plowing, chopping, or harvesting. It had long become accepted that, except in agricultural emergencies, slaves would have Saturday afternoon and Sundays off, either for leisure activities or to work their own garden plots and do their laundry, hunting, and fishing. These working hours seem horrendous to us today, accustomed as we are to 8-hour days, but they were unexceptional either to free white farmers in the South and the North or to early industrial workers. People expected to be physically tired at the end of day, and most went to bed shortly after it became dark. Unlike free workers, however, slaves did not have the option of deciding when or how long to work, nor did they have the freedom to strike out west for a new life when they tired of their present situation. The absence of freedom, not habitual overwork, was the deepest tragedy of slavery.

Since slaves only very indirectly worked for themselves, owners found it necessary to direct slave labor through a variety of management procedures. Slaves on a small farm simply worked with and often alongside the owner, who determined the day's task and allocated chores. On larger farms and small plantations the owner might utilize an elder son, a brother, or, more commonly, a hired white man to be the overseer and supervise slave laborers.

The overseers, who roused the slaves in the morning, set them to their tasks, and used a combination of incentives and discipline to maximize output, frequently insulated the owner from the most onerous aspects of slave ownership. Not only did the owner escape having to discipline the slaves, but the slaves usually aimed their most immediate complaints about work and provisions at the offending overseer; slaves often appealed to the owner about perceived mistreatment, and the owners, wanting to be seen as paternalistic and realizing that in the long run the relative contentment of their slave workforce was more important than the feelings of an overseer who could easily be replaced, often chastised overzealous overseers. Thus the owner felt righteous, the slaves projected their anger onto the overseer, and the overseer felt himself to be in an untenable position. If he maximized income he risked being discharged for driving the slaves too hard; if he were too relaxed in his demands, he risked being discharged for not producing enough. But to many slaves the overseer, not the master, seemed the villain.

Some slaves held managerial positions on plantations, usually the largest ones. On occasion slaves served as the overseer, being authorized by the owner to supervise the operation of a plantation and its black laborers. More commonly, black managers served under a white overseer and as "drivers" were responsible for seeing that other slaves carried out the general tasks determined by the overseer. Drivers, for example, might be in charge of the men, women, and older children chopping cotton, and the driver would take the group to the field, supervise their work, and discipline those who flagged, acting as the arm of the overseer. Drivers were especially common on cotton plantations, where slaves worked in "gangs" for a set number of hours. (On rice plantations slaves were often given a set "task" to perform, with a task being a previously agreed upon amount of labor to be performed as measured in output, not hours. Skilled or industrious slaves could often complete their "task" by early afternoon, and had the rest of the day off for leisure or to pursue their own interests: many had gardens, pigs, boats for fishing, wagons for hire, and so on.)

Black drivers often earned the enmity of their fellow slaves, for while some might strive to protect their charges from abuse or overwork, more were eager to preserve their favored status and consequently pushed the slaves under their purview to greater exertions. As a rule slaves were not worked so hard that their lives were physically endangered, in part at least because the whites came to believe their own stereotype of black laziness and in part because slaves developed subtly effective techniques to control the workpace. And slaves worked harder than we might expect in such a seemingly incentiveless system because they recognized they had a powerful incentive—upon their labor ultimately rested the success or failure of the plantation, and in lean years, when food, clothing, and medicine had to be cut back, they well understood whose rations would be the first to suffer. Moreover, in the event of a severely bad season, if the master felt constrained to pay his bills by selling slaves, it was the slave community who suffered. Indirectly, but very profoundly, slaves were interested in the prosperity of their plantation because, while they had the least to gain, they had the most to lose.

But as with the white overseers, black drivers had to walk a tightrope, balancing their desire to please the owner against the necessity of not seriously alienating their fellow slaves. If the driver pushed the slaves too hard, they would attack him, organize a work slowdown, sabotage draft animals or tools, run away temporarily in protest, or plead their case with the owner—any of which could result in the driver being summarily removed from his position. On most plantations there were also slaves who by their strength, skill, experience, or natural dignity gained the respect and trust of the whites and fellow slaves, and these slave leaders, with or without a managerial title, served as advisers to the owners or overseers, as workers who set the pace for others, and as take-charge leaders of whatever task. Slaves accorded respect to such natural leaders whether or not their masters rewarded them with a putative managerial title.

Yet no slave, even the most skilled or responsible in the sight of the owner, was ever fully removed from the possibility of discipline. Perhaps nothing so symbolizes the raw subjection of the slave as the image of flogging. The actual frequency of whippings is disputed and probably exaggerated. This was an age when white school children, soldiers, and sailors were corporally punished to an extent that staggers us today. Clearly most slaves, whether they felt the sting of the lash themselves or not, witnessed members of their community being publicly flogged. Every slave on a plantation was vicariously punished when another was, for when one watched a companion wince as the whip hit his back and heard the sound of the lash as it bit into the flesh, leaving at first great welts and then open, bleeding cuts, one could imagine the sting of the lash on one's own back. Such anticipated horror magnified the effect of each whipping, and every slave lived with that image as an ever-present reality. Slaves were also disciplined by having privileges withdrawn, by being humiliated in front of others, by being assigned to particularly unpleasant tasks, and by being sold away from family and friends. In order to demonstrate that slavery was evil, it is not necessary to argue that slaveowners were demons. The system allowed the dehumanization of interpersonal relationships, and even in the hands of good masters slaves lived precariously amid potential disaster. Like skating on thin ice, slaves even in the best of situations were deprived of essential freedoms and could, by sale or the death of a master, be easily cast, to change the temperature of the metaphor, into a living hell bereft of loved ones and support systems. It was the random potential for horror, not its prevalence, that made slavery so wrong.

Similarly, to condemn slavery for the housing or food or health care provided slaves is to misdiagnose the malady. Slave cabins were comparable to those of poor whites, but unlike whites, slaves were not free to use their skills and ingenuity to seek a better life elsewhere. Slave food was monotonous, even though slaves, through their gardens, poultry, pigs, and prowess in hunting and fishing, significantly augmented the staple goods distributed and accounted for by their owners. There may have been occasional dietary deficiencies in the long winter months when fresh vegetables were unavailable, but slaves were not as a matter of purposeful treatment kept semistarved and undernourished. Simple economic self-interest, not to mention rudimentary humanity, led owners to see that their slaves had sufficient food and shelter. For like reasons owners wanted to keep their human property healthy, and, understanding that disease was no respecter of class or race, they resorted first to home remedies, patent medicines, hints from self-help medical books, and then professional doctors when all else failed—the same progession that obtained when they or their own family was ill—but the state of medical knowledge was so poor that most people of either race remained sick until they either got well or died. Slaves also practiced, as did the whites, their own folk medicine along with presumably scientific medicine, but illnesses often lingered and people were often bothered by a bad tooth or a hernia or an incorrectly mended broken bone for years. For complicated reasons of genetics blacks suffered more from some diseases, and less from others, than did whites, but no one understood why even if they noted the differential toll.

Some slaves also suffered debilitating social and psychological damage as a result of bondage. The records irrefutably reveal black violence against blacks, theft perpetrated against fellow slaves, slave men abusing slave women and children, women fighting among themselves, occasional child abuse. Slavery was obviously a labor and social system that produced great stress, anger, and frustration for its victims, and the reality of white power often forced blacks to project their anger on nearer, relatively powerless victims— the owner's livestock, the omnipresent dogs, or their spouse or children. Certainly some slaves also internalized the image of themselves suggested by the whites' racism, and such self-deprecation helped produce more than a few slaves who approximated the white stereotype of the Sambo—the childlike, fawning, dependent, irresponsible, naturally servile slave who by all appearances was content to accept his status in life. Yet the expected pathological consequences of slavery, which every student must recognize, are in the final analysis less consequential than the myriad ways that blacks as a people managed to survive bondage with their essential humanity intact. The most fruitful result of recent scholarship has been to reveal the social construction of the black community and a black culture in the American South.

The plantation South was not run with the rigorous discipline of a modern penal establishment, and analogies with prisons and Nazi death camps have little interpretative value. The whole system was much looser, much more casual, than in theory it might have been, and both the slaves themselves and the owners were responsible for how the system evolved. Owners simply didn't have the energy, the time, or the manpower to supervise every aspect of slave life, and saw no benefit in doing so. Certain expectations of labor and demeanor existed that, in general terms, blacks and whites accepted, and whites employed discipline or its threat to enforce minimal compliance. Slaves learned a thousand and one ways to shape their work environment and to "put on Old Master," and while there were sure limits beyond which they could not go, it would be a mistake to assume that slaves were passive automatons in the hands of omnipotent owners. Slaves knew what the owner wanted, or, rather, they discoved by push and shove, give and take, just how far short of the owner's ideal they could go without being punished, and they then set the perimeters of their work effort and outward behavior just inside the danger point. Slaves were quite conscious of the serious game being played, and by "going along to get along" they were less coopted than skilled at maneuvering their lives between the Scylla of Samboism on the one hand and the Charybdis of self-defeating rebellion on the other. Surviving one's bondage with a degree of self-respect and the love and support of kith and kin, not heroic but suicidal acts of defiance, made life worth living.

In the immediate arena of their home plantation or farm, slave men and women lived out unthreatening lives of subtle rebellion, right under the noses of their owners; and yet few whites were ever aware—in part because slaves were masters of the art of dissimulation—of the significance of the counterculture their slaves created. Severe restraints lay in the path of complete cultural autonomy, of course, and slaves naturally borrowed ideas, foods, and social practices from those around them—blacks from differing African traditions, American Indians, and the polyglot white population. Even those slaves who remembered their African traditions or were taught them by their parents could not exactly replicate rituals in the new land, and when they borrowed concepts from each other and utilized the indigenous flora and fauna of America in attempts to approximate Old World ways, the result was necessarily a hybrid creation. Done in response to remembered cultural expectations but adapted to the reality of the present situation, these expressions of slave culture were a New World creation—something old, something borrowed, something new—an African–American culture different from African ways but different from the ways of the white man as well.

The most profound protests against slavery were the successful attempts of slave men and women to construct a frame of reference, a ground of being, a source of meaning separate from the demands and expectations of their owners. The incremental way black attitudes toward work, food, clothing, folk tales and beliefs, music and dance, kinship and religion were combined, layer after layer, to produce a culture separate from the whites allowed slaves to persevere as a people with a remarkable degree of psychological wholeness. Pathology did exist in the slave quarters, and psychological damage occurred, but in the midst of a system that deprived them of essential freedoms and in which whippings, separation from loved ones, and personal debasement was a constant possibility, the basic humanity of black people proved unextinguishable. Many slaves seem to have found in their ability to perform certain tasks with unusual skill a way to express their worth as special humans even as the task—perhaps plowing an arrow-straight row—met their owner's desire.

Contemporary whites were unable to see how blacks managed to hold a part of their life away from the control of whites. The rice planter commanded his slaves to make baskets with which to winnow the rice, and the black borrowed from Indians knowledge of certain grasses and reeds to weave into baskets, but when one examines the patterns in the baskets, one sees unmistakeable African designs. Slaves took discarded pieces of the whites' clothing and reassembled them in individualistic fashion, thereby making a sartorial statement about their personal independence. From bits and pieces of cloth slave women sewed quilts, and while whites mistook the asymmetrical patches of rectangular color as an indication of the blacks' artistic primitiveness, the blacks were following an African conception of the appropriate pattern of color and shape. In the aftermath of Mozart and Beethoven, whites found slave music hauntingly strange and exotic, but they also thought the tonal pattern and the rhythms so different as hardly to qualify as music, never fully comprehending the complexity of the beat and the role of improvisation. Whites heard snatches of African folk tales and animal stories but never realized how such tales helped explain allegorically the nature of life and the slave's response to it. Folk tales and Uncle Remus stories were more than entertainment; they taught survival behavior and provided vicarious examples of slaves triumphing over tragedy and white power at the same time that they warned of communally destructive action by other slaves. In ways we are still discovering—the loose gait and style of dancing, peculiar naming practices that differed from the white even when the same English or Biblical names were employed, attitudes about kinship and matriarchal conceptions of child rearing, methods of food preparation and consumption, dietary preferences—blacks carved out a world somewhat of their own even as they became increasingly acculturated to the ways of the whites.

Yet one should also appreciate the extent to which whites and blacks came to participate in much the same culture. Southern whites and blacks shared many of the same attitudes, and indeed it was that community of shared values that made so important to blacks the ways in which their beliefs and practices differed. Whites (and especially the huge majority of nonaristocratic whites) and blacks ate much of the same food, shared the same work routines, had similar attitudes toward family and kin, especially compared to nonsoutherners, enjoyed the same outdoor recreations (hunting and fishing), loved music and dancing, believed the world to contain ghosts and practiced a degree of white magic—good luck charms, behavior to avert bad fortune, and superstitious consulting of astrological "signs" before planting gardens or castrating a shoat. At least to outsiders, southern whites and blacks seemed to share similar speech accents. But perhaps nowhere was the antebellum culture more nearly biracial than in religion, and this unexpectedly so.

From the very beginning of the evangelical movement in the South, the evangelical churches had welcomed black worshipers. In fact, in the early decades the evangelical churches had been critical of the institution of slavery, but as they grew in membership and began to attract converts from a broad spectrum of society, including wealthy slave owners, and then their own members increasingly began to own slaves, the evangelical stance toward slavery evolved. By the second quarter of the nineteenth century practically all Baptists, Methodists, and Presbyterians, along with the Episcopalians, had come to terms with slavery, backing into a biblical defense of the institution on the grounds that Jesus never specifically attacked it and finding a positive theological justification of African bondage as the means God devised to introduce Africans to the Gospel. There had always been slave members of the churches, and following the rise of modern antislavery in the 1830s, the evangelicals created a specific missionary effort to church the blacks in their midst. The so-called mission to the slaves was directed toward those regions with a very high black-to-white ratio, like coastal Georgia and South Carolina and portions of the cotton-rich black belt in Alabama and Mississippi. But outside these atypical regions, blacks had long worshiped with whites in church services that were essentially biracial.

In most parts of the South in the nineteenth century, substantial numbers of slaves were participating members of the dominant—Baptist, Methodist, and Presbyterian—churches, not infrequently actually outnumbering white members. Whites preferred such biracial worship for several reasons: they clearly believed that Christianity was too important to be left up to the slaves themselves—they might misunderstand or corrupt the message of Christ—and they believed biracial worship was simply prescribed by the Bible. Moreover, they feared that religion "improperly" handled could lead to potential resentment or even insurrection. White believers tended to support biracial religion because, despite their racism and support of the institution of slavery, they nevertheless believed that in the eyes of God all were (spiritually) equal; slaves, they were quite sure, had souls just as did white people, and their souls too were precious to God. The white conception of blacks as permanent children carried over into the church, for while whites and blacks sat in the same building and heard the same sermons and sang the same hymns, eventually took communion together, and even later would be buried in the same cemetery, in most church services there apparently was a moment when the minister turned to the slaves and in a condescending tone, much like a children's sermon, admonished them to obey their earthly masters and be good slaves. Slaves heard this self-serving homily and in large part dismissed it contemptuously, but they also heard the full sermon with its message of salvation and hope. From church services slaves gained an invigorated sense of self-worth, found meaning and purpose and even joy for their lives, and often emerged feeling morally superior to their owners.

Looking back at how the slaves were segregated in the balcony and subjected to a demeaning sermonette of obedience, one is tempted to misunderstand what slaves received from religion. Yes, they were forced to sit with other blacks. Does anyone think they would have preferred to sit with their white masters instead? But such church attendance was a safe and unsuspicious way to socialize with slaves from other farms and plantations, and as much gossip and courting went on with blacks at church as with whites. In a sense, the larger slave community had part of its origin in these kinds of black assemblies. And while the ministers' narrow admonitions were annoying, in the totality of the worship service slaves were indirectly treated as persons and were held to substantially the same moral code as were whites. In terms of address in the church record books blacks and whites were alike called "Brother" and "Sister," and slaves asking for admission were expected, like whites, either to come upon profession of faith or submit a written letter of dismissal from their prior church. In the normal disciplinary proceedings of the antebellum churches blacks were not punished out of proportion to their numbers, and in their ability to testify in the church courts, even against whites, slaves church members found a greater degree of equality than they did in the civil courts, where no blacks could testify against whites. Blacks were appointed deacons, they sometimes preached to mixed audiences, and whites often indicated genuine respect for black faith. Suffice it to say that in the churches antebellum whites and blacks met more as equals than anywhere else in their slave society, yet whites were careful to say that a black's legal status was not effected by the quality of his faith.

In the immediacy of the local church, surrounded by a community of believers, and held accountable to a moral standard far higher than their owner's rules, slaves found a purpose to life beyond avoiding the overseer's lash; a life well lived, even a life of suffering, could bring the reward of inner contentment on earth and, it was believed, eternal happiness in heaven. This eschatological hope helped many slaves cope with life in bondage, but the ability to find peace and a comforting sense of self-worth even amid the squalor, toil, and suffering of slavery in the here and now made Christianity an essential part of slave culture. Religion helped arm many slaves to survive their bondage without being driven to hopeless acts of violence. In that sense, and in a way whites seldom fully realized, Christianity served to minimize slave rebellion or channel it in unthreatening directions. But religion was only one part of slave culture that, by helping blacks cope with bondage, provided them with the psychological breathing space necessary to maintain a felt sense of wholeness.

Slave rebellion occurred along a broad spectrum of behaviors, ranging from a lethargic passivity on the one hand to acts of violent insurrection on the other. To think of rebellion only in the sense of violence is to miss the most profound kind of rebellion, cultural. Maintaining one's self-respect and dignity and abiding by a moral code one accepted on one's own volition was both a deeper rejection of slavery and a safer course of action than was angry retribution. Yet in the realm of outward behavior slaves had recourse to a range of actions to protest a general opposition to bondage, but more often they protested less slavery itself than white transgressions against what on any plantation the slaves had come to accept as their right or their due within the slave system. There were very few slave insurrections in protest of slavery per se—Nat Turner's rebellion in Southampton County, Virginia, in August 1831 was an exception. When slaves protested, it usually was against a particular act or series of acts by a particular master; a slave felt himself unfairly punished, or forced to work on a Sunday, or long mistreated by a peculiarly cruel master. The typical protest was more immediate and of less moment than insurrection. A slave or group of slaves would stage what amounted to a work slowdown, infuriating the owner, or they would perform secret acts of minor sabotage, but nothing so extreme as to evoke punishment. A cook might spit, or worse, in the food; a plowhand would leave the gate open and let the mules run away; a seemingly careless hoe would chop down some of the offending master's cotton plants.

On other occasions slaves would feign illness or injury; the planter often suspected the ruse, but he could never be sure and was loath to risk permanently injuring valuable property. Slaves who felt especially misused would run away temporarily, never expecting to leave for good but at least having the satisfaction of depriving the master of at least several days' labor. Such running away was so common that owners did not advertise for them until they had been gone several weeks, and occasionally masters did not even bother to punish runaways when they returned, seemingly considering such short-term labor losses as a normal part of slave management. What usually kept slaves from running away to freedom was their families. A single slave might successfully escape capture long enough to get to Ohio or Pennsylvania, but not an entire slave family, and to leave them in a desperate attempt at freedom was to risk having them punished in response. If the escape were successful, the runaway would almost certainly never see his or her loved ones again. The slave family proved to be the owner's surest safeguard against his slaves' running away.

Geography also seemed to conspire against potential slave rebels. In

Latin America or in the Caribbean Islands, where the overwhelmingly male slave population was worked harder, fed less, and had far fewer opportunities to live as a family than slaves of the Old South, the level of frustration often led to the flash point of rebellion. Slave rebels could escape either into the remote jungle interior of the Amazon River basin or the almost impenetrable mountainous centers of the islands and there establish maroon societies of escaped slaves, far beyond the effective reach of their erstwhile owners. The existence of maroon societies offered a standing example of successful rebellion and served as a very real precedent to disgruntled slaves considering action. Except for extremely limited regions of Virginia and North Carolina near the Great Dismal Swamp and several other similiarly atypical areas, such as the Florida Everglades, southern slaves had no isolated or impenetrable wilderness into which to disappear. From the early eighteenth century onward, slave runaways found at first Indians only too glad to capture them to sell back to their owners or, later, slaveless whites in the Piedmont or in Appalachia happy to have an opportunity to seize them and hold them as their own slaves. Blacks' indelible color made rebels and runaways instantly identifiable in regions beyond the normal sway of plantations. Some slaves revolted by escaping to Florida and becoming assimilated into the Seminole Indians, but this was a unique situation in the American South.

On occasion southern slaves driven to utter despair physically responded to the transgressions of an owner. But the penalty for such acts was extremely severe: terrible whippings, branding, being sent out of the state and away from loved ones—Virginia, for example, banished "criminal" slaves to be sold in the deep South to unsuspecting buyers—and death. Occasionally a slave, absolutely fed up with his plight, would resort to self-mutilation, thereby depriving his full labor (and full selling price) from his owner. Angry slaves at times struck their owner or overseer with their fists or with a weapon—sure punishment did not deter their physical statement of resentment. In rare cases slaves resorted to killing whites, perhaps with poison, when memories of such African techniques were fresh, but in later decades killings were done by traditional American means, a knife or gun. Arson apparently was sometimes meant to kill too, though more often it was intended to punish the owner by destroying his property in a way that made it impossible to detect the perpetrator. In a handful of cases—the Stono Revolt of 1739, the Pointe Coupe rebellion in Louisiana in 1795, the abortive Gabriel Revolt of 1800, the Denmark Vesey Plot of 1822, and Nat Turner's famous insurrection of 1831—slaves conspired together to mount larger assaults against the institution of slavery, but given whites' overwhelming control of the police powers of government, such armed insurrections were doomed to failure and were brutally put down. Most slaves chose other means of escaping the worst effects of slavery. Never did whites think that the institution of slavery was actually threatened by the behavior of the slaves, but the simmering resentment just below the surface testifies to the slaves' peren-nial desire for freedom and revealed itself afresh when, during the Civil War, the presence of Union Armies made escape and liberty seem within reach. Then whites were shocked by the strength of the slave hunger for freedom.

URBAN AND INDUSTRIAL SLAVERY AND FREE BLACKS

The antebellum South had an agricultural economy, and most of its population was rural, but where there was industry there were slaves engaged in industrial, and often skilled, labor, and where there were cities there were urban slaves—140,000 of them in 1860. Most southern industry was extrac-tive—lumbering and mining (iron ore, coal, gold, salt)—or subsidiary to the production and marketing of the staple crops. Slave labor proved remarkably flexible, and wherever there was work to be done in the South, slaves toiled. Teams of slave foresters were sent into the swamps to cut cypress trees, for example, working under minimum white supervision, and slaves labored in the turpentine industry of North Carolina, slashing the pine trees and collect-ing their resin. Blacks were employed at the southern iron works from the seventeenth century on, and in the Georgia and North Carolina goldfields slaves mined and worked sluices, sometimes with the incentive of keeping a tiny portion of their finds. Particularly in the iron works it became traditional for slaves to be able to do additional labor for extra pay. Slaves ran sawmills, supervised rafts of logs floating down the Mississippi for sale in New Orleans, operated the boilers for making salt, and performed highly skilled and dan-gerous jobs in a Baltimore chemical factory. At cotton gins, cotton presses, tobacco factories, hemp factories; as stevedores loading and unloading the ships; as gandy dancers maintaining the railroads that eventually connected the agricultural hinterland to the port cities, slaves, in activities far removed from the cotton fields, helped make the southern economy thrive.

In the widely dispersed southern cities urban slaves performed a variety of jobs. Richmond, Charleston, and Savannah, for example, were one-third slave in 1860. Richmond, because of the dominance of tobacco factories and the Tredegar Iron Works, had a majority of male slaves, but in every other southern city female slaves predominated. They often served as domestic workers or labored in hotels, restaurants, and laundries. Merchants owned or hired slaves to haul and move heavy merchandise; slaves worked in livery sta-bles, blacksmith shops, tanneries, ropewalks, brickworks, and printshops; slaves were disproportionally represented in certain crafts, ranging from bar-bering and catering to carpentry and masonry. Much of the handsome wrought iron scrollwork in New Orleans was molded by slave craftsmen. Even the finest homes were often built at least in part by slaves, who also occasion-ally did exquisite cabinet work and fabricated elegant furniture. The carts and wagons that filled the busy city streets were often driven by black draymen, and the city markets, where produce was bought and sold, were filled with slaves both working in the booths and purchasing goods for their owners. Slave women prepared and cooked food for many urban white families, washed the clothes, cleaned the houses, and watched over the children. The point is that slaves participated in practically every aspect of urban life, and slavery was well adapted to the city. In the 1850s the prolonged cotton boom allowed planters simply to outbid urban employers for slave labor, in part because immigrant workers could more easily be substituted for slave workers in the cities. As a result, in several of the old southern cities the relative size of the urban slave population decreased slightly. But there was nothing about city life that was ultimately inimical to the institution of black slavery.

Just as all slaves were not simple agricultural workers and not all slaves lived in the rural countryside, not all southern blacks were slaves. From at least the mid-seventeenth century some blacks were free; they either arrived in America as free, or, in the same manner as white indentured servants, they were granted freedom after a period of service, or they were given freedom as a reward for especially meritorious service, or, as the mistress or children of a white owner, they were eventually freed by the terms of their deceased owner's will. At the time of the American Revolution there were somewhere between three and four thousand free blacks in the upper South, and, because of the presence of mulattoes, they tended to be lighter skinned than the slave population as a whole. Following the Revolution and the rise of the evangelical movement, significant numbers of owners in Maryland and Virginia particularly, following either the dictates of natural rights philosophy or the image of a God who saw all persons as equals, freed their slaves—all of them, not just light-skinned mistresses and their offspring. The result was both a substantial increase in the free black population and a free black population that in terms of visible characteristics was more representative of the slaves as a whole. Over the three census decades of 1790, 1800, and 1810, the South's free black population increased from 32,357 to 61,241 to 108,265, the bulk of them living in the upper South. The smaller deep South free black population was in the decade of the 1790s also augmented by free mulattoes fleeing the Haitian Revolution. This rapid increase soon ceased, and thereafter the free black population grew almost exclusively by natural means, reaching a total of 261,918 in 1860.

Region-wide, about two-thirds of all free blacks lived in rural areas, and most were farmers. Although they were never prohibited from owning property, relatively few free blacks ever became landowners. In North Carolina, for example, fewer than 4 percent of the free blacks possessed land. Most rural free blacks were tenants, hiring out their labor to white farmers and planters who used them to augment their work force in times of peak demand like harvest. A tiny minority of free blacks owned slaves, usually their wives or children, purchased to prevent the white owner of their spouses from selling them away. A handful of prosperous free blacks became plantation owners or conducted large-scale businesses and bought slaves to work. Rural free blacks by and large lived scattered across the countryside, but in southern cities, where one-third of the free blacks lived, genuine free black communities developed. Often free blacks lived on the outer fringes of the cities, but those who were more prosperous (some became quite wealthy as barbers, builders, caterers, and owners of various shops) lived intermingled with whites of a similar economic level. Residentially, antebellum southern cities were better integrated than northern cities in the mid-twentieth century. Urban free blacks were more likely to be property owners than were rural free blacks.

Free blacks in cities such as Charleston and New Orleans constituted a social class unto themselves and created their own subculture, with organizations and clubs restricted to *free* blacks and sometimes lightskinned ("brown") ones at that. Most southern cities had several large independent black churches, usually controlled by free blacks, that provided a variety of religious and social functions. New Orleans "free people of color" often spoke French, had their own newspapers and militia troops, went to the opera, and had a moral code, which many white men were only too happy to accept, more Gallic than evangelical. Northern and European visitors to the major coastal southern cities, about 40 percent of whose population was black, seeing free and slave blacks in the streets and shops, driving the wagons, working at every conceivable craft, often understandably felt they were in a black nation. Even the domestic architecture in cities like Charleston, with enclosed interior gardens and slave quarters, were adapted to the institution of slavery.

Many prosperous free blacks ran thriving businesses. They often owned slaves or hired free black, and even white, workers. On good terms with their white clientele, some of the wealthiest free blacks, such as the barber William Johnston of Natchez, socialized with whites, frequented the race tracks, exhorted their black employees to work hard and be thrifty, and even purchased a plantation in conscious imitation of the road to white respectability. Of course, most free blacks were poor though hard-working. Competing with southern whites, urban slaves, and, toward the end of the era, with immigrant artisans, they had to scramble for a living. Often they lived on the margin of legality, trading surreptitiously with slaves and traveling and peddling their skills or wares in violation of increasingly harsh restrictions placed upon their freedom of action. The more skilled were often dependent upon the support and patronage of whites and suffered the opposition of vocal white competitors; the less skilled caterers and grogshop keepers depended upon a slave clientele and were constantly criticized by those whites who feared the consequences of increasing black autonomy. The most skilled, prosperous, and influential free blacks, those who might have become the leaders of a united black community, were too aware of their limited privileges, and thus conscious of what they had to lose, to identify fully with the slaves. For that reason free blacks were often a conservative force, more likely to report rumored slave rebellions than, like Denmark Vesey, to lead one.

In a more subtle way, the presence of free blacks in the cities may have defused potential slave rebellion in the countryside by offering an urban escape opportunity for discontented rural slaves. When frustration and anger reached the boiling point, a plantation slave could sometimes run away and emerge in a southern city—still within visiting distance of loved ones left behind—and in the anonymity of the city's black population could, utilizing his plantation-learned skills, emerge as yet another free black. Even though blacks were presumed to be slaves and the burden of proof of freedom lay with them, enforcement was so lax, and free blacks sufficiently skilled at forging documents and artful in subterfuge, that many successfully carried off their escape to freedom. Those who were particularly lightskinned might, through such a move, emerge as whites, "passing," as the phrase had it, the racial boundary. Far more slaves achieved this kind of self-created deliverance from bondage than successfully followed the North Star to freedom in the North by way of the so-called Underground Railroad.

At times the upper-class free blacks consciously copied white society; at other times they remained truer to their own culture. But ironically, as sectional tensions between North and South increased in the 1850s and white southerners grew more paranoid about the survival of slavery, they came to worry more about the living contradiction to slavery that the free blacks represented. If blacks were natural slaves and permanent children, how did one explain free blacks who often prospered because of their not inconsiderable skills? The growing white population, augmented by foreign immigration, eased the urban labor shortage and produced white craftsmen and artisans who objected to black competition; calls were made for colonizing all free blacks or pushing them back into slavery. This never happened, in large part because their economic contribution was too great, but it highlighted the precarious social and legal position free blacks occupied. Categorized increasingly in the late 1850s with the slave masses, free blacks began to accept their racial identity. During the Civil War and Reconstruction, former free blacks emerged as the leaders of a remarkably united common black front. Class divisions existed, as did those based on color, but they were minimal outside of Charleston and New Orleans. More important was the extent to which prewar free black leaders became the political, cultural, and business leaders of the freedmen. This was especially true in the older southern states that had a substantial free black population and not true, for example, in Texas, which had almost no free blacks in 1861. In the same way that antebellum urban whites, in their legal restrictions against urban slaves and free blacks, were unknowingly learning the rudiments of a later, more elaborate Jim Crow exclusionary system, antebellum free black craftsmen and business-men were gaining experience for that day when segregation forced them to do business among and for a black clientele. Out of the prewar free black population largely came the postwar black middle and professional classes.

WHITE WOMEN IN THE OLD SOUTH

No figure has held a more exalted position in the pantheon of southern historical stereotypes than the plantation mistress, she of slender waist, light complexion, pure virtue, and selfless, sacrificial devotion to husband, chil-dren, and slaves. Contemporary prescriptive literature and present-day popu-lar fiction have combined to create a persona that both obscures and illumi-nates real southern women. The image was an ideal that some women tried to live up to and defined themselves in terms of, but the image has been applied so universally and uncritically to southern women that it has misrep-resented the life situations and aspirations of the large majority of them. Over and over again historians find themselves having to correct the oversim-plifications of commonly believed stereotypes. All whites were not planters, all blacks were not slaves, and all slaves were not simple agricultural workers. One essential task of historians is to "complexify" the past, to point out the diversity, the particularity, of the human condition. Usually stereotypes have a grounding in truth, or at least what people have wanted to believe was true, and the difficult part is showing that things were not as simple, as easily cate-gorized, as the stereotype suggests, without leaving the contrary impression that the past was so complex, so varied, so dependent upon multitudinous factors that no possible generalizations can be drawn. A rapidly increasing body of scholarship now allows us to understand the history of southern women with a degree of sophistication impossible a generation ago, and although the bulk of the scholarship emphasizes upper- and upper-middle-class white women, the portrait coming into view differs substantially from that of the plantation mistress of legend and lore.

The myth of the plantation mistress led historians to misinterpret the history of southern women over the long term, from 1619 to the Civil War, as a story of decline. Scholars studying the role of women in the colonial South rightfully noted that, especially in the seventeenth century, when there were often severe labor shortages, women's work was essential to the economic sur-vival of farms and communities. Not only did white women, free and inden-tured, do the necessary household work, but they were involved in every aspect of food production as well, and in addition to washing and mending clothes, they were responsible for producing the thread and cloth. Mortality was high (though declining) throughout the colonial period, and women often became widows; in so doing they on many occasions took over the running of their departed husband's farm or business. Certainly most remarried, but others chose to remain single and operated their former husbands' store, tannery, ferry, tavern, newspaper. In fact, women, again mostly widows, could be found in practically every occupation in the colonial period, and this apparent access to occupations beyond the household has been interpreted as respresenting an era of relative economic equality for women. From this view it was an easy logical jump to the conclusion that antebellum plantation mistresses, supposedly doomed to a life of idleness and confined to preoccupation with proper manners and spiritual matters, had suffered a precipitous decline in status. Recent historians have drastically revised this interpretation.

Revisionists have challenged both sides of the argument, showing that colonial women had fewer legal rights than commonly recognized and were more dependent on the earning power of a husband than later women were. Moreover, women in the antebellum period were not as removed from the real world of production and management as the stereotype suggested, and at least middle- and upper-class women came to make use of equity law to preserve a degree of economic dependence from their husbands. In addition, new attitudes about women's cultural and social roles emerged in the half century following the Declaration of Independence; these shifts in viewpoint, influenced by new intellectual currents from Europe, by changes in the urban workplace, and by demographic trends, produced in northern cities what has been called a "cult of true womanhood" that emphasized the womanly virtues of domesticity, piety, submissiveness, and benevolence. As women were increasingly removed from the workplace and made economically irrelevant, the argument runs, they were given moral empowerment. The male world of commerce and manufacturing was deemed evil and corrupt; women, by maintaining the home as a moral oasis, could both redeem their husbands from their daily trespasses and train their children in Christian values, an essential task in a Republic because the young boys would eventually grow up and vote. While women's economic importance declined, their spiritual and cultural importance expanded even as they were insulated from the world of business and politics. The peculiarities of the plantation economy meant that these northern-based models of prescriptive behavior did not precisely fit the plantation women, but definite gender-based roles did develop in the South that shaped both how middle- and upper-class white women saw themselves and other women and how southern white men perceived the women around them.

The common law of England, with only very slight revisions until after the Civil War, was the basic law affecting women's property rights in the South. By common law, the single woman was essentially equal to men—she could own and control property as she wished. But upon getting married the woman lost almost all her property rights to her husband; not only did he have legal authority over all the income and property he was able to earn, but he also gained control over whatever property (and associated income) the wife brought to the marriage. The only exception was the wife's dower rights to one-third of the income and property during her lifetime. This was intended to insure the woman's support after her husband's death. Before a husband could convey away his property, real estate, or slaves, the wife had to agree to the conveyance. Still, creditors had the right to seize all the property, including the wife's dower share, in payment of debts incurred by the husband. Nevertheless, the economic opportunities for single women were so limited that practically all of them had to marry in order to survive. As a thirty-year-old female teacher in Georgia complained to her diary, "It is indeed a hard lot for a penniless girl to go forth alone in this wide world to seek maintenance . . . . what can a poor timid woman do?"

Most widows remarried, and soon. On occasion a woman could improve her lot by a good marriage—as could a man by marrying a wealthy widow—and a widow with children and property by dower sometimes (by equity law) drew up a marriage contract with her future husband that protected her independent property (and income) by placing it in a separate estate, but such contracts were rare in colonial days. They became much more common in the last three decades of the antebellum period, especially for single women who expected to inherit substantial property from their parents or for widows with property from their prior marriage or marriages. The increased use of marriage contracts gave some antebellum women more control over their economic future than their colonial forebears had held. Yet the intended purpose of marriage contracts—and dower rights too—was not to enhance the economic power of women but to keep property in the family and to provide for the subsistence of women and their children. Both dower rights and marriage contracts were seen as a hedge against irresponsible or unlucky husbands who might otherwise squander a family's wealth and leave his dependents adrift in a heartless world.

By the common law, single women and widows did have legal equality with men and could use or dispose of their property as they saw fit. Under equity law, those married women who held property in separate estates could also handle it as they wished. One recent study of how free women transferred their property by gifts of deed (effective during the lifetime of the grantor) and by will suggests that women in fact operated out of a different set of assumptions than men. This difference suggests that something like a separate woman's culture existed in the antebellum South. Across the decades of the first half of the nineteenth century southern white women made wills in increasing numbers; indeed, they showed a greater propensity to make wills than men. This may in part reflect women's dominant role in the religious life of the era, for one result of a conversion experience was lessened fear of death, indeed, a willingness to face death frankly, and just such an attitude lay behind deciding to write a will. But women were not simply more willing to think about death; in their wills they differed from men in how they distributed their wealth.

Increasingly in the nineteenth century southern white fathers split their inheritance among their children, including daughters as well as sons, and the property was typically divided equally in value (there was a tendency to give sons land and daughters slaves, the assumption being that the slaves could be moved more easily to her future husband's plantation). In a sense, fathers divided their estate formulaically, with relatively little attention to the particular needs of a given child or other recipient. Women, on the other hand, had a greater tendency to distribute their income differentially in terms of their perception of need or just deserts. Such a pattern of conveyance suggests a greater willingness to discriminate according to affection or loyalty or need. Men seemed to write their wills according to impersonal rules of equal distribution; women seemed to have been more personalistic in their actions, rewarding certain persons more than others according to their own internal calculus of justice or love or discriminating against someone because of anger of lack or affection.

Southerners in general have been described as being more personalistic in their attitudes than other Americans; perhaps it is to southern women that this characteristic owes its origins. Women's greater attention to need than to equality in their division of their estates suggests also their concern with caring for individuals. In other words, in their wills women revealed themselves to be more religious, more personalistic, more nurturing than men. To some degree these characteristics may have represented a conscious effort on the part of women to meet certain gender-prescribed roles, but to a significant degree the role prescriptions reflected a deeper reality based on a separate woman's culture.

The household, the family, and the church were the primary arenas in which white women lived out their lives, and each of these institutions contributed to the making of a woman's culture in the South. We know far more about upper-class women, the literate ones who left diaries and letters, and this discussion for the moment will center on them, although later more will be said about the silent majority of women both free and slave. Because of the limited career opportunities for antebellum women, most of them defined themselves as mothers and wives. Prohibited from participating in the political world, not allowed to serve on juries, uninvolved except in special situations with the commercial transactions necessary to market plantation crops or purchase supplies, women were confined to the household. It was here, in a private domestic world, that they made management decisions, disciplined slaves and children, visited with relatives and friends, conversed, sang or played musical instruments, read, shared feelings and parenting responsibilities with their husbands, indeed, shaped their identity as women.

In this private world relationships with others were personalistic, not formal or dictated by political or economic concerns. In the public world men had to interact with other men from a range of class and economic levels, had to deal affably with men they disliked or barely knew, had to make impersonal decisions about crops, politics, court cases, slave purchases, and the like. Most women's relationships were personal and familial, not public, and even the slaves they normally came into contact with were cooks or house servants seen up close and familiarly, not near-anonymous field hands known vaguely and kept at arm's length. Genuine affection between plantation mistresses and individual slaves was common. The warp and woof of daily life led women to interact with others in an intimate, personal way; life was privatized to a degree almost unimaginable today. In this private domestic world women quite naturally developed personalistic attitudes about human relationships.

Women saw people concretely, as individuals, whereas men had more experience in dealing with people in the abstract; the result was a subtle difference in perception, and that difference helped make men marginally more willing to accept diversity, less prone to made invidious class distinctions, than women. Upper-class women appear to have found their far-less-common social involvement with poor whites much more uncomfortable, even distasteful, than did their husbands, who after all had more experience with persons outside their social class. In fact, the intense personalism of plantation women could make the mistresses more racist than the masters, whose greater diversity of human experience and tendency to see slaves abstractly and, psychologically speaking, at a distance lessened the normal irritations attendant to supervising workers. For plantation mistresses, interactions with slaves in the close private world of the home often allowed minor irritations to be magnified and infractions of rules to be seen as personal slights precisely because the interrelationships were so personal. Upper-class women in the Old South could both be more caring and personalistic in their attitudes toward their children, their friends, and certain slaves than their husbands were, and simultaneously more elitist and racist. Plantation mistresses often grumbled about managing slaves, complaining that they were more trouble than they were worth, but to take such complaints for opposition to the institution of slavery would be a serious mistake. White women were not closet abolitionists; they valued the leisure and standard of living that slavery brought them, and they found it difficult to imagine an alternative arrangement of society. In women's private plantation world personal interrelationships with slaves were often annoying, and the smallness of the domestic arena exacerbated the friction when personalities rubbed one another the wrong way. Even the most pious women who often in their letters and diaries indicated feelings of affection for their house servants could also record moments when anger boiled over and they chastised slaves with a verbal sharpness or a physical blow that later caused them pangs of guilt.

Women's anger often led to guilt because the all-too-human emotion was so at variance with the religious ethic of forgiveness that was a central motif of evangelical Christianity. Protestant evangelicalism in the eighteenth-century South had been a lower-class movement associated with slaveless whites and slaves; it was a religion of the heart, not the head, with a felt sensation of forgiveness by Christ more important than intellectual assent to a series of theological propositions. Central to the attraction of evangelical religion for the plain folk and blacks was a negative evaluation of the material things of the world and an affirmation that even those persons of little apparent merit were accepted and forgiven by Christ. In an age whose upper-class opinion makers valued restraint, order, and rationality, evangelical Christians represented an emotional, intensely personal counterculture, where crying, shouting, hugging, footwashing, and constant talk about love—God's love for sinners, Christ's sacrificial love, Christians' loving fellowship one with another—were fully accepted. As this mode of religious belief and practice spread across the South and, in the aftermath of the Great Revival of 1800 to 1805, gained thousands of new adherents, it broadened its class appeal and helped transform fundamental attitudes about interpersonal relationships, especially with household members.

In some historical situations new ideas, outlooks, and behavior patterns trickle down from elites to find broad popular acceptance, but just as often new ideas, outlooks, and behaviors that first emerge among the folk bubble up to change the lives of the elites. Evangelical religion had that effect in the early nineteenth-century South. By 1825 or so evangelical attitudes characterized not only the Baptist, Methodist, and Presbyterian churches but the Episcopal Church as well, and an evangelical frame of mind—a personalistic, emotional, privatistic conception of religion—had become as common to upper-class whites as to those in the lower order of society. In fact, there is some evidence that by that date evangelical conceptions of Christian behavior were more dominant among the better off, who now associated "proper" behavior—an aversion to profanity, anger, and violence; genteel notions of decorum; opposition to too much concern with making money; "feminine" concepts of meekness, gentleness, and sweetness of character—with role modeling that called for being Christ-like. Significantly more women than men were members of the churches, and the influence worked in both directions; so-called women's virtues helped shape and define the worship practice, and women modeled themselves after the church-defined prescriptions of proper (Christian) behavior and accepted the role of moral exemplars. Women were supposed to be, and women generally were, demonstrably more religious than men, and the personalistic, privatistic, and emotional emphases of evangelical religion found reinforcement in the household worlds of most women. And so did the evangelical emphasis on love, on demonstrable, emotional affection.

Historians of the family have posited that the affectionate, child-centered family and love-based companionate marriage were both products of modernity—declining infant mortality rates and the like. But both developments in the South seem to have been in advance of what modernization theory would suggest, and the influence of evangelical attitudes—authenticating the open display of emotion, of love—might very well have been the motivating force for change. Evangelical religion had both a personalistic and a sentimentalizing influence, both of which made more acceptable the showering of affection on children. Love for children and between spouses became less something persons were afraid to risk or embarrassed to reveal and more the expectation. Men as well as women were often doting parents. Into the second quarter of the nineteenth century considerations of family background and wealth still figured in the calculations both of young people contemplating marriage and their parents, but they were by no means the only desiderata. Detailed studies of familial correspondence and analysis of such factors as the order of marriage among maturing young people in a family suggest that love and congeniality shaped marriage choice more than did calculations of inheritance.

To some extent companionate marriage raised the expectations of conjugal happiness and might thereby have occasionally heightened frustrations and deepened dissappointments when love faded or failed to materialize. Since divorce was practically impossible in the antebellum South (except by special legislative enactment), many women found marriage almost unbearable, especially when their husbands turned out to be brutes or drunks or thoughtless failures, and surely some men were afflicted with hectoring wives as well. Even those spouses who genuinely loved and respected one another were on occasion irritated or disappointed in their partner and sometimes revealed their feelings in correspondence or confided their hurt to a diary. But this is the drama of real life, and we should not rush to conclude from isolated phrases that southern women as a group were terribly unhappy and victimized in marriage. Anyone who fairly samples the abundant collections of personal correspondence that enrich the archives of the South will find moving, heart-felt evidence of the love, trust, and forgiveness that often created insoluble bonds between countless men and women. The family and the home, was for myriad southerners the source of comfort, of warmth, and of happiness in a competitive, risk-filled agricultural society.

The enterprise of women's history has made several important shifts in the last half century. For many years history was seen to be not much more than past politics, with a war thrown in now and then for good measure. History was essentially about what men did—they were the ones who voted, practiced statecraft, were the captains of industry, and dominated the professions. Women were left out, but after all, asked the historians, what else were women doing but raising children, cooking, mending, and going to church? When women's history first began to be taken seriously, its proponents essentially accepted the old views about what was really important in history and sought to document the ways in which women had contributed to politics, or to the professions, or to scholarship. Some women, it turns out, did run businesses, manage plantations, and edit newspapers, for example, all the while keeping the home fires burning. In more recent years the agenda of women's history has expanded to discuss women's culture, the specific ways in which women thought differently about the world and responded to it in ways unlike the ways men did. This new scholarship, a component of social and cultural history more generally, seeks to understand how women lived—the texture and feel of their daily lives; their role models and expectations; the nature of their household tasks; their relationships with spouses, children, slaves, neighbors; their networks of friends; the diverse ways they found meaning, purpose, and dignity for their lives; how they constructed a sense of belonging and an identity within a male-dominant world. The new scholarship moves beyond simply defining women as passive victims of a male society and seeks to understand how women found self-legitimating roles for themselves. Women created a separate culture that in many respects intersected the male culture but nevertheless had a distinct core of different expectations and assumptions.

By women's culture in the antebellum South is meant culture in the anthropological sense, the set of assumptions that represent models of and for living and thereby help explain the world. Antebellum women were not modern feminists, and their culture was not based on membership in gender-specific associations whose goals were to redress the basic injustice of women's situation. Women's self-identification was not as victims of but rather as active participants in their society, and special participants at that. Women usually were more actively religious than men, and both men and women assumed that this was normal. The fashionable literature read by both sexes suggested that women were more gentle, more nurturing, more appropriately emotional or sentimental than men, and evangelical religion and the intimate family-dominated household of most women reinforced these expectations. Women were given and insisted upon the major responsiblity for parenting, especially for young children, although there are examples of nurturing fathers as well. To a degree women also saw themselves as petticoat preachers, concerned for the souls of their children, husband, relatives, and often slaves, and the idealized home environment was practically an adjunct of the church. From a modern perspective these seem to be confining expectations, ones that drew women away from the exciting real world and limited them to personal and household concerns. Women at the time may have seen these as ennobling responsibilities, ones for which women had unique skills and which were ultimately more important than mundane economic and political issues. To what extent if any men allowed women more moral authority in such areas to make up for restricting their economic roles is problematical, as is the extent to which women consciously expanded such nurturing roles in response to losing authority in other aspects of society. Most women may have seen the development as an enhancement of their status in society.

The full proliferation of these values was restricted to a tiny minority of women, the plantation mistresses. Many of them were not as removed from the operational concerns of the plantation itself as northern-based models of women's activities would suggest. To a significant degree the change in scale of manufacturing in northern cities led the husband and the artisans under his direction to move out of the household shop to separate facilities elsewhere, producing a real separation of the workplace from the home, and—or so the argument goes—with this spatial separation came the cultural separation of spheres of influence, with the woman's sphere and the attendant cult of true womanhood essentially restricted to the immediate family. Plantation women, on the other hand, lived amid the scene of production, and their own leisure depended upon the labor of slaves whose supervision in part depended upon the plantation mistress herself. The conception of the plantation household, for the care and nurturing (physical and spiritual) of whose inhabitants women were responsible, also included the slave workforce in a way clearly different from the northern lady's obligations to the factory workers. Plantation mistresses tended to see the slaves as dependents who needed her care, and such attitudes enhanced her feelings of racial superiority and, to the extent slaves accepted her role as nurturer and healer, it reinforced their habits of subservience. The plantation and its slaves fell under the sacred canopy of a woman's traditional domestic duties.

In work, in recreation, and in worship there were culturally accepted definitions of appropriate roles for men and women. On large plantations the mistress would be responsible for supervising the slave labor in the big house, especially the kitchen, and would often be involved with health care and the delivery of babies in the slave quarters. Such household management and nurturing, traditional women's concerns, could be very time-consuming, and even those women who seldom had to become more active in plantation management (when, for example, their husbands were away for days or weeks on matters of business or politics) were often quite burdened with administrative responsibilities. Most southern white women were of course not plantation mistresses, and these farm women were involved to a much greater extent with the actual physical labor necessary to run a household and raise a family in the antebellum period. Even so, in the household division of labor, clear gender boundaries were drawn. Women did the cooking, the washing and mending, the spinning and weaving, and were responsible for the dairy; men did the hunting, the chopping of firewood, and the heaviest field work. Women and men to a significant degree thought of themselves in terms of the work they performed, and hence women's child-centered, nurturing role (and the husband's role as "protector" and provider) was augmented by the unexamined routine of daily chores.

When families visited at home or church, much of the socializing and conversation was done in a manner that reinforced conceptions of the different roles of men and women. While preparing dinner or cleaning up afterwards, women would work together and talk about mutual concerns, and the men would sit apart, perhaps smoking, discussing their mutual concerns, and the conversations were distinctly different. Gossip was especially important to women as a means of enforcing community moral standards. Young women learned from such pointed conversation what kinds of behavior were scandalous and the social repercussions of unladylike or un-Christian actions. One false step, magnified through gossip, could ruin a young woman's good name and her honor. At church men and women often sat on opposite sides and, even though back in the log-cabin world of the small farms both husband and wife worked together at many chores and genteel values were absent, both spouses assumed there were roles within the church and topics of conversation (gossip again) appropriate to each sex. Women could not preach, but they could teach Sunday school; women could not serve on the vestry or board of deacons, but they could raise money with fairs, cake sales, sewing circles, and the like to underwrite expanding the church.

When one family got sick, a neighboring man might plow the field for them and his wife might bring over dinner or nurse the patient. When a woman was about to deliver a child, neighboring women would come over to provide moral support and physical assistance, and the process clearly was a bonding one for all. When a nursing mother had difficulty providing milk for her infant, another nursing mother—black or white, kin or not—would, if available, provide the nurturing assistance only a woman could provide. White women on occasion nursed black infants, and black women often assisted in the delivery of white babies, and vice versa. In such cases gender at least temporarily and to a degree overcame the restrictions of race and class. But women helped other women mostly of the same class, and women in general had less experience in transcending class lines than did men. In practically every situation of antebellum life across the spectrum of social class there were gender-prescribed roles and expectations for both sexes, and in such roles and expectations are to be found women's culture in the antebellum South. In barn-raisings and log-rollings, at corn-shuckings and quilting bees, at the sick bed and in the church, men and women knew what to do, and in that knowing they found a sense of purpose and fulfillment.

All this is not to deny that women (and men) did not sometimes chafe under the restrictions placed on their lives. Educated and articulate women knew their skills had limited outlets, although Mary Boykin Chesnut found a vicarious career through her husband, and the attraction men found toward her, "fat and fortyish" as she described herself, suggests a greater male openness to wit and learning in women than we might expect. Louisa McCord wrote and published penetrating essays on a variety of topics, but she defended both conventional roles for women and slavery. Other educated women found creative outlets and release through correspondence and keeping a diary. For many women church activities were a means of acting in a sphere larger than the household without upsetting role expectations. Women on widely scattered farms and plantations could also be lonely, although some apparently had little time to think much about their plight.

Still, even in the rural South, there were ways to counter isolation. Church attendance was as much a social occasion as religious, as was participation in camp meetings and scheduled revivals, and church sewing circles, committee service, and assorted fund-raising activities were a means of talking and working with likeminded women and no doubt were a respite from monotonous household duties. Visiting played an important social and recreational function as well, breaking down the walls of isolation, but in addition to the welcome news and change of conversation visitors provided, visiting was an important means of cementing family ties, supporting family members temporarily (or, it sometimes turned out, permanently) in need, and renewing friendships interrupted by migrations westward. And of course the good-natured fellowship and fun of a barn-raising or a corn-shucking was fully as important (and desired) as the work accomplished.

To date most women's history has been written about plantation mistresses or urban women, and while we know a good bit about slave women, least is known about the majority of southern women, those who lived and labored and loved on small farms with no slaves, little leisure, and scant claim to "ladyhood." For them life was hard, filled with drudgery and childbearing, and literally their work was never done. Farm women rose early to get the fire started, prepared breakfast for the rest of the family, milked the cow (if there was one), prepared the milk to make butter or cheese, gathered eggs and tended to the chickens, weeded in the garden and gathered a "mess" of peas or squash or corn, and then shelled or peeled or shucked the produce. Nearly everything was hand made, and the farm wife busied herself making soap, cloth, and clothes; canning and cooking and baking the family's food; doing the wash by hand over a huge black pot heated by a wood fire underneath; drawing water from the well and carrying the buckets to the house; nursing the infants, wiping their noses and handwashing their soiled diapers. Because farms were often miles apart and roads bad, many farm wives were isolated, bereft of the support and community of neighbor women. Again, it is easy to appreciate the social attraction of the Sunday meeting—the phrase itself suggests the human hunger church helped minister to.

Few such women were literate, fewer still were self-conscious about their feminine identity. Of their imaginative world we can do little more than hypothesize. But they no doubt understood their "womanly duties" in terms of domestic chores, childbearing and rearing responsibilities, their role as physical and spiritual nurturers. They responded in ways deemed appropriate to their sex to neighbors in need, especially the ill and women in childbirth, but did anything approaching a sense of sisterhood with all women of their class or race or region develop? Probably not. Was there a sense that women's needs, weaknesses, and strengths were different from men's? Definitely yes. To that degree a women's culture existed in the antebellum South, and out of it would eventually grow an expanded vision of women's roles and responsibilities. But that growth both depended on and was a response to economic, social, and cultural changes that came with war, urbanization, and the combination of forces and influences historians conveniently lump together as modernization.

SLAVE WOMEN

Slave women represent a special subset of southern women, and their lives in some measure fall outside the domain of the models and interpretations of women's history. Slave owners saw slave women as both productive and reproductive units of their workforce, and that bifocal view shows that race and class did not obliterate gender considerations. White owners expected slave women to be primarily laborers, set to field tasks even as white women were increasingly imagined as genteel homemakers. But although occasional slave women might plow (some apparently at their own request), typically female field hands did lighter chores like hoeing cotton and thinning tobacco. Women and all available hands would be put into the fields at harvest time, and indeed some nimble-fingered women were the best cotton-pickers. In off seasons or in times of inclement weather male slaves might be employed clearing land, ditching, or repairing barns and fences, and female slaves would be sent to the loom or the spinning wheel. Some women on occasion cleared land and ditched, but men did not sit at the loom. Women assumed primary responsibility for food preparation and for early parenting, but these of course were compatible with African notions of women's duties. In West Africa, too, women traditionally did much of the agricultural work. The point is that women slaves defined their labor and especially their domestic routines to be different from that of men, and their owners enforced similiar expectations. Still, white owners significantly slighted the parenting and domestic roles of slave women and forced them, when there was a conflict between duties, to serve the production needs of the plantation.

As a general rule, owners did not intrude themselves in the slaves' choice of mates, nor did they attempt through force to maximize the number of children a woman bore. This was an era when "fruitful" women of both races were idealized, and white masters often praised and rewarded slave women who were "good breeders." The irrepressible Parson Weems had advocated similar goals for white families—multiply and fill up the empty lands to the west. Planters understood that it made good business sense to allow slaves to live in family groupings and to promote having children, and slaves were obviously more content with their plight when at least they could enjoy the earthly pleasures of conjugal life and the happy patter of children underfoot. Planters would with pride point out to visitors the number of supposed healthy black babies on their plantations. But there is no clear evidence that planters ever operated stud farms, where there was a disproportionate number of childbearing women whose primary role was to produce children for the slave market. A callous forcing of certain slave men upon unwilling slave women for the sole purpose of getting her with child no doubt occurred, but it certainly was not normative behavior both for reasons of Christian morality and practical slave management. Pious masters on occasion tried to enforce evangelical attitudes toward premarital sex on slaves, who had a different concept about continence before marriage but shared the Christian view about fidelity after marriage. The white—in fact, biracial—churches upheld Christian precepts about adultery among slave couples and in various other ways tried to protect the sanctity of slave marriages within a legal system wherein husbands and wives could be separated and sold at the discretion of their owner.

As with many women, black and white, then and now, slave women had to do double duty, laboring long hours in the field then trudging back to the cabin to become mother, cook, and wife. The owner determined how late into her pregnancy she had to work in the field and how soon after delivery she had to return. Nursing mothers were allowed to visit their infants several times during their work days, or older children would bring the hungry baby to the mother at the edge of the field. Elderly women, assisted by children not yet old enough to work in the fields, often cared for the slave infants during the day, and perhaps such primitive daycare centers helped to produce a special bonding among the slave children. Slave mothers did not just concern themselves with the physical growth of their children; like all mothers, they sought to shape them into responsible adults, teaching them both folk wisdom and a good measure of Christianity. Slave mothers and fathers also through folk tales and folk lore helped give their children a means of understanding the natural and social world and socialized them into their world of bondage. Part of being a slave mother (and father, even one who lived on an adjacent farm) was teaching one's children behavior patterns that would lessen their chances of being whipped (or worse) by the white owner without letting such defensive and deferential attitudes deprive them of their own inner sense of worth and individuality. A blend of artful subterfuge and dissembling along with an internalized kernel of self-pride was taught by slave elders to the children, and we get a glimpse of this preparation for life in the Brer Rabbit tales.

A subset of slave women worked in the households of their owners. For that half of slaveholders who possessed four slaves or fewer, many owned only a slave woman who primarily did domestic work. Perhaps a single slave family was owned, or the slave husband and father was owned by a nearby white, but many such small holdings consisted of at least a slave mother with a child or two—the slave children resided with their mother regardless of the location of their father, and some whites seemed to consider the mother and children the basic family unit not subject to separation by sale. On such small farms the slave woman and her child(ren) lived in a lean-to attached to the owner's small house, or maybe slept in the attic. The slave woman would work for the owner's wife, doing most of the gardening, dairying, food preparation, washing, and so on. She and her children would have essentially the same diet as the white family, though they would take their meals separately. Living and working in such close quarters, whites and blacks came to know one another with an intimacy that could lead to affection or hate. Surely on very small farms slaves lived more under the direct supervision of whites, and it was more difficult for slave mothers or fathers so owned to keep alive separate African American folk traditions. Because there was clearly less anonymity for individual slaves on small holdings and fewer opportunities to interact with other slaves and share tales of weal and woe, small-scale bondage may have been more psychologically smothering than life on a big plantation.

On the comparatively few large plantations some slave women spent all or a good portion of their time assigned to the house of the owner, serving as cook, nursemaid to children, and housekeeper. Upper-class plantation mistresses, the women most likely to have left manuscript records, generally had most of their contact with these house slaves. The relationship between races could be relatively harmonious and affectionate; often it was tense and involved an interminable cold war of nerves, one young mistresses especially sometimes lost. Slave women who served as cooks in the big house sometimes wielded real authority over the other house slaves, and these cooks often brooked little meddling management from the plantation mistress and disciplined white children who interfered with her domain. There may have been old cooks who so strongly identified with the white family that they almost forfeited their membership in the slave community; there surely were cooks who used their privileged positions in the slave hierarchy to gain special advantages for certain slaves and family members, either by sneaking food to the quarters or by making entreaties to the master on behalf of one slave or another.

Other slave women who were nurses or nannies to white children practically lived in the big house, relieving the white mother from the unpleasant aspects of child care. Such black nurses often traveled with the white family, dressed better than field slaves, and gained a degree of familiarity with the white family that occasionally shocked northern and foreign travelers. Love and mutual respect could grow between the black woman and the white, and between slave nanny and the white children, but so could aggravation and hostility and bitterness. Many whites might have imagined a degree of love on the part of the accommodating slave women that was nonexistent, although mutual love for the white infants might well have been the catalyst for a degree of bonding between slave nurses and plantation mothers that existed nowhere else in plantation society. It is important to reemphasize that white plantation mothers did not as a matter of course hand over their infants to black wet nurses. Medical guide books pointed out the advisability of mothers' nursing their own children, and the correspondence of mothers shows their strong desire to do so. Only when nursing was impossible for a mother, and the only available woman for nursing was black, was a slave wet nurse used. Just as often the plantation mistress's sister or sister-in-law, a white neighbor, even her mother, stepped in to offer milk to the hungry infant. The idea that southern white men as a type were suckled and reared by black nannies, and that therefrom deep Oedipal complexes arose that led to a postbellum rape syndrome, is patently ridiculous.

Interracial sex did exist in the Old South, but its extent and cause is difficult to measure. In some cases love drew whites and blacks together, commonly a white man and a black woman, and some white men, such as Richard M. Johnston of Kentucky, openly acknowledged their black mistresses. No doubt there were some slave women who used sex as a means to better their own situation or that of their children. But in most cases of interracial sex the white male, from his position of legal and economic power, took advantage of helpless black women and forced them to become his partner of convenience. Just how often this happened is conjecture. Some slave narratives and memoirs—like that of Harriet Jacobs—prove miscegenation existed; many plantation mistresses, at least according to Mary Chesnut, could point out mixed-blood children on every plantation but their own; and some abolitionists described an Old South that was one giant brothel. On large plantations young white males might have considered a dalliance with a comely slave woman almost a rite of passage, but such amoral behavior, tantamount to rape, was not openly bragged about in the South as it was, for example, in Brazil. Surely evangelical attitudes made such sexual activity scandalous and probably lessened its occurrence, as did racial prejudice toward blacks. The presence in the Old South of relatively balanced sex ratios within the white population also worked against the kind of interracial behavior that occurred, for instance, between seventeenth-century French fur trappers and Indian women. Nevertheless, one proslavery advocate partially justified the institution for its providing a sexual outlet for white males, thereby protecting the virginity of white womanhood. Miscegenation obviously occurred and it normally resulted from the disproportionate power white males wielded in the society, but no precise measure of its incidence is possible.

THE CHEROKEE TRAGEDY

Following Andrew Jackson's 1814 defeat of the Creek warriors at Horseshoe Bend and the resulting Treaty of Fort Jackson, most of the Creek Indians had given up their land in the South and been removed across the Mississippi River into what was called the Indian territory, present-day Oklahoma. In subsequent treaties both state and local governments systematically forced other Indian groups, the Choctaws, Chickasaws, and Seminoles, to leave. The story of all these Indian removals is filled with chicanery and dishonesty on the part of government officials and hardship, disappointment, and death on the part of the Indians who saw agreement after agreement broken. But perhaps the most tragic episode of all involving the callous mistreatment of Indians in the South concerns the Cherokee, who more than any other Indian nation tried to follow the white man's beckon and become acculturated. In return they were shamefully betrayed by the white leaders of the South and the nation.

In 1814 the Cherokees, led by their chieftain called The Ridge, had been allies of Jackson at Horseshoe Bend, thinking thereby they could ingratiate themselves with the whites and be allowed to remain on their ancestral lands. But within two years Jackson ignored their assistance and forced two treaties upon them whereby they gave up some three million acres of land for about twenty cents an acre. Tribal leaders tried to resist Jackson by pointing out their recent cooperation at Horseshoe Bend, but Jackson was only interested in the complete removal of all Indians from all lands that white men coveted. The 1817 treaty promised the Indians replacement acreage west of the Mississippi, and Jackson expected the Cherokees would be gone from their lands centered in northeastern Georgia and neighboring portions of North Carolina, Tennessee, and Alabama within two years, but the Cherokees decided to resist politically and culturally.

Even before the end of the eighteenth century it was becoming obvious that the destruction of game meant the traditional Cherokee economy based on the fur trade was ending. Many Cherokees had begun adopting white ways, shifting their economy to agriculture, including cotton, corn, and hogs, and buying black slaves. The Cherokee lands by 1820 were dotted with plantations, sawmills, gristmills, schools, and churches, and the region was a

Christian mission field. The Cherokees developed a method of writing their language. A significant minority of Cherokee leaders spoke English and adopted the white mode of dress. The Ridge himself sent his son John Ridge and several nephews to Connecticut for schooling, and one of the nephews, who renamed himself Elias Boudinot, later became a national spokesman for the Cherokee cause. Between 1817 and 1827 the Cherokees transformed their manner of tribal government into one modeled on the United States, with a bicameral legislature and a written constitution. Their capital was located in New Echota, in northwest Georgia, from which, after 1828, they published a bilingual newspaper, the *Cherokee Phoenix.*

By the 1820s mixed-blood, sometimes mostly white, Cherokees dominated the tribe economically and politically, though they were a minority of the total population. The mixed-blood Cherokees led the movement toward adopting white ways, and they were the leaders in organizing the National Committee that governed under the new constitution. In fact, John Ross, who wrote the Cherokee constitution and became in the mid-1820s the pre-eminent Cherokee leader, was only one-eighth Cherokee. When he decided to forego his business as an Indian trader with the Cherokees and to devote his life to their behalf, he had to take instruction in their oral traditions. Ross always spoke in English. But his identity with the Cherokee cause was total.

During the 1820s Andrew Jackson was no longer in military control of the region, and the presidents—James Monroe and John Quincy Adams— were relatively sympathetic to the Cherokee position. The lecture tours of Elias Boudinot and the editorials of the nationally circulated *Cherokee Phoenix* created more support for the Indians, as did the well-dressed, fluent-in-English mixed-breed spokesmen. But on the state level Georgia was pushing the federal government hard for the Indian lands, based on claims and agreements that went back to 1802. And then, in 1828, Andrew Jackson was elected president. Georgia now had an ally in the White House, the Cherokees a determined foe. The Cherokees, however, were not without supporters, and Daniel Webster, Henry Clay, Davy Crockett, and Jackson's good friend Sam Houston all spoke on behalf of the Indians. But Jackson was able to push his Indian Removal Bill through Congress and signed it on May 28, 1830. Georgia officials did all they could to accelerate the removal process, while the Cherokees and their friends fought it in every nonviolent way they knew how. The Ridge was especially adamant against giving in. The Cherokees even took their cause to the Supreme Court, where William Wirt, who had earlier been attorney general in the Monroe and Adams administrations, argued their case. Chief Justice John Marshall wrote the decision, which sided with the Cherokee Nation in 1832, but neither Georgia nor Jackson decided to abide by the decision. Jackson was reputed to have said, "John Marshall has made his decision; now let him enforce it!" The Court, of course, had no independent mechanism of enforcement.

Within months Georgia had the Cherokee lands surveyed and began to distribute it to whites through a lottery. Whites would move in, force Indians off their farms and plantations and out of their homes and "legally" claim the property. As if Georgia was not already avaricious enough, gold was discovered in the mountainous Cherokee region. Within three years some 40,000 white Georgians were occupying the Cherokee lands, far outnumbering the Indians. Despite having come to accept the white civilization's understanding of private ownership of property, the Cherokees had theirs stolen out from under them. Jackson meanwhile was working on strategies to make conditions in general so unpalatable that the Cherokees would "voluntarily" choose to give up their lands and move west to the Indian Territory. John Ross fought back tenaciously, saying in effect that the Indians would never forsake their ancestral lands. But John Ross was wrong. Conditions had gotten so desperate that some Cherokees now felt they had no choice.

Leading a minority movement to abandon their lands were no less than full-blood John Ridge, son of The Ridge, and Elias Boudinot, who ironically represented the more prosperous, mixed-blood Cherokees. Even the *Cherokee Phoenix* editorially promoted removal westward because further resistance seemed futile. Still the full-blood Cherokee masses backed Ross—himself mostly of Scotch ancestry—and his desperate attempt to hold on to their lands centered in Georgia. Jackson took advantage of the divisions among the Cherokees, which became more bitter as Jackson's pressure intensified. Jackson chose to recognize the treaty party, led by the two Ridges, and negotiated with that group a treaty of removal in 1835. The Ross faction resisted, but Jackson and the national government had the upper hand. The anti-treaty group in effect boycotted the final treaty negotiation parley held at New Echota in late December 1835, but The Ridge himself, now advanced in age, was there and signed the agreement. The US Senate ratified the Treaty of New Echota by a razor-thin margin on May 16, 1836.

General Winfield Scott was put in charge of rounding up the Cherokees and placing them in a series of stockades across the Cherokee lands preparatory to their forced march west. John Ross used his persuasive powers to prevent Indian violence, understanding that opposition at this point would be hopeless and fatal. In fact, once he at last accepted that removal was inevitable, he with the government's blessing took charge of organizing the migration westward. (Several hundred, perhaps as many as a thousand, Cherokees fled northeastward into the Great Smokey Mountains of western North Carolina to escape removal, and their descendants live there yet.) The trip west to the Indian Territory proved long, incredibly arduous, and plagued with shortages of food, shoes, and clothing. Disease and hunger stalked the caravans westward.

By the time the Cherokees straggled into what is now Oklahoma, between January and March, 1839, approximately one quarter of their total population had perished. The survivors would come to call the forced west-ward march "The Trail of Tears." The Cherokees, who had done everything they could to accept the ways of the white man—adopting his language, his dress, his legal concepts, his crops and the practice of enslaving blacks—had been pushed aside. Three decades earlier Thomas Jefferson had suggested that such acculturation would allow Indians to be incorporated into the nation as citizens (albeit at the cost in effect of giving up their Indian iden-tity). Andrew Jackson and many southerners of his generation had a far less tolerant view. They could not imagine Indians in any form ever being assimil-able. The Cotton Kingdom was to be a white empire.

THE SOUTHERN WAY OF LIFE

The South's varied landscape, uniquely peopled as it was in part by occasional planters and many slaves, and supporting crops like cotton, rice, and sugar that could be cultivated nowhere else in the United States of that time, inspired most travelers to describe it as a region markedly distinct from the remainder of the nation. Looking back from the perspective of the late twentieth century at the great Civil War that eventually erupted between the North and the South, it is fashionable to assume that the incompatible cul-tures of the two regions made such a war inevitable. Given the course of events political and economic after 1820, a retrospective reading does suggest a series of causes that seem to make conflict necessary. Certainly by the final decade of the antebellum period both southerners and northerners became accustomed to seeing the South through spectacles that magnified the sense of Dixie's difference. Yet forgetting for the moment that it is known today what happened in 1861 and moving backward in time to the 1820s through the 1840s, how culturally distinct was the South? Was there a characteristic southern "mind," an ineffable southern way of life, a set of attitudes and val-ues and expectations—a culture that clearly made the antebellum South a separate nation that found political expression ultimately in 1861 when the various states seceded? That, in a nutshell, has been *the* central question in the history of the South.

Early on in American history observers noted that there were factors that set the South apart, even though there were disagreements over where one drew the line demarking the boundary of the South. In the colonial period some assumed the colonies to the south of New York were "southern," but this was more a geographical than a cultural notion. By the mid-eigh-teenth century spokesmen from Virginia and South Carolina especially were aware that their colonies' dependence on slave labor and exporting staple crops gave them a set of interests different from, say, Massachusetts, but dur-ing the American Revolution nationalizing sentiments overcame fledgling regional interests even as most citizens continued to identify themselves in very localistic terms. Thomas Jefferson in a famous letter to the Marquis de Chastellux in 1785 listed the divergent characteristics of the northern and southern states, and he ascribed the root cause to climate. The northern states' gradual abolition of slavery in the generation after the Revolution tended to emphasize the South's divergence, but there were also at the time southern abolitionists and colonizationists who called for freeing the slaves and settling them elsewhere. Then, beginning with the controversy in 1819 over the admission of Missouri as a slave state, a steady concatenation of political disputes elicited an ever stronger sense of southern distinctiveness, escalating from sectionalism ultimately to nationalism. But had there been no political pressure, would the North and South steadily have grown apart? Was it politics and economics that drove the wedge between the regions, or was the political controversy simply an inevitable reflection of some quintessential difference that could not be papered over with patriotic rhetoric? To pose the question bluntly, *how* different were the North and the South in the mid-nineteenth century?

Simply to pose the question that way assumes, of course, that they *were* different, and those seeking to explain the difference have offered nearly every conceivable explanation from climate to the so-called Celtic background of many white southerners. Anyone can compile a list of objective factors that document at least surface differences: the South was far more rural than the North, it had far more blacks and far fewer persons of recent European background, it had fewer miles of railroad tracks and less industrial production. But of course there were fundamental differences within the North—Massachusetts was not like Indiana—and within the South—Virginia was very much unlike Louisiana. And as long a list of objective factors documenting how the North and South were alike could be compiled by a dexterous historian. Both spoke English, both followed the English common law, both accepted the primacy of private property, both were predominantly Christian (though the South was more Protestant than the North), both believed in progress.

Yet no matter how many attributes two people share, if they disagree on one thing, and that one thing is important enough, that one dissimilarity can make all the difference in the world. Increasingly, the presence only in the South of a slave economy came to differentiate the North and the South in absolutely fundamental ways. That the two regions shared so much, even a common revolutionary heritage, exacerbated the intensity of the disagreement. The North changed more than the South did in the first half of the nineteenth century, and the concept of an emerging southern distinctiveness must be understood in a bipolar context. A relevant biological simile would be to compare the schism between the antebellum North and South to fission within a unicellular organism, wherein the single cell inside itself begins to split into two independently maturing daughter cells whose connecting link slowly becomes so attenuated that it snaps—think of Lincoln's "mystic chords of memory" trope in his first inaugural address—and the result is two totally separate cells having been created out of one.

Antebellum white southerners were very much Americans, though Americans of a special sort. But their specialness should not blind us to their identification with the United States. Southerners from the 1820s right down to the outbreak of civil war considered themselves heirs of the Revolution; in fact, they often compared secession to the 1776 rupture with Great Britain, interpreting both as efforts to protect the independence of one group of people from the tyrannizing power of a central government located elsewhere. As long as southerners thought that their peculiar institution was safe within the structure of the national political parties—only in the 1850s with the Free Soil party and then the Republican party did they genuinely feel threatened—they identified themselves politically as members of national parties. Throughout much of the antebellum period Whigs and Democrats fought to a veritable draw in the South. In fact, since each national party accepted slavery, local issues were often more controversial than national issues, and southern politicians focused on national issues precisely because the most immediate issues—dealing with personalities, internal improvements, sectional disputes within states—were often too divisive to build political organizations around.

When speaking of Manifest Destiny, or reacting to European condescension toward the nation, or joining in the celebrations of Greek independence or Lafayette's 1825 tour of the nation, or offering eulogies for John Adams and Thomas Jefferson after their almost simultaneous deaths on the fiftieth anniversary of the Declaration of Independence, southerners spoke of themselves as Americans. All Americans read much the same literature, shared in the increasing democratization of politics (still for white males only), had faith in hard work, and aspired to success. Political loyalty is not indivisible; southerners felt a loyalty to their county, their state, increasingly their region, and the nation. National loyalty began to wane only when southerners judged that their local institutions—primarily slavery and the economic and racial implications of that system—were threatened by national politics. The rise of southern separatism was a defensive response to a felt threat, not a logical outgrowth of an indigenous culture.

Yet aspects of the southern way of life helped condition how southerners came to perceive and respond to the changes underway in the North. Within the vocabulary of Americanism southerners slowly began, as it were, to speak with a different accent. In part this was a result of the localistic orientation of most southerners. Living on small farms or plantations scattered across a rural, often densely forested region, with few cities and limited transportation—all the accounts of travel in the region, whether by Fanny Kemble or Frederick Law Olmsted or Solon Robinson, are filled with references to the distance between households, the execrable roads, and the discomfort of stagecoaches, trains, and inns—and no region-wide newspapers, most southerners had little experience with or personal knowledge of the larger world. Large-scale planters understood that the international cotton market determined what they received for their crops, but had no control over it, and the basic marketing decisions were made for them by their factor, located in a port city such as Charleston, Mobile, or New Orleans. For everyday life one's world revolved around one's immediate vicinity—the household, a handful of neighbors, the local church, the crossroads store and mill, the county seat for occasional voting, and perhaps jury duty. There were local newspapers, relatives visited to relieve the tedium of rural isolation, and everyone was eager to learn news of the outside world from visitors, itinerant peddlers, and the paper or periodical often scanned at the country store. But the correspondence, diaries, and account books reveal that most people's attention was on the ordinary, practical details of farm life—the written record is filled with mundane references to the weather, to the progress of crops, to sickness, and to who preached last Sunday.

Southerners were no more localistic or provincial than similarly rural people in Michigan or Indiana, but despite wisps of news from New York or Washington, the intellectual horizons of persons engaged in everyday occupations were extremely limited. The South simply had far fewer cities and fewer opportunities to interact with a wider world. One's neighborhood and county was the locus of most political and economic dealings and of the most concern. Politics were local not only in the sense that sheriffs and justices of the peace were the most visible government officials, but delegates to the state assembly or to Congress in Washington were expected solely to represent the interests of their local constituents—that is what they were elected to do, rather than, because of their greater wisdom or broader perspective, do what was necessarily right for the nation as a whole at the expense of their immediate constituents. Politics became more localistic as they became more democratic, and nowhere in the nation were both features more prominently displayed than in the South.

This intense localism was strengthed by the influence of kinship and the growing emotional commitment to and concentration on the immediate family. Evangelical religion, ever widening its sway over the minds of southerners of all classes, also powerfully tended to narrow the conception of community to the fellowship of believers in a local congregation, with a lessened concern for the larger world. Extra-congregational associations bound like-minded Christians together in limited ways, but the individualism of the evangelical conception of a person's encounter with God and the felt primacy of one's spiritual state worked against what might be called cosmopolitanism. For similar reasons southern white evangelicals in the nineteenth century forsook their earlier antislavery sentiments and came slowly to justify slavery as God's plan for bringing heathen Africans to the South so that they might be converted to Christianity. Northern evangelicals, with a stronger societal dimension to their faith, saw revivals as precursors to a general reform of society; southern evangelicals, more personalistic, saw revivals as a means of converting individuals who might then lead more moral lives and thereby convert others among their kin and household, including their slaves. Reform evangelicalism in the North often led to abolitionism, while in the South it came to defend slavery as a veritable missionary activity toward Africans. From a world perspective both North and South were like regions where evangelical Protestantism was dominant, but from a national perspective that common faith had developed regionally specific characteristics that helped set one section apart from another.

The localism of the plantation world, even though the agricultural crops were being sold in an international market, had predisposed late-eighteenth-century planters to favor the so-called Country party in British political disputes, and as heirs of this republican ideology Revolutionary-era Americans had learned an entire political vocabulary wherein power was evil, money often corrupted, and virtue was a political term denoting disinterested devotion to the common welfare. Commercial and manufacturing development and the transforming power of capitalistic attitudes toward accumulation of wealth, rational division of labor, and maximizing efficiency—a whole congeries of causes and effects that Marxist historians have reified and popularized as "the market"—led many northern spokesmen during the second quarter of the nineteenth century away from classical republicanism in the direction of modern liberalism, with its emphasis on free labor, government-sponsored internal improvements, a national bank, and, by the by, a strengthened role in general for the central government. Politically sophisticated southerners—those opinion-shapers who wrote letters to local papers, gave speeches, and published broadsides—had their old-fashioned republican ideology reinforced precisely as they stood increasingly in opposition to the economic changes remaking the North.

The southern agricultural capitalists feared the rise of cities and industrialism in the North. For them the Bank of the United States stood for northern manipulation of credit to the detriment of the South. Internal improvements often meant taking from one locale to benefit another, and commerce came to mean "southern profits and northern wealth" and tariff programs that gouged importing regions like the South to the benefit of northern merchants and factory owners. The strengthened role of the central government raised the specter of a government whose long arm might reach into the South and interfere with slavery—from the southern viewpoint, a tyrannical exercise of governmental power. Southern localism, dependence upon imported goods, and concern for the defense of slavery led them to apply republicanism not in defense of "liberty and equality for all" but rather in defense of the interests of the white propertied classes. Liberty came to mean the right or freedom of slaveholders to own slaves. Even poor whites, those with little or no property, vaguely identified banking and an activist government with a threat to their vaunted independence. These plain folk may not have recognized the term republicanism, but the basic outline of that ideology had trickled down to them from pamphlets, newspaper editorials, and political stump speeches and helped mold their political views.

John C. Calhoun attacked the federal government and the tariff using language and ideas from the eighteenth century, and other learned spokesmen like him, in quarreling with the North, created a southern version of Adam Smith's capitalism. In a sense, the ultimate division of labor was black slavery, for having a racially distinct permanent lower class "to do the menial duties, to perform the drudgery of life," to be "the very mud-sill of society," as James Henry Hammond said in a speech to the Senate in 1858, made it possible for slaveholders (Hammond ignored what a small fraction of even the white population he was referring to) to devote themselves to the finer things of civilization. And social refinement, not keeping everyone's nose to the grindstone merely to make more money, was, southern apologists argued, precisely what Adam Smith envisioned by capitalism. So in the hands of proslavery spokesmen, true capitalism meant not free labor in urban factories and profit maximization but a system of racial slavery supporting a southern white planter aristocracy.

One other essential component of classical republicanism was the independence of the free man. Independence meant being not subject to control or pressure by another; from this there had developed in the late colonial era the idea that debt was evil, for the debtor was as clearly beholden to his creditor as the landless farmer was to the landholder. A premium was placed on the landed farmers, whom Jefferson had called "God's chosen people," who stood free of entangling debt. The opposite of independence was slavery, being totally under the control of another. For white southerners, slavery was no intellectual abstraction but a palpable fact, for around them were human reminders of what it meant not to be free. Anything that smacked of slavery for themselves caused them to shudder, with the result that white southerners carried their sense of independence like a chip on their collective shoulders. Understandably in the decade of the 1770s southern planters were quick to interpret British imperial actions in the context of republicanism, and, as pointed out in the earlier discussion of the coming of the Revolution, they bandied about the horror of their being enslaved by the minions of the king.

In the North the imagery of independence and slavery faded in the decades after the Revolution, perhaps being replaced with notions of upwardly mobile egalitarianism in the Jacksonian era, but in the South slavery remained a constant reminder to whites of what the absence of independence meant. Southern politicians interpreted many of the political events of the decades after 1820 through this perspective, rendering them supersensitive to any threat, real or implied, against their "right" as free, independent men to own and control slaves. Any government action that might interfere with their independence, or the possiblity of such action represented by a general strenthening of the central government, posed a threat to enslave them. We should not be surprised that southerners in the years after 1820 would occasionally overreact to events, including the election of Abraham Lincoln in 1860.

On a personal level, the slightest indication that a man's independence was at risk—when someone had treated him with disrespect, suggested he accept a servile role, or somehow cast aspersions on his honor—would, if he did not respond appropriately to the threat, result in his being "un-manned," that is, destroy his public stature as an independent actor and thereby enslave him, a fate held literally to be worse than death. Proud, competitive upper-class southern men, their honor slighted, challenged their attackers to a duel, a formalized way of controlling violence. Lower-class men might defend their honor—they would probably use the words "good name" instead— more spontaneously in an eye-gouging, ear-biting, no-holds-barred fight. And, it should be pointed out, a great many men of every class, devout evangelical Christians, denounced dueling and fighting and rested their dignity— their good name—upon their godly reputations.

Republicanism, capitalism, and evangelicalism were systems of belief that northerners and southerners subscribed to in differing degrees, but conditions in the South led to distinct ways of interpreting those beliefs both in the abstract and in application to their peculiar society. It should be emphasized that there were thinkers in the South who used these ideas and others to understand, analyze, sometimes critique, and often defend their society. For decades it was fashionable to say that antebellum southerners had no collective intellectual life. At the beginning of the twentieth century New Englander Henry Adams, discussing in his famous autobiography the antebellum southerners he had known at Harvard, wrote that "strictly, the Southerner had no mind; he had temperament . . . . he could not analyze an idea, and he could not even conceive of admitting two. . . ." Perhaps Adams intended the remarks to be no more than a sardonic literary conceit, but the view nevertheless became a central motif of much writing in the field of intellectual history. In part at least that erroneous judgment has held up because intellectual life has been primarily associated with the production of imaginative literature—poetry and fiction. But if we appropriately widen our definition, then a southern intellectual life does reveal itself to us in newspaper and periodical writings, mainly in the form of essays, addressing topics dealing with politics, slavery, agriculture, religion, science, and reviews of books both

American and European. The paucity of large cities with universities and libraries limited scientific achievement in the South, but southern scientists like Joseph LeConte, William Barton Rogers, and Henry William Ravenel made the most of their opportunities and gained recognition in the world-wide fraternity of scientists.

Intellectual life was not completely moribund in the Old South, and neither was it only reactive and defensive. Journals like the *Southern Quarterly Review*, the *Southern Review, Southern Literary Messenger, De Bow's Review,* and the *Southern Presbyterian Review* carried learned critical essays on current topics in theology, philosophy, literature, and economics, written often by urban southerners but read more widely across the region. Ideas and intellectual styles fashionable in Europe were commented upon and occasionally accepted. Certainly many southern intellectuals were influenced by the Romantic movement and came to see themselves (as unappreciated by the public) and their society in Romantic terms, complete with the melodramatic pessimism that was in vogue. Some southerners recognized the paradoxes and contradictions of life in a slaveholding, market-oriented agricultural society, seeing, for example, that Christian denials of materialism could conflict with speculation in cotton and slaves, that descriptions of Africans as being a separate race conflicted with the account of man's creation in Genesis, that defending white freedom and black slavery required a certain nimbleness of mind, not to say hypocrisy. And out of this intellectual tradition there did grow a corpus of writing in defense of slavery that in many ways has come to characterize "the mind of the Old South."

Proslavery writing was more than simply a knee-jerk reaction to abolitionist attacks. While it was a defense of the South's use of slave laborers, it took the form of a coherent social philosophy. The first proslavery writings had appeared in the colonial period, and in fact practically all the arguments later rehearsed in defense of the peculiar institution were first advanced in the eighteenth century. Proslavery literature was not confined to the South, and antebellum defenders of the status quo often borrowed ideas from and cited both New England and West Indian writers. These early proslavery works were produced before slavery was under moral attack and suggest that factors other than guilt motivated at least many proslavery authors, including an unexceptional desire to legitimate the world as they found it. Yet this is not to deny that events after 1831—the beginning of modern abolitionism, Nat Turner's revolt that same year, increasing sectional tensions, and England's abolition of slavery in her colonies—intensified the interest in constructing defenses of slavery and gave the enterprise an intellectual significance it had not had before. The literature became more extensive, more carefully argued, more widely read, less abstract, and more contextualized to fit the situation the South found itself in.

Widely acknowledged as the first of the new defenses of slavery was

Thomas R. Dew's *Review of the Debate in the Virginia Legislature,* published in 1832 in response to the 1831 emancipation debates in Richmond. Dew was less concerned with arguing the merits of slavery in some utopian, abstract sense than in considering it in the context of Virginia and the South. Slavery as practiced in this particular time and place—a Christian society—was good. The practical difficulties of changing the status of slaves outweighed in his mind the admitted abstract evil of slavery. He argued that society evolved gradually over long periods of time, that relations between classes and races were in organic relation to the whole of society, and that schemes for a quick fix of theoretical imperfections would likely result in catastrophe. He counseled not only a frank defense of slavery in the South but argued that it benefited the blacks and, refuting Thomas Jefferson, Dew argued that it was (read should be) conducive to making whites more responsible and benevolent toward others. Dew also used every argument at his command, drawing from the Bible, from history, from economics, to defend the institution, suggesting by so doing that the sources for proslavery sentiment were universal and irrefutable.

In the three decades after the publication of Dew's pamphlet the South saw a proliferation of similar efforts, some emphasizing religion, some history, some early sociology, some science and pseudoscience (for example, Josiah Nott's analysis of the cranial capacity of various races and his suggestion that Africans were not genetically related to white men), but religion lay at the center of most proslavery arguments. In more formal proslavery writings the Biblical defense consisted of scriptural exegesis to demonstrate that neither the Old Testament nor the New Testament attacked slavery, that Jesus never condemned the institution, nor did Paul. This literalistic proslavery reading of the Bible was not a theological rationalization but a consistent southern attitude toward what was considered the authoritative Word of God. The Bible did not categorically teach that slavery in every situation was wrong. The prosperity of the Cotton South was seen as further evidence that slavery was in the specific southern setting the recipient of divine approval.

Southerners also held a racially hierarchical view of society, and they found nothing in the scriptures to suggest such a view was wrong. White southerners more interested in the practice of Christianity than in theology also defended slavery as the means to convert Africans to Christianity. Again, neither was this simply a hypocritical response to slavery. Evangelical Christians saw the world as a travail of pain for everyone, with heaven the goal and reward. For them, dismissing the earthly drudgery and suffering of slaves as being inconsequential when compared to an eternity with God was comparable to consoling each other when confronted with hardship and death. To a modern reader the remark in 1809 by Francis Asbury, a Methodist bishop, that "What is the personal liberty of the African which he may abuse, to the salvation of his soul; how may it be compared?" sounds like the most egregious kind of special pleading, but to antebellum white evangelicals it was an honest statement of the belief that exchanging pagan life in Africa for Christian conversion was a good bargain for slaves. It never occurred to proslavery advocates to ask the slaves how they felt about the transaction.

Proslavery writers argued that slavery had existed throughout history; that it provided the leisure necessary for a master class to advance civilization; that it was a more benevolent system for the laboring class than harsh, capitalistic "wage slavery" for free laborers in the North; that it was the best way to prevent the rise of labor unrest and to control a large, submerged worker class of another race; that statistics showed slaves were better off than northern factory workers; that, given the reality of four million blacks living in the South and the impracticality either of transporting them elsewhere or of their living peacefully together with free whites, it was the only real solution to a concrete problem. This last point grew in importance, for whatever southern thinkers in the abstract might have thought about the rightness or wrongness of slavery, they could not imagine any other solution of the immediate situation in the South. Even to suggest ending the institution of slavery was to threaten the South with economic ruin and to risk a genocidal race war that the slaves would surely lose.

Southerners increasingly convinced themselves that they were in an intractable dilemma, which admitted of no solution save cautious attempts to ameliorate the worst abuses of slavery. In some sense proslavery arguments containing references to the responsibilities of masters toward their slaves were backhanded criticisms of slaveholders who mistreated their bondspeople; such arguments were calls for reforming slavery as well as defenses of it. Honest slaveholders acknowledged that some masters were cruel—just as there were cruel husbands and fathers—but such exceptions to the ideal of paternalistic slaveholding no more discredited the institution of slavery in their eyes than less-than-ideal husbands and fathers discredited the institutions of marriage and the family. While admittedly susceptible to evil, like all human institutions, slavery for the most part was simply accepted by southern whites as one of the givens of southern life. The good owner's dilemma was how to preserve slavery and keep it as humane as possible. It was conceded that slavery could be evil—and often, in the world's history, had been—evil, but in the peculiar circumstances of the Christian South it could be both benevolent and redemptive for the slaves.

Southern thinkers came to identify slavery with their regional economy and their personal hopes for prospering, their sense of being responsible Christians, and their self-respect as free men, and defenses of slavery became defenses of the whole southern way of life, especially in its idealized form. Ministers in particular argued that the dominance of the evangelical churches in the region showed that divine providence smiled on the region, and individual Christian slaveholders were further proof of the basic rightness of the institution as it existed in the South. When sufficient numbers of white southerners came to feel that the United States government threatened slavery and all it stood for, secession became a live option. Many of those who cautioned against secession did so because they believed that even with a number of disturbing threats from the North, slavery would have a better chance of surviving if the South remained in the Union and fought tenaciously for the South's "rights" in the federal Congress. Despite the divisions in the South over how best to do it, preserving slavery was the overwhelming concern of white southerners as the decade of the 1850s drew to an end.

THE BEGINNING OF SECTIONALISM

Slavery had seemed secure until the Missouri crisis of 1819; the institution was defended by the clear though implicit language of the Constitution. But once the possibility of interference with slavery by the national government was broached, hypersensitive southerners developed an uncanny ability to find threats against their peculiar institution in any number of quarters. For almost fifty years sectional politics had been kept at bay because of pressing external threats against the nation (in 1776 and 1812) and because of the power of ideas (Jefferson's vision that had led to the withering away of the Federalist party). But the threats that southerners perceived in 1820 were internal, not international, and no strong successor to James Monroe stood in the political wings to keep alive the Virginia dynasty. True, the Federalist party was no longer a rival at the presidential level, but Monroe's second administration was hardly an "era of good feelings." Perhaps "era of rising suspicions" would be a more accurate label, for a series of unconnected events combined to rachet up the tensions of many southerners and an unprecedented scramble began among would-be presidents that roiled the political waters. Until now political parties had existed as only means to an end, hardly institutions to which one gave devotion and allegiance. But a shrewd political operator from New York, Martin Van Buren, pioneered the idea that parties were positive agencies that mobilized the sovereign power of the people and, by stretching across various states and regions, served to minimize factional regionalism. Politics became a profession, and political parties came to be seen as a positive good, a means of expressing the popular will against the narrow, self-serving machinations of political elites and insiders.

The Missouri controversy and the Panic of 1819 were not the only events of that fateful year that southerners saw as frightful portents of the future. Virginian John Marshall had long used his position as Chief Justice of the Supreme Court to strengthen the authority of the central government, and a long trail of decisions—*Marbury v. Madison* (1803), *Fletcher v. Peck* (1810), *Martin v. Hunter's Lessee* (1816), and, later, *Cohens v. Virginia* (1821)—

had set aside the decisions and statutes of state courts and legislatures. In two key decisions in 1819, that of *Dartmouth College v. Woodward* and *McCulloch v. Maryland*, Marshall's conception of the Supreme Court's power over states and his conception of the practically unlimited authority of the federal goverment were emphatically stated. The *McCulloch* decision was especially far reaching, for in defending the constitutionality of the Bank of the United States, Marshall had greatly stretched the definition of what powers were allowed the federal government by the Constitution. Within a month of the decision, a hard-hitting series of critical essays (probably written by Judge William Brockenbrough, a prominent Richmond judge and orthodox Jeffersonian opponent of enhancing the role of the central government) attacking Marshall's "alarming errors" began appearing in the Richmond *Enquirer.* Marshall felt that this Virginia critic would spread the virus of states' rightism throughout the land, so he penned a biting reply under the name of "A Friend to the Union" that appeared in the Philadelphia *Union* in late April. Wary Virginians were ready for Marshall, and an even mightier opponent, Judge Spencer Roane of the Virginia Court of Appeals—and a friend of Brockenbrough—issued a stinging four-part reply under the pseudonym "Hampden" (a not-so-subtle reference back to the eighteenth-century country-party ideologue in England and hero of Revolutionary-era Americans) in the Richmond *Enquirer.* Marshall tried again to silence the Virginia critics in a series of nine nationalistic essays published in the Alexandria *Gazette,* this time signing the articles "A Friend of the Constitution." Neither side convinced the other, but the whole exchange aggravated the fears of increasing numbers of thoughtful Virginians (and by extension, southerners) of the dangers to slavery that inhered in the growing power of Washington. Marshall's brilliance could not still the states' rights rumblings beginning to be heard in the South.

While the South was still reeling from the economic effects of the Panic of 1819, South Carolina was shocked in 1822 by the discovery of a widespread rebellion planned by Charleston slaves, led by a literate free black named Denmark Vesey. In one of the subsequent trials slave testified that Vesey had shown him a copy of an antislavery speech made by Senator Rufus King of New York—concrete evidence, in the eyes of South Carolinians, that northern abolitionist activities literally threatened the lives of white southerners. The lessons, they judged, were that the South could brook no criticism of its institutions and that southerners must stand vigilant to guard against any and every threat. A siege mentality was beginning, and it would soon arch over the South like a great dome, reflecting and magnifying every utterance and action that could be considered unfavorable. In the political turmoil of the early 1820s, as potential presidential successors to James Monroe jockeyed for position, it became clear how important this contest was to the South, whose voters thought that the president set the tone of the central government. For most southerners, the optimum political philosophy was that represented by the Virginia and Kentucky resolutions—a very limited central government with maximum authority residing in the state governments, which, the theory ran, could be expected to protect local interests (i.e., slavery).

As long as there had been a Federalist party in opposition, the Republicans had been unified, especially since Jefferson, Madison, and Monroe had seemed by experience and prestige to be the logical successors to the presidency. But after 1820, with the explicit understanding that Monroe would follow precedent and not run for a third term and with no national opposition party to forge Republican unity, the Republican coalition began to dissolve and reaggregate around a number of rival sectional candidates. Republican congressmen had previously met in caucus to choose the party presidential candidate, who was subsequently elected by the electoral college chosen not by the people but by the state legislatures. However, a popular political movement had arisen after 1820 against this essentially legislative election of the president—spokesmen "for the people" began advocating popular election of the presidential electors—and this democratic sentiment reflected unfavorably on the idea of a party caucus itself. No small group of elected officials through backroom machinations should be able to choose candidates for the American people. But the Republican congressional insiders, largely influenced by the Virginians, favored William H. Crawford of Georgia to succeed Monroe; Crawford was a conservative states' right advocate and a strict constructionist who had served as Monroe's secretary of the treasury. When the party caucused to appoint him the official candidate, only one-fourth of the Republican congressmen attended. Even with the backing of Thomas Jefferson, Crawford could not garner the same congressional support that his predecessors had enjoyed, and the weak caucus vote indicated that a new kind of politics had emerged.

Everyone seeking the presidency in 1824 called himself a Republican, but the different approaches to government represented by the various regional candidates revealed the philosophical diversity that the Virginia Dynasty had been more or less able to control. In truth, under the political labels Quids and Old Republicans, Virginian dissenters like John Randolph and Nathaniel Macon had attacked the nationalizing tendencies of Jefferson and especially Madison and Monroe, who had responded to the humiliating experience of the War of 1812 by attempting to strengthen the federal government. John C. Calhoun as a young congressman and as secretary of war under Monroe had strongly advocated a tariff to improve the national government's fiscal health, and he had energetically sought to rationalize and centralize the military arm of the government. But the events of 1819 and thereafter had caused many southerners to reconsider the advantages of strengthening the central government and increasing its revenues (at, they believed, the expense of the South). Calhoun—never completely separating his presidential ambitions from the changing political climate of South Carolina, a state crippled in the early 1820s by a decrease in cotton prices and frightened by Denmark Vesey's aborted plot—found himself quickly reevaluating his politics as he campaigned for the presidency.

Henry Clay, the gregarious Speaker of the House from Kentucky, with a personality as open and inviting as Calhoun's, was intense and cerebral, approached the presidency with a nationalistic platform that in its calls for economic development revealed a Hamiltonian vision of America. Calling his plan the American System, Clay projected an industrial East that would both provide factory goods for the South and West and be the leading market for the staple crops of the South and the meat and grain of the West. He proposed a far-reaching program of internal improvements that by turnpikes and canals would tie the regional markets together into a national economy. The profitable commercial system that Clay envisioned would be made stable by sound credit based on a strong national bank.

John Quincy Adams, the aloof and learned secretary of state, a firm and principled nationalist, possessed all the qualities of a great president except political instincts, and while he could count on the solid support of fellow New Englanders, his conception of politics did not prepare him for the kind of rambunctious campaigning being perfected on the hustings of the South and West. He never understood that he was about to be eclipsed by a new kind of political phenomenon, the personified expression of mass democracy.

Andrew Jackson did not possess the learning of Adams, the national vision of Clay, or the analytical logic of Calhoun; he had not been schooled at the feet of a previous president as Jefferson, Madison, and Monroe had been. But he possessed enormous name recognition because of his victory over the British at New Orleans in 1815 and his exploits as an Indian fighter. He was a natural politician who seemed instantly to sense the national mood and to project a blend of nationalistic jingoism. Political operators like Van Buren recognized his public appeal and with other supporters helped turn the wealthy lawyer and large slaveholder into a living icon symbolically representing the will of the common people—General Jackson became almost a force of nature, and the masses found him irresistible even though he seemed to have no clear program or position on such critical topics as the tariff. Calhoun—at the time secretary of war—discovered in early campaigning in Pennsylvania the patriotic attractions Jackson had for the voters and pulled out of the presidential race, correctly assuming he could win the vice-presidency instead and likewise assuming (incorrectly it turns out) he would then be safely be in line for the next election. When the nation's votes were cast in 1824, Jackson had far more popular votes than anyone else and also more electoral votes, but he did not have a majority in the electoral college.

According to the Twelfth Amendment, in such a situation the House of

Representatives chooses the president from among the top three vote getters, a rule that eliminated Clay, the popular Speaker of the House, who was fourth in electoral votes. But Clay had great prestige in the House and played the kingmaker in the ensuing vote. Crawford had suffered a debilitating stroke in the campaign year and though he had not pulled out of the race, his candidacy was obviously dead. Clay noted Jackson's popularity but disdained his abilities, once commenting that simply killing a lot of Redcoats hardly prepared one to be president. And Clay recognized that Adams's nationalism closely resembled his own American System. So Clay threw his decisive support behind Adams, who as a result became the sixth president of the United States. As if this loss of the presidency even though he had dominated both the popular and electoral vote was not enough to anger the hot-tempered General Jackson, Adams's prompt appointment of Clay as secretary of state was the excuse to mount a campaign of outraged moralism about the "corrupt bargain" between the so-called Puritan president and the blackleg politician. Clay of course had diplomatic experience, and Adams was too prudish to plot, but Jackson had found an effective campaign issue. He and his supporters instantly began preparing the ground for a popular electoral assault against Adams's presidency, a campaign that cemented the new conception of party politics and essentially destroyed Adams' administration—an administration of expansive vision that called for a national university, a great astronomical observatory, and a national transportation system, but never recognized that its support was dissolving beneath its feet.

As the election of 1828 neared, it became increasingly clear that Jackson's party—now called the Democratic Republican party to distinguish itself from Adams's National Republicans—had mastered the techniques of mass politics. Besides the matter of personalities, the only concrete issue was tariff policy. Southerners like John C. Calhoun had supported the tariff of 1816 in the nationalistic afterglow of defeat of the British, but manufacturing interests in the Middle Atlantic states had won a far higher tariff in 1824, one clearly benefiting them at the expense of other parts of the nation. South Carolina, suffering under falling cotton prices, felt especially burdened by the higher tariffs. Calhoun had reconsidered the pros and cons of the tariff, admitting that he had not clearly differentiated in his own mind in 1816 the merits of a protective tariff versus one essentially to raise revenue for the government. The latter he still supported so long as the rates were moderate, but protective tariffs that benefited a narrow set of interests or only one portion of the nation he now opposed. Jackson's position on the tariff was unclear, but spokesmen for a variety of interests began to lobby for a new tariff in 1828. Jackson's managers concocted a hodgepodge tariff bill that had little logic and seemed to dissatisfy a variety of interest groups. Perhaps Vice President Calhoun, who surreptitiously had a hand in it, secretly intended it to be so unappealing that even normal pro-tariff congressmen would turn it down.

But Senator Van Buren at the last moment effected a minor compromise that satisfied the interests of the woolens manufacturers, and—voilà!—the so-called Tariff of Abominations passed.

Although southern opposition to the tariff was immediate, as Jackson's managers had anticipated, he was not implicated in its passage; he over-whelmingly won the votes of the South in the presidential election of 1828. But no state was more hurt by the tariff than South Carolina, and no state was more politically solid. Slavery was dominant in all regions (except a tiny far-western alpine section), and the upcountry was firmly committed to slavery and cotton and the lowcountry to slavery and rice. Fear that their slave-based agricultural economy was threatened by the tariff fueled feverish opposition to the levy in South Carolina, hotheads began calling for non-consumption of taxed imports and began discussing the most extreme states' rights ideas. Cal-houn had shifted a long way from his 1816 nationalism to accommodate the new situation in his home state, but he was not yet a secessionist. He feared that unchecked central government power, exhibited in such matters as the tariff, might drive an injured region in desperation to leave the union. In 1828, in order to moderate the most radical states' rights advocates in South Carolina, he secretly wrote a document entitled the *South Carolina Exposition and Protest,* which proposed a mechanism for a state to use to check central-government actions that it found unacceptable. Perhaps South Carolina's own experience with the so-called Compromise of 1808, which had effected a rough balance of power between the upcounty and the lowcountry, had sug-gested to Calhoun the efficacy of a system whereby the people of one state, voicing their opinion in a specially called convention, could declare a national law null and void within the boundary of that state. Calhoun was searching for a conservative, undisruptive, orderly, constitutional means to protect state sovereignty without necessitating the state's withdrawal from the federal union.

Jackson did not know that Calhoun was the author of the *Exposition,* but differences in personality and style soon divided them, and the fingerprints of Van Buren were often on the issues that drove a wedge between the two southern politicians. Jackson and his supporters legitimated partisan patron-age politics as appropriate for a democracy, and they adopted from the short-lived Anti-Masonic party the idea of a party convention to replace the out-moded party caucus. But Jackson and Calhoun split less on matters of campaigning than on such symbolic issues as the morality of Peggy Eaton, the saucy wife of Secretary of War John H. Eaton. Floride Calhoun, John C. Cal-houn's wife, considered Mrs. Eaton a woman of compromised virtue and snubbed her. Calhoun realized the touchiness of the situation but accepted his wife's position. Jackson, remembering similar slights against Rachel Jack-son, his beloved wife who died before he became president, instantly sided with the Eatons and, egged on by widower Van Buren who affected to dote on

Mrs. Eaton, came to blame Calhoun for the insult both to her and, indirectly, to himself. His suspicions about Calhoun raised and fed with poisonous ideas by Van Buren, who already saw himself replacing Calhoun as vice-president on the 1832 ticket, Jackson heard fresh rumors that Calhoun—then secretary of war—had objected to Jackson's high-handed military incursion against Florida back in 1818, that Calhoun was the anonymous author of the *South Carolina Exposition,* and that he was at the head of secessionist activitites in that state. Two strong-headed egos clashed, and neither would back down.

The issue was brought to a head indirectly when Senator Thomas Hart Benton of Missouri became the spokesman on behalf of a federal policy to facilitate squatters buying from the government the land they occupied. When easterners, led by Senator Samuel A. Foote of Connecticut, proposed limiting public land sales for a time, Senator Robert Y. Hayne of South Carolina saw a chance to attach the West to the South. Addressing the Senate in long and divisive remarks, he sought to wean the West away from supporting the tariffs and clumsily succeeded in turning the debate over western land policy into a debate over the constitutionality of the tariff. In the course of his harangue Hayne incorporated ideas from Calhoun's *Exposition.* Hayne's speech gained great attention, but even more interest was shown in the reply to it being prepared by Senator Daniel Webster of Massachusetts, the powerful orator with a massive head and puny scruples. The Senate was full on January 20 and 26, 1830, as the mighty Webster sent verbal wave after wave crashing against Hayne's logic, and generations of schoolchildren later memorized the closing of his peroration with its dual vision of two Americas, one "drenched . . . in fratricidal blood" and the other gleaming in peace and prosperity, and then the famous ending: "Liberty and Union, now and forever, one and inseparable."

What was Jackson's position on the escalating controversy over the tariff and, by implication, nullification? Even at this far remove one can feel the tension when all the administration bigwigs assembled on April 13, 1830, at Brown's Indian Queen Hotel in Washington for the annual Jefferson Day Dinner. Two dozen toasts preceded Jackson's, but when his turn came he raised himself to his full height, looked pointedly at Calhoun, lifted high his glass, and declared: "Our Union—It must be preserved!" Calhoun, his turn immediately following, stood up as every eye in the room watched his response. With his hand shaking ever so slightly but with his voice powerful and firm, he returned the challenge: "The Union, next to our liberty most dear!" Then, in a didactic soliloquy that deflated the effect of his toast, he continued: "May we all remember that it can only be preserved by respecting the rights of the States and distributing equally the benefit and the burthen of the Union!" The break between the two men now was irreparable, and confirmation of Calhoun's 1818 criticism of Jackson only deepened the rift.

Shortly afterward Jackson asked for the resignation of his cabinet in order to purge it of enemies to Eaton and himself, and Calhoun could read the handwriting on the wall—Van Buren, named minister to Great Britain, was being groomed to replace him as vice president.

Andrew Jackson was a strong nationalist, but he understood the states' rights argument as well; when he vetoed the Maysville Road Bill on May 27, 1830, it was because, as he pointed out, the road lay entirely within Kentucky and was therefore properly a matter only of that state's concern. When in 1832 Chief Justice John Marshall on the Supreme Court ruled that the Georgia law regarding Cherokee lands was unconstitutional, Jackson, an inveterate Indian hater, ignored Marshall's decision and let Georgia in effect nullify the Court decision. And though Jackson accepted the principle of protective tariffs, he believed that the rates were too high and in 1829, 1830, and 1831 called for lowering the tariff. Finally, after much wrangling, the Tariff Bill of 1832 passed on July 14, lowering the rates substantially. Jackson hoped thereby to take the wind out of the nullificationists' sails, but South Carolinians—with visions of Wendell Lloyd Garrison's screaming headlines in the abolitionist newspaper *Liberator* vivid in their minds and the fright of Nat Turner's 1831 Virginia slave rebellion still making their blood run cold—were now in no mood to compromise. Calhoun, apparently thinking the tariff reduction was an attempt to buy off South Carolina at the cost of its principles, huffily returned to South Carolina and soon resigned the vice presidency.

The state elections in South Carolina were scheduled for October 1832, and the nullification issue dominated everything else. There was a small unionist party comprising upcounty yeomen who were emotionally attached to the idea of the union and Andy Jackson as a patriotic idol without any of the Hamiltonian politics of modern nationalism. The unionists were led by a handful of wealthy, cosmopolitan, conservative lowcountry planters and Charleston merchants who simply feared precipitous action, but the nullifiers controlled the state and carried the elections. The newly elected legislature then called for the election of delegates to a special state convention—the traditional way of going back to the people for direction on issues of fundamental importance—to consider nullification. On November 19 the convention delegates assembled at Columbia and debated the tariffs of 1828 and 1832. Drawing on the logic of Calhoun's *Exposition* whereby a state had the right to exercise its limited sovereignty in opposition to federal authority, the convention on November 24 adopted an Ordinance of Nullification declaring the contested tariffs unconstitutional and hence "null, void, and no law, nor binding upon this state." The state legislature met subsequently and forbade the collection of tariff duties after February 1, 1833, threatening, if federal troops were sent to try to enforce the payment of duties, that the state would secede from the union. The legislature, in an in-your-face mood, then chose fiery Senator Robert Y. Hayne the new governor and appointed Calhoun to succeed him as senator.

Calhoun's motives in all this were complex, made even more so by the personal animosity between himself and Jackson. Calhoun still believed himself a true nationalist (he held on to his presidential ambitions) and saw nullification as a way to forestall more extreme "fire-eaters" in South Carolina whose *first* response was secession. He feared that a federal tariff and other centralizing policies would soon endanger slavery, giving the southern states no alternative but to leave the union. Calhoun saw nullification as a legal means within the bounds of the Constitution of protecting essential southern interests, thereby preserving the fundamental nature of the union without sacrificing the South. He and fellow South Carolinians expected other southern states to follow suit, but though other deep South states opposed the tariff and feared northern abolition, they revered Andrew Jackson and the union and considered nullification simply a radical pretext for secession. Had Jackson been less popular or Calhoun more a southwide hero, additional southern states might have bought into nullification and played a moderating role on South Carolina. But increasingly isolated even from its slaveholding neighbors and out of step with the emerging national party system that exercised some control over eccentric states, South Carolina was intensely preoccupied with its "endangered position" and like a runaway steam engine puffed and hissed and rushed ahead with nothing to stop it but a great collision.

For the moment Andrew Jackson provided the unmoveable force that slowed the secession express. No intellectual giant and a man of inconsistent nationalism—witness his opposition to Clay's American System and his rebuff of John Marshall—Jackson nevertheless would accept no threat to the union for which he had suffered as a child in the Revolution and for which he had fought at New Orleans. When push came to shove, Jackson used an iron fist. The audacity of the Nullification Ordinance incensed him, and he responded in kind with a Proclamation to the People of South Carolina (drafted by Louisianian Edward Livingston, secretary of state) on December 10: "I consider . . . the power to annul a law of the United States, assumed by one State, incompatible with the existence of the Union, contradicted expressly by the letter of the Constitution, unauthorized by its spirit, inconsistent with every principle on which it was founded, and destructive of the great object for which it was formed." Shortly thereafter he sent General Winfield Scott with US Army troops to reinforce Castle Pinckney and Fort Moultrie in Charleston Harbor and asked Congress to pass a Force Bill giving him express authority to use military force to compel obedience to federal law in South Carolina.

While Congress was debating the Force Bill, Henry Clay was persuaded to use his unique legislative skills to push through a compromise tariff bill. Assisted by Senator Calhoun, Clay was able to get through Congress a significant tariff reduction to take place over nine years. It passed on March 1, 1833, the same day the Force Bill was passed. President Jackson signed both into law the following day. The South Carolina legislature, having won a tariff reduction but not having attracted additional southern support (slavery was not yet the controlling issue that overwhelmed every other consideration in southern politics), and facing the reality of Jackson armed by the Force Bill, soon met and on March 15 rescinded the Ordinance of Nullification. Three days later, to save face, it passed another ordinance nullifying the Force Bill, but of course this was an empty gesture that Jackson was wise enough to ignore. Both sides claimed victory. South Carolina got the tariff lowered, and President Jackson smashed the Ordinance of Nullification and defended the supremacy of the union. A potential national conflict had been averted. But South Carolina did not feel chastised and perhaps learned too well another lesson: nullification was no option for discontented states, which left only secession.

THE POLITICS OF SECTIONALISM

Although the compromise tariff settled one issue for the time, worried southerners remained paranoid about criticism of slavery, fearing not only slave unrest and rebellion—they could point to the examples of Nat Turner and Denmark Vesey—but the possible evaporation of support among those whites who owned no slaves. Most white southerners foresaw a threat in abolitionist materials indiscriminately circulated throughout their region and wanted to ban what they considered inflammatory matter from the mail. Jackson and his successor as president, Martin Van Buren, sympathizing with the southern position and treasuring the southern vote, effectively pressured postmasters to restrain such literature from being sent to the South. Enough northern Democrats sided with their southern colleagues to maintain what was called the "gag rule," which automatically tabled abolitionist petitions to Congress and squelched the possiblity of divisive congressional debate. A lid was thus placed on the simmering pot of abolition, but everyone understood that the heat could be turned up, and one of the major goals of political parties for the next generation was to dampen the fire of slavery controversy.

Slavery was not the only issue in American politics. Even by 1832 two divergent approaches to the future were emerging. One view, following in the activist government tradition of Alexander Hamilton, John Quincy Adams, and Henry Clay, saw opportunity in terms of economic development and diversification, internal improvements, and the use of national resources to shape and reform social behavior. Supporters of this tradition came to oppose Andrew Jackson because his vision of America appeared to them to be backward looking. The view of Jackson and his followers was of a restricted role for the national government in economic planning, was more concerned with the perceived loss of personal independence to big government and big financial institutions, and stressed westward expansion rather than economic modernization. His enemies were infuriated by Jackson's imperial vision of his own role as president, seeing himself as the unique embodiment of the people's will by virtue of his popular election. (It was at this time that Jackson's managers changed the name of his party from the Democratic Republicans to the Democratic.) To Jackson's supporters he was their defender against "the interests." This fundamental difference of opinion about the proper role of government—and divergent vision of the course of empire—came to be focused on the rechartering of the Second Bank of the United States (BUS).

The friends of the bank and the enemies of Jackson hoped to put him in an untenable political position in 1832 by proposing congressional rechartering of the BUS four years ahead of schedule, but Jackson parlayed popular fears of huge and distant banks in general into a horror of "the monster" Bank of the United States in particular. The chimerical appeal to many voters that election year of the short-lived anti-Masonic party indicates how pervasive was a vague fear generated by a series of unsettling economic and social changes. Even had third party candidate William Wirt not drained away some of challenger Henry Clay's vote, Andrew Jackson with his image of bold and fearless leadership would have still swept the election. His veto of the bank bill thus approved by the people, Jackson moved to dismantle the offending institution. He had to fire two secretaries of the treasury until he found obliging Roger B. Taney who would do his bidding and remove federal funds from the BUS and place them in specially selected "pet banks" in several states. The BUS's able director, Nicholas Biddle, responded by calling in loans, hoping to cause a depressionary panic that would force the business community to pressure Jackson to back down. Jackson was too stubborn to retreat; besides, he had a typical westerner's animosity to a Philadelphia bank controlled by northeastern investors. Biddle relented, but by then the pet banks were lending money so freely that an uncontrolled boom had begun, fueled by the administration's opening up of vast public lands for sale. Then, just as suddenly, this reckless boom collapsed when on July 11, 1836, Jackson issued his Specie Circular, which required that after August 15 federal land be paid for only in gold or silver. Aggravated by the Bank of England's curtailment of British capital flowing to America, the land boom soon collapsed, as did many banks and associated activities, but not before Jackson's handpicked successor, Martin Van Buren, had won the White House. Jackson's political enemies, who had taken to calling themselves Whigs in an attempt to paint him a tyrannical "King Andrew"—thereby utilizing the rhetoric of the American Revolution—ran a team of regional presidential candidates against Van Buren, but the Whigs had not yet learned how to counter Jackson's appeal to the common man.

Van Buren had hardly assumed office before the panic of 1837 hit with a staggering blow, causing severe economic problems throughout the nation until the early 1840s. The Whig party could smell victory in the next election; and its leaders, Clay and Webster, began to maneuver, essentially cancelling each other out to the benefit of a dark horse, William Henry Harrison, an old Indian war hero. Through a blatant use of campaign gimmicks, symbolic imagery, and demagogic appeals that rival present-day presidential politics, the Whigs beat Van Buren in 1840 at his own game. After several years of turmoil and internal adjustment, and despite the strategy of the campaign, the Whig party now clearly represented the interests of those who had a more modern, more cosmopolitan view of the interrelationships between commerce, industry, internal improvements, and stable fiscal institutions. The Democratic party, with a 1790s attitude toward states' rights and a lingering republican/country/party fear of governmental power and the corruptive possibilities of government money, became increasingly the party of outsiders, small farmers, urban artisans, and newly arrived immigrants, who valued their "independence" and freedom of individual opportunity more than national economic planning. In his opposition to Jackson, Calhoun had been an early Whig, but with Jackson out of the way Calhoun moved to his more natural position back in the Democratic party.

The leadership of both the Whigs and the Democrats understood that on one issue, slavery, there could be no debate if southern votes were desired. This conspiracy of silence allowed both parties to be national parties; while the Democrats were more successful in winning the White House, for the period from 1832 to 1852 the Whigs and the Democrats were equally balanced rivals in southern congressional elections. Large planters, along with merchants and bankers in the South's cities, tended to support the Whigs. Smaller planters and yeomen farmers tended to vote Democratic. Both southern Whigs and Democrats saw themselves as representing the interests of the South and protecting the institution of slavery. The personality and character of the candidate was important, but so were national issues, and elections were hard fought and attracted an increasingly high turn-out as property qualifications were ended and the presidency became a matter of popular election. As long as slavery was avoided, the emergent two-party system facilitated a growth of democratic participation in government and provided, through the national parties, a workable means of moderating regional extremism in politics. Eventually, however, slavery would become an issue on which it was impossible to compromise.

THE TEXAS QUESTION

The controversy over whether Texas should be admitted to the union as a state, then the consequences of its admission, proved to be a wedge that threatened to irreparably break apart the convenient compromise on slavery. Texas, a part of the Mexican state of Coahuila, had lain almost completely neglected by the Spanish colonial government for a half century. By the early nineteenth century there were only a handful of small mission settlements, several thousand non-Indian inhabitants, and a pitiful economy. Land-hungry adventurers and desperate men one step ahead of the US law began to trickle into Texas in the first decade of the century, illegally settling and trading between Louisiana and eastern Texas. There were several abortive attempts to seize portions of Texas and found new empires, none of which were successfull but all of which worried authorities in Mexico City. By the terms of the Adams–Onis Treaty of 1819 the United States government gave up all claim to Texas, but southerners with visions of virgin soil for the taking paid little heed to diplomacy. Then Spain changed its mind, deciding to allow some settlers in and, by treating them well, hoped to tie their allegiance to Mexico and thereby form a buffer against future United States expansion. Once Mexico gained its independence from Spain in 1821, it pursued this policy more aggressively, even legalizing commerce with the United States.

Moses Austin, whose lead mining business in Missouri had been ruined by the panic of 1819, was alert to new opportunity. Through connections in Louisiana he heard rumors of the richness of Texas land and the possibility of a change in Mexican attitudes toward "gringo" settlers. Austin promptly went to San Antonio, where, after a confusing period of talk and rebuff and reconsideration, he was awarded in January 1821 a grant of 200,000 acres if he would settle 300 families in some as-yet-unspecified region of Texas. Moses Austin died before he could effect his plan, but his son, Stephen F. Austin, took up the mantle to become the founder of Anglo Texas. In the next few years the terms of the Austin grant changed several times, and other land promoters—people such as Sterling C. Robertson and Green DeWitt—also worked out agreements with Mexico and brought settlers in. Mexico required that the settlers accept at least nominally the Catholic faith, and the constitution of Coahuila prohibited slavery. The settlers from the mostly Protestant South effectively ignored the Catholic requirement and found a vague loophole in the law whereby they pretended to lease the labor of their slaves whom they styled indentured servants. The new Mexican constitution of 1824 was liberal, the burdens of government were light, and the officials lax. Consequently white southerners came west, bringing slaves and cotton with them, and the "Texans," as they called themselves, prospered.

By 1830 the Mexican government began to fear it had created a threat of its own, for the Texans were growing in numbers and in autonomy, and the Jacksonian press began making noises about annexation. Perhaps it would be better to stop additional settlement from the United States, which an act on April 6, 1830, attempted to do, and attract a variety of European settlers to try again to form a buffer against the United States. Some British reformers saw Texas as the possible site for a free-labor experiment in growing cotton, and Quaker Benjaman Lundy envisioned Texas as a refuge for free blacks from the slave states. A smattering of Swiss, French, English, and other settlers were attracted, but southerners continued to come too. The situation in Texas was clearly getting out of hand when the Mexican democratic government fell to the centralizing dictatorship of Antonio Lopez de Santa Anna; he abolished the liberal constitution of 1824 and began a process to put outlying regions like Texas under his firm control. The Texans of both Anglo and Hispanic heritage resisted what they labeled tyranny.

In defense of the constitution of 1824, not in a quest for independence, 187 Texans inside the Alamo, an old Spanish mission in San Antonio, held off for thirteen days in late February and early March, 1836, a Mexican army of 6,000 commanded by the hated Santa Anna. The Texans, led by William B. Travis, James Bowie, and Davy Crockett, decided not to surrender, and Santa Anna decided to offer no quarter. Before dawn on March 6, with their band playing "El Deguello," the centuries-old song calling for total destruction of enemies, the Mexican army made its final assault, ultimately killing all the defenders and burning their bodies in a great pyre. While the siege of the Alamo was underway, a convention of delegates from the various settlements in Texas met at Washington-on-the-Brazos and drew up and signed on March 2, 1836, a Texas declaration of independence—the men of the Alamo never knew they were fighting for Texas independence. The convention then named Sam Houston, former governor of Tennessee and close friend of Andrew Jackson, commander-in-chief of the army and began framing a constitution. Houston took charge of the remnants of the army and, playing a waiting game as reinforcements joined up, retreated eastward from the vicinity of San Antonio with Santa Anna in pursuit. When Santa Anna divided his superior forces near the present site of Houston, General Houston turned around and surprised the Mexican forces at siesta time on April 21. In a climactic battle at San Jacinto lasting seventeen minutes, Sam Houston's troops completely routed the Mexican army and captured Santa Anna himself, quickly ending the Texas revolution.

The Texans soon voted to join the union, and Andrew Jackson would have liked to accommodate them; indeed, he wanted Texas, California, and everything else. But critics of slavery instantly suspected a southern plot to increase the extent and political power of slavery, and they mounted a ferocious opposition. Even Jackson backed down, not wanting to jeopardize the election of Van Buren. Texas meanwhile had begun its career as an independent nation, complete with an army, a navy, and foreign consulates of France and Great Britain in the capital city of Austin. Britain hoped to support Texas, wean it away from slavery, and mold it into a British satellite like Canada that would both hem United States expansion and offer a refuge for runaway slaves. This only made southern politicians more intent on getting Texas safely inside the union as a slave state. John Quincy Adams, then a congressman, carried on a one-man filibuster against statehood in 1838, and Van Buren was too dependent on votes in the northeast to aid Texas. William Henry Harrison of Ohio won the presidency in 1840, but within weeks he was dead and Virginian John Tyler assumed the presidency.

Unwilling to follow the direction of Clay and Webster, Tyler was essentially read out of the Whig party. More a southerner than a Whig anyway and eager to court southern Democrats' support and possibly their nomination for the presidency, Tyler warmed to the annexation of Texas but could not convince Congress. On February 28, 1844, a tragic cannon explosion aboard the warship *Princeton* killed among others Secretary of State Abel P. Upshur; two weeks later President Tyler appointed Calhoun his new secretary of state. A little over a month later Tyler submitted a treaty of annexation, drawn up by Calhoun, to the Senate, but an intemperate defense of slavery by Calhoun served to put northern antislavery forces on guard, and the Senate turned down the treaty in June. Calhoun had injected slavery into national politics in the most dramatic form since the Missouri crisis of a generation earlier, and this new crisis would disrupt American politics until another great compromise six years later.

Expansion was the main issue in 1844, but the ghost of slavery lurked behind every discussion of territorial acquisition. Southerners and westerners in the Democratic party ultimately spurned Tyler, rejected Van Buren because they suspected his ties to the Northeast made him unsafe on the issue of slavery in Texas, and ended the deadlock in the party convention by choosing as their presidential candidate Congressman James K. Polk of Tennessee, Speaker of the House, master politician, and friend of Andrew Jackson. Polk was an avid expansionist, but he also understood the depth of the North's objection to expansionism as a pro-slavery plot by southerners. The Whigs nominated Henry Clay, who had opposed the annexation of Texas because he too had gauged the strength of the northern and Whig sentiment against the spread of slavery. Polk skillfully attracted northern expansionist support by advocating the "reoccupation" of Oregon. There were strong northern commercial desires for Oregon both to keep Britain from gaining a toehold in the West and for establishing ports opening up potentially lucrative trade with the Orient. Polk secretly had his eyes on California, but he did not mention this publicly because he hoped to purchase the territory from Mexico and did not want to alert Mexico to his ambitions and thus have her raise the price. Many in the North had similiar eyes on California. Webster even said San Francisco alone, with her great harbor, was worth twenty Texases.

As Polk began to build a national consensus for expansion, Clay, at heart an expansionist too, began to weasel in his opposition. This equivocation won him no expansionist votes anywhere but only led principled Whig opponents to shift their support to third-party candidate James G. Birney, whose anti-slavery Liberty party remained solidly against the annexation of Texas. The vote for Birney was critical, because it siphoned off just enough support from Clay in New York and Michigan to deliver the November presidential election to Polk. Polk would not take office until March 1845, and lame-duck President Tyler, generously interpreting Polk's narrow victory (he won less than 50 percent of the total vote) as a national mandate for the annexation of Texas, reintroduced the issue to Congress. There the northern and southern Democrats, seeking to cement a new-found unity, cooperated with Tyler and accepted his proposal to annex Texas by a joint resolution. Such a resolution required only a majority vote, not the two-thirds vote required in a Senate treaty. Nowhere did the Constitution allow annexing an independent nation, much less without benefit of a treaty, but the resolution passed on February 28, 1845, giving the Republic of Texas until January 1 of the following year to respond.

France and Britain began to woo Texas, preferring an independent nation friendly to them rather than an enlarged United States. But the Texans had too strong a sentimental and cultural attachment to the United States. Anson Jones, the president of Texas, called the Texas Congress together and proposed a resolution accepting annexation and called for a convention to draw up a new state constitution. The annexation resolution passed without opposition, the convention drafted a constitution in short order that was quickly accepted by Congress in Washington, and on December 29, just before the deadline, President Polk signed the act making Texas the twenty-eighth state in the Union, and a slave state as well. Two months later, February 19, 1846, a crowd of Texans stood at attention in Austin as the Texas flag was lowered, the Stars and Stripes was raised, and Anson Jones resigned as president of the Republic of Texas and handed over the reins of power to the new state governor, J. Pinckney Henderson. Polk had gained Texas, but his sights were higher. The upshot of his ambitions ultimately split the union.

THE WAR WITH MEXICO

Even as events in Texas were underway leading to congressional acceptance of its annexation, and while Polk was still talking in bellicose terms to Britain about US claims to the Oregon Territory, Polk sent a secret agent, John Slidell of Louisiana, to Mexico to inquire about the possibility of buying California and the New Mexico territories for $25 million and $5 million respectively and US assumption of all claims of American citizens against Mexico. In addition to these new territories, Mexico was asked to surrender its claims to Texas territory between the Rio Grande and the Nueces River. But information about Slidell's potential deal had leaked by the time he arrived in Mexico City, and the fragile Mexican government could not risk offending public opinion by appearing to bargain away a part of the country with such an extraordinary envoy.

Meanwhile, Polk, who feared British ambitions for California, was addressing Congress about a reformulation of the Monroe Doctrine that implied no European country had a right to prevent any American territory from being annexed by the United States. On December 16, 1845, the Mexican government informed Slidell that it would not receive him; Slidell sent word to Polk, who received the message on January 12 and on the very next day sent an order to General Zachary Taylor (previously ordered to go from Fort Jessup, Louisiana, to the southern bank of the Nueces River, in the disputed territory) to advance to the bank of the Rio Grande. Taylor arrived there in late March, much to the consternation of Mexican officials who correctly saw his presence as an invasion. Polk hoped for a provocation by an overzealous Mexican defense force, and the moment came on May 3. Eight days later President Polk indignantly informed Congress that Mexico had invaded American territory "and shed American blood upon the American soil." On the same day the House overwhelmingly declared war on Mexico; the next day, May 12, the Senate declared war with only two nay votes and three abstentions, including that of John C. Calhoun.

Polk's war with Mexico was extremely unpopular in the North, where it was rightly seen as aggressively imperialistic and proslavery. Opposition to this war was the occasion for Henry David Thoreau's being jailed rather than pay taxes, resulting in his "Essay on Civil Disobedience," a philosophical stance that would find application in the South more than a century later during the civil rights movement. The sentiment Thoreau represented was the very reason that Calhoun had opposed the war: he correctly foresaw divisive northern opposition and, in the event of military success and the conquering of Mexico, clamoring by some southerners for the annexation of Mexico. Calhoun understood that war would increase the size, authority, and expense of the national government; he feared northern opposition could escalate dangerously and threaten the union; and he believed that the potential incorporation of "inferior" Mexican nationals would subvert "the genius and character" of the American republic. Calhoun by his own lights was still a nationalist. He jettisoned his presidential ambitions and risked repudiation in the South for his stand. Actually Polk himself had no desire to annex Mexico, and the success of his policy of talking tough to the British and then accepting less expansionist boundaries had won a treaty settlement in June 1846 of the Oregon Territory.

But the war against Mexico went embarrassingly well, and by 1847 Generals Zachary Taylor and Winfield Scott and almost the whole younger varsity of the later Union and Confederate officer corps—Lee, Grant, Sherman, McClellan, Beauregard, Stonewall Jackson, even Jefferson Davis—essentially had their run of Mexico. The succeeding Mexican governments were too unstable to accept a peace treaty. After a fitful round of negotiations and a recall by Polk, resourceful Nicholas Trist discounted the American conquests and reached a settlement in 1848 similar to what Slidell had proposed before the war: purchase of California and New Mexico and acceptance of the Rio Grande as border in return for a total payment of $15 million and the assumption of American nationals' claims against Mexico, significantly less than Slidell had offered in 1845. Polk was angered by Trist's Treaty of Guadalupe Hidalgo but realized the northern opposition to the war required its acceptance; Polk submitted the treaty to the Senate, which promptly ratified it on March 10, 1846, ending the Mexican War.

TERRITORIAL EXPANSION, CONFLICT, AND COMPROMISE

As Calhoun foresaw, the problems Polk unleashed by declaring war on Mexico could not be solved by peace, and like the story of Pandora's opened box, the consequences eventually overwhelmed the best efforts of a generation of politicians. The lid was first lifted by a young congressmen from Pennsylvania, David Wilmot, at a sultry Saturday-night session of the House of Representatives on August 6, 1846. Polk had sent an ordinary request for a $2 million authorization to underwrite negotiations with Mexico. Wilmot stood, explained that he was no foe of expansion per se, but he went on in moralistic terms to attack the expansion of slavery. Then, explicitly borrowing words from the Jefferson-inspired Northwest Ordinance of 1787, he attached a rider to the appropriation bill; referring to land that might be acquired from Mexico, "neither slavery not involuntary servitude shall ever exist in any part of said territory, except for crime, whereof the party shall first be duly convicted." Wilmot's words went through the House and the entire political establishment like a surge of electricity. His amendment passed the House, but it failed to pass the Senate before that body adjourned on August 10.

The issue would not go away. The existence of slavery in the individual states had been accepted as a matter of local authority since the northern states had abolished the institution in the decades following the Revolution. Precedent for prohibiting slavery in territories had been established in 1787 and followed in the settlement of the Missouri crisis in 1820, but the issue had lain dormant for a generation in part because party leaders knew how explosive it could be. Now it was in the open, for an undeniable result of the war with Mexico and diplomatic pressure on England would be new territory. What would be its disposition? Southerners knew Iowa and Wisconsin were on the verge of statehood, and that Minnesota was waiting in the wings. The political balance was obviously tipping toward the North, even without the new territory that, if Wilmot's Proviso were obtained, would all eventually be in the North's column. Pandora's box, once opened, could not be shut.

When Congress reconvened in December, Polk was able to persuade Wilmot to restrain from offering his amendment to the now $3-million administration request, but when Preston King of New York attached an even stronger version of the original rider, Wilmot and many other northern Democrats and Whigs went along (though the amendment did not pass the Senate). In all this controversy John C. Calhoun espied danger to the South and to the union. From his perspective, if the North successfully applied anti-slavery restrictions on the territories and otherwise harmed southern interests, real or theoretical, eventually the South would have no recourse but secession. The only way to save the union, Calhoun thought, was to shock politicians with the danger of imminent secession so that they would make solid guarantees of the South's right to hold slaves and take them anywhere. Accordingly Calhoun devised a strident defense of the southern position and set it forth to the Senate on February 19, 1847, in the form of four resolutions.

Repudiating the logic of the Ordinance of 1787, Calhoun argued that the territories belonged equally to all citizens of all states and that to prevent any citizen from safely taking his property (read slave property) there would be to deprive him of his Fifth Amendment privileges, which forbade Congress from depriving any citizen of his life, liberty, or property. Calhoun was not really interested in reclaiming the states of the Midwest for slavery, or for throwing out the Missouri Compromise. Rather, he wanted to gain a rock-solid defense of southern rights as he saw them, and he wanted to disrupt politics-as-usual and create a regional, pro-slavery political party whose presence would force the national government to accept a balance of regional interests at the risk otherwise of breaking up the union. By forcing the issue, Calhoun in a kind of desperation move hoped to preserve the South's peculiar institution from future interference by the national government. Calhoun tried in vain to raise funds to establish a southern newspaper to be published in Washington, and friends of his, having bought the *Southern Quarterly Review* in Charleston, replaced its northern-born editor with a southerner (eventually William Gilmore Simms became editor) and used it to provide an intellectually respectable defense of the southern position on all things cultural, social, and political.

Compromise lubricates the wheels of American politics, but the Wilmot Proviso envisioned no compromise on the issue of expanding slavery and Calhoun's resolutions (which did not win Senate approval) allowed none on limiting expansion. Both national political parties scrambled to find some means of disarming the issue of its explosive potential. President Polk and other Democratic regulars proposed simply extending the Missouri Compromise's (36° 309) line, but hardliners in both expansion and restriction camps opposed the idea because it satisfied neither. Senators Lewis Cass and Stephen A. Douglas proposed the idea of "squatter sovereignty" or popular sovereignty that, in the time-tested tradition of local democracy, would let the actual settlers of a territory decide the issue, thus removing it from the arena of national politics. But when would territories decide, when applying for statehood? Would not the possibility of such a decision against slavery discourage potential slaveholding settlers from entering a territory? The Democrats tried to evade the issue in the 1848 presidential election by nominating Cass of Michigan but not mentioning slavery in the party platform—a return to the old strategy of simply avoiding the problem. The Whigs hoped to finesse the issue by nominating a Mexican War hero and southern slaveholder, General Zachary Taylor, who was blissfully apolitical and avoided taking a stand on any issue. But many northern "Barnburner" Democrats and "Conscience" Whigs refused to blink at the central issue facing the nation; they, and a remnant from the 1844 Liberty party, coalesced into the Free Soil party with the memorable slogan of "Free soil, Free speech, Free labor, and Free men" and nominated Van Buren. Here was a truly regional party, but not one to Calhoun's liking, and it eerily presaged the future of national politics. The Free Soil party won enough votes in New York to deprive Cass of victory, ensuring the election of "Old Rough and Ready" Taylor as president.

The election, of course, settled nothing. Already Oregon was organizing for statehood, and antiblack sentiment there led territorial leaders to restrict slavery and prohibit free blacks from living in the territory. In January a mechanic erecting a sawmill for Johann A. Sutter near Sacramento discovered gold, and the news when it spread eastward produced a tidal surge of population westward. These prospectors included southerners experienced in the gold fields of Georgia and North Carolina, and some of the southern "Forty-niners" brought their slaves with them to California, and free black prospectors migrated as well. Hostility quickly arose in the gold fields against the black competitors, hostility that further predisposed California against slavery. The sentiment in both Oregon and California was more antiblack than antislavery, but southerners saw it ominously as abolitionism. President Taylor, never much one for abstractions, believed that slavery (which he associated with cotton, sugar, and rice) would never be a real factor in the arid Southwest or in California. He seems not to have suspected that slaves could be employed in mining and herding. Dismissing metaphysical arguments from principle, he simply proposed asking California and New Mexico to write constitutions and apply for instant statehood, not mentioning the theoretical issue of slavery. Most southerners just as quickly opposed Taylor's position; Calhoun urged ideological purity—no compromise!—and proposed a future meeting of southern delegates at a convention in Nashville in 1850 to promote secession as the alternative to anything short of a congressional guarantee that slaveholders had the right to take their slaves anywhere. The forces of slavery and antislavery were clashing, and to many observers the nation seemed threatened in late 1849 as never before. Younger politicians in particular seemed willing to hold to their principles even if it cost disunion.

At this moment two old Senate warhorses, Henry Clay and Daniel Webster, put aside their generation of political differences and joined forces to try to save the union. Clay, with his unparalleled parliamentary skills, introduced in the Senate in late January 1850 a series of eight resolutions that he thought were sufficiently balanced to satisfy warring elements in both the South and the North, and on February 5 and 6 he addressed the Senate, appealing for concessions from both sides and attacking the notion of secession. Calhoun, the third aged warhorse, once more saw compromise as tantamount to southern surrender, with secession the only real alternative, and he garnered his strength to make one last great effort for total southern victory on the right for slavery to expand. On March 4 a gaunt Calhoun, his eyes

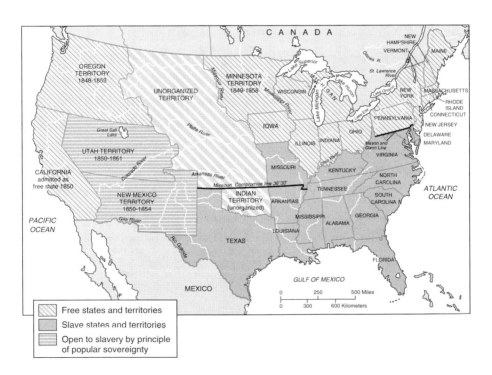

The Compromise of 1850

even deeper sunk than normal and his great mane of hair wildly pushed back, entered the Senate chamber too ill to speak. He sat, wrapped in his black cloak, looking like death itself, as Senator James M. Mason of Virginia read Calhoun's morose words of no compromise, of giving the South veto power over national legislation. It sounded like the death rattle of the union even as Calhoun professed to believe it was the only way to save the union. Three days later Webster's turn came, and the chamber was crowded as the powerful orator, speaking slowly, almost painfully it seemed, with perspiration glistening on his forehead, began: "Mr. President, I wish to speak today, not as a Massachusetts man, nor as a Northern man, but as an American. . . . I speak today for the preservation of the Union." There is, he insisted, "no such thing as a peaceable secession." Four hours later he closed with an eloquent paean to the nation, "Never did there devolve, on any generation of men, higher trusts than now devolve upon us for the preservation of this Constitution, and the harmony and peace of all who are destined to live under it."

Opposition to Clay's proffered compromise began to melt as each side looked the possiblity of secession and war squarely in the face. Calhoun died on March 31, his posthumous *Disquisition on Government* spelling out his ideas on balancing regional interests through what he called concurrent majorities. President Taylor unrealistically held to his own position and opposed Clay's resolutions, but on July 9 Taylor too died. Vice-President Millard Fillmore of New York ascended to the presidency; a long-time supporter of Clay and Webster, he put the administration's power and prestige behind the forces of compromise. Clay, exhausted from the struggle, handed over leadership of his resolutions to Senator Stephen A. Douglas, his nearest equal in parliamentary prowess. Breaking the resolutions apart from the one-package format, Douglas cajoled and bargained the separate resolutions through Congress by effecting a series of shifting coalitions. Between September 7 and 17, 1850, five distinct but interrelated acts passed Congress. California was admitted as a free state; the New Mexico Territory was organized without restrictions against slavery (and Texas gave up significant territorial claims in present-day New Mexico, Colorado, Wyoming, Kansas, and Oklahoma in return for $10 million); Utah was organized similarly as a territory; the slave trade but not slavery was ended in the District of Columbia; and a strengthened Fugitive Slave Act was passed to facilitate southern slaveholders' recovering slaves who had escaped to freedom in the northern states.

THE COMPROMISE BREAKS DOWN

Sanguine unionists thought the plural Compromises of 1850 solved the divisive sectional issues for all time. Little did they foresee how the Fugitive Slave Act, by allowing southern slavecatchers to come into the North to seize

runaway slaves who had escaped to freedom, as well as outrageous examples
of unscrupulous southerners kidnapping bona fide free blacks and selling
them into slavery, would bring home to countless northerners the evils of
bondage in immediately vivid fashion. Little did they anticipate that the issue
of slave property in New Mexico and Utah would be a constant rubbing of
salt into the wounded pride of southerners. They could not have known that
in late 1850 Mrs. Edward Beecher, incensed over what she saw as Congress's
unprincipled compromising with slavery and in particular Daniel Webster's
succumbing to the forces of evil, would write an impassioned letter to her sister-in-law, an obscure writer and minister's wife in Brunswick, Maine, Harriet
Beecher Stowe. "Hattie," she wrote, "If I could use a pen as you can, I would
write something that will make this whole nation feel what an accursed thing
slavery is." Supposedly Mrs. Stowe rose from her chair, crumpled the letter in
her fist, and resolved, "I *will* write something . . . I will if I live." In June 1851
the Washington *National Era* began serializing the results of her defiant resolution to the acclaim of a growing northern audience. On March 20, 1852,
Uncle Tom's Cabin was published in book form. Soon it was dramatized across
the nation, pirated editions appeared in London, and it became the publishing sensation of the century. In moving prose, touching the heartstrings of
evangelical Protestantism and replete with the popular belief in the sanctity
of the home and the special virtue of women, the book painted a devastating
and memorable indictment of the intrinsic evils of slavery even in the hands
of "good" owners. The book infuriated the South even as it emboldened
northern abolitionists and widened their appeal. The great sectional conflict
over slavery was not ended by the Compromises of 1850.

The national political parties, with candidates and supporters from all
regions, had served an essential unifying role in the decades before 1850, but
in the next half decade national politics was transformed. The Whig party disintegrated, the Democratic party became primarily a sectional party representing the South, and a new northern sectional party, the Republican,
emerged. Young voters, who came of age in the late 1840s and early 1850s,
had no memory of the earlier nationalizing role played by the Whig and
Democratic parties in the 1830s and early 1840s, and they were more willing
to support narrow interest-group politics that placed principles above compromise. Politics hardened and became more partisan as both sides came to
believe their vision of America depended upon one set of policies—no
longer could the most divisive issues be ignored. The Whigs approached the
election of 1852 seriously divided over the Compromises of 1850, with northern Whigs bothered by what they interpreted as acquiescence to the demands
of the South. They refused to support the renomination of Millard Fillmore,
whom they saw as a lackey to the slave interests. This of course made southern Whigs suspicious, and many deserted the party even though Virginian
Winfield Scott, another Mexican War hero, was the presidential candidate,

but he was no slaveholder. The Whigs had somehow failed to satisfy either of their major constituent interests. The Democratic party platform supported the 1850 compromises more forthrightly and emerged more clearly prosouthern, and even though its lackluster presidential nominee, Franklin Pierce, hailed from New Hampshire, he was deemed eminently safe on slavery. Pierce of course won the presidency, but already the Whigs were coming unglued and the Democrats were becoming sectionalized. The explosive political events of 1854 completely disrupted the practice of normal politics, and the chain of events was set underway that culminated in southern secession.

THE KANSAS AFFAIR

Senator Stephen A. Douglas of Illinois had a vision of nationalism that was expansive, and he envisioned an empire of trade stretching from the Atlantic to the Pacific, bridging the gap between booming California and Chicago with the first intercontinental railroad that would bring both prosperity to and exclude potential British interests from the western half of the continent. One problem was the vast, vaguely defined territory west of Missouri and Iowa all the way to the Rockies populated mostly by Indians. For a railroad to be built through this region and prosper, there needed to be settlers, towns, and farms along the route, and for this purpose the territory had to be organized and set on the path to eventual statehood. But all of this region lay north of the Missouri Compromise line, and hence should have been nonslave territory. When Douglas first broached the subject in the early 1850s, several southern politicians, fearful of the safety of slavery in Missouri if a free state developed directly to its west, allowed as to how they had rather see Nebraska "sink in hell" than be organized as free. Besides, southern railroad promoters already planned a southern line to the Pacific, and in fact the Gadsden Purchase was negotiated with Mexico in December 1853 whereby 46,000 square miles of northern Mexico were purchased to facilitate the optimum southern route. Douglas let visions of locomotives and telegraph wires overcome his political judgment. He seized upon the popular sovereignty provisions for New Mexico and Utah in the 1850 compromise as the mechanism to finesse the 1820 prohibition of slavery from the northern reaches of the Louisiana Purchase and to gain southern support of a northern route in return for voiding that venerable compromise. Partially in Douglas's defense it should be pointed out that he really believed popular sovereignty was correct democratic procedure, and he could not conceive of slavery actually existing in the climate and terrain of the territory under discussion. Nevertheless, he failed to foresee the magnitude of the controversy he was about to unleash.

Douglas introduced his Nebraska bill to the Senate on January 4, 1854, and although northerners were instantly outraged by his reopening the possibility of slavery in the region, southerners were slow to nibble at the bait because they knew that popular sovereignty could also lead to prohibitions against slavery. The bill failed to pass. Douglas scouted the political terrain and on January 23 reintroduced his proposal as the Kansas–Nebraska Act, designating two territories to be organized––with Kansas as a sop to the South—and making explicit that the 1820 ban on slavery north of the fateful Missouri Compromise line was void. These concessions to the South, after almost three months of fierce debate, led to victory for Douglas and his bill, but the consequences were catastrophic for American politics. Old Free Soilers, former Liberty party men, Conscience Whigs, and northern Democrats, were all outraged. Within a day of Douglas's second version of the bill, on January 24, the *National Era,* which had serialized Harriet Beecher Stowe's eye-opening novel, published an "Appeal of the Independent Democrats in Congress to the People of the United States," written by six antislavery congressmen, including Senator Charles Sumner of Massachusetts. In purple prose the appeal attacked the bill as a part of a southern slave-power plot, and editorials and addresses across the North took up the theme. Abraham Lincoln, a former congressman from Illinois, was aroused as never before, and Senator William Pitt Fessenden of Maine confided that "It needs but little to make me an out & out abolitionist." Southerners of course replied in kind. Douglas's bill had fallen like a bomb in the midst of American politics, and its concussion shook the political establishment for months.

The events of late 1853 and 1854 lent credence to northern fears of a slaveholders' plot to expand the limits of slavery. Several times between 1849 and 1851 a colorful expatriate Cuban adventurer named Narciso Lopez had garnered southern support for filibuster attacks on Cuba, hoping to conquer the island with its half million slaves for southern annexation. After Cuban officials captured and killed Lopez in 1851, southern expansionists waited until a more friendly president took office. Franklin Pierce became president in March 1853 and for a while supported southern calls for annexing Cuba. His minister to Spain, Louisianian Pierre Soule, incautiously trumpeted American claims to acquire Cuba. In late 1853 and early 1854 Pierce encouraged firebrand John Quitman's quixotic filibustering plot to invade Cuba and precipitate a revolutionary movement there that would presumably result in calls for annexation by the United States. After the political turmoil of the Kansas–Nebraska Act, Pierce tried to rein in such filibustering efforts, but he did authorize Soule in Madrid to offer Spain as much as $130 million for the sugar-and-slave-rich island. In October 1854 the volatile Soule met with the American ministers to Britain and France at Ostend, Belgium, and persuaded them to sign a document—the so-called Ostend Manifesto—calling Cuba a necessary adjunct to the United States and claiming a divine right to buy or otherwise obtain the island. When word of the memorandum leaked to the press, northern newspapers and public opinion were livid. Pierce had to back down, recall Soule, and abandon all Cuban schemes. But the damage had been done, for southern proslavery expansionism seemed to have no limits.

In March 1854 a Virginia slave named Anthony Burns had escaped from his bondage and arrived in Boston, where he found employment in a clothing store. But an indiscreet letter written to his brother, who was a slave, fell into white hands, and Burns's former owner came to Boston to reclaim his human property. The Fugitive Slave Act gave Burns's owner licence to recapture him, and, moreover, that act required that local officials aid the slave catcher. Burns was arrested in May, charged on bogus grounds, and jailed. When a commitee of abolitionists protested and even attempted to batter down the jail door, President Pierce sent federal troops to Boston to enforce the unpopular law. Friends of liberty raised money and tried every legal maneuver they knew to win Burns's case, but Pierce and the US attorney were set on carrying out the letter of the law. Burns's owner even agreed to sell Burns to the committee (who of course would set him free), but the US attorney would not allow the issue to be so evaded. At the conclusion of the trial in June federal troops marched Burns to the sound of tolling bells through Boston streets lined with black-draped buildings, silent protestors, and upside down American flags to the federal revenue cutter waiting in the harbor to whisk him back to slavery.

Wealthy textile manufacturer Amos A. Lawrence spoke for many when he wrote that "we went to bed one night old fashioned, conservative, Compromise Union Whigs & waked up stark mad Abolitionists." In Massachusetts, Ohio, Michigan, and Wisconsin strong personal liberty laws were passed to try to counter the Fugitive Slave Act by giving blacks increased legal protections and rights. The North increasingly saw southerners as manstealers and rabid slavery expansionists, and the South saw the North as incorrigible opponents of slave owners' legal rights. It was in the vortex of this swirling passion that the Kansas–Nebraska Act was to take effect, and southerners and northerners both saw Kansas as emblematic of the future of slavery. Either slavery or freedom would be victorious in Kansas, and neither side was willing to leave the results of popular sovereignty to chance. "Bleeding Kansas" was the result.

Following the House's approval, the Senate passed Douglas's Kansas-Nebraska bill on May 22, 1854. In June President Pierce appointed Pennsylvanian Andrew H. Reeder territorial governor of Kansas and opened the territory for settlement even before treaty arrangements were worked out with the Indians. The result was a land rush by settlers from neighboring states, eager to claim the best farm sites and stake out future towns. Most of the settlers were probably more interested in scrambling for land than the future of slavery, but the symbolic issue Kansas represented aroused people elsewhere who were fervently interested in slavery's prospects. Back in New England, Amos Lawrence, his consciousness raised by the recent Anthony Burns affair, helped fund the New England Emigrant Aid Company to promote the migration to Kansas of free-soil settlers. Senator David Atchison of Missouri, a proslavery extremist, fanned anti-abolitionists' fears and, as the November date neared for the election of Kansas's first delegate to Congress, Atchison organized a temporary invasion of "border ruffians" to insure the success of the proslavery candidate. Atchison intended not merely to win the election but to extirpate northern sympathizers from the region. Writing to Pierce's secretary of war, Jefferson Davis, Atchison admitted that "we will be compelled to shoot, burn & hang, but the thing will soon be over. We intend to `Mormonize' the Abolitionists"—a reference to Missouri's earlier violent confrontation with Joseph Smith's followers. New Englanders were sending in boxes of rifles called "Beecher's Bibles" (the reference was to a quip made by the Reverend Henry Ward Beecher, Mrs. Stowe's brother), and violence was imminent.

Because a majority of the settlers in Kansas were from nearby Missouri, the proslavery forces could have won the delegate election fairly, as they could have the election of a territorial legislature slated for March 1855. But Atchison was in no mood to gamble on the results of true popular sovereignty. Hundreds of "border ruffians" crossed the imaginary line dividing Missouri and Kansas and cast approximately five thousand fraudulent votes, illegally electing a proslavery legislature. Territorial governor Reeder denounced the election but did not contest it. He felt powerless without the support of President Pierce, who was cravenly dependent upon southern Democratic support. Once the Kansas legislature met it expelled the several antislavery delegates, passed a harsh slave code, and made even expressing sentiments unfavorable to slavery punishable by fine and imprisonment. But ongoing immigration had created a free-soil majority in the territory's population, and this majority responded vigorously, calling for an extralegal election to a constitutional convention to be held in Topeka in October. That convention drafted a constitution that outlawed both slaves and free blacks from Kansas (many free soilers were antislavery but racist and wanted no competition from blacks); applied for admission as a free state; and set an election date in January 1856 for choosing a (presumably) free-soil governor and legislature for the territory—a rival government to the preexisting proslavery one. Kansas became even more of a powder keg waiting for a spark.

As settlers poured into the territory in the spring of 1856, hate and tension increased. A proslavery judge urged a jury to indict supporters of the rival government for treason, and many of the antislavery settlers lived in Lawrence, the town named after the Massachusetts textile manufacturer cum abolitionist. Deciding to take matters in their own hands, a mob of border ruffians attacked Lawrence on May 21, burning buildings—including the home of the free-soil governor—destroying antislavery newspapers, and "sacking" the town. Outrageous as this wanton destruction was, the northern press exaggerated it further. But no one was more outraged than John Brown, a fanatical, possibly mentally unbalanced abolitionist who thought he had God's mandate to smite the forces of slavery. Gathering together an avenging force of seven men, including four of his sons, on the night of May 24 John Brown attacked several reputedly proslavery households, dragged the men folk out of their beds, and maniacally cleaved their heads with broadswords. Full-scale guerilla war broke out in Kansas, and by the time a new territorial governor, John W. Geary, backed by federal troops, quelled the disorder, over two hundred Kansans lay dead. Across the nation southerners and northerners took sides, attitudes hardened, and the rhetoric escalated. Events were racing out of control as partisans on both sides found themselves taking positions that allowed no retreat. Moderates in the North and South felt their positions crumbling.

The day before the sacking of Lawrence, pompous Charles Sumner had taken the Senate floor to deliver a two-day-long attack on the slaveholding interests entitled "The Crime of Kansas." A self-righteous man with extraordinary powers of vituperation and an honest recognition of the evils of slavery, Sumner lit into slaveholders like Samson armed with the ass's jawbone, and no one suffered worse from his verbal blows than the elderly senator from South Carolina, Andrew P. Butler. Sumner labeled the proslavery border ruffians in Kansas "hirelings picked from the drunken spew and vomit of an uneasy civilization," then, warming to his subject, he aimed his invective at Senator Butler. Even antislavery senators were taken aback by Sumner's rhetoric, especially when, mocking old Senator Butler's imperfect control of his lower lip, Sumner spoke of Butler having "discharged the loose expectoration of his speech." Many southerners felt personally assaulted by the intemperance of Sumner's remarks, especially Congressman Preston Brooks, a young cousin of Senator Butler. Disdaining to challenge Sumner to a duel—one only dueled social equals—Brooks waited two days, his anger boiling. Then, after adjournment of the Senate on May 22, Brooks entered the almost empty Senate chamber and walked up to Sumner, who was bent over his desk writing letters. Gold-headed cane in hand, Brooks told the startled Sumner that his speech had libeled both South Carolina and Senator Butler "who is a relative of mine." With that Brooks began beating Sumner on the head with the cane—Sumner was trapped between his seat and his desk, which was bolted to the floor. The cane broke, but Brooks kept up the beating until the blood-splattered Sumner finally ripped the desk away from its mooring and fell in a heap on the Senate floor.

By then news of the sacking of Lawrence also had splashed across newspaper headlines, to be followed within three days by the news of John

Brown's massacre of purported slaveholders. Northerners and southerners were coming to see each other as fanatics who would stop at nothing to achieve their purpose—Yankees determined to destroy slavery versus a slave-power conspiracy determined to rule the nation. Northerners were particularly appalled by the extent to which the South lionized Brooks, receiving him home with a brass band, showering him with compliments, and even sending him dozens of replacement canes.

These were not normal times, and normal politics failed. Pierce's pro-southern excesses in Kansas had lost the Democrats much northern support, further sectionalizing the party. The Whig party had already disintegrated, but its constituent elements still swirled about in search of a new vehicle for expression. The decade before 1854 had seen the most prolific European migration of any period heretofore, and immigrants represented a higher proportion of the total US population in 1854 than ever before or since. The Whig party had always had a tinge of Protestant moralism, a willingness to control economic growth and the laboring masses to create America in its image, and the specter of Catholic, often Irish, immigrants sinking the nation in a morass of drunkenness and servile obedience to the Pope frightened northern Protestants, already competing with immigrants for jobs. Many former Whigs, set adrift from party discipline, were seized by an antiforeign and antiCatholic hysteria. A virulent nativist party resulted with explosive suddenness. Members of the movement, officially named the American party, were called Know-Nothings because they professed ignorance when asked about their intentions.

Catholic immigrants appeared the great monster about to devour freedom and the American experiment, and the Know-Nothing party showed astounding success across New England and the Midwest in the midterm elections of 1854. There were pockets of Know-Nothing strength in the South as well. But almost as suddenly as it erupted the nativist hysteria subsided, in part at least because events in Kansas revealed a new and nearer danger to the American nation, the slave-power conspiracy. The 1854 "Appeal of the Independent Democrats," written in response to Douglas's revised Kansas–Nebraska bill, offered a compelling indictment of the proslavery position and outlined a principled opposition to the expansion of slavery. This document proved to be the rallying cry and rationale for the formation of the new Republican party in Jackson, Michigan, on July 6, 1854. Events in Kansas loomed larger than possible papal plots in mid-1856, and "border ruffians" and "Bully" Brooks seemed, to many former Whigs, one-time nativists, and antislavery northerners much the greater threat to freedom. The Republican party ballooned in strength as the Know-Nothing party slowly deflated. The Know-Nothing party in the South after 1857 became a factor only in scattered local elections, where the issues were local and often idiosyncratic.

Revealing also their Whig and Free Soil roots, the Republicans nominated a charismatic explorer and soldier, John C. Frémont, as their 1856 presidential candidate, with the alliterative campaign slogan of "Free Soil, Free Labor, Free Men, Free Speech, and Frémont." Indicative of the role of the Whig party's remnants in the nativist movement, Millard Fillmore—Whig president after Zachary Taylor's death—was the American (Know-Nothing) party candidate for president in 1856. And the Democrats, recognizing that the Kansas debacle had destroyed Pierce's hopes for reelection, nominated for their candidate a presumably cautious party functionary, James Buchanan, a Pennsylvanian absolutely safe enough on the slavery issue to satisfy southerners. Most of the Republican platform dealt with slavery, and the party suporters campaigned with the moral zeal of crusaders to protect their vision of a free America.

The Democrats tried to paint the Republicans as wild abolitionists, problack fanatics who were more interested in elevating blacks than protecting the rights of northern whites. Moreover, the Democrats charged, the Republicans' fanaticism would, if they won, necessarily drive the South out of the union. Hence true nationalism demanded a vote for Buchanan. This dual campaign of racism and nationalism was effective. It put the Republicans on the defensive—and it probably won the election for Buchanan. Fillmore carried only one state, Maryland, but the returns for Frémont and Buchanan were clearly sectional. Buchanan won every southern state besides Maryland, Frémont every New England state plus New York, and while Frémont took four Midwestern states, Buchanan's nationalist appeal persuaded enough northern Democrats and old-time Whigs for him to win Pennsylvania, New Jersey, Indiana, Illinois, and California and hence the presidency. But Buchanan polled a minority of the total vote, and the Republicans evidenced remarkable strength for a new party. That strength, and the stark sectionalism of the vote, was a forecast of the future.

Franklin Pierce's Kansas policies had been a comedy of errors. Buchanan, eagerly seeking a way to escape the divisive issue of the potential expansion of slavery into a territory, made similar misjudgments and ran into a buzz saw of controversy. A fateful Supreme Court decision presented the first problem that Buchanan fumbled. Dred Scott, a Missouri slave owned by an army surgeon, John Emerson, had been taken by his owner in the course of a military assignment first to the free state of Illinois and then to a remote part (now Minnesota) of the Wisconsin Territory, a nonslave region by virtue of the Missouri Compromise. There Scott met and married Harriet Robinson, a young slave woman owned by the local Indian agent. The agent either sold her to Emerson or gave her to Scott, and the agent, Major Lawrence Taliafero, as justice of the peace, performed the marriage ceremony. Eventually Emerson died and the Scotts found themselves back in St. Louis, where abolitionist friends urged them in 1846 to sue Emerson's widow Irene for their freedom on the grounds that their long-time residence in a free state and then a free territory had voided his bondage.

At first separate but related cases were brought on behalf of each of the Scotts, but in 1850 to save expenses it was decided only to pursue the case in Dred Scott's name, with an explicit understanding that Harriet would have applied to her the ultimate decision. A long journey from court to court, from decision to appeal, brought the case to the US Supreme Court in 1854, where it languished until arguments were heard in 1856. But the justices— possibly to avoid having the decision become a political football in the presidential election—held it over for rearguments in the 1856–57 session. There was widespread newspaper coverage of the arguments, and politicians closely followed the case and awaited the judgment of the southern-dominated

Dred Scott. (New York Public Library)

Court. Buchanan had hoped the court would resolve the issue of slavery in the territories and get him off the hook in Kansas. After the decision was leaked to him in advance by two justices, Buchanan in his inaugural speech on March 4, 1857, called attention to the importance of the imminent decision and recommended that citizens accept the opinion of the court.

Two days later Chief Justice Roger B. Taney, a Marylander, announced the court's tortured decision. All nine justices wrote separate opinions, but Taney crafted the final "Opinion of the Court" that in theory at least represented a vague majority view. First, the court ruled that, as a black, Scott was not a citizen in the eyes of the framers of the Constitution and thus was not eligible to bring suit in a federal court. Second, the court accepted the principle that a slave's status was determined by the laws of the state to which he returned, not the laws of the state in which he had been only a sojourner. Moreover, Taney wrote, the Missouri Compromise prohibition of slavery in certain territories was unconstitutional for it infringed upon a citizen's guaranteed rights (the Fifth Amendment) to own property. Congress could not give away that right. Then, moving beyond the substance of the case, the court ruled that neither could a territory—inferior to the Congress—violate a citizen's right to hold (slave) property. In other words, both the Missouri Compromise and popular sovereignty were unconstitutional violations of a slaveholder's "right" to take and enjoy the labor of his slaves in any territory of the United States. Rather than settle the dispute over Kansas, the Dred Scott decision sparked a firestorm of controversy. Outraged antislavery forces saw it as further evidence of a proslavery conspiracy to push slavery to the farthest bounds of the nation, and cocky southerners were jubilant over their legal victory. But even Stephen A. Douglas, desirous of southern Democratic support yet honestly committed to the principle of popular sovereignty, objected to the decision. At a speech in Springfield, Illinois, in June 1857 Douglas admitted that the Supreme Court determined the law, but he suggested that the sovereign people of any territory could in practice prohibit the existence of slavery simply by refusing to pass the local police and regulatory legislation necessary for its operation. Taney had solved nothing for Buchanan. Matters would only get worse.

The fraudulently elected proslavery legislature in the Kansas Territory called for the election of delegates to a constitutional convention to be held at Lecompton in October 1857 in preparation for a request of admission to the union as a state. But because the election would obviously be rigged in favor of proslavery supporters and because there was no provision for submitting the planned constitution to the voters, Territorial Governor Geary vetoed the measure. The legislature overruled Geary's veto, who resigned when Buchanan took office. Buchanan appointed Robert J. Walker, a former senator from Mississippi, to the position of territorial governor. Thinking he had the president's support and really believing both in popular sovereignty and the union, Walker pledged to the antislavery minority that the constitution would be submitted to the voters for ratification. The antislavery majority boycotted the convention election despite Walker's attempt to get them to vote, but Walker was able to pressure the proslavery politicos to make a slight concession—the convention gave the people the right to vote not on the constitution itself but rather on one clause in it, "with slavery" or "with no slavery." But even if the latter carried, it would not affect those slaves already in Kansas. Senator Douglas was incensed by this travesty of popular sovereignty, as was Walker, who expected to be supported by President Buchanan. Buchanan, however, was afraid to risk losing the support of the South, so he reneged on an earlier pledge to Walker (who then resigned) and backed the Lecompton Convention.

Republicans and many northern Democrats were infuriated—Buchanan was completing the sectionalizing of American politics—and as expected the Lecompton constitution passed the rigged election held on December 21 with the proslavery clause although at least three-fourths of the population was opposed to it. Walker had been able, before he resigned, to persuade the proslavery minority to vote in the fall elections for the territorial legislature, which as expected turned out to be antislavery and opposed to the Lecompton constitution. The newly appointed governor, Frederick P. Stanton, called the new legislature together and it proceeded to call for yet another election on the constitution. This time the antislavery majority participated, and the Lecompton constitution went down to a decisive defeat. Stubborn Buchanan continued to support the Lecompton constitution and tried to get it, and statehood for Kansas, accepted by Congress. The Senate followed the administration line, but with many northern Democrats siding with the Republicans in the House, the bill was amended to prepare for a full and fair vote on the proposed constitution in Kansas. This time, on January 4, 1858, the antislavery voters cast their votes and the constitution was resoundingly defeated even though the voters knew such a vote would delay statehood. For most Kansans, slavery had become a moral abomination about which one could not compromise.

Kansas now moved off the stage of national events and did not gain statehood until 1861. But, like the Dred Scott decision, it had served to harden the lines between the North and the South and between the Republicans and the Democrats. Republicans considered slavery a moral evil and a flaw in American democracy, defended by a power-hungry slaveholding aristocracy. Southerners considered slavery a divinely ordained institution and the North a section increasingly dominated by fanatical abolitionists and unAmerican foreigners, Catholics, and power-hungry industrialists. The virulence of the political rhetoric obscured from both sides the values they shared and emphasized their differences. When the Panic of 1857 devastated the North and left the South relatively unscathed, southerners' already exaggerated sense of the power and importance of King Cotton was increased. Southern Democrats were unwilling to accept interference in their "peculiar institution" by the numerically dominant North, and southerners faced the perilous future with a defiant chip-on-the-shoulder resolve.

THE FAILURE OF POLITICS

The Republican party had influence only in the northern states, and the Democratic party—its northern support attenuated after the Lecompton debacle—remained the only semblance of a national party. Slowly the cords that stretched across the Mason-Dixon line to hold the nation together were either being cut or were snapping under the stress. In 1845 the two most numerous denominations in the South, the Baptists and the Methodists, had split, over slavery and theological issues, from their northern brethren to become sectional churches. (The Presbyterians had split in 1838 specifically over revival measures, but the effect was two essentially regional churches, although an explicit North-South break did not occur until 1861.) In 1858 Stephen A. Douglas was the only political figure who could possibly generate support in both regions, but his stance in opposition to the Dred Scott decision and the Lecompton constitution severely strained his appeal in the South. Could he straddle the fence so that somehow he could still support a version of popular sovereignty and appear sufficiently proslavery to secure the South? Privately Douglas was opposed to slavery. But when push came to shove, he treasured the union more than he abhorred slavery. He was willing to sacrifice moral principle on slavery for what he took to be the greater public good of the nation. Douglas believed that he could traverse the political minefield of slavery and win the presidency in 1860, thereby possibly saving the union. But to do so he had to win reelection to the Senate in 1858, and the Illinois Republicans chose a tall, lanky lawyer with a homespun image and a mind as quick as a steel trap to contest the election with Douglas.

No country bumpkin by a long shot, Abraham Lincoln possessed masterful stump-speaking skills and a writing style of spare elegance that blended a biblical cadence with down-home pungency. Lincoln did not support social and political equality with blacks, but to the deepest recesses of his soul he believed slavery was morally wrong. How could one remain neutral on such an issue, as did Douglas with his unsullied confidence in local self-determination? For Douglas, the issue would be solved simply by allowing the people to vote slavery either up or down. For Lincoln, slavery was a moral issue that allowed no such moral complacency. Lincoln began his campaign by raising the controversy to a higher plane of morality. Quoting Jesus, Lincoln reminded his audience that "A house divided against itself cannot stand." He went on to warn that "I believe this government cannot endure permanently half slave and half free. . . . It will become all one thing, or all the other." Lincoln's position was that slavery must not be allowed to expand and that somehow slavery limited to its present position would ultimately become extinct. When pressed he did not know how this would come about, but actually southerners believed the same thing. That was precisely why they fought so hard to insure that slavery could expand.

Douglas agreed to debate the issues with Lincoln at seven sites in Illinois. In spirited verbal sparring the two great orators argued their case. Douglas was aware that the entire South was looking over his shoulder, so he tried to paint Lincoln as a raving abolitionist whose fanaticism would surely sunder the nation. Lincoln, though, was intent on raising the floor of the debate from political expediency to Christian morality. The point for him was more the evil of slavery than the good of the union. At the debate in Freeport Lincoln forced Douglas to reiterate his previous argument that the people in a territory could, by simply refusing to pass necessary police legislation, in effect prevent slavery, whatever Chief Justice Taney might decide. But this was not a new admission by Douglas, and Lincoln stressed the immorality of slavery more than Douglas's inconsistency of trying to appease both the South and the North. Douglas's reiteration of what came to be known as the Freeport doctrine further harmed him in the South. But in a narrow election the Democratic delegates won a majority in the Illinois legislature, and in November they—this was before senators were popularly elected—again chose Douglas to be their senator. Lincoln had lost the contest but incidentally succeeded in widening the split both between Douglas and the southern Democrats and between the Republicans with their increasingly moral stance on slavery and the northern Democrats who sought political compromise for the sake of the union.

With the Kansas issue settled in early 1858 and the Illinois Senate race decided in the fall, and with prosperity returning during the winter and spring of 1859, the political fever cooled. In December 1858 William Walker, filibuster extraordinaire, failed in his third harebrained attempt to seize Nicaragua for American annexation, although by then even the most extreme southern expansionists were tiring of his escapades. Less than two years later, captured once again, Walker's scheming was ended by a Honduran firing squad. Yet just beneath the seemingly placid surface of economic and political good times lay hidden magma of hot political passion. Fissures in the thin compromise of political expediency vented hissing steam of violence and burning rhetoric that hinted frightfully of the volcanic eruption sure to come. One particularly destructive fissure was opened by John Brown at Harpers Ferry, Virginia (now West Virginia), in October 1859 when the mountains were adorned in their finest fall colors.

In the tumultuous years after the Pottawatomie Massacre in Kansas in 1856, John Brown, his sense of being God's arm of vengeance in no wise weakened, plotted to strike a blow at the heart of slavery. Living near and sometimes passing over the boundaries of both legality and sanity, Brown perused topographical maps of the South, studied census data to ascertain in which counties slaves were concentrated, raised funds from prominent northern abolitionists who did not seem to want to push him very far on his plans, collected weapons, and put together a biracial group of followers willing to risk their lives in an invasion of the South. His plan began to center on Harpers Ferry; apparently after taking the federal arsenal there Brown expected to move down the mountain valleys deep into the South, distributing weapons to willing slaves who fled to his cause. Whatever his intention, on the night of October 16, 1859, Brown and twenty heavily armed supporters, black and white, slipped into Harpers Ferry and seized part of the arsenal guarded by only one watchman. Sending out a patrol to inform the neighborhood slaves, Brown and his men waited at the arsenal for the black population to rise up. A few hours later a train came by, enroute to Washington; Brown delayed it for a while, then let it go, spreading word of the raid.

By the next morning the citizens of Harpers Ferry had awakened to the plot; sharpshooters kept Brown's men penned down and killed eight of them (including two of Brown's sons). Militia from Virginia and Maryland arrived soon, and from Washington President Buchanan sent a company of US marines, led by Colonel Robert E. Lee and Lieutenant J. E. B. Stuart. By then Brown's remaining force, along with several prisoners, were holed up in the brick engine house of the arsenal. Lee ordered the marines to attack with only their bayonets so as not to risk harming the prisoners. After spirited hand-to-hand combat the marines killed two of the raiders and captured Brown and six followers. In less than two days the military phase of the affair was over. But the passion and outrage of the South boiled for months. The governor of Virginia arranged for a quick trial. Within days Brown was convicted of treason and conspiracy to incite insurrection, with his hanging scheduled for December 2 in Charles Town, Virginia. Shortly before the trial, a barnful of pikes was discovered in Maryland. The weapons were to have been distributed to rebellious slaves. Southern extremist and agricultural reformer Edmund Ruffin had one of the pikes sent to each southern state capital to be displayed as a visible reminder of what Brown had in mind for the white people of the South.

For most southerners John Brown represented the logical outcome of abolitionism and the principles of the Republican party. It mattered not that Lincoln and most reputable leaders of both the Republican party and the northern wing of the Democratic party condemned Brown and his methods. Brown's relatives claimed he was insane, but Brown accepted his sentence with dignity and an eloquent defense of his actions. For many northerners he was instantly transformed into a Christ-like martyr on behalf of freedom: "Now, if it is deemed necessary that I should forfeit my life for the futherance of the ends of justice," Brown declaimed, "and mingle my blood further with the blood of my children and with the blood of millions in this slave country whose rights are disregarded by wicked, cruel, and unjust enactments, I say, let it be done." Southerners saw him as a raving madman. But from the pens of northern intellectuals like Theodore Parker, Ralph Waldo Emerson, and Henry David Thoreau came a string of encomiums sprinkled with phrases like "not only a martyr . . . but also a SAINT," "the gallows as glorious as the cross," and "a crucified hero." These Massachusetts writers were wildly unrepresentative of northern sentiment, but southerners were past careful discrimination. In southerners' minds, John Brown, Abraham Lincoln, Horace Greeley, and the Republican party merged as murderous foes of the South, willing to condemn every white man, woman, and child to a horrendous death if it took that to destroy slavery. The times, the issues, admitted of no compromise. No middle ground remained. Only the firmest national guarantees of the rights of slaveowners could hold the nation together.

The new Congress convened in Washington three days following John Brown's hanging, and the southern Democrats were in no mood for reconciliation. The House fought brutally over the speakership, and early in the session, on February 2, 1860, Senator Jefferson Davis of Mississippi, a tall, slender man with an aristocratic mien, introduced a series of strongly worded resolutions that in effect demanded an iron-clad federal slave code protecting slavery everywhere and in every form. Davis's resolutions touched off extensive Senate debate, but Davis could hardly have expected Senate passage. Rather, he intended his slave code resolutions to be a litmus test for Democratic senators, to measure the doctrinal purity of Douglas and his supporters. Douglas deplored such "abstract resolutions" and recognized that they threatened "the integrity of the Democratic party," but the deep South insisted upon precise, narrow, and absolute conformity to its defense of slavery. The Democratic presidential conventon was portentously scheduled to be held in Charleston, South Carolina, in April 1860, and for most southern Democrats a willingness to compromise was no virtue.

THE ELECTION OF 1860

Jefferson Davis was not a demagogue. The forcefulness with which he argued for what was in effect a federal slave code that defended slavery in the territories only suggested the mood of truculence that was abroad in the South. In the months following John Brown's raid on Harpers Ferry and into the spring of 1860 there had been a rising cacophony of voices calling for secession, stating that the election of any government that did not stand foursquare behind slavery would be just cause for the South to leave the nation. One heard angry speeches about Black Republicans and abolitionism and rumors of slave revolts. Several southern states passed appropriation bills to buy arms and raise military forces. April was the month when Charleston was its most beautiful, with its azaleas and wisteria blooming and the warm sea breezes whisking away the last faint traces of winter. But as Democratic delegates began to assemble in the proud city in April 1860, ominous storm clouds were building on the horizon. The Senate Democratic caucus, dominated by southerners, had adopted resolutions essentially calling for the federal government to enact Jefferson Davis's pro-slavery guarantees, and the northern Democratic backers of Stephen A. Douglas felt honor bound to support Douglas's basic concept of popular sovereignty, modified as it was by the existence of the Dred Scott decision and the so-called Freeport Doctrine.

The salty sea air of Charleston seemed to elicit extreme statements, for as each side argued its position, tempers rose and the rhetoric heated. In the corrosive political atmosphere people began to take stands beyond where reason dictated, but in the heat of the moment few seemed to notice that moderation and compromise were the first victims of the debate. The Douglas forces had enough votes to block a platform plank that followed the Davis resolutions introduced in the Senate but not the two-thirds necessary for nomination. That deadlock if anything increased the frustration level of all the delegates. None were more fervent in support of the most extreme position on southern rights than a disparate group of individuals collectively called fire-eaters. And the most zealous of these zealots was William L. Yancey of South Carolina, who even went so far as to castigate the northern Democrats for not actually defending slavery as a positive good and blaming them for the South's felt necessity as a consequence to demand a federal slave code. Yancey provoked Senator George E. Pugh of Ohio at last to warn the "Gentlemen of the South" that "you mistake us—you mistake us. We will not do it." When the controversial platform plank failed to pass, Yancey rose from his seat and began to walk out of the convention. Time seemed to stand still for several interminable seconds as all eyes watched Yancey and wondered who, if any, would follow. Then delegate after delegate from the deep South got up and deserted the convention too, personally seceding from the last truly national political party that existed in 1860. But this mini-secession was intended as a bluff. The deep South delegates thought their bold gesture would shock the northern and Border State delegates and force them to compromise, but it did not. Yet Douglas still could not win a two-thirds vote of confidence. (It had to be, ruled the convention chairman, two-thirds of the original number of delegates.) On the tenth day of the prolonged convention Douglas and his supporters, recognizing the deadlock was unbreakable, by majority vote adjourned the convention and called for it to reconvene in Baltimore on June 18. Perhaps compromise would emerge in a border-state city.

Before the divided Democrats could reconvene, other forces were at

Jefferson Davis. (Eleanor S. Brockenbrough Library, The Museum of the Confederacy, Richmond, Virginia)

work. Many older Democrats, most of them former Whigs, were staunch unionists and fearful of the effect of rabid proslavery on the future of the nation. Frightened of the danger the Lecompton constitution posed to the nation, southerners like Senator John J. Crittenden of Kentucky had, as early as 1858, begun to promote a new party to bridge the widening chasm between the regions. Joined by northern conservatives, the movement had grown during 1859. In December of that year about fifty Congressmen met to form a "Constitutional Union" party, and by January 1860 the plans had jelled. Attacking both existing parties and, on George Washington's birthday, calling for unconditional support for the union, the new party announced its existence and called for a convention to open in Baltimore on May 9 to nominate presidential and vice-presidential candidates.

Subsequently, at a brief, somber convention, delegates from some twenty-three states, fearing to risk the controversy of writing a party platform, simply called for adherence to the Constitution, support of the "Union of the states," and enforcement of the laws. A candidate as bland as the party program, John Bell, a moderate slave-owner from Tennessee, was nominated for president, and Edward Everett of Massachusetts was put forward for the vice-presidency. The new Constitutional Union party hoped to divert its eyes from the practical problems of the day—fugitive slave laws, territorial controversies, possibly reopening the African slave trade, as some of the fire-eating extremists were then calling for—and focus with single-minded determination on the preservation of the union.

A week after the Constitutional Union convention, the Republican convention opened in Chicago on May 16 at the huge amphitheater called the Wigwam. Front-runner William H. Seward was hampered by having been politically prominent and outspoken for too long and by the shady reputation of his principal backer, Thurlow Weed. Abraham Lincoln proved to be an ideal second choice for most delegates, and when Seward failed to win on the first ballot, Lincoln's stock began to rise. Lincoln was sufficiently antislavery to attract the party zealots but cautious enough on what could not be done about slavery where it at present existed to satisfy party moderates. His homespun image as Honest Abe was a salutary contrast both to Thurlow Weed and the scandal-ridden Buchanan administration. Lincoln was aided by having political maestro David Davis as his manager. Davis packed the galleries with leather-lunged partisans who on command could turn the assembly into pandemonium, and having assiduously courted votes among state delegates and perhaps dangled the promise of political appointments, Davis set the stage for a political upset.

When Lincoln's vote total rose on the second ballot, Davis and his assistants began pulling all the wires, and amid the noise and the assurances and the promises the third vote began. As the end neared, and the noise rose, Lincoln stood a scant one-and-a-half votes shy of the nomination; suddenly a mad scramble began among the state delegations to switch their votes. Ohio was first, changed four votes, and then Lincoln had the Republican nomina-ton for president. For political balance a former Democrat from Maine, Sena-tor Hannibal Hamlin, was named the vice-presidential nominee. The Repub-lican platform contained a firm statement against the expansion of slavery into the territories, but it appealed to those other than abolitionists with calls for a high tariff, a transcontinental railroad, and free homesteads (for all resi-dents, including not-yet-naturalized immigrants). The North was becoming economically united; wheat from the Midwest went east on railroads to feed the urban areas, and manufactured goods from eastern factories traveled west in return. Cheap land and a welcome hand to immigrants to populate the West had potent political appeal, erased some of the nativist taint from the Republicans, and guaranteed a Lincoln sweep across the North.

As the Democrats gathered in Baltimore on June 18, their political opposition was in place. Lincoln was clearly going to be a viable candidate only in the North (his name did not even appear on the ballots of ten south-ern states). Bell's support would primarily be in border states. Only the Democratic party had a chance to mount a national campaign for the presi-dency, but Douglas and his supporters alone seemed to understand the point. When the convention majority had voted back in Charleston to meet again in Baltimore, the delegates who had already bolted the assembly decided to meet in convention in Richmond a week before the Baltimore gathering. But they could decide on nothing in Richmond, so the deep South delegates journeyed to Baltimore. There was some dispute over admis-sion, because in their absence the Douglas Democrats had, with some suc-cess, organized new state parties and had new delegates elected to the Balti-more meeting. The Douglas forces controlled the convention, and a committee ruled to accept most of the new, pro-Douglas delegates.

The anti-Douglas delegates had a rule-or-ruin determination, and see-ing the writing on the wall, they again withdrew from the convention. This time most of the upper South delegates followed the deep South members. One third of the total delegates walked out; they reconvened as a separate convention, and with no moderates remaining to temper their actions, they adopted a strong slave-code platform and on June 28 chose the sitting vice-president, Kentuckian John C. Breckinridge, as their proslavery presidential candidate. The regular convention, absent the southern hardshells, and full of foreboding about the upcoming election, went ahead and nominated Stephen A. Douglas on a platform still calling for popular sovereignty. (Sena-tor Joseph Lane of Oregon was named Breckinridge's vice-presidential run-ning mate, and former Georgia governor Herschel V. Johnson became Dou-glas's.) The Democratic party was now formally split, and the Breckinridge supporters must have known what that did to Democratic chances. But for them there was no longer room for compromise: perhaps some even hoped to deliver the election to the Republicans, seeing that as the way finally to effect a southern secession.

The presidential campaign that followed was hardly a normal presidential election. The Constitutional Union party often found itself having somehow to assure the proslavery forces that it was safe on slavery, and of course this only drove many northern ex-Whigs to the Republican party. Breckinridge and the southern Democrats campaigned as invincible defenders of slavery, painting Lincoln and the Republicans as dangerous abolitionists whose victory would doom the South. Newspaper editorials fanned rumors of slave unrest and abolitionist plots, and Lincoln began to loom in the minds of many southerners as a fifth horseman of the apocalypse. Douglas tried in vain to convince southerners that a politics of intransigence would destroy the nation, but few southern listeners seemed either convinced or concerned. In the North, Douglas Democrats used racist attacks against Lincoln in a futile effort to win the white vote. Lincoln's managers had the stroke of genius to run him as the spokesman of the common man, the rail splitter, with whom any free-soil northern white farmer could identify. Lincoln sat out the campaign in good Whig form, but his managers whipped up political enthusiasm with torchlit parades, supporters carrying rails through city streets, and a steady barrage of surrogate speakers.

The resulting election was in effect two elections, Lincoln versus Douglas in the North, Breckinridge versus Bell in the South. The campaigns have proven difficult to discuss without engaging in several might-have-beens. Had Breckinridge campaigned in the North, perhaps the Republicans would have gauged the utter intransigence of the southern Democrats. Having no way to judge the matter, Lincoln especially regarded southern talk of secession as simply a bluff to wring concessions out of the Republicans. And Lincoln was determined to call their bluff. He continued to hold that interpretation of events until the actual firing on Fort Sumter began. But in truth, what concessions short of total capitulation would have satisfied the southern Democrats in late 1860? Had Lincoln campaigned in the South, or had spokesmen for him been active there, southerners might not have mistaken him for a rabid abolitionist, a John Brown in stovepipe hat. But Lincoln had over and over again made clear that he did not believe the federal government had constitutional authority to touch slavery in the states where it already existed, and reading him, the South still did not understand. How else could Lincoln's rather moderate stand have been communicated?

The South ultimately decided it would accept the union only on its own terms, and those terms, many northerners came to believe, were incompatible with humanity and justice. As Lincoln had prophetically stated in 1858, "a house divided against itself cannot stand." When the votes were finally cast, they simply ratified the sectionalism of the campaign. Breckinridge carried the popular vote of the South from North Carolina to Texas (along with

Maryland and Delaware) and won the section with seventy-two electoral votes. Bell won the fewest popular votes, but they were concentrated in the upper South, and he won the thirty-nine electoral votes of Virginia, Kentucky, and Tennessee. Douglas had almost as many popular votes as Bell and Breckinridge combined, but they were scattered across the nation, and he won only Missouri's nine electoral votes and three electoral votes from a divided New Jersey. Lincoln tallied 39 percent of the total popular votes, but only 26,388 of his 1,838,347 votes came from the southern states. With his support concentrated in the northern states, Lincoln won 180 electoral votes and hence the election. Had the other three candidates effected a fusion, and had one candidate run against Lincoln, his popular vote was so focused in the northern states that he would still have won the electoral count. That as much as anything else frightened the South. Lincoln proved conclusively that the North could control the federal government by winning the presidency, and the South was helpless to stop it.

THE CRISIS OF SECESSION

The electorate cast its votes for the presidency on November 6, and by November 7 news of Lincoln's victory had sped across the telegraph wires to inform the nation. What would happen next? Southern fire-eaters had been ranting for months about secession if a "Black Republican" won the presidency, but would actions follow talk, or had this been a kind of political blackmail? South Carolina had acted precipitously several times before and been burned by her solo stance. This time the South Carolina legislature met immediately after the election results were known and called for an election on January 8 of delegates to a secession convention that would convene a week later. South Carolina leaders hoped the two-month delay would give other southern states an opportunity to assess their situation within a nation controlled by a slavery-hating Republican party and move for separation too. The January date was chosen to allow fellow southern states time to act so that South Carolina would not be out front alone again. But on November 9 a large group of Georgians arrived in Charleston to celebrate the completion of a rail line linking Charleston and Savannah, and in the celebrative, expansive atmosphere of the moment secessionist talk simply got out of hand, with Senator James Chesnut even boasting to drink all the blood that might conceivably be shed as a result of secession. Chesnut, like many other southerners, did not believe the North would really contest the South's departure. The lesson many southerners had drawn from such prior events as the irenic separation of the region's major evangelical churches from their national organizations more than two decades earlier was that secession could be peaceful. Few southerners saw secession as the prelude to years of bitter war.

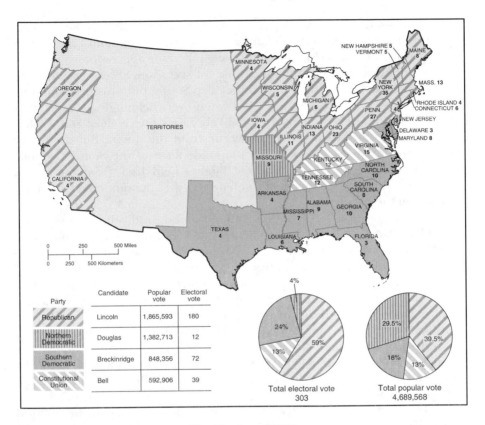

The election of 1860

Emboldened by the heady talk in Charleston on November 9 and by news that the governor of Georgia advocated a secession convention in that state and that secession rallies had occurred in Alabama and Mississippi, the South Carolina legislature decided that the tide had already turned and there was little use in waiting two months for a show of southern sentiment. Accordingly the legislature met on November 10 and pushed through a bill calling for an election of delegates on December 6 for a secession convention to meet on December 17, 1860. This time South Carolina's leadership position produced a domino effect, for within a month Alabama, Florida, Georgia, Louisiana, and Mississippi called for similar elections. The refusal of Unionist Governor Sam Houston to call the legislature slowed developments in Texas. When the South Carolina delegates met in Charleston on December 17 two days of flaming rhetoric resulted in the unanimous passage on December 20 of a secession ordinance voiding "the union now subsisting between South Carolina and other States."

Within days the other deep South states chose delegates to their respective secession conventions. In January a group of secessionist leaders in Texas, stymied by Sam Houston, informally called for a secession convention that soon returned an overwhelming vote for secession. Secession sentiment was by no means unanimous even in the deep South, but prosecessionist delegates dominated the conventions and voted overwhelmingly for separation from the Union. Between January 9 and February 1 the six deep South states joined South Carolina in voting to secede from the union. But the upper South and Border States—with the preponderance of the South's population, food production, and industrial might—held back from the fateful break. The future of the incipient Confederacy, and the sundered nation, lay hanging in the balance.

The motivation for secession differed among individuals, among the individual states, among the deep South states and the upper South states, and between regions within states. No simple generalization suffices to explain this second epochal rupture in American history, although the institution of slavery was apparently involved, somehow, in every decision. Perhaps for the sons of plantation patriarchs, there was a powerful psychological motive. Raised on the image of strong, assertive slave masters, each of these sons had to be subservient to the patriarch until his death—a kind of forced subservience that thwarted their sense of manhood and independence. For young men suffering from delayed maturity, secession was a bold, manly stroke of assertive independence that would quickly offer them the opportunity to command.

The continuing relevance of republican ideology shaped the political perceptions of many southerners in a way that made secession a principled defense of their own liberties against the overweening power of a distant federal government. In both North and South republican ideology contributed to a style of political thinking that attributed evil intent and conspiratorial power to agents foreign to their region, agents antithetical to order, freedom, and self-government. Northerners had feared the impact on their democratic institutions of the increasing number of foreign, especially Catholic, migrants, and then a menacing image of slaveholders conspiring to rule the nation in their interests became a motivation to oppose further compromise with slavery. White southerners who had earlier feared the supposedly antirepublican tendencies of the "Monster Bank" now associated abolitionism and the Republican party with the major threat to their interests. In 1860 as in earlier times of crisis white southerners identified their liberty with the right to enslave blacks and saw an attack upon slavery as an assault against their own freedom. The conspiratorial mode of political analysis that inhered in the republican ideology borrowed a century earlier from English dissenters worked against a spirit of compromise in 1860 and gave a sense of moral earnestness to Americans on both sides of the Mason–Dixon line.

White southerners across the economic spectrum had always associated easy access to inexpensive land to the west with freedom and upward mobility. The entire history of the South had been one wherein younger sons, devoid of landed opportunity in their ancestral county, moved west to the Piedmont, to Mississippi and Alabama, and to Texas in search of prosperity. This prosperity, it was assumed, would normally be based on slave labor. The shifting of the slave economy southwestward had also provided a steady market for the surplus of slaves in Virginia and Maryland, and, after 1830, for the Carolinas and Georgia. Wealthy slaveholders in the older southern states depended economically on selling their surplus slaves, and there was a related fear that the inability to send slaves westward would result in dangerous concentrations of slaves in the older states, leading possibly to insurrections. Most whites, slaveholders and small farmers alike, saw the right of slavery's unimpeded movement west to new territory as an essential guarantee of their and their region's prosperity and a safeguard against unsafe concentrations of slaves in the future. Northerners like Lincoln also believed that if slavery were confined to the existing South it would be on the road to extinction. In fact there were millions of acres in the existing South that had not by 1860 been set under cotton cultivation, as the doubling of cotton acres in the region by 1880 attests. But the fear was real, though unfounded. The Republican party's insistence on preventing the expansion of slavery—while acquiescing to its current presence—was no acceptable compromise to most southerners. Instead, to them it was a sure recipe for economic disaster and potential revolution.

The economic impact of slavery was far broader than the percentage of whites who owned slaves would indicate. A substantial portion of the white population, even those far removed from the geographical region where most slaves lived and labored, had an economic stake in slavery. As we have seen before, whites in the "nonslave" regions marketed their goods—wheat, corn, oats, barley, apples, hogs, and mules—in the slave regions. The economic nexus was real, substantial, and recognized. Appalachian farmers, for example, understood that the price they received for their products was related to the price of cotton. Moreover, even outside the so-called slave regions some whites owned slaves and others aspired to ownership. Those who did not but wanted to own slaves also accepted slavery as a necessary method of controlling the existing slave population. Most southern whites could not envision their society without the presence of African slaves, and, to the extent that the ascendency of the Republican party threatened that vision, southern whites were willing to countenance secession. These southerners supported the idea of the union also, but conditionally: only a union that guaranteed their right to hold slaves secured their allegiance. If support for the union conflicted with the right to own slaves, most southern whites would leave the union.

But there were southern whites who did not share the slaveholders' imaginative worldview, and hence there were in the South pockets of strong unionism based on opposition to slavery and slaveholders. In the mountainous far western region of Virginia many small farmers practicing mixed, subsistence agriculture were opposed to slavery for a variety of reasons, including racial opposition to competition with blacks. Long opposed to the disproportionate political power of the Tidewater and Piedmont planters in the state assembly, western Virginians had decades of antagonisms built up against the slaveholding power to the east. Many of the western farmers' contacts with the outside world ran northward along the river valleys into western Pennsylvania, and they shared more with the northern free-soil pattern of life than with the slaveholders' pattern.

Further south along the mountain chains there were also substantial divisions. The farmers in western North Carolina had prospered in the final decades of the antebellum era by selling their products back east and southeastward to the towns or plantation-dominant regions of their own state and South Carolina. Moreover, increasing numbers of wealthy lowcountry Carolinians were visiting vacation sites in the mountains. With their present economy tied to the wealth of the cotton and tobacco planters, and expecting that their future prosperity would increase as their economy became better integrated with the plantation economy, the Appalachian counties of North Carolina saw their future tied to that of the South. After mid-April, when federal troops surrendered Fort Sumter to the Confederacy and Lincoln called for 75,000 volunteers to join the army, the mountain folk of North Carolina sided with the forces of secession.

In contrast, the mountain counties of Tennessee remained unionist even though in terms of demography, terrain, climate, and agricultural products they were similar to western North Carolina. The difference seems to have been in perception. Whereas the North Carolina mountain region saw its future in optimistic terms as increasingly sharing in the growth and prosperity of the plantation regions to the east and southeast, east Tennessee, the earliest settled region of the state, had seen the tide of empire skip over it to the flatter, more fertile land of middle and western Tennessee. As slaves and cotton brought wealth and population growth to that region of the state, eastern Tennessee became increasingly a backwater, felt politically discriminated against, and harbored antagonism against rather than identified with the Old South portion of the state. When Tennessee seceded following Fort Sumter, the mountain counties remained a unionist stronghold.

Northwest Arkansas was another region of the South where unionist sentiment remained strong. Most of the settlers in the mountainous section of Arkansas had migrated from the upper South, bringing with them a lifestyle similar to that of eastern Tennessee. Farming small acreages in the mountain valleys, practicing mixed agriculture with little dependence on outside markets, utilizing almost no slave labor, the plain folk of northwest Arkansas dominated the state's population until 1850 and differentiated the state from its southern and southeastern neighbors, Louisiana and Mississippi. In the final decade of the antebellum era planters and slaves from those two states began to migrate in large numbers to the flat, delta sections of southeastern Arkansas, introducing the cotton economy to the state. This substantial migration changed the political and economic center of gravity of Arkansas, transforming it by the slimmest of margins into a slave–cotton state by early 1861. In a very close election held after a majority of the unionist-controlled secession convention had voted for separation following Fort Sumter, the Arkansas people voted to secede. Even so, significant unionist feelings persisted in the Ozark Mountains and eventually flared up to form peace societies during the Civil War.

Eastern Texas had boomed in the 1840s and 1850s with the migration of deep South planters and slaves, and cotton production skyrocketed. Identification with the deep South was strong, and visions of a continuing empire based on slavery and cotton danced in the heads of most white Texans. Some unionist sentiment persisted in the northwestern part of the settled portion of the state, along the Red River, where migrants from the upper South predominated and where grains were a major crop. But the union stronghold in Texas lay in a band of counties sweeping from a hundred miles west of Houston to Austin, San Antonio, and just beyond. Here heavy migration from Germany had created a distinct region of politically liberal farmers whose culture, language, religion, folk architecture, and mores set them apart from the society of the Old South to the east. There were German farmers to be sure who bought slaves and selectively adapted American ways, but ten counties in the German belt of Texas voted against secession in the popular referendum on the issue held on February 23, 1861. Statewide the vote ratified the action taken three weeks earlier by the secessionist convention. Governor Sam Houston, an old-line Jacksonian unionist, refused to take an oath of allegiance to the Confederacy, so the secession convention declared the gubernatorial office vacant and elevated the lieutenant governor, Edward Clark, to the governorship. Abraham Lincoln offered Houston federal troops if he would oppose secession with force, but Houston, foreseeing a bitter civil war within the state, refused the offer. Houston had earlier proposed that Texas, if it insisted on leaving the union, simply become an independent nation once more, but the pro-Confederacy sympathies were too strong.

There is a tendency to identify the seven deep South states that voted for secession by February 1 with the ultimate eleven-state Confederacy, but to do so incorrectly minimizes the extent and depth of Unionist sentiment in the whole South. No state other than Texas had as distinct a subregion as the ten German counties and a governor who was so determined a foe of separation. But in other southern states there were areas, such as eastern Tennessee and western Virginia, where slavery was almost nonexistent and many farmers had limited identification with the planters who politically and economically dominated their states. One might expect that secessionist sentiment would be weak in those portions of the states. Yet throughout the deep South there were regions of high slave concentrations and huge plantations where the slaveholders, former Whigs, also doubted the wisdom of secession precisely because they feared secession would surely lead to war, and they had the most to lose. Such Unionist slaveholders argued that the best defense of slavery's future was to remain in the Union and pressure for political guarantees of slavery's protection where it presently existed and enforcement of the Fugitive Slave Act. Yet this was for the most part a conditional Unionism, calculated on the basis of what was best for the preservation of slavery. For most Unionist slaveholders and ex-Whigs, Lincoln's call for arms after Fort Sumter and his attempt to coerce the seceded states ended their conditional devotion to the Union and made them reluctant secessionists. The overwhelming prosecessionist vote of the secession convention delegates exaggerated the strength of secession feeling throughout the deep South before Fort Sumter.

Despite the exceptions that must be noted—the many nonslaveholders who supported slavery and secession because they aspired to slave ownership and considered slavery to be a means of controlling blacks, and the many large slaveholders who at first opposed secession because they expected it would lead to war and destruction of their way of life—the fact remains that the states with the largest concentrations of slaves were the foremost supporters of secession. Secession represented a rational analysis of their economic prospects and the policy implications of the Republican platform, not a maddened overreaction to fears of abolitionism. But the political situation in the deep South was exacerbated by the total hegemony of the Democratic party and the absence of any second party. Without party competition there was no moderating influence, and candidates vied with one another on the sincerity of their support for slavery. In the upper South and border states there remained at least the semblance of two-party competiton—the remnant of the Whig party, expressed either as Douglas Democrats or, at the very end of the antebellum era, as the Constitutional Union party. In either form the absolutist demands of the southern Democrats were moderated, or at least another viewpoint was expressed and debated. There were no countervailing tendencies in the Democratic party of the deep South.

Interstate unity had long been the bugaboo of South Carolina's secessionist extremists. Even in the final secession crisis there was debate: should the deep South states try to effect a quasi-union on principle and then secede en masse, or should each state stand alone on secession and hope later to form a confederacy of individually seceded states? Fire-eaters pushed for instant secession while the shock of Lincoln's election was fresh; waiting for complete regional agreement on the exact rationale for secession would cause unnecessary delays, confusion, and in fact might let the magic moment pass, quieting the secessionist urge. Some so-called secessionists urged waiting until a united secession could be effected because they hoped that such a wait would still the urge. But in the rush of events following Lincoln's victory and South Carolina's bold move, six states in quick succession cut the tie that bound them to the union. Even before other states acted, South Carolina elected commissioners to future seceding states, instructing the commissioners to call for a convention for the purpose of creating a provisional southern government. Accordingly the commissioners appointed a convention to meet at Montgomery, Alabama, on February 4. Even before the Texas delegates arrived the convention began work.

Within three days the delegates adopted a provisional constitution for the Confederate States of America closely modeled on the US Constitution but with firm guarantees of slavery expressly written in. Two days later Jefferson Davis of Mississippi was chosen the provisional president of the Confederacy, Alexander H. Stevens vice-president, and on February 18 the two were inaugurated. The Confederacy of seven deep South states was underway. (The Montgomery convention, after the Confederacy was established, drafted a permanent constitution and later submitted it to the states for formal ratification; Davis and Stevens were likewise formally elected by a Confederate plebiscite in the fall of 1861 and reinaugurated on February 22, 1862.) Meanwhile, in the North, James Buchanan still resided in the White House as the lame-duck president, and Abraham Lincoln stayed close to his home in Springfield, Illinois, saying as little as he could about the course of events. What would the upper South states do? When asked to say something conciliatory to wavering southerners in the upper South, Lincoln refused, saying his views were already well known. Apparently still believing secession was a ploy to force the Republicans to make significant concessions to the slavepower forces, Lincoln kept an extremely low profile in Springfield throughout the tension-filled weeks, causing even many Republicans to wonder if he had the wisdom and character to be an effective president.

A hesitant Buchanan declared secession illegal but quickly said he had no Constitutional power to coerce states who left the Union. Some northerners were unwilling to contest secession, in fact, had a "good riddance" attitude toward the seceded states, and certain northern business interests were afraid that attempts to pressure either the seceded or upper South states might cause a "secession panic" that would be bad for business. Others, either more aware than Lincoln of the seriousness of the occasion or more sanguine about the possibility of meaningful compromise, or more willing than Buchanan to act, sought to intervene. The Senate organized a Committee of Thirteen to try to prevent additional states from seceding. Perhaps if some conciliatory concessions could be gained, even some of the seceded states might be weaned back to the Union.

Senator John J. Crittenden of Kentucky took the leadership role in the committee, eventually proposing a series of amendments that, though labeled moderate, in fact caved in to the South's demands. Among other things Crittenden's amendments called for barring slavery "in all the territory of the United States now held, or hereafter acquired," north of the old Missouri Compromise line but permitting and protecting it south of the line, enforcing the Fugitive Slave Act, allowing any future states to enter the Union, slave or free as they wished, and amending the Constitution so it could never in the future interfere with slavery either in the District of Columbia or in any state where it now existed. But southerners refused to support the Crittenden amendments unless the Republicans accepted them in advance, and Lincoln advised them not to. Neither he nor most Republicans would compromise on letting slavery expand into additional territories. Moreover, the phrase about territory "hereafter acquired" conjured up images of southern filibustering attempts in the Caribbean. Such an amendment "would," in Lincoln's words, "amount to a perpetual covenant of war against every people, tribe, and State owning a foot of land between here and Tierra del Fuego." Lincoln understood what a Republican compromise would mean, and he dug in his heels. With Republican opposition and hence little southern support, the Crittenden amendments went down to defeat on the Senate floor by the end of December.

By the end of the year Buchanan's resolve was slightly strengthened on behalf of the Union because several of his southern cabinet members resigned as their states prepared to elect delegates to secession conventions and were replaced in the cabinet with Unionists. South Carolina began to seize federal property, and Buchanan's response to his Constitutional obligations intensified the struggle within his mind. In late December Major Robert Anderson of Kentucky, the commander of fewer than ninety US soldiers at Fort Moultrie in Charleston harbor, followed the vague orders of his superior officers and moved his men under cover of night the short distance from that indefensible position to Fort Sumter. The fort, which was still under construction, was a massive, thick-walled fortification on a speck of an island in the middle of the entrance to the harbor. Outraged Charlestonians considered the move an act of war and demanded that Buchanan send the troops back to Moultrie. But in the absence of his southern cabinet advisers, Buchanan stiffened his back and sent reinforcements and provisions to the harried Anderson via an unarmed merchant ship, the *Star of the West*. The effort was marred by a comedy of errors, and when the ship, not expected by Anderson, approached Fort Sumter on January 9, the Charleston artillery opened fire and sent the supply ship back to sea. In truth these were probably the opening shots of the Civil War, but Major Anderson, not having orders to do so, did not fire back. Then Buchanan's backbone softened once again. He returned to his passive mode, and Lincoln continued in his. (Three months later, when Lincoln took office, he was given a memorandum from Major Anderson indicating that his supplies were running out and a critical decision had to be made.) But to James Buchanan on January 9, as the *Star of the West* left Fort Sumter, tomorrow was still another day, and the future another president's responsibility.

FORT SUMTER

Throughout January 1861, one after another of the deep South states voted to secede and then seized federal property—forts, post offices, customs offices, and the like—within their boundaries. An impasse was rapidly approaching. What would the upper South states do? The Virginia legislature, hoping to effect a compromise that would contain secessionist sentiment and generate Unionist support in the upper South and Border States sufficient to insure the perpetuation of the Union, called for a Peace Convention to meet in Washington on February 4, which was, coincidentally, the date that the Confederates met in Montgomery to draft their constitution. Twenty-one states, including all the undecided southern states, sent delegates, and they met in secret at the Willard Hotel under the chairmanship of former president John Tyler of Virginia. But once again the compromises sufficient to mollify the South had no chance of winning Republican approval. The delegates, mostly older men of the previous generation, even met with President-elect Lincoln, but Lincoln would not compromise on his opposition to slavery in the territories. After three weeks of negotiation the convention in effect only slightly modified the Crittenden amendments, and the Peace Convention proposals also went down to defeat in Congress.

Ironically, on February 27, the same day that the final Peace Convention proposals had been presented to Congress, a resurrected amendment from the Crittenden committee mustered the necessary two-thirds votes to pass both the House and the Senate. This proposed amendment guaranteed slavery where it presently existed from any future interference by the federal government. The next step in the normal process was to submit this Thirteenth Amendment, which explicitly protected slavery forever, to the states for ratification, but events intervened. Four years later, after a calamitous Civil War, another Thirteenth Amendment would pass and be ratified. That Thirteenth Amendment would abolish slavery forever in the United States.

With Jefferson Davis already in office and the last of the compromise efforts dead, Lincoln's rendezvous with history neared. Traveling by train from Springfield, he was forced to slip through Baltimore by night because of rumors of an assassination attempt. No president had seemed so to slouch toward his inauguration, but Lincoln had philosophical and rhetorical depths as yet unplumbed. Aware that upon his words hung the fate of the nation, Lincoln carefully repeated his position that he had no Constitutional authority to interfere with slavery where it existed at present. He reiterated his support for the Fugitive Slave Law, disavowed any intention of invading the South, and said no blood need be shed. Yet he emphatically stated his opposition to secession, saying the "Union of these states is perpetual." In that context he reported that he would "hold, occupy, and possess" federal property lying within the seceded states but would do so in an unprovocative manner. Lincoln was trying not to provoke the South. To a group of Virginia Unionists calling on him in late February he had hinted at withdrawing from Fort Sumter if Virginia would cancel its secession convention. And in the key sentence of his inaugural address he had silently stricken the word "reclaim" from the list of verbs.

Lincoln wanted to project an image of firmness tempered with moderation. He urged all Americans to be calm, to think carefully about their actions at this critical moment in time, and he told the southerners point blank that there would be no conflict "without being yourselves the aggressors." Secretary of State William H. Seward had pushed Lincoln to be even more conciliatory and had suggested a conclusion to the inaugural address. Lincoln took the suggestion and recrafted the words into an eloquent ending: "I am loathe to close. We are not enemies but friends. We must not be enemies. Though passion may have strained, it must not break our bonds of affection. The mystic chords of memory, stretching from every battlefield, and patriot grave, to every living heart and hearthstone, all over this broad land, will yet swell the chorus of the Union, when again touched, as surely they will be, by the better angels of our nature."

But the better angels were silent, and discordant voices drowned out the chorus of the Union. Southerners in the seceded states heard Lincoln to be calling for coercion, and the issue of Fort Sumter hung, like Damocles' sword, above Lincoln's desk in the Oval Office. Major Anderson had written that at least twenty thousand troops would be required to reinforce his position and that his supplies would be exhausted in four to six weeks. Until he received Anderson's memorandum Lincoln had felt that delay was on his side, and the longer action could be put off, the better chance that the states of the upper South would reinforce their attachment to the Union and perhaps even some of the seceded states would reconsider their position and drift back to the Union. Now there seemed to be an outer limit to delay—six weeks. Meanwhile many in the northern press were calling for action now. Lincoln seemed far too passive and weak. Others, like Secretary of State Seward, hoped to buy more time even at the price of giving up Fort Sumter. Seward was secretly telling southerners that Lincoln would abandon the fort, and Seward even suggested picking a war with a foreign power in a last-gap effort to rekindle nationalist feeling in the South.

Lincoln, however, felt a Constitutional and moral obligation to hold and protect federal property; if the Union seemed so weak and vacillating that it could not hold federal forts, might not the resolve of the secessionists in the unseceded states be so strengthened that they would seize power and take the upper South out of the nation? Would Lincoln not risk the loss of his own party's support if he were seen to acquiesce in the fall of Fort Sumter? But to move aggressively to hold the fort would surely provoke a war, and in the face of northern aggression there would be no hope of keeping the upper South states in the Union. After much turmoil, debate, and conflicting advice, Lincoln hammered out a plan. Provisions, not arms or men, would be sent to Major Anderson in hopes of continuing indefinitely the federal occupation of Fort Sumter, a militarily insignificant position since the fort was unfinished and Anderson's forces were miniscule. Sitting off at sea would be ships with arms and soldiers, but these would be called into service only if the supply ship was rebuffed.

An explicit message would be hand delivered to Governor Francis W. Pickens of South Carolina describing the peaceful, nonthreatening nature of the effort: "I am directed by the President of the United States to notify you to expect an attempt will be made to supply Fort-Sumter with provisions only; and that, if such attempt be not resisted, no effort to throw in men, arms, or ammunition, will be made, without further notice, [except] in case of an attack upon the Fort." Apparently Lincoln thought there was a slight possibility that the Confederacy might accept such a reprovisioning peacefully. If so, the uneasy peace would be continued. Lincoln assumed the probability was that the South Carolinians would reject the offer and attack the fort, but by so doing the onus of firing the first shot would be on them. In that case, the North would be unified behind Lincoln's cause, and there was a possibility that some of the yet unseceded southern states would reject the Confederate claims.

Fort Sumter, squatting dark and low in the mouth of Charleston's harbor, stood tall in symbolic importance. If its fall to the forces of secession boded ill for the prospects of Lincoln and the Union, even more did its continuation in the hands of federal forces threaten the Confederacy. What did it say about the strength of the Confederate States of America if the enemy occupied a fort in the very bosom of its spiritual capital? How seriously would potential European allies take the new nation if it could not or would not rid itself of such an irritant? The future status of the upper South states was even more important to the nascent Confederacy than to the Union. The Confederacy's prospects looked dim without Virginia especially. Deprived of the populous upper South and its resources, would the resolve of the seceded seven slowly evaporate, soon to ask to return, tail between their legs, to the Union?

Southern hotheads were demanding that President Jefferson Davis act, and do so decisively. Fort Sumter presented Davis with more of a dilemma than it did Lincoln. Lincoln believed that delay might restore the departed states; Davis believed inaction would seal the death of the fledgling southern nation. Davis and other southerners interpreted Major Anderson's late December move from Fort Moultrie to Fort Sumter to have been both provocative and aggressive. To acquiesce passively to the reprovisioning of his forces now would be to admit helplessness. Lincoln could risk war for the chance of peace. Davis and his advisors risked war for the chance of nation-hood—perhaps Lincoln and the Black Republicans would back down. After all, nothing had happened after the January 9 firing on Buchanan's half-hearted attempt to bring supplies to Fort Sumter. If Lincoln flinched, Davis and the Confederacy would look invincible, and the reluctant upper South and even the Border States would join the Confederate States of America.

So, when on the night of April 8 Jefferson Davis in Montgomery received a telegram from General P. G. T. Beauregard, commander of the recently strengthed Confederate forces in the Charleston area, informing him of the message from Lincoln to Governor Pickens of South Carolina, Davis wired back: "Under no circumstances are you to allow provisions to be sent to Fort Sumter." Feverish consultations followed between Davis and his cabinet during the next two days. Should Beauregard attack now, or wait to see if provisioning would really be attempted? Was the so-called message from Lincoln genuine? In the midst of these talks on April 10 came a telegram from Texas fire-eater Louis Wigfall, visiting in Charleston. Lincoln was surely preparing for war, Wigfall said. Delay was inadvisable. Virginia was excited about the turn of events, and secessionists there awaited the outcome in Charleston. "A bold stroke on our side" would turn the tide of events in Virginia, and she would cast her lot with the Confederacy. Davis made his decision, and he wired a message back to General Beauregard: "If you have no doubt of the authorized character of the agent who communicated to you the intention of the Washington Government to supply Fort Sumter by force you will at once demand its evacuation, and if this is refused proceed, in such manner as you may determine, to reduce it."

The next day, April 11, Beauregard sent a demand to Major Ander-son—ironically an old friend and former teacher of Beauregard at West Point—to surrender, requesting an answer by 6:00 P.M. Anderson later in the afternoon sent a written refusal to surrender, but pointed out that in several days the lack of food would force him to lay aside his arms. Informed by tele-graph of Anderson's response, Davis advised by Secretary of War Leroy P. Walker that, if Anderson could give a precise date of this future surrender, before Lincoln's provisions arrived, then Beauregard should wait and avoid unnecessary bloodshed. But Anderson's final reply proved unsatisfactory. The Confederates had just intercepted a letter from Anderson to Washington in which Anderson acknowledged the supplies being sent. Anderson had added, "My heart is not in the war which I see is to be thus commenced."

Unwilling to wait any longer, Beauregard made final preparations to begin the attack on Fort Sumter. The next morning, precisely at 4:30 A.M., the shelling began, one of the first shots fired by secessionist fanatic Edmund Ruffin. For thirty-three hours the artillery pounded the island fortress. "These long hours the regular sound of the cannon roar," wrote Mary Boykin Chesnut in her diary, "—boom—still go these terrible guns." In mid-afternoon of April 13, the fort partly in flames, his men exhausted, Major Anderson surrendered. The next day the American flag was lowered and the Confederate flag was hoisted to wave over the ruins of Fort Sumter. Lincoln was right. If there had to be war, the South would have to fire the first shot. It had, the North knew where to place the blame, and when Lincoln the very next day issued a proclamation declaring ominously that there existed "combinations too powerful to be suppressed" by ordinary police powers in the seceded states and called for 75,000 volunteer forces from "the several States of the Union" to "suppress such combinations," the northern response was overwhelming. So, fatefully, was that of the South.

Unionists in the upper South and border states had watched events during the months after Lincoln's election with a growing sense of sadness, hoping against hope that somehow critical decisions could be put off indefinitely and maybe time that heals all things could even salve the nation's political wounds. Many of them were Unionists only if the Union supported slavery where it existed with an enforced Fugitive Slave Law, but they were not precipitous secessionists. Virginians such as Jubal A. Early blamed the seven seceding states for having put them "in this perilous condition." They were angered by South Carolina's actions on April 12, realizing that the attack on Fort Sumter would quickly force the issue that the Unionists did not want to have to face. But the conditional Unionists, in addition to supporting slavery, were adamantly opposed to the North's coercing any southern state. Coercion smacked of tyranny, of the loss of independence of action, and the near-century-long influence of Republican ideology raised warning flags in most southerners' minds whenever a threat to white liberty was suspected. Even more than Fort Sumter, Lincoln's call for troops to "suppress" the insurrection in certain southern states was the issue that pushed the conditional Unionists and reluctant secessionists over the edge. The secessionist minority in the upper South had of course exulted over news that South Carolina had acted. The American correspondent of the *Times* of London was in Baltimore on April 12 enroute to Savannah, and in Baltimore, Norfolk, and Goldsboro, North Carolina, before Lincoln's proclamation he heard wild jubilation and bellicose boasting. The gunfire in Charleston's harbor and the northern call for soldiers cemented southern sentiment in Virginia, Arkansas, Tennessee, and North Carolina.

In Virginia the secession convention had been meeting off and on for two months and on April 4 had once again voted down secession; in the furious aftermath of Lincoln's call to arms the convention met on April 17 and passed an ordinance of secession by a two-to-one vote. The issue was formally put to a statewide referendum on May 23, but for all practical purposes Virginia—the South's most populous, most industrialized state, with leaders such as Robert E. Lee and with the great Gosport Navy Yard and the Tredegar Iron Works—had joined the Confederacy. Without Virginia it is hard to imagine the Confederacy not quickly collapsing. Before the popular vote Virginia had placed her army under the direction of Jefferson Davis, and the Confederate Congress had accepted Virginia's invitation to move the Confederate capital from Montgomery to Richmond. The example of Virginia's secession, following as it did the specter of thousands of Union troops marching south to coerce seceded sister states, quickly and overwhelmingly turned the tide of political opinion in Arkansas and Tennessee, despite pockets of tenacious Unionism in their mountainous regions. On May 6 Arkansas voted to secede, and on the next day Tennessee was taken out of the Union by action of her governor and legislature without waiting for a secession convention. The decision in North Carolina awaited the action on May 20 of the secession convention, but the vote was a foregone conclusion. The governor had already used the state militia to seize several federal forts and an arsenal. By late May, then, the Confederacy, eleven states in all, was complete, though the ultimate disposition of Maryland, Kentucky, and Missouri was still problematical. Tiny Delaware, with only 2 percent of its population enslaved, had already in January voted "unqualified" opposition to secession.

If the secession of Virginia was essential to the hopes of the Confederacy, keeping Maryland and Kentucky within the Union was essential to the North. Had Maryland seceded, Washington, DC would have been surrounded by enemy territory, and the Baltimore mob that on April 19 attacked the 6th Massachusetts Regiment as it marched through the city was a harrowing premonition of what might lie in store for Washington. Lincoln acted decisively in this case, setting aside delicate concerns about civil liberties, suspending habeas corpus, and preemptively jailing suspected secessionist leaders. Southern Maryland and the Eastern Shore had strong secessionist feelings, but Baltimore with its commercial ties to the North, and the wheat growing sections to the West, leaned toward the Union. Lincoln's shove tilted the state against secession, much to the relief of the citizens of Washington, DC, and those charged with its defense. Lincoln also knew how important Kentucky was to the Union cause, and Kentucky itself felt tugged in both directions. But strong commercial links with Cincinnati and the Midwest, and the assurance of Lincoln that the North had no intentions to use military force against the state, persuaded the legislature to keep the state in the Union. Confederate armies later invaded the Bluegrass state, and Union armies responded, and slightly more Kentucky volunteers fought in blue than in gray. Again Lincoln's political skills and judgment served the Union well.

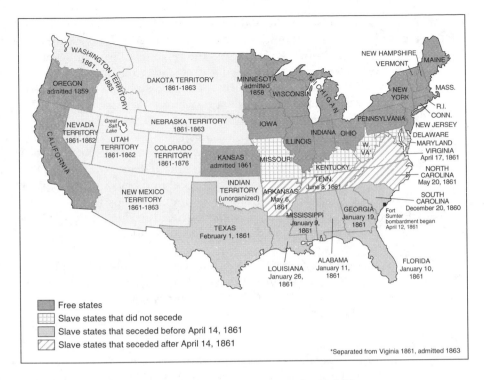

The United States on the eve of the Civil War

The fight over secession was especially bitter in Missouri. The Unionist proponents ultimately proved to be better organized, and they were well served in Washington by Congressman Francis P. Blair, Jr. In effect an extralegal Unionist rump section of the erstwhile secessionist convention governed the state throughout most of the war, keeping Missouri in the Union. A mini-civil war broke out in Missouri between Unionist and secessionist forces, with sections of the state sinking into virtual guerrilla warfare. Confederate diehards like the notorious William Quantrill and his raiders (including Jesse and Frank James) terrorized portions of Missouri, and their bushwacking activities led to Unionist "Jayhawker" guerrilla fighters who matched them atrocity for atrocity. Missouri was devastated by this internecine fighting, and the bitterness lasted for years, but the state did officially stay in the Union.

The westernmost counties of Virginia, which had almost no slaves, also balked at the decision in favor of secession made in Richmond. Delegates from those counties met on June 11 in Wheeling, rejected secession, and established a counter-government. Union troops had already moved into the region from Ohio to disrupt the Baltimore and Ohio Railroad, and soon there were twenty thousand federal troops in the trans-Allegheny counties of Virginia. Confederate troops later contested the region, but with military support the Unionist proponents established a rival state government to that in Richmond. On May 23 this rival government, which obtained in approximately fifty counties, created the new state of West Virginia, provided for gradual emancipation of its slaves, and became the thirty-fifth state on June 20, 1863. The Confederates had better success in the Indian Territory (later Oklahoma), where many members of the Five Civilized Tribes owned black slaves. The Confederates matched the annuities the federal government had paid the Indians, and the Indians provided a good number of troops for the southern cause. (A much smaller number of Indian troops fought on the Union side.) Brigadier General Stand Watie, a Cherokee chief, would fight in several major Civil War battles and did not in fact surrender until two months after Appomattox.

Had Virginia, Arkansas, Tennessee, and North Carolina remained in the Union, the Confederacy might well have shriveled and the crisis of secession been surmounted. Had the Border States of Maryland, Kentucky, and Missouri seceded, the strength of the Confederacy might well have made the North more open to compromising with slavery, or the war that resulted might have ended in genuine stalemate. But no one at the time fully appreciated the momentousness of what was happening, and no one foresaw that the next four years would bring the deadliest war in American history. Hindsight gives us a false sense of wisdom. The exigencies of political life afford few occasions for reclaiming decisions or choosing the interplay of men and events. The Union of 1776 was sundered, and storm clouds were building on the horizon of history. The future, as always, was opaque to the participants.

THE WAR BEGINS

Standard procedure for Civil War historiography requires a list of the advantages the North had over the South. The North's population stood at about 22 million, while the Confederate South's was 9 million, 3.5 million of whom were slaves. In industrial production, arms manufacturing, railroad mileage, food production, and the like the North far outranked the South. But no one at the time foresaw a lengthy war that would be determined by the size of the North's military and industrial pantry. Jefferson Davis and the Confederate government went about establishing the infrastructure of nationhood in a spirit of misinformed optimism. Cabinet officers had to be appointed, government bureaus had to be established to do everything from delivering the mail to handling the Confederacy's finances, and an army had to be raised and backed up by a support and command system. Jefferson

Davis had served as the secretary of war in Franklin Pierce's administration, and that, along with his own experience in the Mexican War, provided him with enough military expertise to seduce him into interfering with the Confederacy's secretaries of war. Within little over a year he had appointed and lost three war secretaries before settling on James A. Seddon in November 1862. Seddon looked permanently ill, but he was a good administrator and knew how to identify talented subordinates.

None of Davis's appointees was more skilled than Josiah Gorgas, the head of the Confederate ordinance bureau, who, like a soldierly Rumplestiltskin, magically created guns and ammunition out of the South's miserly larder of resources. As essential as military ordinance was the wherewithal to pay for the war, and Secretary of Treasury Christopher G. Memminger faced an impossible task. The Confederate government was especially aware of the importance of respecting the rights of the individual states and moved hesitantly toward taxation. Early in the conflict a war tax was passed, but the states were simply asked to provide their prorated share, and most of them borrowed the money rather than levy a tax. The Union embargo deprived the Confederacy of significant resources. A tiny fraction of the wartime monetary needs were raised from European loans, but in short fashion the Confederate government came to depend upon paper money backed by the presumed success of the Confederacy. Hundreds of millions of dollars of Confederate money were printed, and its value plummeted in ratio to the amount in circulation and the prospects of eventual victory. As the war dragged on, the Confederate money depreciated till in the end it was worth scarcely more than one penny on the dollar.

But these problems were in the future in the summer of 1861. In the excitement of the moment publicists of all sorts, from politicians to preachers, were extolling the political and moral virtues of the Confederacy. It was as though, sensing that a new nation had been born, spokesmen believed its character and legitimacy could be established by an act of the will. Secession led to self-conscious Confederate nationalism, not vice versa. And nothing seemed more to justify the rightness of the Confederacy than Lincoln's call to arms with its explicit intention of coercing the seceded states to return to a normal relationship to the Union. Early battlefield successes nourished Confederate nationalism as a natural and proud response to victory, but as the war ground on, Confederate officials employed nationalism as a means of maintaining morale and a willingness to sacrifice for the cause of the South.

Few expected much sacrifice would be called for in the heady days of 1861. Many southerners continued to doubt that Lincoln and the North would long persist in an effort to reunite the states. Moreover, southern statesmen had great confidence in the power of King Cotton to attract British and European diplomatic and economic support. Jefferson Davis was not pleased with his first two secretaries of state, Robert Toombs and R. M. T.

Hunter, but in Judah P. Benjamin, the third Confederate secretary of state, who was graceful and persuasive, Davis found a kind of alter ego who also trusted the economic power of the South's great staple. But no one in the South adequately understood that cotton's influence would be weakened first by Britain's stockpiles and then by new sources in Egypt, or that the diplomacy of England and France would be determined by those nations' notions of larger self-interest. Grain imports from the North proved at least as important to European powers as the lure of cotton from the South, and the promise of emancipation on January 1, 1863, clarified the North's moral position with regard to slavery and doomed the hope of Confederate alliances with European powers. The future of the South would be decided on the fields of battle, not by the fields of cotton.

Particularly in the early days of the Confederacy, Jefferson Davis was his own military strategist. His views largely determined government policy. Davis and southern leaders in general did not desire a war of conquest against the North. Rather, in their opinion the South had peacefully seceded and simply wanted to be left alone. Consequently the southern military policy would be defensive. The North, if it persisted in its intention to contest secession, would have to be the aggressor, come south, and defeat the southern armies who would be protecting their heartland. Few southerners expected the North to have much stomach for hard, bloody fighting deep within the South against spirited southern defenders.

Abraham Lincoln had no military background and in the opening months of the war did not presume to make military strategy. Lincoln accepted the logic of his general-in-chief, aged Winfield Scott, who proposed surrounding the South by holding the Border States, winning control of the Mississippi River to its mouth, and enforcing a stiff maritime blockade on the coastal South from the mouth of the Chesapeake to the Rio Grande. Slowly this great noose would close around the South and gradually strangle it. Then offensive attacks could be made with surgical accuracy on limited southern targets to bring about the cessation of the war with minimum casualities. On April 19, 1861, Lincoln proclaimed a blockade of the South. Southerners quickly labeled it merely a paper blockade and appealed to British precedent in an attempt to persuade British and European diplomats to ignore the embargo. But Secretary of Navy Gideon Welles soon made the blockade far more effective. Within months the South's foreign trade diminished to a fifth of its prewar scale, and though small, swift blockade runners continued to slip goods into isolated ports, the loop around the South became increasingly tight and produced crippling wartime shortages of supplies in the Confederacy. Even so, the blockade runners prolonged the life of the Confederacy by months, perhaps a year.

Much of the northern press, along with a noisy group of Radical Republicans, had long thought Lincoln moved too slowly on every aspect of the

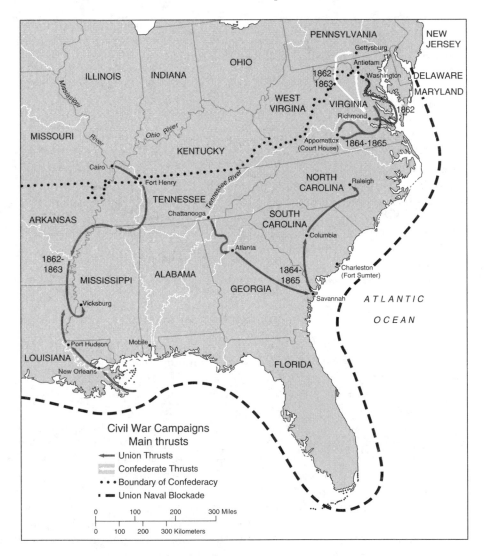

Military Strategies of the Civil War

problem with the South, and they demanded military action against the southerners. Perhaps in a sudden move Richmond itself could be captured. Under a barrage of political attacks, Lincoln in early July 1861 ordered General Irvin McDowell to move his army of thirty thousand men toward Richmond. Delays constantly wracked McDowell's army, but it finally set out southwesterly on July 16. By this time the Confederate army through its network of spies knew the Union intentions, and President Davis had ordered

General P. G. T. Beauregard to move toward the oncoming northern forces and set up a defensive position. Beauregard's army dug in along the southern bank of a small stream called Bull Run that ran between the town of Centreville and the railroad connection at Manassas Junction. The Union army moved into position and readied for an assault. Beauregard decided to attack first on July 21, but he was awakened before dawn by the sound of artillery—McDowell had beaten the surprise Confederate attack. For most of the morning the Union forces were victorious and pushed back the southern troops. Both sides fought surprisingly well for this early in the military season, and for a while it seemed McDowell would gain a major victory. Exultant telegrams were dispatched back to Washington, and the ladies and gentlemen from the capital who had journied out to picnic and watch the battle felt gratified.

But the northern advance slowed as the fighting surged up Henry House Hill. With the southerners fighting desperately, the battle lines surged back and forth. At one critical point a southern officer pointed to the strong defensive stand being made by the forces under the command of General Thomas T. Jackson and shouted: "There is Jackson standing like a stone wall!" Thus rallied by "Stonewall" Jackson's men and his example, the southerners held their ground until that afternoon when General Joseph E. Johnston's fresh troops, having given the slip to the Union general in the upper Valley of Virginia, Robert Patterson, and come by train to Manassas Junction, arrived to turn the tide decisively for the Confederates. By now the Union troops were thirsty and exhausted. The imminent end of their ninety-day enlistment period made a last-ditch stand unusually unappealing, and when thousands of Confederate troops, screaming at the tops of their lungs, surged forward in counterattack, the Union lines broke. Panicked soldiers dropped their weapons and gear and fled the field of battle, soon to become snarled in the rush of carriages hurrying the picnickers and sightseers back to Washington. The southern army became almost as disorganized in its advance as the northern army was in its retreat. Although Jefferson Davis himself, who had come up from Richmond to watch the activity, urged pursuit of the fleeing Federals and the possible capture of Washington, DC, Generals Beauregard and Johnston argued against further advance. Later much mutual recrimination resulted from the ultimate decision not to follow up the victory at Manassas, but McDowell did pull together enough troops to establish a defensive position near Centreville that night. Pounding rains the next morning turned the roads into an impassable quagmire. An advance might not have gone as easily as at first seemed possible.

So the two armies backed away from each other in the fashion of older military strategy, licked their wounds, and proceeded to draw lessons from the just-finished conflict. As with many instant analyses, each side probably drew the wrong conclusions. The South, cocksure to begin with, now believed its military prowess so invincible that it could engage in limited offensive war. The North, with a tail-between-the-legs sense of defeatism, overestimated the skill and effectiveness of the Rebel forces and determined never to move against them unless the North had overwhelming superiority in numbers and material. Cautious General George B. McClellan replaced McDowell as head of the Union forces that were soon named the Army of the Potomac. Both armies did correctly perceive that they had organizational and logistic problems to overcome. In the aftermath of First Manassas the active theater of war shifted to the West for the next six months.

The Union strategy was to move southward from Kentucky toward Alabama and Mississippi and simultaneously move northward from the mouth of the Mississippi River, effectively cutting the Confederacy in two. In January 1862 a Confederate force at Mill Springs, Kentucky, near the Appalachians, fell to Union troops commanded by General George H. Thomas, and to the west General Ulysses S. Grant followed up that initiative by relentlessly pushing up (southward) the Tennessee and Cumberland rivers. Making skilled use of iron-clad river boats, Grant attacked and defeated Fort Henry on the Tennessee (February 6), then marched overland to besiege Fort Donelson on the Cumberland. The southern forces proved their mettle, but their officers soon realized Grant's advantage. Confederate General Simon Buckner sent a proposal to Grant to discuss terms for surrender, but Grant brusquely replied that only "unconditional and immediate surrender" would be accepted. Faced with a potential slaughter or surrender, Buckner handed over thirteen thousand men to Grant. Grant then pushed further south, as did General Don Carlos Buell, making his way from Louisville through Nashville, later to rendezvous with Grant's forces at Pittsburg Landing on the Tennessee River near the state line just above Mississippi. The whole heartland of the South seemed about to be in Union hands.

A feeling of desperation stalked the statehouse in Richmond. Davis understood the strategic significance of Union control of the region and the breaking of supply and communication lines. A diversionary attempt in the Far West failed when Confederate General Henry H. Sibley was defeated at Glorieta Pass in New Mexico and had to limp back into Texas. General Earl Van Dorn's plan to sweep through Arkansas, cross the Mississippi River, and catch Grant's army from the rear while General Albert Sidney Johnston moved north from his base in the state of Mississippi foundered when Van Dorn's forces were scuttled by Union troops at Elkhorn Tavern, Arkansas, in the most one-sided Federal victory of the war. Before the entire central Confederacy came unraveled, Johnston thought he saw an opportunity to scotch the Union advance and perhaps change the course of the war. Grant's army of about forty thousand was debarking at Pittsburg Landing, expecting any moment to be joined by Buell's 35,000 additional troops. Johnston's army of 27,000 at Corinth, Mississippi, barely 30 miles away, had just been augmented by Braxton Bragg's 15,000 men, and Johnston decided to strike at Grant before Buell's reinforcements arrived.

As usual, unforeseen delays slowed the army's march, but on the morning of April 6, 1862, in the vicinity of Shiloh Church, the fierce battle began. Grant had been surprised, and the Rebs, ably led by Johnston, who lost his life there, threatened to smash the Union army. Grant's army was pushed back toward the Tennessee River, and it seemed for a moment that the South was about to win a signal victory. But approaching nightfall and physical exhaustion halted the southern advance. The most fierce fighting so far in the war had occurred that day, and darkness found both armies battered, with 10,000 casualties lying in the field during a stormy night of pelting rain.

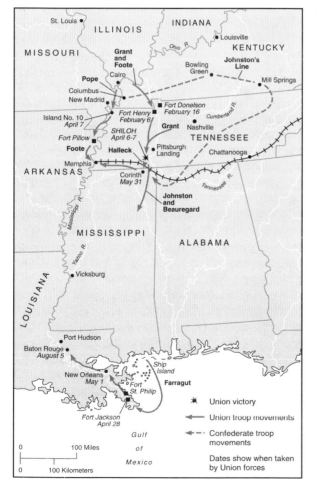

War in the West, 1862

But General Buell had arrived late in the afternoon with fresh troops and was ferrying them across the river to join Grant's bedraggled forces. With Johnston dead, Beauregard now commanded the southern army, and Beauregard, sleeping four miles away in General William T. Sherman's captured tent, thought victory was imminent. Grant and Sherman, though, were tenacious fighters, and the next morning it was the Confederate's turn to be surprised by an attack. Regrouped Union forces drove the southern regiments backward, their morale broken by the realization that they had not won the battle the day before. By mid-afternoon Beauregard authorized a retreat, so the two armies slowly separated. By dark the first really big battle of the war had haltingly come to an end. In the mud and the blood lay more than twenty thousand casualties, dead and wounded, about evenly divided between the two armies. (For comparison, the total Allied casualties on D-Day, June 6, 1944, were forty-nine hundred.)

Little seemed to have been settled except that perhaps the South could find some solace in Grant's march southward having been stopped for the time being. But within two months of Beauregard's retreat, Union forces controlled the important rail center of Corinth, Mississippi. No one understood that the awesome size and destructiveness of the battle at Shiloh presaged the scale of the battles that lay in the future. Everyone did sense the true horror of modern combat and recognized that this war would afford no easy victory to either side. Gone were the days when officers' wives visited them and took up residences in homes near winter sites. Could the South dare to admit that Union forces would be able to seize and to hold significant sections of the South and disrupt critical rail connections between the western Confederacy and the eastern Confederacy?

That reality was driven home again in only three weeks when Captain David G. Farragut with a flotilla of warships and gunboats broke through the Confederate defenses at the mouth of the Mississippi and began an inexorable push up the river. Fending off attacks from southern forts, cutting a chain stretched across the river, narrowly escaping burning rafts floated downstream, Farragut's ships with 15,000 men aboard bore down on the Crescent City. On April 29 New Orleans, the South's largest city, its leading banking and financial center, home of the valuable Leeds Foundry Works, surrendered to Farragut. Two days later the soon-to-be-eternally hated Benjamin Butler arrived with Federal troops to begin the Union occupation of the city. Jefferson Davis well knew the strategic importance of this loss, the loss of the Mississippi River, to the Confederate cause, and no one understood better than Davis the diplomatic blow abroad that the South had suffered by this turn of events. Within two months both Baton Rouge and Natchez had also surrendered to Farragut, and Grant had captured Memphis and both sides of the Mississippi south almost to Vicksburg, high and supposedly safe on its bluffs overlooking the river. In mid-1862 the war in the West looked almost lost to the Confederacy.

In late August Confederate General Bragg began an invasion of Kentucky. He expected a series of easy victories would liberate Kentucky from Union hands—a political miscalculation of the first order, because most Kentuckians with southern sympathies had already joined the Rebel army. General Buell had a large army present to defend the state, and both forces moved, countermoved, and feinted toward one another. Finally a bloody battle occurred at Perryville, south of Louisville, on October 8, 1862. Casualties were high for both sides, and neither commanding general distinguished himself. In a sense neither army "won," but Bragg, who had risked the most by invading Kentucky, had to abandon his plan of winning the state. He retreated back to Chattanooga. Buell frittered away a number of opportunities really to smash Bragg's army. Lincoln soon replaced him with General William S. Rosecrans. Still, Bragg had made the larger blunder.

The South had been out-generaled in the West, but in Virginia it was a different story. General McClellan had drilled his army of one hundred and fifty thousand to perfection, and though Lincoln wanted a direct overland assault of Richmond, McClellan persisted until his own plan was accepted. He would ferry his troops down the Chesapeake Bay to the peninsula formed by the James and York rivers, land them there in early April, and begin a slow, powerful march up the thick finger of land till he captured the Rebel capital. This plan was thwarted by southern strategy. Robert E. Lee was now military adviser to Davis, and Lee accepted Stonewall Jackson's plan to move his army up the Shenandoah, threatening Washington from the northwest even as he thrashed Union armies en route. A worried Lincoln withheld some forty thousand of McClellan's troops to guard Washington. McClellan, already obsessed with caution and always imagining the southern army to be far larger than it was, now moved with a snail's pace up the peninsula. By the end of May he had drawn within five miles of the Confederate capital.

Suddenly the southern defender of Richmond, General Joseph E. Johnston, saw McClellan divide his forces near the Chickahominy River and decided to strike. The southern attack proved to be disorganized and the battle at Seven Pines indecisive, but it did halt McClellan's advance and, since Johnston was severely wounded, he was replaced by the incomparable Robert E. Lee. Understanding that Stonewall Jackson's successes to the north had many Union forces looking away from Richmond, Lee then called for Jackson swiftly to move toward the Confederate capital. Combined with Lee's forces, the strengthened southern army engaged McClellan's sluggish troops first at Mechanicsville, June 26–27, 1862, then in a week of battles (in which both sides suffered heavy casualties) called the Seven Days forced the Army of the Potomac into a painful retreat back down the peninsula. Richmond was safe. Jefferson Davis had the superior generals in Virginia. Lee, Jackson, and cavalryman extraordinaire "Jeb" Stuart, whose horsemen had completely cir-

Robert E. Lee. (Library of Congress)

cled McClellan's army in a tour de force of reconnaissance, made the Army of the Potomac even more unsure of itself.

Lincoln, still preferring a direct Washington-to-Richmond attack, ordered the northern army to withdraw from the peninsula and join up in northern Virginia with a smaller force commanded by John Pope in preparation for an assault on the Confederate capital. General Lee anticipated these moves and pushed overland to smash Pope before McClellan could arrive. The armies collided on August 29 and 30 in the Second Battle of Manassas, and in a series of brilliant maneuvers Lee utilized the generalship of Stonewall Jackson and James Longstreet to rout Pope's troops. Once again Union forces, spent and demoralized, fled back toward Washington from the vicinity of Bull Run. Three months before McClellan had been on the outskirts of Richmond; now Lee's army looked invincible hardly twenty miles from the suburbs of Washington.

ANTIETAM AND THE EMANCIPATION PROCLAMATION

Davis and Lee both knew that Washington was too well defended to risk attacking. They also knew that, following a string of defeats in the West, the South needed to follow up its recent successes in Virginia with such vigor as to prop up southern morale and demoralize the northern public. Davis and Lee recognized, too, that a sensational victory might so impress the diplomats in France and England such that they would finally recognize the South as a bona fide new nation. For those reasons, in the late summer of 1862 Lee mulled over a bold plan. On September 4 Lee's strategy was revealed when his troops crossed the Potomac and began an invasion of Maryland. Stonewall Jackson's army moved on a parallel course slightly to the west, with plans of taking Harpers Ferry with its rich cache of munitions. At first things went as projected. Lee's men entered Frederick on September 6 singing "Maryland, My Maryland," and Jackson moved toward Harpers Ferry. A frustrated Lincoln ordered McClellan toward Maryland and tried to light a fire under him, but McClellan was cautious as ever. Lee divided his army, sending a portion toward Harpers Ferry to help bottle up the bluecoats there, intending thereafter to reunite these men, and Jackson's, with the remainder of his troops preparatory to an invasion of Pennsylvania. Lee expected thereby to gain needed supplies, further demoralize the North, impress the Europeans, perhaps even persuade the northern public to demand a cessation of the war and acquiesce in the secession of the South. But this daring plan failed because of an incredible fluke of good luck for McClellan.

On September 13 two Union soldiers found a piece of paper wrapped around three cigars; unrolling the sheet, the paper was found to be a copy of Lee's orders—fallen from a Confederate officer's pocket. McClellan now

The Peninsular Campaigns
and the Battle of Antietam

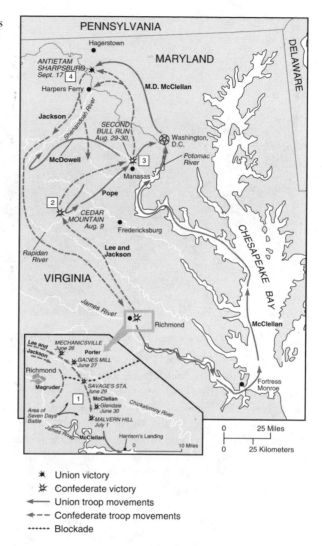

* Union victory
※ Confederate victory
◄········ Union troop movements
◄─ ─ Confederate troop movements
+++++++ Blockade

knew that Lee's forces were divided, Jackson was miles to the West, and the
Union army far outnumbered the individual pieces of Lee's invading army. If
McClellan moved quickly, he could knock off Lee's divided forces one after
the other before Lee could recombine his troops. But as usual McClellan
moved cautiously and wasted much of his advantage. Jackson took Harpers
Ferry on September 15; Lee learned what McClellan knew and began to
gather his forces behind Antietam Creek near the small town of Sharpsburg,
Maryland. Jackson was approaching posthaste. On September 17, just as Jack-

A view of the Union casualities at Antietam. (Library of Congress)

son arrived to help, McClelland's eighty-seven-thousand-man army began battering the fifty thousand Confederate troops.

Never had anyone seen such intense fighting. For hours the terrible slaughter continued, at the Dunker church, at the cornfield, in a sunken farm road accurately renamed Bloody Lane, beside the stone bridge that arched Antietam Creek where thousands of Union soldiers died in futile attempt after attempt to push well-defended Confederates back. Armies could not long sustain the kinds of casualties suffered that day. By nightfall, with over twenty-three thousand wounded and dead, those alive almost stupefied by the horror and bloodshed and senseless butchery, both sides stumbled to a moratorium in the fighting. The next day Lee remained in place in a defensive posture, but neither army was militarily or psychologically fit to resume hostilities. On September 18 Lee's forces, what were left, began a painful retreat back to the South, with a regimental band playing "Carry Me Back to Old Virginny." McClellan was insufficiently bold, or ruthless, to attack again and crush them before they escaped. One can hardly say that McClellan won at Antietam (Lincoln replaced him as commander of the Army of the Potomac with Ambrose E. Burnside two months later), but Lee certainly lost, and for reasons besides the toll in lives.

Lincoln had despaired of Union military successes in the early summer of 1862, and he had come increasingly to appreciate the advantageous military use the Confederates were making of slaves in building fortifications and in a wide variety of other noncombat duties. Confederate officers often brought along their personal slaves who did their cooking, laundry, and in general helped ease camp life, sometimes to the annoyance of the enlisted men. Slaves at home working in the fields and munitions factories also freed thousands of white southerners for army service. Lincoln's moral opposition to slavery had also grown, but he saw no Constitutional way to strike against slavery simply because he and others were convinced it was repugnant. Not only did Constitutional scruples constrain him, but he feared northern sentiment would not yet support such an effort and might tip the political balance toward antiwar Democrats or possibly even cause secessionist movements in several Border States.

Yet southern military successes pressed Lincoln to consider other ways of solving two problems: he could both attack slavery and deprive the Confederacy of a signal manpower asset and could do so on the justifiable grounds of military necessity. The war powers clause of the Constitution offered him his legal warrant. On July 22 Lincoln broached these thoughts to his cabinet, where there was only one objection, although Secretary of State Seward advised waiting for "military success" so the action would not look like a desperate move by an almost defeated nation. Lincoln accepted that advice and waited for the right moment. The news from Sharpsburg of a muted northern victory—Lee's invasion of the North had been squelched—provided the opportunity. September 22, five days after that bloody victory near Antietam Creek, Lincoln notified his cabinet and released his Preliminary Emancipation Proclamation.

Intending to give the South due warning, Lincoln announced that three months hence, on January 1, 1863, he would designate which states were still in official rebellion and that in the portions of those states under Confederate authority "all persons held as slaves . . . shall be then, thenceforward, and forever free." As predicted, this pre-announcement generated some Democratic and racist opposition in the North, and most southerners were outraged, seeing it as an invitation for slave rebellion against helpless women and children whose male protectors were off at war. And when on New Year's Day 1863 the actual Proclamation was released, southerners were further shocked to see that Lincoln had added a clause declaring that the freed slaves "will be received into the armed services of the United States." Northern abolitionists were on the whole enthusiastic, as were blacks. Suddenly the war seemed a genuine moral crusade, a battle for righteousness' sake. Certainly that was how it was perceived abroad. No longer did British liberals and workingmen's groups have doubts about which side they favored. Moreover, until Sharpsburg the South had been seen by sympathizers in England as a region that did not really want war and suffered northern military aggression. Now the South looked to be the aggressor, subtly changing the moral equation.

The Emancipation Proclamation destroyed any chances that the South could win essential diplomatic concessions from England, and without England's support, France offered none. Southern desires for help from John Bull were slow to fade. As late as October 1862 remarks such as those by William Gladstone, Chancellor of the Exchequer, "Jefferson Davis and . . . the South have made an army; they are making . . . a navy; and they have made what is more than either—they have made a nation," fueled southern hopes, but Gladstone was unrepresentative of British opinion. Northern moral, diplomatic, and economic pressure continued to build, and by the end of 1863 Britain moved to prevent private shipbuilders from constructing and outfitting streamlined blockade runners and powerful ships armed with rams. Jefferson Davis had no way of foreseeing on the eve of Sharpsburg the full dimensions of the defeat to the South's ambitions.

Lincoln and northern public opinion fervently wanted the Union army to follow up the victory at Sharpsburg with hard blows to Lee's crippled forces. The new northern commander, General Burnside, attempted to mount an offensive against Richmond, but to do so he chose to cross the Rappahannock River at Fredericksburg, heavily defended by the Confederates. General Longstreet had his troops well positioned on high ground overlooking the town, with a wide open field especially vunerable to Confederate gunfire from men behind a stone fence on what was called Marye's Heights. Burnside, following older military strategy, believed his superior numbers would enable him to smash the Confederate defense. When the Blues began crossing the river on December 13 and charging up the hill, devastating southern gunfire destroyed the Union army. Within minutes thousands of dead and wounded men carpeted the field of brown grass. Burnside's plans were crushed, and he had to withdraw. The year came to a cruel close.

A NEW KIND OF WAR

The year 1862 brought home to both sides, but especially to the South, that this war would demand sacrifices of everyone, military and civilian, that no one had ever experienced or imagined before. A new kind of war had emerged, and the size of the armies alone required a revolution in logistics, in manpower, and in food and materiel that strained the sinews of southern society to the breaking point. Technology also changed the pace of war, with troops moved rapidly by rail and information flashed instantly by telegraph. Could the South's more conservative social system meet the challenge?

At President Davis's urging the Confederate Congress in April 1862 passed the first conscription act in American history, calling up all white southern males between the ages of eighteen and thirty-five for three years of military service—later the eligible years were expanded to seventeen through fifty. Exemptions were made for persons in certain occupations considered essential to the war effort. One white man was exempted on each plantation for every twenty slaves, and substitutes could be hired. These exemptions, the so-called "twenty-nigger rule" in particular, created much ill will among average southerners, who came to call the conflict "a rich man's war and a poor man's fight." Conscription was never popular, but it proved to be the whip that drove tens of thousands of southern men to volunteer so they could escape the ignominy of being drafted. Some governors, such as Joseph E. Brown of Georgia and Zebulon M. Vance of North Carolina, were such rigid advocates of states' rights that they tried to undermine central government acts like conscription, almost fatally crippling the South's war effort. Davis proved less creative than Lincoln in bending the rules of government to meet the exigencies of war, but even so the bugaboo of states' rights paralyzed the kind of ruthlessly efficient centralized government policy necessary to fight total war. Could anyone have done significantly better with the South than Davis?

Already by the end of 1862 southern civilians were experiencing severe shortages of everything from coffee to corn, from salt (important as a meat preservative) to medicine. Prices shot skyward; by 1864 a pound of butter in Richmond cost more than an army private's monthly salary. The blockade was by now creating real problems, but even worse were the disruptions and dislocations within the South. Food production collapsed as hundreds of thousands of men were pulled from farming to join the armies, and agricultural production collapsed as young boys, old men, and women unaccustomed to farm management tried to plant the crops and supervise the slaves. Labor shortages plagued regions where there were few slaves. Large portions of the South were under Union control—much of the central heartland, most of the rich bottomland lining the Mississippi River, and wealthy coastal enclaves in South Carolina. Whites with their slaves fled from such regions and became refugees elsewhere in the South, upsetting agricultural production further. The rail lines that were not overused and worn out by transporting troops could hardly move even the available supplies from less disrupted regions like Texas to war-ravaged areas. Soon the southern war effort and the agricultural economy were crippled by a growing shortage of both horses and mules, caused in part by Union occupation of Kentucky and Tennessee, the major sources of draft animals.

Southern armies and civilians alike began to suffer hunger, and nothing dispirited the soldiers in gray more than plaintive letters from their wives and mothers describing hardships and starvation at home, nothing was more conducive to desertion, if only for a few months to get a crop planted or harvested. Armies not only marched on their bellies; they also moved on the supportive will power of their womenfolk. In the first year of the war women had often been exuberant supporters of the Confederate cause. They organized a wide variety of creative fundraising events. They made socks, bandages, and quilts for soldiers, sewed handsome flags and regimental colors for local troops, gladly gave up luxuries and "made do" with substitute goods—all for the sake of the Confederacy. But fatigue, hunger, desperation, and loneliness exacted at last a terrible toll, and hope began to evaporate. When in the later years of the conflict women came to question the incredible sacrifices the war effort demanded of them—food, shelter, safety, and loved ones—the true impact of total war came home to the South.

Southern soldiers learned too that older attitudes about courage and heroism and the romance of war were largely invalid. At the war's beginning—and First Manassas seemed to confirm the conceit—southerners assumed any one of them could whip a passel of Yankees, the war would be filled with manly adventure, and combat set individual against individual in an arena where courage offered assurance of success. But the common soldier learned more quickly from sad experience than did the commanding generals that the new scale of combat, with the new technology of killing, made outmoded earlier concepts of war. Current military strategy was based on the relative ineffectiveness of the Mexican War-era single-shot, muzzle-loading musket. Slow and cumbersome to load, with an effective range of eighty to one hundred yards, and notoriously inaccurate, the musket equipped with bayonet gave the advantage to offensive troops massed together. Since attackers could draw within one hundred yards of defenders before being at much risk, the survivors of the first volley could then charge with bayonets drawn and be upon the defenders before they could reload. Hence concentrated offensive charges were, according to the West Point manuals that most generals had studied, effective against defensive positions, and both sides insisted on employing the tactic in the first two years of the war. But the rifled musket drastically changed the odds against offensive warfare.

Both armies in the Civil War began using muskets that had rifled barrels, meaning that instead of being smooth-bored, the inside of the barrels were grooved in such fashion as to give to the emerging conical "minie ball" a spin that—like a spiraling football—significantly enhanced both its accuracy and the distance it would carry. Rifled muskets had an effective range of upwards of four hundred yards. Now charging troops came into the range of defensive troops at such a distance that defenders could get off three or more shots before the attackers were upon them. The increased accuracy meant that more of the shots actually hit oncoming infantrymen. The result was that well-positioned defenders could literally mow attackers down with successive rounds of fire before the attackers got close enough to wield their bayonets. Practically no offensive charge could succeed unless their numbers were sufficient to absorb catastrophic casualties. At Shiloh, at the stone bridge over Antietam Creek, at Marye's Heights, this lesson was absorbed by Johnny Reb and Billy Yank, but seemingly not by their commanders. In six of the nine largest battles of the war in 1862 and 1863, the Confederates made tactical offensive charges, and while they won half the battles, southern casualties exceeded those of the North by twenty thousand men (eighty-nine thousand to sixty-nine thousand). The South could little afford such prolific expenditure of men. Grant and Sherman would go on the offensive in the later stages of the war, but they had the manpower and the raw will to overcome their losses.

Moreover, the inadequacies of medical science exacerbated the horrors of the new technology of killing. Doctors did not understand about germs and went from wounded patient to wounded patient unintentionally spreading infection. Almost the only treatment for gunshot injuries to limbs was amputation, without the benefit of anesthesia. The head-high piles of arms and legs outside the surgeons' tents did little to improve the morale of soldiers. Common diseases like dysentery and diarrhea often made camp life a living hell, with deaths from injuries and illness probably double the actual combat deaths.

In January 1863, after Burnside's defeat at Fredericksburg, Lincoln sacked the general (whose predilection for facial hair gave us the word *sideburns*) and replaced him with arrogant Joseph "Fighting Joe" Hooker (whose predilection for loose women, legend has it, gave us a synonym for prostitute). Hooker thought that he could drive toward Richmond, feint a movement near Fredericksburg that would isolate a portion of Lee's troops, and proceed to roll up the Army of Northern Virginia. But Lee proved too smart, too bold, for Hooker, and with Stonewall Jackson at his service Lee divided his troops, sent Jackson on a swift flanking movement, and there in the scrub-oak region locally called the Wilderness smashed Hooker's larger army at Chancellorsville. Again, as at the Battle of Seven Days, Lee utilized quick shifting of troops, bold offensive assaults, and screaming Rebel fighters to demoralize and defeat ill-positioned northern troops—a lesson inappropriate, it would turn out, for the next great battle that would take place in Pennsylvania when the Union forces had protected positions above the southern onrush.

GETTYSBURG AND BEYOND

Lee could not foresee the future, but on the evening of the first day of hostilities at Chancellorsville, May 2, 1863, he did glimpse a frightening portent of destiny. Stonewall Jackson, on a moonlight reconnaissance of the battlefield, returned toward the Confederate camp. Jackson was challenged by a sentry, and before he could convincingly identify himself a volley of shots was fired. Mighty Stonewall was struck in the hand and arm, and later that night surgeons amputated his left arm. Lee summarized the situation: "He has lost his left arm, but I have lost my right." The Confederate victory several days later at Chancellorsville seemed empty when, on May 10, Jackson died from complications including pneumonia. Twelve thousand southern troops were also lost in the victory—a hard victory indeed. Nevertheless, the tactical success here, and continued rumors of Confederate malaise in the West—generals quarreling with one another, no satisfactory command system, and the mounting shortages of basic supplies—led Lee to plan a daring gamble in the fleeting hope that the war could still be won.

Lee knew that Grant was bearing down on Vicksburg, the Gibraltar of the Mississippi. After months of skirmishes and thwarted attacks, Grant presently had the city under siege after a brilliant dash downriver and a sweep below and to the east of the city. At the moment Grant was pressing in on Vicksburg from the east. Holding Vicksburg was absolutely essential for Confederate prospects in the West, but Lee knew that before troops from Virginia could get there the siege would be over one way or another. So Lee looked elsewhere to take the pressure off the West. A quick thrust to the north, through Maryland into Pennsylvania, might, if successful—and Lee believed his army of nearly 75,000 battle-tempered soldiers could achieve anything he requested—further strengthen Peace Democrats in the North, discredit the Republicans, possibly lead to capture of Philadelphia, reopen the prospects of diplomatic success abroad, and perhaps force the North at last to acquiesce to the South's desire for separate nationhood. After the recent victory at Chancellorsville, might not another stunning Confederate victory—this time in Pennsylvania—thoroughly demoralize the North before the South ran completely out of the resources necessary to wage war? Lee pushed his ideas with Davis, who soon accepted the desperate logic of Lee's gamble.

Lee began the bold campaign in the first week of June 1863, first moving west, then turning north in the Valley, crossing the narrow neck of Maryland through Hagerstown and invading Pennsylvania. Fighting Joe Hooker thought he saw a chance to capture Richmond with Lee pressing north, but an exasperated Lincoln—now understanding the point of the war better than most of his generals—tutored Hooker that he had to defeat Lee's army, not capture territory! Lincoln ordered Hooker north to keep himself between Lee and Washington, DC. Meanwhile Lee's advance troops were nearing Harrisburg, with his men under strictest orders not to harass civilians and forage for food with the kind of wild abandon northern armies had been inflicting on the South. But Rebel soldiers could not always resist the temptation. By late June, Lee was studying maps and scouting out terrain for the ideal site to turn on the Union army—Lincoln had removed Hooker and put General George G. Meade in control—for another one of his patented victories.

On June 30 a Confederate division under General A. P. Hill, searching

Fredericksburg to
Gettysburg, 1862 to 1863

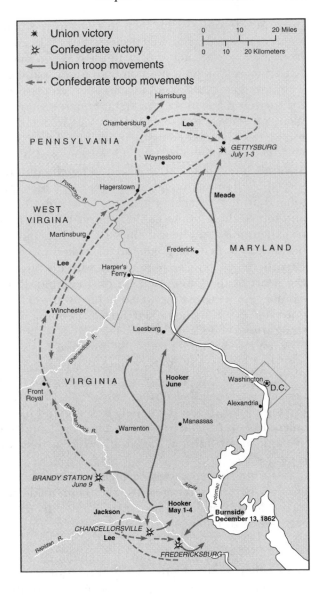

for boots and saddlery, accidentally came upon a Union patrol near the little
college town of Gettysburg. Shots were fired, both sides promptly sent reinforcements, and events quickly got out of hand. Neither Lee nor Meade had
wanted a battle here. In fact, Jeb Stuart, Lee's mounted reconnaissance
genius, was off toward Baltimore raiding Union supply lines. Nevertheless, in
the hours following the first day's skirmishing north and northwest of Gettys-

burg, Meade ordered his men to take up positions on a high, rocky ridge south of town; his men, well protected by rocks and stone fences, looked west from a convex arc allowing both good vision and internal communication. Lee's forces took their position on a lower, parallel ridge about a mile away. They faced east, and swept in a broader, concave arc that made it impossible for the left flank to see the right. Squarely across the slightly rolling open field, up the rocky rise, rifled muzzles in hand, stood determined Union forces, this time defending their homeland from invasion.

Did Lee fully recognize the weakness of his position? His subordinate generals surely did. Did he have too much confidence in his intrepid men, incredible fighters though they were? Did he expect too much of the prolonged artillery exchange that rent the quiet of the countryside on July 2 and rattled the windows of Gettysburg? Was his normally sharp mind dulled by exhaustion and physical illness? Casualties mounted throughout that day, but on July 3, Lee had come too far, risked too extravagantly, to back down. He ordered General George Pickett with his fifteen thousand men to assault the heart of the Union defense on Cemetery Ridge in a glorious, reckless frontal charge across the wheat fields. About 3:15 that afternoon the gaunt gray soldiers launched their attack, keeping in cadence as they walked straight into the face of death. The forces in blue held their fire until Pickett's men were within range, then opened fire with deadly effectiveness. By now the Rebs were running, yelling, in a flurry of guns and bayonets and battle flags, but the fusillade of Union gunfire cut the men down like an invisible but terribly lethal scythe. One small contingent momentarily reached the top of the Union ridge, only to be forced back. Then the entire charge failed, like an exhausted wave on the beach, and swept back down the slope in panic and confusion and death while artillery and muskets raked their retreat.

Of the fifteen thousand men who had begun the charge only thirty minutes before, a meager five thousand made it back to safety. Lee was forced to pull back and managed to rally his stunned troops. Meade, however, failed to follow up with a clinching assault that might have ended the war on July 4, 1863. The next day Lee began his slow, demoralized retreat back to Virginia, his caravan of ambulance wagons stretching seventeen weary miles. Twenty-eight thousand men of the Army of Northern Virginia were killed, wounded, or missing. The mood of Richmond was as somber as that of Washington was joyful. Some four months later, at ceremonies dedicating a national cemetery near the Gettysburg battlefield, Lincoln—in a stunningly eloquent 272-word address used the occasion to redefine the whole national purpose—the achievement of equality for all persons. Coming as it did after the Emancipation Proclamation, the Gettysburg Address would soon join the Declaration of Independence and Constitution as the essential charters of purpose for the ultimately reunited nation, though the goal of equality has yet to be fully met.

But Gettysburg was not the only momentous news that Fourth of July. Telegrams arrived from Vicksburg, a thousand miles to the west. After a siege of six weeks, during which its citizens suffered unspeakable hardships, General John Pemberton surrendered the city and his whole army, thirty thousand men, to General Grant. Along with the men went thousands of stands of arms, caches of gunpowder, and the hope of the West. Within a week Port Hudson in Louisiana also fell, giving the Union uncontested control of the entire Mississippi River and effectively cutting off most of the men and supplies in Arkansas and Texas from the desperate Confederate armies to the east. The combined news of Gettysburg and Vicksburg shattered southern confidence, and at Vicksburg Lincoln knew he had finally found a general who knew how to fight. Lincoln quickly put Grant in command of all the Union troops in the West and ordered him to push Confederate General Braxton Bragg out of central Tennessee.

A series of battles in the early fall pitted Union armies under General William S. Rosecrans against Bragg's forces, and at the Battle of Chickamauga near Chattanooga Bragg seemed about to turn the tide once more in favor of the South when General George H. Thomas (the "Rock of Chickamauga") made a heroic stand, forcing Bragg into launching a protracted siege of Chattanooga. Before Bragg could effect a victory General Grant, with fresh troops, arrived and drove the frustrated Confederate army back into Georgia. Here was a victory almost as important as Vicksburg. The Union now controlled the entire southern heartland and the Tennessee River system. The South's only remaining choice was to hang on by sheer will power and courage, and hope it could absorb and wear down the North's incentive to fight. But southerners did not anticipate the tenacity of Ulysses S. Grant and William T. Sherman. In the spring of 1864 Lincoln brought Grant east to become general in chief of all Union forces, and Grant named Sherman his successor in command of the armies in the West.

Conditions continued to deteriorate in the southern economy, and both the army and civilians on the homefront suffered grievously. Soldiers in the forthcoming months would sometimes march shoeless, without guns, starved to the point of collapse. The South's transportation system failed, and while there were warehouses and depots with food, there was simply no means of distributing the rations. Necessary medical supplies were gone, making the suffering in the hospitals and on the battlefields indescribable. Men who had earlier felt warfare glamorous now saw it as a kind of gnawing, unyielding cancer, and many of the rules and restraints of military etiquette were abandoned in a bitter effort to survive. Famished, half-naked "Johnny Rebs" were now driven to scavenging the uniforms, even the rations, of dead and dying Union soldiers lying on the ravaged fields of battle. Women and children back home struggled with starvation, and conquering Union troops, embittered too by the continuing war, made fewer exemptions for civilians, depriving widows and families of food, draft animals, even fence rails, which they used for making campfires.

Thousands of slaves, sensing freedom in the air, fled to the Union armies when opportunity offered itself, sometimes almost overwhelming by their numbers the logistic capabilities of the military. After the Emancipation Proclamation the Union army made increasing use of black laborers and then black soldiers, infuriating racist Confederates who often refused to accept captured black soldiers as prisoners of war and shot them instead as traitors. But blacks proved to be a valuable augmentation of Union forces, further tipping the scales toward Union victory.

Desertion grew as a problem for Jefferson Davis. Women became desperate for food, leading even to bread riots in Richmond itself. Peace societies developed in several mountainous regions, with areas essentially withdrawing from the Confederacy. Class conflict began to emerge as segments of the population felt they were paying a disproportionate share of the human and economic burden. Davis and the Confederate government tried to respond to the exigencies of war, but to do so required central government regulations that flew in the face of states' rights sentiment. Centralization, a degree of urbanization and industrialization, and economic controls—the very things required to fight a modern war—threatened to transform the South into what it had to some extent gone to war to avoid becoming. Political carping at Davis at times drove him to distraction. The Confederacy had no political parties, no mechanisms by which Davis could garner political support and chastise opponents. When events went badly, he was an easy scapegoat, but despite the blame heaped on him, no one supported the southern cause more assiduously than Davis did.

With planters and many white men in the armies, the authority structure essential to slave control also began to break down. Blacks rejected bondage for the promise of freedom and escaped to the Union armies—even slavery seemed to be dissolving in the midst of the war. Patriotism waned as farmers with cotton illegally traded it to northern agents in the regions captured by the Union. This especially became a problem along the Mississippi valley. Southerners with stockpiles of cotton but deficient in everything else found that they could pledge loyalty to the Union, sell cotton to the North, and then purchase food and medicine. The desire for survival proved stronger than nationalism, intensifying class conflicts and lowering morale further. Defeat was creeping over the South as surely as the tide raises the sea, but resolute Confederate officials and military officers were determined to resist what they refused to accept. This refusal to face the absolute inevitability of defeat cost the South needless thousands of deaths and did not change the outcome of the war.

CONFEDERATE DEFEAT

The South was running out of everything, and with hardship and spreading defeat came a loss of morale and will, but what really turned the fortunes of the southern armies was the strategy of the North now that Grant was in command. Grant (and Sherman) understood that the point was to destroy the other side's armies and the other side's ability to sustain the war. Grant proposed two brutal sweeps: he would take the Army of the Potomac, 115,000 men, and push toward Richmond, crushing whatever stood in his way, no matter now long it took or how many casualties it cost. Sherman would take his 100,000 men and push from northwestern Georgia to Atlanta. By now the northern economy was going full blast, bountifully providing Grant and Sherman with supplies and manpower. Grant began his campaign in the spring, beginning in May west of Fredericksburg at the Battle of the Wilderness (May 5 to 7). Lee again proved a brilliant campaigner, stopping Grant momentarily at a terrible cost, with gunfire catching the thick woods on fire and horribly burning to death the wounded who could not be rescued or escape on their own. Even though Grant lost over 17,500 men in the two days, he kept pushing onward relentlessly. Days later (May 8 to 12), the two armies met again in savage battle at Spotsylvania Court House. Here the fighting became hand to hand; at one particularly hard fought section Union survivors found 150 dead southerners in an area no larger than a modern bedroom. Men could barely comprehend such profusion of noise and blood and death. Soldiers fought half-dazed, suffering what later ages would call shell shock. In one week of battle butchery Grant suffered 32,500 casualties, but still he kept coming.

Grant looped east and south, but Lee moved quicker and got into position behind the North Anna River. Grant pulled back again and looped south again, about to approach Richmond from the east. But again Lee performed logistical miracles and got into position first at Cold Harbor, where his engineers constructed an elaborate system of earthworks and trenches. Now the southerners were fighting defensively, and the North spent thousands of men on courageous and deadly assaults. Despite frightful casualties on both sides for a month, they both somehow got reinforcements and were almost back to full strength at Cold Harbor. Grant's men now were in awe of Lee's resolute soldiers who simply did not know when they were beaten. When Grant ordered an assault on Lee's trenches on June 3, hundreds of

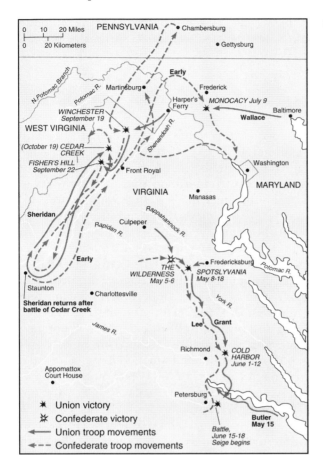

War in the East, 1864

Grant's men fatalistically pinned pieces of paper with their home address to their uniforms so their next of kin could be notified of their deaths. The southern gunfire was so constant it sounded, Lee would remark, like sheets being ripped by the wind, and in minutes 7,000 bluecoats lay dead and wounded.

The northern press was outraged by Grant's profligacy with men, but Grant was determined to purchase victory whatever the cost. Realizing this frontal attack was foundering, Grant once more made a great loop south, then west, hoping to take Petersburg by surprise—Petersburg, Richmond's back door and rail connection to the hinterland. P. G. T. Beauregard, terribly undermanned, performed defensive miracles to hold the city. Tardily, but in time, Lee discovered Grant's intention and rushed additional troops into place at Petersburg, getting solidly entrenched before Grant could carry the day. By mid-June both forces, exhausted and bled by more than six weeks of the bloodiest warfare the world had yet seen, settled into a stalemate and siege that dragged horrible month into horrible month. Both armies found trench warfare to be a new definition of hell, but neither side would call retreat.

Beginning on May 7 General Sherman embarked on his march through North Georgia. Joseph E. Johnston, a masterful defensive strategist, contested his every step. Sherman learned quickly that he could not sustain direct attacks on Johnston, so he bobbed and weaved his way southeastward as Johnston fell back, took strong defensive positions, and forced Sherman again to feint first one way, then jab another. Both commanders were skilled, and Johnston kept up a brilliant delaying tactic. But Jefferson Davis and other Confederate officials wanted to stop the slow yet relentless advance of Sherman ever closer to Atlanta. They wanted a southern commander who would attack, not defend, so on July 18, 1864, Davis replaced Johnston with John B. Hood, who was more aggressive than he was wily. In three separate battles during the week of July 20 to 28 Hood attacked Sherman, heedless of the advantages defensive forces now possessed. Hood did little more than suffer 15,000 casualties to Sherman's 6,000. Sherman simply outfoxed Hood, utilizing speed and skill to outflank him, then swept to the south of Atlanta to disrupt its essential rail connections. Atlantans hardly knew what had hit them in the final days of August when Hood had to retreat precipitously to avoid capture and torched Atlanta as he left. On September 2, Sherman's forces triumphantly took the city and the victorious general telegraphed Lincoln, "Atlanta is ours." Nothing since the fall of Vicksburg so shook the South, and the fall of Atlanta came just in time to boost Lincoln in the fall presidential election. A veil of doom spread stealthily across the Confederacy like a heavy fog. Little did southerners know that Sherman was about to rewrite the manuals of war at their expense.

The hostilities then entered an unprecedented level of intensity. Grant and Sherman realized that not simply did opposing armies have to be destroyed if there was to be an end to the seemingly endless conflict. The South's ability to support a war had to be destroyed. The entire infrastructure of the region—at least a section of it for demonstration purposes—had to be destroyed utterly. Sherman was the man for such work. Several months earlier Grant had sent General Philip H. Sheridan and the Army of the Shenandoah on a mission up the Valley with instructions to turn it into a waste so barren "that crows flying over it for the balance of this season will have to carry their provender with them." Now Sherman was to perfect that kind of warfare of obliteration, and having dispatched General George H. Thomas to hold Tennessee and keep Hood occupied, he commenced his infamously devastating march through Georgia. Meeting almost no resistance, like a giant lawnmower sixty miles wide Sherman's forces cut down everything of

Final Campaigns of the Civil War, 1864 to 1865

value in the 285 miles from Atlanta to Savannah, destroying barns, burning crops in the field, killing cows and horses, sacking homes, melting train tracks and tying them around trees, and completely demoralizing and embittering the citizens of Georgia. As he neared the beautiful city of Savannah, its defenders had the good judgment to surrender to avoid total destruction. On December 21, 1864, Sherman wired Lincoln, "I beg to present you, as a Christmas gift, the city of Savannah." Meanwhile, near Nashville, Thomas had destroyed Hood's Army of Tennessee. In early January Sherman turned north, heading by way of Columbia and through North Carolina to join with Grant and overpower Lee near Richmond. How much longer could the South hold out?

The South was being exhausted of everything—food, munitions, manpower, morale. Initially it was less a matter of losing the will to fight than simply losing the wherewithal to engage in the new kind of warfare. But the resulting despair began to enervate the will. By the end of 1864 huge portions of the South were under Union control. The blockade had become so tight that the ratio of ships that successfully eluded Federal patrollers had fallen from nine out of ten in 1861 to barely one in two, and these were much smaller ships. For several years British-made cruisers like the C. S. S. *Alabama* had sailed the seven seas wreaking havoc on Union merchant shipping—the *Alabama* alone sank almost seventy northern ships—but the seemingly unconquerable *Alabama* herself had been sunk on June 19, 1864, outside a French port. On August 5, 1864, Union Admiral David Farragut had withstood a ferocious bombardment from three forts guarding the entrance to Mobile Bay and led his fourteen wooden ships and four iron-clad monitors through a network of mines to the heart of the bay. In the midst of the battle, after one of the monitors was blown up by a mine, Farragut shouted "Damn the torpedoes! Full speed ahead." After three weeks of battle the three forts fell, closing the last major blockade-running port on the Gulf Coast east of Texas. By January 15, 1865, the South's last open port of significance, Wilmington, North Carolina—the best of the blockade-running ports—was closed by a Federal armada commanded by Admiral David D. Porter. The noose was drawing ever tighter even as Lee's stubborn defenders of Richmond, enduring the almost mind-numbing hardships of trench warfare, kept Grant's army at bay.

At the beginning of the war effort the southern clergy had been influential supporters of the Confederate cause and nationhood. In sermon after sermon they defended slavery as a providential institution, secession as a necessary separation from a corrupt and sinful North, and the battle for southern independence as a kind of sacred crusade. But the reality of defeat on the battlefield had started to sink in. Since their theology did not allow for God to be wrong, clergymen began to wonder if their cause was pure. They began to chide their fellow southerners for sinfulness, for wartime corruption and price gouging, for not properly treating their slaves and living up to the high moral standards implied by the definition of slaveholding as a divine obligation.

Perhaps southern moral failures had caused God to withdraw his protective hand and allow the South to suffer chastisement. Clergy mounted reform efforts, pushed to ameliorate the institution of slavery and prohibit its worst abuses, and began subtly to suggest that defeat was possible. Military reverses led to sinking morale, which in turn contributed to a species of religious resignation to defeat as somehow God's plan. But such acceptance of the probability of defeat only decreased morale further. Religious confidence in military and political victory dissipated, and ministers would, after the war, seek to find solace by preaching repentance and revivalism and otherworldliness with renewed enthusiasm. Out of secular defeat they sought to find spiritual triumph.

After the Emancipation Proclamation thoughtful southerners had also understood that the presence of black soldiers and black noncombatants gave Lincoln's army additional advantages. In the months following Gettysburg and Vicksburg, scattered southern newspapers suggested that the South should arm slaves to fight on behalf of the Confederacy, freeing them in the process. This was still an unthinkable idea for most southerners, but bold men, counting up the casualties, proposed hitherto unthinkable actions. General Patrick R. Cleburne in January 1864 formally proposed such a move to his commanding officer, General Joseph E. Johnston. Johnston took no action other than forwarding Cleburne's letter to Jefferson Davis. Other Confederate generals protested what they considered the outrageousness of freeing and then arming slaves, arguing that it contradicted the traditional southern view that slaves were permanent children, not potential "men" in the nineteenth-century meaning of the term. If slaves could be soldiers, then the whole southern logic of slavery and secession was wrong. Davis cautioned against public discussion of the controversial issue, but he too was coming to understand that only such a bold casting aside of tradition might be able to secure the South's independence. By late 1864 a number of southern spokesmen believed similarly. On November 7 Davis sent Congress a message calling for increased utilization of blacks by the army, with the government buying the slaves so impressed, presumably prior to freeing them. This measure encountered violent objection in Congress, and not until Robert E. Lee himself in a letter on February 18, 1865, supported the arming and freeing of slaves was passage of the bill ensured. On March 13, 1865, five days before it adjourned forever, the Confederate Congress passed and President Davis signed "An Act to increase the military force of the Confederate States." The act did not actually provide for freeing the black soldiers, but the orders eventually issued by the War Department made emancipation clear. Several weeks later recruiting and training of black troops began in Richmond and other Virginia towns, but it was too late. The end came before any black Confederates saw military action.

As this extreme action suggested, by early 1865 the South was willing to give up slavery to save the Confederacy, a switch from 1861 when secession had seemed a move primarily to save slavery. But northern war aims had shifted too, from simply preserving the Union to ending slavery. On February 3, 1865, three southern emissaries, Vice-President Alexander H. Stephens, R. M. T. Hunter, and Joseph A. Campbell, had persuaded President Davis to let them meet with Lincoln to discuss terms for peace. After some confusion and delays the Confederate peace commissioners met with Abraham Lincoln and Secretary of State William H. Seward aboard a Union transport ship, the

River Queen, in the waters of Hampton Roads off Norfolk. Lincoln would accept nothing less than the end of slavery, the cessation of all hostilities, and the South's rejoining the Union—terms that Jefferson Davis and the South were not yet willing to accept. The previous month Davis had sent special envoy Duncan Kenner to Europe to confer with Confederate diplomat James M. Mason. Mason subsequently was granted an interview with British Prime Minister Viscount Palmerston in which Mason dangled an offer: would England recognize the Confederacy in exchange for the South's willingness to emancipate the slaves? But it was too late. Palmerston had been reading the war bulletins, and the time for a British diplomatic rescue was long past.

As the final Confederate winter slowly began to show signs of spring, Sherman was marching through North Carolina. General Joseph Johnston still resisted and slowed the bluecoats here and there, but there was no stopping Sherman. Conditions grew ever more hopeless in Richmond. Lee knew he could not remain long in the city—perhaps he could make a dash west, then hurry south to join up with Johnston's forces in North Carolina. On April 2, Sheridan seized the last railroad into Petersburg and forward units began to batter through the thin Confederate lines on the outskirts of the city. At best Lee could hold on till darkness gave him cover to lead his army away. Jefferson Davis sat worshiping in church that sunny blue Sunday morning when suddenly a messenger rushed in and whispered in his ear; silently, hurriedly, Davis rose and left. All over town the same little drama occurred. Davis scurried around, giving orders amid the confusion, trying to gather up the government's essential papers. That evening the Confederate government and its archives, what could be thrown in boxes, was on a train to Danville, escaping just before the capital fell to Grant. Lee's army fled west too. Their clothes in tatters, famished, they marched only out of respect for General Lee, but Grant was on their tail. The long war was winding down with a whimper, not with a bang.

Lincoln journeyed to Richmond just hours after Davis and Lee had departed; he was surrounded by throngs of thankful blacks who understood that freedom was very near. So was Confederate defeat. Six days later, after several minor skirmishes, Lee accepted reality. A last-ditch effort to escape Grant's clutches was thwarted near Appomattox Courthouse. One officer suggested the army disperse into the mountains and continue guerrilla warfare, but Lee knew the South was already devastated and such marauding would "take the country years to recover from." No, it was time to call a halt at last to the futile bloodshed. Lee sent Grant a note. Later that day, April 9, 1865, Palm Sunday, Lee and Grant met in the parlor of William McLean's house— ironically, McLean's first house, near Manassas Junction, had been used as Beauregard's headquarters in the war's first significant battle in July 1861. Grant was his usual informal self, Lee his usual immaculate self. Each in his own way was dignified and courteous. They began with a few words about old times back in the Mexican War. Then they discussed terms, and Grant was generous. The Army of Northern Virginia would lay down its arms, and no reprisals would be made. Lee asked that his men be allowed to keep their horses; Grant agreed. Lincoln had ordered him to "give them the most liberal terms," and Grant was a magnanimous victor.

Later that day Grant sent rations to Lee's hungry troops and ordered that his own troops stop hurrahing and firing festive salutes. Soldiers in blue and gray mingled with a surprising lack of animosity, their hate having been expended in combat. Three days later, on April 12, exactly four years since the attack on Fort Sumter, the southern troops marched across the field, heads down, to stack arms, the symbol of surrender. But the men who had fought so long and hard against one another held each other with mutual respect at the very end. The northern officer in charge of the ceremony, Joshua Chamberlain, who had heroically defended Little Round Top at Gettysburg against the Confederate forces, ordered a bugle call. The Union soldiers shifted their arms to an honor salute. The southern commander, General John B. Gordon, instantly recognized the stance, saluted in return, and ordered his men to march forward in honor formation. The war, which had in its fighting turned brutal and savage, ended with dignity.

The curtain quickly fell over the remaining combat zones. Six days later, near Durham Station, North Carolina, General Johnston surrendered his remaining troops to General Sherman. On May 4 the last of the Confederate troops east of the Mississippi surrendered at Citronelle, Alabama, and on May 26 General Edmund Kirby Smith, who had often roamed the trans-Mississippi South as though it were his own fiefdom, yielded in New Orleans. There were scattered minor skirmishes after peace began breaking out, and here and there even more final surrenders. Edmund Ruffin, the proslavery fanatic who had fired the first shot at Fort Sumter, penned a note proclaiming everlasting hatred for Yankees and committed suicide on June 18. Jefferson Davis, defiant to the end, refused to accept defeat and urged southern soldiers to become partisan fighters in the hills and woods. But the southern people could not bear any more fighting; Davis himself was captured May 10 at Irwinsville, Georgia. So the war was essentially over after Appomattox. The toll of total wartime casualties was staggering—360,000 Union dead, 258,000 Confederate dead—the combined equivalent of 15 million in terms of the 1990 United States population. On April 14, 1865, four years to the day after he had surrendered, Major Anderson once again raised the American flag above Fort Sumter. That evening President and Mrs. Lincoln, looking forward to celebrating at last the happy conclusion of the killing, went to Ford's Theatre for a bit of well-deserved relaxation.

✣ CHAPTER 4 ✣

The Colonial South

There are times in the life of a nation, as with some individuals, when tragedy seems to know no bounds. President Lincoln's death on April 15, 1865, from an assassin's bullet at Ford's Theatre was a bleak omen for a peace without rancor, and many southerners sensed that their last best hope for an easy reconciliation with the North died with Lincoln. That premonition proved to be correct, though no one at the time foresaw the curious twists events would take. Indeed, Andrew Johnson, the new president, could have been expected to direct a vengeful Reconstruction that would fundamentally transform class and racial relations in the South. But history seems to delight in upsetting expectations and confusing predictions, and contingency is more the rule than the exception. The decade or so following the end of the Civil War remains as difficult to decipher as it was important, and the South struggled with the unresolved problems of the era for more than a century. Probably no other period in southern history has been as insistently misunderstood. The general reading public has been slower to accept the conclusions of revisionist scholarship on Reconstruction than on any other topic in American history.

At the heart of Reconstruction was the continuing dilemma of working out the proper destiny of blacks within the nation. From the date of Lincoln's Emancipation Proclamation on, everyone understood that chattel slavery would be ended by northern victory, but few agreed on the role blacks should or could play in the restored nation. And how were the states of the defeated

Confederacy actually to be brought back into the nation? What would be the political role of former Confederates? Were they to be punished for their actions, or nurtured back to support the Union? How would the South's war-ravaged countryside be restored and its economy be revived? What kinds of animosities between the regions, and between residents of the regions, might poison efforts at reconciliation? No one knew the answers to these questions in the spring of 1865, but the euphoria that warfare had finally ended was soon punctured by the pressing reality of insoluble problems. The era of Reconstruction is doubly tragic because solutions did not turn out well, and also—given the assumptions and passions of the age—no outcome that was possible would have been truly satisfactory in hindsight. The ultimate measure of that tragedy would be revealed in the history of the South over the next century.

By pedagogical convention, history courses and their accompanying textbooks divide the past into discrete units of time, but the flow of history is not as discontinuous as semester divisions imply. Slavery did not end, nor did the Old South, with Fort Sumter, or with the Emancipation Proclamation, or, to a very significant degree, even with Appomattox. Slavery did cease with the conclusion of the war, though the racial attitudes that underpinned bondage persisted, especially among white southerners, for generations more. Many of the values, economic assumptions, and mores associated with the Old South lingered for decades into the postwar period. And Reconstruction did not begin only after Appomattox. Instead, from the moment Union forces occupied regions of the South, the problems of Reconstruction were thrust upon the North even though no one had yet fully defined the nation's options or goals. Policy was makeshift, attitudes were in flux, and long-range social planning was overwhelmed by short-term military needs.

LINCOLNIAN RECONSTRUCTION

During the first summer of the Civil War the US House of Representatives had overwhelmingly passed the Crittenden Resolution, which specified that the purpose of the war was solely to defend the Constitution and to preserve the Union; the Senate had passed a similar resolution. But for Lincoln personally and for the North collectively the war aim gradually shifted, with the Emancipation Proclamation evidence of that evolution. In the beginning the status of the seceded states, not that of the slaves and freedpeople, was Lincoln's primary concern. After all, Lincoln accepted the Crittenden philosophy and was faced, as early as 1862, with the capture of significant portions of Louisiana, Tennessee, North Carolina, and South Carolina. Lincoln's attention at the time was focused on winning the war, not constructing an elaborate blueprint for remaking southern society.

Thus Lincoln's so-called Plan for Reconstruction never had the larger purpose of addressing the issues that came to bear so heavily on the nation after 1866. Rather, Lincoln wanted to weaken the Confederacy and strengthen the northern military effort, and he wanted to do so quickly and with a minimum of controversy. He also believed that there were significant numbers of former Whigs and reluctant secessionists in the South who might be wooed to the Union cause. Social engineering with regard to blacks was not only foreign to Lincoln's way of thinking in 1862, but it would also interfere with his war policy of attempting to attract influential white southerners to a Unionist position and thereby drain support from the Confederacy. He also realized that he risked alienating many in the North if he boldly redirected the war aim against slavery. So Lincoln's initial policy statements on occupied states should be seen in the light of winning the war, not reshaping the South.

By mid-1862 Lincoln had to establish some policy concerning the regions of Tennessee, Louisiana, and the Carolinas over which Union forces had control. He had long insisted that the southern states had no right to leave the Union, and, consistent with his theme of the inviolability of the Union, he sought to ease them back into a normal relationship with the Union as efficiently as possible. Thus he appointed military governors in a stopgap measure to restore the captured states to the nation. Lincoln formalized this procedure on December 8, 1863, with the issuance of a Proclamation of Amnesty and Reconstruction, but again he was not attempting to solve all the outstanding questions regarding such matters as the rights of blacks, confiscated land, and Confederate debt that existed then and later loomed large as divisive issues. Lincoln was thinking pragmatically about the immediate problem of shortening the war when he offered a general amnesty to all white southerners who would take an oath pledging loyalty *now and in the future* to the Union, to the Constitution, and to the wartime proclamations (including emancipation) of the federal government. Lincoln assumed that most oath-takers would have in the recent past been supporters of the Confederate cause. Only high military and civil officers would be excluded from amnesty. All confiscated property except for slaves would be returned, and once the number of oath-takers equalled 10 percent of the number who had voted in the 1860 presidential election, that state would be allowed to draft a new constitution and elect state officials and members of Congress. There was, however, still the constitutional proviso that the US Senate and House ultimately had the privilege of judging the qualifications of their own members.

No further provisions were made for the freedpeople—for example, the right to vote and to equality before the law—although Lincoln expressed a hope that white southerners would pass laws guaranteeing permanent freedom and, perhaps for a few skilled, property-owning blacks, the right to vote. He issued a vague statement to the effect that he would not oppose southern legislation appropriate for a "laboring, landless, and homeless class." Southerners did not need instruction on devising laws to control the black population, as they showed in the infamous "Black Codes" at the conclusion of the war. Lincoln's, and the North's, opinion on the appropriate status of freed slaves proved to be in flux, but throughout the war he occasionally mentioned colonization of free blacks as a solution to racial problems.

Arkansas, Louisiana, and Tennessee followed Lincoln's general prescription and in early 1864 formed loyal governments, only to have Congress reject their representatives and their electoral votes in the presidential election of 1864. Clearly Congress, unlike Lincoln, was acting on the assumption that the seceded states were still out of the Union, and Congress gave notice that it intended to be involved in any plan of restoration. The term Radical Republicans is more pejorative than descriptive, and the label covers a variety of viewpoints, but there was a loosely identifiable group of Republican Congressmen who fundamentally differed with Lincoln on how the conquered South should be treated. Vengeance was not their primary motive; rather, they intended to remold the South so a future secession would be impossible. They wanted to ensure that new leaders, who did not harbor secessionist sentiments and who were more in harmony with northern attitudes, would control the new state governments; and while they differed on exactly what guarantees and rights should be extended to blacks, they sincerely believed Lincoln had been too sanguine in his expectations of what white southerners might voluntarily do and too insensitive to the interests of the freedpeople themselves. A larger group of Moderate Republicans joined the Radicals in mid-1864 in an attempt to seize the Reconstruction initiative. On the Fourth of July, 1864, the Radical-Moderate coalition passed the Wade–Davis bill, cosponsored by Senator Benjamin F. Wade of Ohio and Representative Henry Winter Davis of Maryland, outlining in some detail Congress's plan for dealing with the conquered South.

While Lincoln may have felt that whether the seceded states were really in or out of the Union was a "pernicious abstraction" that simply got in the way of restoring the Union proper, Congress operated on the assumption that the southern states in fact were out and should be treated by Congress as any other territory, whose admission or readmission to the Union was a matter of strictly Congressional jurisdiction. The Wade–Davis bill rejected Lincoln's lenient 10 percent plan and specified that a presidentially appointed provisional governor in each state should conduct a census. When a majority of the white males pledged loyalty to the Union, the governor should then call for an election of delegates to a new constitutional convention. Only those southerners who could swear that they had never been disloyal to the Union could vote for the constitutional delegates—a provision that obviously disenfranchised the overwhelming majority of all white southerners. Moreover, these new constitutions that were to be drafted would specifically have to abolish slavery, repudiate all Confederate and state debts, and take away the right to vote from former Confederate civil and military leaders. Then the national Congress would decide whether or not to accept these reconstructed states back into the family of the Union.

From the viewpoint of many northerners, who had seen the Union sundered by southern proslavery forces and who had suffered tens of thousands of deaths to restore the Union and end slavery, such an approach was merely sound policy to prevent a possible recurrence of the present difficulties—along with an understandable degree of repudiation and punishment meted out to the leaders who had precipitated the current unpleasantness. The Wade–Davis bill came in the midst of the 1864 presidential campaign, but Lincoln refused to let the Radical philosophy define either the party platform or his new policy. Disingenuously saying that the South could follow the Wade–Davis prescription if it wanted, but refusing to make it mandatory, Lincoln took advantage of the adjournment of Congress to kill the bill by use of a pocket veto, outraging the bill's authors.

Yet the Radicals had nowhere else to go that year, angry as they were, because they did not want to jeopardize Lincoln's election. After his reelection they again pressed their claims, particularly to safeguard the results of the Emancipation Proclamation. Aware that the Constitution allowed slavery and that the Emancipation Proclamation was a war measure that could in theory be revoked when the war was over, Congress moved to change the Constitution by adopting the Thirteenth Amendment—abolishing slavery—in January 1865. It would eventually be ratified in December of that year by counting the votes of eight former Confederate states, accepted for the nonce as states for the purpose of ratifying the amendment. Consummate politician that he was, Lincoln sensed the ground shifting under him and seemed willing to compromise, to adjust, to experiment with Reconstruction in the Spring of 1865. But John Wilkes Booth's madness closed off that promising possibility.

JOHNSONIAN RECONSTRUCTION

Andrew Johnson became the fifteenth president of the United States following Lincoln's death. Like Lincoln, Johnson had been born in a Border state and had been reared in poverty, but there the similarity ended. The school of adversity had taught Lincoln humility, humor, and flexibility; Johnson was tactless, unskilled in interpersonal relations, and stubbornly dogmatic. It is difficult to imagine a president faced with more intractable problems, or one less well equipped by temperament to handle those problems, than Andrew Johnson. Yet few anticipated his political clumsiness, especially those northerners who knew of his distaste for secession and his hatred of planter aristocrats. In the rough-and-tumble world of Tennessee politics, Johnson had risen to the Senate by galvanizing the yeomen of East Tennessee with his strictures against the cotton nabobs. But Johnson attacked the slave-holding aristocrats for reasons of class, not because he opposed slavery; in fact, he wished every white family had a slave or two to do their menial labor, and his attitudes toward blacks were conventionally racist. It was his antiplanter sentiment that made Johnson the only southern senator not to resign his seat after secession, and that dogged attachment to principle attracted Lincoln, who named Johnson military governor of Tennessee in March 1862 when Union forces captured part of the state. Johnson put Lincoln's moderate Reconstruction plans into action in Tennesee, and in 1864, even though he was a lifelong Democrat, the Republican party named Johnson to the ticket in a successful attempt to attract pro-war Democrats to the Republican camp. The strategy worked, Lincoln was reelected, and Johnson ascended to the presidency as a result of tragedy in 1865 with the South prostrate at his feet.

Johnson's abstract dedication to the idea of the indestructibility of the Union, which was why he felt secession was treason, also led him to disavow that the southern states had ever really been out of the Union; rather, they had been in an imperfect relationship to the Union, and they required only minor adjustments, as directed by the president, to restore them to the Union. Following that logic, and with little sensitivity to the interests of freedmen, Johnson moved swiftly to end the separation of the southern states. Within weeks he recognized the governments that had been established in Arkansas, Louisiana, Tennessee, and Virginia under the terms of Lincoln's so-called 10 percent plan, then Johnson appointed military governors to the remaining seven states. On May 29, 1865, he issued a Proclamation of Amnesty offering a pardon to all white southerners who would now pledge present and future loyalty except for a minority of high-ranking military officers and civil officials and those persons who owned more than $20,000 worth of property—presumably the former slaveholding aristocracy who had perpetrated secession. These leaders of the Confederacy would have to receive individual pardons from the president himself.

The white population that received the general amnesty (no set percentage of the total population or 1860 vote was mandated) would elect delegates to constitutional conventions and draft new state constitutions that would expressly abolish slavery, revoke the ordinance of secession, ratify the Thirteenth Amendment, repudiate the state and Confederate war debts, and, when all this was done satisfactorily, elect a new state government and new members of Congress. The eleven ex-Confederate states, after some haggling, complied with Johnson's prescribed plan, and Johnson, pleased by the progress according to his terms, liberally handed out pardons to the erstwhile plantation elite with abandon, perhaps receiving some kind of psychological boost from the ability magisterially to dispense pardon to those he had formerly hated and to whom he had felt socially inferior. White southerners found Johnson surprisingly generous and seized the opportunity to regain control of their state governments and, it was reasonably assumed, the freedpeople. Dared they hope that the results of the defeat would not be as politically debilitating as they had at first feared? To the extent that Johnson fostered that sentiment among white southerners, he contributed mightily to his own fall and multiplied the tragedy of Reconstruction.

Many white southerners acted badly at this juncture of history, but our task is less to condemn them than to try to understand their motivations. Certainly most white men—the women we will address later—initially accepted the results of the war in the sense that they understood that slavery was now ended and that the South needed to get about the business of resuming normal life—planting crops, restoring commerce, reestablishing order, and solving immediate emergency situations of hunger and homelessness. As with any society facing crisis, white southerners turned to their putative leaders for guidance and authority, but they did so with a degree of discrimination. They largely recognized that secessionist firebrands were inappropriate for political office; in fact such extremists now seemed culpable for the South's economic and political destitution. It was unthinkable to turn to nonleaders, to people so bereft of prewar or wartime respectability or prominence that they had not participated in any political or military capacity, for direction and leadership in such a momentous occasion as post–Civil War adjustment. Other prewar leaders were so clearly identified with the Unionist position that they in effect forfeited their right to govern afterwards. Elisha Marshall Pease of Texas, governor of the state from 1852 to 1857, was such a man. He had been a Unionist Democrat firmly opposed to secession, and he retired from public life rather than serve during the Confederacy. All was not forgotten after 1865, for he was rejected by postwar voters when he ran for the gubernatorial position again (although he later won military appointment as Republican governor in 1867).

But more moderate traditional leaders—men who before the Civil War had been Whigs and reluctant secessionists and who had sided with the Confederacy simply because they could not make war on their own state—were precisely the men southerners expected to help them deal pragmatically with the problems of defeat and restoration of normality. These neo-Whigs were exactly the people Lincoln and Johnson hoped would now rule the South, confident that their pledge of future loyalty would cement them to the cause of the restored Union. But to most northerners, the election of many former Confederates, even if they had been Johnny-come-lately-Rebs, looked suspiciously like southerners were trying to void the outcome of the war. How otherwise can the election of former Confederate vice-president Alexander H. Stephens as US senator from Georgia be explained?

What strengthened this northern suspicion was even the moderate southerners' attitudes toward the freedpeople. As southern military fortunes had waned in the latter years of the war, influential Confederates had come to defend the idea of using slave troops who, by virtue of their military service, would earn their freedom, but beyond the press of felt necessity few white southerners could imagine, must less countenance, a world in which blacks were the equals of whites. They might admit of individual exceptions here and there, but the mass of white southerners had so internalized a conception of black inferiority that they could not comprehend a world in which blacks were not disciplined and controlled by whites. They believed that blacks would not work, would not police themselves, and probably would not be able to survive physically without paternalistic (and not so paternalistic) white supervision. Operating on these racist assumptions, whites saw as one of the first social priorities the development of governmental regulations regarding freedpeople that would replace planter authority with state authority.

The result, in 1865 and early 1866, was a series of Black Codes passed in one southern state after another. The freed blacks were guaranteed some rights that had not existed under slavery: the right to own property (except for a while they could not own land in Mississippi), sue and be sued in civil courts, have their marriages legally recognized, and testify in courts against whites in six states. But in no state could freedmen vote, hold political office, or legally bear arms. Freedom of assembly after dark was often limited. And in most states there were severe restrictions against blacks leaving their jobs: labor contracts bound them annually except under rare conditions. Vagrancy laws also allowed white officials to arrest blacks whom they judged to be insufficiently employed and, if the blacks were convicted, they could be bound over to work on chain gangs or contracted out to white planters. White southerners were moving only as far away from black slavery as they felt they had to, and northerners were quick to understand that the result was the wolf of slavery disguised by the sheepskin of vagrancy laws.

The South's reaction to events is more difficult to explain than the North's. Even well-meaning, moderate southerners said and did things that seemed infuriatingly defiant to the North. Yet by their lights the southerners had repudiated the secessionist extremists and turned, on the whole, to leaders who had been moderates in the past—men who had opposed secession. Again, in their view they had accepted the end of slavery and extended significant new rights to blacks, only holding back from full legal, economic, and social equality because to do so was absolutely unthinkable for the overwhelming majority of white southerners (and northerners, for that matter) in 1865. President Johnson neither requested nor demanded that they make further concessions, so most white southerners believed they had responded responsibly to the nation's mandate. To ask them to do more—either to repudiate all their wartime leaders or give up any more regulatory authority over the black population—white southerners saw as vengeful—trying to rub their noses in the stench of defeat. Defeated they were, and to some extent willing to accept modifications in their society, but they insisted on salvaging their honor. But it was precisely this southern unwillingness to acknowledge the dishonor of their late cause, to accept the moral right of northern victory and the moral wrong of slavery, that caused northerners to read in southern actions a streak of insolence that threatened to undo the results of the war. That the North would not countenance.

Congress met again in December 1865, and it had to face the Johnson-ordained southern state governments and the newly elected southern congressmen. Complicating the issue of the Confederate tinge to the fresh congressmen was that the South, now that slavery had ended and the three-fifths compromise was void, would have a larger congressional representation. Fearful that the fruits of victory were slipping away, the Radicals in Congress established a Joint Committee of Fifteen—six from the Senate, nine from the House—to review the credentials of the southern congressmen and to evaluate Johnson's Reconstruction policies and advise Congress on alternative policies. The committee quickly moved to change the direction of Reconstruction, first by refusing to seat the southern congressmen and secondly by moving to continue the Freedmen's Bureau, which had been established in March 1865 to protect the rights of and supply food and clothing to refugees and freed slaves. Johnson, who felt southern whites should be left alone to handle the freedpeople, vetoed the bill; Johnson believed Reconstruction policy was wholly within the jurisdiction of the executive office. The Radicals, observing the harsh Black Codes, could well imagine what leaving the status of ex-slaves to southern whites meant, and their judgment that Johnson was inadequate to the task of truly reconstructing the South instantly hardened.

The bill to renew the Freedmen's Bureau had widened its authority to include the settling of labor disputes (intended to address the problem of the vagrancy laws but often working to the opposite effect, pressuring blacks to obey white labor contracts). On April 9, 1866, Congress passed a Civil Rights Act that bestowed citizenship upon blacks and granted them the same civil rights that whites enjoyed; again, a direct response to the extremes of the Black Codes. When Johnson vetoed this bill too, Moderate and Radical Republicans coalesced to override the veto and then repassed the Freedmen's Bureau bill. Realizing that these guarantees of the rights of freedpeople depended upon who controlled Congress and were hence potentially impermanent, the Joint Committee of Fifteen began work to put the guarantees in the Constitution, beyond the vagaries of congressional or court opinion. Violence in the South toward blacks gave impetus to the movement to amend the Constitution to protect the rights of all citizens.

A small race riot occurred in Norfolk in mid-April, 1866, but at the end of April and for several days in May, a full-scale race riot broke out in Memphis, and after almost a week of mindless violence forty-six blacks and two whites were dead, about eighty persons were injured, five black women were raped, and black churches, schools, and homes were torched. Southern whites pointed the finger at "uppity" blacks—black males in Union uniforms were especially irritating to former slaveholders—and felt force was justified to establish boundaries around acceptable black behavior; northern whites saw only intransigent former rebels determined to keep blacks down. Throughout the early spring constitutional amendments were discussed, revised, and introduced to the Senate. In April the Joint Committee of Fifteen drafted an amendment to protect the citizenship of blacks; debate was intensified by news of the violence in Norfolk and Memphis. On June 13, 1866, the Fourteenth Amendment passed Congress and three days later was submitted to the states, including the southern states, for ratification, which would not come for more than three long years. This amendment proved to be a turning point for Reconstruction.

The first section of the Fourteenth Amendment extended citizenship to all American-born blacks and said that no state could "abridge the privileges or immunities of citizens . . . nor shall any State deprive any person of life, liberty, or property, without due process of law; nor deny to any person within its jurisdiction the equal protection of the laws." The intent of this section was to redress the Black Codes that so grossly deprived black individuals of "equal protection of the laws," though it later was applied to "legal persons" such as corporations. Section 2 did not require that states allow freedmen to vote, but it did mandate a proportionate reduction in the congressional representation of those states that did not allow all males the franchise. Actually, southern states would rather accept the congressional penalty than enfranchise their former slaves. Section 3 disallowed from federal or state political office, or from participation in the electoral college, any person who had once taken an oath of office to support the federal Constitution and then had supported the Confederacy. This disability, which affected practically all southern leaders, could be removed only by a two-thirds vote of both houses of Congress, not by individual presidential pardon. Section 4 specifically validated the federal debt and invalidated all Confederate debts, including claims for compensation for slaves. The final section gave Congress the power "to enforce, by appropriate legislation" the provisions of the amendment.

The Fourteenth Amendment represented a series of compromises between the Moderate and Radical Republicans. It did not, for example, actually give the vote to black males, nor did it disenfranchise for years every person who had supported the Confederacy. Had the southern states ratified the amendment promptly, Congress would have seated their representatives, the states would in effect have been readmitted to the Union, and Reconstruction would have essentially been over. Tennessee, which had been captured early by Union forces, was the home of many Unionists. Led by strongly pro-Union governor W. G. "Parson" Brownlow, Tennessee promptly accepted the amendment. But every other former Confederate state found section 3, which disfranchised most former Confederate leaders, an insurmountable stumbling block. Since many such leaders had been reluctant secessionists and now accepted the results of the war, albeit grudgingly, white southerners interpreted section 3 as unnecessarily vindictive.

President Johnson, disputing Congress's role in Reconstruction, advised the southern states not to ratify the offending amendment, advice they were only too glad to accept. For most of the North, however, southern opposition seemed absolutely intolerable intransigence, and when, in the midst of the ratification debates, another bloody race riot occurred in New Orleans with over 150 casualties, northern public opinion turned solidly against the South. President Johnson knew that the fall congressional elections would determine his fate, so during the summer he and his friends organized a National Union Party in an effort to unite the handful of Conservative Republicans, northern Democrats, and southern whites. He then set out to campaign for his supporters in a number of key northern cities, but the more he traveled and talked the more intemperate he became. In the end Johnson made a sorry spectacle of himself, discrediting his office and his cause. When the votes were tallied, the Republicans had veto-proof majorities in both houses of Congress. A new phase of Reconstruction was about to begin.

CONGRESSIONAL RECONSTRUCTION

Emboldened by their success in the fall elections, the Radicals in Congress decided to strike while the iron was hot. Even before the newly elected congressmen took office, the old Congress voted to move the convening of the new Congress up from December 1867 to March 4, 1867. Then, just two days before the old Congress expired, on March 2, 1867, it pushed through three measures that would determine subsequent events. Many Radicals wanted a thoroughgoing reshaping of the South—giving black males the right to vote, disenfranchising former Confederates for the foreseeable future, providing public education for blacks, and confiscating former rebel land and redistributing it to freedpeople. But Moderates were unwilling to go so far, restrained by racism, considerations for the rights of property ownership, and the basic commitment to majority rule in the various states. The resulting Military Reconstruction Act was a blend of constantly shifting Radical and Moderate elements, for neither group could control Congress on its own.

The Military Reconstruction Act declared that no legal state governments existed among the ten seceded states. (Tennessee had already accepted the Fourteenth Amendment and been readmitted to the Union.) While respecting the state boundaries, the act divided the South into five military districts, each under the control of a military commander backed by a small contingent of troops. The military commanders were authorized to use military tribunals in place of the civil courts (which were controlled by local whites) if necessary to maintain order and protect the "rights of persons and property." But the primary task of the district generals was to prepare the states under their authority for readmission to the Union. Several steps were required. First, the military commander would conduct a registration of voters, including all black adult males and white adult males who were not disqualified from officeholding by the terms of section 3 of the Fourteenth Amendment. (About 10 percent of whites were so disenfranchised—perhaps another 25 percent did not vote for reasons of apathy or disgust with the whole political process.) The voters additionally had to take a complex loyalty oath to the Union. After this was done, the military commander was to call for the election of delegates to state conventions that would then draft new state constitutions, one provision of which had to be the extension of suffrage to black males. Once these constitutions were ratified by the registered loyal voters, then elections could be held for new state governments. If the new state legislatures accepted the Fourteenth Amendment, and if Congress accepted the new state constitutions, the states would be restored to the Union once the Fourteenth Amendment had been ratified by the mandatory three-fourths of all the states.

Quite obviously, Congress did not intend to leave the post–Civil War settlement up to ex-Confederates. But Congress's determination to thwart President Johnson and to guarantee that the South underwent at least minimal change was also revealed in two other acts passed on March 2, 1867. The Tenure of Office Act prevented the president from removing from office without the consent of Congress persons whose original appointment had required the consent of Congress. This act was intended to protect Secretary of War Edwin M. Stanton, the only member of Johnson's cabinet who favored congressional Reconstruction and supported protecting and expanding the rights of blacks. Congress also passed the Command of the Army Act, which required that all military orders issued by the president go through the commanding general of the army (Ulysses S. Grant), whose headquarters were restricted to Washington and who could not be removed from office or assigned elsewhere without Senate approval. This act was meant to prevent Johnson from subverting the intentions of the Military Reconstruction Act. These three acts were frontal assaults on the president's power to influence Reconstruction.

As some Radicals had predicted, several southern states chose not to act, preferring to remain under military rule rather than write new constitutions enfranchising the blacks on the often correct assumption that racist military officers would probably deal more favorably with southern whites than with freedpeople. The Military Reconstruction Act had no mainspring to push events forward, a failure that three supplementary acts passed later in 1867 were intended to correct. These additional acts required the military commanders to initiate the actions aimed toward the drafting of reform constitutions. By 1868 six of the seceded states—Arkansas, North Carolina, South Carolina, Louisiana, Alabama, and Florida—had met the prescribed procedures and were readmitted to the Union. And with the mandatory approval of the former Confederate states, the Fourteenth Amendment was declared ratified on July 28, 1868. The remaining four states—Mississippi, Virginia, Georgia, and Texas—were back in by 1870. By then Congress had passed and submitted to the states the Fifteenth Amendment, guaranteeing black men everywhere in the Union the right to vote; the last four states to be reconstructed had to accept the Fifteenth as well as the Fourteenth Amendment before they were readmitted to the Union.

By mid-1868 Johnson's ability to act as a roadblock to congressional Reconstruction had been eliminated. As early as 1867 Radicals had feared Johnson would willy-nilly turn control of the South and the freedpeople back to the former Confederates, and Radicals were suspicious that he would use the power of his office to delay, weaken, and destroy congressional plans for Reconstruction. And Johnson did replace several military governors who favored Radical policies with conservatives who predictably sided with white state leaders. On several occasions half-baked charges and preliminary impeachment attempts were begun, but although Johnson clearly opposed the Radical version of Reconstruction, he was hardly guilty of "high crimes and misdemeanors," the Constitutional grounds for impeachment. Then in August 1867 Johnson rebuffed Congress by removing Secretary of War Stanton from office without congressional approval. Technically, since Stanton had been appointed by Lincoln, his position was not protected by the Tenure of Office Act, but in the superheated political atmosphere Johnson seemed to be flagrantly defying the will of Congress. House Republicans, glad to have a pretext to attack the obstructionist Johnson, rushed through a resolution of impeachment.

The trial in the Senate elicited harsh attacks and bitter recriminations. There was no doubt that Johnson cared little about the plight of the freed slaves, vilified the Radicals, and undermined congressional Reconstruction at every opportunity, but by the Constitution's precise terms he was not guilty of impeachable offenses. Johnson's lawyers clearly were superior to the Grand Old Party (GOP) impeachment managers when it came to the fine points of the law, but more important than technical arguments was the doctrine of separation of powers. Moderate Republicans might have been incensed at Johnson's recent policies, but they feared to create a precedent whereby a two-thirds majority of Congress could impeach any president with whom it disagreed on policy matters. The whole principle of the separation of powers, not just Johnson's plight, seemed to be at stake. Moderate members of the

GOP made overtures to Johnson, seeking some sort of compromise. Johnson must have listened, because he conducted himself with uncharacteristic dignity thereafter and promised no longer to be obstructionist toward congressional Reconstruction policies. The implict understanding worked. On May 16, 1868, enough Republican senators voted with the Democrats to prevent, by one vote, Johnson's conviction on impeachment charges, though there is evidence others were prepared to oppose his conviction if their vote was necessary.

Johnson was spared impeachment, but in his successful attempt to win support he had agreed no longer to oppose congressional Reconstruction and had forwarded to Congress the newly written constitutions of Arkansas and South Carolina. After his ordeal in the Spring of 1868 Johnson ceased being a significant factor in Reconstruction. His own party rejected him as its nominee for the presidency later that year, while the Republicans, determined to win, nominated the popular war hero, Ulysses S. Grant, who had no known political ambitions or skills. The Republicans waved the bloody shirt to remind voters of the human costs of the late war, while Democratic candidate Horatio Seymour, courting western farmers who had agricultural debts, campaigned in favor of issuing cheap money—the so-called greenbacks. But the memories of the recent intersectional hostilities were stronger than the attraction of greenbackism, given Grant's martial fame and the Republican rhetoric about a Confederate resurgence. The Grand Old Party captured the White House in the fall of 1868 to go along with its control of Congress.

RECONSTRUCTION AT THE LOCAL LEVEL

For the white South, however, the real issues were, and had always been, local. The devastation and demoralization of the war had embittered many white southerners, but most of them primarily wanted to put their lives together again after four years of conflict. Hardly a southern family stood untouched by death or injury in 1865, and slaveholders had lost their $2.5 billion investment in slavery, a severe economic loss despite the gain for humanity. The southern banking system was ruined, the South's railroads were almost beyond repair, and tens of thousands of homes, barns, bridges, public buildings, colleges, and churches were destroyed or badly damaged. Fences were gone, tools and wagons worn out, hundreds of thousands of head of livestock had been butchered to feed both invading and friendly armies. Land values plummeted too. But the economic losses were matched by the public despair. Gaunt Confederate veterans, thousands of them with missing limbs, returned home to find their farms in ruins, their cattle and hogs gone, and their wives utterly exhausted by the ordeal.

Often the women felt more frustrated than the returning Rebel soldiers, who at least had had the opportunity to express their feelings on the battlefield. Women without number had suffered loneliness, hunger, and endless toil trying to hold body and soul together while maintaining the family farm, supervising the slaves, and feeding their own children. Time and again soldiers from both armies had marched through, taking whatever foodstuffs they needed despite the pleas of the distraught women. On many occasions soldiers had treated southern women with respect and sensitivity; just as often, and especially so in the last years of the war and even more especially for those in the path of General William T. Sherman's march to the sea, Union soldiers had taken their anger for the horrors of the war out on southern women by cursing them; wantonly destroying crops, farm animals, and household larders; smashing household furnishings even to the extent of cutting portraits out of their frames; and purposely humiliating the women—whose smoldering anger Union troops rightfully translated as unrepenting support for the Confederacy—by scattering their clothes and undergarments. Little wonder that many postwar travelers commented on the unforgiving scorn southern white women often held for occupying Union troops.

Though the return of peace found the South in a state of shock, most white southerners recognized that there was much work to be done. Husbands and wives had to come to know one another again, a task complicated by the wrenching ordeal both had lived through. Many women had lost their husbands and had to scramble to make a living by taking in boarders, teaching school, or becoming seamstresses or milliners. Farms had to be repaired, crops put in the ground, and livestock replenished. The economic and transportation infrastructure had to be rebuilt and marketing systems reestablished. How would blacks be controlled, disciplined, set to work, in the new age? How would whites get along without slaves to do much of the menial labor? No one had all the answers, but as the white South began to pull itself together, a consensus began to emerge. Some acceptance of the new political realities must be made. When first Lincoln and then Johnson outlined a process for restoring the seceded states within the nation, calling for men to pledge their present and future loyalty to the Union, moderate southerners accepted the call. Few were willing to repent for the past, to condemn their Confederate experience, but more, understanding that they had fought a good fight and had lost, were ready to accept the consequences of the war and follow the direction of the president. Grudgingly acknowledging that slavery had ended, but unsure of how much equality had to be extended to freed people, southern whites after mid-1865 were ready to face the future on their own terms.

The southern white leaders elected according to the terms laid out by Lincoln and Johnson were not drawn from the tiny minority of wartime Unionists, but rather from the ranks of Confederate political and military officialdom, though few of them had been secession leaders. The great majority had been reluctant secessionists at best, and though they had served the Confederacy, they had joined the cause only after the election of Lincoln or after their states had actually seceded. These leaders, moderates in the southern universe, now sought to restore the southern economy. They understood the need for diversification away from a complete dependence on cotton. Consequently they passed legislation to encourage banking, factories, and railroads. In fact, in their willingness to issue bonds to support railroad construction and in other ways promote industrialization, the moderate southern leaders of the Johnson governments acted almost identically to the later so-called Radical state governments, as well as the modernizing New South spokesmen who led the South after Reconstruction. The moderate ex-Confederate leaders were not diehard secessionist fanatics with their heads buried in the sands of the past. Their tragic flaw was that they could not conceive of a world in which blacks were allowed substantial control of their own lives. Nor could they repudiate in the abstract the principles of the Confederacy. The result was a public relations debacle, and the North felt justified in rejecting Johnsonian Reconstruction.

Once Reconstruction came under the control of Congress in the spring of 1867, many southern whites lost interest in state politics and turned their concerns inward, to devising plans to determine exclusively local politics and to managing their farms with free black laborers. Racism toward the freedpeople had increased significantly during the Civil War, and the animosity would be racheted up several notches in Reconstruction. While most antebellum whites had considered blacks a permanently inferior race, relations with their own slaves, and especially with certain favorites, whites had felt were quite cordial. Most slaves interpreted differently the merits of slavery, and when the opportunity offered itself during the war, they ran away by the thousands to join the Union liberating forces, sometimes threatening to overwhelm the logistic capacities of the army. Whites, who had convinced themselves that blacks were happy, natural slaves who felt affection at least toward their owners, were shocked by this turn of events. Rather than see it for what it was, evidence of slaves' hunger for freedom, many whites saw the slaves as ungrateful wretches, repaying whites for the care, food, and clothing provided during slavery times by running away to the Yankees the first chance they had. Disbelief was replaced with anger as again and again slaveholders saw their most favored slaves—the house servants, overseers, drivers, and artisans—leave the plantation in search of freedom. This anger escalated beyond general resentment to wrath toward black soldiers wearing the uniforms of the North. Military defeat, economic deprivation, and then the division of the postwar South into military districts turned the region into a pressure cooker of political racism.

Racism lay behind the writing of the infamous Black Codes, racism undergirded the southern opposition to the Fourteenth Amendment, racism made the Military Reconstruction Act of 1867, with its enfranchisement of black males and disenfranchisement of many whites, anathema even to most moderate southern whites. Many boycotted the elections mandated for the drafting of new state constitutions, and the constitutions were opposed more for their origin and authorship than for their content. In fact, these constitutions were in many ways the best the southern states had ever had; they modernized the systems of governance, outlawed imprisonment for debt, more fairly apportioned representation, made more offices elective, and provided for public education. But most southern whites never gave the new state governments a chance, for they were interpreted as the dictatorial results of a vindictive, race-mixing northern tyranny. Moderate northern hopes for a resurgence of pre-war Whiggism were dashed by the southern opposition, giving credence to the Radical belief that black participation in southern politics, mandated and protected by Congress, was the only way to safeguard the fruits of victory in the South.

Of course there were anti-Confederate, consistently pro-Union whites in the South, predominantly in the mountainous regions, but their numbers alone were hardly sufficient to build a Republican party that could govern the region. Many of these loyal whites had been nonslaveholders, had opposed the political hegemony of the planters, and had even organized peace societies during the Civil War. To the white majority in the South the loyalists seemed traitors to their native region. Few of these true Union loyalists had enjoyed political prestige or positions of leadership in their states, but after the war they were often joined as supporters of the Republican party by former lowcountry planters, native urban merchants, and political newcomers from the North. These groups have, in the mythology of southern Reconstruction, been consigned to the lowest level of hell. Native southern whites who joined the Republican cause were labeled "scalawags," a term originally referring to scrawny, inbred ponies on the Scottish island of Scalloway and later used to describe worthless, trash livestock in general, and the suggestion was that scalawags were shiftless ne'er-do-wells who opportunistically sold out their southern heritage for a mess of political porridge from the Republicans. Despite the prevalence of this image in American popular culture, it grossly misrepresents the social origins and political outlook of the native whites who cooperated with the Republicans.

During the middle decades of the antebellum period the Whig party had competed equally with the Democrats for political control of the South. Primarily the party of the large planters and the numerically small urban merchant and banking class, the Whigs had been more reformist, more modernizing in general approach than the Democrats. With the national demise of the Whig party, southern Whigs became men in search of a party, and some had flirted with Know-Nothingism. In the secession crisis most former Whigs had recommended caution, had favored the Constitutional Union movement, and only most reluctantly had supported the Confederacy after secession, Fort Sumter, and Lincoln's call for volunteers made fence-sitting politically impossible. From this prewar party of wealthy planters and urban commercial interests came the leadership of the scalawags. On the whole these were hardheaded, practical men who understood that the postwar South's infrastructure had to be rebuilt, its economy and social conditions stabilized, its agricultural system reestablished. Their considered judgment was that cooperation with the Republicans, in part at least in order to control the mountain loyalists and the black masses, was necessary if the region were to regain prosperity. Moreover, they found the national Republican party position on economic matters compatible with their prewar Whig philosophy. A surprising number of former Confederate officers—including General James G. Longstreet, Lee's "Old War Horse"—eventually joined the southern Republican party. Lincoln and Johnson put much faith in a reemergent Whig movement to restore the South to order and the Union; they simply overestimated the numbers of former Whigs. As a group the southern whites who became Republicans were neither vindictive nor unusually corrupt. They wanted the South, a reformed South, to rise again.

Another group of whites living in the South who became natural allies of the Republican governments were newcomers to the region. According to southern mythology, these interlopers were unprincipled opportunists who came south carrying all their worldly belongings in a cheap duffel bag made of carpet. These so-called carpetbaggers have been portrayed as economic vultures, flocking to buy up war-damaged plantations auctioned for nonpayment of taxes and conspiring with traitorous mountain Republicans and unscrupulous scalawags to use ignorant black voters to govern the defeated South for their private advantage. The stereotype fit some northern men who moved to the South, but it presents a glaringly distorted view of history. For one thing, the image often did not discriminate between men who had come before the war and those who came much later, and it misrepresented the motives of most who came in the immediate aftermath of the conflict.

Northern men had long come south because they saw the region as a land of opportunity. Many hoped to become cotton planters, while others brought their skills in commerce or merchandising or banking or industry to the South because they recognized those skills were in short supply there. In other words, for the same reasons people went west, they came south. The motive was the American dream of getting ahead. During the Civil War several thousand northerners bought land in the South and set up farming, expecting northern work habits and Yankee thrift would reap them fortunes and, by the way, teach southern whites and blacks modern agricultural meth-

ods. Northern arrogance was often defeated by the vagaries of cotton growing, and southern workers of both races resisted Yankee industry, but southerners often welcomed the capital and job opportunities northern landowners provided. Southern cities and industries, such as the textile mills, had
long been dependent upon northern marketing and technical know-how.

This northern migration to the South accelerated in the immediate
aftermath of the war. For one thing, many former Union soldiers who had
served in the region liked the climate; they saw firsthand the fertile soil, towering forests, evidence of rich deposits of coal and ore, and streams and rivers
available both for water power and inexpensive transportation. They also
understood that the region was capital-starved and short of people with entrepreneurial talent. There was present a streak of northern arrogance—the
South needed northern skill and direction to prosper. But the basic motive
was traditionally American—to make money. Northern land purchasers,
would-be cotton planters, merchant capitalists, and captains of industry came
south in the spirit of the times to make money, not to crush, defraud, mongrelize, or humiliate the already defeated South. They recognized the Republican party with its national business orientation as more conducive to their
interests, and they allied with loyal southern whites in support of the Reconstruction governments. Only when their economic ambitions faltered—
northern agricultural experience did not guarantee success with cotton, and
the animosity of local southern whites sometimes deprived carpetbaggers of
business opportunity—did many northerners in the South out of a sense of
desperation turn for their livelihood to political careers. Southern white
Democrats called the result an attempt to impose alien rule on the poor,
defeated South.

Republicans in Congress and loyalists in the South knew that without
almost complete disenfranchisement of all former Confederates—a step
some Radicals desired but most Republicans realized was counter to the
basic American commitment to majority rule—there was no way white
Republicans could maintain control of southern state governments. So the
issue of black enfranchisement was as much one of Republican political
expediency as high principle. There were a few moderate southerners who
acknowledged that some blacks, educated and propertied, might indeed
deserve the vote, and some Republicans had racist doubts about the propriety of blacks voting. But for most southern white Republicans, no matter
how recent their conversion to the party, the black voter, disciplined and
controlled by the party, was essential to the reforming of the South. Nothing
else so infuriated the majority of southern whites as the spectacle of former
slaves voting while former Confederate leaders were prevented from holding
office; nothing else so poisoned race relations and made native whites
absolutely determined to resist Republican rule with whatever means at their
disposal. The result was a reign of violence unmatched in American history.

White southerners conducted what can only be called a prolonged terrorist campaign against black voters.

The prevalence of black voting and its impact on southern politics was greatly exaggerated at the time, and inflated perceptions of "black rule" have been perpetuated by racist novels like Thomas W. Dixon's *The Clansman* (1905) and the movie it inspired, *Birth of a Nation* (1915). Popular history books with titles like *The Angry Scar* and the cinematic masterpiece *Gone with the Wind* have continued the stereotypical views. But nowhere did blacks rule the South; nowhere was a black elected governor (P. B. S. Pinchback served for five weeks [December 12, 1872 to January 13, 1873] as governor of Louisiana after the duly elected governor, Henry C. Warmoth, was impeached); nowhere did the number of black officeholders match their percentage of the population, nowhere did blacks control a state legislature, nowhere was legislation passed that flagrantly discriminated on behalf of blacks. During the entire course of Reconstruction only fourteen blacks were elected to the US House of Representatives, only two to the Senate—and both senators were distinguished and educated men.

Most of the approximately two thousand black officeholders served at the local level—sheriffs, justices of the peace, county tax collectors, members of city councils and boards of aldermen, and the like. The blacks elected to more elevated offices had disproportionally been free before the Civil War and had, as artisans, small businessmen, ministers, and teachers possessed demonstrable skills, including literacy, that prepared them to be credible officeholders. In the immediate aftermath of Reconstruction blacks who had been free before the Civil War also dominated officeholding, particularly in states such as Virginia, South Carolina, and Louisiana where there had existed sizable free black communities, but as political mobilization and orga-nizing spread, former slaves gradually came to dominate local black office-holding, and they proved capable students of politics as well. Many of these freedmen had gained leadership ability through wartime service in the Union army or by working in some capacity for the Freedmen's Bureau as soon as the war was over.

Black voting did not unleash on the South a torrent of corrupt, igno-rant, self-serving black politicians who rode roughshod over common decency, honesty, and fairness. Taken as a whole, black officeholders were overwhelmingly literate, and a very significant number either before the war as free blacks had been property holders, or after the war became so as freed-men. Most black politicians before they entered politics had careers that pro-vided them with experience readily applicable to public service. The largest single prepolitical occupation was that of minister, with teacher second, fol-lowed by carpenter. Hundreds more had been storekeepers, merchants, edi-tors, lawyers, barbers, blacksmiths, masons, and other artisanal trades. Still, most black officeholders represented very modest wealth, but nearly all represented the interests of their constituencies effectively, honestly, and with a concern not to flagrantly irritate conservative whites. But of course with black officeholders as with the Reconstruction constitutions, it was the mere principle of black participation that drove some southern whites almost to frenzy.

Many black officeholders—perhaps as many as 10 percent—were the victims of Reconstruction violence, and after the end of the era some left the region. Harry M. Turner, a Methodist minister and member of the Georgia legislature until blacks were excluded in 1871, after his officeholding career ended began a life-long campaign for blacks to migrate to Africa. Turner made four trips to Africa and lectured widely both in this country and in England on behalf of black nationalism and black culture. Other blacks moved North, or gave up politics entirely. Still others had to submerge their sentiments, only to emerge briefly during the Populist movement in the 1890s. Others regained their voices to protest the efforts to disenfranchise blacks at the end of the century. Black participation in southern politics essentially ended by 1900. But for several years toward the end of the era of Reconstruction hundreds of blacks served their region in politics, and although they were often disparaged by their contemporaries and forgotten by historians, they performed ably, without vengeance, and helped craft new state constitutions that were far better than the ones they replaced.

FISCAL RECONSTRUCTION

White southerners then and since have wanted to point accusing fingers at the so-called black-dominated Reconstruction governments for outrageous corruption. And, as is always the case in the course of human affairs, there were examples of moral and judgmental lapses. In the lower house of the South Carolina legislature, where for two years blacks were dominant, were found obvious cases of misrule, corruption, and extravagant misuse of public funds—two hundred porcelain spittoons purchased for the statehouse, for example. Louisiana also exhibited corruption, though of course political chicanery and venality were as traditional in that colorful state, before Reconstruction and since, as a good roux. But Reconstruction-era corruption looks different when examined more closely. Corruption had existed in the all-white Johnson state governments; it was much worse in the Democratic urban political machines of the North, such as the notorious Tweed ring in New York City; and the southern Democrats, after they regained control of the South, exceeded the worst examples of Reconstruction corruption. Placed in historical context, in an era of loose political morality, the Reconstruction state governments were relatively clean. For example, the total cost of congressmen voting themselves stationery allowances that somehow paid for hams and champagne pales alongside the subsidies paid railroad companies for track never built, but in the latter case the malefactors were the rail magnates, not the Republican legislators. The magnates pocketed the profits and defrauded the states both before and after Republican Reconstruction. This was the baroque age of corporate corruption nationally, and it is manifestly unfair to single out southern Republicans or black officeholders for the failures of capitalism rampaging out of control.

Government expenditures went up significantly during Radical Reconstruction. However, this was evidence not of misgovernment but rather of attempting to meet the extraordinary needs of the times. Government buildings, bridges, and the like had to be rebuilt and enlarged. And the scope of government responsibility expanded, pushed in part by the black politicians, to provide needed hospitals, asylums, orphanages, and prisons for society. Eleemosynary institutions were also provided for the black populace, a flagrant misuse of funds in the eyes of most whites. But the most important reform of the Republican state governments was the development of systems of public education for all the children of the states. Southern whites were occasionally skeptical of public schools even for their own children, but the idea of educating black children seemed hopelessly inappropriate. State governments floated bonds to raise the funds necessary to build the needed railroads and public works, and due to the unsettled economic situation, they had to offer northern creditors outrageous discounts, sometimes more than 50 percent of the face value of the bonds, to raise the required monies. Any fair examination of state budgets of the South during the period will conclude that most of the expenditures were justified and indeed represented more responsible government than had existed in the antebellum era. That did not preclude southern white conservatives, looking for reasons to attack Republican rule and black participation, from attacking the regimes as extravagant examples of misrule that had to be ended.

Along with the justifiable increase in state expenditures came an increase in taxation. Again, given the real social needs of the region, these taxes were understandable. But southern whites, still suffering from the economic disruption of the war and struggling with reestablishing the profitability of their farms, considered the rise in taxes as but another example of Republican fraud, waste, and malfeasance. The majority of southern whites in the antebellum South had paid practically no taxes except for an inconsequential poll tax. The tax structure was not intentionally progressive, for most taxes were levied on property. However, the slaveholding minority owned most of the property in the form of the slaves, which meant that the majority, nonslaveholders, had a very light tax burden, and, given the lingering Republican ideology from the era of the American Revolution, they considered taxation a close cousin to tyranny. But the Thirteenth Amendment had ended slavery, forcing the tax burden to shift much more heavily toward land.

This meant, in effect, a significant increase in the tax liability of small farmers, most of whose property was land. To make matters seem worse, wartime destruction had resulted in a drastic lowering of the assessed value of southern farm lands, which in turn required that the tax rate increase. Small farmers—the overwhelming majority of the population—would have felt a double whammy even if there had been no need to increase total state revenues to meet the postwar exigencies. The justifiable expansion of government services exacerbated the tax bite the farmers felt, which likewise magnified the outrage directed toward the Reconstruction governments. Farmers not yet completely recovered from the war simply did not have the cash to pay their increased taxes, and the newspaper listings of farms being auctioned because of back taxes became a constant reminder to white Democrats of what they considered the injustice of Republican rule. The real rise in taxes also struck a devastating blow against the mountain Republicans, who never anticipated that the end of slavery and the provision of public schools would have so disproportionate an impact on them. The Republican state governments lost badly needed loyal white supporters because of taxation, many of whom felt somehow doublecrossed. No one was really to blame; the times were simply out of joint.

The reality of higher taxes and black participation in the political process and the perception of unparalleled corruption and scandal in state government were a tragic combination that ultimately doomed Reconstruction. The white majority in the South determined to end Republican rule. In no state did a majority of the whites support the Reconstruction governments; only through the disenfranchisement of supporters of the Confederacy and the organization of black voters were the Republicans able to maintain tenuous control of state politics. In three states (Louisiana, Mississippi, and South Carolina) blacks were a majority of the population, and in several other states there were significant black minorities that—with the addition of relatively few white voters—could have controlled state elections. White Democrats saw that the path to regaining political hegemony lay through intimidating their opponents (especially the blacks) and reacquiring the right to vote. The latter came without bloodshed, both through presidential and congressional pardons. The basic national commitment to democracy meant that even the most radical in Congress had no stomach for depriving the majority of southern whites of a voice in their government. The pardoning process was substantially complete even before the Amnesty Act of 1872 restored political rights to the 150,000 or so ex-Confederates who remained unpardoned, leaving only several hundred outside the political system. In many regions of the South political organizing by the white Democrats was sufficient to wrest political control away from the Republicans, especially after higher taxes caused leakage from GOP support.

THE END OF POLITICAL RECONSTRUCTION

Native whites also used violence, social ostracism, and economic pressure to persuade many scalawags and carpetbaggers to withdraw from politics, change parties, or leave the region. Much of this political pressure was localized and ad hoc, but southern Democrats also developed racist organizations intended to terrorize Republican whites and especially black voters. The best known terrorist group was the Ku Klux Klan (KKK), first organized in Pulaski, Tennessee in 1866, apparently as a social club. But its possibilities for harassing blacks after the beginning of Radical Reconstruction led to a transformation of the organization, and by 1867 provisions were made for various local dens, linked hierarchically from neighborhood to county to state to the entire South, with leaders bearing frightening titles like Grand Cyclops and Grand Wizard. Secret rituals, ceremonies, and the distinctive wearing of white sheets as ghost-like disguises contributed to the effect, and with a kind of mystical fervor the KKK members roamed the South under cover of dark, disrupting Republican political rallies, threatening Republican officeholders, and intimidating black voters with torches and burning crosses, random beatings and killings, and several massacres.

A virtual guerrilla war erupted; hundreds of blacks were murdered for exercising the right of assembly or for voting. Other vigilante groups emerged, with euphemistic names like rifle clubs and the Red Shirts; their purpose was to drive the blacks out of politics. Grant, the Radicals in Congress, and even some decent people in the South were outraged by the lawlessness, and Congress in 1870 and 1871 passed a series of Enforcement Acts aimed to quell the KKK and similar organizations, such as the Knights of the White Camellia. Eventually Grant declared nine counties in South Carolina to be under martial law in 1871, suspended habeas corpus, set up special courts, and sent in troops. This had some effect, but the KKK simply went underground and suspended its activities. The southern Democrats had essentially achieved their purpose and were able to ease up on their campaign of brutality, though the potential of violence remained to keep blacks in line after the federal presence was withdrawn. The North never had the willpower to smash southern violent opposition. To have done so would have required a commitment of troops and money less than a decade after the end of the Civil War, and would probably have been impossible without a suspension of Constitutional rights for the majority of southern whites.

The North also had its own political and economic agenda to pursue, its public was tired of involvement with the South, and northern racism limited the willingness to interfere with southern racial mores—the North became morally exhausted and turned "the black problem" over to the South. In part this followed from an ideological attachment to the idea that freedom alone should be sufficient to solve the freedpeople's dilemma. And in part north-

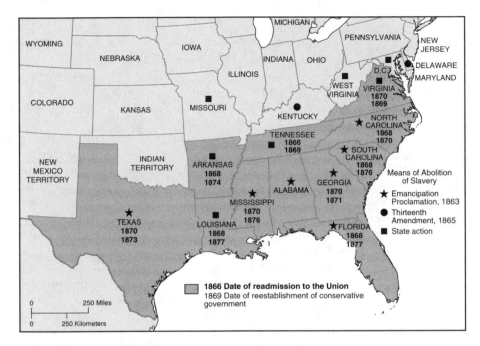

MICHIGAN

WYOMING

IOWA

PENNSYLVANIA

NEW JERSEY

NEBRASKA

INDIANA   OHIO

DELAWARE

ILLINOIS

D.C.

MARYLAND

WEST
VIRGINIA   VIRGINIA
1870
1869

COLORADO

KANSAS

MISSOURI

KENTUCKY

★ NORTH
CAROLINA
1868
1870

TENNESSEE
1866
1869   1868

★ SOUTH
CAROLINA
1868
1876   Means of Abolition
of Slavery

NEW
MEXICO
TERRITORY

INDIAN
TERRITORY

ARKANSAS
1868
1874

★
ALABAMA   ★ GEORGIA
1870
1871

★ Emancipation
Proclamation, 1863

MISSISSIPPI
1870
1876

● Thirteenth
Amendment, 1865

★
TEXAS
1870
1873

LOUISIANA
1868
1877

★ FLORIDA
1868
1877

■ State action

1866 Date of readmission to the Union
1869 Date of reestablishment of conservative
government

0   250 Miles

0   250 Kilometers

After the war: reconstruction and restoration

ern business interests became disillusioned with the lack of progress in "reconstructing" the South and the continuing violence and disorder so disruptive to business investment. Powerful northern interests were willing to sacrifice the rights of the blacks in order to buy stability. Given the terrorism and the erosion of northern support, loyal southern whites wilted away from the Republican party, black political participation plummeted, and resurgent, pardoned southern white Democrats regained control of their state and local governments. Republican rule ended as early as 1870 in Virginia, North Carolina, and Georgia; in Texas, in 1873; in Alabama and Arkansas, in 1874; in Mississippi, in 1875; and in South Carolina, Louisiana, and Florida, in 1877.

Political Reconstruction ended that year in the resolution of the famous disputed presidential election of 1876. Samuel J. Tilden, the Democratic candidate, won 184 electoral votes, 1 vote short of victory, and Rutherford B. Hayes, the GOP candidate after scandal-plagued Grant had been refused the nomination, held 165 electoral votes. At stake, though, were the disputed 19 electoral votes of the last three states with Reconstruction governments, Florida, South Carolina, and Louisiana (and also one disputed electoral vote in Oregon, which Hayes had won and which involved a legal technicality). There is no way of knowing how many potential black voters were frightened away from the polls, but Tilden surely won the majority of the white vote that was cast. Since southern whites considered the elimination of black votes both normal and acceptable, they believed the Democrats had won the states fair and square. In the confusion and fraud that resulted, however, each state reported competing Democratic and Republican vote tallies. With but one additional vote Tilden would become president and break the Republicans' sixteen-year hold on the White House. To settle the dispute Congress established a special fifteen-member Election Commission consisting of five members from the House, five from the Senate, and five from the Supreme Court—eight Republicans and seven Democrats. Every issue was decided by the same eight-to-seven vote, with the result that when the dust had settled, Hayes had picked up all twenty votes and was declared the winner. So while the Democrats stole the original election, the Republicans stole the recount.

Yet the Democrats peacefully accepted the results, evidently because of additional bargaining that took place behind the scenes—in the Wormley House hotel, to be precise. Apparently the Republicans promised that if Hayes were accepted, he "would deal justly and generously with the South," code language meaning he would remove the few remaining troops from the region and acquiesce in the Democratic takeover of the state governments of South Carolina and Louisiana. (Florida had been won by the Democrats several months earlier.) Moreover, Hayes or his agents promised that he would not use his patronage to defeat Democratic candidates in the region, would support federal appropriations for rebuilding much needed levees along the Mississippi River, and would support a southern route for a second intercontinental railroad. In return Democrats pledged to recognize the basic rights of blacks as outlined by the Thirteenth, Fourteenth, and Fifteenth Amendments, to stop the quasi-warfare against southern Republicans, and to agree to Republican James A. Garfield as Speaker of the House. Neither side ultimately lived up to the complicated secret bargain, but with the troops removed and Democrats in control of all southern state governments, Reconstruction had really ended. Perhaps it hardly needs saying that southern Democrats also reneged on their promise to protect the constitutional rights of the blacks.

BLACK RECONSTRUCTION

What had the South's four million blacks gained by the Civil War and Reconstruction? The easy answer is that slavery was destroyed, although neither the Emancipation Proclamation nor the Thirteenth Amendment ended bondage with the ease and finality of a magic wand. Slavery slowly disintegrated over the course of the Civil War, but vestiges of the institution lingered into Reconstruction and long afterward in sharecropping and racial segregation. Slavery began dying by degrees as soon as Union troops began moving into the South, and as soon as wartime mobilization drew planters away from the plantation to the battlefield. Union armies were the symbol of liberty, enticing slaves to risk escaping to freedom. The breakdown of plantation authority emboldened slaves, long schooled in caution, to dare to take that risk. The reality that slaves desired freedom and would act to gain it pressured the Lincoln administration to change its policies, leading to the Emancipation Proclamation.

An important part of slave culture had been learning ways to push at the boundaries of white discipline to gain advantages, but to do so in a manner that would minimize the chances of punishment. Slaves became masters of dissembling, hiding their real motives and feelings as they pushed and delayed, cajoled and played the childlike Sambo to persuade their master or mistress—or wear them down to the point of giving in—to make an accommodation. No one misunderstood that ultimate power stood with the whites, but every white when honest also understood that slaves carved out a degree of autonomy over their workplace that could be transgressed by the master only at the cost of trouble. Whites misread the slaves' accommodationist mien and their dissimulation as genuine contentment with their bondage. Whites would occasionally acknowledge that other planters' bondspeople were unhappy and might run away, but they seldom could see the same discontent in those they called their own people. Perhaps some ignorant field hands, they reasoned, duped by abolitionist propaganda, might run away; certainly the trusted mammy or the head driver would never do such a thing. Confederate mythology preserved a special place in its pantheon of heroes for the trusted slave who hid the family silver from the Yankees or stayed on the plantation to the very end, trying to void emancipation by pledging eternal loyalty to their sainted white owners.

Some slaves did show such faithfulness to the old order, or at least to their old owners, just enough to give some substance to the myth, and stories of the faithfulness of former slaves were especially treasured during Reconstruction when it seemed to white southerners that all the old verities of racial etiquette were being overturned by freedpeople. But many more slaves ran toward freedom when a good opportunity offered itself than stayed as the loyal retainers that supported the myth. Plantation discipline eroded with the planters off to war and with wives, younger sons, or elderly men left in control—few had the mark of authority the male head of household had exhibited, and slaves took advantage of the cracks in the command structure. Even so, slaves knew how important it was to be cautious, to avoid precipitate action that could result in capture and punishment. Armies moved forward and sometimes retreated. One had to be careful about running away to join the Union because if the Bluecoats retreated, one could be left stranded.

Many slaves, sensing toward the later days of the war that the end was near, preferred to wait safely for Confederate defeat rather than make a possibly dangerous dash toward freedom. Yet despite all the experience that urged caution, tens of thousands of slaves left their plantations and fled to the Union armies. Long before Lincoln, Congress, or the army had developed a policy for dealing with refugee slaves, the slaves by the press of their numbers forced northern authorities to come to terms with their presence. Union armies very early in the war captured Confederate territory, and, especially in the sea islands of South Carolina, the wealthy white planters rushed to the interior leaving their slaves to the invading Union forces. Here too, as with runaways, the Union had to come to grips with the basic question of Reconstruction: what was to be the proper role of blacks within the captured, and later defeated, South?

The Civil War was barely a month old when three slaves escaped to Union forces at Fort Monroe, Virginia, near where the first blacks had been introduced to Virginia in 1619. General Benjamin F. Butler, knowing the Confederates had been employing them as war laborers, accepted the runaways, called them contraband, and refused to return them as the normal operation of the fugitive slave laws provided. Yet Butler's ad hoc decision did not set national policy, and for months to come commanders in the field were left to improvise. In June General Henry W. Halleck decided to return fugitive slaves to their owners, but on July 9 the House resolved that it was not the duty of federal troops either to capture or to return them. A week later General Winfield Scott requested permission to allow the owners of slave runaways to seek and recover their claimed property behind Union lines. The Crittenden Resolution of July 22, which stated that the war was not being waged for the purpose either "of overthrowing or interfering with the rights or established institutions" of the seceded states, seemed to confirm the Halleck–Scott position. Then on August 6 Congress passed the first Confiscation Act, authorizing the federal government to seize any property used to aid the rebellion and to free slaves employed either as soldiers or workers against the United States.

Neither the northern public nor Lincoln as president were ready to endorse emancipation as a war aim; Lincoln was restrained by his racism, conventional for the era, and by his concern that any emancipationist noises by the North might convince the skittish border states to lurch toward secession. But the realities of war made Lincoln's arm's-length stance toward slavery increasingly awkward. What was to be done with slaves who came to Union forces or were seized by the advance of Union troops? On August 30, 1861, General John C. Frémont declared Missouri to be under martial law and proclaimed that all the slaves belonging to persons resisting the Union were free. This clearly went beyond the Confiscation Act and threatened the fragile war consensus in the North, so Lincoln quickly ordered Frémont to observe the narrow emancipation parameters of the act.

Still, it did not seem right to turn away slaves seeking their freedom, and military officers became more aware of how the South's use of slave laborers in effect increased the number of white men ready for combat. Both military necessity and morality suggested that policy had to evolve. In October 1861 General Thomas W. Sherman was authorized to "employ fugitive slaves in such services as they may be fitted for," but the secretary of war made sure that the order not be construed as a general arming of slaves for military duty. And when, the following March, General David Hunter issued a proclamation freeing slaves in Georgia, Florida, and South Carolina, Lincoln promptly countermanded the proclamation. The legal demise of slavery would be as unplanned and evolutionary as its origins had been in the seventeenth century.

In May 1862 General Hunter, elaborating on the orders given General Sherman, began calling upon blacks to form what he called the First South Carolina Regiment, but again the idea of organizing black troops went beyond what Lincoln deemed possible, and he ordered the regiment disbanded. As emancipationist sentiment gained ground in the North, aided by the activities of prominent black abolitionists, and the number of slave runaways threatened in places to inundate Union forces, Lincoln and Congress were forced to experiment with policy. On March 13, 1862, Congress prohibited the use of military force to return runaways. With Lincoln's support, Congress on April 10 promised compensation to the former slave owners of any Border State that developed a plan of gradual emancipation.

Less than a week later slavery was abolished in Washington, DC, and on May 20 the United States agreed to cooperate with England in suppressing the international slave trade. The pace accelerated; on June 19, 1862, Lincoln signed a bill abolishing slavery in the territories, and in less than a month Congress passed a strengthened Confiscation Act that proclaimed free all those slaves belonging to disloyal masters who found themselves, either because the slaves had escaped to the Union lines or because the advancing army had occupied the region where they lived, within territory controlled by northern troops—whether the slaves were being directly involved in the war effort or not. As the Union slowly began to capture and hold sections of the South, it created pockets of black freedom. For those geographical regions, Reconstruction began months and years before the end of the war.

It was in this context, within a week of the revised Confiscation Act, that Lincoln advised his cabinet that he intended, come January 1, 1863, to issue a general Emancipation Proclamation declaring free all the slaves within rebellious states, hence extending emancipation in the abstract far beyond the confines of conquered southern territory. His plan was publically announced on September 22, 1862, after the abortive southern invasion of the North was squelched at Antietam. That announcement shifted the whole stated purpose of the war, eliminated any chances the South might have had of garnering significant British support, heartened northern abolitionists, and horrified white southerners even as it infused an almost millennial hope among the slaves. But after the announcement, it became impossible to continue the restraints against freedmen serving as military laborers and even soldiers, and the federal government had to begin making plans for solving the problem of what to do with freedpeople in the South.

During the autumn of 1862 Lincoln began to permit the enlistment on a limited basis of black troops. General Butler in New Orleans promptly mustered a troop composed of free men of color and ex-slaves; General Rufus Saxton reconstituted the South Carolina regiment that General Hunter had earlier formed only to have Lincoln dismiss. From the viewpoint of white southerners, nothing more symbolized the revolutionary—the horrendous— potential of defeat than the specter of armed black troops. White soldiers' response to their presence was nearly frenzied; a group of black Union soldiers, attempting to surrender, was massacred by Confederates at Fort Pillow, Tennessee, in 1864. When the Confederates defined black troops as slave insurrectionaries subject, if captured, to reenslavement or death, Lincoln responded that for every black soldier so treated, a white rebel soldier would

After the Emancipation Proclamation freed slaves fled to the Union army. (Library of Congress)

be executed. Whether it was Lincoln's threat or better judgment on the part of the Confederate government, southern troops as a matter of official policy never killed black soldiers in violation of the code of war. Even so, there were clearly incidents—Fort Pillow being the worst—where black soldiers were not allowed to surrender.

By late fall of 1862 the number of fugitives coming into Union lines increased as northern forces pushed deeper into the South. In November General Ulysses S. Grant attempted to deal with the growing number of refugees in Tennessee by appointing Chaplain John Eaton, Jr., to be in charge of fugitives. A refugee camp was established at Grand Junction, and later moved to Memphis, where shelter, food, and a modicum of medical attention were supplied. Able-bodied freedpeople were hired out to loyal whites who had leased abandoned plantations. Henceforth the emancipators were to deal with the refugee problem by adjusting the plantation system to the new realities of wage labor. This technique had been pioneered earlier in the vicinity of Port Royal, South Carolina, and the prospects of combining social control of the blacks with the profitable production of staple crops proved too enticing for northern reformers to resist. Seeing therein a way to teach newly freed slaves middle-class Yankee habits of self-discipline and industry, hard-headed military commanders and visionary reformers agreed on the utility of this gradual transformation of dependent slaves into independent farmers.

But Yankee notions of efficiency clashed with black notions of autonomy, and utopian dreams foundered as misunderstanding flourished. Freedpeople in general were never given the wherewithal to prosper—they had neither land, draft animals, tools, nor capital—and racism put limits on the patience of whites. In several locations, such as the Davis Bend, Mississippi, properties of Jefferson Davis and his brother Joseph, freedpeople were allotted land directly, planted food and cotton, and practiced virtual self-government under the watchful eye of army-appointed superintendents of Negro affairs. Despite localized success stories, most freedpeople who farmed behind Union lines did so as wage laborers on white-leased property.

At the very end of the war, on March 3, 1865, the Freedmen's Bureau (officially the Bureau of Refugees, Freedmen, and Abandoned Lands) was established, and it was primarily responsible for handing out emergency supplies to destitute freedpeople (and whites left impoverished by the war). But the disposition of abandoned lands was also one of the responsibilities of the Freedmen's Bureau, and during the final days of the war several thousand blacks were settled on land abandoned by southern planters, particularly in the coastal regions of South Carolina and Georgia, and throughout the South the federal government had gained control of hundreds of thousands of acres of abandoned land. On a limited scale, in isolated regions, freedmen were granted ownership of small parcels of land. Partly because of this, and partly because of a much-discussed speech by Representative Thaddeus

Stevens of Pennsylvania advocating that ex-slaves be given forty acres, the "forty acres and a mule" rumor swept across the South. Yet there never was an explicit plan to confiscate and redistribute the property of wealthy planters—the respect for the Lockean right to property ownership prevented the federal government from seriously entertaining the idea of widespread land confiscation. Even the relatively small-scale efforts undertaken by the Freedmen's Bureau to provide land to freed slaves were aborted by President Johnson, who ordered all property returned to the Confederates, whom he pardoned with abundant generosity. Johnson's actions ended the best hope most freedpeople had for genuine financial independence.

So the return of peace in the late spring of 1865 found blacks betwixt and between slavery and real freedom. Legally they were slaves no longer, but they did not possess the necessary means to begin life anew as free farmers. They faced a southern white population more racist than ever and determined to regain through legal means—the infamous Black Codes—almost complete white control of the blacks in their midst. While blacks were soon introduced to political participation, they just as soon learned that their Republican friends did not have the power to protect them from southern whites' violence. In fact, for most blacks what was happening in Washington or in the state capitals was of less moment than immediately local events. Black men and women knew that by the fiat of law they were free, but precisely what that freedom meant in real-life terms was yet to be decided.

The great majority of southern whites had experience dealing with blacks only as slaves, and most blacks had dealt with whites only in the unequal position of slave to master. A strict racial etiquette had placed firm boundaries around acceptable black behavior, and blacks had been socialized to observe those restraints. Blacks understood that freedom meant a breaking down of old barriers, but southern whites manned the barricades to prevent as much erosion of old habits as possible. Blacks wanted to experiment, to push at the old limits, but not to risk retribution any more than they had to. Yet what did freedom mean if it did not change the old ways of behavior? The ability to choose one's place of work seemed essential to freedom, but whites read such freedom of choice as detrimental to crop production and as evidence of black irresponsibility. The ability to travel, to move about, seemed to blacks at the heart of personal liberty, but again whites saw it as inefficient vagrancy.

Black Codes, with their labor contracts and antivagrancy provisions, struck against these simple manifestations of black freedom. Blacks did want to travel about, but the roaming was mostly neither random nor the result of laziness. Thousands of black families had been broken up and dislocated by the whites moving their work forces out of the way of invading Union armies, and many blacks were searching for loved ones from whom they had been separated. Blacks also desired to move to southern cities and towns, expecting to receive from the Freedmen's Bureau both provisions and protection from white violence. Action that seemed rational to blacks seemed to whites symptomatic of black irresponsibility. From the white viewpoint, agricultural recovery depended on blacks remaining steadily at work on farms from early spring planting through the final picking of cotton that occurred as late as December.

Early Reconstruction was a time of confusion, anger, and violence, but it was also a poignant time when whites and blacks were experimenting with how to act toward one another. How far could a black move away from earlier models of deferential behavior without being charged with uppity behavior that might bring retribution? How much equality in demeanor was a white required to accept? Such matters as terms of address, deciding on housing arrangements and crop choice, hiring and being hired, were fraught with problems even for cautious blacks and well-meaning whites. Who gave way on a crowded town sidewalk? How would plantation mistresses, never accustomed to the hard chores of cooking and washing, survive without easy access to black workers? Some mistresses kept up a brave front as they struggled to get the housework done, while others whined and cursed their fate. But for most blacks, as for most whites, the central problem was economic. The whites owned the land, the draft animals, and the tools, but what good were these without laborers? The freed slaves were propertyless, but their labor potential gave them some bargaining power. The crux of black–white relations during the first few years of Reconstruction was working out an acceptable arrangement for blacks to work on the land growing the self-same crops, but as people possessed of some degree of freedom. The ultimate result was the system of sharecropping that would come to dominate the southern countryside for over half a century, involving in time the majority of white farmers as well as black.

BLACK SHARECROPPERS

In some ways black emancipation was a mighty revolution, but in other ways, the more things changed the more they stayed the same. The same actors were present, carrying many of their old attitudes with them, the climate and soil were unchanged, cotton still loomed as the great money crop, and the power relationships between blacks and whites remained unequal. With the war over and thoughts turning to making a living, people of both races primarily thought of the old staple-crop standbys: rice, sugar, tobacco, and especially cotton. Convinced that blacks would not work unless forced to, whites began to experiment with methods of exploiting them just short of slavery. Whites accepted with resentment that freedpeople now had to be paid wages in cash, but landowners expected the blacks to continue dwelling in the former slave quarters grouped together for ease of supervision near the big house and to continue working together in the fields in gangs under the direction of white overseers or foremen. Sometimes the wages were paid monthly (perhaps $10 per month for an adult male), but usually at least half the wages were payable after the crops were harvested.

The system of cash wages proved unsatisfactory for everyone involved. Aware that without a stable workforce available through harvest their prosperity was in jeopardy, whites required their farm laborers to sign contracts that severely limited their freedom of movement, often specifying the landowner's right to control the laborers' working hours and determine their chores and requiring strict obedience to the landowner. The contracts also contained limited guarantees of the rights of blacks, and for that reason— and because they shared the local whites' attitudes both toward blacks and toward the necessity of having workers in place throughout the crop year— Freedmen's Bureau agents often helped to persuade or force reluctant freedpeople to sign the agreements and keep their contractual obligations. Even some southern whites came to admit that the generally despised Freedmen's Bureau served the whites' own interests. Blacks obviously resented the heavy overtones of bondage associated with such labor contracts and work routines and resisted by shopping around for landowners who gave them marginally better terms.

In the midst of the postwar labor shortage, this limited ability of blacks to choose their employers gave them considerable leverage, and they used it to gain greater autonomy. After all, they understood too well how much the emerging system smacked of slavery, and they resisted precisely those arrangements that most affected personal freedom. Blacks pushed for the right to live apart from the old slave quarters, out from under the landowner's watchful eye. They wanted their houses on separate acreage, scattered around the landowner's property, so they could grow their crops as an independent family unit, not as members of work gangs laboring on common fields. Moreover, because landowners devised numerous methods of shortchanging illiterate blacks when payday came—even firing them a few days ahead on trumped up charges and telling them they had thereby forfeited their wages—freedpeople preferred payment in the form of being allowed to keep a fractional share of the crop they produced. In a sense blacks then felt they were paying a portion of their family agricultural output as rent rather than receiving a wage from the landowner. By receiving a specified percentage of their harvested crops, their skill and hard work would be rewarded.

Landowners too were quickly dissatisfied with the wage system that first evolved. Since it gave freedpeople no incentive to work hard, a great deal of costly, irksome supervision was required to maximize production. Occasionally blacks would depart in midseason, with or without their cash wages, leaving the landowner precariously short of manpower to harvest his crops at the most labor-intensive period of the year when temporary workers were impossible to hire. Primarily, however, white landowners—the former planters—desired a shift away from cash wages because there was a drastic shortage of money in the postwar South. Planters, even wealthy ones, were land poor and simply had no ready cash with which to pay monthly wages. For that reason they welcomed the development of a system of payment in crop shares, with settlement after harvest, for not only did it lessen their cash requirements, but it also placed an equal share of the crop risk on the freedpeople. Moreover, without really ever openly acknowledging it and despite all their expectations of black laziness and irresponsibility, whites discovered that blacks could and would work productively without substantial supervision when they and their families were allowed a measure of incentive. Ironically, what blacks desired and pressed for—the right as individual families to control their own labor on plots of land assigned to them—whites began to accept, too, as the best possible compromise. Sharecropping emerged as another form of mutual accommodation.

Most black families, without an opportunity to possess their own land in fee simple, came to see their assigned sharecropper's "farm" as the next best thing, for at least they had more control over their own work schedules and had privacy in their home life. The landowners' prewar unified plantation became in effect a collection of small farms cultivated (but not owned) by individual black families. In addition to their greater freedom, the ex-slaves in the years immediately after the war received more than twice as high a proportion of the agricultural output of the large agricultural units (an aggregate of many sharecroppers' plots, the new form of the old plantation) as they had in the days of slavery. If fact, considering the total standard of living, the basic material income of these blacks increased by about a third as a result of emancipation, though their plight may have later worsened as a consequence of the long-term decline in the price of cotton that occurred in the last decades of the nineteenth century. But what freedpeople valued more than their slight increase in income was their increased control over their own lives, over their patterns of consumption, over their leisure time.

On their individual agricultural units of from twenty to forty acres, black families could choose to maximize output by keeping the women and children in the fields as during slavery times, or they could accept a somewhat lower material standard of living by withholding a portion of the family members' labor. On the whole black families preferred to withdraw the mother from the field except at periods of peak labor needs and let her perform more the role of mother and housewife than that of field hand. Similarly, children were exempted from some labor when public schooling was available. Because blacks chose for cultural reasons to withdraw some percentage of their labor force from the fields, at least for portions of the year, the total productivity of the black population—as compared with slavery times—decreased somewhat. From all accounts, blacks showed an intense interest in education, with children, their parents, and white-haired elders crowding the primitive classrooms hungry to learn to read. Literacy was associated with freedom and getting ahead economically. Southern whites condemned blacks' pursuit of learning as inappropriate for their station in life, an unnecessary government expense, and an impediment to maximum agricultural output. Blacks eventually learned the sad reality that in an impoverished, racist society, literacy alone did not promise progress.

Sharecropping never became the exclusive system of agricultural organization in the postwar South, and in some areas the transition to it lasted for a decade or longer. A variety of systems existed: plain renting of land (tenant farmers), work for cash wages or wages paid in crop shares, and so on. The largest landowners would have some of their land cultivated by wage laborers, and perhaps a tenant farmer or two, in addition to several sharecroppers. Some blacks, utilizing the entrepreneurial or craft skills they had developed as slaves, combined hard work, skill, and luck to scrape together enough money to buy small parcels of land, and by 1880 about one-fifth of the black farmers in the South owned their land—a substantial achievement, even though the average size of the farms was less than half the size of those owned by whites. But for the majority of blacks, some variant of sharecropping was their lot. Those who owned their own mules, plows, and enough capital to provision themselves for the year needed a landowner to supply the actual land, a house, and usually firewood. In return the blacks, called in this case share tenants, would pay the owner one-third of the corn and one-quarter of the cotton; this was called "working on thirds and fourths."

Most blacks, however, could offer only their labor. The landlord supplied everything else but food and clothing and for his efforts received one-half the cotton and grain production. For their essential food and clothing the sharecroppers had to find a supplier who would extend them credit, the balance being due when the cotton was sold. Thousands of small country stores mushroomed across the cotton South in the years immediately following the war to perform this service, and many large landowners also began to offer their and their neighbors' sharecroppers store supplies on credit. These "furnishing merchants" cum planters charged the sharecroppers exorbitant "credit" prices that included interest rates averaging as high as 60 percent per annum on the provisions bought.

The stores were able to charge such rates because the sharecroppers usually had no alternative supplier. Stores were sparsely scattered across the rural South and transportation was primitive, so the stores had little competition. The merchants justified the charges by the high risk of offering credit to penniless farmers dependent upon an unreliable crop affected by the vagaries of the weather and the selling price. To make things worse, the large northern wholesale houses that supplied the local stores on credit routinely charged them enormously high interest rates because of the risks involved in their business. Even well-disposed furnishing merchants had little choice but to pass the interest charged them on to their customers. Because of the inflated prices of necessary provisions, hundreds of thousands of sharecroppers found that their one-half of the cotton would not even cover their debt at the local store. So at the end of the year, at settling up time, the sharecroppers had no choice but to ask for credit for yet another year, in the futile hope that an extraordinary crop yield would finally boost them over their debt hurdle and allow them to buy a little patch of land. Another year's labor, another year's crop, usually left them deeper in debt.

Merchants quite understandably wanted collateral from the sharecroppers for the credit extended them, but the landless farmers had no assets except the expectation of a crop. In the early postbellum years the state legislatures passed crop-lien laws, which allowed merchants to require that the sharecroppers given credit sign a lien bond that legally bound the future crop to the merchant, and the merchants often stipulated that cotton be grown almost to the exclusion of grain crops. The lien laws had several effects. First, of course, the croppers were tied to the merchant by the legal promise of that year's harvest, and the merchant had first claim to the crop. If the sharecroppers' harvest did not cover what they owed the merchant, they ended the year further in debt. They had to get credit for the following year, often having to take a reduction in the amount loaned (and hence a cut in their already low standard of living), and by the lien that secured the credit were tied once more to cotton and farming on the shares. There simply was no escape; every year many slipped further behind, locked ever more firmly into an endless circle of cotton, credit, and economic catastrophe. Secondly, since the merchant demanded that they maximize cotton production because he expected to receive his payment from its sale, farmers on shares had to reduce the labor and land devoted to food crops and livestock, thus forcing them to buy more canned goods from the store, pushing them even deeper into debt. For hundreds of thousands of sharecroppers, black and white, King Cotton had become a tyrant from whose grasp there was no escape.

WHITE SHARECROPPERS

Sharecropping in one guise or another was never a phenomenon confined just to blacks. Before the Civil War, even stretching back to the colonial period, there had been thousands of landless white farmers who had worked as farm laborers for payment in kind. Yet the sharecropping system that developed after the Civil War became more firmly entrenched, and the marketing and provisioning system, secured by the lien laws, made it harder to escape. Changes in both local commerce and the international staple market also brought far more poor white farmers into the clasp of sharecropping and, by encouraging overproduction, produced lower prices and greater poverty. Sharecropping became more dominant in the post–Civil War South than the plantation had been in the antebellum South, and its social and political consequences were as great. The image of the poor benighted South largely owes its origin to the evils of sharecropping and the prevalence of essentially one-crop agriculture, and that image—alive even today—aptly characterized the South down to World War II. By the early twentieth century a majority of white farmers had become landless sharecroppers, and they outnumbered black sharecroppers.

The large majority of southern whites had been landowners in 1860, and many who were not were children and relatives of landowners who could expect to inherit property in the near future. Small landholders, especially in the regions that because of terrain or inaccessibility to transportation were not dominated by staple-crop production, had practiced mixed farming, growing most of their foodstuffs along with some surplus or specialty goods they could either sell or barter—mules, hogs, corn, honey, apples, and barley. Often a few acres were devoted to cotton or tobacco to earn some cash, but these small farmers lived in a relatively cashless society, where goods or labor were bartered for supplies either with neighbors or with crossroads stores. The South as a whole before 1860 had been self-sufficient in terms of food production. Most of the household furnishings, clothing, and shoes were made in the home or by neighborhood craftsmen who exchanged them for a combination of cash and produce or labor. Slowly, almost imperceptibly at first, changes in the regional economy and transportation system after the Civil War began to disrupt this localized world of home consumption.

The great increase in property taxes, which had to be paid in money, and the fact that with the end of slavery the brunt of the tax assessment fell on land, meant that now small farmers had to be able to come up with more cash at one time than they had earlier been accustomed to handling, and this required that they exchange substantially more of their goods or services for money. In addition, the development of a railroad network allowed huge northern wholesale and merchandising houses to penetrate the rural southern countryside, both underselling local craftsmen and substituting a modern, commercial economy for the earlier, community-centered, barter, or low-cash society. Sharecropping itself contributed to the proliferation of crossroad stores. In the southern plantation district during the antebellum period, the planter had not only sold all the cotton grown on his land but had done the central purchasing of goods which he then distributed to his slaves; the planter's factor was his connection to the market in coastal port cities both to sell his crop and to purchase his goods (and those of his slaves) from wholesalers.

But with the rise of sharecropping, individual black families made their own purchases. This disaggregation of purchasing ended the dominance of the old-fashioned cotton factor, who was replaced with local furnishing merchants scattered throughout the countryside. The total value of their store assets was small—hence they represented a major risk to their suppliers—but they did offer aggressive northern wholesalers access to an expanding market. Highly competitive northern wholesale houses took advantage of this new marketing device and the penetration of the southern hinterland by railroads to spread the influence of modern commerce across the entire South. In the 1870s railroad mileage expanded greatly, the number of country stores more than doubled, and the modern world of commerce swept beyond the old cotton-dominated black belt South to areas that before the Civil War had been characterized by mixed agriculture. This was not all bad, for it meant that isolated farmers now had easy access to goods—shoes, sewing needles, canned food, ready-made clothes, and commercial fertilizer—that had before been more expensive or hard to find.

But these goods had to be paid for in money. People came to prefer the new goods, and as local craftsmen found themselves undersold and quit their trades, people became dependent on store-bought goods paid for in money. Obviously, as the modern commercial system replaced the older system of self-reliance, barter, and cooperative labor, the cash nexus became supreme. Farmers who had previously been mostly self-sufficient now found that they needed a cash crop to be able to pay their infernal taxes and afford the goods available at crossroads stores. And in order to earn cash, farmers had to shift away from production for home consumption to production for the cash market. No longer was the South self-sufficient in foodstuffs. In 1880 the region as a whole had to import more grain and livestock than it exported—a dramatic shift since 1860. Thus across the South small farmers were sucked into the cotton trap. There was a world market for cotton, there was a pricing structure, there were agents who stood ready to purchase, gin, transport, and sell abroad even cotton grown in the remotest hinterland. No readily available market structure existed for other southern farm products, such as corn or barley, for example.

Cotton-buying agents used country stores to purchase the staple, and improved transportation at first increased the price cotton growers received for their crop, further enticing them to shift acreage away from food crops to cotton. So countless thousands of small, land-owning white farmers found themselves inexorably drawn into the commercial cultivation of cotton, resulting in a doubling of the acreage given over to cotton between 1859 and 1879. The number of bales produced went up accordingly as the relative self-sufficiency in foodstuffs plummeted. The tragedy was that the price of cotton soon fell to a fraction of its immediate postwar high, meaning that farmers grew ever more but got less and less in return.

Unfortunately, as the South produced more cotton, so did other regions of the world. The opening of the Suez Canal in 1869 made Indian cotton more competitive in price for the mills of England, and vast cotton fields (sometimes managed by ex-southerners) also opened up in Egypt. At the same time that the worldwide supply was increasing, the global demand for cotton, which had risen almost uniformly for seven decades following 1790, flattened out in the postwar period. The result of worldwide overproduction was a constant decline in price. When individual southern sharecroppers and small farmers who had shifted to an emphasis on cotton production found out at settlement time that they had not broken even, they simply arranged another line of credit and did what to them seemed rational—they determined to work harder and plant more acres of cotton in hope that a bountiful harvest would allow them to pay out and escape their debt. But practically every cotton grower did the same, production increased accordingly, prices fell still further, and the poorest suffered the most. The crop lien tied the unfortunate sharecropper to cotton, and the merchant, who bought his goods on credit too from northern wholesalers and was thus also in debt to his suppliers, had to insist that his creditors plant the one sure money crop. The system could not be budged off center.

Hundreds of thousands of white farmers, including many who began the postbellum era owning their land, were brought into the circuit of commercial agriculture, growing cotton for cash, and found themselves falling ever deeper into debt with the country store. First they lost money, and then their land, to the clutches of the cotton market. They too, by the hundreds of thousands, became landless sharecroppers, eventually outnumbering the freedpeople who never escaped from the grasp of the system. Even had blacks during Reconstruction been given the fabled forty acres and a mule, chances are that they, too, having even less experience with money management and credit arrangements than the white farmers, would have backslid into sharecropping. Almost no one in southern agriculture, except perhaps some of the largest furnishing merchants, really prospered. The South's great lack of captital linked sharecropper to merchant to northern wholesaler, with enormous, though often hidden, interest rates extracted at each successive stage. Profits flowed to the North, poverty flourished in the South. By 1880 the per capita income of the southern states was about one-third that of the rest of the United States. The racism and political irrationality that marked so much of the South's history in the half century following Reconstruction are inextricably linked to the region's poverty, as were the several efforts at significant political reform. But until the South escaped the paralysis of dependence on one crop, its economic and human potential was severely crippled.

THE FIRST NEW SOUTH

Even during the antebellum period the South had not been aggressively anti-industrial. Occasionally well-to-do planters had invested in factories, railroads, mining, and a variety of decidedly nonagricultural pursuits. Many of these industries, such as cottonseed oil plants, cotton compresses, jute bag (used to cover cotton bales) manufacturers, and so on, served agricultural interests. Sawmills, gristmills, ironworks, and saltworks also dotted the region. Southern industrialists like William Gregg worked tirelessly and with some success to plant textile mills across the region, and Joseph R. Anderson's Tredegar ironworks in Richmond pointed toward the later southern steel industry that would bloom in the vicinity of Birmingham, Alabama. Still, in 1860 the South had produced only 15 percent of the nation's iron and about 25 percent of the textile goods. Southern banks and private individuals serving as lenders provided much of the credit and funds for investment, but the South remained overwhelmingly agricultural.

In part this was due to the South's competitive advantage in growing certain marketable crops like cotton, tobacco, sugar, and rice. As long as these crops could be reasonably expected to provide a safe and profitable return, there was little incentive to risk money on alternative investments. A substantial portion of the southern population—the slaves—could not be avid consumers, and this lessened the market for locally produced goods. The southern transportation system in the antebellum era had been primarily designed to transport bulk agricultural products to port cities and as such was not conducive to facilitating the transportation of raw materials to industrial cities and the distribution of manufactured goods throughout the region. Moreover, the small-scale southern manufacturers were ill-equipped to compete either in the region or in the nation with larger, more efficient northern manufacturers. But the point is that there was a not insignificant industrial presence in the Old South. Many antebellum planters, merchants, and bankers were quick to respond to potentially profitable opportunities whether they were rich cotton lands or industrial schemes. Southern legislatures passed laws dealing with such matters as incorporation that, even if they did not unfairly favor manufacturing enterprises, did not discriminate against them either. Shareholders in corporations were also extended the advantage of having limited liability. In other words, the Old South was not intrinsically hostile to all industry.

During the course of the Civil War the South's industrial potential was stretched beyond the breaking point, but in the process the South underwent an almost miraculous temporary industrial transformation, developing munitions factories, ironworks, armories, shipbuilding facilities, and the like. The output was never enough to meet military and civilian needs, and in the end shortages of nearly everything compounded the misery of death, disease, and emotional exhaustion that climaxed with Lee's surrender at Appomattox. The South did not undergo a permanent industrial revolution as a result of trying to meet wartime exigencies. But neither were southern leaders so hidebound in their infatuation with agriculture that they could not appreciate the importance of industrialization, which, along with crop diversification, promised to rescue the region from overdependence on one crop. The northern victory in itself showed how essential industry was not merely for military prowess but, by implication, for prosperity.

While southerners may have been slow to acknowledge the moral superiority of the North's cause in the first months after the war, they fully appreciated the success of the northern economy. J. D. B. De Bow, whose *De Bow's Review* in New Orleans had been the Old South's leading journal of political economy, led the chorus of voices calling for the recuperating South to purge itself of addiction to cotton and strengthen itself through industrialization and crop diversification. The first post–Civil War state governments formed in the South in accordance with Andrew Johnson's directives made initial efforts to promote a more modern economic base in the region, but these efforts were soon swept aside by the torrents of Reconstruction politics. The issues of how to regulate the freedpeople and how to regain control of local politics were of paramount importance to white southerners, and their decisions on those matters—reasonable as they seemed to most white southerners themselves—suggested to national observers that the South had in mind repudiating the outcome of the war. The resulting political turmoil, which as we have seen soon descended to violence and fraud, obscured the South's initial efforts to modernize its economy.

During the periods of presidential and congressional Reconstruction efforts were made to forward the industrialization of the region; Republican politicians, less wedded by tradition and experience to agriculture and more committed to commerce, industry, and the need for change in general, often advocated legislation that would benefit the South (and, in tune with the times, occasionally themselves). Legislatures passed bills and issued bonds to underwrite railroad construction, but southerners had done the same both in the antebellum era and in the immediate aftermath of the Civil War. The underlying motive in each case was the stimulation of prosperity—seen as some industrialization along with an enhancement of commerce—with improved transportation. Some railroad enterprises went bankrupt, others swindled the taxpayers' money, and unscrupulous individuals on occasion lined their pockets, but all in the grand old American tradition of unregulated capitalism. Corruption was neither automatic to the process nor endemic among Republicans. Well-meaning Republicans from the North, ex-Confederates who wanted to put the past behind them and find prosperity for the region, and go-getters of all sorts saw in southern forests, mineral deposits, available cheap labor, and amenable climate the ingredients for economic growth. Nothing conspiratorial or anti-southern need be assumed in the emerging movement to modernize the South and renew its prosperity.

The rationales for development were many. For some advocates there was a strong element of regional chauvinism, a desire to see the South share in national prosperity and be independent of northern manufactured goods. Other spokesmen, while not unaware of regional implications, were primarily local boosters who urged that their town garner the rail route or the new textile mill so as to keep up with the spirit of the times and perhaps a rival, upwardly mobile town. Would-be industrialists and capitalists were more than willing to prosper personally, and they justified the desire for economic gain both as getting in step with the rest of the nation and as a way to uplift the impoverished whites in their midst by providing manufacturing jobs. Suffice it to say that most of the jobs turned out to be low-skill, low-pay, dead-end work, and poor whites (and blacks) usually found themselves simply exchanging rural poverty and backbreaking labor for long, monotonous hours of environmentally hazardous work in factories or mines with little or no improvement in living standard.

The managerial and industrial elite of the postwar South evolved from the antebellum planter class, but the evolution required less of a break with the past than sometimes recognized. While most prosperous planters liked to imagine themselves as paternalistic agriculturalists who treated all their dependents—white and black—in benevolent fashion, they on the whole made hardheaded business decisions about crops, land and slave purchases, and even relocations to other sections of the South with a keen eye on profits and what they called getting ahead. When times and conditions changed, as they surely did in the 1860s, able planters changed with the times. Even the fictional Scarlett O'Hara, surely a plantation stereotype, became a sawmill operator when the need and the opportunity presented themselves.

In the real world too countless planters and sons of planters (and occasionally daughters) reassessed the opportunities facing them in the 1870s and determined to cultivate industrial prospects rather than agricultural crops. They expected at least to maintain and hoped to improve their social position. They expected to control cheap labor with a paternalistic rationale that shielded them from facing their exploitation of their employees, but their flexibility on matters of occupation and regional economy did not extend to matters of race and politics. Much had changed, but much remained unchanged. The shift from antebellum planter to postbellum industrialist required a change in investment strategies, but it neither required nor produced a fundamental change in ethos. Younger sons of prewar planters, with one foot still in the soil, eagerly stepped with the other foot toward industrialization and the siren song of modern prosperity. Without ever repudiating the past they lunged for new ways of advancing both themselves and their local community. And just as the prewar planter class had been open to able young men on the make (either through hard work and good luck or advantageous marriage), the southern planter-cum-industrial class welcomed northern investors and promoters who promised to enhance profits and maintain the racial and class status quo. The business and industrial elite fully intended, in cooperation with the agricultural elite, to control politics for their mutual benefit. Both wanted low taxes, a docile labor force, and "stability" in order to attract northern investments.

In truth there was a substantial increase in industrial activity in the South in the two decades following Reconstruction. Railroad mileage grew fourfold between 1865 and 1890, and there was an even greater increase in the number of cotton spindles as at last the textile mills, seeking cheap labor and reduced transportation costs from the cotton fields, began relocating with a vengeance from New England to the cotton-producing states. By 1900 the South was the nation's leading producer of textiles. Lumber production multiplied, an iron industry developed in the vicinity of Birmingham, Alabama, and new deposits of coal began to be exploited. Yet the real southern attractions were cheap labor and raw materials; a handful of owners and managers (many northern) prospered, but the laboring masses toiled with little hope of ever achieving a satisfactory standard of living.

If the growth in investment in southern industry or the value of southern manufactured goods is compared with the rest of the nation, then the industrial boom in the South seems more a bust, for after more than two decades of activity the South's share of the national output remained constant. But when one remembers that this was a period of phenomenal industrial growth nationwide, then the South's ability to stay in the same relative position meant that the South was industrializing at a brisk rate. A comparison not with the nation but with southern output in 1860 or 1865 reveals the dimension of that growth. This economic revitalization of the South was in part the result of a concerted policy of a number of southern businessmen, would-be industrialists, promoters, and publicists who advocated the development of a so-called New South of progress and prosperity to replace the lamented and admittedly irrecoverable Old South of slavery and defeat.

A number of newspaper and magazine editors took the lead in this effort, and at first it seemed a rational, matter-of-fact analysis of the present state of the regional economy and an evaluation of the South's human and natural resources, with an eye to attracting substantial northern investment both of money and know-how. Editors such as Henry W. Grady of the Atlanta *Constitution,* aided by staff writer Joel Chandler Harris, who collected Uncle Remus tales for pleasure but wrote promotional editorials at work, Frances W. Dawson of the Charleston *News and Courier,* and Henry Watterson of the Louisville *Courier-Journal,* tirelessly promoted the advantages of crop diversification, industrialization, and the wider acceptance of Yankee-like, get-ahead attitudes. Richard H. Edmonds of Baltimore published in his *Manufacturer's Record* an unending paean to factories and investment, and his pages paraded seemingly every broom factory and wagon shop established from Maryland to Texas, with each opening memorialized as a step toward progress and prosperity. Talk of steel mills in Anniston or the discovery of coal deposits in Tennessee led to rhapsodic discussion of how that region was the coming Ruhr of the United States, Birmingham the next Pittsburgh. According to the *Manufacturer's Record*, every mountain city had a healthful climate to go along with its sparking prospects.

Within a decade of the end of Reconstruction this New South journalism had ceased being exhortatory and had begun being congratulatory. The New South spokesmen subtly convinced themselves that the South had become what the spokesmen had so ardently called for. One notices a shift in the tone of the editorials; by the 1880s articles on new factories or plans for a new town were offered as proof that the South had become prosperous, the industrial heartland of the nation. Was this really only an effort to persuade northern investors to invest their dollars in a stable, progressive region, or did that intention evolve from conscious strategy to unconscious myth? The evidence seems to suggest the latter, wish being father to belief. The best known spokesman became Henry W. Grady, who in a famous address in 1886 to the New England Society of New York at Delmonico's Restaurant in New York City captured the mythical essence of the finished New South message.

Following William Tecumseh Sherman, the scourge of Georgia, on the program, Grady artfully gained the favor of his audience by stating that while once there had been "a South of slavery and secession—that South is dead. There is a South of union and freedom—that South, thank God, is living, breathing, growing every hour." He went on to assure his northern listeners that southerners had "sowed towns and cities in the place of theories, and put business above politics. . . . We have fallen in love with work." Reaching out for capital, he insisted that "we have smoothed the path to Southward, wiped out where the Mason and Dixon's line used to be, and hung out our latch-string to you and yours." Thundering applause sealed his audience's approval of his sentiments, and Grady and likeminded New South promoters seemed convinced that a new age of prosperity and racial and class harmony had arrived. Those northerners who had wanted to remake the South in the image of the North in the aftermath of the Civil War could believe that Grady and others were doing just that. But the New South spokesmen implicitly assumed that a business-industry-planter oligarchy would rule southern politics, with taxes and government services kept low and wages dampened. Blacks would be held "in their place," performing the most menial or distasteful jobs, and all would supposedly work together in harmony and efficiency to create a truly New South with the same elite as always in control. With the North safely assured that the South had accepted northern attitudes, the federal government could relax its concern about the plight of the freedpeople in the South, a message most northern whites were only too willing to believe. The shadow of the Old South lay over the New South, and prosperity proved as illusory in the 1880s and 1890s as Confederate success had proven in the 1860s.

URBAN GROWTH

One of the most striking features of the Old South had been its relative lack of urbanization. In 1860 only 7.1 percent of the region's population had lived in urban areas (defined as 2,500 people or more), roughly one-third the percentage for the North. New Orleans was the only large city in the South, and it ranked only sixth in size among the nation's cities. New Orleans was more than four times as populous as Charleston, the second largest southern city. Moreover, the ten major southern urban areas were all river or seaport cities. Since 1840 the urban share of the South's total population had been declining, but that decline was halted immediately after the Civil War, in large part because of a very significant migration of rural blacks to the region's cities both to seek the protection of the Freedmen's Bureau officials and to seek improved job opportunities. The nationally depressed economy of the 1870s, along with the South's peculiar cotton depression, slowed urban growth in that decade, but the 1880s saw a renewed acceleration of the growth of cities. This development would continue into the twentieth century, resulting in a doubling of the proportion of the South's population that were urban dwellers, to 15.2 percent in 1900. Despite this marked growth, the South lagged even further behind the nation as a whole that year—New Orleans, for example, had slipped to fifteeth among America's largest cities. But the truly remarkable urbanization of the nation as a whole should not be allowed to obscure the rise of an urban South during this period.

Several aspects of this postwar southern urbanization are noteworthy. It came about less because of the rapid growth of older cities than as a result of a new generation of cities located in the interior of the South and to the west. While the sons of pre–Civil War commercial and planter interests tended to dominate the leadership of the older, slower growing cities, the new cities were led by a newer class of southerners, less tied by kinship and viewpoint to the past. Family name counted for less in the emerging cities than skill, hard work, and drive. By 1890 the list of ten largest southern cities included such new marketing and manufacturing centers as Nashville, Atlanta, Dallas, and San Antonio, with Houston and Birmingham on the rise. These cities, and dozens not so large in the region, grew not as the result of immigration from Europe but mainly from internal southern migration. The depressed agricultural economy gave an added attraction to southern cities, dreary though they might have been. Blacks, young men on the make, widows, and single women saw towns and cities as places of opportunity. With the exception of Birmingham, most of these urban seats were closely related to the region's cotton economy.

Typically, small marketing towns would have cotton gins and a handful of stores; slightly larger towns would have, along with their rail depot, cotton compresses, where the cotton bales were reduced in size for ease of transport, and cottonseed oil mills that extracted oil by crushing the seeds that were a byproduct of ginning. The oil was marketed for illumination and lubricating purposes. Still larger towns, small cities, would combine these functions and also collect the compressed bales from a wide hinterland and ship them, by water or rail, to manufacturing centers in the South, the North, or England. In return, linked by rail to northern or regional wholesale houses, the marketing cities would initiate the distribution of manufactured consumer goods, usually from the North, back down the trade network to agents and storekeepers in towns and ultimately to small stores at the village crossroads. Commerce and agricultural services, not manufacturing, were the chief functions of southern urban places.

No particular city had a special advantage over another, or a way to increase significantly the size of either its cotton servicing or consumer-goods market. Consequently, although a number of southern towns grew into small cities, with the largest of them having populations ranging from 40,000 to 100,000, none of them came close to rivaling the really large cities that were emerging in the North. Dozens of marketing towns of 5,000 to 10,000 people came to dot the South, and while many of the towns were ambitious and the town promoters active, few ever grew into real cities. Nevertheless, much that was progressive in the South centered in the urban areas. Here congregated southerners of talent, of entrepreneurial ability, with a desire to change the region for the better. Here were most of the region's lawyers, doctors, and other professionals. "Boosterism" was the word of the day, and business enterprise was assumed to be the magic key to growth, progress, and prosperity. The economic development that occurred—whether the appearance of textile mills or steel mills, or the attracting of a new railroad line—usually came because the urban business class advocated it. The results might have seemed puny to a visitor from New York City or Chicago, but for the son or daughter of a small farmer, the commerce and ambition of a regional marketing city symbolized the first step out of lethargy and poverty. Business progress, women's civic reform efforts, black middle-class prosperity, all originated in the South's postwar cities.

Because the railroad was the necessary link to the markets of the North, often the largest and grandest building in a city on the make was the train station. In antebellum cities church steeples had been the tallest symbol of a city's pride, but now the cathedrals to rail commerce were what inhabitants proudly pointed to. Soon showcase government and civic buildings followed in their wake. The office and storefront buildings were still low—two to four stories. Not until the 1890s did the first skyscrapers begin to appear in the very largest southern cities, Atlanta leading the way in 1892 with the Equitable Building. Cities touted their hotels, expecially their one grand hotel, and most managed to have an opulent opera house, both assumed to be sure symbols of a progressive city with a get-ahead attitude. These cities, for all their hunger for growth and modernity, were by present-day standards amazingly backward at the beginning of the 1880s. Most of the roads were unpaved, almost no modern sewer systems existed, pure city water was a thing of the future, police forces were unprofessionalized and crime was rampant, and fire protection was primitive. Practically every city had at least one disastrous fire during the period, with scores of homes and businesses destroyed. There were almost no public parks and few public schools, and the provisions for black education were shockingly inadequate.

Cities like New Orleans and Memphis in particular were regularly plagued with horrendous epidemics of yellow fever or cholera, with deaths mounting into the thousands. The Memphis yellow fever scourge of 1878–79 alone took almost six thousand lives. On several occasions the entire city had to be quarantined, bringing commerce to almost a complete halt. The infant mortality rates were high, especially for blacks, but all races and classes suffered from a broad range of illnesses. Cities were a public health nightmare, with privies and sewers emptying onto the open ground or streets, along with tons of horse manure and urine (the pollution of horse-drawn transportation) with little thought given to the location of water wells. Urban dwellers often kept chickens, hogs, milk cows, and horses penned behind their homes or in stables, contributing to the rural look and smell of late-nineteenth-century cities.

It was not until the 1890s that cities began systematically to build sewer systems, construct modern water works to replace private wells and cisterns, and pave more than just a few blocks of streets in the heart of the cities. By the 1870s most southern cities had horse-drawn street cars linking the outskirts to the central business district, and by the late 1880s southern cities actually outpaced their northern counterparts in pioneering the development of all-electric trolley systems. This improved transportation began to make possible a spatial rearrangement of the class and racial structure of the cities, with those of higher income now able to move out and commute in to work. The first so-called streetcar suburbs then developed in Atlanta, Birmingham, Houston, and other cities. Also, by the 1890s, electric lights became the *sine qua non* of the self-consciously progressive cities, and hundreds of municipalities developed their own public power plants. Telephones were not far behind, with local telephone companies providing the miracle of modern communication to small networks of subscribers. The South was somewhat slower in becoming integrated into the larger Bell networks than was the North because the region's commitment to localism retarded the process. Population growth as measured by the decennial national census was taken as a promise of better things to come by town boosters, and cities often annexed adjacent areas simply to augment their census numbers, not to provide better urban services to the neighboring regions.

Some of the stories of urban growth and development were remarkable. Birmingham had been founded in a cornfield in north-central Alabama in 1871, near iron ore and coal deposits. Promotors like the Louisville and Nashville Railroad quickly linked it by rail to Atlanta and points northward. The investors came both from the North and from the region—Henry De Bardeleben, who had married one of the daughters of Old South textile manufacturer Daniel Pratt, was a local entrepreneur who pushed the manufacturing and successful marketing of Birmingham steel, despite fighting freight rates and pricing strategies imposed from without that penalized southern production. The population of Birmingham swelled from 3,086 in 1880 to 26,178 in 1890, 38,414 in 1900, and an incredible 132,685 in 1910. No other southern city could claim such meteoric growth, but Birmingham was not the only beneficiary of development schemes. A concerted campaign to build cotton mills along the route of the Southern Railroad in North and South Carolina resulted not only in the rapid rise of small cities like Charlotte, Greenville, and Spartanburg, but in the South's overtaking of New England as the nation's textile center by 1900. Railroad connections also led to the rapid expansion of Atlanta, Dallas, and Houston, and made possible the burgeoning growth of the port of Norfolk.

For no group of southerners did the cities produce greater change than for blacks. While many arrived in early Reconstruction to escape the violence of the countryside, blacks quickly came to associate urban areas with enhanced opportunity and freedom. The older southern cities, whose residential neighborhoods had been integrated before the Civil War, retained that pattern, although by the end of the century totally black neighborhoods had developed. The newer cities that were springing up in the South's interior tended much more quickly to segregate the races, a process accentuated by the exploding black urban population. By 1890, 15 percent of the South's blacks had moved to cities and towns, where they represented fully one-third of the region's total urban population and a remarkable 70 percent of the nation's urban black population. Whites seemed both resentful of and frustrated by the growing black numbers, and spatial separation by race became far more pronounced and rigid. Blacks now were often excluded from theaters, restaurants, and railroad station waiting rooms. Blacks were not excluded from the street cars, though efforts at the end of the period to require them to sit in back seats (or give up their seats to whites) occasionally caused blacks to boycott the transportation systems, with some success. As a result, urban street car systems tended to be less segregated than other aspects of city life.

Before the Civil War blacks had often dominated certain skilled trades, such as carpentry and masonry, and they were well represented in many others. In the harsher racial environment of the New South, and particularly so in the newer cities, white craftsman and artisans pushed black males out of most traditional skilled trades and did not allow them to find employment in new occupations like plumbing and electrical work. The result was a very significant de-skilling of the black male workforce, with black men increasingly concentrated in low-skill, low-pay jobs. Many whites, frightened by the competition with the growing number of urban blacks and worried that the countryside would soon have a shortage of black agricultural laborers, strongly advocated that the proper place for blacks was in the cotton fields, As a result of the de-skilling of black male job opportunities in the cities, many males did have to leave their wives and families and seek at least temporary work elsewhere on railroad construction crews, in lumber camps, and as temporary harvest laborers. Black women could usually find urban employment as domestics, beginning the phenomenon of female-headed families in the cities. By 1890 as many as a quarter of urban black households had only the mother present.

The growth of the black population in the towns and cities, and their increasing segregation, brought about the rise of a separate black economy. Most cities saw the rise of black business districts featuring black-owned stores, cafés, undertaking establishments, and shops and services of every sort that catered to the black population. Whites often rejected black customers or treated them poorly, which only drove blacks to prefer their own establishments. An indigenous professional class of black lawyers, teachers, doctors, dentists, and pharmacists began to emerge, the result either of blacks going north for education or graduating from the black colleges and medical schools established across the region during the era of Reconstruction—institutions such as Howard University, Hampton Institute, Fisk University, Atlanta University, and Meharry Medical College. These black business and professional people had an all-black clientele, and while many blacks were proud to be able to confine their business to fellow blacks, the black entrepreneurs and professionals often prospered. As a result of white prejudice and black opportunism, a black elite began to develop in the cities. Many of these well-to-do blacks possessed not only skill and business acumen but a strong sense of obligation toward their people. Such black leaders often pioneered a number of organizations that nurtured and served the black community. Blacks founded and managed their own hospitals, schools, and other institutions; during the antebellum period blacks had often been actively excluded from such facilities. Separate, segregated facilities were seen in the post–Civil War era by blacks as an improvement of their situation, and whites preferred the growing degree of racial separation in the cities. Excluded from white organizations, black men formed clubs and fraternal organizations like the Colored Masons, the Colored Odd Fellows, and the Knights of Pythias. Black women likewise found community and performed service in the United Daughters of Ham, the Ladies' Benevolent Society, and Order of the Eastern Star. Black savings banks, burial societies, and insurance companies were organized to benefit both urban and rural blacks, often filling a void that white businesses ignored. In all the cities black community and social life often revolved around the churches, and ministers were important social and often political leaders in the black community. The intensification of racism and separatism in the era affected blacks every day of their lives, but the simultaneous growth of manifold community institutions, especially the churches, helped the black population survive. The black professional class would, in coming decades, discover new ways both to minister to their people in a Jim Crow age and ultimately begin to chip away at the entire racist edifice. But before the region saw the color code recede, race relations would grow still worse.

THE POPULIST CHALLENGE

Despite all the New South rhetoric about industrialization, agriculture was still the backbone of the southern economy, and all was not well down on the farms. Sharecroppers and tenant farmers, white and black, seldom prospered, but neither did most small landowners. Dependence upon one crop—though the crop varied from region to region—made the entire South hostage to the vagaries of the climate and the international market. The biggest black-belt planters and their business and industrial allies controlled state and local politics, and the interests of the poor hardly concerned the New South politicos. Low wages, low taxes, and minimal government services were what the development crowd wanted and got, and the sharecroppers and small farmers had little say in the affairs of state. Hard times were endemic, but poor white men—perhaps accustomed by their Civil War military experience to follow the command of their leaders—were afraid to risk upsetting the Democratic party's control of racial matters by protesting economic policies strenuously, and of course the blacks had practically no influence on such matters.

Several times in the 1870s and 1880s discontent from the lower orders bubbled up, with real political impact in the case of the Readjuster movement in Virginia. Money was dear, taxes on farm land relatively high, schools and most social services woefully inadequate, and the conservative Democrats blithely unresponsive to the people's needs. In this situation a gifted politician and former Confederate general, William Mahone, led a reform movement that burned brightly for several years on either side of 1880. Before the Conservative Democrats were able to mount an effective counterattack by raising the specter of a Republican comeback and black rule, the Readjusters—so-called because one of their major causes was scaling back or readjusting the state debt—politically dominated the state and revised the tax system, increased funding for education, reformed aspects of the penal system, and in general tried to make government more responsive to the needs of a broader spectrum of the populace. But the Democrats put an end to "Mahoneism" by the mid-1880s.

The Virginia situation was unique in terms of the success of the reformers; yet most southern states had flurries of political protest in the 1870s and l880s. Greenbackism flourished in many areas, and it spoke to farmers' desires for inflationary monetary policies to ease their burden of debt. Local reform movements aimed to end the domination of courthouse gangs who ruled county politics for the aggrandizement of the few at the expense of the masses. Protests over such things as high taxes or unfair valuation, exorbitant railroad rates, and outrages in the convict lease system were common but produced no general remedies. Agricultural reform was a perennial cause, and farmers supported first the Grange then a variety of organizations like the Agricultural Wheel that blended community-building social functions with the dispensing of useful economic and scientific advice. Ideas associated with reform movements that originated outside the South, such as the Knights of Labor and the Single Tax crusade of Henry George and Edward Bellamy's Nationalist movements (which arose as an outgrowth of the popularity of his futuristic reform novel, *Looking Backward* [1881]), also filtered southward and gained scattered adherents. Still the plight of the plain folk seemed to worsen, and, what made it more painful, who noticed or understood or cared? A number of mostly short-lived utopian movements, religious and secular, sprang up in this age of dissatisfaction. Many southerners also became disillusioned with mainstream religious denominations and either found comfort in a world-denying holiness movement in Methodism or joined new sects that sought to reject this world and pursue spiritual perfectionism.

As this range of responses suggests, the farmers' sad condition, real and perceived, was not narrowly economic. Farmers felt unappreciated, forgotten, and condescended to by the shapers of national opinion. Their own political leaders neglected their needs and governed to please northern investors and southern busincssmcn-industrialists. Farmers in the more isolated, fringe regions of the South felt particularly abandoned. Their hard work earned them little money and no respect from the larger world. They were ridiculed as hayseeds and country bumpkins while well-dressed financiers whose hands never toiled to produce anything real dictated the laws and reaped the profits. It did not seem right that hard-working, God-fearing tillers of the soil should suffer while eastern and urban philistines prospered. The farm protestors shared with industrial laborers a commitment to producerism, an old idea that stretched back to the republicanism of Thomas Jefferson and beyond. According to producerism, the actual producer (a farmer, artisan, or industrial worker) deserved the fruit of his or her labor. Groups with special privileges—monopolists, railroad interests, and purchasing cartels—should not interfere with the natural, legitimate, and, the farmers would say, God-given right of the producer to benefit fully and fairly from his or her labors.

As railroads and ready-made goods penetrated the countryside and undercut traditional crafts—making obsolete old habits of barter and the sharing of skills and labor, and putting everything on a cash basis determined by unseen wholesale houses—an entire way of life was threatened with destruction. The price fetched by the primary money crop, cotton, was determined not by a farmer's skill but by the vagaries of an impersonal international market. New phosphate fertilizers became available for purchase because of railroads and country stores, and although the chemical fertilizers improved crop yields and hence were almost mandatory to buy and apply, they also increased farmers' costs (debts) and the corresponding risks of failure. Southern farmers in the generation after Reconstruction lived in times of wrenching change, and the political establishment failed to understand and address the pain and cognitive dissonance many farmers felt. Tens of thousands of white farmers sank deeper and deeper into debt, bankruptcy, then loss of their land. Black farmers, and sharecroppers, already living at the very edge of desperation, found their plight worsening still. The result was a long season of despair that led to a period of unprecedented political protest.

In a profound sense the farmers were responding to modernity, which from their perspective victimized them and the ethos of their local communities. There were objective reasons for farmers' discontent—the prices for staple crops fell in the 1880s and early 1890s, for example—but in some inchoate way the farmers felt their decline in social status and the constant slights to their dignity more than the pinch in their pocketbooks. This acute sense of loss, economic and cultural, first began to reveal itself on the farming frontier of northwestern Texas, in Lampasas County, where obscure farm clubs began to organize in the mid-1870s into a fledgling Texas Farmers' Alliance. Charles W. Macune, a self-taught practitioner of pharmacy, medicine, and law, and organizer par excellence, emerged as head of the group in 1886. Meanwhile similar farmers' organizations—the Arkansas Wheel and the Louisiana Farmers' Union—had arisen, and Macune persuaded the sister groups to merge themselves with the Texas Farmers' Alliance to form the National Farmers' Alliance and Cooperative Union. Macune was an enormously skilled leader and educator whose speeches and editorials shaped the thinking of increasing numbers of southern farmers because he so accurately captured their mood and prescribed remedies that seemed both to tame the impersonalism and greed of modern capitalism and harken back to a cooperative world of the past.

If Macune had an equal in appealing to the farmers' sense of discontent in order to mobilize them for change, it was Leonidas Lafayette Polk of North Carolina. With a military and political career spanning from the Civil War era and a commitment to agricultural reform beginning in 1877, when he was named North Carolina's first commissioner of agriculture, Polk knew his state and its farmers' problems intimately. In 1886 he had founded the magazine *Progressive Farmer* to urge scientific agricultural practices, and when the following year the Farmers' Alliance appeared in North Carolina, Polk quickly saw its promise and rose to its leadership. By 1888 Polk and Macune had through effective advocacy and personal charisma helped fold all the southern farm organizations, from Texas to the seaboard, into the Southern Farmers' Alliance (called the Southern Alliance), with headquarters in Washington, DC. (There was a roughly parallel organization of black farmers, called the Colored National Farmers' Alliance and Cooperative Union, which the Southern Alliance now and again reached out to and timidly cooperated with.) Macune was the first president of the Southern Alliance, but soon Polk succeeded him as president, and Macune served as the pithy, shrewd editor of the association's primary educational organ, the *National Economist.*

The Southern Alliance sponsored traveling speakers, a variety of local newspapers, and a steady procession of state conventions and local picnics and rallies that had much of the look and feel of a religious camp meeting. Both men and women were charter members of the fledgling Southern Alliance. The women were often more radicalized than the men were, for no one suffered longer or harder from the numbing poverty and bone-aching exhaustion of farm labor than did the womenfolk. The result was an intense period of what we call today consciousness-raising. Farmers found a new sense of community and purpose through meeting with others and reading and hearing about their plight and their social and moral worth. It was always somehow comforting to know that one was not alone in misery. The Southern Alliance became a movement of over a million farmers, men and women, and their evolving prescription of what should be done represented a radical challenge to the New South advocates of limited government and unchecked capitalism. The Alliance developed the most sustained mass critique of unrestrained free-market capitalism in American history, and it was by far the most far-reaching and radical protest political movement in the South from Reconstruction to the 1960s. The heart of the Populist movement, the incubator of its most profound challenge to modern capitalist America, lay in the South.

The Southern Alliance was simultaneously backward looking and uncannily modern in its program. Its myriad local social gatherings attempted to rekindle the sense of community and belonging that many farmers, especially the more geographically isolated ones, longed for. In an era of dog-eat-dog competition and laissez-faire economics, the Alliance spokesmen called for harmony and cooperation in society. In a period when local politics were often controlled by courthouse gangs and efforts were already beginning to limit the franchise, the Alliance promoted an increase in participatory democracy. Faced with distant monopolies that set policies and prices and rates with callous indifference to how they affected small farmers, the Alliance called for government price and rate controls. Aware that overproduction pushed prices down, the Alliance called for government limitation of crop acreage. Battered by interest rates and monetary deflation, the Alliance demanded government intervention both to bring down the cost of borrowing money and to increase the money supply. At the mercy of crop prices when harvest times bloated the immediate supplies, the Alliance—and in all these suggested remedies Macune was the primary inspiration—advocated a series of government warehouses that would store nonperishable crops until the prices went up, and in the meantime would give farmers negotiable subtreasury notes worth 80 percent of the local market value of the warehoused crop.

In sum, the Southern Alliance represented a frontal assault against the governing principles of the regnant big planter-businessman-industrialist class, who, not unexpectedly, responded to the Alliance as though it were the bubonic plague. Even so, across the South between 1887 and 1890 the Alliance, finding here and there seemingly cooperative Democrats, elected six governors and gained control of eight state legislatures. But the Alliance supporters were soon disappointed by the so-called friends of the farmers they elected. Most Democratic politicians were more interested in gaining the Alliance vote than enacting their program after they were elected.

Agrarian discontent and reform was not limited to the South; farmers in the Midwest, from the Dakotas though Kansas, had been devastated by crop failures and price collapses, and the Northern Alliance that developed there—its way prepared by the organizing and teaching efforts of the Southern Alliance— mirrored the growth of the farmers' rebellion in the South. Farmers had been lulled by several years of atypically bountiful rainfall and wildly optimistic promotional literature—some of which argued that rainfall followed the plow—into moving onto the high plains and adapting agricultural practices there not really suited to the climate. When the rainy years ended, farmers found themselves bankrupt, often hungry, and with absolutely no resources left. False promises of prosperity were replaced by terrible hardship. In the northern prairie states the Republican party was entrenched, and finding it as unresponsive to their needs as southern

Alliance members found the Democrats, northern farmers pioneered the formation of a third party to carry their banner. The issue of a third party was
extremely controversial in the South, where the memory of Reconstruction
still made any threat to the Democratic party practically unthinkable to most
southern whites. Hard-pressed Kansas farmers actually first organized a third
party with the name the People's party, soon called the Populist party, and
third-partyism spread across the central plains, initially provoking anguish
and argument among Southern Alliance members in Texas and elsewhere in
the South.

By 1890 the People's party had begun to incorporate into its membership all sorts of disillusioned farmers and reformers—old Grange members,
former Greenbackers, and current Alliance spokesmen. The Populists represented a broad synthesis of protest attitudes: some were advocates of producerism, a view reminiscent of an earlier age; others shared much with modern
capitalist America and simply wanted a quick economic fix, the monetization
of silver; still others were strongly antimonopolistic and supported a communal, noncompetitive society. All were gathered under the broad tent of Populism, and this breadth of opinion often led to division within the ranks. Still,
the communal/producer ethos represented the cultural center of gravity of
the Populist movement in the South. By 1891 the People's party was planning
a national convention to be held the following year that would represent the
aggregate of all these reform ideas—many of which were more relevant to
farmers on the northern prairies than to those in the creek bottoms and
among the red clay hills of the South. The formal organization of the People's party as a nationwide institution occurred in St. Louis in February 1892,
and a presidential nominating convention was scheduled that July to meet in
Omaha, Nebraska.

Although the Southern Alliance officially supported the transformation
of the farmers' movement into a political party, many southern Alliance
members, such as Charles Macune himself, bitterly opposed the formation of
a third party. Another leader, Leonidas L. Polk, suddenly died, and with him
died the Populists' best chance of bridging the sectional and ideological divisions that existed within the movement. The Southern Alliance was splin-
tered by the controversy over entering partisan politics, and many sincere
friends of reform could never bring themselves to leave the Democratic
party, especially after the Senate Republicans in 1890 and 1891 had tried to
pass a so-called Force Bill that would give the federal government supervisory
control of elections, raising again in southerners' minds the bugaboo of a
revival of Reconstruction. Other Alliance members, convinced that only a
third party could deliver the needed changes, made the break. The Populist
presidential candidate was James B. Weaver of Iowa, and the party platform,
though it did endorse Macune's idea of a subtreasury plan, was more attuned

to the needs of midwestern prairie farmers. Consequently the Populists won slightly more than a million votes nationwide, and even elected governors in Colorado, Kansas, and North Dakota, but most southern voters remained loyal to the Democratic party. Still, no third party had ever done so well in its initial presidential campaign. When in the following year the nation plunged into the worst depression in its history and the administration of Grover Cleveland, the recently elected Democratic president, seemed paralyzed over how to respond, agrarian reformers and third-party advocates felt vindicated and emboldened.

In the mid-term elections of 1894 the People's party did surprisingly well in the South, particularly in Alabama, North Carolina, and Georgia, and in a number of regions Populist leaders began cautiously to explore both cooperation with black voters and the idea of combining or "fusion" with southern Republicans. The aim was to break the Democratic stranglehold on southern politics. In North Carolina a coalition of Populists and Republicans actually gained control of the general assembly, and Texas Populists were forthright about the need to put aside meaningless racism and work together with blacks to improve everyone's economic condition. A superbly skilled black orator, John B. Rayner, was employed to speak to Texas whites in an attempt to defuse their fear of blacks' participating in politics and to speak to blacks about their need to support Populist candidates. But the Democrats proved a wary foe, both adopting some of the reforms of the Populists— again, especially in Texas and North Carolina—and employing fraud and brutality to maintain their political dominance. The stakes were high, and the presidential election of 1896 loomed as an epochal battle that might well determine the future of southern politics and the southern economy.

The nation itself approached the election with foreboding. Depression, bloody industrial strikes, and agricultural unrest had marked Cleveland's term, and while no one really knew the solution to the myriad problems facing the nation, one chimerical idea had emerged. The Silver Purchase Act of 1890, which had in effect monetized silver through the issuance of treasury notes, had been repealed in 1893 at the urging of Cleveland. The resulting deflation had exaggerated the hard times of many farmers. Western mining interests had pushed the idea that the remonetizing of silver would, by effectively expanding the money supply, bring inflation that would benefit farmers who suffered under a heavy burden of debt. The national Republican party tried to evade the issue, but at the insistence of eastern banking and commercial interests it came out against silver and in support of the gold standard as the only basis of a sound economy. In preparation for the 1896 presidential election Republican political operators handpicked William McKinley of Ohio to run a front-porch campaign that kept him away from reporters and controversial statements, and the party used its ample financial resources and its influence over urban factory workers to either buy or command votes.

The conservative Democrats wanted to run Cleveland again on a strict gold standard platform, but reform Democrats had had enough. Persuaded almost against their good sense that the monetization of silver would be a panacea for the nation's problems, they succeeded in nominating a Nebraska agrarian reformer and silverite, young William Jennings Bryan, for the presidency after he had electrified the Democratic convention with a soaring oration against the evils of gold-based deflation and in favor of the "producing masses of this nation"—a phrase that farmers particularly felt described them as opposed to the evil money changers in faraway big city banks. In one deft stroke the reform Democrats had skewered the Populists, for if they put forward their own candidate (who most certainly would have to be a silverite, too, to attract the western votes) the Populists would divide the prosilver vote and hand the election to the Republicans.

But when the Democrats, with a strong platform plank calling for the unlimited coinage of silver at the rate of sixteen ounces of silver to one ounce of gold, opportunistically reached out to the eastern Democratic goldbugs and nominated conservative Maine banker Arthur Sewall for the vice-presidency, it was more political inconsistency than the Populists could stomach. The national Populist convention went along with the Democrats and also nominated Bryan as its presidential candidate, but repudiating Sewall, the Populists nominated a true southern radical, Thomas E. Watson of Georgia, as their vice-presidential candidate. So William Jennings Bryan was saddled with two vice-presidential nominees who represented opposite visions of America. Bryan's response was to barnstorm the nation, preaching old-time virtues and the redemption of the body politic through silver. Populists in the prairie states could in good conscience urge a fusion with the Democrats because the party in local control was the Republican; for many southern Populists, faced with the memory of several years of conflict with the locally dominant Democrats—who had used fraud and violence to steal elections from the Populists in 1894—the idea of fusion with the Democrats was ideologically bankrupt.

Populist purists in the South disparaged the idea of cooperating with their erstwhile enemy, and in a number of states Populist leaders urged the faithful to fuse with the Republicans instead. The fight was especially bitter in Texas, where Populist leaders tried to convince their followers to put aside Reconstruction memories and racial fears and combine with blacks to throw the Democrats out for the sake of Populist orthodoxy. But racism proved stronger than reform, and the Democrats had learned too well in the aftermath of Reconstruction how to steal an election. Democratic demagogues stirred up old fears with farfetched warnings of black domination. Populist efforts at fusion and at building biracial coalitions failed, and Democratic–Populist voters nationwide were confused by the opposing vice-presidents that were linked to Bryan. When push came to shove, too many southerners were hesitant to break with the entrenched Democratic party and its essentially conservative political leaders they supported as much out of a habit of deference as for fear of racial change. Perhaps more important nationally, the Republicans had superior organizational skills and money galore, and their power over industrial workers allowed them often to dictate their vote. The result was a resounding victory for McKinley, a devastating defeat for the Democrats, and a movement-ending debacle for the Populists.

Southern Populists in particular were crushed. The Democrats responded in two ways. One was to perfect several schemes already underway to limit the participation of blacks in politics. The ill-fated Populist effort to form biracial coalitions in support of political reform frightened Democrats and in their minds justified their use of shocking electoral fraud in 1896. The solution to fraud, argued the Democrats, was to remove the possibility of black voting, and some disillusioned Populists like Tom Watson now agreed. The majority of Populists continued to advocate the widest possible franchise and the truest possible democracy, but the conservative, racist forces carried the day. In state after state ingenious methods of disenfranchising blacks were enacted, and new requirements that voters be literate and be able to interpret the state constitution, pay a poll tax, and have grandfathers who had been eligible to vote were transparent attempts to hide the raw anti-black motives of the election "reformers." The result, by 1900, was the almost complete disenfranchisement of southern blacks and—not completely unintentionally—a substantial reduction in the number of poor whites who could vote. The conservative Democrats had devised a sure method of maintaining themselves in firm control of southern politics.

The other way Democrats shored up their control was, once blacks were safely excluded from the franchise along with the poorest and potentially most radical whites, to open up the Democratic party to popular participation. Party rules were liberalized, United States senators were directly elected by the people rather than by the state legislatures, and statewide primaries, in which only whites were permitted to vote, were developed to give voters a voice in the selection of party candidates. Now that the threat of voter rebellion was no more, the Democrats approved making elections more honest, with rules about regularizing polling places and ballots, outlawing bribes, and even accepting the secret ballot. Many old Populist reformers were both too tired and too disheartened to protest much any more. Restrictions on voting drastically shrank the number of people participating in elections, and in several states there emerged Democrats of modest reform intentions, such as Governor James S. Hogg of Texas, who adopted some Populist reform ideas.

With this combination of opening up politics to safe white voters and depriving blacks of the right to vote, seasoned with a sprinkling of reform, southern Democrats had learned the recipe for control; they ruled the region almost unchallenged for the next half century. This was the era of the Solid South.

WOMEN IN THE POST–CIVIL WAR SOUTH

The Confederate South was forced by wartime necessity to undergo remarkable changes—its cities grew, its industrial base expanded, and its central government strengthened and sought to control aspects of life southerners had always thought beyond the law. But these revolutionary changes were temporary. White women too found their lives only momentarily changed in some ways, while in other respects their lives were transformed. At the heart of the transformation was the demise of slavery. White women living on plantations, who were a small minority of southern women, suddenly found themselves without maids, cooks, washerwomen, and the like. For wives of yeoman with few on no slaves, the prospect of making do without black labor was less daunting; such women had always worked long and hard to keep their families' tables set and their husband and children in clothes. For plantation mistresses, emancipation meant they had to garden, cook, wash, mend, and keep house themselves, and many found such unending and often monotonous labor a disheartening postscript to Confederate defeat. Many held up bravely and professed to being glad they were free of the responsibility of disciplining and caring for slaves, but most missed the luxury of having others perform the humdrum chores of everyday life. Some at first took their anger and frustration out on any Yankees they happened to meet. Time did not heal these wounds, but plantation mistresses came to terms with their changed world and learned to make do.

Of course, many erstwhile plantation mistresses still had husbands who were landowners, or were landowners themselves, and over time, and through such arrangements as sharecropping, many southern white women in short order again had the wherewithal to have black women, now free but still poor and powerless, back in their houses cooking and washing and caring for the babies. White women had also, during the course of the war, learned they had skills and money-earning capacities they had never before had to use; with husbands dead or lame, and with low cotton prices putting financial pressure on even the owners of many acres, women found ways to augment the family income. Sometimes they did sewing, became postmistresses, took in boarders, taught school, sold eggs and butter to merchants in local towns, or found any number of ways to supplement what the crops brought in. Probably in most cases women used the money they earned to pay for their families' necessities, but certainly such income augmentation also helped on occasion to pay for the black woman who daily had first to care for the white family before she could care for her own.

Freedwomen had minimally more freedom than before the war, and they along with their husbands had the benefit of a slightly larger portion of their agricultural output. The sharecropping system—despite the hard work, poverty, and constant moving from farm to farm—meant a greater control over their lives than they had enjoyed as slaves. Black families were more intact in freedom than in slavery, and black mothers did not have to fear losing their husband or children through sale. Still, most black women could look forward to lives filled with back-breaking toil, long hours, and extremely limited upward mobility. Yet poverty was far better than slavery.

For many white women, the net economic result of the Civil War was a fall in their standard of living. The price of cotton fell, state and local taxes increased, and many of their husbands and sons either did not return from battle or came home missing a leg or an arm and found their productive capacity lessened. White women, particularly the increased number of war widows, were often forced to find employment, but even when they had to earn money, their domestic duties did not lessen. They still had hungry mouths at home to feed and the laundry to do. Women's lives were no longer confined to the home, but their lives were enriched little by their gainful employment. One of the common justifications for attracting textile mills to the South was that they would provide badly needed job opportunities for women and children; factory work, however, meant long hours, boredom, danger, bad pay, and little or no upward mobility. Perhaps one of the reasons southern white males so glorified the image of southern womanhood was because they somehow understood how dreary and unrewarding the reality of life was for their mothers and wives.

From a modern perspective, farm women of both races had a very confining existence. Most days and early evenings were filled with the unending chores associated with running a household in days before modern conveniences (which, it later has turned out, are not as liberating as futurists had once hoped). All the food had to be home grown or at least processed at home. All the water used in a household had to be drawn from a well or spring and carried to the home. The cooking was done on wood stoves, and of course wood had to be cut, brought into the house, loaded in the stoves, the fires tended, the ashes taken out. Washing and ironing clothes required arduous labor, with clothes agitated in a huge pot over a low fire using a stick, complemented with hand-rubbing the wet clothes over a corrugated "rub board." The clothes were wrung by hand, then hung on lines or fences or obliging tree limbs to dry. Those that were to be ironed had to have starch added, and the irons were heavy "iron" devices that were heated on the stove or fireplace and had to be held with a rag. The whole enterprise was hot, tiring labor that was especially hard on the back, making many women stooped at an early age.

Childrearing in an age before paper diapers or diaper service, preprocessed baby food, or supplemental infant formula, was equally arduous. Women performed these duties without ceasing, having seen their mothers so burdened, and expected little relief in the future. Economically better-off white women turned, as we have seen, to black women for help; but most white women could not afford paid assistance, and black women often had to do double duty, for they had responsibilities at their own home. Older children as a matter of course were involved in the work of childrearing and running a household.

Rural farm women's lives revolved around their domestic duties. There was no money or leisure time for extensive traveling or the kind of drawing room culture associated with upper-middle-class women in northeastern cities. What few diaries exist reveal preoccupation with the affairs of everyday life: comments about when the peas will be ready to be picked, the setting hen about to hatch, a neighbor's child sick with the croup, and the number of jars of jelly and jam put up. This represented a body of concerns separate from men's, and to that degree a separate women's culture existed, but it was more matter of fact than self-conscious, and little theorizing was devoted to it. Even in music there seems to have been some gender differentiation, with women usually singing ballads and sentimental parlor songs in domestic situations, while men occasionally sang humorous and bawdy songs outside the home. It was also usually the men who played the fiddle or banjo. But certainly when families sat around on long evenings and sang for their own entertainment, both men and women (and children, too) knew, loved, and sang together most of the common repertoire. Women especially were involved in the church, and not just as hearers of the word but as doers too. They taught Sunday School classes, organized themselves into societies to visit the sick and raise money for various church needs, and planned days to beautify the graveyard. By some form of alchemy women combined their courage, grit, and love for family members to produce an often surprising zest for living. Such women discovered hope, purpose, and joy in their mundane endeavors. In their church participation, through songs and tales, by the comforting ties of kinship and friendship, and by means of simple forms of folk recreation, ranging from camp meetings to quilting parties, they found a way partially to overcome the dreary vicissitudes of poverty and unceasing labor. These were not women without spunk, and they often overcame in spirit what they lacked in worldly wealth.

Even while women in the late nineteenth century could not vote and were presumed to have no expertise in politics, they were at least as aware as their husbands were of their family's economic plight in days of falling cotton prices. Women as well as men understood that the economic system was not working well when a season of hard work left them further in debt at the country store. The Grange movement had offered farm women an opportunity to visit and commiserate with neighboring women, and the Farmer's Alliance meetings were often family affairs. Farm women read the Alliance and later Populist newspapers, occasionally wrote pungent letters to both, and emboldened their husbands to work for reform. The economic injustice associated with sharecropping in an age of agricultural surplus, high interest rates, and both restricted markets and sources of credit, served to bend rigid gender roles. But while farm women were morally outraged at injustice, advocated economic change, stiffened their husbands' reform backbones, and sometimes wished wistfully for the vote themselves, an aggressive women's rights movement did not develop among southern farm women.

Urbanization in the South lagged far behind that of the Northeast and Midwest, but there was a proliferation of marketing towns in the South after the Civil War and gradual growth of the old port, river, and railroad cities. Southern women in towns and small cities had many more opportunities to interact with other women and organize themselves as various interest groups. There had long been women's societies attached to churches and benovelent societies of various kinds, including temperance societies. The Woman's Christian Temperance Union (WCTU), the best known of these, first began in the North in the mid-1870s, and by the early 1880s WCTU clubs began being organized across the South. Even earlier, women in several northeastern cities had formed women's clubs of various names but aimed less at societial ills than at the self-improvement of their individual members. By the final two decades of the nineteenth century the women's club movement had spread to the South, and every small town soon had an organization of women seeking self-education in literature, music, new developments in science, and the like. Black women had separate but similar clubs for self-improvement. In an age when there were few opportunities for women to get post-secondary education, these women's clubs answered to a strong hunger for learning, a sense of community outside the household and more inclusive than the members' own church, and a seldom articulated discontent with the limits placed on women's lives by social habit.

State federations of women's clubs were soon organized, and after 1890 state federations in the South affiliated with the General Federation of Women's Clubs, a national association. To some degree this national tie broadened the agendas of the southern clubs, but primarily their purposes evolved in relation to local concerns. The appeal of these clubs to informed, energetic, upper-middle-class women was in direct response to the limits they found elsewhere in society. By the turn of the century the club women sought ways to inject their values into the larger society. They held to traditional women's values in that their concerns dealt with matters of health, aesthetics, education, cleanliness—attitudes normally associated with women's nurturing responsibilities in the household. But with their increasing self-confidence in these values, women broadened their concept of the household, recognizing that good health, good morals, good education, and "higher" values should not be confined to the home.

Women began to seek ways to extend their nurturing skills to the community around them, and as such their clubs evolved in purpose from self-culture to community service. By 1900 women's clubs in the South were advocating health reforms in the schools, clean water fountains in towns, playgrounds, city beautification projects, and cleanliness standards for dairies and city markets. They worked with male politicians, pressuring them through increasing public awareness of their aims and raising funds to begin pilot projects that they then shamed the men into taking over as public responsibilities. Long before they won the right to vote, southern white women in particular organized and committed, worked for civic improvement, and both helped usher in the Progressive movement in the South and represented the ethos of the movement. Black club women were also avid promoters of efforts to benefit their race.

Historians have long been aware that the churches offered an important arena for women's activity in the South. Even in the antebellum era southern white women through their churches had organized for benevolent purposes, raising money for charity, for funding Sunday Schools, and for supporting church programs of many sorts. In the postbellum period church women expanded these activities, and in many cities female leaders in evangelical churches progressed from efforts on behalf of their local churches to broader denominational activities to work ultimately on behalf of such inter-denominational movements as the Woman's Christian Temperance Union and general programs focused on community uplift and social betterment. Frustration engendered by the discrepancy between such women's community-improvement agendas and their political disenfranchisement often led to support for women's suffrage.

Yet clearly the progression was not always thus from evangelical churches to the campaign to vote. Research on women's reform activities in Galveston, Texas, for example, suggests that at least in older, more established southern urban regions, elite women from Episcopal and Presbyterian churches first responded to the social problems associated with urban growth. These women organized a variety of church-based associations that addressed a range of urban ills. When, in the case of Galveston, the great hurricane of 1900 in effect wiped the slate clean, in the face of that unprecedented challenge elite women with strong connections to the male political establishment pioneered a broad range of responses that prefigured, promoted, and institutionalized what historians have labeled Progressivism. Such white-gloved elite women identified urban community ills, diagnosed solutions, and worked to achieve both short-term and permanent reforms and regulatory agencies. Ultimately many of these women from the social and economic elite became effective proponents of their right to vote. Women's involvement in politics, reform, and suffrage was both varied and complex, but women were heard, and they learned how to be effective.

PROGRESSIVISM, SOUTHERN STYLE

The election "reforms" devised by the various southern states in the final decade of the nineteenth century had been rationalized as precursors to honest politics by removing the possibility of black votes being bought or stolen to promote one party or another. We have already seen how devastating these new election procedures—poll taxes, registration requirements, literacy or grandfather clauses, and the like—were on black participation in politics. Not incidentally, hundreds of thousands of white voters, too—the very ones who had been most apt to support political radicalism—were also eliminated from voting. Soon most states completed the process by developing white Democratic primaries. In one sense, the primary was more democratic than the old procedure of having a caucus of party bigwigs pick party candidates, and initially primaries were used only on a local or county level. South Carolina first began the procedure on a statewide basis in 1896, but the development rapidly spread throughout the South.

Since the majority of southern voters were Democrats, and blacks had been largely eliminated from voting, the white primary effectively became *the* election that counted in most of the South. Most counties did not even have an active Republican party organization or, if one existed, it was an empty shell of a party that continued mainly as a way to get patronage jobs (at the post office, for example) from Republican presidents. Hence the winner of the Democratic primary was a shoo-in in the official election and, in fact, all the competition, hoopla, and enthusiasm associated with politics revolved around the primary. The official election was anticlimactic, with the turnout only a tiny percentage even of the reduced vote of the primary.

With blacks effectively eliminated as voters and the Republican party uncompetitive almost everywhere and practically nonexistent in most places, the locus of political conflict shifted to the Democratic white primary. In fact, by doing away with party caucuses, the primary opened up white politics to influence by organized pressure groups, and by disenfranchising blacks and most dispossessed whites, politics was rendered safe enough to allow spirited debate among competing factions of white Democrats. The result, in every southern state, was the emergence of a bifactional politics that pitted a variety of reform forces against the forces of status quo. The South was a region of one-party politics, but under the umbrella of that one party there was significant protest, competition, and pressure for change. Yet the most effective promoters of change, aware of the bitter controversies of the Reconstruction and Populist eras, tried to throttle radicalism and modulate the call for reform by appealing to southern tradition. The perceived necessity to work safely within the confines of the possible often cast a conservative shadow even over the most significant reform efforts of the period, particularly with regard to race. To an unfortunate degree, Progressivism in the early twentieth-century South was for whites only.

Yet there were some restraints on reform everywhere in nation, and the social drag of racism and tradition in the South did not completely thwart the reform impulse. There was a notable Progressive movement in the South—a recognition that the region had severe problems and needed an effort to solve them. Every historical event has antecedents, and Progressivism was obviously related to its rural predecessor, Populism. Yet the relationship between the two was not always obvious, and the sources of support, even the desired social outcomes, were often quite different. Populism at its most radical sought to repudiate the competitive basis of modern capitalism and return society to an earlier model of political economy founded on cooperation and face-to-face relationships. The stinging and demoralizing defeat of 1896, accompanied by fraud, violence, and broken promises, caused many Populist supporters simply to withdraw from politics, more disillusioned than ever with the modern market economy. But then farm income improved in the several years following 1896, taking even more of the edge off political protest. Muted prosperity associated with urban growth, an increase in manufacturing—particularly textiles in the Southeast, iron and steel in Alabama, and the beginning of the oil industry in Texas, Louisiana, and Oklahoma— and the gradual rise of an urban-commercial-professional-industrial middle class in the South created new support for change.

All the problems of farmers had by no means been solved, and a significant portion of the Populist agenda was taken up by the new breed of reformers, especially the call to regulate railroad rates in many states and to control monopolistic purchasing practices for certain crops, such as the effort to end the domination of the tobacco trust in the Black Patch tobacco region of Kentucky in the early twentieth century. But there was a different tone, a different vision of the future, among Progressive reformers. In large part because of where they lived and how they made their living, the urban middle-class reformers were not at war with modernity. They accepted the idea of competition, large-scale industry, and the market economy; they simply wanted the system to work more fairly, more efficiently, and to the maximum benefit of the majority. In other words, the Progressives believed in what at the time was called good government.

This concern with the commonweal had several origins. The genuine excesses of unregulated capitalism—brutalization of employees, vicious competition, environmental destruction, exploitation of child laborers, and nightmarish unconcern with cleanliness in food processing—produced a counterreaction in the South as well as in the nation, and national magazines and published exposés fueled indigenous anticorporation sentiment among many southerners. Humanitarianism burgeoned, and many comparatively well-off urban dwellers became sensitive to the poverty and injustice surrounding them but not actually impinging on their own lives. This growth in moral consciousness came in part from the moral outrage that had often marked Populist reformers in the recent past and in part from a handful of urban ministers and denominational leaders and publicists who developed a new social consciousness that represented a mild regional variant of the Social Gospel. And, almost phoenix-like, the old ideology of southern progress first articulated in the New South movement of the 1880s reemerged, chastened of its easy optimism and now recommending a series of reforms necessary to facilitate prosperity and progress. This new ideology of progress emphasized the aspects of southern life that had to be improved if the South were to enjoy abundance and partake of the American dream.

The result of these various and often complementary sources of reform was a cornucopia of efforts, large and small, to remake the South. Farmers should diversify their crops and practice scientific agriculture, hence the promotion of agricultural colleges and the development of model farms and the farm extension service. Education was seen to be a prerequisite to economic growth, so many efforts arose to improve schools, train better teachers, and enforce school attendance. Diseases such as hookworm and pellagra were slowly recognized to be sapping southerners of both races of the energy necessary to be efficient workers or students, so agencies arose to promote cleanliness, sanitary toilets and water supplies, uncontaminated meat and dairy products, and to attack infestations such as hookworm. Urban experts were called upon to make cities cleaner, provide the rudiments of a public health system, and develop efficient governing mechanisms for urban areas—the commission form of city government, for example, developed in Galveston in 1900 after the great hurricane had almost destroyed the city and forced its leaders boldly to consider new ways of meeting unprecedented problems. Staunton, Virginia, in 1908 pioneered the use of the city manager system of municipal governance.

The reform message, usually argued with the benefit of scientific data and advocated both for economic and humanitarian reasons, covered a broad range of activities. Farmers were taught new techniques and new crops; housewives learned improved ways of preserving and canning food; towns and cities developed sewage and water works and attempted to control the indiscriminate spitting of tobacco juice and the use of a common dipper at water fountains. Prostitution, drunkenness, abandoned children, victims of disease and industrial accident—all forms of evil and misfortune—found groups and agencies armed to combat them. Prohibition was a particularly divisive cause. The movement had begun in earnest in the 1880s with local option laws; supported strongly by women, rural voters, and evangelical Protestants, the movement in the early twentieth century began to focus on statewide prohibition. Georgia was the first state (in 1907) to become legally dry, and thereafter states were often in turmoil over the issue, with some states reversing their positions in subsequent elections. However, by 1919, when the Nineteenth Amendment passed with overwhelming southern support, every former state of the Confederacy except Louisiana had adopted state prohibition. Of course, no one should think that drinking alcoholic beverages ceased in the region. As always, many southerners had a casual or selective attitude toward the law, and some saw prohibition more as a way to restrict drinking by blacks than by respectable citizens such as themselves.

Businessmen addressed ways to improve the efficiency of their workers and, with an educated, healthy workforce, attract additional northern investment. Religious leaders dispensed charity to the destitute and battled such enemies of moral behavior as the whiskey distillers, though unlike northern Social Gospel ministers, they seldom constructed a theological critique of the social institutions that produced or allowed poverty and injustice. Women organized first in church societies or in culture clubs came to expand their conception of their proper nurturing role to include not just their homes but their communities. The result was an effective phalanx of female reformers who both identified social problems—in schools and food processing plants, for example—and worked for solutions. Most of these southern reformers were white, and most of them were blind to racial injustice and the special needs of the blacks, but despite their limitations the southern progressives produced a significant body of reform.

Reform proposals of course required changes in the social policies of industries, institutions, and individuals, so in the end reform led to politics. Reform meant pressure to change, meant regulation, meant developing standards and seeing that they were met. So whether the source of Progressive ideas was religion, general humanitarianism, the ethos of scientific efficiency, organized women's groups, or the lingering influence of Populism, the result came to express itself in the political arena. And the peculiar, changed politics of the post-Populist era—a shrunken plebiscite and the procedures of the white primary—contributed ironically to an effervescence of political debate and reform. Beginning on the local and state levels, southern Progressivism eventually partook of the national movement, eventually playing an essential role in Woodrow Wilson's congressional efforts to enact reform legislation. For the first time in over fifty years, southern legislators, whose seniority gave them disproportionate power in Congress, played a positive role in national policy.

The conservative Democrats and disillusioned Populists who had supported restricting the right to vote had been more interested in removing blacks from politics and preventing a recurrence of popular reform than in cleaning up politics—as the ostensible rationale had it—so whites could freely discuss the real issues facing their region. But once more history had a way of producing unexpected results. As discussed before, the development of the party primary and the abolition of the party caucus in fact made the Democratic party responsive to issue-oriented groups, as long as they were white. And the Progressive era generated many groups who had strong concerns about the ills of southern society, men and women who were motivated, informed, and willing to unite to effect change. Politics became the arena in which the issues of the day were debated, coalitions formed, and policies proposed to correct whatever various groups identified as societal problems. Southern political contests were hard-fought because the stakes were high—or so they seemed to highly motivated and committed reformers at every level of society. The Democratic party in local and state elections witnessed a new level of issue-oriented politics in the early twentieth century and a new kind of political leader.

A significant number of Progressive mayors, governors, and legislative leaders represented the southern genteel tradition, except that now they tended to be from urban areas. Educated, moderate, they calmly, almost scientifically studied southern problems and advocated cautious, rational solutions. They established boards to evaluate the conditions of various aspects of society and called upon experts to suggest proper action. Boards of health were one result, and commissions were formed to study and make recommendations. Urban Progressives—governors such as Andrew J. Montague of Virginia, Hoke Smith of Georgia, and Braxton B. Comer of Alabama—were genuinely motivated by a sense of *noblesse oblige* to serve the people of their state and thereby usher in progress and prosperity, and they intended by doing so to prevent potentially more radical change—the specter of a Populist revolt run rampant.

Such governors in fact did push through far-reaching legislation that improved the public schools and the public health, expanded the range of governmental services, and prevented the worst excesses of exploitative capitalism. Several states passed child labor laws and rules to regulate working hours and safety conditions in coal mines and textile mills. But perhaps even more important than the legislation passed were the boards and commissions that resulted, agencies that attempted to regulate railroads, insurance companies, and public utilities. Regulatory commissions often failed to meet expectations because commission members frequently were too close to the interests they were supposed to regulate, but the commissions usually prevented the worst abuses. Local civic organizations and state-funded agencies also did everything from providing agricultural extension services and demonstration farms to home economics instruction to hookworm eradication programs. Government on the state and local level gained a new importance and became far more pervasive in its influence for the public good. Government was, in the eyes of the urban Progressives, society's helpmate, not its enemy. But another type of Progressive politician emerged too, one whose roots clearly went back to Populism and whose appeal was more visceral and less dependent upon experts.

Like some effervescence from the agrarian radicalism of the past, in several southern states popular leaders arose who used an emotional appeal to the interests of the common people to win political office and push through legislation that was narrowly progressive. In fact, in programs that they advanced these more rough-hewn leaders differed little from their more genteel urban counterparts who used expert opinion to promote their causes, but the often outrageous stump behavior of these popular leaders has frequently obscured their genuine and substantial reform efforts. With flamboyant rhetoric and resort to a politics of symbols, these skilled mass politicians, dismissively called southern demagogues, used their ability to win popular support to push against the obstacles to change. Conservative political leaders and institutions resistant to reform saw these politicians as unprincipled manipulators of the unwashed, and in truth occasionally these so-called demagogues blurred the line between truth and propaganda, honesty and corruption, public service and self-aggrandizement, but no more so than the opponents of reform did. In the rough-and-tumble world of southern politics, reformers did not always play by Sunday-School rules, and neither did their opponents. We should look more at results than process, but the demagogues were often so colorful that their antics deserve description.

Mississippi produced two popular leaders who revolted aristocratic planters. The first was James K. Vardaman, a tall, dramatic-looking man with his long black hair hanging to his shoulders, wearing a trademark white Prince Albert coat, a big black hat, and riding to rural political gatherings aboard an eight-wheeled log wagon pulled by twenty yoke of oxen. From the speaker's stand he held his audiences spellbound, his powerful oratory rolling out over the crowd and by turn inspiring them, angering them, and empowering them to believe they amounted to something. With the persuasive tools of the country revivalist, Vardaman—the Great White Chief, he was called—employed stark racism and class divisiveness to battle the establishment and push forward a remarkably progressive program for whites only. "He looked like a top-notch medicine man," Delta aristocrat William Alexander Percy said in derision, but Vardaman was governor of Mississippi from 1904 to 1908 and in 1911 rose to the US Senate.

One of Vardaman's protégés, Theodore G. Bilbo, after a short interlude followed the White Chief to the governor's office. Bilbo was a small, feisty, rat-terrier of a man, whose ability to employ invective and scurrilous sarcasm at his opponents' expense recalls John Randolph of Roanoke back in the Age of Jefferson. William Alexander Percy might call Bilbo a "pert little monster, glib and shameless, with that sort of cunning common to criminals which passes for intelligence," but Bilbo was the hero of the back-country rednecks with whom he cultivated an identity. Less an overt racist than Vardaman, Bilbo too shepherded modest progressive reforms through the Mississippi legislature.

The campaign style of Vardaman and Bilbo helped popularize the stereotype of the southern demagogue as a stock character in American political culture, but to the extent that the stereotype presents a one-dimensional portrait of the demagogue as simply a racist, it is false. Racist they were, as indeed was the society in which they thrived, but the so-called demagogues often understood the needs of the common man, even sometimes the blacks, and practicing politics as the art of the possible, they used Negro-baiting and verbal pyrotechnics to budge the status quo. The Mississippi pair, of course, were not the only such practitioners of mass politics.

In state after state there arose masters of political harangue who understood the common people and often articulated their needs and fears. Not all these so-called demagogues who became governors ever developed a program of progressive legislation. Some, like South Carolina's Pitchfork Ben Tillman, divided class against class mainly to get control of the Democratic party, but others were like Tillman's successor, Coleman Blease, who used his power to sway the textile workers to advocate changes that benefited the poor. Jeff Davis of Arkansas espoused radical reforms on behalf of the common folk and wore a Confederate-gray frock coat to complete the symbolism suggested by his name, but he was ultimately ineffective in the state legislature. And Georgia's Tom Watson had been a heroic figure battling the establishment in the heyday of the Populist revolt, but in the early twentieth century the meaner angel of his personality became dominant and he became a bitter, racist, Jew-baiting, anti-Catholic professional hater.

There were also significant reform politicians such as Governor John M. Parker of Louisiana, who hailed from the planter class (he was a prominent New Orleans cotton buyer as well) and showed that the Progressive impulse ranged from hillbilly radicals to planters and urban patricians. All in all, in the early twentieth-century South Progressivism was a multifaceted movement that lent Woodrow Wilson support on the national level. Yet in the final analysis the Progressive reforms that were enacted and the innumerable agencies and institutions that developed on the state and local level made only incremental progress in solving the deep-rooted economic and racial problems of the South. Even Franklin D. Roosevelt's more thoroughgoing New Deal found the impoverished South a daunting project.

INDUSTRIALIZING THE SOUTH

For most readers, any discussion of so-called southern demagogues and southern poverty in the early twentieth century produces ready images of woebegone sharecroppers and mountain hillbillies living in unkempt shacks amid eroded cotton fields or beyond the forks of the creek. The South was still poor and still primarily agricultural into the 1930s, but that stereotype of rural destitution insufficiently recognizes the degree to which industrialization had begun to change the economic landscape of the region. Cotton textile mills had, of course, begun to develop in the late antebellum era, but by the closing decades of the nineteenth century the textile mill village had become commonplace along the Piedmont of Virginia, the Carolinas, Georgia, and into Alabama. Powered by water, made profitable by cheap labor—much of it supplied by women and children—and often controlled by autocratic, if paternalistic, owners, textile mills provided dead-end jobs for almost one hundred thousand southerners in 1900, roughly one-third of the nation's textile workers. The pay was low, the hours long, the air filled with lint, and the employment precarious, but for many poor whites the prospects in the factory seemed brighter than in the cotton or tobacco fields.

Town leaders and investors saw cotton mills as a visible symbol of modernity and an object of civic pride even as they hoped to profit; occasionally, advocates of mills actually believed that providing factory jobs was a species of philanthropy. Yet, too often, poor whites merely traded agricultural poverty for mill poverty, and even though community support structures emerged in both the mills themselves and in the mill villages, they were seldom as strong and complete as those in rural agricultural settings. Textile mill workers' low salaries made them weak consumers, and the resulting low tax base hindered the development of such basic institutions as adequate schools. Agricultural poverty had similar results. The point is that a significant increase in industrial employment in much of the South should not be automatically equated with emergent prosperity.

Since colonial days many southerners had worked in the mines and the forests, but not until the end of the nineteenth century did the South engage in both extractive industries in truly large-scale fashion. Both northern and southern military engineers and topographers noticed evidence of significant coal reserves during the Civil War, but many of the best sources were too remote to be economically feasible. Only when railroads began to penetrate the Appalachian mountains in western Maryland, West Virginia, western North Carolina, and eastern Kentucky and Tennessee did southern coal find ready access to fuel northern industrial growth. One of the profound ironies of southern history is that about the same time that the national press discovered Appalachia and portrayed it as a region suspended in time—a sort of cultural fossil where our "contemporary ancestors" lived as they might have lived centuries ago—the region was being delivered to the industrial interests of the North.

Coal agents traveled through Appalachia buying for a pittance mineral rights, rails snaked up river valleys into the innermost recesses of the region, and ill-paid miners began their dangerous borings into the hearts of the mountains to cart out the fuel that fed the blast furnaces and factories of the nation. Even the small-scale efforts of the 1880s and 1890s had environmental consequences, but as the equipment and demands of the new century grew in size, mountains were literally devoured. The cost in both human and ecological terms was catastrophic. Grimy company coal towns dotted the region; miners died from cave-ins and noxious gases; and violence met workers' efforts to earn more than starvation wages. Some fortunes were made, but few of the fortunate lived permanently in the South. Cheap coal, low wages, and intimidated or sold-out governing officials made much of Appalachia an angry wound—hardly the romantic land of folk ballads and primitive customs described in travel and local-color literature. Bitter labor strikes, such as the one in the 1930s that caused Harlan County, Kentucky, to become known as "Bloody Harlan," finally brought to much of the nation's attention the complicated and often tragic results of untrammeled modernization and exploitation of a fragile human and natural ecosystem.

Like mining, the lumber industry had existed in the South since the colonial days. But also like mining, the scale and ecological effects of lumbering changed dramatically between 1880 and 1920. Of course the people of the South had long made their houses and barns and fences of wood, burned it for fuel, and laid ties under the rails that were increasingly binding the region into a nationwide economy. But in the final two decades of the nineteenth century, as northern urban growth mushroomed even as the forest reserves of the Northeast and Midwest dwindled, the demand for southern hardwoods in particular boomed.

Earlier logcutting had been almost a family activity, performed by fathers and sons and brothers when agricultural tasks allowed. Increased markets began to change the industry; in the Piedmont and coastal South logs were cut and hauled to railheads or rivers by ox-drawn wagons. In the mountains of Appalachia logs were cut and floated downs streams and rivers; sometimes when the water level was too low, loggers waited for spring rains or even built dams to stockpile water for scheduled releases. In these cases the rampaging logs gouged out the banks and damaged the natural water courses, but few involved in the lumber trade had strong environmental scruples. Agents for giant lumber companies roamed the South, buying timber rights. Much of the South's virgin forest still stood in 1880, with mighty hardwood trees of four to eight foot in diameter soaring 150 feet or more in the sky. In early logging days only the tallest, straightest trees were cut, trimmed, then pulled out by mules or oxen to the streams or wagons. But after 1900 train tracks increasingly reached out from huge hardwood and yellow pine mills into the surrounding forest. Steam-powered skidders replaced animals to pull the logs to waiting railcars, and improved band saws sped the process of felling logs. In 1900 about one-fifth of the southern industrial workers were employed in some aspect of the timber industry.

Clear-cutting techniques left the land denuded, producing problems of erosion. From Appalachia to East Texas, gigantic hardwood mills would enter a region, reach their rail tentacles out, quickly cut the forests, then close the mill and take up the rails and move on. Almost a century later embankments in second-growth forest are often a mute reminder of rail lines that once served a lumbering boom of giant proportions. On the eve of World War I southern lumber mills turned out billions of board feet annually. By the 1930s, with national demand at low levels and the great forests cut over, southern lumber production plummeted. Now primarily second growth trees were available, and on cotton-exhausted lands scrub yellow pine was a pale reflection of the forest that once swept almost unbroken from Maryland past East Texas.

On the very eve of the depression, chemist Dr. Charles H. Herty, working for the US Forest Service, perfected a process to produce pulp and newsprint from southern yellow pine. A prototype paper mill was constructed in Lufkin, Texas, in 1939, with production beginning in 1940, and a new southern forest industry was launched. Southern pine was the most ubiquitous of southern trees; it grew rapidly on poor, worn-out soil—often abandoned cotton fields; and the paper mills required small, short logs easily lifted by hand onto inexpensive bobtail trucks. With cotton production dying because of the boll weevil and many former sharecroppers underemployed because of farm mechanization (the tractor and the mechanical cotton picker), thousands of rural men to supplement their income cut pulpwood in off season and hauled it in old trucks over the network of farm-to-market paved roads that was being built in the South. The pulpwood truck became as much a symbol of the post–World War II South as had the cotton wagon earlier, and by mid-century the South was producing more than half the nation's basic pulp paper stock.

In 1861 everyone considered Texas a part of the South; a century later its regional identification was debatable, while Texans themselves often claimed with what had become typical braggadocio that Texas was a world unto itself. What made all the difference was oil, black gold, an unctuous combustible liquid that brought untold wealth to the state and transformed its economy and cities. As early as the mid-sixteenth century a remnant of Hernando de Soto's men, wrecked ashore eastern Texas, had used a gooey petroleum substance found floating in the water to caulk their boats. Later observers noted traces of oil and tar balls in the gulf waters, and on occasion oil seepage ruined water wells. Perhaps the first oil found on purpose was discovered in a shallow well near Nacogdoches, Texas, in 1866, but there was little or no market for the substance. Neither as lubricant nor as the basis of various patent medicines was oil in great demand. The first real production came in Corsicana, Texas, in 1894 as an incidental result of a well driller to provide artesian water for the town. Within several years the local glut of oil proved a minor environmental disaster; town leaders even attracted J. S. Cullinan from Pennsylvania in 1897 to develop the state's first commercial refinery, but still the economic viability of the petroleum was problematical. Slowly markets developed, with, for example, trains switching from coal to oil-fired boilers, but before the automobile with its gas-guzzling internal combustion engine, oil seemed a natural resource of minor significance.

The twentieth century would come to be known as the age of the automobile, and, auspiciously enough, the century had barely opened when the modern petroleum era began in southeast Texas. Captain A. F. Lucas, a military engineer who had worked in the salt domes of Louisiana, reasoned that great reservoirs of oil might be found trapped beneath the giant salt domes west of Beaumont, and with money raised from a variety of sources, including the Mellon fortune in Pittsburgh, he hired a small drilling company from Corsicana to bring their new rotary rig to a salt dome known locally as Spindletop. On January 10, 1901, the bit dug through the surface and hit the oil that was contained under great pressure in a cavernous chamber. The pressure blew the bit and rig out of the hole and a mighty geyser of oil spurted more than a hundred feet into the air. For more than a week 70,000 to 100,000 barrels of oil gushed forth each day, capturing the nation's attention. In the resulting oil rush drillers and investors swarmed to southeast Texas, with roughnecks, roustabouts, and wildcatters adding new terminology to the vocabulary of southern occupations. Hundreds of oil companies were incorporated within several years, including the predecessors of Mobil, Gulf, Exxon, Texaco—the industry behemoths. By 1902 Texas oil production totaled twenty-one million barrels, refineries sprang up across the region, along with the firms that provided oil tools, drilling mud, and technical know-how. Discoveries in the next decade added names like Sour Lake, Humble, and Goose Creek to the roll call of oil fields. The modern petroleum industry had been born; by 1930 huge oil deposits had also been found in Oklahoma and Louisiana, state legislation provided for a modicum of control of runaway production, pipe-line laws made access to refineries open to small producers as well as the established giants, and the South produced two-thirds of the nation's oil.

Oil fueled the growth of Houston, which came from practically nowhere in 1900 to become the South's largest city in 1950. Houston was one-sixth the size of New Orleans in 1900, and Galveston was the center of Texas commerce and ocean shipping. Then in September 1900 a hurricane devastated the island city, killing 6,000 people—the greatest natural disaster in American history—and Galveston was still suffering from this catastrophe when, barely three months later, oil was discovered at Spindletop. Galveston was in no position to respond to this new opportunity, so Houston investors seized the moment. Since its founding in 1836, Houston had had an inadequate link to the sea via a crooked, shallow, tree-overhung Buffalo Bayou, but years of lobbying finally paid off. In 1914 President Woodrow Wilson pushed a button in Washington, thereby firing a cannon that officially opened the Houston Ship Channel, a straightened, widened, deepened version of the bayou with a basin near downtown where ocean-going ships could be turned by tugs. At last Houston had direct access to the Gulf of Mexico. With both oil and shipping, Houston began a prolonged boom that would not cease until the mid-1980s. It became not only the South's largest city but the national and international center of oil production, technology, refining, and petrochemicals—and it was the nation's third-ranked port as well. Houston was the most spectacular example, but in similar fashion oil reshaped much of the region from Baton Rouge to Midland.

SOUTHERN FARMERS AND THE NEW DEAL

By the early decades of the twentieth century the South had achieved what a generation ago was called the take-off point for industrialization, but low-wage jobs in textile mills and extractive industries like coal mining and lumbering did not work an economic transformation of the region. Oil brought more wealth, but to a tiny minority in a limited subregion. Despite the economic changes, the growth of new industries and new cities, the South before World War II remained—as it had been for almost a century—the nation's poorest section. The South was still largely dependent upon the production of several staple crops, mainly cotton, rice, and tobacco; its farms were still far smaller than the national average; and the majority of its farmers were impoverished, possessed little equipment or machinery, were poorly educated, and worked as landless tenant farmers or sharecroppers. The major railroads, mining and petroleum companies, and lumbering interests had northern owners, and while the low wages remained in the South, the corporate profits flowed northward. Three generations after the Civil War, the South was an economic colony of the North, a source of cheap labor and raw products, dominated by an inefficient agricultural system that seemingly could not be budged off center. When Franklin D. Roosevelt called the South "the Nation's No. 1 economic problem" in 1938, the description would have been accurate for practically any date since 1865. And at the heart of the problem was an antiquated agricultural economy that had trapped millions of southerners, white and black, in abject poverty for generations. Simply too many people were trying to eke out a living on too little—and overused—

land. There seemed to be no escape from the vagaries of the fluctuating prices that agricultural crops fetched, farmers' debts, occasional drought and boll weevil infestation, and small, underequipped farms that offered no chance for profitability. The impoverished South of 1938 bore an unmistakable resemblance to the South of 1870.

In the aftermath of the Populist debacle of the 1890s, various spokespeople addressed the problems of southern agriculture. Reformers advocated crop diversification in the pages of farm journals and magazines and at agricultural fairs. Large, prosperous farmers in state after state experimented with improved breeds of livestock, crop rotation and diversification, and improved plows for deeper plowing and better cultivation techniques, but despite their demonstrations of the undeniable benefits that would result when their practices were followed, most small farmers were in no position to emulate their successes. The United States Department of Agriculture (USDA) similarly advocated improved farming techniques, and agricultural scientist Seaman H. Knapp of the USDA, using demonstration farms, proved to small numbers of agriculturalists the merits of reform. State experiment stations, colleges of agriculture, extension services, and editors like Clarence H. Poe of the *Progressive Farmer* all worked in vain to transform southern farming practices. The Smith–Lever Act of 1914 institutionalized along with the Federal Extension Service the kind of educational efforts Knapp had promoted, and the Smith–Hughes Act of 1917 provided federal grants-in-aid to support agricultural education in the region's high schools. Land-grant universities developed major agricultural research programs as well.

None of these well-intentioned efforts had significant success for the simple reason that the farmers who most needed to reform did not have the economic wherewithal to change their practices. Almost half of the farms had less than fifty total acres, and the improved acreage was even smaller. In 1920, for example, the average farm in North Carolina harvested only twenty-one acres, the average farm in Mississippi twenty-three acres. Most farmers had only one mule, practically no modern implements, a handful of chickens, perhaps a half dozen pigs, and many had a cow or two, although fully a quarter of the farms did not have a source of milk. How could such a farmer selectively breed his livestock? Which land could be removed from planting in the money crop to facilitate crop rotation or the cultivation of food crops?

Even had the acreage allowed, the landowner and the country store insisted that the farmers maximize cotton (or tobacco) production in order to pay off the sharecropper's debt for goods purchased on credit throughout the year. Certainly the worn-out soils needed more chemical fertilizers, but how was this to be paid for? How could a farmer dependent upon the credit of the local store for his very sustenance opt out of the cotton system and instead experiment with another crop? To make matters worse, no marketing mechanisms existed for other potential crops. Even for those small farmers who learned about alternative agricultural techniques and understood the benefits to be gained, such knowledge lay in the realm of impossible theory; there was insufficient economic freedom to experiment with improvement. Few, if any, small farmers, and no tenant or sharecroppers, could ever hope to save up enough money to buy and equip a dairy farm, for example.

Moreover, improved efficiency, deeper plowing, and increased use of fertilizer promised bigger crops, but that was as much problem as solution. Farmers were always plagued by overproduction that reduced the prices the crops brought. World War I temporarily stimulated the markets for all the South's agricultural products, and the year or two following the war promised unprecedented farm prosperity, but the prosperity proved dishearteningly short-lived. Cotton prices shot up, farmers calculated their profits and planned expanding their acres, then overproduction ushered in years of falling prices, bankruptcy, and debilitating poverty. Plagued at the end of the year with being unable to pay up at the store, farmers determined the following year to work harder and plant still more acres, with the result that prices fell further. Like ants in a doodlebug hole, climbing out of their economic trap was impossible for small-scale southern farmers. Slowly farm organizations and state politicians began to advocate voluntary acreage reduction, but no workable, region-wide enforcement mechanism was ever devised by the states. Effective crop reduction required that all states and all farmers participate. Louisiana governor Huey Long proposed a Cotton Holiday for a year, but when Texas refused to go along, the experiment failed. And if some farmers reduced their cotton acreage but others did not, the uncooperative farmers would benefit doubly. Even southern politicians, who had been suspicious of the national government for a century, began to understand that the problem of overproduction had only a national solution.

The South's agricultural dilemma was exacerbated by the stock market collapse of 1929 and by a prolonged drought that began in late 1929 and lasted through the following year. The region's crops were devastated by the most severe shortage of rainfall in the nation's climatological history. Output fell by more than half in many states, but even worse than the decline in cash crops was the loss in feed and food crops. The severity of southern poverty, even hardship and hunger, shocked outside observers. Insensitive novels, such as Erskine Caldwell's *Tobacco Road* (published in 1932) portrayed white sharecroppers as ignorant, physically and morally deformed, socially irredeemable trash, and this image was seared in the American imagination, but more thoughtful persons recognized the human tragedy in the region. The South's land, plowed for generations and subject to the summers' normal assault of thunderstorms that washed away the topsoil, was depleted of nutrients; nature was now sending a drought, but earlier, in the 1890s, the boll weevil had invaded south Texas from Mexico and, year after year, had marched slowly but inexorably northward and eastward across the South, a kind of insect version of Sherman, devastating all the cotton fields in its wake. Chronic overproduction, parching drought, inefficiently scaled farms, capital-starved farmers, boll-weevil-ravaged crops—was there no end to southern agricultural misery?

The South had long voted overwhelmingly Democratic, and when Franklin D. Roosevelt ran in 1932, the voters of Dixie gave the New York patrician their strong support. Roosevelt understood that the whole nation was in the midst of an economic crisis, and he was of an experimentalist temperament, willing to try practically anything to effect change. Most of his concerns and most of his advisers were northern, but southern congressional delegations, powerfully placed because of the seniority system, helped push southern issues onto the New Deal agenda. The major response was the Agricultural Adjustment Act (AAA), signed into law on May 12, 1933. The aim of the AAA was to eliminate overproduction by curtailing the cultivation of certain enumerated crops (including cotton, rice, and tobacco) and to prop up the prices of these enumerated crops to match the average purchasing power of the nations' farmers during the relatively prosperous years of 1909 to 1914 (for tobacco alone the base years were 1919 to 1929). The so-called parity prices and the reduced production would, it was hoped, begin to restore if not prosperity, at least survival. To persuade farmers to reduce their acreage, the AAA provided that in exchange for voluntarily reducing the size of their crops, cooperating farmers would be paid directly, and the funds for doing so would be derived from levies placed on the processors of the various farm products. Moreover, to help relieve the credit crunch that habitually crippled farmers, the AAA also established the Federal Land Banks.

Farmers had their cotton planted by the spring the AAA became law, and even though many farmers had previously felt there was something unnatural, almost irreverent, about plowing under crops, by the summer of 1933 they were desperate enough to try anything. The mules, however, long trained to walk between the rows avoiding the plants, were less flexible, and farmers reported great difficulty in persuading the stubborn draft animals to cast aside training and perhaps conviction and plow up the cotton plants. Nevertheless, almost 10.5 million acres of cotton were removed from cultivation in 1933, farmers received $116 million in direct payments, and—true to the forecasts—the price of cotton increased.

But the AAA was unable to save the small cotton farmers and bring relief to the hundreds of thousands of sharecroppers before it was declared unconstitutional in 1936. For small landowners the benefit payments (ranging roughly from $7 to $20 per acre), even with the slight increase in prices, did not spell the difference between poverty and prosperity. But for the large landowners whose acres were worked by tenants and sharecroppers, the AAA proved a bonanza. They could cut back on the cotton they planted, receive the AAA benefits, and evict croppers from the land because their labor was no longer needed. The landowners took the money and the landless laborers were left homeless. In theory some of the money should have gotten to the sharecroppers, and landowners were not supposed to reduce their number of workers, but the law provided no effective means of enforcement. Some argued that the benefits should only be paid to the small farmers, but the real purpose of the AAA was to reduce crop production, and that could only happened if the largest producers were involved. By the mid-1930s New Deal planners had devised the Federal Emergency Relief Administration and the Resettlement Administration, among other agencies, and although some farmers did get loans and were helped to acquire their own farms, the dimensions of the South's agricultural illness completely swamped the planners' tentative efforts to throw the sinking farmers a governmental lifeline. The intentions were good, but the immediate despair of the South's farmers was largely unsolved by the New Deal's direct relief programs.

Yet in other ways the New Deal helped set into motion a number of forces that would eventually help lift the South out of its economic mire. And other developments, incidental to New Deal policies, that helped reshape the South's economy and demography were going on apace. Imperceptible at first, the foundations for change began to be set in place during the 1930s that would make the decade of the 1940s a true watershed in the region's history. The point here is that New Deal programs, many of which were not directed specifically at the South, nevertheless helped transform the land of cotton.

Congress established the Soil Erosion Service in 1933, later renamed the Soil Conservation Service. This agency had no special southern agenda, but its services were especially needed in the region. The hilly farm lands, planted unremittingly in cotton and subject to the harsh downpours of summer thunderstorms, were badly eroded and leached of their nutrients—the South had more acres of badly eroded soil than all the rest of the nation combined. The Soil Erosion Service taught farmers the importance of contour plowing and terracing the hillsides, and provided funds for doing so. Crop rotation schemes were developed, with legumes and pasturage replenishing the exhausted soils. After World War II thousands of southern farmers improved their livestock-raising facilities by removing scrub timber from pastures and digging stock ponds, and the cost of these improvements to the farmers was reduced by subsidies from the Soil Conservation Service. By 1950 cattle had replaced cotton on many acres in the southeast. The Soil Conservation Service also engaged in a major and very successful effort to reforest the South, concentrating on planting hardy pines on abandoned cotton fields. The development of the pulp-paper industry beginning in the late 1930s proved the economic wisdom of reforestation and provided employment and supplemental income to many small farmers who learned to cut and haul pulp wood after crops were laid by.

Another grandiose government scheme was the Tennessee Valley Authority (TVA), which Congress established in 1933 to address the human and ecological problems of a large portion of the southern heartland. The purposes of TVA were flood control, soil conservation, reforestation, recreation, improvement of agricultural practices, and the generation of cheap electricity. Government studies of small mountain communities that were moved in order to avoid inundation by the system of TVA lakes produced a valuable by-product: sociological, economic, and demographic analyses of the southern poor. Begun with a spirit of idealism, TVA aroused much controversy from conservatives who feared government planning and involvement with local life. And, in truth, the economic payoff to the region did not really occur until after World War II. But TVA was one of the nation's first coordinated efforts to improve the socioeconomic well-being of the people of a large region. It exemplified the expansion of the accepted role of government.

The TVA was not the federal government's only effort with electricity. Of far greater importance was the Rural Electrification Administration (REA), written into law in 1935. Utilizing cooperatives whereby the rural recipients of electrical service also belonged to and supported the local electrical co-ops, REA brought low-cost electricity to rural areas where private enterprise had been hesitant to enter. Perhaps nothing since the development at the beginning of the century of Rural Free Delivery of the mail so changed southern life. Now farms could have electric lights, refrigerators, radios, water pumps, and indoor plumbing. Refrigeration made possible better food in the winter months, lessening the prevalence of niacin- and protein-deficiency diseases like pellagra. Rural mail delivery, radios, and the good roads movement—which had begun in the first decade of the century, received a powerful stimulus in 1916 with the Federal Highways Act, and proliferated in part because of state aid in the 1920s and 1930s—took hundreds of thousands of farmers out of the mud and rural isolation and helped them enter the American mainstream. Often the states utilized the labor of convicts to build the roads, an effort whose purpose was captured in the phrase "bad men make good roads." In truth, conditions in the road gangs were commonly brutal, and the workers were disproportionately black, but many Progressives believed such labor could be socially rehabilitative for the men at the same time that it improved the roads.

Better roads also meant that farmers could have part-time jobs in small towns and commute to and from their farm, thereby augmenting their income. Farmers could also sell their truck crops in neighboring towns more easily via paved roads, often accurately called farm-to-market roads, and growing truck crops helped many small farmers cope with the collapse of the cotton crop. As the boll weevil, crop reduction programs, and, later, farm mechanization reduced the number of full-time farm laborers needed, improved and especially paved roads often meant the difference between deprivation and a modicum of well-being for farm families.

The New Deal also produced a variety of relief agencies that provided many southerners with either a low-paying job or direct relief benefits. The great Mississippi River flood of 1927 followed by the unprecedented drought of 1930 had attracted national Red Cross attention. Relief payments then prevented widespread starvation and helped significant numbers of the poorest southerners come to accept the idea of relief. The Federal Emergency Relief Administration spent hundreds of millions of dollars in the South, but only scraped the surface of poverty there. The Civilian Conservation Corps with its Tree Army, the Works Progress Administration, and the National Youth Administration not only performed very worthwhile public services—building parks, lakes, recreation buildings, and so on that still benefit the region—but provided absolutely essential wages that literally saw many families through the nadir of the Great Depression. For the first time, millions of southerners came to see the federal government as a friend indeed. A hyperenergetic young Texas administrator, Lyndon B. Johnson, made that state's National Youth Administration a model agency, and he learned in the process powerful lessons about how the government could transform for the better the lives and hopes of distressed people.

Meanwhile, far-reaching changes were underway in the agricultural economy. The citrus industry began to prosper in the Florida peninsula and in the Rio Grande Valley region of Texas. Farmers forced away from cotton by the boll weevil and the AAA shifted to peaches, peanuts, soybeans, cattle and—increasingly after the 1930s—large-scale broiler production. Flue-cured tobacco was slow to mechanize and impervious to the boll weevil, and, in part because the market was controlled by several large tobacco companies, that industry managed its 1930s crop reductions better than cotton growers did. Tobacco farmers suffered in the Great Depression, but not to the extent that cotton farmers did. Cotton was already beginning to shift west to the drier soils of West Texas and later New Mexico, Arizona, and California. Boll weevil infestation was minimal there; the huge, level, irrigated fields were more accommodating to mechanization; and as a result the center of the cotton industry shifted away from Dixie to the New Southwest, but the full effects of this movement became visible only after World War II. Between 1900 and 1920 rice cultivation had also shifted west, away from the tidal areas of South Carolina and Georgia to the prairies of southwestern Louisiana, southeastern Texas, and the delta regions of Mississippi and Arkansas. Pioneered in this region by midwestern farmers who adapted reapers and giant tractors to rice cultivation, rice plantations were truly factories in the field. Well capitalized, organized by producers' groups, and amenable to AAA reduction plans, the southwestern rice industry managed to survive the Great Depression relatively intact.

Cotton, which had long dominated the South, was more traumatically affected by the forces of change in the 1930s than any other major agricultural industry. The boll weevil and AAA acreage restrictions proved a double whammy, and the result was a halving of the cotton acreage between 1930 and 1940. The source of agricultural poverty in the cotton regions of the South had been too many laborers and farms that were too small to be profitable. The shattering poverty of the depression years, combined with the expectation of jobs in the North (occasioned in part by post-World War I laws that increased the restrictions on foreign immigration), pushed and pulled the southern farm poor toward northern destinations. Southern blacks had the added incentive of escaping the virulent racism of Dixie. The result, over the whole first half of the twentieth century, was the largest internal mass migration in American history. Between 1900 and 1950 almost ten million southerners (equally divided between the two races) fled the region.

Black and poor white ghettoes developed in every northern city and in cities such as Bakersfield, California. The "Okie" phenomenon was much more widespread, in terms of both origins and destinations, than the powerful depression-era novel *The Grapes of Wrath* (1939) suggests. Southern culture, white and black, gained outposts far beyond the confines of the former Confederate States where cotton had once been king. While owners of larger, more prosperous southern farms had begun to purchase tractors in the 1930s, and, after years of experimentation, a workable mechanical cotton picker was finally developed at the very end of the 1930s, significant farm mechanization came only after World War II and was more a result of sharecropper migration than a cause of it. In fact, the vaunted mechanical cotton picker really depended upon new strains (hybrids) of cotton plants on which bolls grew higher up on the stalk and opened more evenly and upon chemical defoliants that caused the leaves to fall off so they would not contaminate the lint sucked into the trailers. Modern pesticides, huge tractors, and high-tech cotton farming really prospered on the giant agribusiness farms of the Texas plains and further west in the 1960s, not on the exhausted soil of the suffering South in the 1930s.

THE NADIR OF RACE RELATIONS

In agricultural practices the South of 1930 or so seemed almost indistinguishable from the South of 1900 or 1870. Poor black and white farmers walked behind mules in dusty cotton fields; lived in small, unpainted shacks made simply of planks nailed to a frame, without inner walls or ceilings; and stayed in hock to the furnishing merchant—powerless to change their lives for the better. The southern journalist Walter Hines Page returned to his homeland in 1902 after an absence of two decades and found life and labor practically unchanged; "pickled" was his phrase. "Southern rural society," he wrote, "has remained stationary longer than English-speaking people have remained stationary anywhere else in the world." But in one area there was change, and in large measure for the worse. Perhaps it should be no surprise that in an era of increasing agricultural poverty and the disillusionment following the Populist collapse, white racism increased. Blacks became the scapegoats for the frustration, poverty, and bitterness of poor whites, and the white establishment harnessed this displaced anger to thwart threats to its power. This was the nadir of race relations in post-slavery America.

Blacks were almost completely disenfranchised by the end of the century, but disenfranchisement is only one index of the dilemma. Lynching had long been a weapon of vigilantes in the South. Well into the 1880s it was frequently used against whites, but the race of its victims changed. In 1885, for example, of the 184 lynchings in the nation (almost all of which were in the South), 110 of the victims were white, 74 black. By 1900 the ratio had drastically reversed; of 115 total lynchings, 9 were of whites and 106 victims were black. Two blacks a week were lynched in the South. The numbers of lynchings decreased in the next three decades, but the overwhelming majority of victims remained black—53 blacks and 5 whites in 1920; 20 blacks and 1 white in 1930. Prominent white southerners, men and women, publicly and privately defended the lynching of blacks as necessary to defend Western civilization, the sanctity of womanhood, and the southern way of life. In fact, a distinct minority of lynching victims were accused of raping white women, yet in the rhetoric used to defend the heinous practice of lynching, rape was almost always the alleged crime being punished or being prevented.

Many lynchings were not secret affairs, conducted surreptitiously under cover of darkness or sheets. On the contrary, lynchings often became public spectacles, with huge crowds, voluntary participation, refreshments served, innocent blacks terrified, law enforcement officials averting their eyes. At some of the more outrageous events, any interested party could shoot, stab, hit, burn, or otherwise brutalize the victim. In the largest sense the respectable white society condoned such barbarities while members of the lower order did most of the dirty work. In 1898 Rebecca Latimer Felton of Georgia, a leading Methodist layperson, journalist, prohibitionist, feminist, and the first woman appointed to the US Senate, exhorted white men that "if it takes lynching to protect woman's dearest possession from drunken, ravening human beasts, then I say lynch a thousand a week if it becomes necessary."

Popular stereotypes and literary depictions of blacks revealed the heightened racial animosities during the 1890s and thereafter. The iconography of blacks degenerated. Children's books, cartoons, face mugs, miniature

Scene from a lynching. (National Archives)

statues for lawns, knick-knacks, and advertising all exaggerated the black phenotype. Every black male had grossly oversized lips, bulging eyes, and awkward posture; every black woman was rotund, with a shiny black face and a turban; every black child seemed to cavort unharmed with jungle animals and eat watermelon and appear not fully human. Often these images were not consciously vicious, although on occasion black males were depicted with razor in hand as though a quick slice was as natural as a handshake. Blacks were shown as decidedly comical or dangerous or ridiculous, never as mature, thinking, self-possessed adults; even the images that whites insisted were lovable were inherently demeaning to blacks.

Popular literature and film expressed identical images, as did vernacular humor. One of the more vicious literary portrayals occured in Thomas Dixon, Jr.'s, lurid bestsellers, *The Leopard's Spots: A Romance of the White Man's Burden, 1865–1900* (1902) and *The Clansman: An Historical Romance of the Ku Klux Klan* (1905). These two novels represented the darkest interpretation of Reconstruction, a vengeful period in American history when evil outside forces attempted to destroy southern white Christian civilization and mongrelize the population. Every imaginable stereotype was given memorable form: opportunistic, corrupt carpetbaggers hoping to enrich themselves; mousy scalawags bent on humiliating former planters; ignorant, smelly, barbarous blacks whose votes were manipulated by the carpetbaggers; beautiful white women, pious and genteel, subject to the animalistic desires of black beasts; and heroic southern white men fighting against all odds for civilization. The obvious stereotypes ring hollow today, but such images seemed to many white southerners at the turn of the century to capture essential truths about the last generation. Blacks were the foulest villains: no longer smiling, shuffling Sambos, but evil beasts. Such images lay behind the white defenses of disenfranchisement and lynching. *The Clansman* was loosely adapted as the story line for the 1915 movie *Birth of a Nation*, breathtakingly innovative cinematographically but reactionary in message. When Woodrow Wilson first saw this film with its stark portrayal of Reconstruction, he is said to have commented that this was history written with lightning. The racist portrayals of blacks, larger than life on the silver screen, were seared into the southern white psyche.

It is difficult for readers today to grasp how rigid and far-reaching segregation became in the South during the two generations after 1900. Blacks went to separate schools and churches, lived in separate parts of town (often called "nigger town" or "nigger quarters"), used separate water fountains and restrooms, and had separate waiting rooms; they were often prohibited from parks, playgrounds, and music halls; and they could not sit in a restaurant and order a meal—perhaps they could enter through a back door and eat in the kitchen with the cooks. Blacks had to sit at the rear of trolleys and in special train cars; they often could not try on clothes in department stores; they could not stay at "white" hotels but had to try to find black relatives or an obliging black family to stay with when traveling across the South, a dangerous trip even when not inconvenient. Curfews were enforced in some cities—Mobile in 1909, for example, required blacks to be off the streets by 10:00 PM. In every personal interaction with a white, blacks had to be careful to be properly deferential, to "know their place." The retribution for being "uppity" could be both economic and physical, and, if a white woman was involved, a black male even rumored to have breached in the slightest regard the racial etiquette was very likely to be severely beaten, castrated, or killed. Black prison inmates were victimized by the cruel system of leasing them out to private employers, and when that was reformed and replaced by the chain gang—building and repairing roads for the state—the violence was only moderated, not stopped. Violence toward blacks was the reverse side of southern gentility. Blacks often had no practical recourse but to grin and bear it or to flee the region; and millions fled. In 1910, fifty years after the Civil War, nine out of ten American blacks still lived in the South; by 1960, only six out of ten blacks lived in Dixie. In that half century, 4,473,300 blacks migrated from the South to the North and the West.

Blacks in the South constituted a society within a society. Blacks lived in segregated sections of cities, and black-owned businesses and a black professional class arose to serve their needs. Black leadership came disproportionately from this business and professional class, especially from ministers. Following the organization of the National Association for the Advancement of Colored People (NAACP) in 1908, black leaders joined the NAACP in hopes of advancing their race. Efforts in the South had to be cautious, gradual, and piecemeal. For most American whites, and probably most southern blacks, the preeminent black leader was educator Booker T. Washington.

Washington had been born a slave in Virginia in 1856, and after the Civil War his family labored in the salt works and coal mines of West Virginia. Eventually, through drive and ambition Washington graduated from Hampton Institute, and although he briefly considered other careers, a stint teaching at Hampton convinced him that education was to be his mission in life. In 1881, following the Hampton example, he founded Tuskegee Normal and Industrial Institute in Macon County, Alabama. All the staff at Tuskegee were black, and Washington promoted the college and his conception of a black self-help philosophy throughout the nation with great success. Undervaluing courses in the arts and humanities, Washington advocated a practical curriculum, essentially vocational. He believed that learning a trade and habits of self-discipline were the avenue to prosperity for blacks, and this prosperity, based upon their economic utility to the larger white community, he believed would eventually earn blacks the respect and support of whites.

In a famous speech in Atlanta in 1895 Washington had galvanized his audience with his vivid image of blacks and whites working together for common economic prosperity but remaining separate in social matters. Washington tacitly accepted social segregation and political disenfranchisement in return for white acceptance of limited black economic opportunity. This was precisely the message that whites wanted to hear (Washington's 1901 autobiography, *Up From Slavery*, became an instant classic in the up-by-the-boot-strap tradition begun by Benjamin Franklin's autobiography at the end of the eighteenth century), and Washington became the leading spokesman for blacks. Consequently, Washington became also the most powerful black man in the nation, and he used his power craftily and ruthlessly to maintain his position vis-á-vis the white establishment by undermining potential black rivals and opponents. Privately and secretly, Washington was more critical of segregation and worked to affect change in a wide variety of ways, but he accurately gauged the temper of racial sentiment in the white South and judged that a frontal assault on racism would be counterproductive.

New Englander William E. B. Du Bois, who was the first black to earn a PhD at Harvard (1895), disdained such temporizing and argued that a talented minority of blacks should work for enhanced opportunities in matters cultural and social as well as economic. Du Bois argued that Washington insufficiently appreciated black culture and history and was too deferential toward the regnant ideas of business capitalism. Du Bois's eloquent book of

Booker T. Washington. (Office of Public Relations, Hampton Institute)

essays, *The Souls of Black Folk* (1903), a kind of antidote to *Up From Slavery*, also became a classic and was particularly venerated by black intellectuals. The black community itself was divided on the proper response to segregation, but maneuvering room for southern blacks was extremely limited.

In the early twentieth century, as in slavery times, some blacks did learn ways to carve out more autonomy and freedom of action than the system would seem to allow. Black ingenuity, creativity, and an inextinguishable desire to maximize control of their own lives resulted in a limited degree of black progress, prosperity, and cultural expression in a desperately racist society. Black businessmen in certain trades, especially those with an all-black clientele, occasionally prospered, and the National Negro Business League by 1915 had dozens of chapters across the South. Throughout the region there were prosperous black stores, pharmacies, and funeral homes. Black banks, though usually small and prone to failure because of their depositors' weak resources, nonetheless sprouted across the South. Several black-owned and -operated insurance companies were founded, the largest of which was the North Carolina Mutual Life Insurance Company of Durham, established in 1899 by John Merrick.

Black churches grew rapidly in size and influence in the decades after Reconstruction, and frequently they were the largest religious institutions in southern cities. The churches ministered to a broad spectrum of human needs—social, educational, economic, cultural, and recreational, not just spiritual. Black women especially found in the churches an opportunity for service and growth, although the male ministers were often authoritarian. Black fraternal organizations and social clubs offered additional ways for finding an arena for self-expression and community service. Perhaps the most impressive self-help community organization was the Neighborhood League, founded in 1908 in Atlanta by Mrs. Lugenia Hope, the wife of Atlanta University president John Hope. The Neighborhood Union success-fully advocated street, sanitation, and educational improvements in the city's black neighborhoods. But while it is important to recognize black victories over the system, one should never minimize the prejudice, poverty, injustice, and violence that afflicted southern blacks in the midst of what was ironically labeled the Progressive Era.

During the course of World War I approximately fifty thousand Ameri-can blacks, most of them from the South, served in the military. Most of them had auxiliary duties, but some were combatants and, due to their bravery and ferocious fighting, they suffered casualties out of proportion to their num-bers. When black soldiers returned home after the war, they found racism just as entrenched as before. The war might have been intended to make the world safe for democracy, but democracy was for whites only in the American South. Black soldiers were less willing after their military experience to turn the other cheek to repeated insults and injury. The result, in response usually to unprovoked assaults by whites, was a series of deadly race riots in Longview and Houston, Texas; in Knoxville, Tennessee; in Elaine, Arkansas; and in Tulsa, Oklahoma. The North, too, was wracked with a string of bloody con-frontations, and a newly emergent Ku Klux Klan found as strong an accep-tance in the North and West as in the South. Catholics, immigrants, and out-siders in general, not just blacks, were the victims of the resurgent KKK of the 1920s.

Southern rural blacks in particular, though, were pummeled with repeated blows of hateful racism, random violence, and a cotton economy ravaged by boll weevils and overproduction. Blacks were hardly in a position to withstand the collapse of the sharecropping system. When, during the Great Depression, planters reduced their crop acreage and kept the government reimbursements to themselves, blacks had no means of defending their interests. When white government officials disbursed welfare payments and severely discriminated against blacks, no effective black challenge could be mounted. Whites, often ravaged by the depression themselves, could rarely find within themselves the moral resources to be magnanimous toward the poor blacks in their midst. In this context, the effort of the NAACP to chip away legally at the monolith of segregation is a tale of heroism and persistence.

One of the first efforts of the NAACP was through research and publication to reveal the extent of lynching in the South. A study was issued in 1919, but had little effect, and in 1929 Walter White, executive secretary of the NAACP, published *Rope and Faggot: A Biography of Judge Lynch.* The NAACP, with the help of northern liberals, tried to push federal antilynching legislation through Congress. Southern congressmen fought these efforts hard and successfully. Although Eleanor Roosevelt encouraged her husband to propose racial reform, Franklin D. Roosevelt thought his New Deal programs too dependent on southern Democratic support to risk alienating southern congressmen on the lynching issue. The concern of southern whites—especially the Association of Southern Women for the Prevention of Lynching, organized in 1930 by Jessie Daniel Ames from Texas—over the damage to the South's reputation caused by lynching gradually limited the evil. By the late 1930s the number of blacks lynched annually fell to eight, then six, then two, in 1939.

The NAACP attacked discrimination in voting and higher education. A series of cases mounted in Texas in the 1930s culminated in 1944 in a Supreme Court decision, *Smith v. Allwright,* that outlawed the white primary. And in Maryland Thurgood Marshall, a black attorney on the staff of the NAACP, successfully challenged state laws that prevented an otherwise-qualified black applicant, Donald Gaines Murray, from attending the University of Maryland's law school. A Baltimore municipal court in 1935 and the state supreme court the following year agreed with Marshall's logic, and the law school was desegregated. A similar case originated in Missouri with the application of Lloyd Gaines to the all-white University of Missouri law school. Marshall ultimately won this case in the US supreme court in 1938. These two cases dealt only with postgraduate education, but Marshall and the NAACP were encouraged to hope that careful legal argument carried all the way to the highest court of the land would eventually be the key to desegregating the nation's entire educational system.

As storm clouds of war rose over Europe at the end of the decade, few observers of the South fully understood the significance of the changes underway. Blacks were leaving the South in record numbers, propelled by crushing rural poverty, the constant threat of violence, and continuing racial discrimination. The boll weevil, crop limitation policies, and the bare hint of farm mechanization suggested that real agricultural change was imminent. The courts seemed to reformers to be the mechanism to break the nearly fatal hold of legal segregation. But taken as a whole, the South still seemed to be pickled in time, as Walter Hines Page had described it, rather than a region on the edge of transformation. W. J. Cash, a North Carolina journalist who had a morbid fascination with the South and a penchant for overripe prose, summed up his critical evaluation of the South's entire history and—in *The Mind of the South*, published in 1941, now universally considered a classic—deemed the region's history tragically marked by continuity with the past. But he was writing of the South he had known. Even so probing an analyst as Cash could not foresee as the decade of the 1930s closed that the South was nearing the end of an era. Events in the next decade and a half would reconstruct the South more completely than had the Civil War and Reconstruction four score years earlier.

EMERGENCE OF A SOUTHERN LITERARY TRADITION

Southern blacks hardly dared hope throughout much of the first four decades of the twentieth century that their condition would improve; for them, change usually meant a decline. And most southern whites, given the rigidity of their intellectual and religious worldviews, could not imagine a South significantly different from what they had experienced. For complex reasons the South was a world apart from the rest of the nation during this period, aggressively resistant to outside criticism and with an underdeveloped tradition of self-criticism. In the North, Protestant theologians in the several decades following 1880 developed a penetrating religious critique of the social institutions that produced poverty and injustice, but such analysis was almost completely absent among southern Protestants. Most of the historical and memoir writing that followed the Civil War defended the Confederacy and its leaders and, even when the end of slavery was accepted as ultimately beneficial to the South, the institution was remembered, by whites at least, as benevolent on the whole. In the words (1929) of the first great historian of slavery, Georgia-born but Yale-teaching Ulrich B. Phillips, "their [planter] despotism, so far as it might properly be called, was benevolent in intent and on the whole beneficial in effect."

The imaginative literature of the generation following the war consisted on the whole of sentimental, romantic fiction about plantation life, with happy darkies and gentle planters. Thomas Nelson Page perfected this genre of writing, and through such stories as "Marse Chan," published in *Century* magazine in 1884, he perpetuated the memories of white southerners of a lost utopia and catered to a growing acceptance by white northerners of the southern idyll both as an implicit criticism of northern industrialism and urbanization and as a reflection of their belief that southern whites knew best how to handle the race problem. In several novels and many stories, the best of which were collected as *In Ole Virginia* (1897), Page portrayed the blacks of the Old South as dependent Sambos who revered their masters and mistresses. Joel Chandler Harris, on the other hand, in his Uncle Remus stories that retold in dialect black folklore and folktales, presented, along with a panoply of stereotypical images of plantation blacks, a counterimage of blacks who often possessed a sensitivity, an ability to care for others, and a depth of folk wisdom that made them seem more authentically human than the hegemonic whites.

Yet another popular genre of southern belles lettres was local color, a form that was enormously successful. Despite the popularity of many of these writers, a surprising number of whom were women, this literature is little known today and even less read. But authors such as Frances Courtenay Baylor, Sarah Barnwell Elliott, James Lane Allen, Mary Murfee, Sherwood Bonner, and Augusta Evans Wilson (with her spectacularly best-selling *St. Elmo* [1866]) dominated southern reading habits during the generation following the Civil War. These local-color writers emphasized story, narrative, description, and character sketch. Seldom were their works experimental, psychologically probing, or critical of the region, the society, or middle-class values.

George W. Cable was one of the few exceptions to the conservatism of the local color school, for his depictions of Creole life in antebellum Louisiana (*Old Creole Days* [1879] and *The Grandissimes* [1880]) contained subtle criticisms of Creole racial mores, and his later essays on civil rights, *The Silent South* (1885) and *The Negro Question* (1890), were pointed in their critique of southern racial attitudes. Cable predictably became a persona non grata in New Orleans, and left the region. Another Louisianian, Kate Chopin, used the local-color medium to explore more boldly the contradictions of multiracial sexual mores in *The Awakening* (1899), the story of a woman who, dissatisfied with her marriage to a businessman, had an extramarital affair. Public outrage at such frankness practically made her a recluse, and she had difficulty publishing subsequent work.

Not until the very end of the nineteenth century did writing critical of the South, its racial views, its stultifying political establishment, and its continuing economic backwardness come to appear with some degree of regularity.

Walter Hines Page, a native North Carolinian, with safe editorial and publishing positions in Boston and New York City, led this appraisal of the South. By virtue of his editorship of such prominent national journals as *Forum* and *Atlantic Monthly*, he published his own essays and those by fellow southerners, like Edgar Garner Murphy, Edwin Alderman, William P. Trent, and John Spencer Bassett, that criticized aspects of southern life. Page, later in his life a prominent diplomat and US ambassador to Great Britain, was actually quite restrained, even diplomatic, in his censure of southern ways, and he hoped, by pointing out errors, promoting regional education, and prodding gently, to lead the South away from the errors of its ways. William P. Trent, who taught at the University of the South in Sewanee, Tennessee, was more blunt. His scholarly biography of William Gilmore Simms, the antebellum Charleston novelist, was scathing in its portrayal of the Charleston aristocracy and its arrested intellectual life. Trent founded the *Sewanee Review* in 1892 as a forum for open-minded, critical analysis of southern life and letters. Trent left Sewanee for Columbia University in 1900, but the journal he founded there is extant.

In 1902 another young southern academic, John Spencer Bassett, founded an even more South-focused journal, the *South Atlantic Quarterly*, at Trinity College, the predecessor of Duke University. In those pages Bassett forthrightly rebuked the South for its racial attitudes, its intolerance, its absence of a critical spirit, and its politics of reaction. A storm of criticism arose over Bassett's essays, with demands that he be fired from Trinity College. The college boldly and successfully stood up for academic freedom, but Bassett understood the intellectual climate of the state. In 1906 he resigned and moved to Smith College, in Massachusetts. While some southerners were able to see the faults of their region and were courageous enough to publish their views, the region at large had no tolerance for criticism.

It was precisely that touchiness about criticism that made the South extraordinarily sensitive to the national coverage, in 1925, of the trial in Dayton, Tennessee, of a young school teacher charged with teaching biological evolution in defiance of a state law that forbade teaching "any theory that denies the story of the Divine Creation of man as taught in the Bible, and to teach instead that man has descended from a lower order of animals." Actually the act that made teaching evolution illegal had little support, but few legislators, clergymen, and educated laypersons cared to attract the antipathy of single-issue fanatics by criticizing a law they expected to be more honored in the breach than in the observance. Then the American Civil Liberties Union advertised that it would provide free legal services to the first person charged with breaking the antievolution statute. John Thomas Scopes, science teacher and football coach, believed that evolution and the Bible were reconcilable, and since he used the state-adopted textbook that discussed evolution, he anticipated no problem with the law. In fact, there is little evidence he really taught scientific evolution as opposed to biblical creation. But town leaders, egged on by a northern engineer who managed a large mining operation locally, and hoping to put Dayton on the map, decided to protest the state law and convinced Scopes to take up the challenge. The case exploded into a major national press extravaganza.

Clarence Darrow, the great Chicago courtroom orator and self-professed agnostic, came to defend the right to teach evolution (and only incidentally to defend Scopes), and William Jennings Bryan, the aging three-time candidate for the presidency and defender of old-time religion, headed the prosecution team. H. L. Mencken, the outrageously iconoclastic columnist for the Baltimore *Sun* and coeditor of the *Smart Set* magazine, led the flock of journalists who came to Dayton to cover what was soon described as the great war between the forces of modernity (Darrow) and blind fundamentalism (Bryan).

When the trial opened, movie cameras were there to record the spectacle, and radio station WGN of Chicago broadcast live the epic battle. With Mencken labeling the case the "Monkey Trial," reporters from around the world rushed to describe, sensationalize, and ridicule the courtroom drama. Bryan willingly accepted the role of defender of the faith, although he, like most southerners, was not a fundamentalist in the modern sense of the word but rather was simply a biblical literalist. For Bryan, however, at issue was the true faith, especially when the antagonist, Clarence Darrow, was modern unbelief personified. Bryan was hardly a sophisticated Bible scholar, and was clearly past his prime; nevertheless, he let Darrow put him on the witness stand.

Darrow had no equal at interrogation and he annihilated Bryan by catching him in contradictions and forcing him to admit that there were parts of the Bible that even Bryan himself did not take literally—neither did most other southern literalists, who were conservative Christians, not fundamentalists, a northern-based strain of Christianity that did not really penetrate the South until after World War II. Though Bryan was made to look ridiculous and died several days later—a sure sign, thought the secularists, that modern views were correct—Scopes himself, practically forgotten by the mighty contenders and the press, was convicted and fined $100. The Baltimore *Sun* promptly paid his fines, Scopes was never sentenced to jail, and shortly the state supreme court overturned the verdict on a technicality. But the outcome of the case was less important than how the national and international press, following Mencken's lead, had used the Scopes trial to portray the town of Dayton, the state of Tennessee, and the South at large as the land of ignorance, prejudice, and reaction. Even more so than Darrow, Mencken was the master of ridicule, and with his acid pen he created and disseminated a devastatingly negative portrait of the South.

Mencken's diatribe against the South had begun in 1917, when he published a scathing essay entitled "The Sahara of the Bozart" in the New York *Evening Mail*, reprinted with access to a far broader audience in his book *Prejudices: Second Series* (1920). With hyperbole and acerbic wit the Baltimore critic surveyed the state of the mind in the South: "Down there," he wrote, "a poet is now almost as rare as an oboe-player, a drypoint etcher or a metaphysician." But worse yet, as for "critics, musical composers, painters, sculptors, architects . . . there is not even a bad one between the Potomac mudflats and the Gulf. Nor an historian . . . sociologist . . . philosopher . . . theologian . . . scientist. In all these fields the South is an awe-inspiring blank." Warming up to his subject, Mencken concluded that "In all that gargantuan paradise of the fourth-rate there is not a single picture gallery worth going into, or a single orchestra capable of playing the nine symphonies of Beethoven, or a single opera-house, or a single theater devoted to decent plays, or a single public monument (built since the war) that is worth looking at, or a single workshop devoted to the making of beautiful things."

Given Mencken's attitude, the Scopes "Monkey Trial," with all its attendant excesses, provided him with abundant ammunition to fire at the backward, provincial South, and fire away he did. But southerners far removed in geography and sophistication from the townsfolk of Dayton, Tennessee, read Mencken's dispatches, and as they did, anger and determination arose defensively in their breasts. None reacted more effectively than a group of poets, writers, literary critics, and historians loosely associated with Vanderbilt University. Several of them, including John Crowe Ransom, Donald Davidson, Allen Tate, and Robert Penn Warren, had begun meeting in 1920 to read and critique each other's poetry, and in the process they developed a methodology that later became known as the New Criticism. Between 1922 and 1925 they published some nineteen issues of an enormously influential little magazine, the *Fugitive*, and the writers themselves became known as the fugitives. The attitudes, styles, and talent of the group varied and evolved, but most of them, joined by other southern academics of similar spirit and men of letters, responded vitriolically to Mencken's regional put-down.

Led by Tate, Ransom, and Davidson, and joined by others—historian Frank L. Owsley, political scientist H. C. Nixon, and novelist Andrew Lytle— these self-styled Agrarians defended the South, its people, character, religious traditions, and folk culture from the likes of Mencken by portraying the region as a humane, people-centered folk culture as compared to the cold, urban–industrialized modern culture that had, sadly, they felt, emerged in the North. Twelve Agrarian authors published as their manifesto in 1930 a powerful book of essays, *I'll Take My Stand*, but this volume was more a heartfelt defense of the traditional South than a prescription of how that South might be nurtured and, God forbid, follow the path of the North. Yet the book was partially successful in trying to turn the South's localism and sense of family and place into sources of strength and pride, not symptoms of social pathology. The South should not become an undifferentiated part of the American urban–industrial behemoth. Barely beneath the surface of the debate was the reality of change. The forces of modernity, of shifting attitudes about race and economics and gender and politics—as well as literature—were beginning to tug and pull at a South stuck in the mud of poverty, racism, and religious and political conservatism. Some, like Mencken, wanted to throw out both the past and the present South and jerk the region into the future; others, like the Agrarians, understood some of the present problems, feared an all-new future, and desperately tried to mediate between the two. Yet another group of southerners were willing to usher in the future South with comparative alacrity.

If Nashville was the center of the orbit of the Agrarians, then the Regionalists revolved about Chapel Hill. The movement had begun in 1920 when Howard W. Odom came to the University of North Carolina as head of the Department of Sociology and the School of Public Welfare. Odom developed these academic divisions into centers for applying the methods of modern social science to the life and problems of the South, all with the intention of reforming, improving, and modernizing Dixie. Soon joined by an equally able colleague, Rupert B. Vance, Odom and coauthor published a series of influential books—*Human Factors in Cotton Culture* (1929), *An American Epoch: Southern Portraiture in the National Picture* (1930), *Human Geography of the South* (1932), and *Southern Regions of the United States* (1936)—that helped define what was called the Regionalist position. Sectionalism smacked of conflict and carried the aroma of the Civil War; Regionalism, on the other hand, suggested diversity within a cooperative context.

Odom founded the *Journal of Social Forces* and the Institute for Research in Social Science, both of which put the University of North Carolina in the national forefront of such studies and generated a powerful impulse for southern reform. Actually, both Vance and Odom liked more aspects of the traditional South than they were willing to admit even to themselves, but their work called for southern industrialization and urbanization, improved schools, public health measures, and rational politics. One of Odom's associates, W. T. Couch, editor of the University of North Carolina Press, edited in 1934 a volume entitled *Culture in the South* that, while it tended to refute H. L. Mencken, tended also to combine the Agrarian and Regionalist viewpoints, even to the point of containing essays by several Agrarians.

H. L. Mencken could hardly have imagined in 1917, when he first published "Sahara of the Bozart," or in 1920, when it was reprinted in *Prejudices*, or in 1925 when he covered the Scopes trial, that, partly in response to his writings, two such movements as Agrarianism and Regionalism would have resulted. But had he recognized yet another development, Mencken would have been alert to the irony that at almost the very moment he was attacking the literary output of the South, a magnificent outpouring of southern literature was just begining. That movement in general has gained the sobriquet of "the southern renascence."

Nobel Prize–winning novelist William Faulkner (born William Falkner in 1897) came to symbolize the rich tradition of southern literature that effloresced in the decades after 1925. Faulkner employed a dense, convoluted, hauntingly beautiful prose style to probe the human tragedy in "Yoknapatawpha," a fictional county in Mississippi. Not all his novels and stories were set in that imaginative distillation of Mississippi geography and history, but Faulkner cultivated the South's history and racial complexities to create out of local materials plots and characters involving universal dilemmas. The southern past, present, and future at times seemed to intermingle and war with one another in Faulkner's writing, and during the decade following 1929 he produced single-handedly a bookshelf of distinguished novels: *The Sound and the Fury* (1929), *As I Lay Dying* (1930), *Sanctuary* (1931), *Light in August* (1932), and *Absalom, Absalom!* (1936). Yet Faulkner had gained comparatively little fame or profit from his novels until Malcolm Cowley's *The Portable Faulkner* in 1946 introduced his complex fiction to a broader audience. And then the Nobel Prize for Literature in 1950 ensured Faulkner's fame. Before his death in 1962 he was universally recognized as one of the world's greatest literary artists.

But Faulkner was not alone. Thomas Wolfe in North Carolina in 1929 published *Look Homeward, Angel,* beginning a torrent of words that exemplified his intense love–hate relationship with his native region. Richmond, Virginia, had its own mini-renascence, beginning with Ellen Glasgow, two of whose later books, *Barren Ground* (1922) and *The Sheltered Life* (1932), were masterpieces in their own right. More exotic was James Branch Cabell, whose *Jurgen* (1919) was the only book Mencken had excepted from his attack on the aridity of southern literature. Erskine Caldwell wrote blisteringly critical portrayals of poor white culture, while Stark Young and Marjorie Kinnan Rawlings wrote more sympathetically.

Black writers, too, participated in the southern literary outpouring, with Langston Hughes, Jean Toomer, Countee Cullen, James Weldon Johnson, and perhaps especially Zora Neale Hurston with her *Their Eyes Were Watching God* (1937) making particularly noteworthy contributions; each of these authors used the black experience in the South as material for their artistic achievements. The outstanding black writer of the time, Richard Wright, published his most famous books just as the era was ending. Born, like Faulkner, in Mississippi, the child of sharecroppers whose father abandoned the family, Wright spent most of his youth in Elaine, Arkansas; Jackson, Mississippi; and Memphis, Tennessee living with relatives. His first book appeared in 1938, but it was *Native Son* (1940) that gained him instant acclaim. The major protagonist of the novel, Bigger Thomas, is one of the most memorable characters in all of American literature. Though the novel is set entirely in the North, it is a scathing portrayal of the racial tragedy of pre-World War II America. Five years later Wright's semi-autobiographical *Black Boy* presented a searing depiction of the violent racism he had encountered growing up in the urban South. Wright's South and the racial dilemma it represented haunted all his best books. In 1946 Wright and his wife and daughter moved to Paris, France, and, sadly, his subsequent writing, cut off from its sources, suffered.

All these authors—from Faulkner and Wolfe to Wright— were serious writers, the kind whose life and oeuvre constitute courses in university English departments. But the blockbuster novel of the 1930s has only recently been raised to the category of even semi-serious literature. On June 30, 1936, *Gone with the Wind* was published with an unheard of initial printing of one hundred thousand copies, yet the demand far outpaced the supply. Within six months one million copies had been sold, and the book continues to sell tens of thousands of copies annually more than a half century later. On December 15, 1939, the movie version by David O. Selznick premiered to enormous acclaim in Atlanta. The movie has been the most popular movie in the history of the media. No other novel/movie has so entered the national and regional imagination, becoming the central image in popular culture of the Old South, the Civil War, and Reconstruction. This stunningly successful work of fiction, a bulky novel of 1,035 pages, was written by a one-time Atlanta newspaper woman, Margaret Mitchell, in part for self-amusement as she recuperated from a lengthy illness. Little could she know that the long manuscript she had practically completed by 1930—and the only book she ever wrote—would transform her life.

On one level, the secret of *Gone with the Wind*'s success was its story line, a fascinating and engagingly told tale of war and tragedy and love and courage peopled with memorably sketched characters, all of whom quickly became part of American folklore: Scarlett O'Hara, Rhett Butler, Ashley Wilkes, Melanie Hamilton, Mammie, and Gerald and Ellen O'Hara. Even the plantation house, Tara, has become as much a part of American folk memory as Mount Vernon or Monticello. At the popular level *GWTW*, as it came to be called, was marvelous escapism for a South and nation mired in the Great Depression, with Scarlett's indomitable will to overcome the post–Civil War poverty and destruction a metaphor for contemporary impoverished readers striving to pull themselves up from destitution.

Yet at another level Margaret Mitchell had written a novel that represented the inner struggle for the soul of the South that had been going on for several decades. Even as early as the propaganda of New South spokesmen like Henry Grady in the 1880s, there had been an implicit conflict between reverence for the Old South and a recognition of the need for industrial development. In different ways both the Agrarians and the Regionalists of the 1930s addressed this issue. The South was undeniably the least economically advanced region of the nation, with a particularly distressed agricultural economy. How could prosperity and urbanization—modernization, in short—be brought to the region without a loss of certain older values and without acceptance of the imagined crassness and impersonalism of the industrial North? This inner tension that played itself out in the works of Edwin Mims and Howard W. Odom provided the deeper mainspring to the story that Margaret Mitchell spun. *Gone with the Wind* depicted less a moonlight-and-magnolia romance of the Old South than a hard-fought conflict between modern and traditional values in the post–Civil War South, and that fictional controversy that mirrored historical experience elevated the novel above being simply escapist literature.

The characters of Margaret Mitchell's book were representations of images and aspects of the South: Ashley Wilkes was the idealistic but impractical Old South; Melanie the sentimentalized southern belle cum plantation mistress; Rhett Butler the hard-headed critic of the antebellum South's fire-eating arrogance, who nevertheless ultimately could not accept the New South's modernizing trends; Scarlett O'Hara, in her willingness to cast aside the ruffles and pretensions of aristocracy and do whatever was necessary to regain prosperity—including running a sawmill and hiring and firing employees in decidedly "unladylike" fashion—to a degree personified what the New South had to do to escape its past of backwardness and poverty. And yet Scarlett longed for the love of Ashley, and when, finally, she recognized that Rhett was her true love, he had already rejected her and the new ways she represented and returned to the myth of the older South. So the novel does not end with the two lovers living happily ever after—nor had the South quieted the war within. But that is not *GWTW*'s only departure from pedestrian historical romances. Scarlett O'Hara is ultimately depicted as a strong, take-charge woman, no wilting southern belle. She takes her life and her situation in her own strong hands and creates her own destiny. As such, Scarlett takes the southern woman off the pedestal and puts her in the middle of history. The movie version is far more traditional, stereotypical, and romantic in its portrayal of changing southern ways than Margaret Mitchell's book, and she was justifiably upset by the liberties movie producer Selznick took with her creation. The book *Gone with the Wind* is a pioneering work of fiction that deserves more than popular success.

SOUTHERN MUSIC

Southern writers in both the high and popular art forms—from William Faulkner to Margaret Mitchell—gained readers and admirers in the North and throughout Europe. The South as a historical place and as an imaginary construct became familiar to readers outside the region. Yet the South thus understood did not always bear close resemblance to reality. Even more problematical was the movie version of the South. Most of the early film portrayals of Dixie were unrelentingly romantic—*Hearts in Dixie* (1929), *So Red the Rose* (1934), *Steamboat 'Round the Bend* (1935), and *The Littlest Rebel* (1935) starring Shirley Temple—escapism for Depression-era viewers with blacks presented as loving, comically simpleminded, deferential Sambos skilled at little beyond soft-shoe. Perhaps this was some improvement over the vicious imagery of *Birth of a Nation,* and it gave employment to some gifted black actors and actresses, but it indicated that neither southern nor northern audiences, nor the movie moguls behind the productions, had a very sophisticated historical understanding of the South, past or present. And the movies, even while they reflected sentimental southern white attitudes about the region, were Hollywood productions, not genuine southern cultural artifacts. Through the cinema the North and the world got a secondhand version of the South that seldom provided a glimpse of the real folk and folkways of Dixie.

However, one quintessential southern folk art found its way beyond the region and came to have an enormous worldwide impact. Southern literature found audiences above the Mason–Dixon Line and across the seas, but southern music has proved even more universal. The first southern style of music to move beyond the region and become part of American popular culture was ragtime, a highly rhythmic, syncopated style of music whose origins lay on the old plantations. The fiddle and the banjo, complemented with foot stomping and hand clapping, had been an energetic, joyful kind of dance music, and in the latter part of the nineteenth century, as the piano became increasingly popular, innovative black musicians adapted the form to the keyboard. With a new instrument and an old musical style, so-called ragtime music was especially popular in the barrelhouses of lumber camps, in bawdy houses, in saloons, and in honky tonks.

Scott Joplin, a classically trained black musician and composer from Texarkana, Texas, heard the music and incorporated it into short compositions called piano rags. His most famous piece was the 1899 composition "Maple Leaf Rag," named after a club in Sedalia, Missouri, where he occasionally performed. The sheet music version became a best seller, the first of many ragtime compositions that proved profitable to publishing houses. (Many people today know Joplin only through the music in the movie *The Sting,* although the Houston Grand Opera's 1970s version of his folk opera *Treemonisha* was seen on public television nationally and toured several US and European cities to great critical acclaim.) By way of published sheet music, ragtime piano compositions entered homes across America, and a variety of composers, many white, absorbed the style and began to write popular pieces, one of the most famous of which was the national hit, "Alexander's Ragtime Band," by Irving Berlin. Other black writers and musicians, such as Eubie Blake, kept ragtime alive for audiences of both races, rural and urban, throughout the nation. At first proper white audiences were scandalized by ragtime, but it soon became sanitized, domesticated, and harmless, though in such popular form it was a far remove from its bawdyhouse roots.

Black blues, too, spread beyond its southern black roots in the field hollers, work shouts, and spirituals of the slave community, but it never moved as far from its origins as jazz did. Blues songs were secular, individual rather than group performances the way slave spirituals had been, and they usually spoke of personal despair, racial injustice, crushing poverty. But when the individual blues singer performed, his or her listeners could identify with the singer's plight and feel the desperation, anger, and sense of release. Often the solo performer accompanied himself with a guitar, with the instrument—sometimes its sound transformed by sliding a bottle or pocket knife along the strings—used almost as a second voice to accentuate the singer's words or answer them. Such blues arose almost simultaneously in the Mississippi Delta and in East Texas, and in Texas the style was influenced by cowboy, German and Czech, Cajun, Mexican, and other styles. The rural blues was almost always a solo male singer accompanying himself on the guitar.

Singers such as John Hurt in Mississippi and Blind Lemon Jefferson in Texas were extremely influential, but it was another trained black musician who, like Scott Joplin with ragtime, really broadened the appeal of the blues. William C. Handy's band was playing in the Mississippi Delta when he first became aware of the power of rural blues, and, absorbing the raw style, he began to write music for his largely brass band that incorporated the new music. Handy soon moved to Memphis and found employment in the clubs and brothels associated with Beale Street, and the rural blues, moved to an urban context and adapted to a wider range of instruments, found a popular audience among the blacks who had crowded to the cities for jobs. Handy's most famous composition was "St. Louis Blues," and others began to write urban, band-backed versions of the once rural blues, with singers male and female singing lyrics that touched black listeners.

In 1920 a young black woman from Ohio, Mamie Smith, recorded two songs, and the record proved enormously popular with southern blacks. Then when Columbia Records in 1923 began recording Bessie Smith, usually accompanied with a brass-dominated band (once including a young trumpet player named Louis Armstrong), the blues found its first superstar and one whose extraordinary popularity with black audiences nationwide awoke the recording industry to the size of the black market. Bessie Smith, originally from Chattanooga, Tennessee, became a blues singer known around the world.

If the roots of ragtime and blues were rural and black, the origins of jazz were urban and more ethnically complex. Jazz represented a creative blending of music of many types and from many peoples: African, Caribbean, and European; religious music, secular music; minstrelsy, ragtime, blues, and brass marching bands. This heady mixture most often occurred in cities, and most often of all in New Orleans, and it was primarily instrumental music. While the instruments were mainly of European derivation, and the occasion for playing was often to accompany social dancing, which had become a national pastime at the turn of the century, the black urban musicians in particular drew upon African-American traditions to create a new blend of music that was characterized by syncopation, antiphony, polyrhythm, blues notes, and especially virtuoso instrumental improvisation. Perhaps the first to perfect a recognizably distinct sound that came to be called jazz was the black New Orleans trumpeter Charles "Buddy" Bolden in the period from 1895 to 1907. But almost simultaneously, musicians, black and white, in New Orleans, Memphis, St. Louis, and other river towns connected by the Mississippi River and its showboat bands, contributed to and helped develop the style.

This infectious, individualistic, and improvisational style of music spread through several white bands to Chicago and thence to New York. First spelled *jass* and considered lascivious because of its association with bawdyhouses, the music was domesticated, popularized, had its spelling standardized to *jazz*, and became a national vogue soon after records began to be pressed in 1917. Hence Americans in general first came to know essentially white "Dixieland" jazz that was one step removed from the music as it originated in New Orleans. It was not until five years later that the initial recordings of black jazz musicians were made, with Joseph "King" Oliver and Louis Armstrong leading the way. The music took the nation by storm, hailed by many as a fresh, energetic, liberating art form and attacked by others as indecent and undisciplined. But for many people, George Gershwin's adaptation of the form in 1924 with his "Rhapsody in Blue" represented the legitimating of a powerful, distinctly American style of music. Louis Armstrong in particular became practically a national icon, and his trumpet playing and scat singing (nonsense syllables) made him world famous. Today jazz is played, listened to, and loved around the globe, from Russia to Japan, and it has continued to evolve, absorbing still newer influences.

Recording had first been the medium whereby southern folk musical expression reached a large public, but it was the development of commercial radio broadcasting that created a national awareness, then a market for the broadest form of southern music, variously called hillbilly or country music. Southern radio stations began broadcasting in 1922, and, eager to fill their programming hours, they sought local entertainers. When local singers and instrumentalists began to perform, local listeners immediately responded, and this response led to more entertainers, more recordings, more broadcasts, and the proliferation of the musical form. Commercial record producers often incorrectly portrayed the music and the performers as the product of either the southern mountains or western ranches, and the performers just as often accepted the commercial image, even adopting appropriate costumes and stage names untrue to their origins. This was true for the music of all areas of the South.

This was also truly the music of the white folk, with voices and styles influenced by a broad catholicity of traditions. It was the kind of music that families sang in their parlors or to friends; it was heard at house parties and at barn dances; it represented the values, the ethos, the pains and joys, of the plain folk of the rural South. This music did not arise in a vacuum but rather it grew out of sentimental parlor songs, variations upon ballads and dance music from the British and European past, and every new kind of music with which the folk came into contact—jazz, Tin Pan Alley, minstrel melodies, brass bands on steamboats plying the southern rivers, Hawaiian music, blues, and Mexican and Cajun music. White southerners had always been eclectic about music; they simply accepted music they liked from whatever source and made it their own. They little cared, for example, that "Dixie" was the composition of an Ohio-born minstrel singer, or that "Carry Me Back to Old Virginia" had been written by a Long Island black songwriter. The lyrics themselves are an index to the complex concerns of the folk: conflicting opinions toward modern ways and modern inventions; expressions of wanderlust and carousing and love for home and dear old mom; protests about working conditions and irreligion and a lost way of life; and unrequited love and love casually offered. Country music lyrics represented a wide range of political viewpoints too, from praise of new inventions, such as Mr. Ford's Model A, to conservative opposition to change to radical protests of economic injustice, bad working conditions, and environmental destruction. The voices were seldom polished; rather, in raw, unaffected ways this was the authentic expression of the plain white people of the South, who, though mostly rural, even when they had moved to the towns and cities retained the outlook of the countryside. In the music of the Carter family, of Jimmie Rodgers, and myriad others, southern families in the 1920s and 1930s found spending evenings by the side of the radio to be not only entertainment but also a means of achieving self-awareness.

Programs such as the "Grand Old Opry" and the "Louisiana Hayride," and various barn dances, created an industry in response to the folk music of the white South, and entertainers and songs entered the mainstream. The music evolved and grew, from the simple mountain music of Appalachia to Bob Wills's Western Swing, with its broad range of instruments, and its use of jazz and the big band swing sound. In the south of Texas, Mexican influences produced "Tex-Mex music"; in Louisiana there developed a distinct Cajun form of music; as a result of the increasing use of electrical amplification in the noisy beer joints of the Texas oil fields there emerged loud, often rambunctious "honky-tonk" music. In 1934 a gifted singer from Tioga, Texas, named Gene Autry, made the first of the singing cowboy movies, creating a popular new form of cinema and reinforcing the western image of what would soon be known as "country and western" music. Americans everywhere came to know this wide range of music, and like jazz, it effected popular music of all styles in this nation and spread throughout the world.

Closely related to so-called country music, if not a subset of it, was gospel music, a genuine expression of the folk piety of the region. A variety of influences created gospel music, and black composers and singers made major contributions. Songbook publishers had traveling quartets that introduced new songs, peddled the newest song books, and absorbed the newest musical trends. Radio programs, all-day singings, and singing schools conducted by the itinerant song masters were other means of promoting gospel music, and many young people who learned to sing in their church quartet—like Elvis Presley, who was born in Tupelo, Mississippi, in 1935—later moved to blues, country, and, in the 1950s, rock. The influence was two-way, with the gospel sound identifiable in much secular music and vice versa. The piano-banging secular singers and hell-raisers Jerry Lee Lewis and Mickey Gilley are cousins of piano-banging religious singer and pentecostal revivalist Jimmy Swaggart. The music spanned the spectrum. As in the other forms of southern music, gospel has entered the American mainstream, with songs like Thomas A. Dorsey's "Precious Lord, Take My Hand" and "Peace in the Valley" and Albert E. Brumley's "I'll Fly Away" becoming special favorites. Dorsey was black, Brumley white, but listeners of both races loved their songs and seldom knew the racial background of the composers.

One of the greatest cultural productions of the South, indeed the nation during the first four decades of the twentieth century, was its varieties of folk music. In the same way that Mencken in his "Sahara of the Bozart" diatribe of 1917 and in later writings had not foreseen the literary outpouring now known as the Southern Literary Renascence, his snide comments about music showed no awareness of the richness of the folk music traditions. In fact, Mencken had in mind when he bemoaned the state of culture in the South the institutionalized high culture of museums, symphony orchestras, and grand opera. Yet their relative absence in the South of 1920 or so was not an indication of congenital southern backwardness but rather was a symptom of the poverty and rurality of the South. Museums, symphonies, and opera companies require the wealth and numbers of supporters that only big cities can offer, and the South of 1920 had no big cities other than New Orleans. The Crescent City had the size, but Mardi Gras absorbed the money and leisure that elsewhere flowed into high art. So Mencken's observation about the absence of a certain kind of high art was accurate, but his analysis of why was wrong. In more individualistic, less expensive art forms—a writer writing, a singer singing—the South's creativity blossomed. Only later, after World War II, would rapid urbanization and greater wealth lead to major southern museums, orchestras, and opera companies. But in its literary productions and in the music of its folk, the South left its impress on the world.

NEW DIRECTIONS IN POLITICS

When Walter Hines Page had written in 1902 that southern life had been "pickled" for decades, by which he meant that it seemed impervious to change, politics was one of the key factors he identified that kept the South stuck in the ways of the past. It is easy to accept the general features of such an argument. Southern politicians had had little national influence and a scant national role since 1861—the Wilson presidency being an exception— and with the largest arena closed to them, it was only natural that politicians tried to identify and promote provincial interests. No candidate running from the South had sought the presidency since 1860. What did it benefit a leader to advocate a national agenda if in so doing he risked losing his office? In a region with only one viable party, how did one differentiate oneself and gain public support? An often accepted way was to use rhetorical excess to gain attention, a ploy that worked especially well if the oratory attacked safe enemies and promoted policies that promised to help the economically depressed masses.

Here was a situation primed to allow a proliferation of demagoguery, and leaders skilled in invective and empty promises arose in plenty. Certainly some politicians were serious and tried to deliver on their promises, but on occasion promises were more a means to gain political office than to help the needy. Racism was always the convenient means to galvanize political supporters. As blacks were increasingly disenfranchised, antiblack political rhetoric intensified. Now no potential black votes were to be lost, and antiblack sentiment could be counted on either to keep supporters in line or to threaten and destroy political enemies.

Too often, all a politician had to do to gain and stay in office was rant about blacks, recall for his listeners the threat of northern domination and Republican rule, and hoodwink the poor white voters at the same time that the entrenched business interests were surreptitiously served. The losers were the white majority, all the blacks, and ultimately the South as a whole. Despite not inconsiderable Progressive-era reforms, most of the region's people were left untouched by the policies of good government advocates. Often the business environment was more improved than the quality of life of the average person, and Progressive reforms were far more evident in the large marketing towns and cities than in the countryside, where most southerners lived.

It is difficult for modern readers to comprehend the quality of life that was obtained for most southern folk practically down to World War II. Imagine a region whose per capita income was less than half the rest of the nation; a region where the average white child attended school for fewer than three months annually, and the black child even less; where modern medical care was unavailable; and where the incidence of disease, tooth decay, illiteracy, infant mortality, murder, and practically all other bad social indices were significantly higher than elsewhere in the nation.

The typical farmer, white or black, was a sharecropper, living in a shotgun shack two or three rooms deep. Many such farmers did not even have an outdoor privy. Shallow water wells, unscreened windows, and incomplete acceptance of the idea of using soap helped the spread of micro-organisms. The typical shack was a wooden frame building, sitting off the ground on sections of tree stumps; the exterior walls were wide boards nailed to the frame, with narrow slats nailed over the cracks—tongue-and-groove planks were too expensive to use. Most such houses had neither a ceiling nor interior walls. Sometimes newspapers tacked or glued to the walls served as makeshift wallpaper to help keep out the wind. In cold weather the family huddled around a wood heater or stove for warmth and slept crowded together in bed. Drafts of cold air defeated even the hottest stoves, and through the cracks in the floor one could see the chickens and dogs and feel the chill wind blow.

The families living together in such uncomfortable homes, accustomed to hard work and little reward, often found succor in their religion, their love for one another, and their music and stories. They did not wallow in self-pity and through their folk art and culture persevered with their basic humanity surprisingly intact. But their poverty, their limited political and cultural vision, the degree to which they were trapped in their station in life, all contributed to a sense of quiet desperation. Yet hope for a better existence was never completely extinguished. It was that yearning, and that desperation, that both fueled racist demagoguery and occasional reformist crusades. And it was out of that milieu that three politicians would arise who would represent the transformation of the region from the post–Civil War colonial South of poverty and prejudice to the post–World War II South of relative prosperity and racial moderation. Huey P. Long, Lyndon B. Johnson, and James Earl (Jimmy) Carter both led and symbolized the emergence of the American South in the last half of the twentieth century.

Huey Pierce Long was born in 1893—in the midst of the deepest economic depression of the century—in Winn Parish, Louisiana, a county in the north central portion of the state that had been a stronghold of Unionist sentiment in 1861 and that gave the Populists the highest percentage of votes of any county in the South in 1896; a county, moreover, that on the eve of World War I saw a socialist slate of candidates elected in the county seat of Winnfield. This tradition of dissent has often been suggested as somehow influential in the gestation of Huey Long as a political leader, but that is far too deterministic. Long was, to continue the biological metaphor, a sport. He was, in his own words, *sui generis*, and it would be a mistake to see him as a twentieth-century version of the Populist revolt. But Long did understand how the poor people of Louisiana suffered, how the political establishment cared more about staying in power through serving the interests of the wealthy and powerful than addressing the serious economic and racial maladies of the state. Long understood the folk, knew how to harness their frustration, could ignite their hope for a better life and use it to promote his policies the way no one else could, and he was an absolute genius at speaking their language and gaining their vote. Whether he truly believed in their cause is problematical; what is certain is that he believed in his cause.

Even as a child Long impressed everyone with his energy, his brains, his sass, and his desire to be in the limelight. His rebelliousness kept him from being allowed to graduate from high school, but after a quick succession of salesman positions and several months of reading law at Tulane University, he was able to pass the state bar exam. As a lawyer his personality traits soon made him successful, but it was his race to become a member of the state railroad commission that first really indicated that he would be a force to be reckoned with. Barnstorming across the multicounty district in a secondhand Oldsmobile at a time when a car still attracted attention, Long drew upon his sales experience (and his phenomenal ability seemingly to remember every face and name he had ever known) to win a spirited runoff campaign. And once in office, Long began attacking Standard Oil and other big corporations and promoting the welfare of the common farmers. He quickly showed a flair for winning publicity, deflating his enemies with colorful nicknames, skewering them with pithy invective. He successfully presented himself as the selfless protector of the poor, doing battle against the powerful forces of Wall Street. Although he lost his first campaign for the governor's office in 1924, his ruthlessly efficient political machine was being perfected, and four years later he won the gubernatorial race. Baton Rouge had never seen anything like Huey Long before, nor had the nation, and the state would never be the same again.

Long took over the governor's office and the huge state bureaucracy like a man possessed. He would stop at nothing to get his programs through. If that required taking over the assembly with a combination of bluster, bribery, bullying, wily parliamentary maneuvering, and ruthless hardball politics, then so be it. Huey Long was not concerned with civics-class politics. He took Louisiana government by the neck and wrung out of it the results he wanted. His first priority was political power—staying in office—and Long understood that that was best achieved in a state accustomed to corruption, misrule, and poverty by catering to the palpable needs of the voting masses. Long correctly identified the interests of the people and capitalized on the pent-up desire for government help to solidify his position. The delivery of services was the means, through the agency of democracy, for Huey Long to rule Louisiana with the ironlike grip of a tyrant.

For the people the cost of preserving Long's power often seemed a bargain. The governor provided entertaining rhetoric, got in good licks against the traditional enemies of the poor—"pour it on, Huey" was a common refrain at his political rallies—and delivered real benefits: several thousand miles of paved roads, bridges across the state's numerous rivers, free textbooks for school children, and hospitals financed largely by increased taxes on the large corporations that were headquartered elsewhere but extracting Louisiana's mineral wealth. But the larger cost was in the principles of fair play, honesty, the rule of law. Long's political machine extorted huge sums of money ("deducts," short for deductions) by requiring that state employees give a certain set percentage of their wage as a mandatory contribution. Opponents, even principled ones, were crushed. Long manipulated the assembly with an utter disdain for rules and orderly procedures; he had contempt for anyone who stood in his way.

Long was not above using racist charges and innuendos when it served his political purpose. Unlike some earlier southern demagogues, ugly race politics was not Long's primary method, perhaps because he knew how to use other issues so effectively. But neither was Long very interested in providing significant government benefits to blacks, in part because they could not vote. We should not expect Long to have been anything other than a person of his times; however, his outrageous political corruption and ruthlessness have been excused because he supposedly did not use race-baiting and saw to it that blacks benefited from his programs. When they did so, it was only incidentally. In balance, Long was more concerned with maintaining his power than benefiting the poor, white or black. He was a populist by political strategy, an autocrat by temperament.

But Long did control the state the way no governor ever had, anywhere else in the nation. Even after being elected to the United States Senate in 1930, he spend an inordinate amount of time in Baton Rouge and thoroughly controlled his hand-picked successor, O. K. Allen. Long withstood an impeachment attempt, the concerted opposition of all "good goverment" types, and in essence was a Dixie dictator. "I'm the Kingfish," Long said, referring to the character on the popular "Amos and Andy" radio show. In the Senate, Long continued to gain press attention by extravagant antics. He soon broke with Franklin D. Roosevelt, proposed more radical solutions to the Great Depression with his redistributive scheme called "Every Man a King," and caused Roosevelt to call him one of the two most dangerous men in America (the other was Douglas MacArthur). Partly in response to Long's perceived threat, Roosevelt's New Deal policies shifted slightly leftward to preempt some of the Kingfish's appeal.

But Long's great self-described trajectory to become president came crashing down in a quick, bloody encounter in the corridors of his new capitol building in Baton Rouge one muggy September evening. Long had long been at odds with Judge B. Henry Pavy of St. Landry Parish, who remained a steadfast opponent of the Long political machine. During 1935 Long had apparently threatened the judge that if he did not prove more cooperative,

Long would spread an old rumor (dating from an earlier scurrilous opponent of Pavy's in 1910) that Pavy had "coffee blood"—a Louisiana euphemism for saying that some black blood coursed through Pavy's veins. A young Baton Rouge surgeon, Dr. Carl Austin Weiss, had married Pavy's daughter Yvonne. Somehow Dr. Weiss heard of the threatened smear both to his father-in-law and, by implication, to Weiss's wife.

On Sunday evening, September 8, 1935, shortly after tucking their infant in bed, Dr. Weiss told his wife he had to go out to see a patient. Slipping a cheap .32 automatic pistol into his coat pocket, he drove toward the spire of the thirty-two story capitol, parked his car, walked inconspicuously into the building, and stood behind a column. Shortly Huey Long came walking briskly down the hallway, accompanied by his retinue of bodyguards. Suddenly Dr. Weiss stepped forward with his hand outreached. Just as he fired a bodyguard slapped his hand, causing the bullet to enter Long's abdomen. A barrage of bullets from the guards then slammed into Weiss, and apparently a ricochet from that attack hit Long in the lower spine. In seconds it was all over—Dr. Weiss, his corpse riddled, lay dead in a pool of blood; Long was fatally wounded and died some thirty hours later. An inglorious era in Louisiana politics had come to an inglorious end.

For decades after Long's assassination the state's politics largely consisted of Long and anti-Long factions. The roads remained, the bridges stood, the children had textbooks. But the state's tolerance of political corruption still set it apart. Class and racial conflict marred the political process; Long had not promoted the idea that the purpose of government was to solve problems and to deliver services because people had a right to them. Rather, Long suggested that it was he personally who provided necessary services. Long did not attempt to persuade the citizens of Louisiana that the federal government had a legitimate role to play in their lives. In a sense Long did not routinize government; instead, governing for him was the means to personal power for no greater end. It would be another southern politician, equally energetic, equally concerned with power, who would promote the idea in the South that the purpose of government (and the purpose of power) was to improve the lives of constituents. Lyndon B. Johnson appreciated the positive role of the federal government, but despite the surface similarities to Long, LBJ was a very different kind of politician.

In 1908 Lyndon Baines Johnson, the first child of Sam and Rebekah Johnson, was born in Gillespie County, Texas, just west of Austin, the state capital, in a semi-arid region of rolling hills, springtime bluebonnets, outcroppings of limestone, and stark beauty. For his whole life Johnson had great affection for the county and its inhabitants, later purchasing a ranch there on the Pedernales River and turning it into his Texas White House. Sam Johnson, LBJ's father, was a tall, lanky, compassionate man, given to great outbursts of anger but possessing enormous personal charm. A farmer early in his life, Sam was, by 1904, a Populist-minded state legislator who traveled to Austin to represent his rural neighbors. But after marrying Rebekah Baines in 1907, Sam reluctantly did not run for reelection in 1908; instead, he had to support his wife and then their baby boy. Rebekah was an impressive person in her own right. She was smart, determined to make something of herself and her children, strong willed, and an unusually nurturing mother. Much of Lyndon's genuine compassion for the plain folk of his region, state, and nation and his fascination with politics came from his parents.

In 1918 Sam again became a state legislator, and he often proudly brought Lyndon with him to Austin. Little Lyndon, just ten years old, roamed the state capitol, listening to speeches and absorbing the bustle, the bombast, the camaraderie, and intrigue of Texas politics. When Sam went out on the hustings to seek votes, Lyndon was in his glory. If ever a child grew up in politics, it was Lyndon B. Johnson. He discovered how empowering it was to feel one was doing important things, to solicit and win public approval, to be a person of influence. Politics to him was the noblest profession, and from his parents he learned that the purpose of the political process was to serve constituents, to use government to improve the lives of the decent hill country farmers eking out a hard-scrabble existence on the rugged landscape. And Lyndon learned that to be effective one had to be noticed, had to be heard.

Everyone who knew Lyndon as a child remembered him for being a show-off. He was always wilder, or louder, or dressed flashier than anyone else, and in every classroom he did whatever it took to stand apart. Such behavior did not win everyone's favor, but everyone did sense that Lyndon was also, to use Huey Long's phrase about himself, *sui generis*. By the time he graduated from high school and entered Southwest State Teachers College in nearby San Marcos, certain of Lyndon's lifelong characteristics were well formed: he was a consummate political animal, he could persuade almost anyone to do what he wanted by talking right into their face, at times charming and beguiling and at times pleading and angry, and then again logical and impressive with factual analysis. When Lyndon got involved in campus politics, he was like a man among boys. He even had the highest school administrators on his side, and his political opponents felt that they had been both steam-rollered and snookered. Leaving behind him a trail of devoted friends and smoldering enemies, Lyndon graduated in 1930 with his political calluses well formed.

Lyndon had barely been able to scrape together enought money to attend college, and he borrowed money, worked odd jobs at the college, and had to drop out in 1927–1928 to teach school in the tiny town of Cotulla, near the Mexican border. There he taught in a segregated elementary school for Mexican children, and their poverty touched Lyndon's heart. He threw himself into the task with the kind of Johnsonian energy that later became legendary. He came to love the children and abhor their situation; he determined to enhance their self-image, inspire them to study, and motivate them to change their lives. He drove himself, the other teachers, and the students, but the children and their families loved him for his obvious devotion to them.

After graduating from Southwest Texas State Lyndon began teaching speech and debate at Sam Houston High School in Houston. Again he completely threw himself into the task; he inspired, cajoled, pushed the students to excel and win debate tournaments. He became their coach, their father figure, their champion. And again Lyndon found his heart going out to the children from poor families. He fervently came to believe that the government had a responsibility to its citizens; government should be a friend, a helpmate, not a distant, impersonal force. With his earlier political instinct and his experience teaching, Lyndon Johnson saw government as the means to an important end—improving constituents' lives. But of course one had to be in politics and win elections to help achieve that purpose.

In the fall of his second year of teaching, Lyndon's opportunity came. The newly elected congressman from his home district, Richard Kleburg, a member of the wealthy King Ranch family, was only nominally interested in the legislative, political aspects of his new position, and when an adviser suggested that old Sam Johnson's boy—an energetic political whiz kid—be appointed his secretary, Kleberg sent word to Lyndon to meet him in Corpus Christi. So excited he could hardly function, Lyndon came to the interview, got the job, secured a leave of absence from Sam Houston High School, and arranged to move to the US capital. On December 2, 1931, Lyndon Johnson was Washington bound, to a city he essentially never left again.

In everything but name Lyndon Johnson became a congressman in 1932. He was the hardest working, most driven, most compulsive congressional secretary and aide anyone had ever seen. He had an unquenchable hunger to know how the institution worked; he practically worked to death the office staff, but no one worked as long and hard and with as much intensity as he did. Kleberg let Johnson make decisions and handle constituent matters and intervene with various government agencies far beyond what his age and title suggested was appropriate, but Johnson was up to the task. He learned whom to contact to get a constituent's problem solved; he learned which congressman's office was effective; he asked questions and talked and absolutely mastered the art of congressional politics. Lyndon quickly impressed the power wielders in the capital, especially Sam Rayburn and eventually President Roosevelt. When Roosevelt pushed through the National Youth Administration (NYA) in 1935 to alleviate the problems of the youthful poor, Johnson used all his connections to win appointment as head of the NYA in Texas.

Once he became Texas director of the NYA, Lyndon poured his almost superhuman energy into the agency, determined to do all that was possible to improve the lives of young Texans. He seemed consumed both by the immensity of the job to be done and by the potential for good of targeted, compassionate, government action. Individuals, families, communities, and eventually the entire state, region, and nation would be the beneficiaries. At a time when most southerners were still suspicious of the federal government, Johnson understood the role it could play in addressing the ills of an impoverished region. Johnson's ambition for political power—for his own inner needs and for what he could do for the people—would not long be satisfied by the NYA, however, and when he saw an opportunity to run for a seat in Congress in 1937 after the incumbent congressman died, he threw himself into the campaign with the all-consuming energy with which he now seemed to approach every task he considered important. Cloaking himself with the support of Franklin D. Roosevelt and promoting the successes and connections he had gained through the NYA, young Lyndon won the election.

No sooner was he in Washington than Johnson showed he understood how political power was wielded. He quickly became a friend of such influential congressmen as Carl Vinson of Georgia and Sam Rayburn of Texas, majority leader of the House. The rough-and-tumble political practices of Texas were second nature to Johnson, and he campaigned with the compulsive zeal that was his trademark. In his first and most famous Senate race in 1948 he campaigned by helicopter, still a novelty and a sure attractor of crowds in small-town Texas. Politics in the Lone State were hardfought and often corrupt, and Johnson followed conventional political ethics in winning his Senate runoff election by the landslide margin of eighty-seven votes. But Johnson, once firmly in power, used the federal government as a tool to advance the interests of his district and state. He never lost sight of the political implications of any act, but he pursued power for a purpose larger than himself. Johnson was perhaps the first modern southern politician to understand that the South had to change its attitude toward the federal government if it wanted economic redemption. For Johnson a growing federal government meant the potential for good for the whole South, not something to be feared because it might interfere with southern institutions (i.e., segregation). In a very fundamental way the central government in the years following 1941 remade the South more completely than either the Civil War or the first Reconstruction did. Lyndon B. Johnson represented a new, forward-looking generation of southern politicians who understood that some changes had to come gradually, some could be pushed forthrightly, but that the lives of whites and blacks in the South would be improved as the whole economic pie enlarged. Johnson intended to profit too, and he surely did, but he never lost sight of the raison d'etre of national political power. As such he was the first modern southern politician.

But Lyndon Johnson had won the presidency with the identity of a Washington insider and a bigger-than-life Texan, not exactly as a southerner.

And Woodrow Wilson had successfully run for the presidency in 1912 as the able reform governor of New Jersey and former president of Princeton University. The honor of being the first clearly identifiable southern post–Civil War president would ultimately fall to a young Georgian who only came of age at the end of World War II. But as a child in the 1930s Jimmy Carter learned the lesson that the federal government could bring benefits. His father, like Johnson's, was an avid politico who often took his son Jimmy to hear campaign speeches. From his father and from family stories he heard about his maternal grandfather, Jim Jack Gordy, who supposedly had first suggested the idea of Rural Free Delivery of the mail, Jimmy Carter too learned that government could and should be a helpmate to its citizens. He remembered how, when he was 13 years of age, the New Deal-sponsored Rural Electrification Agency (REA) brought electricity to the Georgia countryside. But the change was not merely in running water and electric lights. As he wrote in his campaign autobiography, *Why Not the Best?* (1975), "Farmers began to have county and regional meetings to discuss the changes that were taking place in their lives, to elect REA directors, to discuss national legislation, to determine rate structures, to bargain with the Georgia Power Company on electricity supplies, and to determine which new areas would be covered next by the electric power line. In general our families' horizons were expanded greatly."

The perverse localism of the rural South was being changed; southerners came to understand that there was more to politics than race-baiting. But World War II was to bring even more of a transformation, both in economics and race, and Carter himself, a generation later as governor of Georgia (1971–1975), would announce to his state that it was time to put an end to discrimination. He symbolically hung a portrait of civil rights leader Martin Luther King, Jr., in the Georgia statehouse. A new age in the history of the South had begun. The era of World War II would be a major watershed in the history of the South, making possible at last a New South. The election of Carter in 1976, and even more so of William Jefferson Clinton as president and Al Gore as vice-president in 1992, represented the coming of age of the American South.

✵ CHAPTER 5 ✵

The American South

Hundreds of millions of television viewers around the world sat nervously watching their screens on July 20, 1969, listening with incredulous attention to radio transmissions of the conversation of three American astronauts as two of them, inside an ungainly lunar module, prepared to land on the moon's surface. The crackling radio communications described the lunar module's uncouplingly from the command module, then its gradual, almost science-fiction-like descent to the moon's cold surface, blowing up lunar dust before the final touch down. The first word uttered from the moon was "Houston," followed by "the eagle has landed." Who would have anticipated, two generations earlier, when H. L. Mencken made the South a byword for scientific ignorance and backwardness, that a southern city would one day be associated around the world with the greatest high-tech adventure to date in human history?

Who could have imagined, in the midst of the Depression-era South, that less than a half century hence Atlanta would be identified worldwide with Cable News Network, the most advanced communication network in the world? Or who, aware of those haggard faces in the 1930s Works Progress Administration documentary photographs of southern sharecroppers, could have foreseen that little more than a generation later the South would be associated with the gleaming skyscrapers of Atlanta, Dallas, and Houston? Who, appalled by the spectacle of public lynchings in the 1920s and 1930s, could have anticipated a South two generations later with more elected black public officials than any other region of the country, several of its largest

cities having black mayors, and Virginia having a black governor—the grandson of a slave? The ugliest race riots in recent times have occurred in Los
Angeles, Detroit, and Washington, not New Orleans or Charlotte.

Clearly to even the most casual observer of the American scene, the
South of the 1990s was profoundly different from the South of the 1930s and
before. In fact, southerners of 1930 would have felt more at home in the
South of the 1830s than in the South of 1970 and later. It might reasonably
be argued that the era of World War II initiated more far-reaching change in
the South than did the Civil War. How had Dixie been transformed in the
generation after 1940, and which aspects, if any, of that older, distinctive
South remained in the so-called Sun Belt South of the 1990s? Was there anything still identifiably southern about the genuine New South that had
evolved over the past half century? Or had the region finally reached the end
of its peculiar history? The making of the American South represents the
coming full circle of the story.

THE SOUTH AND WORLD WAR II

In retrospect the New Deal was more of a transition period than most
contemporaries could understand. From the Tennessee Valley Authority to
the Soil Conservation Service, the federal government had acknowledged a
responsibility for addressing the economic, agricultural, environmental, and
human problems of the poorest region in the nation. Slowly a new breed of
southern politicians, such as Lyndon B. Johnson, began to see the national
government not as the enemy of the South but as a legitimate helpmate. President Franklin D. Roosevelt was careful to protect his political flanks in the
region, because he knew that he needed Solid South Democratic support for
his programs—consequently he never actively campaigned for federal antilynching legislation and he cooperated with entrenched Democratic
machines. But he did convene a national conference in 1938 that identified
the South as the nation's premier economic problem.

Roosevelt and other New Dealers understood that poverty lay at the
root of many southern maladies, including persistent racism, and they also
saw that the South's low wages exacerbated the problem. Much of the southern political and business establishment supported the concept of lower
southern wages, arguing that low wages was the South's most telling competitive advantage in trying to attract northern investment and industry. Moreover, most southern business and industry leaders profited in the short run
by paying their employees wages as much as 40 percent lower than those paid
for comparable jobs outside the South. They often justified their policies by
pointing out that southern workers, especially blacks, were unskilled and
lacking in motivation. New Deal economic planners saw the relationship

between southern poverty and unskilled laborers on the one hand and sub-standard wages on the other. Better wages would begin to break the back of poverty, and, of course better wages also meant that wage earners became consumers who could purchase goods and pay taxes that could improve schools and infrastructure. Wages earned would be spent locally, and each additional dollar in a given community turned over several times, multiplying the effect. Over the opposition of local interests, Washington pushed for uniform national wages in government-related programs and, although some compromises to southern political stubbornness were necessary, the New Deal began the process that ultimately raised southern wages above the poverty level. The southern worker and the region were the beneficiaries.

Southern state governments also slowly came to the realization that the regional economy had to change if prosperity were ever to return to the region. Reliance on the old standbys of cotton cultivation and extractive industries (such as lumber production) did not seem to herald good times, especially since most of the South's first growth of timber had been cut by 1930 and cotton had been devastated initially by the boll weevil and then by overproduction and reduced acreage. Mississippi, a state peculiarly bereft of natural resources, possessing no major port, and correctly seeing that future cotton prosperity was a chimera, led the way in seeking new economic development. In 1936 Governor Hugh L. White pushed through the Mississippi legislature the Balance Agriculture With Industry Act (BAWI). Through this act communities would use local government bonds to construct factories to be leased at a cut rate to industries that would in turn commit to hiring a requisite number of employees for a prescribed number of years. Other tax benefits and promotions were also devised to persuade industry to locate in Mississippi. Before World War II a dozen plants had been attracted to the state, and after the war the BAWI program was renewed and strengthened.

Soon states across the region were competing with one another as well as with northern states to increase industrial investment and manufacturing jobs. Within a generation every southern state had commissions and was sending representatives around the globe promoting industrial development. Unfortunately, the only comparative advantages that much of the South had to dangle in front of prospective investors were comparatively low wages, low taxes, nonunion labor, and lax pollution laws. As a consequence, many of the jobs that were created produced minimum income, scant tax receipts, environmental problems, and continued regional poverty. Manufacturing, states like North Carolina came to realize, did not automatically mean middle-class prosperity for its industrial workers.

But, far more than state industrial agencies and New Deal wage equalization programs, World War II-related investments began to create a new South. The South's climate—relatively mild winters and long growing seasons—had earlier contributed to the South's staple crop production, and after 1941 its climate played an important role in defense expenditures. It obviously made military sense not to have all essential war materiel plants in the Northeast or Midwest, and military training bases would be more efficient if located in all-season locations. On both counts the South stood to gain. The result, helped along by southern congressional seniority, was a proliferation of defense-related industries and a huge expansion of military bases. The Marines had long trained at Parris Island in South Carolina, but now from Virginia to Texas, the South gained more than its share of military expenditures. In addition to the meager salaries of the military personnel, every base generated construction jobs, clerical and support staff employment, and the related growth of stores, schools, and churches. For tens of thousands of southerners who had always been dependent upon agriculture or extractive industry for jobs, military bases meant steady, indoor, and relatively high-paying work. Tens of thousands of rural or small town migrants moved to southern cities or near bases for wartime employment.

Across the South—Newport News, Charleston, Pascagoula, New Orleans, and Houston—the government supported shipbuilding activities, and in each case the initial construction investment, the new wages for southern skilled workers (such as welders and pipefitters), and salaries for thousands of auxiliary workers brought pockets of prosperity to the region. B-24 bombers were built in Fort Worth, B-29s in Marietta, Georgia, bringing defense plant jobs to the southern interior also. Many southern women for the first time found in munition plants and defense factories paid work outside the home and off the farm. Spin-off employment again multiplied the effect on local economies of defense expenditures for equipment and salaries. In all the federal government spent more than four billion dollars on actual military facilities in the South, and another four billion dollars in contracts was awarded to privately owned military construction firms.

Suddenly the South began producing entrepreneurs like Andrew Jackson Higgins in New Orleans. With military support he transformed his small boat-building firm into a giant, modern, efficient producer of Liberty ships, eventually employing 20,000 workers at eight plants in and near New Orleans. Higgins cooperated with unions, paid his black employees the same as white, and loved to stroll through his shipyards shouting encouragement to his workers with a bullhorn. His employees loved him, and the federal government appreciated his managerial acumen. In 1942 he won a huge contract to build over a thousand cargo planes in a gigantic factory that he built in Michoud, just east of New Orleans. A generation later the Michoud Plant was chosen by the National Aeronautics and Space Administration (NASA) as the assembly site for the Apollo rockets in another spree of government-related expenditures that would promote high-tech employment in the South from Cape Canaveral to Huntsville to Houston.

A similar story unfolded in Houston with the construction firm headed by George and Herman Brown. (The original co-founder, Dan Root, had died in 1929, but his name was retained by the company.) An early supporter of Lyndon B. Johnson, George R. Brown utilized his political contacts to win a large contract in June 1940 to construct the Corpus Christi Naval Station. America's entry into World War II required enlargements to the facility, which quadrupled the value of the contract to Brown and Root. With this major success under its belt the firm soon won a series of contracts to build destroyer escorts and landing crafts at a newly formed subsidiary, Brown Shipbuilding Company, near Houston. This company eventually employed 25,000 workers, built 354 combat ships, and acquired total government contracts of about one billion dollars. Brown and Root remained major supporters of Johnson, and in 1961, when he was Vice-President, Houston was chosen as the site for NASA's Manned Spacecraft Center (later renamed the Johnson Space Center). Not surprisingly Brown and Root won the construction contract. In the three decades after 1961 NASA programs would pour additional billions of federal funds into the South.

During the course of World War II more than four million southerners served in the armed forces. This often involved training at a variety of sites, occasionally outside the South, and training introduced young southern men to skills, techniques, managerial practices, and worldviews far removed from what they had known on the farms and in the small towns of Dixie. After training, most southern enlistees served throughout the United States and abroad, further introducing them to ideas, technologies, and attitudes greatly at variance with their prewar experience. Much of the actual wartime experience was unpleasant: boring, tiring, lonely, confusing, dangerous, even deadly. But many southern soldiers had, through the military, their first introduction to a larger, potentially more exciting, liberating, and lucrative world.

They returned home after the war with, figuratively speaking, money in their pockets, new-found skills under their belts, confidence in their nation and their own ability, and broader horizons beckoning. Their world view had changed; they were now less provincial, less fatalistic, and more comfortable with large-scale enterprise and centralized authority. Few would have been able to put their fingers on precisely how they had been transformed by involvement in a world war, but perhaps a shorthand expression would be to say that millions of southerners, white and black, had been modernized to some degree by the events of the last four years. Blacks in particular came to understand their own experience differently as a result of their participation in the war effort. Serving in a war for justice and liberty and in opposition to Nazi theories of racial superiority highlighted for blacks their second-class citizenship in the nation, particularly in the South. The discrepancy between stated ideals and lived reality became more obvious to many whites, too. The military was in advance of other American institutions in breaking down the color line, and southerners of both races came to appreciate that change might be not only possible but possibly salutary. That membership in the National Association for the Advancement of Colored People increased from 50,000 in 1940 to 450,000 in 1946 suggested the change in outlook—even a new militancy—that was underway and heralded a legal transformation in racial practices in less than a decade.

By every index of measurement, the South's economy took off during World War II. The value added from industry tripled, personal income more than doubled, and the number of industrial workers grew by better than 50 percent. The South even narrowed the gap between its per capita income and the national average. With soldiers returning home no longer content to return to a sharecroppers' existence, the economic future was unclear. But what had happened in the previous five years was exactly what the region had needed. The tremendous infusion of capital, managerial talent, and industrial skills primed the South for sustained industrial growth. During the decade and a half of depression and war more than two million southerners, many of them former agricultural workers, had left the region. In fact, it was largely in response to that wartime and immediate postwar shortage of agricultural workers that southern landowners had begun the rapid shift to farm mechanization that ended the regional identification with sharecropping.

The end of the war brought a downsizing of the military forces, but the almost simultaneous outbreak of the Cold War soon guaranteed the continued advantage for the South of huge military expenditures. The presumed threat of Russian missile attack gave further credence to the practice of scattering defense plants and military training installations across the nation, and the South prospered disproportionately from such practices. The former bomber factory at Marietta, Georgia, for example, was reopened by Lockheed in 1951 and ultimately became the biggest industrial employer in the Southeast. Other prominent players in what was soon called the military–industrial complex—companies such as McDonnell–Douglas, General Dynamics, and Rockwell International—opened and operated large plants in the South, at such places as Fort Worth. San Antonio was ringed with Air Force bases; Columbus, Georgia, and Fort Hood, Texas, were temporary homes to tens of thousands of Army draftees. Well-placed southern congressmen used their seniority to gain military benefits for Virginia, North Carolina, and such cities as Charleston and Savannah, in particular, whose powerful congressmen won one Pentagon plum after another for their district. The Tennessee Valley Authority, which had begun in the New Deal with utopian visions of providing good jobs and bucolic family recreation for the people of southern Appalachia, had by the 1950s almost become an arm of the military as a cheap source for the enormous electrical needs of aluminum production for airplanes and nuclear materials for bombs at the Atomic Energy Commission at nearby Oak Ridge, in eastern Tennessee.

National companies, seeking comparatively low wages and docile (nonunion), semiskilled workers, now flocked to the South. Textile manufacturing boomed in North and South Carolina; plywood, lumber, and paper production prospered on second-growth timber; and tourism produced plentiful but low-salaried jobs, particularly in Florida. The modern petrochemical industry grew by leaps and bounds in Texas and Louisiana, fueled by the long American love affair with the personal automobile. Improved economic conditions and bountiful paved roads caused a remarkable expansion in car ownership in the South. During the Eisenhower administration another huge government project, the federal interstate highway system—justified for reasons of national defense—generated billions of dollars of construction jobs in the region and for the first time created a modern, efficient transportation system linking the South internally and to national markets. Trucking replaced the railroads as the major transporter of goods, and northern tourists and would-be manufacturers found Dixie more accessible as a result of multi-lane, divided superhighways.

THE IMPACT OF TECHNOLOGY

A technological breakthrough also made the southern climate more bearable in the summertime. As early as the nineteenth century, inventive southerners had experimented with fans blowing air across ice and various Rube–Golderg contraptions to cool the hot, humid air. The modern air conditioner is a marvel of efficiency and reliability, but it requires a complex combination of electrical motors, thermostats, and leak-proof tubes filled with an inert gas called freon. The first skyscraper to be air conditioned was the Milam Building in San Antonio in 1928, but the cooling system was too large, cumbersome, and costly to be practical. In 1939 Willis Carrier, a pioneer in the field, developed the system of pushing cooled air with powerful fans through small ducts to the various rooms of a building, and the first buildings so air-conditioned were the Bankers Life Building in Macon, Georgia, the Durham Life Building in Raleigh, North Carolina, and the United Carbon Building in Charleston, West Virginia. This system, essentially the same as in use today, was soon common in the newest office buildings throughout the South. By the 1950s hospitals, banks, and movie theaters became some of the first public facilities to offer climate-controlled comfort. Motels springing up along the interstate highways advertised that they were air conditioned, a luxury that was expected to gain them appreciative customers. Many older southerners can remember what a treat it was on a sweltering summer evening forty years ago to go to a theater and enjoy the cool air as much as the color movie on the screen.

Almost no private homes were air-conditioned before World War II, and in the immediate postwar years home units were still too bulky and expensive to be common. In 1951 small window units were perfected, and the air-conditioned house became the realizable dream of the upwardly mobile southern middle class. By 1960 almost one-fifth of the homes in the South were air-conditioned, and by 1980 almost four-fifths were. No one appreciated the new comfort possible more than old-time southerners; electric lights, screened windows to keep out the tiny insects that were attracted to the lights, and now refreshingly cool and dehumidified air—southern summers could be quite pleasant after all. It is difficult to imagine the large-scale migration of northerners to southern cities and retirement communities had modern air-conditioning not been available. By the mid-1950s "factory air" was available in automobiles too. In fact, it soon became impossible to buy a non–air-conditioned car in deep South cities unless it was specially ordered from the factory. The American South is now the most air-conditioned society in the world. Public schools, universities, grocery stores, city buses, sports stadiums (in 1965 the Astrodome in Houston showed that it was possible to cool an entire playing field—and the spectators), gymnasiums, outdoor queues at amusement parks, everything is cooled artificially. City skyscrapers are linked by air-conditioned tunnels or over-the-road glassed-in walkways. Except for a quick dash from one's car to the door, one can now completely escape the long, hot summers in Dixie. The air conditioner may not have been as truly important as Eli Whitney's cotton gin was in 1793, but it certainly brought more comfort.

The changes brought by air-conditioning are obvious and well documented, but far less appreciated are the contributions to comfort offered by the availability of two forms of liquefied petroleum gas (LPG), butane and propane. Both these colorless, flammable gases are by-products of the refining of oil to produce gasoline, a process called cracking. Butane and propane were discovered shortly before World War I, although their manufacture did not become commercially feasible until the 1930s. In 1935 safe, practical heaters for domestic use were developed, but military needs during World War II slowed the growth of the domestic market. Peacetime saw an astronomical increase in the production and domestic use of LPG. Both butane and propane become liquid under pressure at normal temperatures. In liquid form they are easily transported in trucks and can be stored under pressure in metal tanks in sizes adaptable to home use. Here was an inexpensive, portable source of heating fuel for isolated farm homes. No longer was it necessary for an expensive, lengthy system of pipes to bring a heating gas from central storage tanks to individual homes—practical only for urban areas. A small butane tank in the back yard, filled occasionally by a visiting tank truck, could, with a minimum of plumbing, provide a safe fuel for cooking and heating.

At first many farm families used butane or propane for their cooking ranges, lifting a heavy burden from farm wives and mothers. Gone forever was the necessity, first thing each morning, of starting the fire in the kitchen stove, with all the attendant trouble of bringing in the wood and kindling and regularly cleaning out the ashes. The appliance that usually first followed the gas range was the gas water heater. Electric pumps could effortlessly bring water into the home; the water heater just as effortlessly warmed the water for bathing or washing dishes. At this point the modern bathroom could become a reality in farm houses, and it is difficult for modern urban readers to comprehend the manifold improvement in southern rural life this small room affected. Both these applications—gas range and water heater—were often followed, very quickly, by the space heater, which replaced the wood heater and fireplace for warming dwelling rooms. Portable butane and propane released southern farmers from the enormous annual chore of cutting, splitting, and hauling small mountains of firewood. For every southern family who lived through the transition from firewood to LPG, the change seemed almost miraculous. A cleaner, safer, easier way to cook and heat brought an unforgettable improvement in quality of life. For many rural southerners LPG—because of its labor-saving and comfort-providing qualities—was an even greater advance than air-conditioning.

The South's sense of isolation from the American mainstream was significantly removed by television, which, beginning in the early 1950s, began to be accessible throughout most of the region. At first television reception was possible only in the largest cities, and rural homes had to erect tall outside antennas, sometimes as high as one hundred feet and supported by guy wires, in order to receive the flickering black-and-white pictures often afflicted by what was called snow. For some in the deep South this was the only snow they ever saw. But southerners of every income level and race shared the national fascination with television, and southerners now heard a bland, accentless English being spoken, saw immediately the newest fashions in clothes and hair styles, heard the same music the rest of the nation listened to, and had brought into their living rooms and dens white and black entertainers performing together.

Critics argued that reading was being replaced by passive TV viewing, while others lamented the loss of the colorful conversation and storytelling that had once graced southern porches and back yards. But most southerners, certainly rural ones, now that they had electricity, television, and soon room air conditioners, were only too glad to join the television generation. In fact, southern musical traditions and life styles, occasionally caricatured but often presented sympathetically, began to be beamed across the nation by the TV networks. From Elvis Presley to "The Andy Griffith Show" and finally "The Waltons," the South was winning a place in the national entertainment supermarket. The region seemed more creative, more wholesome, than the stereotypes presented by H. L. Mencken and Erskine Caldwell in the 1920s and 1930s. The South may not yet have been culturally redeemed in the eyes of the nation by the 1970s, but it seemed far less pathological.

CHANGES DOWN ON THE FARM

By the decade of the 1970s it was clear that a genuine New South was emerging. Solid industrial growth, fueled by low energy prices, low wages, and cooperative state and local governments (the southern states were rated as having "good business environments," which primarily meant low taxes, lax regulations, and weak labor unions), diversified the various state economies. Federal government funds continued to flow south, enhanced by the effort to put an American on the moon and soon further increased by the Pentagon as American involvement in Vietnam deepened. One other great barrier to the South's entering the American mainstream also began to be removed in the 1960s: legal segregation. Sit-ins, the Montgomery bus boycott, the rise of Martin Luther King, Jr., and then the Civil Rights Act of 1964 and the Voting Rights Act of 1965 slowly but surely reshaped the political, cultural, and economic landscape of the former Confederate states. That momentous story— the great story of the modern-day South—is told in greater length later in this chapter, but the gradual process of removing the most flagrant abuses of segregation opened the South up to a welcome and positive invasion by national corporations. With investment came population growth, and both ushered in a prosperity that enhanced tax rolls. With greater tax revenues southern states could begin to address some of their problems: poor schools, too few hospitals, and inadequate public health programs. The stage was set for the next level of southern economic growth.

The two decades following 1965 were the most prosperous in southern history. The century-long population and brain drain from the South reversed itself, and the population flow, including blacks, became positive. The South had long been a region of small towns with no really big cities. Suddenly the migration from the North, and from southern rural areas, brought unparalleled urban growth to Atlanta, Charlotte, Dallas, Houston, Jacksonville, New Orleans, and San Antonio. John Portman with his striking hotel lobbies helped make Atlanta a byword for the prosperous New South, and futuristic skyscrapers like the Pennzoil Building and Transco Tower made Houston's skyline an architectural wonder that attracted urban experts and architects from around the nation to see the new form of spread-out, automobile city with nodes of skyscrapers scattered across hundreds of square miles. In 1971 DisneyWorld opened near Orlando, Florida; it soon became the largest tourist attraction in the world and made Orlando an instant city. As in the Progressive Era, in the recent South cities were the loci of economic advance and political change.

Even the old mainstay of the southern economy and way of life, agriculture, was transformed during the generation following World War II. Of course, the roots of this transformation went back several decades, to the arrival of the boll weevil and the beginning of acreage reduction plans during the New Deal. But changes set underway earlier came to full fruition in the postwar South. Cotton production continued to shift westward to Oklahoma, west Texas, New Mexico, Arizona, and California in part because the boll weevil was less of a problem in the different soil and drier climate, and because the huge, level fields available there, usually irrigated, were much more conducive to the large-scale, completely mechanized agribusiness that now dominated cotton production. By the late 1970s one could see more cotton being grown between Phoenix and Flagstaff than between New Orleans and Memphis. However, in recent years cotton has made a resurgence in the Southeast, stimulated by the new national popularity of natural cotton fibers as opposed to synthetic fibers (hence higher cotton prices) and new developments in pesticides that have virtually eliminated the boll weevil. Between 1983 and 1990, for example, the number of acres devoted to cotton cultivation in the South more than doubled. But no longer is cotton king. Southern agriculture is now much more diversified than at any time in the past.

Tobacco cultivation remained relatively stable, in terms of both acres cultivated and production methods, until the 1970s. Higher costs for land, fertilizer, and fuels had resulted in some consolidation, and large farmers increasingly shifted to tractors for hauling and to seasonally employed extra hands for harvesting. By the early 1970s bulk curers were introduced and began to change the old way of curing tobacco leaves practically leaf by leaf. Also in 1970 a successful tobacco harvesting machine was finally developed by the agricultural scientists at North Carolina State University. Production per acre increased because of new fertilizers and chemicals, and the man-hours of labor required per acre decreased drastically. Luckily, by the mid-1970s paved roads and the migration southward of light industry provided jobs for the thousands of displaced tobacco farmers. Through the political prowess of the congressional delegations from the tobacco-growing states, the federal government still provided subsidies for the crop even though the evidence linking tobacco to cancer—and hence tremendous personal and economic losses nationwide—was incontrovertible.

Rice cultivation continued in portions of Florida and southeast Texas and especially in southern Louisiana and the delta regions of Mississippi and Arkansas. This was highly capitalized agribusiness with a vengeance: huge, flat fields, gigantic machines, and planting and fertilization by airplanes. In fact, the daredevil flying exploits of crop dusters for both rice and cotton production often brought incredulous stares from tourists driving along the interstates in southern Louisiana as well as west Texas. Delta Airlines, the Atlanta behemoth, began as a small crop dusting outfit in 1924 in the Mississippi delta; in 1928 it changed its name from Huff Daland Dusters to Delta. Although passenger service began the following year, the company, having lost a federal mail contract, quickly returned to crop spraying exclusively. But soon the company reinstated passenger service, moved its headquarters to Atlanta in 1941, and earned sufficient profits during World War II to expand greatly after the war. Today it so dominates air travel in the Southeast that a standing joke in the region is that whether one goes to heaven or hell, one will have to transfer at Delta's hub in Atlanta.

Truck farming, the production of fresh vegetables for sale, usually in nearby urban areas, has also boomed in the postwar South, and with modern truck transport over the interstate highway system, southern vegetables now often find their way to the tables of most Americans in the eastern half of the nation. Florida and Texas lead the region in such agricultural production. Florida also emerged in the 1940s as the nation's leading producer of oranges and grapefruit, and simultaneously a lesser center of citrus production developed in the lower Rio Grande Valley of south Texas. (The citrus industry had begun in both regions in the 1920s.) Apples (in Appalachia) and peaches (in Georgia and South Carolina) are also grown in the South, but production of such so-called deciduous fruit does not come near the value of citrus crops. And as Jimmy Carter brought home to the nation, peanuts are also a significant crop in portions of the South, along with, in particular areas, pecans, spinach (there is a statue of Popeye the Sailor Man in Crystal City, Texas), sugar cane, soybeans, blueberries, and sweet potatoes. Many small producers of these crops supplement their income with town or factory employment, made possible by the network of paved farm-to-market roads and the ubiquitous pickup truck.

The modern beef industry bears little resemblance to the small-scale production and scrawny cattle of years ago. From the eighteenth century until the 1930s most southern cattle suffered from a lowgrade infection caused by two parasitic blood diseases, babesiosis and anaplasmosis, spread by a species of tick whose range almost exactly matched the Confederate South. The cause of this cattle disease, often called Texas fever, became understood by the early twentieth century, and a New Deal cattle dipping program—whereby cattle were forced to walk through trench-like vats filled with an insecticide mixed with water—eventually eradicated the tick that spread the disease. Later a vaccine effective against anaplasmosis was developed, and southern farmers could grow healthy cattle, with a weight gain per pound of feed consumed comparable with other regions of the nation.

Beginning in the 1920s plant scientists at a number of southern agricultural schools and experiment stations worked to improve southern pastures. Agronomists at the Coastal Plains Experiment Station at Tifton, Georgia, in the late 1930s developed new grasses that would thrive in the southern soils and climate. Cotton farmers had worked for a century and a half to keep the native bermuda grass out of their cotton fields, and now experts were working at producing a hardier, faster growing bermuda. The result, in 1943, was what plant geneticist Glenn W. Burton called coastal bermuda. By the late 1940s the new grass was being planted across the South, and this higher quality of grass (and hay) made possible significant additional improvements in the southern cattle industry.

Major cattle diseases were controlled, improved grazing was available, and fencing laws that required farmers to keep their livestock confined were almost universal across the region—finally ending the open range in the South. These changes made possible selective breeding of cattle. In the late 1940s and early 1950s farmers throughout the South began to import pure-bred bulls to improve their stock. A variety of Brahman bulls from Texas—a breed noted for its resistance to disease and heat—were imported, especially into Florida, which became a major cattle-producing state. Purebred Herefords, Black Angus, Charolais, and other breeds became common, along with hybrids like the Brangus, which combined the meat quality of the Black Angus with the hardiness of the Brahman. Now all the pieces were in place, and with cow pastures replacing old cotton fields, the South as a region became a leading producer of cattle.

Before 1930 or so poultry production in the South consisted of a handful of broilers raised by the farmer for Sunday dinners and perhaps several dozen hens for eggs. Often farm wives were in charge of the poultry, and they would market their few surplus eggs in the nearest small town for "egg money" to supplement the family's meager income. Before 1920 in the Delmarva peninsula farmers began to develop large-scale commercial broiler production for the urban markets of Washington, Baltimore, Philadelphia, and New York City. During the 1930s, when cotton production decreased, farmers in several southern states—Arkansas and Georgia particularly—thought of broiler production as a viable source of jobs and income. A feed dealer in northern Georgia named Jessie Dixon Jewell pioneered the development of the vertically integrated broiler industry; he built a hatchery, produced feed, contracted with growers, brought the mature chickens to the processing plants, and marketed the fresh meat.

After World War II this new kind of poultry industry, whereby the farmer himself was little more than an employee of large, completely integrated feed companies, spread rapidly across the South. No longer did chickens mean a few laying hens in a small backyard pen; fully automated chicken houses longer than a football field were found on many farms, with a farm family often raising 100,000 to 300,000 broilers at a time. The broiler industry seemed to thrive especially in what had been the poorest, least urbanized portions of the South, bringing a small but steady income to relatively unskilled farmers who otherwise would have fled to cities or remained poor. Of course the growth of the broiler industry required laying farms for fertile egg production, hatcheries, feed mills, and poultry processing plants—all of which produced jobs. Improvements in breeds of chickens and their feed and medication halved the time it took to grow a marketable broiler, and the national consumption of chicken grew phenomenally. "Egg money" had become big business. To a degree that would have been unimaginable in 1930 or even 1940, cattle and chickens had replaced cotton as the quintessential southern agricultural product.

To the casual observer it began to seem by the 1970s that the South had completely escaped its past of poverty, prejudice, and backwardness. Jimmy Carter and Andrew Young, along with Martin Luther King, Jr., and Lyndon B. Johnson, taught the nation something about racial understanding—although the journey toward justice had been long and perilous and was still not complete. Dispelling old national stereotypes about hayseed southerners living on Tobacco Road, television now portrayed oil millionaires in Dallas and the life styles of the rich and comfortable in Hilton Head. H. L. Mencken's "Sahara of the Bozart" was emphatically refuted by distinguished art museums in Richmond, Atlanta, Dallas, Fort Worth, and Houston, and internationally acclaimed ballet and opera companies and symphony orchestras were located in Atlanta, Baltimore, St. Louis, Dallas, and Houston. With urban growth and wealth came the high art whose absence Mencken had bemoaned. The South now even sported major league professional teams in baseball, basketball, and football, perhaps the ultimate American symbol of urban maturity.

EMERGENCE OF THE SUN BELT

In the early 1970s a new sobriquet began to be applied uncritically to the South. In 1969 political strategist Kevin Phillips had argued that the Republican party should tailor its rhetoric and platform to appeal to the rapidly growing southern portion of the United States, a region he called the "sunbelt," and in 1975 journalist Kirkpatrick Sale published an acerbic analysis of the conservative political tendencies of what he termed "the southern rim" of the nation, stretching from Florida to southern California. Suddenly the label "Sun Belt" became the media buzzword for the South, although the definition was so loose that in some hands the putative region was stretched all the way to Portland, Oregon. But by popular consensus the

Sun Belt came to mean a newly prosperous, rapidly growing (and urbaniz-ing) South that was increasingly free of racism and gaining a disproportion-ate share of federal revenues through various government programs. An almost necessary corollary of the Sun Belt was the idea that the rest of the nation (soon tagged as the Snow Belt or Rust Belt) was losing an unfair por-tion of its share of government transfer payments to a politically regnant Dixie. One could hardly pick up a magazine without finding pictures of smil-ing whites and blacks working together in an Atlanta "too busy to hate," with the reflective-glass skyscrapers in the background a not-so-subtle suggestion that Henry Grady's New South had finally arrived.

Southern boosters were only too glad to promote this image, and in truth there was much data to prove that the South had prospered and urban-ized to a remarkable degree in the last generation. The South had narrowed the gap that separated it from the rest of the nation in most measures of eco-nomic and social well being. Neither southerners nor the press could refrain from publishing the happy statistics. In many ways the South now seemed bet-ter and more truly integrated than most regions of the North. Southern per capita income inched toward the national average, and Texas finally went over it for several years before the oil depression of the middle 1980s. By 1990 Florida and Virginia, the latter fueled by burgeoning government salaries, had per capita incomes above the national average.

Even southern higher education, which had long seemed embarrass-ingly weak and a detriment both to regional self-esteem and economic devel-opment, had made significant strides forward. Within the former Confeder-ate states, for example, most admittedly subjective rankings of American universities by 1990 had Duke University, the University of North Carolina, the University of Virginia, and Rice University in the top twenty-five, with Emory University, Vanderbilt University, and the University of Texas just behind. In terms of membership in the National Academy of Engineering and the National Academy of Sciences, the South has increased its share of mem-bers, suggesting again that the academic and research gap was being nar-rowed. For example, no one from the former Confederate states was a mem-ber of the National Academy of Engineering when it began in 1964; in 1970 southern members (defined by institutional affiliation) made up 8.8 percent of its membership, and this had risen to 14.1 percent in 1990. In that year (when the eleven former Confederate states had 28.5 percent of the nation's population) only 6.9 percent of the members of the National Academy of Sci-ences worked in the South, but that number was up from 3.99 percent in 1960 and zero percent (out of 158 members nationally) in 1917, when Mencken's famous diatribe against the South was first published. The average Scholastic Aptitude Test (SAT) score is an indicator of academic preparation, and stu-dents from the southern states do not perform as well as students from other sections on these examinations. But these results are difficult to interpret because a higher percentage of high-school students take the test in, for example, South Carolina than in Iowa, and the correlations for race, urban or rural, and income level vastly complicate comparative interpretations.

The South has not yet produced multipurpose research universities to compare with Harvard or Stanford, but below the world-class level southern educational institutions are now competitive with those elsewhere in the nation. Curricula are similar, and the standards for employment and tenure are essentially the same as for universities throughout the nation. Several southern professional and medical schools also are top ranked: the law schools of Duke, Texas, and Virginia; the medical schools at the University of Alabama at Birmingham, Duke, Southwestern in Dallas, and the huge Texas Medical Center in Houston, the largest and most comprehensive assemblage of medical institutions in the world.

At several locations in the South sophisticated high-tech industries have developed, usually in cooperation with nearby universities. The major example of this phenomenon is the Research Triangle Park in North Carolina, tapping the resources of the University of North Carolina, North Carolina State University, and Duke. Similar concentrations of Ph.D.s and electronic, computer, and biotechnology industries have been spawned on the outskirts of Washington, DC, at Charlottesville, Virginia, and near Atlanta, Dallas, Houston, and especially Austin. Nothing quite like California's Silicon Valley or the Boston Route 128 concentration yet arisen in the South, but such major computer firms as Texas Instruments and Compaq Computer are headquartered in the region. None of these levels of academic or technological attainment were reached before World War II.

These glowing Sun Belt statistics, however, do not reveal the entire picture. Wages are still lower in the South than elsewhere, and although living costs are also lower, they do not completely make up the difference. State agencies were so eager to attract industry to the region that they figuratively gave away the store to win the factory. As a result tax revenues have not increased as they should have, and the environment has suffered more than it needed to. One Louisiana governor openly admitted before a national television camera that the state had traded environmental purity for employment and suggested that it was the responsible course for a job-poor state. A disproportionate number of jobs have come South precisely because wages were low, regulations were few, and unions seemed nonexistent. So the workers have not benefited proportionately. And once southern wages began to catch up with the nation's in the 1980s and southern states—prodded by the national government—became more attentive to the environment, the South's comparative advantage over the North diminished.

Some southern states and cities learned too late that high quality industrial development (paying high wages and not polluting) was drawn by total quality-of-life concerns, not just low wages and taxes. Moreover, the relatively undesirable industrial employment that formerly was attracted to the South was now moving to Taiwan, South Korea, and Mexico, where wages were far lower, pollution laws practically unknown, and government officials cooperative or capable of being made so. The real third world now competes for jobs that the nation's domestic third world—the South—previously gained. In Mexico alone in the early 1990s some 500,000 workers were employed in "maquiladora" factories along the border. Plant equipment and new materials are shipped to Mexico, then finished products are shipped back to the United States with practically no duties paid. These maquiladora workers average from five to seven dollars per day, and they represent Mexico's second leading source of income after oil. But much of this employment and investment south of the border comes at the expense of the US South. Several American industries, for example, the manufacture of typewriters and television, have completely disappeared north of the border. Moreover, with the end of the Cold War, US defense budgets have fallen, and a number of southern locales, heavily dependent upon military jobs, have suffered severely in the early 1990s. Future defense cuts suggest additional blows to once favored cities. Some initial reports in the summer of 1993 projected job losses in Charleston, for instance, of 25 percent, representing a full one-third of the city's wages.

Not only has much of southern industrial development been in low-paying extractive industries or low-value-added manufacturing, such as textiles, but much of the apparent boom has been in the tourist industry. Many Americans only know the South from vacation trips to southern beaches, golf courses, Williamsburg, DisneyWorld, and like attractions, and several old cities that have preserved much of their architectural and historical heritage: Charleston (remarkably so), Savannah, New Orleans, and San Antonio. But tourist-related jobs are notoriously low paying, and the chances for upward mobility are severely limited. New Orleans, despite a thriving tourist industry, is the poorest large city in the South. Furthermore, much of the economic development has been uneven, with concentration near the largest cities or scattered along the interstates—for example, between Atlanta and Charlotte. There is a broad band of light manufacturing stretching from Virginia to northern Georgia, a tourist mecca along coastal South Carolina and portions of Georgia and the Florida peninsula, and an oil belt in Louisiana and Texas. Spread throughout the region are still great pockets of rural poverty where Sun Belt change and prosperity seem nonexistent.

Much of the southern infrastructure was quickly and poorly built in the boom areas by local governments that made a fetish of keeping taxes (and hence services) low. Job growth has slowed, environmental costs are increasing, and roads and bridges are wearing out. The southern cities' growth came so late in the century that they tend to be automobile cities with practically no effective mass transit systems. It has been difficult to keep up with the need for new roads, water and sewerage systems, and schools in several of the region's boom cities, and after several decades the blunders, short cuts, and bad planning are crippling sustained growth. The South still has a disproportionate number of poor and old people, and that is one reason some analyses of government transfer payments suggested a tilt toward the South. A relatively poor region (hence below average federal tax receipts) with above average human needs (hence above average transfer payments) will on the screen of a computer look like a region being given an unfair advantage in the Sun Belt/Snow Belt competition. But the so-called advantage is misleading. Despite all the Sun Belt discussion, and despite undeniable southern gains over the last three decades, the South remains the poorest region in the nation. Most contemporary southerners, however, this one included, remembering (or having read about) how things were before 1940, prefer to see the glass as half full.

No development in the postwar South has been more striking than the growth of its cities, fueled by immigration from the North, Mexico and Latin America, Asia, and especially the rural South. Many rural counties have been steadily losing population since 1940. But the rise of the cities has been more noticeable than the decline of the countryside. Excluding Baltimore and Washington, DC, New Orleans in 1940 was the largest southern city (population 492,282) even though it ranked only fifteenth in size in the nation. No other southern city was in the top twenty, although Houston was twenty-first in size and Louisville twenty-fourth. By 1990 the national and regional rankings had changed considerably. Houston had passed New Orleans during World War II to become the South's largest city, and in 1990 it was the nation's fourth largest. Joining it in the top ten cities were Dallas and San Antonio, while Baltimore (thirteenth), Jacksonville (fifteenth), Memphis (eighteenth), Washington (nineteenth), Nashville (twenty-third), and New Orleans (twenty-fifth) all were in the top twenty-five. Atlanta's city population ranked it only thirty-sixth in size, but when metropolitan population is included it moves up to the third position in the South (behind Dallas–Fort Worth and Houston) and reigns as the capital city of the Southeast. Miami, too, in metropolitan population moves up in the ranks, and with its huge Cuban and other Hispanic population and its vast economic ties to Latin America, it currently is among the most cosmopolitan of southern cities.

Miami is also indicative of how southern cities have become far less provincial as they have become larger. All of the large southern cities have significant numbers of people from Europe, South and Central America, and Asia, and they all have benefited from migration southward of skilled workers from the northern states. Most major corporations have branch offices or branch plants in the South, and the white-collar employees that staff them are drawn from all over the nation. In the affluent sections and suburbs of

Richmond, Charlotte, Atlanta, Tampa, New Orleans, Houston, and Dallas, one finds a cosmopolitan, even international, mix of peoples. The Texas cities in particular have large Mexican populations, Houston has a substantial Asian population as well, and of course Miami's Cuban population gives that city a decidedly Latin flavor. But in all the cities one finds a variety of ethnic restaurants, hears a range of foreign accents, and sees supermarket shelves stocked with herbs, peppers, and tubers that would have been rare indeed a generation ago. Ethnic foods make curious accommodations in the New South. At the New York Coffee Shop in Houston, for example, grits are offered at breakfast along with various kosher items, and even jalapeño bagels are sold. Certain southern romantics have been highly critical of the region's biggest cities, but few southern urban dwellers—enjoying better jobs, better schools, better health care, a wider range of cultural opportunities, and the undeniable excitement of urban life—are choosing to move back to family farms or isolated small towns. A weekend country home is nice, but not permanent residence.

Until 1950 or so most southern cities seemed to be peopled only by blacks and whites and had the character of overgrown towns. Now the largest cities and their school systems represent far more of the world's diversity and sustain a genuine urban ethos. The availability in the largest cities of home delivery of the *New York Times* symbolizes the degree to which the South has become economically and even culturally integrated into the national mainstream. Southern-based corporations, such as Delta Airlines and Holiday Inns and Compaq Computers—and fried-chicken stands in New York City and catfish recipes in the *New York Times*—suggest that, from the national perspective, the South is now much less of a land apart. Southern institutions, musical styles, and folkways have gained currency throughout much of the nation, often in ways seldom recognized. A Memphis grocery merchant named Clarence Sanders, for example, in 1916 invented the modern supermarket with his Piggly Wiggly stores, and another southern merchant, Sam Walton, in 1962 in Rogers, Arkansas, invented another marketing concept, the Wal-Mart discount store, that by 1992, with annual sales surpassing twenty-five billion dollars, had become the nation's largest retailer. The secret of Wal-Mart seemed to be downhome southern folksiness and friendly service combined with high-tech communications, skilled management, efficient distribution, and everyday low prices.

Texas radio pioneer Gordon McLendon, self-styled "The Old Scotsman," first developed or perfected the concept of "Top 40" and beautiful music formats, the all-news station, editorials on the air, and advertising jingles based on the call letters of his radio stations. By 1950 his Liberty Broadcasting System had 458 affiliates across the nation, with listeners estimated at between sixty and ninety million. McLendon's stations—usually the most popular in each city in which they were located—had easily pronounced call letters: KILT in Houston and KEEL in Shreveport. And a southern evangelist, now headquartered in Minneapolis—Billy Graham—is the best known and best loved religious figure of the twentieth century. His crusades in their music, sermon style, and altar call are unmistakably Southern Baptist, and they are skillfully choreographed and nationally televised. To a significant degree the nation's popular culture has been southernized.

Or, to put it another way, the South has been Americanized. Northern tourists traveling now on an interstate highway through the region experience a South far less distinctive than they might have expected. Everywhere they visit in the South has standardized road signs, the same chain hotels, fast food outlets, and national brand-name stores that they are familiar with, and people wear similar clothes and listen to the same music. Only when these hypothetical tourists get off the interstate highway and out of the car and listen to native southerners (if one could be found in Atlanta or Houston) or taste the local food do they begin to realize that the South is not completely an undifferentiated part of the larger nation. Despite all the economic growth and urbanization, despite the standardization and cosmopolitanization of the region, something almost intangible still seems to set the region apart, especially in the small towns and rural areas.

Perhaps it is more a state of mind than anything susceptible to scientific analysis, but most southerners insist the region is still "southern" whether they love or hate what that defining label means, and most northerners, too, profess to see a region still recognizably different from the rest of the nation. The people living in the region, particularly the native-born whites and blacks, struggle with coming to terms with their region and ponder what part of their heritage should be discarded and what should be held on to. Academicians and journalists who study the region also struggle to understand the persistence of southern identity and debate its future. In the end most discussions of the South come around to that topic.

SEGREGATION UNDER ASSAULT

The shift in the national media's stereotype of the South is represented by the difference between the sharecropper shacks and hillbillies, as portrayed in the book *Tobacco Road* and in such comic strips as "L'il Abner" and "Snuffy Smith," and the opening scenes of the popular television series *Dallas* with the skyline of that rich and powerful city towering over the surrounding plains like some giant mountain range; yet the region's most profound change in the last fifty years has occurred in race relations. One must always hasten to say that much yet remains to be done, but nowhere else in this

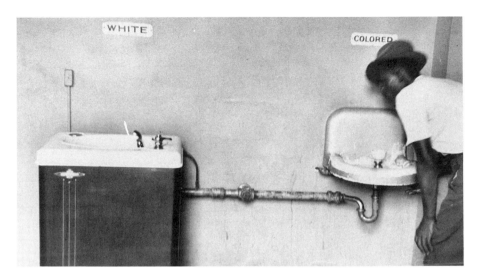

Segregated drinking fountains were seen in the South until the 1960s.
(Elliot Erwitt, Magnum Photos, Inc.)

nation has there been such a shift in basic attitudes. More than in any other aspect, in terms of race relations a New South has indeed emerged in the last generation.

The desegregation of American life in general and southern life in particular is the most significant social movement in modern American history. The movement began to chip away at the prevailing system in the 1930s, gained momentum in the 1940s, saw landmark changes in the 1950s, and by the 1960s had already begun to change forever how blacks and whites interacted in the South. The movement worked at several levels: there was the carefully constructed legal effort on the part of the National Association for the Advancement of Colored People (NAACP), the gradual but ultimately essential efforts of the federal government, and the courageous folk crusade of thousands of black men, women, and children (and not a few whites) in the South, with assistance from people of conscience throughout the nation. To this complex story we now turn.

It is practically impossible for anyone not old enough to have experienced it to appreciate how totally separate blacks and whites were in the South before World War II. Blacks had separate churches, schools, and social organizations; lived in special sections of most towns; could shop in regular department stores, but not try on clothes; could not eat in the dining rooms of restaurants; could not stay in motels unless they happened to find a rare "colored" motel. Blacks could not address a white adult by first name (unless "mister" or "miz" was prefixed), although even white children called black adults by their first names. The slightest infraction of the code of quette by a black brought down punishment by whites—often death, anu even as recently as the mid-1950s. Throughout the deep South, but especially in Mississippi, blacks were routinely cheated, humiliated, abused, deprived of basic human rights, and kept in abject poverty.

The ultimate legal basis of this system of rigid segregation was the 1896 Supreme Court decision, *Plessy v. Ferguson*, based on the case of Homer Plessy. In 1892 he had sat in the white-only car of a train traveling between New Orleans and Covington, Louisiana, only to be dragged off and arrested by policemen. The very light-complexioned Plessy argued that the Fourteenth Amendment guaranteed equal protection under the law and hence made illegal such segregated cars. However, the US Supreme Court ruled in 1896 that the Civil Rights Act of 1875 required only "separate-but-equal" facilities and that a blacks-only railroad car, if it offered equal facilities, met the letter of the law. This decision governed race relations in the South until 1954, but in precious few instances were the facilities available to blacks equal to those provided for whites. By every conceivable measure, the general usage emphasized the *separate* in the dictum, but ignored the *equal.*

In the middle of the Great Depression the NAACP finally decided to mount a full-scale legal battle against segregation in the South, where it was most pronounced. Although earlier a NAACP staff lawyer had argued that the entire principle of separate-but-equal was wrong and based on faulty legal reasoning, the organization believed that a more limited campaign would be more effective. The logic of this campaign, which was directed by Charles Hamilton Houston, dean of the Howard University School of Law and Special Counsel for the NAACP, was to highlight those instances in which southern states clearly failed to offer "equal" facilities as required by the law. Reasoning that it would be less antagonistic to the prejudices of the white South to begin by attacking inequalities in higher education, where the discrepancies were most outrageous, Houston further decided to attack the discrimination rampant in legal education. The first case concerned a young man, Donald Gaines Murray, who was not accepted at the University of Maryland Law School solely on the grounds of race. Arguing the case in the Baltimore and Maryland courts, Houston and his assistant, Thurgood Marshall, showed that sending Murray out of state for his education, which the state was prepared to do, would not be equal training since he wanted to practice law in Maryland. When the state court upheld the decision in favor of Murray, the NAACP knew it had gained an important first breach in the wall of segregation. The following year the team of Houston and Marshall made similar arguments on behalf of Lloyd Lionel Gaines, who sought to attend the University of Missouri's law school, and this case went all the way to the US Supreme Court. Again the decision was in favor of admission of the black candidate to the previously all-white law school.

When Heman Sweatt, a former mailman in Houston, applied for admission to the law school at the University of Texas, the university attempted educational subterfuge. Under the guise of separate but equal, the university proposed to establish a law school for blacks in Houston in three basement rooms, staffed with part-time faculty. The NAACP took up Sweatt's cause and challenged the quality of the education offered—such a pitiful facility for educating black lawyers was in no way comparable to the strong law school in Austin, with its good library, distinguished faculty, and roster of influential alumni. This case became joined with the case of George W. McLaurin, an elderly black professor who had applied for admission to the PhD program in education at the University of Oklahoma and was rejected on the basis of race. Later the university made a compromise of sorts and allowed McLaurin to enroll, but he was required to sit at a special desk with a railing surrounding it, and there were separate tables, for his use only, in the library and cafeteria. With the NAACP's support, both the Sweatt case and the McLaurin case were heard by the Supreme Court in April 1950. This time the NAACP was joined by the nation's Department of Justice, which filed a friendly brief in support of the cause of equal education. But when the Court ruled, on June 5, 1950, in favor of Sweatt and McLaurin, it did so in narrow, technical terms. The University of Texas Law School had to admit Sweatt, and the University of Oklahoma had to stop putting humiliating restrictions on McLaurin's attendance. The opportunity to address segregated education in general was not taken, and the ruling was confined to postgraduate education. It did require, however, genuine equality of educational effort on the part of the states at the postgraduate level. Knowing how difficult the South found it to support higher education in general, the NAACP reasoned that support of dual but truly equal systems would be financially impossible and ultimately repugnant even to diehard segregationists. Slowly but surely Thurgood Marshall and his associates (Charles H. Houston had died.) sensed that the tide of history was on their side, and they had a decade of increasing involvement by the federal government to support that optimistic assessment.

Franklin D. Roosevelt—perhaps in part because of the sensitivities of his wife Eleanor—slowly came partially to understand the situation for blacks in the South; but fearful of political retaliation by southern congressmen, he was extremely hesitant to criticize the South's Jim Crow practices. Once World War II loomed, he feared that any effort to promote the interests of blacks might jeopardize wartime production needs. But blacks were quick to realize that they were not being fairly treated as new war-related job opportunities arose. They were almost always excluded from high-skilled, high-paying jobs and were usually confined to janitorial positions. The discrepancies between national rhetoric about freedom and justice and the reality for American blacks rankled race leaders. A. Philip Randolph, more militant than many NAACP leaders who preferred to work through the court system, began to plan a mammoth March on Washington Movement to dramatize the issue. Roosevelt was worried about how such a visible protest would affect the national image abroad as he was seeking to become the leader of the Allies. When Randolph refused to cave in to Roosevelt's pressure, Roosevelt moved to create the Fair Employment Practice Committee (FEPC) to examine cases of job discrimination in the hope that publicity would discourage such practices. In return, Randolph called off the march. The FEPC proved less efficacious than Randolph would have liked, but at least the federal government had officially taken cognizance of the plight of blacks in the workplace. Conservative white southerners saw the handwriting on the wall. Many of them began to break with Roosevelt and the New Deal because in their minds "the southern way of life" was threatened by such federal interference.

One of the ways the southern white establishment had defended its position was with the white primary, which eliminated blacks from participating in the only election that made any difference in most parts of the South. In 1923 the NAACP had begun to protest legally the white primary in Texas, and Supreme Court decisions in 1927 and again in 1932 had narrowly decided against the Democratic white primary as an official state election institution. But the state had withdrawn its laws concerning the primary, declaring it to be simply the activity of a private party and hence not subject to the provisions of the Fourteenth Amendment. In fact, the Supreme Court in 1935 (*Grovey v. Townsend*) upheld the idea of the primary as a private (not state) matter. Many Texas blacks were outraged. The local NAACP set out to find a way to challenge the decision, and they found a Houston dentist, Lonnie Smith, who agreed to become part of the case after being prohibited from voting in the 1940 Democratic white primary. Almost four years later, in a landmark decision, the Supreme Court in *Smith v. Allwright* ruled that, since in fact the primary was integral to the election process, the exclusion of blacks from it violated the Fifteenth Amendment. Southern states and localities quickly devised other ruses to limit voting, including the previously instituted poll tax and various new literacy or so-called understanding requirements. But *Smith v. Allwright* was another crack in the hitherto solid wall of segregation.

When Harry S Truman from Missouri became president following Roosevelt's death in 1945, many blacks were unsure of his position on race. The significant shift of black votes away from the Republican party to the Democratic party had begun with Roosevelt, but would it continue? The massive migration of southern blacks to northern cities, where their political participation was possible, had begun to make the black vote a significant, sometimes the decisive, factor in local, congressional, even presidential politics. Whatever his previous attitudes toward segregation, Truman could count votes. But he was also frankly appalled at the racism that had continued in the South during the course of and immediately after the war. On several occasions black soldiers, in uniform, were assaulted, discriminated against, or killed. Truman's strong sense of fairness was touched; both his conscience and his political instincts suggested that here was an issue that the nation could ill afford to ignore any longer. In 1946 he appointed a Committee on Civil Rights—with two liberal white southern members—to investigate what Truman was beginning to see as a moral crisis as well as a political opportunity. The following year the committee issued a powerful report, *To Secure These Rights*, which called on the federal government to put its weight behind the campaign to achieve racial equality. In words that dismayed southern segregationists, this official government committee urged "the elimination of segregation based on race, color, creed, or national origin from American life."

In the midst now of a Cold War that rhetorically pitted the free world against Communist slavery, Truman and others were aware of how southern race relations made a mockery of American ideals. And his political advisers suggested to him that the growing power of black voters in northern cities lessened the national Democratic party's dependence on white southern support. Still Truman acted cautiously. Nevertheless, civil rights seemed to be an idea whose time was coming, backed as it was by the great study published in 1944 by Gunnar Myrdal and his associates, *An American Dilemma: The Negro Problem and Modern Democracy*. Black leaders were pushing hard for presidential action. Although Truman addressed Congress in early 1948 on the issue, he again hesitated to advocate a bold program in Congress for fear of alienating southern whites still further. But at the Democratic National Convention that summer, Senator Hubert Humphrey employed his moving oratory and skilled leadership to ensure that the party platform had a strong civil rights plank. Even as diehard southern segregationists abandoned their historic commitment to the Democratic party and turned instead to a new States' Rights party—the Dixiecrats—Truman rose to the occasion and issued two presidential proclamations, one aimed at desegregating the armed forces and the other providing for nondiscriminatory employment practices in the federal government. Truman won a surprise reelection campaign that fall against Thomas E. Dewey, governor of New York, but the loss of southern support contributed mightily, four years later, to the election of military hero and cautious racial moderate, Dwight David ("Ike") Eisenhower, the Republican candidate, as president. On October 5, 1953, less than ten months after taking office, Ike was present when former California governor Earl Warren took the oath of office as Chief Justice of the Supreme Court, replacing the deceased Fred M. Vinson of Kentucky.

The decision makers in the NAACP's Legal Defense Fund had earlier determined in 1950 that the time had come to shift the legal strategy from demanding that the southern states meet the separate-but-equal requirement to attacking the whole legal basis of that doctrine itself. After a planning session in New York City in June 1950 the NAACP set itself the task of accumulating psychological and sociological evidence of the damaging consequences of racial segregation. And they began to search for cases involving secondary schools that lent themselves to a judicial challenge of the 1896 *Plessy* separate-but-equal decision. In Clarendon, South Carolina; in Topeka, Kansas; in Prince Edward County, Virginia; in the District of Columbia; and in Claymont, Delaware, cases emerged. The details of each case differed, but all spoke eloquently to the issue of shocking discrimination and outrageous inequality. With consummate legal skill the NAACP argued and nurtured these various cases through the courts. In June 1952 the Supreme Court announced it would hear two of these cases, then in October it added a third, then, after another delay, the final two cases were added. Consolidating all five under the name of *Brown v. Board of Education of Topeka*, the Court set December 9, 1952, as the day to hear arguments.

Thurgood Marshall led the arguments on behalf of the plaintiffs, his skills honed by years of experience and given added poignance by his evident devotion to the cause. Backed by friendly briefs filed by a who's who of historians and social scientists, and documented with the powerful though controversial evidence of psychologist Kenneth Clark—whose research on black children's attitudes toward black and white dolls gave chilling evidence of the crippling psychological effect of segregation—Marshall faced John W. Davis, a very experienced attorney noted for the vigor of his preparation and presentation. For three days the court heard arguments before convening. Months passed and the justices sent written questions to both sides. Before the court could reach a decision in what everyone understood to be a truly momentous case, Chief Justice Vinson died. Earl Warren, the new chief justice, desperately wanted a unanimous decision in this, his first case, and the final decision was apparently delayed as he struggled to construct a consensus.

Finally on Monday, May 17, 1954—a day segregationists soon called Black Monday—Chief Justice Warren read the ruling. His words would prove to be a turning point in southern and American history: "We conclude, unanimously, that in the field of public education the doctrine of 'separate but equal' has no place. Separate educational facilities are inherently unequal." A new birth of freedom was in the making, but the making proved difficult indeed. The following May the Supreme Court ruled to leave actual implementation of the decision up to southern federal judges and merely urged them to proceed "with all deliberate speed." The ruling meant that hasty changes would not take place in southern racial practices.

The next decade essentially brought racial war to the South, sometimes a hot war, at other times cold, and whites conducted a terrorist campaign throughout. The eleven years between the *Brown* decision in 1954 and the Voting Rights Act of 1965 seemed like a prolonged series of bloody skirmishes and irrational white intransigence, with fervent protestations that the white South would never cave in to Communist-inspired racial mongrelization. Southern whites developed a bunker mentality, tried to eliminate outside influences, and resorted to angry violence to stem the tides of change. But as the old spiritual put it, a new day was a'coming.

In retrospect it is clear that the very outrageousness of segregationist protest not only morally armed a growing black movement, enabling them to overwhelm the forces of apartheid, but also gradually awakened most of the nation to the cancer in its midst. The behavior of southern white segregationists eventually persuaded the nation that legal segregation was wrong. Polls showed that most Americans at the time disagreed with the 1954 *Brown* decision, and President Eisenhower studiously avoided providing any forthright moral leadership on behalf of civil rights; ten years later President Lyndon B. Johnson took up the civil rights motto, "we shall overcome," and used the phrase to win approval in Congress—and in the public opinion polls—for both the Civil Rights Act of 1964 and the Voting Rights Act of 1965. A great watershed had been passed in the nation's history.

There are some indications that the triumphs of 1964 and 1965 might have been accomplished more quickly and with less turmoil and injury had there been courageous white leadership a decade earlier. When the *Brown* decision was announced, governors of several states, including Alabama and Arkansas, expressed regret but said that the law must be obeyed. A *New York Times* poll of southern school administrators suggested that with a minimum of conflict the new ruling would be put into effect. In various communities white political and religious leaders indicated acquiescence in the ruling—after all, the South had once before tried to go its own way, and that had brought failure. Had President Eisenhower immediately and directly used his enormous prestige and popularity, and the bully pulpit of the White House, to insist that the Supreme Court ruling was the law of the land and must be obeyed in spirit as well as in letter, then these glimmers of acceptance might have been nurtured into a groundswell of pragmatic approval. But that leadership was not forthcoming, and once again the meaner angels of the southern body politic took over and produced one tragic encounter after another in the dark and bloody ground of Dixieland.

In July 1954, meeting with a group of friends in the Mississippi Delta town of Indianola, a World War II veteran and plantation manager named Robert B. Patterson organized the White Citizen's Council, a middle- and upper-class version of the Ku Klux Klan that quickly spread across the deep South and eventually had more than a quarter million members. Eschewing the violence of the Klan, however, the Citizen's Council used economic coercion to punish blacks who transgressed the region's strict racial etiquette. Suddenly they would lose their jobs, or have their insurance cancelled, or find it impossible to get a bank loan or a home mortgage. The result was less bloody but almost as dispiriting as Klan terrorism. Another Mississippian,

Judge Tom P. Brady, wrote a pamphlet vigorously attacking the logic of the *Brown* decision, and his argument soon became part of the verbal artillery of militant segregationists across the region. Prominent journalists like James J. Kilpatrick of the Richmond *News-Leader* used their pens and editorial pages to criticize the idea of integration. In the absence of powerful countervailing voices, these voices of hate—sometimes vicious, sometimes restrained— quickly came to dominate white public opinion in the South. An opportunity had been missed.

As southern segregationist attitudes hardened, many white southerners felt besieged, their traditional ways threatened once again by the lengthening and strengthening arm of the national government. At a time when the nation itself was caught up in Cold War hysteria, it was easy for desperate segregationists to see a Communist conspiracy behind integrationist efforts. Even otherwise good southern whites lost all sense of proportion when they felt what they called "the southern way of life" (i.e., strict racial segregation) was in the least bit endangered. Otherwise kind and decent white men and women would countenance unspeakable evil to support segregation; would lie to protect murderers; and would ignore their consciences to keep solidarity with the white community. Even the slightest acknowledgement that perhaps segregation was wrong could bring down upon the heretic the smashing fist of community authority. An unforgiving curtain of racial conformity descended around much of the South, producing what one historian–participant called a "closed society." Not even a child was allowed to transgress.

Emmett "Bobo" Till, a fourteen-year-old boy from Chicago, was visiting his relatives in Money, Mississippi, in August 1955. Emmett attended an all-black school on the Chicago South Side but was innocent of the rigors of the racial etiquette of Mississippi. To make matters worse, he was a lively, almost swaggering youth who enjoyed impressing his country-bumpkin Mississippi relatives with his big city wiles. He even showed his Mississippi friends a wallet photo of a white girl back home whom he claimed was his girlfriend. One of the local boys doubted that Emmett was bold enough to have a white girlfriend, and taunted him by saying that there was a white girl working in the small country store nearby. Words to the effect that "I bet you won't talk to her" were said. The brash Chicago teenager then went into Bryant's Grocery and Meat Market, bought a piece of candy, and apparently said something to Carolyn Bryant, the wife of the store's owner. There is conflicting testimony over whether he called out "Bye, baby" as he left, or whether he whistled at her (Emmett had a slight lisp and often seemed to whistle when he talked.) Whatever happened inside that store on Wednesday afternoon, August 24, 1955, the local blacks standing outside who heard the encounter immediately understood the danger.

For some reason Carolyn Bryant—a native of Indianola, Mississippi— did not tell her husband of the incident when he returned from driving a truck load of shrimp from Louisiana to Texas. But Roy Bryant was no sooner back at his store than another black, having heard of a "Chicago boy" who had spoken out of place, regaled Bryant with a probably embellished version of Till's encounter with Bryant's wife. That fateful conversation set the brutal plot unfolding, because Bryant considered his honor, and his wife's virtue, at risk. After the close of business late Saturday evening Bryant, accompanied by his brother-in-law J. W. Milam, drove in a pickup truck out to Mose Wright's house, where the Chicago visitors were staying. They asked Wright for the youngster, and Wright pleaded with them that the boy was young, that he wasn't from Mississippi and didn't know any better, but the two white men drove off with Emmett, who was probably too naive to know the danger he was in.

After a vicious beating, the teenager was shot in the head, weighted down with a heavy piece of metal tied to his body with barbed wire, and dumped in the nearby Tallahatchie River, which soon washed up the body. There was overwhelming evidence against Bryant and Milam: Mose Wright risked his life to testify against the murderers and pointed to Milam in response to a question from the prosecutor asking him to identify the kidnappers and said, in his imperfect English, "Thar he." The court, in a flagrant mockery of justice, failed to convict the murderers. (Bryant and Milam later confessed for pay to a journalist who published their unrepentant story.) Much of the nation was aghast, especially when Emmett's mother insisted on an open-casket funeral and a national publication printed a shocking photo of the child's face battered beyond recognition. Mississippi was not accepting desegregation peacefully.

The next civil rights skirmish that captured national attention occurred in Montgomery, Alabama, and it resulted in a signal victory for blacks. Montgomery, where the Confederacy had been established in 1861, was like most southern cities in that its buses were segregated. In Montgomery whites began seating row by row at the front of the bus, working backward, while blacks began at the back and worked forward. However, if a white boarded and there were no more white seats available, then the entire next row of black riders had to relinquish their seats so that the white would have a white row in which to sit. Moreover, black riders had to enter the bus at the front to pay the driver, step back out, and walk to the back door to enter and sit. It was not unknown for white drivers to pull away from the curb before the black could reenter the bus. The result was a constant inconvenience and humiliation to the black community.

On December 1, 1955, Rosa Parks, tired after a long day's work as a seamstress at a downtown department store, was resting in her seat on the way home when several white men boarded the bus, more than the existing white section could hold. The bus driver then yelled to the blacks, "Niggers, move back." Rosa Parks, who had recently attended a race relations workshop at the Highlander Folk School—a pioneer institution advocating peaceful desegregation—refused to budge. The bus driver stopped the bus, and called the police, who promptly arrested Mrs. Parks and took her to jail. The white authorities expected no repercussions from their unexceptional response to what was, in their terms, a black person getting out of line.

But Rosa Parks was exceptional; she had a high-school education, she had an excellent reputation, and she was an active member of Montgomery's very active NAACP. The head of the local NAACP branch, E. D. Nixon, knew Mrs. Parks well and quickly sized up the situation: she was the perfect person, and this was the right occasion, to challenge in the courts Montgomery's segregated buses. Jo Ann Robinson, a black English professor at the city's Alabama State College, was head of the Woman's Political Council and an organizer extraordinaire. Nixon, Robinson, and Fred Gray, a black lawyer, decided to put together a community-wide black boycott of the bus system Over the following weekend Robinson mimeographed 35,000 handbills and with a small group of students distributed them all over the city. Monday morning only a handful of blacks rode the buses. The white officials expected the boycott to fade in a day or two, but they did not appreciate Robinson's skills or the commitment of the blacks. An incredible network of car pools, makeshift taxis, and a remarkable willingness to walk simply wore down the city authorities. For month after month blacks walked and car pooled, regardless of the weather or the distance.

Early on in the campaign E. D. Nixon realized that the boycott needed support from local black churches. He understood that he and Robinson had reputations for radical protest that might put off some blacks; the ministers, though, had unparalleled influence in the black community and they were largely insulated from white economic pressure. At that moment a new minister had just arrived at the Dexter Avenue Baptist Church—so new that he had no enemies among the other ministers. This young minister, despite personal hesitation, had leadership of the movement forced on him, and, unbeknownst to anyone at the moment, the civil rights movement found its leader. Martin Luther King, Jr., accepted the mantle of leadership, found himself invigorated with the moral power of the endeavor, and utilized his growing eloquence as a speaker to electrify the black crowds in his church. It was as if a mighty moral force had been unleashed. The black community discovered a sense of pride, purpose, and power it had not known before, and with that came a feeling of confidence that overrode the physical exhaustion of walking. "Yes, my feets is tired," said one elderly black lady in response to a query, "but my soul is rested."

The whole nation took note of what these blacks had discovered within themselves, and after almost twelve months of boycott, on November 13, 1956, the Supreme Court ruled that the city's segregated bus system was unconstitutional. Montgomery blacks had won a great victory, and the civil rights movement had found itself a great leader. Two years later, in 1958, King and others founded the Southern Christian Leadership Conference

(SCLC), in effect adding the powerful influence of the black church and its ministers to a civil rights movement that had previously been led by lawyers. Perhaps even more important, black people had discovered the self-empowerment and exhilaration of meaningful political involvement. King knew about Mohandas Karamchand Gandhi and his philosophy of nonviolent resistance in India; King was also well read in Christian theology; consequently he could put the black movement in a universal context and articulate the desire for justice in universal language of great power.

Nineteen fifty-six proved to be an explosive year in Montgomery. It began with Martin Luther King Jr.'s home being bombed in January, and it concluded in December with another bombing at the home of Fred Shuttleworth, a black minister, who survived by what he considered a miracle. There were other boycotts in other cities. After Autherine Lucy enrolled at the University of Alabama on February 3, a full-scale riot erupted and the officials suspended her from school. When she protested, the college expelled her. Less than six weeks later, in Washington, DC, Senator Sam Ervin of North Carolina turned his considerable legal talents to drafting a so-called Southern Manifesto attacking the constitutionality of the *Brown* decision. The overwhelming majority of southern legislators signed the document, with only Tennessee's senators Albert Gore and Estes Kefauver refusing; by prior arrangement Texas senator Lyndon B. Johnson and Speaker of the House Sam Rayburn were not asked to sign. That fall Eisenhower was easily reelected president.

Ike was certainly no racist, though by experience and temperament he was not very sensitive to the implications of legal segregation. But as a military man he was committed to the rule of law, and, whether he agreed with the Supreme Court or not, his constitutional duty was to enforce the law. He feared to push the South too fast, although from the black viewpoint the commitment to equality had already been delayed almost a century. Ike's attorney general, Herbert Brownell, was more attuned to the black viewpoint. Moreover, he was dismayed by the continuing southern violence and total intransigence. After the Emmett Till case and in the midst of the Montgomery bus boycott Brownell proposed a major civil rights package to Congress. Eisenhower hesitated but finally accepted Brownell's proposal, only to have it defeated by Congress.

Following the 1956 election Ike found an unlikely ally in the Senate Majority Leader, Lyndon Johnson. Johnson had a real commitment to society's underdogs. He also wanted to assume a political posture that would make him a national figure, and he understood that, given southern congressional strength, only a moderate version of Brownell's program had a chance of being approved. The opponents of segregation had not yet learned what a master of the Senate Lyndon could be, and with masterful manipulation and cajoling and calling in of chits, Johnson pushed through Congress on August

29, 1957, the nation's first civil rights bill since Reconstruction. Eisenhower quickly signed the watered-down bill. In that moment of victory there was no way Ike could know that his biggest civil rights crisis was just in the offing.

Little Rock was a racially progressive city in a racially progressive southern state. In fact, promptly in 1954 two school districts in the state desegregated. Within a week of the *Brown* decision the Little Rock school board indicated its willingness to comply. On May 24, 1955, the school board approved a plan to begin integration in September 1957 by admitting black students to the city's Central High School. Affairs looked promising; after all, Arkansas governor Orval Faubus was himself a racial moderate and political progressive. But segregationist sentiment began to rise in the state, led by a young politician named James Johnson who tried to have the state constitution revised so as to prevent school integration. Faubus intended to run again for the gubernatorial office in 1956, and he feared Johnson would use race-baiting against him. As so many earlier southern demagogues had done before and later, Faubus opportunistically decided to pick up the racist banner and champion that cause. In early 1956 he began to say that the citizens of the state were opposed to integration and he had no intention of going against their desires. In effect Faubus legitimated the protest of racist fanatics, who then began to harass local NAACP leaders, such as Daisy Bates. But according to the school board's plan, Central High was scheduled to open, integrated, on September 3, 1957.

The day before integration was to take place, Faubus deployed the Arkansas National Guard to encircle Central High, ostensibly to prevent violence from breaking out but in reality to prevent nine black students from entering. Faced with the troops, the school board asked the students to stay home the next day and sought a ruling from federal judge Ronald Davies; Davies ruled that school officials should follow the integration plan. So the next day the black students came to the school and found it surrounded by a screaming, hateful mob of white segregationists. One of the black students, Elizabeth Eckford, had missed a message to rendezvous with the others and came alone, only to find herself engulfed by an angry sea of whites. She had to turn back, rescued by two kind whites, one a *New York Times* reporter and the other a local woman. The other eight students were prevented by the National Guard from entering the school. A series of telegrams passed between Faubus and President Eisenhower, who pressed the governor to obey the law. Faubus even met with the president in Rhode Island, but Faubus refused to budge.

Judge Davies then issued an injunction ordering Faubus to remove the guardsmen; Faubus did so but replaced them with policemen. On September 23 the black students again approached the school, but the mob had grown in size and worsened in demeanor. Faubus had become a segregationist hero, and the city was nearly out of control. At that point President Eisenhower, recognizing duty if not morality, honored the request of the mayor and sent in a thousand federal troops from the 101st Airborne Division, the first time since Reconstruction that federal military forces were employed in the South to protect the constitutional rights of its black citizens. The Arkansas National Guard was also federalized and commanded to protect the students.

As the world watched on television, the whole force of the national government was directed to allow the matriculation of nine black students in a southern high school. Military bodyguards were assigned to each, and for the rest of the year an uneasy peace ensued. The students survived taunts and stares, but that spring the only black senior, Ernest Green, graduated. The following year Little Rock closed its public schools rather than have them integrated. The Supreme Court then ruled that closing illegal, and in August 1959 Little Rock began a new school year with integrated classrooms. By no means had the forces of segregation been defeated in the South. Yet Eisenhower, despite his caution and lack of passion for the cause, had made a fundamental decision: the federal government had entered the fray on the side of racial change. It was very clear that without such federal involvement, racial segregation in the South would persist far into the future.

By the late 1950s some progress had been made in school desegregation in the southern fringe areas of Kentucky, Tennessee, Arkansas, and western Texas—at least in regions in those states where there were few blacks. But in the rest of the South white segregationists dug in their heels. The whites of Prince Edward County, Virginia, even shut their public schools in 1959 for five years rather than integrate. In other areas school boards experimented with various student assignment gimmicks to void the effects of desegregation. Throughout the region parents resorted to private schools—so-called "seg" academies—rather than send their children to integrated public schools. Often these segregated private schools were associated with churches, and the parents claimed tax deductions for the tuition "contributions." When New Orleans in November 1960 prepared to integrate its public schools, a crowd of angry white mothers, soon tagged "the cheerleaders," surrounded the schools and shouted their opposition: "Two, four, six, eight; we don't want to integrate!" Mob violence threatened to tear the city apart. The spectacle of hate personified was shocking; so much so that city business leaders, fearing the loss of tourist dollars, insisted on peaceful and gradual integration within several months. In more progressive southern cities like Atlanta, Tampa, Charlotte, Houston, and Dallas, that desire to protect the business climate overcame the more retrograde forces and promoted acceptance of integration in order to avoid ugly racial confrontations. By the early 1960s many southern urban school systems, particularly in the border and western states of the South, had at least begun a gradual, grade-by-grade process of integration, and soon the rural areas followed suit. The focus of desegregation then shifted to other aspects of the Jim Crow system.

The civil rights movement took a different tack beginning in 1960, one based more upon mass participation than upon legal briefs. The shift had unpremeditated origins. Four male students at North Carolina Agricultural and Technical College in Greensboro, in a bull session on the evening of January 31, 1960, began to reflect on one of them having been refused counter service at a bus station snackbar. The conversation led to a decision that the next day they would go to a downtown Woolworth store to challenge the refusal to let black customers—who could purchase anything else in the store—sit at the counter and eat a sandwich or drink a cup of coffee. So on February 1, 1960, four polite, neatly dressed college students inadvertently started a movement that eventually shook the foundations of segregation. As expected, the waitresses would not serve them; even the white policeman who was called seemed nonplussed by the event. Word spread back to the college and more students arrived to continue the sit-in; soon white students came also to protest the discriminatory policy. Within several days a thousand students were involved, crowds surrounded the store, and hecklers began to harass the students. Many otherwise conservative whites suddenly had brought home to them one of the more ridiculous points of southern race etiquette.

The sit-in movement spread—and it spread like wildfire; within two weeks to fifteen other cities, within two months to over fifty cities throughout the South, and by the end of the year to one hundred cities. At stake were not abstract constitutional arguments and arcane legal points but rather the simple absurdity of being willing to sell a student a package of Juicy Fruit but not a glass of Coca Cola. Black students and black laypersons now had a visible way to act out their protest. Inspired by the opportunity, Ella Baker, an energetic woman who had been a pioneer in SCLC, called together some two hundred student leaders in Raleigh over the Easter week of 1960 and organized the Student Nonviolent Coordinating Committee (SNCC, pronounced Snick) to marshal student activists against segregation. The control of the civil rights movement was slipping still further away from the more conservative NAACP.

The new emphasis on demonstrating the injustice of segregation by putting live bodies at the point of contest took still another form the following year. Twenty-five years before, in 1946, the Supreme Court had ruled against segregated seating on interstate bus systems, but the law was not enforced in the South. In May 1961 thirteen brave riders, seven black and six white, boarded two buses in the nation's capital and set out to test the law. The ultimate destination was New Orleans, where they hoped to arrive on May 17, the anniversary of the *Brown* decision. The trip was uneventful through Virginia and North Carolina, and the bus terminals voluntarily desegregated as the so-called freedom riders arrived. There was a minor altercation in Rock Hill, South Carolina, but then there was clear sailing all the way to Atlanta. There the two buses split up, with the Greyhound bus routed through Anniston, Alabama, and the Trailways through Birmingham.

As the Greyhound pulled into the Anniston terminal an angry crowd of protesters attacked the bus, slashing at its tires and pummeling it with rocks. The bus pulled away and headed down the road, only to have multiple flat tires a few miles away. When the bus stopped, the mob caught up. Someone threw a fire bomb through a window, and in seconds the bus was aflame. The freedom riders barely escaped in time and were rescued by a car caravan, headed by the Reverend Fred Shuttlesworth, that arrived from Birmingham just in time. When the Trailways bus pulled up to the Birmingham station, all seemed peaceful. In a flash the scene changed as dozens of thugs and Klansmen came out of nowhere and proceeded to beat the bus riders with a wild vengeance. Newspaper headlines and television images spread the sickening story worldwide, embarrassing the Kennedy administration but not moving them to intervene effectively. The Congress of Racial Equality (CORE), the Chicago-based organization that had sponsored the freedom riders, could not find bus drivers willing to continue the journey, and so the original freedom riders were flown by the Justice Department to New Orleans.

SNCC, fearing the long-term effects of a defeat, found new volunteer riders who were willing to risk their lives for the cause. President Kennedy and his brother Robert, the nation's attorney general, were simultaneously moved and annoyed by the black persistence, but they used their influence to obtain a bus driver and extracted a promise from the Alabama governor, John Patterson, that the freedom riders would not be harmed as they drove from Birmingham to Montgomery. The twenty-one freedom riders noted the police protection as they drove along, but when they neared Montgomery, the protection disappeared. When the riders disembarked at the terminal, a mob crazed with anger attacked the students with frenzied violence. Hundreds of screaming people swarmed around the bus, and even John Seigenthaler, a presidential aide sent to observe, was knocked senseless by a pipe-wielding assailant.

Finally the Kennedys began to realize the gravity of the situation, and the president sent in six hundred federal marshals. When the city threatened to explode in violence the next day, Governor Patterson declared martial law and—with the eyes of the world looking on—employed the National Guard to protect the freedom riders. The Kennedys then arranged for the freedom riders to leave and be allowed to pass peacefully through Mississippi. (By prior arrangement they were quietly arrested in Jackson, Mississippi, but not assaulted—the best compromise the Kennedys could arrange with Mississippi officials.) The freedom riders had not reached New Orleans, but they had reached the consciences of millions of Americans, and they drove home to the Kennedys the necessity of action by the federal government. By early autumn, 1961, the Interstate Commerce Commission ordered the desegregation of all interstate bus facilities.

In retrospect 1962 seems the lull before the next big storm. Martin Luther King, Jr., had been called in to Albany, Georgia, to help lead a protest, but the wily sheriff there, Laurie Pritchett, also knew about Gandhian protests and understood that police overreaction only brought publicity and helped the blacks' cause. So he devised a policy of passive counter-resistance whereby the protesters were politely treated and jailed without violence. He reserved cells for a hundred miles in each direction so that the protesters could never completely fill the available jail spaces. Pritchett essentially defeated King at his own strategy, and King began 1963 despondent and fearful that the movement was stalled and that he had lost his leadership role.

Events continued to ensnare the Kennedy administration and force it to take an increasingly active role in desegregation. On September 3, 1962, a federal judge ordered the University of Mississippi to enroll James Meredith. The state's governor, Ross Barnett, rose to the occasion to champion again the racist cause. Before a football crowd's chants of "Never, never, never, never . . ." he perorated on his love of Mississippi's customs. But by now President Kennedy was willing to play hardball with the racist demagogues of Dixie. On Sunday evening, September 29, as Meredith arrived at campus, a full-scale riot broke out. In the midst of the chaos Governor Barnett spoke about the rights of Mississippians being trampled by federal power, but as the destruction, injuries, and then deaths increased, the federal government responded by sending in troops in the early morning hours. An uneasy order was restored, and on Monday morning, protected by federal marshals, James Meredith walked to his first class—American history. Again, the courage of blacks, reinforced however reluctantly by federal power, was successfully challenging segregation in the very heart of Dixie.

Birmingham, a muscular, tough city with the smell of its blast furnaces suggesting the racial hate that smoldered and occasionally erupted into flame, was called the most racist city in America. The Reverend Fred Shuttlesworth had been battling that reputation for years, and now, in early 1963, he was pressuring Martin Luther King, Jr., to come and lead a protest. Shuttlesworth had done the hard preparatory work; it was time for King to lend his charisma. King worried about the city and its notoriously racist police commissioner, Eugene "Bull" Connor. But after the failure in Albany, King needed a success. Bull Connor was exactly the type of arrogant policeman who could be counted on to act outrageously, so outrageously that he would, against his will, both inspire black courage and create international publicity for the cause of integration. With these considerations King and SCLC planned Project C—C standing for confrontation.

The campaign began on April 3 as the city government was in turmoil over a recent disputed election. The city council got an injunction to halt the SCLC-sponsored protests, but King ignored the order. On Good Friday he was arrested and jailed. With time on his hands, and in response to a group of white clergy who objected to his efforts, King sat down over the Easter weekend and penciled around the margins of a newspaper his reply to the white remonstrance. This "Letter from a Birmingham Jail" was an eloquent defense of the religious and moral necessity to work against the racial status quo, and like the Declaration of Independence and Gettysburg Address, the brief essay spoke to the heart of the world. "There comes a time," King concluded, "when the cup of endurance runs over. . . . I hope . . . you can understand our legitimate and unavoidable impatience." King was released on bond from jail on April 20 and immediately made preparations to continue Project C. Now a bold new strategy was hatched. One of the factors that crippled mass black protest was the economic coercion the white establishment could wield against black adults. But black school children did not hold jobs. Did the movement dare to use children as protest marchers? Would Bull Connor be so unyielding as to use violence against helpless children? Would parents consent? Would the children be willing? The answer to all these questions was yes.

The first day, May 2, the police were restrained. But the following day Bull Connor reverted to form. His policemen tore into the defenseless black children, hitting them with clubs and siccing their vicious German shepherd dogs against the school kids. Black adults rushed to defend their children, and the police went berserk. Connor ordered firemen to turn their fire hoses, with water pressure at one hundred pounds per square inch, against the blacks. The powerful stream of water knocked people down, tore the bark off trees, rolled screaming, terrified children across the ground and over curbs. Three days later it happened again, with more black adults—enraged—participating. Finally, faced with the possibility of genuine race warfare, the city business leaders intervened. The city agreed to desegregate the downtown lunch counters, remove the hated "white" and "colored" signs, and employ more blacks. Racists fumed, but the movement had won another victory.

But the larger victory was not in Birmingham. For millions of Americans, the television images of attack dogs and high-pressure water hoses, employed against small children, became one of the defining moments of the twentieth century. Bull Connor's hateful excesses finally awakened the nation to the cancer in its midst. No longer could decent people pretend things were okay, pretend that blacks would accept their traditional place, pretend that no great moral principles were at stake. Still Alabama continued defiant. Governor George Wallace on June 11, 1963, in response to a court order that the University of Alabama integrate, sought political mileage from the state's white majority by symbolically standing in the doorway to a university building to block the entrance of black students. When faced down by the nation's attorney general, Nicholas Katzenbach, Wallace—by then out of range of the television cameras—stepped aside. Nevertheless, Wallace had solidified his position as a feisty defender of "segregation today, tomorrow, and forever." The next day in Jackson, Mississippi, in a completely unrelated incident, Medgar Evers, field secretary of the NAACP, was murdered on his front doorsteps by an assassin. President Kennedy, forced by this series of intolerable events to enlarge his commitment to civil rights, introduced a strengthened civil rights bill to Congress on June 19.

CIVIL RIGHTS AND VOTING RIGHTS

Capitalizing on the moment, and wanting to keep the pressure on the president and the Congress, King and other race leaders began to plan for a march on Washington to make concrete the demand that justice be done in the South. There was some dissension among various civil rights organizations; recent events had radicalized some for whom the pace of the NAACP and the SCLC seemed too slow and too mild. However, the disagreements were papered over for the sake of the march. On the appointed day, August 28, 1963, upwards of 250,000 marchers—a quarter of them white, and with blacks arriving by bus from all over the nation—came together in the nation's capital. At the biggest protest meeting in American history thousands listened to the speakers and entertainers, and everywhere the strains of the anthem of the civil rights movement—"We Shall Overcome"—could be heard. The climax of the march, televised throughout the nation, was an extraordinarily powerful oration by Martin Luther King, Jr., at the foot of the Lincoln Memorial. With the moving cadence of the black preacher style, King captivated the audience and the world, concluding with the image of his dream of a nation undivided by race. "And when this happens and when we allow freedom to ring," he said in words that produced goose bumps on listeners, "when we let it ring from every village and every hamlet, from every state and every city, we will be able to speed up that day when all God's children, black men and white men, Jews and gentiles, Protestants and Catholics, will be able to join hands and sing in the words of the old Negro spiritual: 'Free at last. Free at last. Thank God Almighty, we are free at last.'"

Seldom had the nation been so moved by words. Opinion polls showed that a majority of Americans now desired to redress the racial problems. But the heady optimism was quickly brought up short less than three weeks later. On Sunday morning, September 15, a mighty explosion tore through the Sixteenth Street Baptist Church in Birmingham. Buried beneath the rubble were four young black girls, killed by white hate. Kennedy's proposed civil rights bill was soon bogged down in Congress, stymied by a Senate filibuster led by Strom Thurmond—the former Dixiecrat—of South Carolina and James Eastland of Mississippi, the Senate champions of racism. Then the nation was to be stunned again. On November 22, riding in a motorcade in Dallas, Texas, a citadel of right-wing politics, President Kennedy himself was

Martin Luther King, Jr. (Library of Congress)

killed by an assassin's bullet. Much of the nation was in mourning as Lyndon B. Johnson, newly sworn in as president, came to Washington and sought to assure a shocked Republic that stability was restored. Johnson went out of his way five days later to say to the nation at a joint session of Congress that the programs and policies of Kennedy would be continued and that nothing would so honor the slain president as the passing of the civil rights bill.

Johnson had begun his political career almost four decades earlier as a racial moderate in central Texas, and although political considerations had caused him to take a conservative detour in the late 1940s and early 1950s, events of the early 1960s recalled him to his original principles. Through the spring and early summer his civil rights bill was tied up in Congress; despite Johnson's masterful maneuvering, progress was slow in breaking the segregationists' opposition. At a critical juncture the diehard South once again produced an outrageous act that demanded national action. Beginning in 1962 a coalition of civil rights groups—the Council of Federated Organizations (COFO)—had organized to register voters in Mississippi only to be met with unrelenting terroristic violence intended to intimidate them. To dramatize the desire of Mississippi blacks to enjoy an elemental privilege of democracy, COFO arranged a mock election in 1963 in which 80,000 blacks cast their "Freedom Ballot."

COFO leader Bob Moses also put out a call for northern college students to come to Mississippi and do voter registration during a 1964 "Freedom Summer" campaign, recognizing that the national media would pay more attention to them than to local blacks. Almost on cue, three of the COFO workers disappeared, a local black (James Chaney) and two northern college students (Andrew Goodman and Michael Schwerner), murdered on June 21, 1964, in Neshoba County, Mississippi. An extensive FBI searched some six weeks later to the discovery of the bodies in an earthen pond dam near Philadelphia, Mississippi—the work of the local Klan in collaboration with local law enforcement officers. The abduction and murder of the three civil rights workers provided the immediate background against which, in late June, Lyndon Johnson labored hard to defeat the opponents of the civil rights bill. Finally breakthrough came, the bill passed, and Johnson signed the Civil Rights Act of 1964 on July 2, two days before the national celebration of freedom. The year ended with Martin Luther King, Jr., being awarded the Nobel Peace Prize.

The new year began with King and the SCLC planning a major voter registration drive in Alabama, centering on the notorious region near Selma in Dallas County where almost no blacks were allowed to vote. In February a black teenager was killed in a racial incident, and King matured plans for a protest march from Selma to Montgomery, the state capital. Sheriff Jim Clark of Dallas County looked like a character from a civil right's worker's nightmare: pot bellied, wearing mirrored sunglasses and a short Eisenhower jacket, and walking with a swagger while he tapped his nightstick against his open palm as if itchy to club a black head. On Sunday, March 7, as the black marchers reached the apex of the Edmund Pettus Bridge that crossed the Alabama River at the edge of town, they saw Sheriff Clark's policemen and an army of state troopers. After a momentary warning the policemen attacked the marchers, swinging their clubs, using electric cattle prods, tear gas, and even flailing the defenseless blacks with short lengths of chains and loops of rubber hose encircled with barbed wire. As the blacks fled back down the bridge and sought refuge in their homes, the policemen followed, continuing their brutal attack. ABC News television cameras were on hand, and suddenly Sunday evening television viewers had ABC break into their feature program of the evening—ironically, the movie *Judgment at Nuremberg*—to broadcast live shots of the carnage at Selma. Again the conscience of the nation was shocked by the violence meted out to citizens in a southern state.

Two days later, before King could reorganize a full-scale march, Lyndon Johnson worked out a compromise whereby King—much to his chagrin—would only symbolically cross the bridge and then turn around and return to Selma. But Johnson's response did not stop there. Six days later, on March 15, he made a rare presidential address to a joint session of Congress. To the members of Congress, and to a national television office, he gave the most impassioned and eloquent speech of his career. Making vivid reference to the brutality against blacks in the last ten days, Johnson in his slow Texas accent told the nation: "Their cause must be our cause too. Because it is not just Negroes, but really it is all of us who must overcome the crippling legacy of bigotry and injustice. And we *shall* overcome." He sent his voting rights bill to Congress two days later. Then Johnson notified Alabama governor Wallace that the state's national guard would be federalized to protect the marchers. Later, augmented by volunteers from around the nation, 25,000 marchers walked across the bridge named for a Confederate general through central Alabama to the steps of the state capital, from which Jefferson Davis had taken the oath of office as president of the Confederacy on February 18, 1861. There, on March 25, 1965, joined by such heroes of the movement as Rosa Parks, Martin Luther King, Jr., addressed the crowd and the nation by television. Back in Washington, Johnson continued his efforts and on August 6 signed the Voting Rights Act of 1965. The great ship of southern race relations had finally been slowed and turned. The South would never be the same again.

Of course the victory was neither instantaneous nor complete. Thereafter in hundreds of different places and at a variety of paces the dead hand of the past was gradually lifted from the South. Residential segregation and the concept of neighborhood schools eventually made total integration practically impossible in the South's cities; ironically many of the smaller towns, which could support only one school, more nearly achieved complete integration. The South's private universities on occasion found the transition more complicated than did state universities. One, Rice University, actually had to sue the state in 1963 to have its 1891 charter of incorporation revised to allow it to integrate. And there were occasional backwater counties (McIntosh in Georgia and the notorious Delta region of Mississippi) where integration's arrival was delayed a decade. But throughout most of the South the changes at last came so quickly as to belie the vehemence with which they had been opposed.

The changes were more far-reaching than merely a revision of laws. Black people found a new self-respect, a sense of importance and worth, that had not always been possible in a segregated society. This feeling of respect often led them to embrace political participation. Blacks were organizing, winning political office at the local level (and higher), and serving on boards and commissions. The civil rights breakthrough of 1964 and 1965 had emboldened blacks to step forward and seize political and economic opportunities that had been nonexistent several years before. By the early 1970s, for example, Mississippi had more black elected officials than any other state. Throughout the South blacks found jobs as clerks, secretaries, and in low-level management; they could sit in restaurant dining rooms and attend movies and concerts; and their children could become Boy Scouts and Girl Scouts and participate on school athletic teams. In truth, in fundamental ways a New South had arisen from the ashes of banished legal racism.

Yet the hopes awakened in the early 1970s have been only imperfectly realized. While many remarkable successes have been achieved in integrating southern life and society, unanticipated developments have once again made the historical outcome problematic. Very significant numbers of urban whites have fled to the suburbs seeking larger homes, bigger yards, better schools, less crime, and fewer blacks. The center-city populations of most southern cities have declined (as have those of the North) along with the tax base and general economic prospects. The resulting downward spiral of weakening schools, failing infrastructure, and increasing crime has worsened living conditions for many of the region's poorest blacks, which has only further accelerated white flight, undermined majority white support of government assistance and reform programs, and contributed to the resegregation of southern cities by class as much as by race. The black ghettoes in most large cities of today are much less supportive communities than were the black ghettoes of the early twentieth century, where there were usually present at least some positive middle-class role models and job opportunities. No solutions for the plight of the black underclass seem politically feasible in the final decade of the century.

Small southern cities and towns, not large enough for substantial suburbs and multiple high schools, have more successfully weathered the desegregation storms and emerged as the best integrated areas of the South. Yet amidst this paradox of ugly urban ghettoes and systematic resegregation, every southern city also has growing minorities of well-educated, upwardly mobile black professionals and middle-class workers who live in integrated neighborhoods, send their children to integrated public schools, and move freely and easily in the affluent, comparatively cosmopolitan world of the modern South. And yet again there are pockets of rural black poverty in the region that remind one of the Third World. The gap between prosperous and poor blacks is widening.

Most southern whites today see racism as essentially a thing of the past, but most blacks perceive it as still present and something extra that blacks must strive to overcome. Conservative whites increasingly think special government programs for blacks are no longer needed, while most blacks see government as the primary and still necessary benefactor of their people. Suspicions between the two races appear to be on the rise as the century ends. These differences in perception, these conflicts, sharpened political debate in the years following 1980. Between these two versions of reality lie the hard business of determining the domestic political agenda of the South in the future. Short of achieving a utopian New South, how does a society reconcile such incongruous understandings or cope humanely with such diversity, economic disparity, and unequal social outcomes? The nation's experiment with liberty, of which Abraham Lincoln spoke so nobly at Gettysburg in 1863, remains open-ended.

THE SOLID DEMOCRATIC SOUTH AND SEGREGATION

The vital political role of southern blacks in the 1970s and the election in 1976 of Jimmy Carter from the deep South to the presidency suggest something of the changed nature of politics in the region since World War II, but perhaps the popularity in Louisiana of David Duke in 1991 cautions southerners from too quickly assuming that the old racial ghosts have been completely banished. The Democratic Solid South of the 1920s and 1930s was replaced with a Republican Solid South in the 1970s and 1980s, unless extraordinary events intervened—as they did in 1976 in the aftermath of the Watergate scandal and the presence on the Democratic ticket of a born-again candidate from Georgia. However, the Republican dominance obtains only for presidential elections; at the state and local level a surprising degree of biracial cooperation has continued the supremacy of the Democratic party—albeit a very different Democratic party from that of 1940. Along with the newfound regional prosperity and the breakdown of the worst vestiges of racial segregation, post-World War II southern politics completes the triad of change that has largely remade the recent South. As so often in American history, southern issues have had a major impact on national politics—largely causing the Republican party to reshape itself over the last generation.

To a dismayingly large degree, the primary purpose of Democratic party politics in the decades before World War II was to maintain the racial status quo. The Republican party was effectively nonexistent in most of the region, and one of the South's defenses of one-party politics was that it allowed, through the congressional seniority system, disproportionate southern power in Congress—power especially to protect regional racial mores. Even so masterful a political operator as Franklin D. Roosevelt felt constrained to acquiesce to southern racial feelings lest his programs in Congress be blocked. Likewise, through the requirement in the Democratic party that nominees at its quadrennial conventions receive a two-thirds vote for nomination, the southern Democrats normally had the power to prevent the nomination of presidential candidates whom they considered especially unfriendly.

The first indication that the national Democratic party would in the future not be so cozy with the conservative forces in Dixie came in the midst of the New Deal. The southern politicos were receiving the programmatic benefits of Roosevelt's administration and felt comfortable with their influence. They were caught unaware at the 1936 Democratic convention when, by voice vote, the delegates adopted a simple majority vote rule. Diehard southern states' rightists were alarmed, and more so in the later years of the New Deal as Roosevelt's relief programs began to threaten local control. Moreover, increasing support by northern labor unions and urban blacks made Roosevelt less beholden to the votes of southern Democrats. Southern politicians, now alert to the slightest indication that their power in national political circles was diminishing, began to be more critical of Roosevelt and his New Deal reforms. But the specter and then the reality of war delayed a significant southern revolt against the national party in 1940 and 1944.

As we have already seen, political pressure and increasing sensitivity to the nation's racial problems—magnified in the midst of a war against Nazi ideas about racial superiority—brought home not simply to American blacks but to national politicians the necessity of redressing the worst abuses of the Jim Crow system. Harry S Truman had become president in 1945 following Roosevelt's death, and the man from Missouri surprised black leaders by showing a depth of humanity and an ability to change his attitudes toward black rights. His appointment of a Committee on Civil Rights and his issuance of presidential proclamations desegregating the armed forces and providing for fair employment practices in the federal government were the last straw for many southern Democratic segregationists. After Truman had called for "effective federal action" against discrimination in his 1948 State of the Union address, southern party leaders seethed.

Truman understood that he faced a difficult election in 1948, and he momentarily hesitated to risk a break with the southerners, but when advisors—incorrectly as it turned out—told him he could push forward against segregation without losing the support of southern Democratic leaders, Truman moved ahead boldly. Pushed by the liberal Americans for Democratic Action and such senators as Hubert Humphrey from Minnesota, the Democratic party became the champion of civil rights. As angry southern delegates were outvoted time and again at the 1948 convention, a strong civil rights plank was accepted. Although Texas congressman Sam Rayburn, the presiding officer, tried to prevent a wholesale southern walkout, in the end some thirty-six southern delegates—13 percent of the southerners present—did bolt. Nevertheless, the national Democratic party and its president were on record as favoring significant action to reform the nation's racial practices.

Three days after the Democratic convention, six thousand southern white Democrats gathered in Birmingham, organized the States' Rights party (popularly known as the Dixiecrats), nominated Governor Strom Thurmond of South Carolina as its presidential candidate and Governor Fielding Wright of Mississippi as its vice-presidential candidate, and mounted a forthrightly racist campaign to preserve every last vestige of segregation against what they termed a Communist-integrationist onslaught. In the deep South states of South Carolina, Alabama, Mississippi, and Louisiana, whites cast the overwhelming majority of their votes for this party of the past, but in the South as a whole Truman won almost eight out of ten votes and upset Thomas Dewey to win the presidency in his own right. But the future was foretold: southern whites, especially in states where blacks were most numerous, would break with their traditional party over the race issue. In what might be called the peripheral or rim South many whites still voted for the Democrats as much by habit as by conviction, but a crack had been made in the wall of the Solid South, and that fissure would widen until the wall collapsed in the aftermath of the civil rights advances of the 1960s. Race would be the key to the rise of the Republican party in the South.

Actually, southern Democratic committee chairmen still had inordinate power in Congress, and for that reason among other concerns that occupied him—such as the rising tensions in the Cold War—Truman did not seek a full-scale legislative attack on segregation. In fact, for a decade the major battles would take place in federal courts, and race receded somewhat as the paramount issue in presidential politics, in part also because national Republicans were not yet noticeably less supportive of civil rights than Democrats were. The saliency of the issue remained, however, as illustrated by the upset defeats of Claude Pepper of Florida and Frank Graham of North Carolina in the senatorial elections of 1950. Graham's defeat in the Democratic primary was particularly prescient of the future campaigns against liberal Democrats: a vicious racist attack, orchestrated by a staff that included a young journalist named Jesse Helms, depicted Graham (a bungling campaigner in the best of circumstances) as an ultraliberal whose values threatened the white South's way of life, which, it was argued, was already under siege by Communists whose ultimate aim was the mongrelization of the white population of Dixie.

But at the presidential level the Republicans rejected the more conservative candidate, Senator Robert A. Taft of Ohio, who opposed federal fair employment and school desegregation efforts, and chose instead war hero Dwight D. Eisenhower. Two southern Democrats, senators Richard B. Russell of Georgia and Estes Kefauver of Tennessee, made a run for the nomination. Kefauver's personable campaign style won considerable success in several early primary states, and he entered the Democratic convention with more delegate strength than any other candidate. But the moderate from Tennessee lost on the third ballot to the more liberal and more eloquent Governor Adlai Stevenson of Illinois. Many southerners who had become increasingly disenchanted with the national Democratic party, yet bound by tradition to the Democrats, found in General Eisenhower an authentic hero who made switching parties at the presidential level palatable. In the fall 1952 elections Ike won 50 percent of the southern white vote and carried the peripheral states of Virginia, Florida, Texas, and Tennessee. In a number of states "Democrats for Eisenhower" movements represented a kind of political halfway house for those who were moving away from the governmental activism of the Democratic party but were not yet ready to quit the party of their fathers.

Eisenhower was a cautious leader in domestic affairs, and he firmly believed that states, not the federal government, should somehow ultimately handle social matters like school desegregation. Nevertheless, Ike believed even more strongly in his responsibility to enforce the law as defined by the Supreme Court. Because the Court had decreed in 1954 that segregated education was inherently unequal, and although he probably regretted the issue having been thus made a concern of the federal government, when the crisis came in Little Rock the former general sent in troops to defend the law of the land. Needless to say, many southern whites felt betrayed. Still, much that Eisenhower stood for—strong defense, limited government, a modified conception of states' rights—appealed to white southerners, and most felt that, the appointment of Chief Justice Earl Warren notwithstanding, Ike was less aggressive on desegregation than any national Democratic president would be. When the national Democrats in 1956 once more put Stevenson up against Eisenhower, Ike swept to an easy victory, winning 53 percent of the South's electoral votes and adding Louisiana to the four southern states that he had carried in 1952.

Despite these Grand Old Party (GOP) victories in the presidential balloting, at the local level the South's politics remained overwhelmingly Democratic. As late as 1960 the Republicans held only forty-eight seats in the South's lower houses (out of more than 1,300) and twelve seats in the upper houses (out of about 450 total). In hundreds of rural counties there were no Republican candidates, no party tickets, no party organization. In the affluent suburbs of the larger cities there were tiny organizations, but these were far more conservative and rabidly anticommunist than the national Republican party. Some of these southern GOP organizations were hotbeds of activity on behalf of paranoid radical-right groups, such as the Christian Anti-Communist Crusade and the John Birch Society, whose founder Robert A. Welch called even Eisenhower a dupe of the Communist conspiracy. At the local level the Republicans were not a factor in southern politics, and most southern racists found state Democratic leaders such as Orval Faubus, John Patterson, Ross Barnett, Strom Thurmond (who had returned to the party after the failure of the Dixiecrats), and senators such as John Eastland and Herman Talmadge to be the leaders of their cause. Particularly after President Eisenhower's sending of troops to Little Rock in 1957, southern segregationists turned increasingly to homegrown Democratic racists to protect the so-called southern way of life.

THE PARTIES SWITCH ON THE ISSUE OF RACE

Precisely because at the national level both political parties seemed mildly progressive on the racial issues, neither party had an automatic advantage in the South in 1960. Although Vice-President Richard Nixon, the Republican candidate in 1960, did not possess the personal charisma that Eisenhower had, Ike had shown southerners that they could vote Republican and not have to hide their faces. But southern conservatives were still angry about the Little Rock intervention and were uncertain that a GOP vote was necessarily a defense of segregation. At the same time the head of the Democratic ticket, Senator John F. Kennedy, a Roman Catholic from Massachusetts, raised religious issues that he only partially settled at a skillful meeting with Baptist ministers in Houston. Kennedy, wary of losing the South, had chosen Lyndon B. Johnson of Texas as his vice-presidential candidate. Still, many southern segregationists, remembering LBJ's support of the 1957 Civil Rights Act and his lack of support for the 1956 Southern Manifesto that defended states' rights principles, were lukewarm toward the colorful Texan because they felt he had betrayed the South. Nevertheless, Kennedy had telegenic charisma in abundance, and Johnson proved to be a skillful campaigner in the South. Nixon himself had long supported civil rights, and though he carefully positioned himself slightly to the right of the Democrats in 1960, such positioning did not allow him to increase the GOP share of the southern white vote. On the other hand, LBJ's residual southernness appealed to even conservative southerners, while Kennedy's telephone call to offer sympathy to Coretta Scott King when her husband, Martin Luther, was in jail, won Kennedy a substantial majority of the votes of the relatively few southern blacks who could vote (and of course it galvanized the many northern blacks in support of the Democrats). The result of these conflicting factors was a razor thin Democratic victory in the South and in the nation. Thanks largely to the presence of LBJ on the ticket, Kennedy reversed the last two elections and won the majority of white southern voters. Together the Kennedy–Johnson ticket carried South Carolina, Georgia, Alabama, and Louisiana in the deep South, and Texas, North Carolina, and Arkansas in the peripheral South. Nixon, however, did win Virginia and Florida, two states with significant in-migration of northerners who had traditionally supported the GOP, and Tennessee, whose strong base of mountain Republicanism stretched back to the Civil War.

The popular election in the South was much closer than the Democratic tally of electoral votes indicated, and Republican strength in Virginia and Florida suggested that population growth and emergent prosperity could vastly enlarge the GOP base in southern states beyond the small group of right wing radicals who had dominated the party in the 1950s. The concept of the Sun Belt was unknown in the early 1960s, but already in the growing suburbs of Atlanta, Charlotte, Dallas, New Orleans, and Houston there were increasing numbers of middle-class, professional voters who identified with the national Republican party in its opposition to what was called Big Government. Thousands of these new suburban southerners were recent migrants from the North, life-long Republicans with no regional devotion to the Democratic party.

An entire constellation of values associated with the GOP had first arisen in opposition to the New Deal, and newly prosperous white southerners, no longer seeing themselves or their relatives as benefiting from government relief programs, came to identify with the conservative Republican agenda. Central to this agenda was opposition to taxes, opposition to federal government involvement in any local matters, a strong belief that the least government was the best—indeed, that government was the enemy of freedom and prosperity—and a patriotic defense of a strong military establishment. Race per se was seldom mentioned as a central issue, although calls for less government intervention indirectly attacked the only agency that seemed to advance black interests in the South. Vicious race-baiting was not a characteristic of this country-club Republicanism. The powerful rural Democratic domination of southern state politics had long thwarted the development of the suburb-based Republican party in the region by rendering urban districts politically impotent, but the Supreme Court's one man, one vote decision in *Baker v. Carr* in 1962, amplified by a series of like decisions (*Gray v. Sanders* in 1963, *Reynolds v. Sims* in 1964, and *Drum v. Seawell* in 1966), brought about a very significant reapportionment. This resulted in a redistribution of political power in the South, essentially enfranchising the cities and suburbs and providing a window of opportunity for southern Republicans. This potential for growth also meant that the Republican party in the South could move beyond advocacy of extremist policies to join the national party ideologically. Ironically this occurred at the very moment when the national party itself moved away from moderation. As its 1964 standard bearer would say, "Extremism in the defense of liberty is no vice."

The national Democratic party was more publicly identified with support for civil rights than the Republican party was, but President Kennedy had little interest in and less passion for the issue. Yet his administration found itself preoccupied with civil rights because southern blacks had made their cause a folk movement and forced the nation to face southern segregation squarely. The sit-ins, the freedom rides, the fire hoses of Bull Connor in Birmingham, and the deaths of Medger Evers and the four little girls in the church bombing pricked the nation's conscience. President Kennedy, Attorney General Robert Kennedy, and the administration were thereby forced to get involved. Their nemesis, Governor George C. Wallace of Alabama, became nationally prominent as a vocal opponent of integration and helped politicize the issue. Civil rights pushed Cold War concerns aside to become the defining issue of the day, and in the very midst of these troubled times, as President Kennedy traveled to Texas in part at least hoping to temper conservative Democratic opposition to his policies, Lee Harvey Oswald shot and killed the president as he rode in a motorcade through the streets of Dallas on November 22, 1963. Later that day Vice-President Lyndon B. Johnson took the oath of office in Air Force One, the presidential jet, and became the nation's president at a moment of great tragedy.

Johnson was an enormously complex man, simultaneously power hungry, crass, and egocentric, yet caring deeply for the poor and oppressed. He wanted to outdo his hero Franklin D. Roosevelt in improving the life of the average people and wanted to show the northeastern provincials—by whom he had long felt patronized—that he could push programs through a Congress that had completely bottled up Kennedy's proposals. In part, too, Johnson wanted to save the South from its most besetting sins so that it could more completely join the rest of the nation. Johnson was often vulgar and self-indulgent and occasionally corrupt, but he identified with the lowly in American society who had been denied justice and he immediately sensed that this moment of tragedy could be in part redeemed by passing landmark legislation. The most urgent social problem was racial discrimination. Johnson took advantage of the emotional intensity and mood of national introspection following Kennedy's assassination to break the congressional logjam over civil rights legislation. With surprising eloquence and typical legislative skill, putting together a bipartisan, multisectional coalition and winning the cooperation of Republican Senator Everett Dirksen of Illinois, LBJ in the year following his abrupt ascendancy to the Oval Office pushed through not only the Civil Rights Act of 1964 but the greatest amount of progressive social legislation in the nation's history. His Great Society program represented the logical fulfillment of Roosevelt's New Deal, and from Head Start and Medicare to the National Endowment for the Humanities, LBJ reshaped American society. The role of the national government had never been larger, its commitment to racial and economic justice had never been stronger.

Not everyone approved of the direction the national government had taken. George Wallace began campaigning in January 1964 in opposition to the expanding role of the government, particularly in the realm of civil rights, and he took his message to the North and border states with considerable success. Wallace was clear in his aims; he was running to force the national Democratic party to shift back to the right. But just before the Democratic convention, anticipating Barry Goldwater's nomination by the Republicans, Wallace withdrew from the race. Johnson automatically won renomination along with Hubert Humphrey of Minnesota as his running mate. No major party figure had a longer or more forthright identification with integration than Humphrey, who had led the fight for the civil rights plank at the 1948 convention. If the Democratic convention was unambiguously for civil rights, the Republican convention rejected the tide of racial reform. Party conservatives, increasingly from the West and the South, defeated the more moderate northeastern faction of the party and nominated the conservative movement's hero, Senator Goldwater of Arizona, for president, along with a little-known New York congressman, William E. Miller, as the vice-presidential candidate. Goldwater was honest, outspoken, suspicious of the urban Northeast, a rugged individualist, and personally not a racist, but he was a tenacious opponent of the Civil Rights Act of 1964 and a strict states' rightist. In the early part of the campaign Strom Thurmond switched his party allegiance to the GOP and traveled throughout the South speaking on Goldwater's behalf. Goldwater also had a penchant for off-the-cuff militaristic statements, so the national Democratic campaign strategy capitalized on fears that a Goldwater victory would lead to nuclear holocaust. But in the South the overriding issue was race.

All the southern white opposition to civil rights and federal government intervention and increasing black militancy in the South welled up in support of Barry Goldwater. Johnson had said when the Civil Rights Act had passed that "I think we just delivered the South to the Republican party for a long time to come," and as far as white voters are concerned he might have been correct. Nevertheless, Johnson did not back away from his support of civil rights even when campaigning in the South, and Goldwater and his supporters made the issue their cause, too, openly campaigning against government-mandated integration. Segregationist Democrats, the ones who normally supported Wallace and Thurmond, switched by the droves to Goldwater. This proved to be a transitional election for the southern GOP, and Goldwater's primary appeal was to racially conservative whites. He did best in those states and regions of states with the highest percentage of blacks, winning, for example, 91 percent of the white vote in Mississippi. Goldwater's greatest appeal was to former Democrats who had rejected their party's stand on civil rights. No longer was the Republican party strongest in the peripheral states and among affluent suburbs. In fact, Goldwater did less well in those regions where Eisenhower and Nixon had done best. In the deep South the new Republican ascendancy was clearly based on opposition to racial change first and on traditional GOP economic issues second. Goldwater carried only his home state of Arizona and the five deep South states: South Carolina, Georgia, Alabama, Mississippi, and Louisiana. Johnson won the election in a landslide and received practically every vote cast by a black, but in the South as a whole Goldwater won 55 percent of the white vote. Those returns would suggest future political strategies for both parties.

Goldwater was too inept a campaigner, and the Johnson electoral victory too overwhelming, to allow the 1964 election to be called a true realignment election that positioned the Republican party as the dominant party in the South. But the GOP was positioned to gain dominance as the party of white protest in the South. This protest was directly proportional to the national Democratic party's continuing support of civil rights, including the Voting Rights Act of 1965 and the Open Housing Act of 1968. A series of massive urban riots, beginning in the Watts section of Los Angeles in 1965 and erupting in Detroit, Baltimore, Washington, DC, and other cities, frightened many Americans, including those who had been heartened by the civil rights advances of the early 1960s. The rise of the black power movement, the assassination of Martin Luther King, Jr., in March 1968 and then Robert Kennedy in June, the increasing opposition and divisiveness of the war in Vietnam, especially after the Tet offensive by the enemy forces in early 1968 revealed that—Pentagon reports to the contrary—the war was not going well from the American point of view, all made the election year of 1968 chaotic. Senator Eugene McCarthy of Minnesota was mounting a movement against LBJ and the American presence in Vietnam, and Johnson, discouraged about criticism of his war policies and also worried about a second heart attack, announced on March 31, 1968, that he would not run for reelection. Not since the Civil War had American society been so rent by racial, political, and cultural divisions.

THE NEW POLITICS OF RACE

George Wallace, who had stepped aside for Goldwater in 1964, now mounted a national campaign against what he and many conservatives saw as military spinelessness in much of America and racial meddling in Washington. An articulate, capable campaigner with a knack for mobilizing white supporters who felt unfairly taxed by the federal government and discriminated against in favor of blacks, Wallace carried white southern opposition to civil rights to the North. He shocked liberal media commentators by his appeal in states like Illinois, Michigan, and Wisconsin. Attacking federal bureaucrats, "pointy headed intellectuals," and student antiwar demonstrators, Wallace's angry campaign proved to be the most potent third-party protest in over half a century. For years Democrats had fired up their lower- and middle-class supporters by attacking Republican plutocrats; now Wallace was mobilizing these same voters by attacking "elitest" Democratic bureaucrats. His success showed how fluid American public opinion was in 1968.

The Democratic party was itself very conflicted that year. Johnson had assumed that Vice President Humphrey would be the nominee and would continue Johnson's policies, but Vietnam now so dominated Johnson's agenda that his Great Society reforms seemed in the remote past. In 1967 and early 1968 McCarthy and then Robert Kennedy had conducted major challenges to Humphrey, and the Democratic convention in Chicago that summer turned into a bloody riot. Humphrey won the nomination, and with his running mate Senator Edmund Muskie from Maine, emerged from the convention to face a nation that seemed to be coming unraveled. Following Johnson's landslide victory only four years earlier the Democrats had seemed invincible; now they were threatened on the right by George Wallace and his fellow racial reactionaries and on the left by uncompromising antiwar liberals. And, rising like a phoenix from the ashes of 1964 was the Republican party and, even more phoenix-like following his devastating California gubernatorial defeat in 1962, former Vice-President Richard M. Nixon. Nixon adopted a "southern strategy" that made the South the GOP stronghold and the 1968 election a true watershed event in recent southern politics.

The political turmoil of the previous four years, and white southerners' identification of the Democratic party with racial change, had led to a marked increase in the vitality of the Republican party in local politics. In state after state, especially in the rapidly growing suburbs, the GOP was emerging as an effective competitor to traditional Democratic dominance, and the emerging GOP was far more mainstream than the 1950s brand of southern extremism. Republican John Tower had won a special election in Texas in 1961 to replace Johnson in the Senate, and Tower was the first Republican senator elected in the South since Reconstruction. Tower was on the right edge of the party and opposed all civil rights legislation, but he was no John Bircher. In the later 1960s Republicans began to win scattered state and local contests in the South. Nixon and his strategists, such as Harry S. Dent, saw the potential for growth of a conservative but mainstream Republican party in Dixie.

Nixon and Dent understood that the white racial extremists would support Wallace, but more moderate whites who nevertheless wanted to slow the pace of racial change could be appealed to without losing all northern support. Carefully chosen code words substituted for blatant racism but suggested much the same sentiment. Nixon and the GOP learned to announce support for racial equality in abstract terms but oppose governmental policies aimed at achieving that result. Many whites were upset at what was called reverse discrimination and government "give-away" programs that redistributed tax revenues and government benefits downward. Policies that had begun as an attempt to address unfairness in the economic and legal spheres were now themselves under attack for being unfair. Lower- and middle-class whites often felt that the real costs of what was called "social engineering" fell on them; in their language, money was taken from those who worked and given to those who did not. Skilled politicians were quick to seize that anger and make it a potent campaign issue.

Moreover, Nixon's substantial experience in foreign affairs saved him from being compared with the reckless militarism widely associated with Goldwater. In addition, Nixon's vice-presidential years and his identification with traditional probusiness economic conservatism made him acceptable to the kinds of northern mainstream Republicans who had migrated to the increasingly prosperous South. Nixon carefully sized up his niche: appeal to affluent, suburban southerners, position himself slightly to the right of Humphrey on foreign policy issues and slightly to the left of Wallace on racial issues, and bank on the fears of social chaos in a year of rioting and assassination to win mainstream conservative support. After all, Nixon had lost in California in 1962 and, though now living in New York but clearly not representative of the moderate Republicanism represented by Governor Nelson Rockefeller of New York, Nixon had no natural political base in the Empire State. Nixon had to create one for himself among the whites of the South. In effect, the white South would shape Nixon's new version of the Republican party.

The 1968 election was extremely close, with Wallace winning 40 percent of the southern white vote overall, but less than a third in the peripheral South, where Nixon received 45 percent of the white vote. Humphrey did not lead in the white vote in a single southern state, although the growing southern black vote went almost entirely for him. In the last days of the election northern labor and the liberal vote swung heavily for Humphrey, but he carried only Texas in the South. Wallace won Arkansas, Louisiana, Mississippi, Alabama, and Georgia. Nixon's shrewd southern strategy enabled him to win Florida, South Carolina, North Carolina, Virginia, and Tennessee, and with those southern votes Nixon squeaked through to win the presidency with a solid electoral majority but with only a seven tenths of 1 percent advantage in the popular vote. The Democrats had won just one southern state, Texas, partly a sentimental vote for retiring president Johnson.

As president, Nixon nurtured his southern strategy, backpedaling from his comparative racial liberalism of the 1950s and early 1960s. The result was a skillful campaign to capitalize on the racial backlash and fear of change rampant among southern whites in particular. Nixon disavowed busing to achieve school integration, slowed the Justice Department's efforts on behalf of integration, nominated three "strict construction" southern justices for the US Supreme Court (only one of whom was approved by the Senate), advocated "law and order" policies, and supported traditional GOP economic issues to firm up his appeal to conservatives nationally. Seldom was explicitly racist language used; instead, a subtle new political vocabulary of code words and abstractions spoke to the old concerns, but in a way that did not embarrass better educated, more affluent southerners. Nixon consistently defended the principle of equal opportunity as he opposed so-called quotas and affirmative action. In effect, a new kind of conservative populism had emerged that, on the basis of opposition to special privileges for some, attacked government programs on behalf of minorities. With Nixon in the White House the GOP began to replace the Democratic party as the local preserve of whites in much of the South. Republicans now regularly won elections as state legislators, governors, even congressmen and senators. Many of these were essentially mainstream national Republicans, like senators Howard Baker and W. E. Brock; others like Jesse Helms represented the far right end of the GOP's political spectrum. Much of the South in the 1970s experienced true two-party politics for the first time since before the Civil War.

The rise of local, respectable Republican party organizations in the South was not the only significant political change in the South. The southern Democratic party became more liberal and more similar to the national Democratic party partly as a result of the rise of southern Republicanism. Angry at the liberalism of the national Democrats, the most conservative southern Democrats began to leave the party of their fathers and join the GOP, which was seen now as far more supportive of what was euphemistically called the southern way. This tendency reached floodtide in 1972 when the Democrats nominated its most liberal candidate in decades, Senator George McGovern of South Dakota, whom southern conservatives pilloried as unpatriotic, fiscally irresponsible, and prodrugs (the drug culture was widely associated with everything bad in the late 1960s and early 1970s). The southern Democratic party was liberalized by the departure of its most conservative members and transformed by the Voting Rights Act of 1965 and a massive campaign by various civil rights groups to register black voters. The ratification of the Twenty-Fourth Amendment in 1964, prohibiting the imposition of a poll tax for presidential elections, and the extension of that prohibition to

all elections by the Supreme Court in 1966 had made the fundamental democratic act of voting accessible even to the poorest of southerners. By 1972
more than 3.5 million southern blacks were registered to vote, and their vote
was almost entirely Democratic.

A whole new group of southern white politicians understood the
changed nature of the southern electorate and began to put together coalitions of moderate white and liberal black voters, realizing that such coalitions
could often defeat the almost all-white conservative support of the southern
GOP candidates. Large numbers of local black officeholders emerged too,
though mainly in counties or urban precincts that were heavily black. The
result was a new kind of two-party politics at the state and local levels in the
South: economically and racial conservative Republicans and socially and
racially liberal or moderate Democrats who still were quite conservative on
fiscal issues. Nevertheless, though coalition-building could result in the election of Democrats at the state and district level, the GOP emerged as the
dominant party in southern political elections. The election year of 1972
made that point emphatically.

The Republican ticket in 1972 was headed by President Nixon and his
tough-talking vice president, Spiro Agnew of Maryland, who had become the
bête noire of Democrats because of his spirited attacks on liberals, intellectuals, college radicals, and protestors against the Vietnam war. Republican strategy was in large part following the guidelines established by Kevin Phillips,
who had written *The Emerging Republican Majority* in 1969. Phillips had argued
convincingly that the GOP could replace the Democratic party as the permanent majority party by linking national economic and cultural conservatives
with the racial conservatives of the South. That is, if Nixon could capture the
Wallace supporters and add them to more traditional, mainstream Republican voters, then the Republicans could expect to control the presidency for a
generation. Nixon and Agnew pursued policies that were intended to polar-
ize the American public on the cutting issues of the day: school busing to
achieve integration, affirmative action and set-aside programs, the Vietnam
war, and amnesty for those who evaded the military draft. Also appealing to
conservative voters, George Wallace ran for the presidency in 1972. He was
willing to speak more bluntly than even Vice- President Agnew, and Wallace
had every intention of running a national campaign, less to win the presidency than to move both major parties significantly to the right. A string of
stunning primary victories in early 1972 showed that Wallace, a feisty and
effective politician, was not a merely regional candidate. Then the entire
presidential campaign was turned upside down when Arthur Bremer, a
demented would-be assassin, shot and wounded Wallace on May 15 while he
was campaigning in the parking lot of a suburban Maryland shopping center.
Wallace had to withdraw from the election and was left paralyzed for life.
With Wallace out of the race, the conservative vote was Nixon's for the taking.

The Democrats by their choice of the very liberal George McGovern as the party's nominee effectively stampeded the conservative vote to Nixon.

What happened to the Democrats in 1972 can only be understood if the historical context is kept in mind. The national Democratic party, and especially its nominating convention, had been transformed since the mid-1960s—a transformation that severely alienated conservative southern white Democrats and caused many of them to leave the party and join the Republicans. Eight years earlier at the 1964 convention, LBJ had hoped to avoid all controversy because he was trying to maintain the broad coalition that he had put together to pass the Civil Rights Act a few weeks earlier. Johnson had other progressive legislation in the hopper and did not want to risk alienating any possible congressional supporters. But a group of black activists from Mississippi felt conditions back home were simply too offensive to be swept under the rug of political coalition-building. The Council of Federated Organizations, or COFO, had developed in 1962 a concerted plan to register black voters in Mississippi, and the violence and corruption that they fought against had emboldened, not disheartened them. In 1963 they had held a mock "Freedom Election" to demonstrate the black hunger for the franchise, and in 1964 they had created the Mississippi Freedom Democratic Party (MFDP) complete with convention delegates in part to protest Mississippi's all-white delegation to the Democratic National Convention.

The regular Democratic delegates from Mississippi of course resented this black challenge to their credentials, but when members of the MFDP presented their case to the convention, especially in a moving talk by Fannie Lou Hamer, the justice of their cause was evident. However, Johnson at this juncture wanted consensus above all else. He worked out a compromise by promising to name Hubert Humphrey as his running mate (which was probably already decided), agreed to seat two of the MFDP members as at-large delegates, required the all-white delegations from Mississippi (and Alabama) to pledge their support of the Democratic candidates, and stated that at future conventions delegations would not be accepted from states that disallowed black participation. This compromise satisfied neither the MFDP nor the regular white delegates from Mississippi, most of whom went home and voted for Goldwater. But the way was cleared for far greater black participation at subsequent Democratic conventions.

The next major reform of Democratic convention procedures followed the absolute debacle at Chicago in 1968, when Chicago's Mayor Richard Daley controlled events inside the arena with an iron fist even as chaos reigned outside. Though Hubert Humphrey, a liberal stalwart in the past, emerged as the nominee, many Democrats were offended by the convention proceedings, so offended that in response the convention delegates approved (against overwhelming southern opposition) the McGovern–Fraser Commission to study and recommend reforms in the entire process that produced delegates. By 1970 the party had accepted the commission's recommendations. States would have to open up the delegate-selection process. Rules were adopted that guaranteed better representation of minorities, women, and younger delegates, with limitations on the number of officeholders who had seats. The resulting delegates who met in 1972 at the Democratic convention in Miami were 36 percent women and 24 percent black. Reformers, activists, and antiwar liberals had wrested control of the convention away from traditional party power brokers.

The Democratic primaries represented a broad range of candidates, with Wallace on the right, Hubert Humphrey and Edmund Muskie in the center, and George McGovern on the left. Wallace withdrew following his gunshot wound in May, and Humphrey, crippled by his association with LBJ and the increasingly unpopular war in Vietnam, never picked up momentum. Muskie began as the frontrunner, but his calm, dispassionate style did not seem to fit an election year filled with passion. Senator George McGovern, the idealistic son of a Methodist minister and a history Ph.D. from Northwestern University, welded together an enthusiastic reform, antiwar campaign consisting largely of young, college-age supporters and long-time opponents of the continuing war. McGovern's liberalism appealed to the new make-up of the 1972 convention, and he won the nomination. He proved to be by far the most liberal candidate ever nominated by a major party and, along with Goldwater in 1964, the weakest candidate ever put forward by a major party.

McGovern's forthright opposition to the war, his support of amnesty for what were called draft dodgers, his strong support of civil rights and busing, and his proposals for modest income redistribution made him absolutely anathema to most southern white Democrats. Richard Nixon and the proponents of a southern strategy for a new Republican majority had had handed to them the perfect foil for their campaign. The election was a foregone conclusion: Nixon won 79 percent of the southern white vote (86 percent in the deep South states), carried every southern state, and swept to a landslide national victory. McGovern positions allowed the Republicans to put together a powerful coalition. In contrast to the Democrats, the southernized GOP stood for fiscal conservatism, law and order, limited government, strong defense, traditional cultural values, opposition to busing to achieve integration, a sense that civil rights should not be pushed any faster or further, and opposition to affirmative action.

White liberals and blacks might interpret much of this as subtly coded, polite racism, but it was an aggregation of attitudes and policies that perfectly matched majority white sentiment in the South and in much of the nation. Gone were the Depression-era days when the government was seen as a benefactor. Especially for middle-class, upwardly mobile white voters in Sun Belt suburbs, government primarily meant taxes and civil rights and give-away programs that both cost them and favored minorities. The GOP understood those gut-level reactions far better than did the national Democratic party. And as a result, the Republican party has not lost the white vote in the South in a presidential election since 1968. With Nixon's resounding victory in 1972 it is possible to speak of the emergence of a Solid Republican South.

However, the Democratic party was not dead in the South; it was in the process of being transformed. The continuing departure of conservative Democrats to the triumphal Republican party meant that liberals, moderates, and blacks would control the residual Democratic party. In many southern states the so-called independents had grown greatly, made up usually of former Democrats who still hesitated to join the GOP and regional newcomers who were not ready to join either the Republican conservatives or the Democratic liberals. The 1972 electoral victories of Barbara Jordan of Houston and Andrew Young of Atlanta, the first blacks elected to the US House of Representatives from the South since Reconstruction, demonstrated the enhanced political power of black voters when augmented by liberal and moderate whites. Certainly on the state and local level, black votes could often be decisive.

THE NEW SOUTHERN DEMOCRATS

Southern Democratic politicians understood that carefully constructed coalitions of black and white liberal and moderate Democratic voters, with a scattering of moderate independents, could still win elections. Coming on the heels of this discovery was a group of young, attractive, and aggressive Democratic gubernatorial candidates: Reuben O. Askew in Florida, Dale Bumpers in Arkansas—to be followed by David Pryor and Bill Clinton—Jimmy Carter in Georgia, James B. Hunt in North Carolina, and John C. West in South Carolina. Such new style Democrats could prosper in a South whose presidential vote was overwhelmingly Republican. The region seemed to have a split mind: at the presidential level one type of candidate, at the local level another. The South did not completely reject progressive social legislation. Rather, it chose to base such political programs in the hands of politicians closer to home than the White House. Democrats could still win state legislative and gubernatorial office, congressional seats, even election to the Senate.

Could a white southern Democrat possibly win the presidency by finding an ideological middle ground between progressive local interests and conservative presidential politics? Could a southern candidate dare to be liberal enough to win northern labor voters and black voters—old New Deal Democrats—and yet conservative enough to attract moderate Democrats and independents in the South? Perhaps so, when the national Republicans were severely wounded by the Watergate scandal (a break-in to the Democratic campaign headquarters, a presidential coverup, and revelations of a variety of illegal "dirty tricks" and pay-offs). Vice-President Agnew was forced to resign because he had taken bribes, President Nixon was so threatened by revelations and lies that he had to resign to avoid impeachment, and then President Gerald Ford, who had been appointed vice-president and became president when Nixon resigned, pardoned the previous presidential malefactor. This almost unbelievable chain of events made possible the presidential victory of southerner Jimmy Carter of Georgia in 1976, an electoral anomaly in a Republican age.

Carter's election shows both the possibilities for, and the limits to, Democratic presidential politics in the modern South. In many ways Jimmy Carter seemed perfect for a Democratic renewal. His maternal grandfather had been a Populist politician whom family legend credited with originating the idea of rural free delivery of the mail. His father became a regional director of the Rural Electrification Administration, another government program that significantly improved the lives of rural southerners. His mother was a nurse who often had to go to patients' homes and in effect substitute for a doctor. Young Jimmy had grown up in rural Georgia, where his family ran a peanut farm, with this strong family tradition of public service. Like many rural southerners then and since who were inspired by good school teachers, Carter absorbed a strong work and self-improvement ethic. In part because of his father's political influence, Jimmy Carter won a congressional appointment to the US Naval Academy for 1943. After graduating and marrying his hometown sweetheart, Rosalynn Smith, Jimmy Carter was commissioned a naval officer and began what looked to be a traditional southern career in the armed services. Soon he was attracted to the nuclear submarine program and took additional training in nuclear engineering and propulsion, which advanced his naval career. His father died of cancer in 1953, and the felt responsibility for carrying on the family peanut business made Carter decide to leave the navy and return to the small town of Plains, Georgia.

Farming and business success soon led to involvement in local political issues. Perhaps because of the influence of his mother and his naval background, Carter was opposed to racial segregation. His refusal to join a local Citizen's Council caused him to lose business in the mid 1950s, and his comparative racial liberalism set Carter apart from many of his neighbors. Still Carter gained the respect of the townspeople of Plains, and eventually he was appointed to the local school board, his first personal taste of politics. He liked it, and soon began to consider running for a position in the Georgia Senate. Carter had to overcome shocking political fraud to win his first race, but in so doing he was bitten by the political bug—he had long seen politics as a means of serving the people, a duty taught by his parents. In 1964 Carter was elected to the Georgia state senate. By 1966 he was considering running for the US Congress but instead ran unsuccessfully for the governor's office. Lester G. Maddox, a colorfully outspoken defender of segregation, was

elected governor. Carter had not even made the runoff, but he began working immediately for another run in 1970. Following his 1966 gubernatorial
defeat, in a mood of depression and introspection, Carter was, in evangelical
parlance, born again and became far more active in his Baptist church. This
born-again, farmer–businessman who had served in the armed services, all
cardinal southern virtues, threw himself into the gubernatorial campaign of
1970 with almost fanatical devotion. Carter's major opponent, Carl Sanders,
campaigned as the liberal, and Carter ran as the more conservative candidate, appealing to the erstwhile Wallace and Maddox voters. Carter's opportunistic strategy worked; he won the governor's office.

In his inaugural Carter signaled that it was time to put aside old racial
issues: "I say to you quite frankly that the time for racial discrimination is
over. Our people have already made this major and difficult decision, but we
cannot underestimate the challenge of hundreds of minor decisions yet to be
made. . . . No poor, rural, weak, or black person should ever have to bear the
additional burden of being deprived of the opportunity of an education, a
job, or simple justice." In one of his first acts Carter hung a portrait of Martin
Luther King, Jr., the assassinated civil rights leader, in the Georgia capitol.
Then Carter set about reorganizing the state's governmental machinery to
make it more efficient and responsive in order to attract industry, to improve
education, to enact environmental protections, and to establish procedures
for long-range planning. Carter believed that economic growth, civil rights,
equal opportunity, and efficient government would improve the lives of all
Georgia's citizens. But Carter was not long content to confine his ambition
for public service to the state of Georgia. In 1972, midway through his four-
year term as governor, he decided to run for the presidency of the United
States.

No one had ever seen a campaign like that Carter and his major strategist, Hamilton Jordan, devised, and no one had seen a presidential candidate
as indefatigable as the ever-smiling Carter. Although starting with practically
no national name recognition, Carter—carrying his own luggage to counter-
act the media image of Nixon and the imperial presidency and seemingly
shaking every hand in the caucus states—racked up a series of stunning victories. First in Iowa, then New Hampshire, then a major victory over George
Wallace in Florida, and the peanut farmer from Georgia was on his way. To a
nation still upset by Watergate and then President Ford's pardon of Nixon, a
nation upset by the lying and cursing and immorality revealed by secret tapes
at the highest levels of government, Carter—the quiet-spoken Sunday School
teacher from the South, the straight-arrow former naval officer, and the busi-
nessman-farmer—seemed a wholesome throwback to another age of down-
home values. At the conclusion of his triumphant nomination at the Democratic convention at Madison Square Garden in New York City, and after his
rousing, old-time Populist acceptance speech, Carter and other leading

Jimmy and Rosalynn Carter. (Jimmy Carter Museum and Library)

Democrats, black and white, including Martin Luther King, Sr., stood, raised their clasped hands in unity, and sang together the anthem of the civil rights movement, "We Shall Overcome." To many southern blacks and liberal and moderate whites it was a poignant moment. Perhaps at last the South's long estrangement from the nation over race—first slavery, then segregation—was ending. Carter stood as the representative of the new American South.

The election proved extremely close, for Ford had the power of the incumbency behind him, and Carter found it difficult to modulate his appeal so that he could hold on to the New Deal coalition and at the same time not lose conservative and moderate whites. When the votes were tallied, Carter had won by a nose with 51 percent of the popular vote, winning ten of eleven former Confederate states. Yet his southern vote was deceptive. Carter garnered over 90 percent of the black vote but only 46 percent of the southern white vote. The black vote enabled him to win every southern state but Virginia. Yet the loss of the white vote signaled that he had little maneuvering room in the region, little margin for political error. After all, at least some of the white vote was a kind of southern sympathy vote, not an endorsement of the national Democratic agenda. Nevertheless, most southerners took a kind of pride in the inauguration of the first deep South president in over a century. Southern cooking and country music in the White House, southern accents in the Oval Office, and members of the national press attending a fish fry in rural Georgia: it all made southerners feel that a regional albatross had been lifted from around their collective necks.

Yet President Carter found governing more difficult than running for office. Having campaigned as a political outsider, he found it difficult to bargain with Congress. Because of his training as an engineer, Carter seemed to think that the rationality of his programs would automatically recommend themselves to Congress, but of course Congress does not work that way. Though he still taught a Baptist Sunday School class whenever he was in his hometown of Plains, Georgia, Carter favored the Internal Revenue Service putting restrictions on the tax exempt status of many private religious schools that had often begun as segregation academies. This policy alienated the Christian fundamentalist vote and contributed to its shift of support to the GOP by 1980. Manipulation of the international oil markets by the Organization of Petroleum Exporting Countries caused a rapid increase in world oil prices followed by double-digit inflation in all the western nations, and Carter was blamed for inflation in this country. In an absolutely unprecedented act of international terrorism, Iranian fundamentalists seized the American embassy at Tehran and held American personnel as hostages. Carter, valuing the lives of the hostages, was powerless to rescue them. Nightly television coverage made Carter seem as helplessly hostage to events as the embassy prisoners were to their captors.

Supporters might point to the number of blacks Carter appointed to government positions, or to his progressive environmental policies, or to his essential involvement in the Camp David accords that brought peace between Israel and Egypt, or to his willingness to brave public opposition and work for a Panama Canal agreement that all presidents since Eisenhower had supported yet hesitated to advocate, but these policy successes meant naught to the American public in the face of high inflation and Iranian highhandedness. Carter misunderstood the psyche of the nation. In the midst of the energy crisis he warned the nation of the profligacy of consuming far more than its share of the world's energy and cautioned the people about putting self-interest above all other values. "In a nation that was proud of hard work, strong families, close knit communities and our faith in God," Carter said to the American people in a televised speech, "too many of us now tend to worship self-indulgence and consumption. Human identity is no longer defined by what one does but by what one owns." But such homilies to selflessness was not what the increasingly materialistic American public wanted to hear. They wanted lower inflation, cheaper oil, America standing tall in the world wielding, metaphorically, a big enough stick to have its way untrammeled by Third-World anti-American leaders such as the Ayatollah Khomeni, the leader of Iran. Carter seemed as wrong for the political climate of 1980 as he had seemed right in 1976. It took more than decency and intelligence to survive as president; it took political know-how and a great deal of good luck.

Events over which the United States had no control appeared to take over Carter's presidency. Russia's invasion of Afghanistan was simply another example. The Democratic establishment never warmed to the political outsider from Georgia, and now that he was falling in the polls, political sharks began to circle. Carter's presidency seemed out of control, almost in free fall. Democratic Senator Edward M. Kennedy of Massachusetts, never personally attracted to the Georgian, announced that he would challenge Carter for the nomination in 1980, a brutal battle that Carter eventually won only to find himself thoroughly bloodied. Independent John Anderson mounted a third-party challenge, attracting many liberal Democrats and independents who were mildly suspicious of Carter's southernness and disillusioned by his inability to solve intractable problems. By June 1980 Carter's approval rating in the polls had fallen to a dismal 21 percent, even lower than Nixon had ever fallen. The presidency appeared ripe for the picking by a Republican.

DEMOCRATS DISCREDITED

The Republican candidate in 1980 was not just any Republican but the ideological embodiment of the American right, Ronald Reagan. Reagan had had a modestly successful career in the movies, but it was his hosting in the 1950s of a popular television program entitled *General Electric Theater* that made him a conservative icon. For much of eight years he toured the nation giving patriotic, probusiness talks for General Electric, perfecting a script that became known as The Speech. It was this address that he gave at the 1964 GOP convention in support of Barry Goldwater, and The Speech made Reagan, even more than Goldwater, the conservative spokesman for what media pundits in the Nixon era began calling Middle America. The Speech was antigovernment and antitax, enlivened by folksy anecdotes of federal excess. Government was the people's enemy; the free enterprise system, devoid of meddlesome government controls, was the people's truest benefactor. For comfortable, middle-class white Americans, Reagan's speech seemed a breath of fresh air. Reagan had ridden these ideas to two terms as governor of California, the nation's largest state, so he ran for the Republican nomination as an experienced politician, no mere movie star. Mediagenic and with a gift for giving even pedestrian speeches with oratorical flair, Reagan swept aside his more prosaic opponents and handily won the nomination for the presidency.

Reagan and his able strategists understood the importance of rewinning the South for the GOP, and they understood the political potency of the antigovernment, low-tax ideology of The Speech, especially when yoked to flag-waving patriotism. Reagan opened his 1980 campaign in Neshoba County, Mississippi, where the three civil rights workers had been murdered in 1964, and to an audience of 10,000 whites at the county fair he announced "I believe in states' rights." He promised to "restore to states and local governments the power that properly belongs to them." Here was Nixon's old southern strategy of muted racism with a newly honed edge. Carter opened his campaign in Alabama by denouncing the Klan and older racial animosities, but Carter's style never stood a chance against Reagan's in the changed atmosphere of 1980. Carter would give fact-filled lectures about energy and environment and America's need to recognize limits, but listeners, though impressed with his knowledge and insight, left feeling mildly depressed. Reagan spoke optimistically about unlimited potential and freedom and prosperity and America's standing strong in the world, and because it sounded like a pep rally, listeners left feeling proud and upbeat. There was no question who would win the election. Carter captured only 36 percent of the South's white vote and carried only his home state of Georgia. Nationwide, Reagan won forty-four states and 489 out of 538 electoral votes. Carter, his party, and the values he stood for were thoroughly discredited both regionally and nationally.

Exit poll interviews showed that the voters who were most opposed to taxes, government services, and civil rights programs and most favorably inclined toward increased defense expenditures were the strongest supporters of Reagan. By 1980 the antitax crusade had grown to be an almost unstoppable force in American politics. The crusade was fueled both by the decade-long white backlash against paying taxes that were felt to be unfairly transferred to blacks and to support government programs considered wasteful, intrusive, and permissive, and by a genuine rise in the tax rate paid by millions of middle-class voters as their climbing incomes over the past decades had pushed them into higher tax brackets. The antitax movement was crystallized in 1978 when California voters passed a tax limitation bill called Proposition 13. The idea swept like wildfire across the nation. The GOP, far more attuned to white attitudes than the Democrats, understood what a powerful issue lay at hand. And no one saw the issue more clearly than President Reagan. His mandate seemed clear, and so did the dilemma of the Democratic party.

Reagan proved to be a popular president, bringing the people sharply lowered taxes and increased defense budgets. His administration began with a severe recession that led to the highest unemployment since the Great Depression, but it squeezed much of the inflation out of the economy. Also, since energy prices had stabilized, so did inflation. The pump-priming effect of lowered taxes and tremendously increased government expenditures for defense led to a long, steady low-grade boom. European and Japanese investors underwrote the mushrooming national debt, keeping interest rates low. True to his promises, Reagan cut back on government regulation of business and of the environment; civil rights and affirmative action programs were slowed; and strong conservatives were appointed to government positions and the judiciary, many of whom, like James Watt as Secretary of the Interior and Anne Burford, head of the Environmental Protection Agency, were essentially opposed to the mandated mission of the government agency they now headed. Reagan had in effect campaigned to turn back the political clock, the majority of Americans had heartily approved, and New Deal–Great Society expansion of government programs ceased. The budget deficit ballooned as never before and the US became the world's largest debtor nation, but with lower taxes, the average American cared little about long-term economic consequences. Iran had held the hostages till Reagan was inaugurated, then let them go instantly as if to spite Jimmy Carter. After a generation of rule by Cold War troglodytes, Russia got a youthful, pragmatic leader in Mikhail Gorbachev who understood that Afghanistan-type adventurism and the continued Cold War arms race was bankrupting the already weak economy of his nation. Gorbachev sought domestic reforms and a relaxation of international rivalries. The result was an epochal break in the arms race and ultimately the end of the Cold War. Reagan profited from these diplomatic windfalls and the long-term though narrow-gauged prosperity of the 1980s.

During the mid-term elections of 1982, in the midst of the recessionary downturn, the Democrats won a number of state and local victories in the South, as in the nation. But with the return of prosperity in time for the 1984 presidential elections, and with Reagan's mastery of symbolic politics, the election was a foregone conclusion. Inflation was down, the recession was over, and, borrowing Reagan's campaign theme, it seemed to be morning in

America once again. The Democratic candidate, Walter F. Mondale, who had been Jimmy Carter's vice president, was associated in the popular mind with Carter and with liberal Democratic programs. He even said that it would be necessary to raise taxes to balance the federal budget. Consequently Reagan was reelected in one of the greatest landslides in American political history, carrying every southern state, winning 72 percent of the white South's vote, and sweeping forty-nine states. Given the vocabulary of southern politics in the 1980s, Mondale with his calls for New Deal-type progressive government never had a chance against Ronald Reagan.

The dominance of the GOP in southern presidential politics now seemed complete. But Reagan's second term was marred by several scandals, including the revelation that, contrary to stated policy, arms were traded to Iran in the hopes of securing the release of American citizens held hostage by Muslim fundamentalists in the Middle East. Then it turned out that profits from such arms sales were illegally used to support the conservative Contra rebels, who opposed the Sandinista government in Nicaragua. A firestorm of opposition broke out, with the administration quickly responding more for damage control than to get to the bottom of the scandal. A congressional committee suggested that Reagan's administrative style was so relaxed that extralegal, almost freelance policies were undertaken without his knowledge. Yet the immense public reservoir of good will he had created left Reagan relatively untouched, and he was not as injured by this scandal as Nixon had been by Watergate even though the constitutional issues involved were far greater in what became known as the Iran–Contra Scandal. Moreover, after two terms in office, there were a number of indications that the economic miracle of the 1980s was more mirage than reality. Investment was down, job creation per annum was down from the Carter years, workers' annual income, adjusted for inflation, was down, bank failures were up, the federal debt had tripled, the trade balance had gone from positive to negative. The combined tax rate for the poorest one-fifth of Americans rose during the period from 1980 to 1985 from 8.4 percent to 10.6 percent, and it fell for the richest one-fifth from 27.3 percent to 24 percent. For the entire decade, 1980 to 1990, after-tax income for the poorest decile of the population decreased by 10.3 percent, while for the richest decile it increased by 41.1 percent. The wealthy prospered, the poor saw their relative position slip. Would this combination of foreign-policy scandal and economic bad news domestically be enough, as it had been in 1976, to allow a Democratic presidential victory?

Only the Republicans seemed aware that the South was now the nation's largest region, with over one-quarter of the total electoral votes needed for presidential victory. A candidate who won the southern states could win the presidency by picking up only a third of the remainder of the nation's electoral votes. Significantly, no Democrat had ever lost the South and won the presidency. Furthermore, the GOP strategists understood the continuing efficacy of Nixon's southern strategy. The secret was to appeal to mainstreet business-conservative economic concerns and, more important, emphasize cultural-racial issues: law and order, uncritical patriotism (of the "America: Love it or leave it" variety), "family values," and religion; and opposition to busing, affirmative action, welfare, and meddling government "interference." Most Americans, but especially white southerners, subscribed to this set of values. Cultural politics proved more salient than economics, in fact, they could camouflage economic reality. Conservative whites were often genuinely worried about what they perceived as the breakdown in family structure, changing sexual mores, the rise in population groups (black, Hispanic, and Asian) that had different cultural styles, and the obvious increase in crime.

Often this unease was not consciously racist at all but rather a fear of what was happening to the once familiar America that had been depicted in such television shows as "Leave it to Beaver." That fear of loss, though, could be channeled into support of conservative politics. Reagan's vice-president, George Bush, had learned from the master how to evoke these sentiments and appeal to them, and as the Republican candidate in 1988 he faced another Democratic pushover, Governor Michael Dukakis of Massachusetts. Dukakis, a bright, hardworking technocrat, believed that the election was about competence, not ideology, showing thereby how little he and his strategists had learned from the last two elections. It was as if the Democrats had set out to find a candidate and a campaign style guaranteed to fail in the South.

Early in the campaign Dukakis let himself be painted as a candidate who let black criminals out of jail early so they could rape white women, a knee-jerk critic of America who wanted to weaken the military defenses, and a secular humanist who did not support America's religious heritage. Lee Atwater, directing Bush's campaign with a sort of diabolical brilliance, raised negative campaigning to an art form and perhaps changed forever how candidates used the media. The inept Dukakis campaign never recovered from the onslaught. Bush, smarting from liberal jibes that he was a wimp, tore into the seemingly defenseless Dukakis like a man possessed. Before an East Texas audience Connecticut-born and Yale-educated Bush called the Democrat a "'liberal Massachusetts governor' who opposes gun ownership, the Pledge of Allegiance, prayer in public schools, and is weak on crime." Bush and Atwater knew those kind of charges drew blood, so across the nation Bush repeated that "I can't understand the type of thinking that lets first-degree murderers who haven't even served enough time to be eligible for parole out on parole so they can rape and plunder again and then isn't willing to let the teachers lead the kids in the Pledge of Allegiance."

It made little difference that Dukakis's Republican predecessor had developed the parole program or that many states with conservative Republican governors, like Texas, had similar release programs. Dukakis never mounted a sufficient defense, and the Atwater–Bush attack made most white Americans—and southerners even more so—dismiss as irrelevant Iran–Contra issues and such abstractions as the astronomical federal debt. The Republicans knew what kind of cultural issues would keep them in office and solidify the GOP as the new majority party. The national Democrats often seemed stunningly obtuse about the issues the white majority was most concerned about. Hence the Democrats failed to attempt to educate and promote social understanding, and the Republicans capitalized on the visceral emotions of the public. Bush won 67 percent of the southern white vote, all the region's electoral vote, and swept to another Republican landslide victory. Bush won in forty out of fifty states, and he led the electoral vote by 426 to 122. It was not quite Reaganesque, but a resounding victory nevertheless.

Perhaps nothing so demonstrated the political attractiveness of the basic GOP economic and cultural conservatism as the remarkable political career in Louisiana of David Duke. A handsome, suavely dressed, college-educated politician, Duke had a long history of right-wing extremism, having been a leader of the Ku Klux Klan and a neo-Nazi who publicly doubted the holocaust. Yet he shed his sheet, switched his party allegiance from Democrat to the GOP—much to the chagrin and embarrassment of national Republican leaders who quickly repudiated him—and in 1991 ran a highly publicized and surprisingly strong race in the Louisiana gubernatorial election. Duke stressed economic issues in an oil-depressed state; he attacked welfare abuse and affirmative action; he assailed taxing those who he said worked in order to give to those on welfare—a euphemism for blacks; he preached law and order; and he advocated the advancement of the white race. That a majority of white Louisianians would vote for a politician with such an unsavory background testifies to the powerful attractiveness of the set of economic and conservative values he espoused. In this case, after nationwide attention, an infusion of outside money, criticism of Duke by most national Republican leaders, and a remarkable black voter turnout, former Democratic governor Edward Edwards put together a liberal-moderate-black good-government coalition, despite his own unsavory record, and beat Duke in the runoff election. Louisiana liberals put tongue-in-cheek bumper stickers on their cars that read "Vote for the crook."

Although Louisianians, who are usually quick to claim that their state is unique and in this case claimed that the Duke phenomenon could happen practically anywhere that economic distress was high, no doubt the state's peculiar tolerance for political chicanery contributed to his near success. The larger point is that the political tables have been reversed. For the half century preceding World War II, the white South looked to the Democratic party to preserve the region's racial status quo. Following the evolution of the two parties in the region since 1960, present-day white southerners turn to the

Republican party to slow social change. Race, camouflaged by coded language, still dominates southern politics. Economic issues, even when evoked, are secondary. The New South has not completely escaped its heritage, for good and for bad. The past in all its complexity still shapes the course of southern life.

THE END OF SOUTHERN HISTORY?

At first glance the national election of 1992 would seem to suggest that the GOP dominance of presidential politics in the South had ended. After all, the successful Democratic ticket broke with recent tradition not only by having both presidential and vice-presidential candidates, Bill Clinton and Albert Gore, Jr., from the same region, but from neighboring southern states, Arkansas and Tennessee, respectively. (George Bush had lived much of his pre-political adult life in Texas, but he was still considered a New Englander.) And Clinton and Gore carried four southern states—Arkansas, Georgia, Louisiana, and Tennessee—and four border states—Kentucky, Maryland, Missouri, and West Virginia. But these state victories notwithstanding, Bush beat Clinton in the total southern vote, won the southern white vote easily, and in fact Clinton only won two percentage points more in the South than Dukakis had four years earlier and trailed Jimmy Carter's 1976 southern performance by thirteen percentage points. The GOP, despite running in 1992 against two well-financed southern whites who had a masterful campaign strategy and despite bearing the burden of having arguably the most dismal economic record of any administration in over half a century, still won the South as a whole and the southern white vote handily.

Part of the explanation for the poor showing of the Democratic ticket in the South was the surprising success of the third-party candidacy of Texas billionaire Ross Perot, who capitalized on a national feeling of frustration with both major political parties. Perot, with his unorthodox campaign, largely on television, won the second highest vote total of any third-party candidate in American history, with 19 percent of the ballots cast. In the South as a whole Perot garnered 18 percent of the white vote, but most of those were apparently at the expense of Bush, not Clinton. Paradoxically, the election of a southern Democratic President and Vice-President did not indicate that the Democrats had finally broken the GOP conservative stranglehold on the white South.

What, if anything, did the election of a complete southern ticket for the first time since the Andrew Jackson–John C. Calhoun victory in 1828 mean to the region? It suggested once again that the only hope Democrats had of making headway in the region in presidential politics was to run moderate southerners. In fact the ticket's narrow victory margin (after three sound

Democratic defeats) indicated that the national mood of conservatism was still so strong that, even in the midst of severe economic frustration and a strong desire for change, only moderate Democratic leadership could possibly win public approval. It does appear also that the southern-style politics of moderation, pioneered by southern governors, adept at appealing to blacks and other minorities and simultaneously appealing to traditional values of home, place, family, the work ethic, and patriotism, is the key to Democratic success nationally. More aggressive liberal policies in the mold of FDR or LBJ were still out of fashion and discredited. Clinton and Gore exemplified this new kind of southern moderate politics. They were self-consciously southern, yet they symbolized progressive change; they rhapsodized the small town South yet talked about global competitiveness and environmentalism; but all the while they were careful to stake out a position as a new kind—less liberal—of Democrat.

Pundits were quick to call Clinton and Gore the "Bubba" ticket, but these two Ivy League graduates (Clinton a Rhodes scholar from Georgetown, Oxford, and Yale; Gore from Harvard and Vanderbilt) are hardly provincial even though they were quick to offer a southern folk aphorism when the occasion arose. Together they represent how much the New South has changed since World War II. Yet the mixed success in the South of Clinton and Gore also symbolizes how a progressive element in the region coexisted with orthodox forces that were still conservative on matters of race and social change. While Clinton and Gore are every inch modern Americans, they still are very recognizably southern. In that "twoness," both southern and American, they accurately reflect the modern South. The majority of demographically "typical American" cities used to market test new products are now located in the South. In so many outward ways the region appears almost identical with the nation at large, and yet it has a style, a feel, an accent, a pinch of soul that distinguishes it even to the casual observer. Part of the apparent national appeal of Clinton and Gore was their combination of modern images of high-tech American competence with an almost intangible downhome southern folksiness. For many educated southerners who still take umbrage at the often automatic national association of their region with backwardness and racism, the academic panache Clinton and Gore possess also brings a rare public pride last experienced during the early days of the Carter administration.

In the age of George Washington and Thomas Jefferson the South had been the region of progressive nationalism, not defensive regionalism. New Englanders were the secessionists then. William Jefferson Clinton's decision to begin his 1993 inaugural journey to Washington with a tour of Monticello, then essentially replicate by bus caravan Thomas Jefferson's 1801 inaugural journey to Washington, suggests the symbolic connection Clinton wanted to make to that earlier age. It would be tempting to argue that to some degree with Jimmy Carter, but more completely with Clinton and Gore, the South once again represented progressive nationalism, not a defense of retrograde regional institutions. In that sense the South's long estrangement from national norms that at its apex led to Civil War and separate nationhood was finally finished, and the region had at last fully rejoined its rightful place in the nation. Segregation was no longer legal, the South basked in the warmth of the Sun Belt, and two-party politics thrived in the region. Could one imagine that in some sense southern history was finished, Dixie had been vanquished? Would the South soon become an undifferentiated portion of the nation, as culturally flat and un-self-conscious as the Midwest? Could the South as a culturally separate folk region, as a state of mind more than a geographical location, now only be spoken of in the past tense? Had Dixie died?

THE SEARCH FOR SOUTHERN IDENTITY

No other region of the nation has been as concerned with and as compulsive about understanding its identity as has the South, especially since the 1820s when it began to be increasingly evident that the South had an identity, or at least institutions and interests, separate from the rest of the nation. After New England won the cultural battle in the early nineteenth century to define itself as the American norm, with the nation portrayed as New England writ large, the South by definition was the *other* region against which American values and attributes were contrasted. The southern difference was more often simply assumed rather than explained. Jefferson, though, had early posited climate as the determining factor that explained the South's difference, and as late as 1929 so prominent an interpreter of the South as Yale historian U. B. Phillips could begin an interpretation of the South by first talking about the weather. The climatic argument continued to be heard into the 1960s, for example in the writing of historian Clement Eaton, but after air-conditioning practically eliminated the discomfort of the South's long hot summers, the argument about climate's shaping role diminished.

Another perennial explanation of the South's distinctiveness has involved the presence in the region for more than three centuries of large numbers of blacks. This argument has taken a variety of forms, but the most common one, also based on the writings of U. B. Phillips, involves the persistent resolve of whites to dominate the blacks, whether through slavery or segregation or more subtle pressures. Variations of this persuasive view interpret much of southern politics in terms of race, particularly the recurrent desire to minimize white class differences so as to pose a united white stand against the so-called threat of the black underclass. From the aftermath of Bacon's Rebellion in late seventeenth-century Virginia to the appeal of George Wallace and David Duke in the twentieth, white leaders have tried to promote white racial solidarity, a kind of whitefolks democracy, in order to maintain strict racial control. Yet the growing reality of biracial politics in the recent South, especially in the Democratic party at the state level, suggests that this feature of southern politics is less salient now. The politics of racism has not disappeared, as David Duke showed by his near success in Louisiana in 1991, but perhaps more important than his electoral prowess was the forthright opposition to him by the leaders of both the Democratic and the Republican parties. Even the southernized GOP found the starkness of Duke's racial polarizing objectionable. Blatant racism is no longer a political asset in the South, and subtle racism in recent years has seemed as evident in Boston and Detroit and Los Angeles as in Atlanta or New Orleans. Racism no longer defines the Dixie difference.

Another traditional explanation for the South's seeming uniqueness within the nation was that for much of its history the region was more rural and its economy more dominated by agriculture than the rest of the nation. The relative absence of cities and industry was evidence of what in effect was an argument that, compared to the United States as a whole, the South was less modern. A variation of this explanation was the argument that the frontier experience lingered longer in the antebellum South; in fact, the southwestern portion of the Old South at the beginning of the Civil War was barely more than a generation removed from frontier days. Perhaps this explained the absence of cities, the easier acceptance of violence, the undeveloped state of social institutions. But however valid these arguments for rurality and the frontier being responsible for the nature of the southern difference may have been in the past, their utility seemed far less evident for the South after 1960. Now the great majority of southerners live in cities, and more work in industry than in agriculture. Skyscrapers, shopping malls, suburbs, and traffic jams are as much a part of the southern landscape as they are of the northern. So comparative lack of urbanization is no longer a characteristic of the South. Still it could be suggested that the South's large cities, newer and less dense, have a different feel than such cities as Boston and Philadelphia. But it is more a matter of degree than of kind.

Beginning about 1830, as large-scale European migration began to make more diverse the essentially English cultural and social mores of the North, the relative absence of such migration served to set the South apart. Moreover, almost all blacks lived in the southern states. As the white South remained comparatively British and Protestant, the North became ever more ethnically and religiously diverse, particularly in its growing urban areas. As much as anything else, a southern visitor to a northern city in about 1900 would have remarked on the presence of ethnic enclaves and ghettoes there, a babble of languages and cultures that often made portions of the North appear like a foreign country. In turn the South's biracial society often seemed exotic to northern visitors, but at least southern whites and blacks usually shared the same religious faith, spoke the same language, and had similar attitudes on a range of issues. The South, despite the presence of a rigid color line that affected social relations, was probably the more culturally homogeneous society. Southerners black and white shared more ideas about faith, food, and family than did the peoples of the more urban North.

In the almost two generations following the end of World War II, however, very significant northern in-migration to the South, along with the rise of Cuban, Mexican, and Vietnamese communities, have diversified the southern population. Certainly the large southern cities—Miami, Atlanta, New Orleans, Dallas, and Houston—are far more demographically complex than they were a half century ago. Moreover, during the first six decades of this century millions of southern blacks migrated north, mostly to cities. Now one can find soul food almost as easily in Newark or Chicago as in Memphis. Southern cities on the whole still lack the rich panoply of ethnic neighborhoods that characterize cities in the Midwest and Northeast especially, and they tend to be far less densely peopled. Yet the urban South today seems more urban than southern, and in that sense less different from northern cities than it did two generations ago.

For many decades the South's pathological tendencies set it apart. The South was the poorest, the least educated, the most violent, the most racist portion of the nation. Yet in all these measures of the lack of social well being the difference between the South and the rest of the nation has been very significantly narrowed. While the South as a whole still has the lowest per capita income of any region in the nation, it no longer has the social characteristics of a so-called Third World nation. The murder capital is no longer typically New Orleans or Houston, but Washington, DC; Detroit; or Oakland, California, instead. The gap between the South and the nation at large in many areas of social welfare has become small enough to have little apparent explanatory value. Poverty and homelessness and all the attendant social ills are now truly national problems, not stereotypically southern ones.

But if air-conditioning and urban growth and regional prosperity and racial gains have so merged the South and the rest of the nation, can one still usefully speak of a distinctive South? Perhaps it is in the realm of mind and culture that we must today look for the essence of southernness. In fact, that is precisely what modern polling data indicates. Sociologist John Shelton Reed first began to analyze what he called "the enduring South" after informal polls in his University of North Carolina classrooms indicated that southern students used different words to characterize the South than they did the North, and so did northern students, and in fact there was great similarity in the words or values associated with each region by northerners and southerners. Often the words were at best only one remove from stereotypes, but stereotypes indicate social perceptions. As one might expect, the South was described in such terms as warm, friendly, informal, traditional, slow paced, and racist, while the North was seen as cold, rude, busy, progressive, and urban.

The results of these classroom questionnaires led Reed to examine the national Gallup poll data over many decades. The results were instructive. Northern and southern attitudes diverged widely over a broad range of issues in the 1930s, but even though both regions showed marked changes in attitudes over the years, statistically the southern divergence from the national norm was greater in the early 1970s—when Reed did his analysis—than it had been four decades earlier. In other words, across a spectrum of questions, southerners were even more different attitudinally from other Americans in the 1970s than they had been in the 1930s. Controlling for economic status, educational attainment, degree of urbanization, and other factors, people in the South were still regionally distinct. And the better educated, more urban, more widely traveled, and more affluent they were, the more different southerners seemed to be from their fellow Americans in terms of attitudes. That would suggest that as the South as a region continued to narrow the measurable income, educational, and other gaps between itself and the nation as a whole—became more like the nation—the sense of southern distinctiveness might be ironically strengthened rather than dissipated.

John Shelton Reed has made the point that a sense of distinctiveness does not exist in isolation. Rather, one must have some understanding of others who are perceived to be unlike oneself before one can develop a self-consciousness of one's own identity. That is, one defines oneself in relative terms, either positively or negatively, and those southerners who have traveled or worked in the North or abroad, who are educated and who have been exposed to a range of viewpoints, who have become urbanized and experienced in more cosmopolitan social interactions, are the very ones most able to recognize their southernness because they have seen it juxtaposed to other cultures. The least traveled, least educated, and least cosmopolitan persons in the South, on the other hand, have the least self-awareness of their culture. Hence the paradox that those southerners who by education, employment, and lack of provincialism would seem to be candidates for loss of their southern self-identity are in fact most aware and protective of their felt southernness. What are the origins of this resilient sense of mental southernness, and of what does it consist?

Perhaps the most helpful interpreter of the South has been historian C. Vann Woodward. In his presidential address to the Southern Historical Association in November 1952 he suggested that the South was different from the rest of the nation largely because it had had such a different historical experience. The nation as a whole had largely escaped the normal conseqences of history in that, unlike most other nations, it had never been "confronted by complete frustration"—the United States had a "legend of success and victory

. . . not shared by any other people of the civilized world." Southerners, in contrast, knew "that history has happened to our people in our part of the world." In other essays Woodward elaborated this insight, arguing that while in its experience the nation had known mainly success, prosperity, and innocence, the South had struggled with failure, poverty, and guilt. Yet, ironically, what set the South apart from the nation gave it the potential to understand the larger world better, because the South's historical experience was more like that of the rest of the world. That could explain why Europeans, for instance, were so quick to understand and appreciate southern fiction and music.

Woodward was, of course, implicitly writing about the white South, and his analysis of the national experience predated the 1960s "war on poverty" and the 1970s experience with defeat in Vietnam and the guilt of Watergate. Still the burden of his interpretation obtains: the South's entire historical experience—slavery, secession, Civil War, sharecropping, segregation, its variation from the national norms and expectations—is what defines its sense of separateness. The recognition of apartness has often led to a defensiveness that became transmogrified into an apotheosis of southern ways. Few southerners were probably even aware of this process; many simply assumed that southern values and habits and tastes were normative, with other ways less acceptable. Rural, defensive, and comparatively homogeneous for generations, the South's people created unawares a folk culture, an identification with place and family and religion and even gastronomic preference, whereby they understood and defined themselves without premeditation. Rural isolation and loneliness led the southern people to prize kinship, often cemented by visiting; hardship and dislocation caused them to romanticize home and place; evangelical religion offered meaning and hope (and paradoxically fatalism) amidst a life of travail; simple, spicy fried foods provided sustenance; conversation, song, and folk recreations such as hunting and quilting that combined practical results with pleasure in the process brought joy into otherwise humdrum existence. While southern ways were thus grounded in the historical reality of the region, once the mores existed, they came to have a life separate from their origins. Thus reified, these values, habits of mind, and cultural preferences have long outlived their folk roots and become an integral part of a southern consciousness that persists even in the modern urban South. Affluent, educated southern cosmopolites attend church far more frequently than do their northern cohorts; they still express a biracial hunger for so-called soul food, diets be damned; they often reveal an awareness and affection for kin relationships—even to second and third cousins—that leave nonsoutherners befuddled. Southerners still greet newcomers by asking where they are from, revealing that they expect others' identity, too, to be somehow intertwined with their homeplace.

Not every southerner today defends or identifies with every aspect of the region, from stock-car races to country music to fanaticism about football to fervent defenses of a favorite barbecue restaurant. Most understand that certain older characteristics of the region—racism and general close-mindedness, for example—need to be eradicated. But even the most cautious son or daughter of the South who wants not to be stigmatized with certain aspects of the region's past identity will nevertheless defend other southernisms, such as notions about manners or respect for kin. The task of many modern, progressive southerners is discovering what from the stockpile of past southern ways ought to be discarded and what ought to be preserved and nurtured. There remains among many southerners a habit of politeness, a personalism, a patience that sometimes merges into fatalism, a respect for history, that can be very attractive. These values also turn out to be surprisingly biracial; southern whites and blacks are less different from each other in their basic attitudes than both are from other Americans.

This should not really be surprising. Blacks and whites have lived cheek by jowl together in the South for 375 mostly unhappy years, but in so doing they have been shaped by similar forces. In terms of accent, food preference, religious style, music, and attitudes toward kin and home, white and black southerners share far more than they differ. Perhaps it is this centuries-old blending of black and white ways, conscious and unconscious, ignored and denied, that is at the heart of the southern character. These matters of mind and habit, forged together in the southern past, constitute the southern way that both races today largely recognize and label good. As exemplified in the persons and values of Lamar Alexander, Jimmy Carter, Bill Clinton, Albert Gore, Martin Luther King, Jr., Andrew Young, Barbara Jordan, and many others, reformed southern values, drained of racism and violence and drenched in generations of evangelical preaching, can even be redemptive for the nation. Southerners of both races now think the South is the better region of the nation in which to live, and they value highly those aspects of the regional folk culture that they consider essential to themselves as southerners. Now that reformed southern ways are cherished, the occasional fear that their manners of the heart and mind are threatened by societal change or are unappreciated by outsiders or the larger culture only leads southerners to attempt to strengthen them by an act of the will, "Dixiefying Dixie," in the words of journalist Edwin M. Yoder, Jr., Southern identity may now be in significant part a self-conscious evocation, but so is French culture, and neither appear to be headed toward extinction.

Different groups in the South use different ways of revivifying and celebrating their folk roots. College professors attend and promote symposia on the nature of the South and such cultural icons as W. J. Cash and William Faulkner. Other southerners associate stock-car races or college football games or hunting and fishing with their sense of the South. Nostalgic forms of music, primarily country, blue grass, gospel, jazz, and blues, which remain creative but relate to earlier versions of the genre, tie many southerners to a selective portion of the past. Old-time "fiddlin' contests" and radio programs like the "Grand Ole Opry" are self-consciously traditional. Folk crafts are still another popular way to maintain a relationship with older ways, and particularly throughout the mountain South such items as Shaker furniture and the objects made, displayed, and sold at such locations as Berea, Kentucky, and Bransom, Missouri, are almost artifactual fossils from yesteryear. Quilting, military reenactments, a fascination with genealogy, and a rich variety of family and church homecomings with dinner on the grounds, are but representative activities that offer contemporary southerners a connection to what is perceived to be a past that provides stability and meaning to their lives. Certainly many of these activities are not exclusive to the South, but in this region—perhaps more so than elsewhere—they are an important part of regional self-identity.

Fiction, autobiography, and history are also components of present-day southern regionalism. The great works of William Faulkner, Thomas Wolfe, Carson McCullers, Flannery O'Connor, Richard Wright, Robert Penn Warren, and Eudora Welty are still read in the South and often constitute the fare of college literature courses, along with more recent serious authors like Truman Capote, William Styron, Reynolds Price, Ralph Ellison, Ernest Gaines, and Alice Walker. A broader public reads the less serious but equally southern fiction of Bobbie Lee Mason, Harper Lee, Fanny Flagg, Anne Rivers Siddons, Lee Smith, and especially Pat Conroy. National critics label such writers regional novelists, and their works certainly contain much local color. But a great many southerners find themselves and their world reflected in this literary outpouring. Another extremely revealing genre of southern writing has been autobiography. William Alexander Percy's *Lanterns on the Levee* (1941), William A. Owens's *This Stubborn Soil* (1966), Anne Moody's *Coming of Age in Mississippi* (1968), Maya Angelou's *I Know Why the Caged Bird Sings* (1969), and Will Campbell's *Brother to a Dragonfly* (1977) have become beloved books to many southerners wherein they discover something familiar, something new about both themselves and their region. Race is a theme in all these books, a tragic and at times triumphant motif that is central to southerners being who they are.

Movies and television have been powerful creators, propagators, and sustainers of myths about the South—the Old South, the benighted South, the good ol' boy South. In the 1920s and 1930s many of the most popular movies—from *Birth of a Nation* (1915) to *Gone with the Wind* (1939)—continued the moonlight-and-magnolia stereotypes about the region, with a vicious pinch of racism often thrown in gratuitously. These stereotypes were reversed in later films such as *Mandingo* (1975), *Drum* (1976), and *Hurry Sundown*

(1967), where white males are moral monsters. Other films like *Thunder Road* (1958) and *Macon County Line* (1973) feature moonshiners, car races, and law-breaking but good-hearted good ol' boys—a theme that found itself repeated in the popular though mindless 1970s television hit series, "The Dukes of Hazzard." Yet also in the 1960s a spate of more sophisticated films began to suggest ways the South could move, and indeed was moving, beyond its racist heritage. *In the Heat of the Night* (1967) suggested moral growth on the part of a pot-bellied southern sheriff. *Sounder* (1972), a poignant film about a black sharecropper family in depression-era Louisiana, represented a distinct advance over caricatured one-dimensional depictions of blacks— either as Sambos or rebels—in most previous movies. *To Kill a Mockingbird* (1963) showed a white lawyer willing to stand up against racism in a small southern town, and southerners who saw this powerful cinematic drama understood full well with whom they should identify. The 1960s television series named after actor Andy Griffith, who played a wise and kind country sheriff, also offered an affectionate rendering of the small-town South, seemingly all-white but never openly racist or mean-spirited.

In the 1970s the popular television program "The Waltons" (a far cry from the 1960s "Beverly Hillbillies") portrayed a depression-era Virginia family as having wholesome, idealized all-American virtues. In fact, Jimmy Carter in 1976 in many ways seemed to have stepped out of the television screen and onto the political stage. In the 1980s and 1990s such reformed images of the South continued, with television shows like "I'll Fly Away" and movies like *Driving Miss Daisy* (1989) and *Fried Green Tomatoes* (1991). A cultural breakthrough of sorts was achieved with the movie *Broadcast News* (1987), which had actress Holly Hunter playing a southern-accented television news producer from Atlanta who, despite being obviously southern, was simply portrayed as an immensely competent professional. Gone was the automatic identification of attractive southern women with so-called southern belles, empty-headed flirts who cared only about their next date. In real life Rosalynn Carter was a repudiation of the silliness of such outdated and erroneous stereotypes.

History in a variety of forms is another strong cultural adhesive binding the evolving present to a perception of the South's past. Most southern colleges offer courses in the history of the South—as do many colleges and universities outside the region—and the academic discipline supports a scholarly journal and a large annual meeting of historians. No longer is the written history of the South defensive or hagiographic. Rather, it is analytical, often critical of the past, and completely reflects the national trends in scholarship. Every southern state also has an active state historical society and at least one historical journal. All of the southern states have concrete reminders of their past in historic buildings and sites. History in the form of museums, battlefields, restored homes, and recreated structures (such as Colonial Williamsburg) is big business throughout much of Virginia and in Charleston, Savannah, New Orleans, Natchez, and Vicksburg. There is endemic fascination with the Civil War, sometimes even still quaintly called the War Between the States. As one travels across the region, old buildings, rather like geological outcroppings, offer silent evidence of a very different age and society that is now all but vanished. For many southerners these standing physical artifacts are the most vivid expressions of their sense of connection to a past variously and selectively remembered. Organizations such as the Sons of the Confederacy and United Daughters of the Confederacy, along with glorified plantation homes, recall a past often romanticized; while more recently organized civil rights tours in cities like Birmingham and Memphis remind tourists of a very different South that should not be forgotten. Birmingham now has an emotionally powerful Civil Rights Museum, and Atlanta has a museum and memorial celebrating the life of Martin Luther King, Jr. Black and white southerners alike share a belief that who they are is tied up with where they are from, and monuments and shrines serve as symbols that give meaning and value to place. The phenomenal publishing (1976) and television mini-series (1977) success of Alex Hailey's *Roots* illustrates the biracial nature of the southern identification with kin and place.

The South as a distinct region is now mostly a state of mind, a complex reaction to a shared historical experience. Myth and memory, history and fiction are essential ingredients, along with a number of folk practices that keep alive vital links to an otherwise forgotten past. The South's long history incorporates blacks and whites in a common tragedy, while the more recent past offers incentives for regional pride. The occasional scorn directed southward also strengthens a sense of regional community that nurtures southern identity. But the South is no huge living museum. While the past often seems astonishingly close at hand, no other region of the nation has experienced such transforming change during the last two generations. The greatest domestic success story in the nation since World War II has been the civil rights movement in the South. The journey yet to be traveled must not be allowed to obscure the distance already covered. The promise of progressive social change should be the South's offering to the nation. The greatest irony of all would be if the states of the former Confederacy could help heal the racial wounds of the United States. Pain—and history—can be redemptive, and in the South there are grounds for hope.

A Guide to Further Reading

The literature on southern history is immense, and there is no one comprehensive guide. Two historiographical volumes are indispensable for the scholarly literature, Arthur S. Link and Rembert W. Patrick, eds., *Writing Southern History: Essays in Historiography in Honor of Fletcher M. Green* (Baton Rouge, 1966) and John B. Boles and Evelyn Thomas Nolen, eds., *Interpreting Southern History: Historiographical Essays in Honor of Sanford W. Higginbotham* (Baton Rouge, 1987). Because these two volumes provide detailed coverage of the literature on southern history published before 1983, this guide to reading emphasizes books and articles published since then and ones that have shaped my understanding and discussion of the issues. It should be recognized that what follows represents only a fraction of the important works on the South, and I

apologize to those authors whose works I have had to omit because of limitations of space. I have repeated titles when they are relevant to several sections of this book.

In addition to the two historiographical volumes just mentioned, several specialized reference books are also useful for quick information and for pointing the way toward a more extensive literature. Among the most valuable of these are David C. Roller and Robert W. Twyman, eds., *The Encyclopedia of Southern History* (Baton Rouge, 1979); Charles Reagan Wilson and William Ferris, eds., *Encyclopedia of Southern Culture* (Chapel Hill, 1989); Samuel S. Hill, ed., *Encyclopedia of Religion in the South* (Macon, Ga., 1984); Randall M. Miller and John David Smith, eds., *Dictionary of Afro-American Slavery* (New York, Westport, Conn., and

London, 1988); and Louis D. Rubin, Jr., et al., eds., *The History of Southern Literature* (Baton Rouge, 1985). The book reviews in each quarterly issue of the *Journal of Southern History* are a good index of the range of scholarship in the field, and each May issue of the journal contains a detailed, topical bibliography of periodical literature on southern history published in the preceding year. Also useful is Jessica S. Brown, ed., *The American South: A Historical Bibliography* (Santa Barbara, Calif., 1986), which reprints abstracts of almost 9,000 articles in southern history selected from approximately 500 periodicals. Also extremely valuable are Donald B. Dodd and Wynelle S. Dodd, *Historical Statistics of the South, 1790–1970* (University, Ala., 1973), and William J. Cooper, Jr., and Thomas E. Terrill, *The American South: A History* (New York, 1990), which concludes with a long bibliographical essay.

CHAPTER 1:   THE SOUTHERN COLONIES

The history of the Native Americans who predated the first Europeans in the territory we now call the American South has become a field of increasing interest, and historians, not just archaeologists and anthropologists, are currently participating in the ongoing scholarship. A good beginning has been provided by Charles Hudson, *The Southeastern Indians* (Knoxville, 1976) and the volume he edited, *Red, White and Black: Symposium on Indians in the Old South* (Athens, Ga., 1971). See also J. Leitch Wright, Jr., *The Only Land They Knew: The Tragic Story of the American Indians in the Old South* (New York, 1981); Helen C. Rountree, *The Powhatan Indians of Virginia: Their Traditional Culture* (Norman, Okla., 1989); Timothy Silver, *A New Face on the Countryside: Indians, Colonists, and Slaves in South Atlantic Forests, 1500–1800* (Cambridge,

Eng., 1990); James H. Merrell, *The Indians' New World: Catawbas and their Neighbors from European Contact Through the Era of Removal* (Chapel Hill, 1989); Daniel H. Usner, Jr., *Indians, Settlers and Slaves in a Frontier Exchange Economy: The Lower Mississippi Valley Before 1783* (Chapel Hill, 1992); Kathryn E. Holland Braund, *Deerskins and Duffels: The Creek Indian Trade with Anglo-America, 1685–1815* (Lincoln, Neb., 1993); and Peter H. Wood, Gregory A. Waselkov, and M. Thomas Hatley, eds., *Powhatan's Mantle: Indians in the Colonial Southeast* (Lincoln, Neb., 1989). One older study of continuing value is Verner W. Crane, *The Southern Frontier, 1670–1732* (Durham, N.C., 1928).

The essential book for the history of European exploration of the New World is David B. Quinn, *North America from Earliest Discovery to First Settlements: The Norse Voyages to 1612* (New York, 1977), which may be supplemented with his *Set Fair for Roanoke: Voyages and Colonies, 1584–1606* (Chapel Hill, 1985). One should also consult Jerald T. Milanich and Susan Milbrath, eds., *First Encounters: Spanish Explorations in the Caribbean and the United States, 1492–1570* (Gainesville, Fla., 1989); Paul E. Hoffman, *A New Andalucia and a Way to the Orient: The American Southeast During the Sixteenth Century* (Baton Rouge, 1990); and especially David J. Weber, *The Spanish Frontier in North America* (New Haven, 1992).

The scholarship on colonial Virginia is, not surprisingly, voluminous. Perhaps the best starting point is Warren M. Billings, John E. Selby, and Thad W. Tate, *Colonial Virginia, A History* (White Plains, N.Y., 1986), supplemented by Wesley Frank Craven, *The Southern Colonies in the Seventeenth Century, 1607–1689* (Baton Rouge, 1949), whose focus is broader than just Virginia. For the very earliest beginning, consult Alden T. Vaughan, *American Genesis: Captain John Smith and the Founding of Virginia*

(Boston, 1975) and Virginia Bernhard, "'Men, Women and Children' at Jamestown: Population and Gender in Early Virginia, 1607–1610," *Journal of Southern History*, 58 (November 1992), 599–618. See also the relevant essays in Thad W. Tate and David L. Ammerman, eds., *The Chesapeake in the Seventeenth Century: Essays on Anglo-American Society* (Chapel Hill, 1979), which includes essays on the colony of Maryland as well. Edmund S. Morgan, *American Slaves— American Freedom: The Ordeal of Colonial Virginia* (New York, 1975), discusses the evolution of the labor force from white indentured servants to slavery. For indentured servants generally, see David W. Galenson, *White Servitude in Colonial America: An Economic Analysis* (Cambridge, Eng., 1981). Among the valuable local studies are Ivor Noel Hume, *Martin's Hundred* (New York, 1982); T. H. Breen and Stephen Innes, *"Myne Owne Ground": Race and Freedom on Virginia's Eastern Shore, 1640–1676* (New York, 1980); and James R. Perry, *The Formation of a Society on Virginia's Eastern Shore, 1615–1655* (Chapel Hill, 1990).

Aubrey C. Land's *Colonial Maryland, A History* (Millwood, N.Y., 1981) is the most convenient survey of that colony's past. The new social history scholarship on Maryland has been particularly distinguished. Accessible introductions to this work are offered by Aubrey C. Land, Lois Green Carr, and Edward C. Papenfuse, eds., *Law, Society, and Politics in Early Maryland: Proceedings of the First Conference on Maryland History, June 14–15, 1974* (Baltimore, 1977) and Lois Green Carr, Philip D. Morgan, and Jean B. Russo, eds., *Colonial Chesapeake Society* (Chapel Hill, 1988). See also Gloria L. Main, *Tobacco Colony: Life in Early Maryland, 1650–1720* (Princeton, 1982) and Lois Green Carr, Russell R. Menard, and Lorena S. Walsh, *Robert Cole's World: Agriculture and Society in Early Maryland* (Chapel Hill, 1991). Allan Kulikoff's

Tobacco and Slaves: The Development of Southern Cultures in the Chesapeake, 1680–1800 (Chapel Hill, 1986) is an influential study of the whole Chesapeake society.

Colonial South Carolina has been the beneficiary of three unusually good studies; the most general is *Colonial South Carolina: A History* by Robert M. Weir (Millwood, N.Y., 1983), then Peter H. Wood's *Black Majority: Negroes in Colonial South Carolina from 1670 through the Stono Rebellion* (New York, 1974) and Peter A. Coclanis, *The Shadow of a Dream: Economic Life and Death in the South Carolina Low Country, 1670–1920* (New York, 1989), which has a much broader chronological sweep. Carl Bridenbaugh's older work, *Myths and Realities: Societies of the Colonial South* (Baton Rouge, 1952), with its discussions of a Chesapeake, a Carolina, and a backcountry South remains an important interpretation. See also Hugh T. Lefler and William S. Powell, *Colonial North Carolina, A History* (New York, 1973) and A. Roger Ekirch, *"Poor Carolina": Politics and Society in Colonial North Carolina, 1729–1776* (Chapel Hill, 1981).

After its initial founding, Georgia developed following the pattern established by South Carolina. See Kenneth Coleman, *Colonial Georgia, A History* (New York, 1976), Phinizy Spalding, *Oglethorpe in America* (Chicago, 1977); Harvey H. Jackson and Phinizy Spalding, eds., *Forty Years of Diversity: Essays on Colonial Georgia* (Athens, Ga., 1984); and Betty Wood, *Slavery in Colonial Georgia, 1730–1775* (Athens, Ga., 1984). See also Alan Gallay, *The Formation of a Planter Elite: Jonathan Bryan and the Southern Colonial Frontier* (Athens, Ga., 1989).

The evolution of slavery in the American South is analyzed in the previously mentioned works by Edmund S. Morgan, Peter H. Wood, and Betty Wood. There is an enormous body of scholarship on slavery, but for the colonial period, in addition to these three works, see Winthrop D. Jordan, *White Over Black: American Attitudes Toward the Negro, 1550–1812* (Chapel Hill, 1968); Philip D. Curtin, *The Atlantic Slave Trade: A Census* (Madison, Wis., 1969); Ira Berlin, "Time, Space, and the Evolution of Afro-American Society on British Mainland North America," *American Historical Review*, 85 (February 1980), 44–78. A useful survey is found in John B. Boles, *Black Southerners, 1619–1869* (Lexington, Ky., 1983). For the general historiography of slavery, see Peter J. Parish, *Slavery: History and Historians* (New York, 1989).

For the Latin South, see, in addition to the works listed above by Quinn, Hoffman, and Weber, Charles Gibson's *Spain in America* (New York, 1966); John J. TePaske, ed., *Three American Empires* (New York, 1967); and John Francis Bannon, *The Spanish Borderlands Frontier, 1513–1821* (New York, 1970).

The character of the mid-eighteenth-century South is described in many of the books listed above that treat individual colonies. Several additional studies of special value include Edmund S. Morgan, *Virginians At Home: Family Life in the Eighteenth Century* (Williamsburg, Va., 1952); Louis B. Wright, *The First Gentlemen of Virginia: Intellectual Qualities of the Early Colonial Ruling Class* (San Marino, Calif., 1940); Richard Beale Davis, *Intellectual Life in the Colonial South, 1585–1763* (3 vols., Knoxville, Tenn., 1978); Daniel Blake Smith, *Inside the Great House: Planter Family Life in Eighteenth-Century Chesapeake Society* (Ithaca, 1980); John J. McCusker and Russell R. Menard, *The Economy of British America, 1607–1789* (Chapel Hill, 1985); Mechal Sobel, *The World They Made Together: Black and White Values in Eighteenth-Century Virginia* (Princeton, 1987); and Jack P. Greene, *Pursuits of Happiness: The Social Development of Early Modern British Colonies and the Formation of American Culture* (Chapel Hill, 1988).

For the backcountry one can still begin with Bridenbaugh's *Myths and Realities*, previously cited. From there go to Richard R. Beeman, *The Evolution of the Southern Backcountry: A Case Study of Lunenburg County, Virginia, 1746–1832* (Philadelphia, 1984); Robert D. Mitchell, *Commercialism and Frontier: Perspectives on the Early Shenandoah Valley* (Charlottesville, 1977); Warren R. Hofstra and Robert D. Mitchell, "Town and Country in Backcountry Virginia: Winchester and the Shenandoah Valley, 1730–1800," *Journal of Southern History*, 59 (November 1993), 619–46; Robert W. Ramsey, *Carolina Cradle: Settlement of the Northwest Carolina Frontier, 1747–1762* (Chapel Hill, 1964); and Rachel N. Klein, *Unification of a Slave State: The Rise of the Planter Class in the South Carolina Backcountry, 1760–1808* (Chapel Hill, 1990).

CHAPTER 2: THE NATIONAL SOUTH

There is an enormous body of scholarship on the coming of the American Revolution, but here I am emphasizing work that focuses on the South. This scholarship should be read in the larger context of all the colonies. A good beginning book for the political culture of Virginia at mid-century is still Charles S. Sydnor's classic *American Revolutionaries in the Making: Political Practices in Washington's Virginia* (New York, 1965; first published in 1952). A number of biographies of the political leaders also offer an éntrée into the thought and events of the time; one of the most accessible is Merrill D. Peterson, *Thomas Jefferson and the New Nation: A Biography* (New York, 1970). See also Richard R. Beeman, *Patrick Henry: A Biography* (New York, 1974). Jack P. Greene's corpus of work is invaluable for this topic; a good introduction to his viewpoint is "Society, Ideology, and Politics: An Analysis of the Political Culture of

Mid-Eighteenth-Century Virginia," in Richard M. Jellison, ed., *Society, Freedom, and Conscience: The American Revolution in Virginia, Massachusetts, and New York* (New York, 1976), 14–76. T. H. Breen shows the relationship between tobacco cultivation, debt, Anglo-American misunderstanding, and the coming of the Revolution in his *Tobacco Culture: The Mentality of the Great Tidewater Planters on the Eve of Revolution* (Princeton, 1985). For religion's role, see Rhys Isaac, *The Transformation of Virginia, 1740–1790* (Chapel Hill, 1982).

John Richard Alden's *The South in the Revolution, 1763–1789* (Baton Rouge, 1957) remains the essential starting point for understanding the coming conflict, though one should also see more recent accounts of the military aspects, especially John Shy's *Toward Lexington: The Role of the British Army in the Coming of the American Revolution* (Princeton, 1965) and *A People Numerous and Armed: Reflections on the Military Struggle for American Independence* (New York, 1976). Also see Don Higginbotham, *The War of American Independence: Military Attitudes, Policies, and Practice, 1763–1789* (New York, 1971); John S. Pancake, *This Destructive War: The British Campaign in the Carolinas, 1780–1782* (University, Ala., 1985); and Russell F. Weigley, *The Partisan War: The South Carolina Campaign of 1780–1782* (Columbia, S.C., 1970). Henry Lumpkin provides a useful survey in *From Savannah to Yorktown: The American Revolution in the South* (Columbia, S.C., 1981). Several edited books contain important articles on various aspects of the Revolution in the South: Jeffrey J. Crow and Larry E. Tise, eds., *The Southern Experience in the American Revolution* (Chapel Hill, 1978); W. Robert Higgins, ed., *The Revolutionary War in the South: Power, Conflict, and Leadership. Essays in Honor of John Richard Alden* (Durham, 1979); Ronald Hoffman, Thad W. Tate, and Peter J. Albert, eds.,

An Uncivil War: The Southern Backcountry during the American Revolution (Charlottesville, 1985); and Ronald Hoffman and Peter J. Albert, eds., *Women in the Age of the American Revolution* (Charlottesville, 1989).

For the relationship between slavery and the American Revolution, one should perhaps begin with Duncan J. MacLeod, *Slavery, Race, and the American Revolution* (Cambridge, Eng., 1974) and Sylvia R. Frey, *Water from the Rock: Black Resistance in a Revolutionary Age* (Princeton, 1991). But see also the valuable articles in Ira Berlin and Ronald Hoffman, eds., *Slavery and Freedom in the Age of the American Revolution* (Charlottesville, 1983) and Robert A. Olwell, "'Domestick Enemies': Slavery and Political Independence in South Carolina, May 1775–March 1776," *Journal of Southern History*, 55 (February 1989), 21–48. Two older studies remain important, Benjamin Quarles's pioneering *The Negro in the American Revolution* (Chapel Hill, 1961) and Robert McColley's *Slavery and Jeffersonian Virginia* (Urbana, Ill., 1964).

On Indians and the Revolutionary War, consult for background John Richard Alden, *John Stuart and the Southern Colonial Frontier: A Study of Indian Relations, War, Trade, and Land Problems in the Southern Wilderness, 1754–1775* (Ann Arbor, Mich., 1944) and Jack M. Sosin, *The Revolutionary Frontier, 1763–1783* (New York, 1967). James H. O'Donnell, *Southern Indians in the American Revolution* (Knoxville, 1973) is the best available account of its subject.

Perhaps the most accessible introduction to the role of the South in the creation of the new republic is through biography. I can think of no better account than Merrill Peterson's biography of Jefferson, cited above. But see in addition Drew R. McCoy, *The Last of the Fathers: James Madison and the Republican Legacy* (Cambridge, Mass., 1989) and

James Thomas Flexner, *Washington: The Indispensable Man* (Boston, 1974). The ideological background is provided by William J. Cooper, Jr., *Liberty and Slavery: Southern Politics to 1860* (New York, 1983); Lance Banning, *The Jeffersonian Persuasion: Evolution of a Party Ideology* (Ithaca, 1978); Joyce Appleby, *Capitalism and a New Social Order: The Republican Vision of the 1790s* (New York, 1984); and Drew R. McCoy, *The Elusive Republic: Political Economy in Jeffersonian America* (Chapel Hill, 1980). Good on the basic political history of the era are Norman K. Risjord, *Chesapeake Politics, 1781–1800* (New York, 1978); Noble E. Cunningham, Jr., *The Jeffersonian Republicans: The Formation of Party Organization, 1789–1801* (Chapel Hill, 1957); Lisle A. Rose, *Prologue to Democracy: The Federalists in the South, 1789–1800* (Lexington, Ky., 1968); and Margaret C. S. Christman, *The First Federal Congress, 1789–1791* (Washington, D.C., 1989). Two illuminating biographies of second-level figures are Robert E. Shalhope, *John Taylor of Carolina: Pastoral Republican* (Columbia, S.C., 1980) and George C. Rogers, Jr., *Evolution of a Federalist: William Loughton Smith of Charleston, 1758–1812* (Columbia, S.C., 1962).

On the West and Southwest, one can still begin with the work of Thomas Perkins Abernethy, especially *From Frontier to Plantation in Tennessee: A Study in Frontier Democracy* (Chapel Hill, 1932), *Three Virginia Frontiers* (Baton Rouge, 1940), and the relevant chapters of *The South in the New Nation, 1789–1819* (Baton Rouge, 1961). For Kentucky the best brief treatment is Otis K. Rice, *Frontier Kentucky* (Lexington, Ky., 1975). Harriette Simpson Arnow's *Seedtime on the Cumberland* (New York, 1960) is a beautifully written account of frontier life. The best account of a land speculator remains William H. Masterson, *William Blount* (Baton Rouge, 1954). For the Southwest see Arthur P. Whitaker, *The Spanish-American Frontier, 1783–1795: The Westward Movement and the Spanish Retreat*

in the Mississippi Valley (Boston, 1927); Robert V. Haynes, *The Natchez District and the American Revolution* (Jackson, Miss., 1976); J. Barton Starr, *Tories, Dons, and Rebels: The American Revolution in British West Florida* (Gainesville, Fla., 1976); James Leitch Wright, Jr., *Anglo-Spanish Rivalry in North America* (Athens, Ga., 1971); and D. Clayton James, *Antebellum Natchez* (Baton Rouge, 1968). On Louisiana see Jack D. L. Holmes, *Gayoso: The Life of a Spanish Governor in the Mississippi Valley, 1789–1799* (Baton Rouge, 1965); E. Wilson Lyon, *Louisiana in French Diplomacy, 1759–1804* (Norman, Okla., 1934); Alexander DeConde, *This Affair of Louisiana* (New York, 1976); George Dargo, *Jefferson's Louisiana: Politics and the Clash of Legal Traditions* (Cambridge, Mass., 1975); and Chapter 5, "The Purchase of a Trackless World," in Marshall Smelser, *The Democratic Republic, 1801–1815* (New York, 1968), 83–103.

The beginning of cotton cultivation in the South, and indeed all aspects of southern agriculture, are covered in a classic, two-volume study by Lewis Cecil Gray, *History of Agriculture in the Southern United States to 1860* (Washington, D.C., 1933). The indispensable modern studies are by Joyce E. Chaplin, "Creating a Cotton South in Georgia and South Carolina, 1760–1815," *Journal of Southern History* 57 (May 1991), 171–200, and *An Anxious Pursuit: Agricultural Innovation and Modernity in the Lower South, 1730–1815* (Chapel Hill, 1993). For the inventor of the modern cotton gin, see Constance McL. Green, *Eli Whitney and the Birth of American Technology* (Boston, 1956). An excellent illustration of the consequences of the rise of cotton is John Hebron Moore, *The Emergence of the Cotton Kingdom in the Old Southwest: Mississippi, 1770–1860* (Baton Rouge, 1988).

For southern religion in the late colonial period see Rhys Isaacs's *The Transformation of Virginia*, listed above, and Wesley M. Gewehr, *The Great Awakening in Virginia, 1740–1790* (Durham, 1930). For evangelical growth in the early national period see John B. Boles, *The Great Revival, 1787–1805: The Origins of the Southern Evangelical Mind* (Lexington, Ky., 1972) and Dickson D. Bruce, Jr., *And They All Sang Hallelujah: Plain-Folk Camp-Meeting Religion, 1800–1845* (Knoxville, 1974). The implications of this revivalistic tradition are spelled out in John B. Boles, *Religion in Antebellum Kentucky* (Lexington, Ky., 1976) and *The Irony of Southern Religion* (New York, 1994), Donald G. Mathews, *Religion in the Old South* (Chicago, 1977), and Jan Lewis, *The Pursuit of Happiness: Family and Values in Jefferson's Virginia* (Cambridge, Eng., 1983), and Randy J. Sparks, *On Jordan's Stormy Banks: Evangelicalism in Mississippi, 1773–1876* (Athens, Ga., 1994).

Few readers have time to read Dumas Malone's magisterial six-volume biography, *Jefferson and His Time* (Boston, 1948–1981), but Merrill D. Peterson's oft-cited *Thomas Jefferson and the New Nation* provides both biography and context. Insightful studies of this era include Noble E. Cunningham, Jr., *The Jeffersonian Republicans in Power: Party Operations, 1801–1809* (Chapel Hill, 1963); James Sterling Young, *The Washington Community, 1800–1828* (New York, 1966); Norman K. Risjord, *The Old Republicans: Southern Conservatism in the Age of Jefferson* (New York, 1965); James H. Broussard, *The Southern Federalists, 1800–1816* (Baton Rouge, 1978); and Daniel P. Jordan, *Political Leadership in Jefferson's Virginia* (Charlottesville, 1983). Two good general treatments of the era are the New American Nation Series history by Marshall Smelser, cited above, and Norman K. Risjord's *Jefferson's America, 1760–1815* (Madison, Wis., 1991). Jefferson's Indian policy is discussed by Bernard W. Sheehan, *Seeds of Extinction: Jeffersonian Philanthropy and the American Indian* (Chapel Hill, 1973). The background to the troubles with England and France that even-

tuated in the War of 1812 is best described by Roger H. Brown, *The Republic in Peril: 1812* (New York, 1964), Burton Spivak, *Jefferson's English Crisis: Commerce, Embargo, and the Republican Revolution* (Charlottesville, 1979), and J. C. A. Stagg, *Mr. Madison's War: Politics, Diplomacy, and Warfare in the Early American Republic, 1783–1830* (Princeton, 1983).

For the War of 1812 itself, one may begin with Harry L. Coles, *The War of 1812* (Chicago, 1965) and the relevant chapters of Robert V. Remini, *Andrew Jackson and the Course of American Empire, 1767–1821* (New York, 1977). Walter Lord in *The Dawn's Early Light* (New York, 1972) colorfully details the course of the war in Washington, D.C., and Baltimore, and for Louisiana see Frank Lawrence Owsley, Jr., *Struggle for the Gulf Borderlands: The Creek War and the Battle of New Orleans, 1812–1815* (Gainesville, Fla., 1981). The books previously cited by D. Clayton James and John Hebron Moore on Mississippi discuss the onrush of population after the War of 1812. For John Quincy Adams's diplomacy regarding the acquisition of Florida, see Philip Coolidge Brooks, *Diplomacy and the Borderland: The Adams–Onís Treaty of 1819* (Berkeley, Calif., 1939).

Much has been written about the origins of southern sectionalism. The most recent treatment actually begins earlier than its title suggests: John McCardell, *The Idea of a Southern Nation: Southern Nationalists and Southern Nationalism, 1830–1860* (New York, 1979). The standard old study, still indispensable, is Charles S. Sydnor, *The Development of Southern Sectionalism, 1819–1848* (Baton Rouge, 1948). An even older work is Jesse T. Carpenter, *The South as a Conscious Minority, 1789–1861: A Study in Political Thought* (New York, 1930). William W. Freehling, *Prelude to Civil War: The Nullification Controversy in South Carolina, 1816–1836* (New York, 1966), also covers this period. The best study of the Missouri crisis remains Glover Moore, *The*

Missouri Controversy, 1819–1821 (Lexington, Ky., 1953), but see the discussion in Don E. Fehrenbacher, *The South and Three Sectional Crises* (Baton Rouge, 1980). An early indication of emerging sectional crisis is discussed in John B. Boles, "Tension in a Slave Society: The Trial of the Reverend Jacob Gruber," *Southern Studies*, 18 (Summer 1979), 179–97.

CHAPTER 3: THE SOUTHERN NATION

Even though it is more than six decades old, Lewis Cecil Gray's *History of Agriculture in the Southern United States to 1860* (Washington, D.C., 1933) is still absolutely indispensable. But it should be supplemented with Gavin Wright, *The Political Economy of the Cotton South: Households, Markets, and Wealth in the Nineteenth Century* (New York, 1978); Harold D. Woodman, *King Cotton and His Retainers: Financing and Marketing the Cotton Crop of the South, 1800–1925* (Lexington, Ky., 1968); James F. Hopkins, *A History of the Hemp Industry in Kentucky* (Lexington, Ky., 1951); J. Carlyle Sitterson, *Sugar Country: The Cane Sugar Industry in the South, 1753–1950* (Lexington, Ky., 1953); James C. Bonner, *A History of Georgia Agriculture, 1732–1860* (Athens, Ga., 1964); John C. Inscoe, *Mountain Masters, Slavery, and the Sectional Crisis in Western North Carolina* (Knoxville, 1989); Sam Bowers Hilliard, *Hog Meat and Hoecake: Food Supply in the Old South, 1840–1860* (Carbondale, Ill., 1972); and Forrest McDonald and Grady McWhiney, "The Antebellum Southern Herdsman: A Reinterpretation," *Journal of Southern History*, 41 (May 1975), 147–66.

The literature on southern white society is both extensive and impressive. A good brief introduction is found in Bruce Collins, *White Society in the Antebellum South* (London and New York, 1985), though one should also read Frank Lawrence Owsley's classic *Plain Folk of the*

Old South (Baton Rouge, 1949) and James Oakes's *The Ruling Race: A History of American Slaveholders* (New York, 1982) for accounts of yeomen and planters, respectively. The essential monographic literature includes Edward L. Ayers, *Vengeance and Justice: Crime and Punishment in the 19th-Century American South* (New York, 1984); Orville Vernon Burton, *In My Father's House Are Many Mansions: Family and Community in Edgefield, South Carolina* (Chapel Hill, 1985); J. William Harris, *Plain Folk and Gentry in a Slave Society: White Liberty and Black Slavery in Augusta's Hinterlands* (Middletown, Conn., 1985); Robert C. Kenzer, *Kinship and Neighborhood in a Southern Community: Orange County, North Carolina, 1849–1881* (Knoxville, 1987); Daniel W. Crofts, *Old Southampton: Politics and Society in a Virginia County, 1834–1869* (Charlottesville, 1992); and Bertram Wyatt-Brown, *Southern Honor: Ethics and Behavior in the Old South* (New York, 1982). A masterful biography that illuminates much of southern society is Drew Gilpin Faust, *James Henry Hammond and the Old South: A Design for Mastery* (Baton Rouge, 1982). Two older books by Clement Eaton reward a close reading: *The Growth of Southern Civilization, 1790–1860* (New York, 1961) and *The Mind of the Old South* (revised ed., Baton Rouge, 1967).

The topic of slavery has generated more revisionist scholarship over the last twenty-five years than any other subject. The best introduction to the historiography is Peter J. Parish, *Slavery: History and Historians* (New York, 1989). A brief synthesis of the modern scholarship is offered by John B. Boles, *Black Southerners, 1619–1869* (Lexington, Ky., 1983). While the serious researcher will still want to read Ulrich Bonnell Phillips, *American Negro Slavery: A Survey of the Supply, Employment and Control of Negro Labor As Determined by the Plantation Regime* (New York, 1918), and especially Kenneth M. Stampp, *The Peculiar Institution:*

Slavery in the Ante-Bellum South (New York, 1956), most readers could well begin with John W. Blassingame, *The Slave Community: Plantation Life in the Antebellum South* (New York, 1972). Significant books in the development of the modern interpretation of slavery include Eugene D. Genovese's magisterial *Roll, Jordan, Roll: The World the Slaves Made* (New York, 1974); Herbert G. Gutman, *The Black Family in Slavery and Freedom, 1750–1925* (New York, 1976); Lawrence W. Levine, *Black Culture and Black Consciousness: Afro-American Folk Thought from Slavery to Freedom* (New York, 1977); (New York, 1964); Albert J. Raboteau, *Slave Religion: The "Invisible Institution" in the Antebellum South* (New York, 1978); William L. Van Deburg, *The Slave Drivers: Black Agricultural Labor Supervisors in the Antebellum South* (Westport, Conn., 1979); Willie Lee Rose, *Slavery and Freedom* (New York, 1982); Charles Joyner, *Down by the Riverside: A South Carolina Slave Community* (Urbana, Ill., 1984); John Michael Vlach, *The Afro-American Tradition in Decorative Arts* (Cleveland, 1978); Randolph B. Campbell, *An Empire for Slavery: The Peculiar Institution in Texas, 1821–1865* (Baton Rouge, 1989); Peter Kolchin, *Unfree Labor: American Slavery and Russian Serfdom* (Cambridge, Mass., 1987); Ann Patton Malone, *Sweet Chariot: Slave Family and Household Structure in Nineteenth-Century Louisiana* (Chapel Hill, 1992); Eugene D. Genovese, *From Rebellion to Revolution: Afro-American Slave Revolts in the Making of the Modern World* (Baton Rouge, 1979); and Douglas R. Egerton, *Gabriel's Rebellion: The Virginia Slave Conspiracies of 1800 and 1802* (Chapel Hill, 1993).

It is important to realize how diverse the institution of slavery was. Good introductions to the various occupations of southern blacks include Robert S. Starobin, *Industrial Slavery in the Old South* (New York, 1970); Richard C. Wade, *Slavery in the Cities: The South,* 1820–1860 (New York, 1964); Charles B. Dew, "Disciplining Slave Ironworkers in the Antebellum South: Coercion, Conciliation, and Accommodation," *American Historical Review,* 79 (April 1974), 393–418; Ronald L. Lewis, *Coal, Iron, and Slaves: Industrial Slavery in Maryland and Virginia, 1715–1865* (Westport, Conn., 1979); Ira Berlin, *Slaves Without Masters: The Free Negro in the Antebellum South* (New York, 1974); Michael P. Johnson and James L. Roark, *Black Masters: A Free Family of Color in the Old South* (New York, 1984); and Leonard P. Curry, *The Free Black in Urban America, 1800–1850: The Shadow of the Dream* (Chicago, 1981).

The history of women in the South promises to be the topic of the most significant new scholarship in the 1990s. The great pioneering books are Guion Griffis Johnson, *Ante-Bellum North Carolina: A Social History* (Chapel Hill, 1937) and Julia Cherry Spruill, *Women's Life and Work in the Southern Colonies* (Chapel Hill, 1938), followed more than four decades later by Anne Firor Scott, *The Southern Lady: From Pedestal to Politics, 1830–1930* (Chicago, 1970). Two recent brief works of synthesis are Suzanne Lebsock, *Virginia Women, 1600–1945: "A Share of Honour"* (Richmond, 1987) and Sally G. McMillen, *Southern Women: Black and White in the Old South* (Arlington Heights, Ill., 1992). Representative modern studies include Catherine Clinton, *The Plantation Mistress: Woman's World in the Old South* (New York, 1982); Suzanne Lebsock, *The Free Women of Petersburg: Status and Culture in a Southern Town, 1784–1860* (New York, 1984); Elizabeth Fox-Genovese, *Within the Plantation Household: Black and White Women of the Old South* (Chapel Hill, 1988); Sally G. McMillen, *Motherhood in the Old South: Pregnancy, Childbirth, and Infant Rearing* (Baton Rouge, 1990); and Victoria E. Bynum, *Unruly Women: The Politics of Social and Sexual Control in the Old South* (Chapel Hill, 1992). Two recent works that carefully discuss women in a family context are Jane Turner Censer, *North Carolina Planters and Their Children, 1800–1860* (Baton Rouge, 1984) and Joan E. Cashin, *A Family Venture: Men and Women on the Southern Frontier* (New York, 1991). For black women in particular, in addition to the surveys offered by Suzanne Lebsock and Sally McMillen, and the discussion by Elizabeth Fox-Genovese, see Deborah Gray White, *Ar'n't I a Woman? Female Slaves in the Plantation South* (New York, 1985); the first chapter of Jacqueline Jones, *Labor of Love, Labor of Sorrow: Black Women, Work, and the Family from Slavery to the Present* (New York, 1985); Melton A. McLaurin, *Celia, A Slave* (Athens, Ga., 1991); and Harriet A. Jacobs, *Incidents in the Life of a Slave Girl, Written by Herself,* edited by Jean Fagan Yellin (Cambridge, Mass., 1987).

The tragic story of Indian removal should be approached by first reading R. S. Cotterill, *The Southern Indians: The Story of the Civilized Tribes Before Removal* (Norman, Okla., 1954); then John Ehle, *Trail of Tears: The Rise and Fall of the Cherokee Nation* (New York, 1988); Arthur H. De Rosier, Jr., *The Removal of the Choctaw Indians* (Knoxville, 1970); Michael D. Green, *The Politics of Indian Removal: Creek Government and Society in Crisis* (Lincoln, Neb., 1982); Thurman Wilkins, *Cherokee Tragedy: The Story of the Ridge Family and the Decimation of a People* (New York, 1970); Gary E. Moulton, *John Ross, Cherokee Chief* (Athens, Ga., 1978); John R. Finger, *The Eastern Band of Cherokees, 1819–1900* (Knoxville, 1984); William G. McLoughlin, *Cherokees and Missionaries, 1789–1839* (New Haven, 1984); and Anthony F. C. Wallace, *The Long, Bitter Trail: Andrew Jackson and the Indians* (New York, 1993).

The southern way of life is covered, at least implicitly, in many of the works listed above. In addition to the studies that discuss southern religion and south-

ern white society, see Lacy K. Ford, Jr., *Origins of Southern Radicalism: The South Carolina Upcountry, 1800–1860* (New York, 1988); Drew Gilpin Faust, *A Sacred Circle: The Dilemma of the Intellectual in the Old South, 1840–1860* (Baltimore, 1977); Dickson D. Bruce, Jr., *Violence and Culture in the Antebellum South* (Austin, 1979); Larry E. Tise, *Proslavery: A History of the Defense of Slavery in America, 1701–1840* (Athens, Ga., 1987); Eugene D. Genovese, *The World the Slaveholders Made: Two Essays in Interpretation* (New York, 1969); Kenneth S. Greenberg, *Masters and Statesmen: The Political Culture of American Slavery* (Baltimore, 1985); J. Mills Thornton, III, *Politics and Power in a Slave Society: Alabama, 1800–1860* (Baton Rogue, 1978); James Oakes, *Slavery and Freedom: An Interpretation of the Old South* (New York, 1990); Steven M. Stowe, *Intimacy and Power in the Old South: Ritual in the Lives of the Planters* (Baltimore, 1987); Laurence Shore, *Southern Capitalists: The Ideological Leadership of an Elite, 1832–1885* (Chapel Hill, 1986); William W. Freehling, *The Road to Disunion: Secessionists at Bay, 1776–1854* (New York, 1990); George M. Fredrickson, *The Black Image in the White Mind: The Debate on Afro-American Character and Destiny, 1817–1914* (New York, 1971); and Michael O'Brien, ed., *All Clever Men, Who Make Their Way: Critical Discourse in the Old South* (revised ed., Athens, Ga., 1992). I do not find very persuasive the argument, developed most completely by Grady McWhiney, *Cracker Culture: Celtic Ways in the Old South* (University, Ala., 1988), that southern culture is primarily distinguished from northern culture by virtue of many southerners having originally descended from persons who inhabited the so-called Celtic fringe areas of Great Britain.

Any discussion of the sectional crisis must begin with Charles S. Sydnor, *The Development of Southern Sectionalism, 1819–1848* (Baton Rouge, 1948) and

David M. Potter, *The Impending Crisis, 1848–1861* (New York, 1976), the latter being one of the great books in the entire corpus of American history. A number of important monographs treat the issues and events that ultimately rent the nation. Among the best are Kenneth M. Stampp, *America in 1857: A Nation on the Brink* (New York, 1990); Richard P. McCormick, *The Second American Party System: Party Formation in the Jacksonian Era* (Chapel Hill, 1966); Richard E. Ellis, *The Union at Risk: Jacksonian Democracy, States' Rights, and the Nullification Crisis* (New York, 1987); Merrill D. Peterson, *Olive Branch and Sword: The Compromise of 1833* (Baton Rouge, 1982); William J. Cooper, Jr., *The South and the Politics of Slavery, 1828–1856* (Baton Rouge, 1978); Don E. Fehrenbacher, *The South and Three Sectional Crises* (Baton Rouge, 1980); John Barnwell, *Love of Order: South Carolina's First Secession Crisis* (Chapel Hill, 1982); and R. Kent Newmyer, *The Supreme Court Under Marshall and Taney* (New York, 1970).

One very accessible way to understand the issues of the day is through biography, and this topic is replete with superlative studies. Among the major works are Robert V. Remini's three-volume biography, *Andrew Jackson* (New York, 1977–1984); Chase C. Mooney, *William H. Crawford, 1772–1834* (Lexington, Ky., 1974); John Niven, *Martin Van Buren and the Romantic Age* (New York, 1983); and Charles Grier Sellers, Jr.'s, two-volume *James K. Polk, Jacksonian, 1795–1843* (Princeton, 1957, 1966). There are several good biographies of John C. Calhoun, Henry Clay, and Daniel Webster, but for most readers the indispensable study is Merrill D. Peterson's superb *The Great Triumvirate: Webster, Clay, and Calhoun* (New York, 1987).

The best introduction to the literature on Texas history is Walter L.

Buenger and Robert A. Calvert, eds., *Texas Through Time: Evolving Interpretations* (College Station, Tex., 1991). The most useful studies on the background to the Texas Revolution and eventual independence are David J. Weber, *The Mexican Frontier, 1821–1846: The American Southwest Under Mexico* (Albuquerque, 1982); William C. Binkley, *The Texas Revolution* (Baton Rouge, 1952); James W. Pohl, *The Battle of San Jacinto* (Austin, 1989); and Randolph B. Campbell, *Sam Houston and the American Southwest* (New York, 1993). For the diplomatic consequences of the Texas Revolution vis-à-vis the United States, see Frederick Merk, *Slavery and the Annexation of Texas* (New York, 1972) and David M. Pletcher, *The Diplomacy of Annexation: Texas, Oregon, and the Mexican War* (Columbia, Mo., 1973).

The Mexican War is covered in K. Jack Bauer, *The Mexican War, 1846–1848* (New York, 1974) and Robert W. Johannsen, *To the Halls of Montezuma: The Mexican War in the American Imagination* (New York, 1985). No one should miss Bernard DeVoto's imaginative *The Year of Decision, 1846* (Boston, 1943). For the Mexican point of view, consult Gene M. Brack, *Mexico Views Manifest Destiny, 1821–1846* (Albuquerque, 1975). John C. Calhoun's skepticism about the war and potential annexation of territory is portrayed in Ernest McPherson Lander, Jr., *Reluctant Imperialists: Calhoun, the South Carolinians, and the Mexican War* (Baton Rouge, 1979).

On the aftermath of the Mexican War, see Chaplain W. Morrison, *Democratic Politics and Sectionalism: The Wilmot Proviso Controversy* (Chapel Hill, 1967); Holman Hamilton, *Prologue to Conflict: The Crisis and Compromise of 1850* (Lexington, Ky., 1964); Gerald W. Wolff, *The Kansas–Nebraska Bill: Party, Section, and the Coming of the Civil War* (New York, 1977); James A. Rawley, *Race and Politics:*

"Bleeding Kansas" and the Coming of the Civil War (Philadelphia, 1969); Robert W. Johannsen, *Stephen A. Douglas* (New York, 1973); Don E. Fehrenbacher, *The Dred Scott Case: Its Significance in American Law and Politics* (New York, 1978); Stephen B. Oates, *To Purge This Land with Blood: A Biography of John Brown* (New York, 1970); and Allan Nevins, *The Emergence of Lincoln* (2 vols., New York, 1950). Again, on all aspects of the secession crisis from the Mexican War to Fort Sumter, there is no better account than David Potter's *The Impending Crisis*.

At the end, the entire political process broke down, and the war came. There is an extensive literature on the final rupture. After Potter, one may turn to Allan Nevins, *The Ordeal of the Union* (2 vols., New York, 1947) and Roy Franklin Nichols, *Disruption of American Democracy* (New York, 1948). Newer studies of politics include Michael F. Holt, *The Political Crisis of the 1850s* (New York, 1978); Daniel W. Crofts, *Reluctant Confederates: Upper South Unionists in the Secession Crisis* (Chapel Hill, 1989); William L. Barney, *The Secessionist Impulse: Alabama and Mississippi in 1860* (Princeton, 1974); Ralph A. Wooster, *The Secession Conventions of the South* (Princeton, 1962); Robert E. May, *John A. Quitman: Old South Crusader* (Baton Rouge, 1985); Eric H. Walther, *The Fire-Eaters* (Baton Rouge, 1992); and Steven A. Channing, *Crisis of Fear: Secession in South Carolina* (New York, 1970). Two older studies that remain influential are Kenneth M. Stampp, *And the War Came: The North and the Secession Crisis, 1860–1861* (Baton Rouge, 1950) and Richard N. Current, *Lincoln and the First Shot* (Philadelphia, 1963). Excellent modern state studies of the secession movement include Michael P. Johnson, *Toward a Patriarchal Republic: The Secession of Georgia* (Baton Rouge, 1977); Walter L. Buenger, *Secession and the Union in Texas* (Austin, 1984); and James M. Woods,

Rebellion and Realignment: Arkansas's Road to Secession (Fayetteville, Ark., 1987). Older studies exist for every state.

The Civil War has generated more historical scholarship than any other topic in our past. J. G. Randall and David Donald, *The Civil War and Reconstruction* (Boston, 1961), which has been reprinted several times, is the standard textbook account. Two classic multivolume histories are Allan Nevins's *The War for the Union* (4 vols., New York, 1959–1971) and Shelby Foote's *The Civil War: A Narrative* (3 vols., New York, 1958–1974), written with unusual grace. The best long one-volume modern history is James M. McPherson, *Battle Cry of Freedom: The Civil War Era* (New York, 1988). The best brief history is Charles P. Roland, *An American Iliad: The Story of the Civil War* (Lexington, Ky., 1991).

On the history of the Confederacy, see Charles P. Roland, *The Confederacy* (Chicago, 1960); Frank E. Vandiver, *Their Tattered Flags: The Epic of the Confederacy* (New York, 1970); Emory M. Thomas, *The Confederate Nation, 1861–1865* (New York, 1979); Drew Gilpin Faust, *The Creation of Confederate Nationalism: Ideology and Identity in the Civil War South* (Baton Rouge, 1988); and Paul D. Escott, *After Secession: Jefferson Davis and the Failure of Confederate Nationalism* (Baton Rouge, 1978).

The experience of the common soldier has increasingly become a focus of military history. Bell Irvin Wiley began the topic with his *The Life of Johnny Reb: The Common Soldier of the Confederacy* (Indianapolis, 1943), but see two more recent studies: James I. Robertson, Jr., *Soldiers Blue and Gray* (Columbia, S.C., 1988) and Reid Mitchell, *Civil War Soldiers* (New York, 1988). The common attitudes of soldiers have been analyzed by Michael Barton, *Goodmen: The Character of Civil War Soldiers* (University Park, Pa., 1981); Gerald F. Linderman, *Embattled Courage:*

The Experience of Combat in the American Civil War (New York, 1987); and Randall C. Jimerson, *The Private Civil War: Popular Thought During the Sectional Conflict* (Baton Rouge, 1988). For Union soldiers' attitudes toward the southern troops, see Michael C. C. Adams, *Our Masters the Rebels: A Speculation on Union Military Failure in the East, 1861–1865* (Cambridge, Mass., 1978). The best account of black troops in the Union army is Joseph T. Glatthaar, *Forged in Battle: The Civil War Alliance of Black Soldiers and White Officers* (New York, 1990). The Confederate debate over whether to utilize blacks as soldiers is illuminated by Robert F. Durden, *The Gray and the Black: The Confederate Debate on Emancipation* (Baton Rouge, 1972).

On military strategy, see Archer Jones, *Civil War Command and Strategy: The Process of Victory and Defeat* (New York, 1992); Grady McWhiney and Perry D. Jamieson, *Attack and Die: Civil War Military Tactics and the Southern Heritage* (University, Ala., 1982); David H. Donald, ed., *Why the North Won the Civil War* (Baton Rouge, 1960); Richard E. Beringer et al., *Why the South Lost the Civil War* (Athens, Ga., 1986); Gabor S. Boritt, ed., *Why the Confederacy Lost* (New York, 1992); and Frank E. Vandiver, *Rebel Brass: The Confederate Command System* (Baton Rouge, 1956). On the unprecedented violence of the Civil War see Charles Royster, *The Destructive War: William Tecumseh Sherman, Stonewall Jackson, and the Americans* (New York, 1991). The influence of Confederate defeat upon subsequent southern religion and popular culture is the topic of Charles Reagan Wilson, *Baptized in Blood: The Religion of the Lost Cause, 1865–1920* (Athens, Ga., 1980).

Much has also been written about the southern homefront. Old accounts, still valuable, are Charles W. Ramsdell, *Behind the Lines in the Southern Confederacy* (Baton Rouge, 1944); Mary Elizabeth

Massey, *Ersatz in the Confederacy* (Columbia, S.C., 1952); and Ella Lonn, *Salt as a Factor in the Confederacy* (New York, 1933). See also Massey's *Refugee Life in the Confederacy* (Baton Rouge, 1964). The best treatment of women in the Civil War South is George Rable, *Civil Wars: Women and the Crisis of Southern Nationalism* (Urbana, Ill., 1989), but see also Drew Gilpin Faust, "Altars of Sacrifice: Confederate Women and the Narratives of War," *Journal of American History*, 76 (March 1990), 1200–1228, and the discussion in Michael Fellman, *Inside War: The Guerrilla Conflict in Missouri During the American Civil War* (New York, 1989). Not to be missed is C. Vann Woodward, ed., *Mary Chesnut's Civil War* (New Haven, 1981).

Of course there are histories almost without number about specific battles, but of particular value are the following: James Lee McDonough, *Shiloh: In Hell Before Night* (Knoxville, 1977); Stephen W. Sears, *Landscape Turned Red: The Battle of Antietam* (New Haven, 1983); Peter F. Walker, *Vicksburg: A People at War, 1860–1865* (Chapel Hill, 1960); Edwin B. Coddington, *The Gettysburg Campaign: A Study in Command* (New York, 1968); Richard M. McMurry, *The Road Past Kennesaw: The Atlanta Campaign of 1864* (Washington, D.C., 1972); Joseph T. Glatthaar, *The March to the Sea and Beyond: Sherman's Troops in the Savannah and Carolinas Campaigns* (New York, 1985). There are also biographies, often several, of every general. Douglas Southall Freeman's four-volume *R. E. Lee: A Biography* (New York, 1934–1935) should be read in tandem with Thomas L. Connelly's *The Marble Man: Robert E. Lee and His Image in American Society* (New York, 1977). Notable biographies include Frank E. Vandiver, *Mighty Stonewall* (New York, 1957); Richard M. McMurry, *John Bell Hood and the War for Southern Independence* (Lexington, Ky., 1982); James M. Merrill, *William Tecumseh Sherman* (Chicago,

1971); and, on the president of the Confederacy, William C. Davis, *Jefferson Davis: The Man and His Hour* (New York, 1991). The serious student will want to supplement this biography of Davis with the multivolume edition of his papers now underway: *The Papers of Jefferson Davis* (7 vols. to date, Baton Rouge, 1971–), currently being edited by Lynda Crist and associates.

CHAPTER 4:   THE COLONIAL SOUTH

For reasons that are not entirely clear, the lay public has been slower to accept the conclusions of revisionist scholarship on the general topic of Reconstruction than on any other topic in southern or American history, even though the revisionist viewpoint has been overwhelmingly dominant among academic historians for almost a half century. Two extremely effective accounts that popularized—in the best sense—the new understanding are John Hope Franklin, *Reconstruction After the Civil War* (Chicago, 1961) and Kenneth M. Stampp, *The Era of Reconstruction, 1865–1877* (New York, 1965). These two books have had a profound influence, though not as universal as one would wish. The two standard college textbook accounts, which cover the entire Civil War and Reconstruction Era, are J. G. Randall and David Donald, *The Civil War and Reconstruction* (second ed., Boston, 1961), reprinted several times, and James M. McPherson, *Ordeal By Fire: The Civil War and Reconstruction* (New York, 1982). The most up-to-date general account, distinguished by its research in secondary and primary sources and by its vigorous interpretation, is Eric Foner, *Reconstruction: America's Unfinished Revolution, 1863–1877* (New York, 1988). The best treatment of the important legal and constitutional issues raised and sometimes resolved during the entire era are

Harold M. Hyman, *A More Perfect Union: The Impact of the Civil War and Reconstruction on the Constitution* (New York, 1973) and Hyman and William M. Wiecek, *Equal Justice Under Law: Constitutional Development, 1835–1875* (New York, 1982).

For the very beginning of Reconstruction see Willie Lee Rose, *Rehearsal for Reconstruction: The Port Royal Experiment* (Indianapolis, 1964), masterfully written; LaWanda Cox, *Lincoln and Black Freedom: A Study in Presidential Leadership* (Columbia, S.C., 1981); Dan T. Carter, *When the War Was Over: The Failure of Self-Reconstruction in the South, 1865–1867* (Baton Rouge, 1985); and Michael Perman, *Reunion Without Compromise: The South and Reconstruction, 1865–1868* (Cambridge, Eng., 1973). The different positions of Abraham Lincoln, Andrew Johnson, and Congress over the method and pace of Reconstruction have been the topic of very extensive research. Among the essential books are Michael Les Benedict, *A Compromise of Principle: Congressional Republicans and Reconstruction, 1863–1869* (New York, 1974) and *The Impeachment and Trial of Andrew Johnson* (New York, 1973); David Donald, *The Politics of Reconstruction, 1863–1867* (Baton Rouge, 1965); and Eric L. McKitrick, *Andrew Johnson and Reconstruction* (Chicago, 1960).

Much of the most exciting research has focused on specialized topics rather than national or state-level politics. Books that are especially effective at demolishing old stereotypes about the Reconstruction Era are George C. Rable, *But There Was No Peace: The Role of Violence in the Politics of Reconstruction* (Athens, Ga., 1984); Richard Nelson Current, *Those Terrible Carpetbaggers* (New York, 1988); Lawrence N. Powell, *New Masters: Northern Planters during the Civil War and Reconstruction* (New Haven, 1980); Thomas Holt, *Black over White: Negro Polit-*

ical Leadership in South Carolina during Reconstruction (Urbana, Ill., 1977); Eric Foner, *Freedom's Lawmakers: A Directory of Black Officeholders During Reconstruction* (New York, 1993); Allen W. Trelease, *White Terror: The Ku Klux Klan Conspiracy and Southern Reconstruction* (New York, 1971); Joseph G. Dawson, III, *Army Generals and Reconstruction: Louisiana, 1862–1877* (Baton Rouge, 1982); William S. McFeely, *Yankee Stepfather: General O. O. Howard and the Freedmen* (New Haven, 1968); James L. Roark, *Masters Without Slaves: Southern Planters in the Civil War and Reconstruction* (New York, 1977); and Mark W. Summers, *Railroads, Reconstruction, and the Gospel of Prosperity: Aid Under the Radical Republicans, 1865–1877* (Princeton, 1984).

There now exist good, modern studies of the Reconstruction process for each southern state. Representative of the new viewpoints are Stephen V. Ash, *Middle Tennessee Society Transformed, 1860–1870: War and Peace in the Upper South* (Baton Rouge, 1988); William C. Harris, *Presidential Reconstruction in Mississippi* (Baton Rouge, 1967); Ted Tunnell, *Crucible of Reconstruction: War, Radicalism, and Race in Louisiana, 1862–1877* (Baton Rouge, 1984); and Joel Williamson, *After Slavery: The Negro in South Carolina During Reconstruction, 1861–1877* (Chapel Hill, 1965). A model local study is Randolph B. Campbell, *A Southern Community in Crisis: Harrison County, Texas, 1850–1880* (Austin, 1983).

As with slavery, the topics of emancipation and the black experience in Reconstruction have generated a huge body of literature, much of it stunningly good. One may begin with Leon F. Litwack, *Been in the Storm So Long: The Aftermath of Slavery* (New York, 1979); Peter Kolchin, *First Freedom: The Responses of Alabama's Blacks to Emancipation and Reconstruction* (Westport, Conn., 1972); C. Peter Ripley, *Slaves and Freedmen in*

Civil War Louisiana (Baton Rouge, 1976); Ira Berlin et al., *Slaves No More: Three Essays on Emancipation and the Civil War* (Cambridge, Eng., 1992); Janet Sharp Hermann, *The Pursuit of a Dream* (New York, 1981); and Michael Wayne, *The Reshaping of Plantation Society: The Natchez District, 1860–1880* (Baton Rouge, 1983). Most freed persons were soon caught up in the agricultural system called sharecropping. For this process see Roger L. Ransom and Richard Sutch, *One Kind of Freedom: The Economic Consequences of Emancipation* (Cambridge, Eng., 1977); Jay R. Mandle, *Not Slave, Not Free: The African American Economic Experience Since the Civil War* (Durham, 1992); and Harold D. Woodman, "Sequel to Slavery: The New History Views the Postbellum South," *Journal of Southern History*, 43 (November 1977), 523–54. The best account of how white farmers also were pulled into the system of sharecropping is Steven Hahn, *The Roots of Southern Populism: Yeoman Farmers and the Transformation of the Georgia Upcountry, 1850–1890* (New York, 1983). See also Peter Wallenstein, *From Slave South to New South: Public Policy in Nineteenth-Century Georgia* (Chapel Hill, 1987); Gavin Wright, *Old South, New South: Revolutions in the Southern Economy since the Civil War* (New York, 1986); and Gilbert C. Fite, *Cotton Fields No More: Southern Agriculture, 1865–1980* (Lexington, Ky., 1984).

C. Vann Woodward's great book, *Origins of the New South, 1877–1913* (Baton Rouge, 1951), has profoundly shaped how historians ever since have conceptualized the entire era. His overview should now be supplemented with Howard N. Rabinowitz's *The First New South, 1865–1920* (Arlington Heights, Ill., 1992) and Edward L. Ayers, *The Promise of the New South: Life After Reconstruction* (New York, 1992). An extremely helpful historiographical essay is James C. Cobb, "Beyond Planters and

Industrialists: A New Perspective on the New South," *Journal of Southern History*, 54 (February 1988), 45–68. Among the important studies are Jonathan M. Wiener, *Social Origins of the New South, Alabama: 1860–1885* (Baton Rouge, 1978); Dwight B. Billings, Jr., *Planters and the Making of a "New South": Class, Politics, and Development in North Carolina, 1865–1900* (Chapel Hill, 1979); Paul D. Escott, *Many Excellent People: Power and Privilege in North Carolina, 1850–1900* (Chapel Hill, 1985); James Tice Moore, "Redeemers Reconsidered: Change and Continuity in the Democratic South, 1870–1900," *Journal of Southern History*, 44 (August 1978), 357–78; Lacy K. Ford, "Rednecks and Merchants: Economic Development and Social Tensions in the South Carolina Upcountry, 1865–1900," *Journal of American History*, 71 (September 1984), 294–318. Paul M. Gaston in *The New South Creed: A Study in Southern Myth-making* (New York, 1970) shows how quickly the image of a rebuilding South changed from exhortation to myth. The lingering influence of the Confederacy is the topic of Gaines M. Foster, *Ghosts of the Confederacy: Defeat, the Lost Cause, and the Emergence of the New South, 1865–1913* (New York, 1987).

Both Ayers, *The Promise of the New South*, and Rabinowitz, *The First New South*, give ample treatment of southern urbanization following the Civil War. The best analysis of how blacks fared in the process is Howard N. Rabinowitz, *Race Relations in the Urban South, 1865–1890* (New York, 1978). See especially Don H. Doyle, *New Men, New Cities, New South: Atlanta, Nashville, Charleston, Mobile, 1860–1910* (Chapel Hill, 1990) and Harold L. Platt, *City Building in the New South: The Growth of Public Services in Houston, Texas, 1830–1910* (Philadelphia, 1982). The best survey of southern urbanization is David R. Goldfield, *Cotton Fields and Skyscrapers: Southern City and Region, 1607–1980* (Baton Rogue, 1982).

Every student of Populism in the South should begin with C. Vann Woodward's *Origins of the New South* and the biography that began Woodward's distinguished career, *Tom Watson, Agrarian Rebel* (New York, 1938). An impassioned analysis of southern Populists is provided by Lawrence Goodwyn in *Democratic Promise: The Populist Moment in America* (New York, 1976); a more balanced survey is offered by Robert C. McMath, Jr., *American Populism: A Social History, 1877–1898* (New York, 1993). See also Bruce Palmer, *"Man Over Money": The Southern Populist Critique of American Capitalism* (Chapel Hill, 1980). An important interpretation of how Populism was a response to far-reaching social changes is Steven Hahn's previously cited *The Roots of Southern Populism*. A fascinating debate that arose from this book is illustrated by the exchange that takes place between Hahn and two critics, Shawn Everett Kantor and J. Morgan Kousser, in the *Journal of Southern History*, 59 (May 1993), 201–66. For the collapse of Populism see Robert F. Durden, *The Climax of Populism: The Election of 1896* (Lexington, Ky., 1965). Two important articles are William F. Holmes, "Populism: In Search of Context," *Agricultural History*, 64 (Fall 1990), 26–58, and Gregg Cantrell and D. Scott Barton, "Texas Populists and the Failure of Biracial Politics," *Journal of Southern History*, 55 (November 1989), 659–92. Cantrell has since published *Kenneth and John B. Rayner and the Limits of Southern Dissent* (Urbana, Ill., 1993) on race and political reform in North Carolina and Texas.

Anne Firor Scott's work is essential for understanding the life experiences of women during the post–Civil War South. See *The Southern Lady: From Pedestal to Politics, 1830–1930* (Chicago, 1970) and *Natural Allies: Women's Associations in American History* (Urbana, Ill., 1992). An illustrative diary is Margaret Jones Bolsterli, ed., *Vinegar Pie and Chicken Bread: A*

Woman's Diary of Life in the Rural South, 1890–1891 (Fayetteville, Ark., 1982). A model monograph is Marjorie Spruill Wheeler, *New Women of the New South: The Leaders of the Woman Suffrage Movement in the Southern States* (New York, 1993). Much of the best work on women in this period is still in dissertation form; for example, see Megan Seaholm, "Earnest Women: The White Woman's Club Movement in Progressive Era Texas, 1880–1920" (Ph.D. dissertation, Rice University, 1988) and Elizabeth Hayes Turner, "Women's Culture and Community: Religion and Reform in Galveston, 1880–1920" (Ph.D. dissertation, Rice University, 1990).

The place to begin studying the Progressive movement in the South is Dewey W. Grantham's impressive survey, *Southern Progressivism: The Reconciliation of Progress and Tradition* (Knoxville, 1983), which is detailed, analytical, and well written. Sheldon Hackney minimizes the connections between Populism and Progressivism in *Populism to Progressivism in Alabama* (Princeton, 1969), but see the corrective offered by Samuel L. Webb, "From Independents to Populists to Progressive Republicans: The Case of Chilton County, Alabama, 1880–1920," *Journal of Southern History*, 59 (November 1993), 707–36. There are a number of other relevant state studies and many biographies. For representative biographies see Robert C. Cotner, *James Stephen Hogg: A Biography* (Austin, 1959) and William F. Holmes, *The White Chief: James Kimble Vardaman* (Baton Rouge, 1970). Of the many specialized, topical studies, William A. Link's *A Hard Country and a Lonely Place: Schooling, Society, and Reform in Rural Virginia, 1870–1920* (Chapel Hill, 1986) is of particular interest.

Southern industrialization is a major theme of C. Vann Woodward's *Origins of the New South, 1877–1913* (Baton Rouge, 1951). An important study that supplements Woodward's interpretation is David L. Carlton, *Mill and Town in South Carolina, 1880–1920* (Baton Rouge, 1982). Dwight B. Billings, Jr., *Planters and the Making of a "New South,"* previously cited, is a strong challenge to Woodward. The best survey of southern industrialism is James C. Cobb, *Industrialization and Southern Society, 1877–1984* (Lexington, Ky., 1984), but do not miss his important article, "Beyond Planters and Industrialists: A New Perspective on the New South," previously cited. The essential work for Appalachia is Ronald D. Eller, *Miners, Millhands, and Mountaineers: Industrialization of the Appalachian South, 1880–1930* (Knoxville, 1982). Allen Tullos presents a sensitive analysis of how industrialization effected people in *Habits of Industry: White Culture and the Transformation of the Carolina Piedmont* (Chapel Hill, 1989).

The New Deal was an incomplete blessing for the South. A brief interpretation is offered by Frank Freidel, *F. D. R. and the South* (Baton Rouge, 1965), but more detailed studies that emphasize the farmer's plight include David Eugene Conrad, *The Forgotten Farmers: The Story of Sharecroppers in the New Deal* (Urbana, Ill., 1965); Donald H. Grubbs, *Cry from the Cotton: The Southern Tenant Farmers' Union and the New Deal* (Chapel Hill, 1971); and Paul E. Mertz, *New Deal Policy and Southern Rural Poverty* (Baton Rouge, 1978). Two unusually good histories of recent southern farming exist: Pete Daniel, *Breaking the Land: The Transformation of Cotton, Tobacco, and Rice Cultures since 1880* (Urbana, Ill., 1985) and Jack Temple Kirby, *Rural Worlds Lost: The American South, 1920–1960* (Baton Rouge, 1987). See also D. Clayton Brown, *Electricity for Rural America: The Fight for the REA* (Westport, Conn., 1980) and the discussion of New Deal agricultural policies in James C. Cobb's powerful *The Most Southern Place on Earth: The Mississippi Delta and the Roots of Regional Identity* (New York, 1992). The impact of the New Deal on the South's cities is portrayed in Roger Biles, "The Urban South in the Great Depression," *Journal of Southern History*, 56 (February 1990), 71–100.

The shameful story of race relations in the late nineteenth- and early twentieth-century South has been the subject of a series of important books. One should still begin with Rayford W. Logan, *The Negro in American Life and Thought: The Nadir, 1877–1901* (New York, 1954), and August Meier, *Negro Thought in America, 1880–1915: Racial Ideologies in the Age of Booker T. Washington* (Ann Arbor, Mich., 1963). Joel Williamson provides a sweeping interpretation in *The Crucible of Race: Black–White Relations in the American South Since Emancipation* (New York, 1984), and Jack Temple Kirby's useful *Darkness at the Dawning: Race and Reform in the Progressive South* (Philadelphia, 1972) is an excellent survey of developments. The most important study of black disenfranchisement is J. Morgan Kousser, *The Shaping of Southern Politics: Suffrage Restriction and the Establishment of the One-Party South, 1880–1910* (New Haven, 1974). Three excellent state studies are John Dittmer, *Black Georgia in the Progressive Era, 1900–1920* (Urbana, Ill., 1977), Neil R. McMillen, *Dark Journey: Black Mississippians in the Age of Jim Crow* (Urbana, Ill., 1989), and John William Graves, *Town and Country: Race Relations in an Urban-Rural Context: Arkansas, 1865–1905* (Fayetteville, Ark., 1990), but no one should miss William Ivy Hair, *Carnival of Fury: Robert Charles and the New Orleans Race Riot of 1900* (Baton Rouge, 1976). There are many topical studies, but see especially Walter B. Weare, *Black Business in the New South: A Social History of the North Carolina Mutual Life Insurance Company* (Urbana, Ill., 1973) and Willard B. Gatewood, *Aristocrats of Color: The Black Elite, 1880–1920* (Bloomington, Ind.,

1990). Essential biographical studies include Louis R. Harlan's *Booker T. Washington: The Making of a Black Leader, 1856–1901* (New York, 1972) and *Booker T. Washington: The Wizard of Tuskegee, 1901–1915* (New York, 1983) and Elliott M. Rudwick's *W. E. B. DuBois: A Study in Minority Group Leadership* (Philadelphia, 1960). Dan T. Carter's beautifully and powerfully written *Scottsboro: A Tragedy of the American South* (Baton Rouge, 1969) vividly demonstrates the power of racism. The most influential book in the entire history of post–Civil War race relations remains C. Vann Woodward, *The Strange Career of Jim Crow*, third revised edition (New York, 1974), a book that had an enormous influence on a generation of white southerners.

An indispensable source for southern literary history is Louis D. Rubin, Jr., et al., eds., *The History of Southern Literature* (Baton Rouge, 1985). Several important works in intellectual history are essential for putting the literary developments in context. See Daniel Joseph Singal, *The War Within: From Victorian to Modernist Thought in the South, 1919–1945* (Chapel Hill, 1982); Michael O'Brien, *The Idea of the American South, 1920–1941* (Baltimore, 1979); and Richard H. King, *A Southern Renaissance: The Cultural Awakening of the American South, 1930–1955* (New York, 1980). Paul K. Conkin's brief *The Southern Agrarians* (Knoxville, 1988) is a cogent interpretation of that literary movement. For women writers in general see Anne Goodwyn Jones, *Tomorrow Is Another Day: The Woman Writer in the South, 1859–1936* (Baton Rouge, 1981), and for the creator of *Gone with the Wind*, see Darden Asbury Pyron, *Southern Daughter: The Life of Margaret Mitchell* (New York, 1991). A huge critical literature exists for William Faulkner, but historians can usefully begin with David Minter, *William Faulkner: The Writing of a Life* (Baltimore, 1980), and Joel

Williamson, *William Faulkner and Southern History* (New York, 1993). W. J. Cash, *The Mind of the South* (New York, 1941), is part history, part diatribe, part artifact of the age, and it is still necessary to read, but one doing so should balance Cash against James C. Cobb, "Does *Mind* No Longer Matter? The South, the Nation, and *The Mind of the South*, 1941–1991," *Journal of Southern History*, 57 (November 1991), 681–718, and Paul D. Escott, ed., *W. J. Cash and the Minds of the South* (Baton Rouge, 1992).

My discussion of southern music is drawn almost entirely from the scholarship of Bill C. Malone. See his *Country Music, U. S. A.* (Austin, 1985), *Southern Music, American Music* (Lexington, Ky., 1979), and *Singing Cowboys and Musical Mountaineers: Southern Culture and the Roots of Country Music* (Athens, Ga., 1993). One should complement Malone with Eileen Southern, *The Music of Black Americans: A History* (New York, 1971); William Ferris, *Blues from the Delta* (Garden City, 1978), and Lawrence W. Levine, *Black Culture and Black Consciousness: Afro-American Folk Thought from Slavery to Freedom* (New York, 1977).

T. Harry Williams in his book of lectures, *Romance and Realism in Southern Politics* (Athens, Ga., 1961), first argued that Huey Long pioneered a realistic attitude toward Louisiana politics, but his magisterial biography, *Huey Long* (New York, 1969), ultimately becomes a rather romanticized portrait of the Louisiana phenomenon. I find William Ivy Hair's recent study, *The Kingfish and His Realm: The Life and Times of Huey P. Long* (Baton Rouge, 1991), far more persuasive. See also an even more critical study, Glen Jeansonne, *Messiah of the Masses: Huey P. Long and the Great Depression* (New York, 1993). For Lyndon B. Johnson, Robert A. Caro's multivolume biography in progress is powerfully written, but Caro has so demonized Johnson that the

books ultimately lose credibility. See *The Years of Lyndon Johnson: The Path to Power* (New York, 1982) and *The Years of Lyndon Johnson: Means of Ascent* (New York, 1990). Robert Dallek also has in progress a multivolume biography of Johnson, and though his writing style is plodding, his analysis is both more sympathetic and more persuasive than Caro's. See Dallek's *Lone Star Rising: Lyndon Johnson and His Times, 1908–1960* (New York, 1991). For Jimmy Carter, see his own *Why Not the Best?* (Nashville, 1975) and *Turning Point: A Candidate, a State, and a Nation Come of Age* (New York, 1992). James Wooten surveys Carter's background in *Dasher: The Roots and the Rising of Jimmy Carter* (New York, 1978).

CHAPTER 5:   THE AMERICAN SOUTH

Two brief works of synthesis offer the best introduction to the history of the recent South. See Charles P. Roland, *The Improbable Era: The South Since World War II* (Lexington, Ky., 1975) and David R. Goldfield, *Promised Land: The South Since 1945* (Arlington Heights, Ill., 1987). The best account of the events leading up to the changes that came in the wake of World War II is George Brown Tindall, *The Emergence of the New South, 1913–1945* (Baton Rouge, 1967). For southern industrialization, see James C. Cobb, *The Selling of the South: The Southern Crusade for Industrial Development, 1936–1980* (Baton Rouge, 1982) and *Industrialization and Southern Society, 1877–1984* (Lexington, Ky., 1984). There are a number of valuable essays in James C. Cobb and Michael V. Namorato, eds., *The New Deal and the South* (Jackson, Miss., 1984). The indispensable study of World War II's economic impact on the South is Bruce J. Schulman, *From Cotton Belt to Sunbelt: Federal Policy, Economic Development, and the Transformation of the South, 1938–1980*

(New York, 1991). An essay not to be missed is Raymond Arsenault, "The End of the Long Hot Summer: The Air Conditioner and Southern Culture," *Journal of Southern History*, 50 (November 1984), 597–628.

The transformations in southern agriculture are spelled out in three excellent books: Gilbert C. Fite, *Cotton Fields No More: Southern Agriculture, 1865–1980* (Lexington, Ky., 1984); Pete Daniel, *Breaking the Land: The Transformation of Cotton, Tobacco, and Rice Cultures since 1880* (Urbana, Ill., 1985); and Jack Temple Kirby, *Rural Worlds Lost: The American South, 1920–1960* (Baton Rouge, 1987). James C. Cobb's account in *The Most Southern Place on Earth: The Mississippi Delta and the Roots of Regional Identity* (New York, 1992) is geographically limited, but it offers a vivid analysis of the impact, for example, of tractors and cotton-picking machines. The incompleteness of the agricultural transformation is revealed by comparing a classic, first published in 1941, James Agee and Walker Evans, *Let Us Now Praise Famous Men: Three Tenant Farmers* (Boston, 1960) with Dale Maharidge and Michael Williamson, *And Their Children After Them: The Legacy of Let Us Now Praise Famous Men, James Agee, Walker Evans, and the Rise and Fall of Cotton in the South* (New York, 1989). This reading experience should be balanced with J. Wayne Flynt, *Dixie's Forgotten People: The South's Poor Whites* (Bloomington, Ind., 1979) and *Poor But Proud: Alabama's Poor Whites* (Tuscaloosa, Ala., 1989).

David Goldfield and Charles P. Roland in their surveys of the post-World War II South provide a good description of the rise of the so-called Sun Belt. But one should also see Kirkpatrick Sale's angry analysis, *Power Shift: The Rise of the Southern Rim and Its Challenge to the Eastern Establishment* (New York, 1975). A more temperate interpretation is offered by Bernard L. Weinstein and Robert E. Firestine, *Regional Growth and Decline in the United States: The Rise of the Sunbelt and the Decline of the Northeast* (New York, 1978). See also the relevant essays in John B. Boles, ed., *Dixie Dateline: A Journalistic Portrait of the Contemporary South* (Houston, 1983). George Brown Tindall, "The Sunbelt Snow Job," *Houston Review* 1 (Spring 1979), 3–13, debunks exaggerated accounts of Sun Belt prosperity. For Sun Belt urbanization see David C. Perry and Alfred J. Watkins, eds., *The Rise of the Sunbelt Cities* (Beverly Hills, Calif., 1977); Richard M. Bernard and Bradley R. Rice, eds., *Sunbelt Cities: Politics and Growth Since World War II* (Austin, 1983); and Randall M. Miller and George E. Pozzetta, eds., *Shades of the Sunbelt: Essays on Ethnicity, Race, and the Urban South* (New York, 1988).

The great story of the modern South concerns the improvements in race relations. The result has been a great outpouring of scholarship. The most useful introductions to the subject are Juan Williams, *Eyes on the Prize: America's Civil Rights Years, 1954–1965* (New York, 1987), intended to accompany the wonderful Public Broadcast System television series of the same name; Harvard Sitkoff, *The Struggle for Black Equality, 1954–1980* (New York, 1981); David R. Goldfield, *Black, White, and Southern: Race Relations and Southern Culture, 1940 to the Present* (Baton Rouge, 1990); and Steven F. Lawson, *Running for Freedom: Civil Rights and Black Politics in America Since 1941* (Philadelphia, 1991).

Two massive works fully repay reading: Richard Kluger, *Simple Justice: The History of Brown v. Board of Education and Black America's Struggle for Equality* (2 vols., New York, 1975) and Taylor Branch, *Parting the Waters: America in the King Years, 1954–1963* (New York, 1988). Among the many monographs, I have found the following most helpful: Morton Sosna, *In Search of the Silent South: Southern Liberals and the Race Issue* (New York, 1977); Jacquelyn Dowd Hall, *Revolt Against Chivalry: Jessie Daniel Ames and the Women's Campaign Against Lynching* (New York, 1979); William H. Chafe, *Civilities and Civil Rights: Greensboro, North Carolina, and the Black Struggle for Freedom* (New York, 1980); Numan V. Bartley, *The Rise of Massive Resistance: Race and Politics in the South During the 1950s* (Baton Rouge, 1969); Jack Bass, *Unlikely Heroes* (New York, 1981); Howell Raines, *My Soul Is Rested: Movement Days in the Deep South Remembered* (New York, 1977); Clayborne Carson, *In Struggle: SNCC and the Black Awakening of the 1960s* (Cambridge, Mass., 1981); Charles W. Eagles, *Outside Agitator: Jon Daniels and the Civil Rights Movement in Alabama* (Chapel Hill, 1993); Hugh Davis Graham, *The Civil Rights Era: Origins and Development of National Policy, 1960–1972* (New York, 1990); and Stephen J. Whitfield, *A Death in the Delta: The Story of Emmett Till* (New York, 1988). The story of the Montgomery bus boycott is best told by J. Mills Thornton, III, in "Challenge and Response in the Montgomery Boycott of 1955–1956," *Alabama Review*, 33 (July 1980), 163–235.

All discussion of southern politics begins with V. O. Key, Jr., *Southern Politics in State and Nation* (New York, 1949), and the following recent accounts test his interpretations: William C. Havard, ed., *The Changing Politics of the South* (Baton Rouge, 1972); Numan V. Bartley and Hugh D. Graham, *Southern Politics and the Second Reconstruction* (Baltimore, 1975); Jack Bass and Walter De Vries, The *Transformation of Southern Politics: Social Change and Political Consequence Since 1945* (New York, 1976); and Earl Black and Merle Black, *Politics and Society in the South* (Cambridge, Mass., 1987). See also the Blacks' *The Vital South: How Presidents Are Elected* (Cambridge, Mass., 1992), which is indispensable. Also very useful is Alexander P. Lamis, *The Two-Party South*, expanded edition (New York, 1988).

Two of the best state-level studies are Numan V. Bartley, *The Creation of Modern Georgia* (Athens, Ga., 1983) and Chandler Davidson, *Race and Class in Texas Politics* (Princeton, 1990); see also Davidson's earlier *Biracial Politics: Conflict and Coalition in the Metropolitan South* (Baton Rouge, 1972). Steven F. Lawson has written two books that are essential for understanding how the Voting Rights Act revolutionized black political participation; see *Black Ballots: Voting Rights in the South, 1944–1969* (New York, 1976) and *In Pursuit of Power: Southern Blacks and Electoral Politics, 1965–1982* (New York, 1985). Another indispensable study is Earl Black, *Southern Governors and Civil Rights: Racial Segregation as a Campaign Issue in the Second Reconstruction* (Cambridge, Mass., 1976). For the conservative white reaction, see Neil R. McMillen, *The Citizens' Council: Organized Resistance to the Second Reconstruction, 1954–1964* (Urbana, Ill., 1971). For the pivotal election year of 1968 I have relied upon Lewis Chester, Godfrey Hodgson, and Bruce Page, *An American Melodrama: The Presidential Campaign of 1968* (New York, 1969).

The capitulation of the Republican party to racial politics is analyzed in Earl Black and Merle Black, *The Vital South*, previously cited, and even more explicitly in Thomas Byrne Edsall and Mary D. Edsall, *Chain Reaction: The Impact of Race, Rights, and Taxes on American Politics* (New York, 1991). The southern strategy of the Republican party was spelled out by Kevin P. Phillips, *The Emerging Republican Majority* (New Rochelle, N.Y., 1969). See also Dan T. Carter, *George Wallace, Richard Nixon, and the Transformation of American Politics* (Waco, Tex., 1992). For a unique

Louisiana example of racial politics, see Douglas D. Rose, *The Emergence of David Duke and the Politics of Race* (Chapel Hill, 1992).

A perennial topic in southern history has been the search to define the South. Pioneering articles whose influence has been immense include Ulrich B. Phillips, "The Central Theme of Southern History," *American Historical Review*, 34 (October 1928), 30–43; David M. Potter, "The Enigma of the South," *Yale Review*, 51 (Autumn 1961), 142–51; and George B. Tindall, "The Benighted South: Origins of a Modern Image," *Virginia Quarterly Review*, 40 (Spring 1964), 281–94. William R. Taylor, *Cavalier and Yankee: The Old South and American National Character* (New York, 1961) shows how both North and South often defined themselves in relation to the other.

C. Vann Woodward has been the most influential interpreter of the southern identity; the various essays reprinted in the most recent edition of his *The Burden of Southern History* (Baton Rouge, 1993) are required reading for anyone who wants to understand the South. See in relation to these essays Woodward's retrospective of his career and writing, *Thinking Back: The Perils of Writing History* (Baton Rouge, 1986). Among the books that explore the defining nature of the South are twelve Southerners, *I'll Take My Stand: The South and the Agrarian Tradition* (New York, 1930); Louis D. Rubin, Jr., and James Jackson Kilpatrick, eds., *The Lasting South: Fourteen Southerners Look at Their Home* (Chicago, 1957); Harry S. Ashmore, *An Epitaph for Dixie* (New York, 1958); Charles Grier Sellers, Jr., ed., *The Southerner as American* (Chapel Hill, 1960); Francis Butler Simkins, *The Everlasting South* (Baton Rouge, 1963); Frank E. Vandiver, ed., *The Idea of the South* (Chicago, 1964); Howard Zinn, *The*

Southern Mystique (New York, 1964); John Egerton, *The Americanization of Dixie: The Southernization of America* (New York, 1974); George Brown Tindall, *The Ethnic Southerners* (Baton Rouge, 1976); Carl N. Degler, *Place Over Time: The Continuity of Southern Distinctiveness* (Baton Rouge, 1977); fifteen Southerners, *Why the South Will Survive* (Athens, Ga., 1981); and John B. Boles, ed., *Dixie Dateline: A Journalistic Portrait of the Contemporary South* (Houston, 1983), particularly the introduction and the essay by Edwin M. Yoder, Jr. Richard Gray, *Writing the South: Ideas of an American Region* (Cambridge, Eng., 1986), is an interpretation of southerners' long attempt to understand and explicate their region.

The national media has long been fascinated with the South. The one essential study is Jack Temple Kirby, *Media-Made Dixie: The South in the American Imagination* (revised ed., Athens, Ga., 1986), but three other very useful books are Edward D. C. Campbell, Jr., *The Celluloid South: Hollywood and the Southern Myth* (Knoxville, 1981); Stephen A. Smith, *Myth, Media, and the Southern Mind* (Fayetteville, Ark., 1985); and Karl G. Heider, ed., *Images of the South: Constructing a Regional Culture on Film and Video* (Athens, Ga., 1993). In recent years the most often quoted, and the most quotable, interpreter of the South has been the historical sociologist John Shelton Reed. His several books are necessary for anyone interested in the question of the continuity of southern distinctiveness. See *The Enduring South: Subcultural Persistence in Mass Society* (Lexington, Mass., 1972); *One South: An Ethnic Approach to Regional Culture* (Baton Rouge, 1982); *Southerners: The Social Psychology of Sectionalism* (Chapel Hill, 1983); *Southern Folk, Plain and Fancy: Native White Social Types* (Athens, Ga., 1986); and *Whistling Dixie: Dispatches from the South*

(Columbia, Mo., 1990). Anyone interested in the South should also become familiar with the fiction of such literary giants as William Faulkner, Richard Wright, Eudora Welty, and Flannery O'Connor, as well as such autobiogra-phies as those of William Alexander Percy, Anne Moody, Maya Angelou, and Will D. Campbell. The South is a topic of everlasting interest, and there is no indication that the tide of writing about it is about to subside.

Index